Baudelaire

Other books by the author include

Princess Mathilde
Verlaine
Judith Gautier

Baudelaire

JOANNA RICHARDSON

St. Martin's Press
New York

BAUDELAIRE. Copyright © 1994 by Joanna Richardson. All rights reserved. Printed in the United States of America. No part of this book may be used or reproduced in any manner whatsoever without written permission except in the case of brief quotations embodied in critical articles or reviews. For information, address St. Martin's Press, 175 Fifth Avenue, New York, N.Y. 10010. ´

Published by arrangement with John Murray (Publishers) Ltd.

Library of Congress Cataloging-in-Publication Data

Richardson, Joanna.
Baudelaire / Joanna Richardson.
p.   cm.
ISBN 0-312-11476-1
1. Baudelaire, Charles, 1821–1867—Biography.   2. Poets, French—
19th century—Biography.   I. Title.
PQ2191.Z5R47   1994
841'.8—dc20
[B]   94-19660   CIP

First published in Great Britain by John Murray (Publishers) Ltd.

First U.S. Edition: November 1994
10 9 8 7 6 5 4 3 2 1

For
Michael Shaw

. . . Et vous, Seigneur mon Dieu! accordez-moi la grâce de produire quelques beaux vers qui me prouvent à moi-même que je ne suis pas le dernier des hommes, que je ne suis pas inférieur à ceux que je méprise!

Charles Baudelaire:
'À une heure du matin' (*Le Spleen de Paris*)

Vous avez trouvé le moyen d'être classique, tout en restant le romantique transcendant que nous aimons.

Gustave Flaubert to Charles Baudelaire,
22 October 1860

Contents

Illustrations

The author and publishers would like to thank the following for permission to reproduce illustrations: Plate 18 (top), Bibliothèque Nationale, Paris; 3, 4, 5, 11, 18 (middle and bottom), 19 and 20, © Collection Viollet; 8, 9, 12, 13, 14, 15 and 17, Nadar/© Arch. Phot. Paris/SPADEM; 10, © Arch. Phot. Paris/SPADEM; and 1, 2, 6, 7 and 16, author's collection.

Introduction

The title of this book, *Les Fleurs du mal*, says everything. The book is clad, as you will see, in a cold and sinister beauty. It was created with rage and with patience. Besides, the proof of its positive worth lies in all the ill that they speak of it. The book enrages people . . . They deny me everything, the spirit of invention and even a knowledge of the French language. I don't care a rap about all these imbeciles. I know that this book, with its virtues and its faults, will make its way in the memory of the lettered public.

So Baudelaire assured his mother in 1857, on the eve of his prosecution for offences against public morality. He saw his poems as revenge for his destiny. He had staked his life on his work. Some twenty years later, Théodore de Banville declared that, 'for all the young generation of today, Baudelaire has become the poet with whom one lives, the poet one never leaves, the one from whom, in all the agonies and tribulations of life, one asks for consolation and help.' In 1954, nearly a century after its publication, Yves Bonnefoy insisted: 'This is the master-work of French poetry . . . These *Fleurs du mal*, "fleurs maladives", are an almost sacred book.'

In *Les Fleurs du mal*, Baudelaire had sought for poetry in a realm which had until then been unexplored. He had found the poetry of Hell. It had been the poetry of tedium, of nightmare, of moral anguish: the poetry of isolation and despair, that of a man misunderstood by his contemporaries, a Catholic who was aware of the wages of sin. For Baudelaire was concerned not so much with evil as with sin, with man's frailty and with his repentance. The satanism of Baudelaire was only a pose. The anguish of Baudelaire was real and absolute.

Baudelaire made it a duty to confront the mysterious reality of evil. He shuddered with horror, while he felt invincibly attracted by the depths of sin and misfortune, shot through at times by strange enchantments. From his childhood, he had known this feeling of

ambivalence. For him, the poet was at once the most experienced and
the most spiritual of men. Baudelaire created his glory from his misery;
he endured situations which he felt obliged to endure and to trans-
figure. For Baudelaire, who cast himself head first into his destiny, who
determined never to be duped, who knew that he would meet his own
destruction, there was no poetry without this unappeased, unappeas-
able lucidity.

Baudelaire, said Rémy de Gourmont, 'is the master *par excellence* of
all the minds which have not allowed themselves to be contaminated
by sentimentalism.' Only the isolation and suffering of Vigny begin to
compare with Baudelaire's isolation and despair. As Gautier observed,
the poet of *Les Fleurs du mal* 'has no indulgence whatever for vice,
depravity and monstrousness, which he records with the composure of
an artist in an archaeological museum . . . Pitiless for others, he judges
himself no less severely; he sets down his errors, his failings, his per-
versities, with manly courage.' A writer's work often represents the
translation of wishes which cannot be fulfilled in his life. Whatever his
failures, Baudelaire was a man in his attitude to love, religion, suffering
and death: to the ultimate facts of existence.

He recorded, time and time again, the misery of Parisian life, the
longing for escape, for the unknown, even for annihilation. He was
contemptuous of himself, of his own imperfect body, his own tormented soul; and yet he felt obscurely that his torment was his spiritual
capital, his wealth, which was to fructify. 'You must have suffered
greatly, my dear child,' observed Sainte-Beuve. 'This particular sadness which rises from your pages, this sadness in which I recognise the
final symptom of a sick generation, . . . is also what will be esteemed in
you.' The sadness of Baudelaire went beyond the sadness of his contemporaries. As Yves Bonnefoy was to write:

> Baudelaire chose a fatal path, a path which led to death. It was a series
> of decisive events, each leading to the other, and each of them hastening
> death . . .
> Baudelaire chose death, he chose that death should grow in him like
> a conscience, and that he should understand through death. A harsh and
> sacrificial decision. And hazardous, too, with regard to the poetry itself.
> Apart from living misunderstood because he is so profoundly different,
> and with no friends in whom he can confide, Baudelaire can indeed see
> the death of his intelligence, for which he has risked so much. That this
> is possible is proved by the many difficulties in his work, and by the final
> aphasia. And that this was conscious is said in *Fusées*. There is worse.
> The ultimate danger is that this poetry, . . . at the height of the ordeal,
> can only utter words of misery and bereavement.
> But we know that the truth was not refused to Charles Baudelaire.

What was significant about him, suggested T. S. Eliot, was his theological innocence. He was discovering Christianity for himself. Baudelaire did not deny the existence of God; in moments of despair he longed to know that God existed, and that He was concerned with His creation. Whether Baudelaire felt damned, or whether he was afraid of being so, his thoughts revolved around damnation. Claudel observed that Baudelaire 'celebrated the only passion which the nineteenth century could honestly express: Remorse.' Remorse, affirmed André Suarès, was the key to his soul. His need to do penance, his cries for help, were a proof of his Catholicism.

He wrote not only of faith, but of love. As Verlaine observed, it was 'the love of a Parisian of the nineteenth century, something both feverish and analysed . . .' It was the passionate love of the poems to Jeanne Duval: intensely erotic poems inspired by her physical splendour, and perhaps by his own frustrated desire. It was the spiritual love of the poems to Apollonie Sabatier, addressed to the fallible woman whom he had transformed, in imagination, into his ideal. It was the variable love of the poems to Marie Daubrun, some of them affectionate, some erotic, and one, said Maurice Barrès, which introduced a vein of crapulence into French literature. Baudelaire wrote of love with prostitutes, and of love between women, perverted and condemned.

Yet his love poetry was more than a celebration of women: it was an opportunity for him to escape to the distant lands which he had seen on his early voyage to the East, to countries he had only known in books and pictures or in reverie. The warm aroma of a woman's breast, the fragrance of her hair, recalled exotic worlds. Baudelaire sought for spiritual and terrestrial beauty, he sought their relationship to one another. In his exploration, he touched on the correspondences between sound and hearing and sight. He went beyond them, and explored the Platonic correspondence between earth and heaven. In this, as in his concern with the poetry of modern Paris – and he was an intensely urban poet – in his concern with the grandeur of nineteenth-century man, the heroic misery of the poor, a misery which he too often shared, he was significant in his century.

His poetry was written painfully, many times revised. Some of it, towards the end, suggests the tension of determination, rather than imperious inspiration. Yet in *Les Fleurs du mal* there is a voice which cannot be mistaken, a voice not heard before in French poetry. Baudelaire, said Pierre-Jean Jouve, 'is a beginning. In the first place, because he creates a French poetry after centuries of vapidness and speeches; but also because his creation heralds the great change of values – from the rational to the irrational, from the prosaism of thought to the mystery of invention.' Baudelaire, wrote Ernest

Raynaud, 'restored poetry to its true destiny . . . With Baudelaire, poetry became once again, as it had been in the days of the Greeks, a divine manifestation, a ravisher of the soul; but the originality of Baudelaire is that he remained superior to his intoxication, and that he controlled it.' Few poets before him had discovered such powers of suggestion, of incantation, in the French language. To use a language skilfully was, so he said himself, to practise a kind of evocative magic. There was no chance in art; imagination was the most scientific of faculties. Baudelaire remained a classic in his exactitude, in his respect for words and syntax, for the smallest details of punctuation; yet he remained, as Flaubert said, transcendently romantic. He faced the perpetual problems of humankind. He also created a new, enchanted world.

Baudelaire had all the romantic sorrow, but he invented a romantic nostalgia which had been unknown in French poetry. As Eliot observed, a derivative of his nostalgia was the *poésie des départs*, the *poésie des salles d'attente*. He recalled – like Wordsworth – the innocent, lost paradise of childhood: the paradise to which he longed to return. There lay his intimations of immortality.

The visions Baudelaire creates add a new dimension to French poetry. Of his poetic revolution, and of the new world it opened to us, he was absolutely aware. He was drawn to the Romantic; he dreamed of an art which blended all effects and all expressions: which drew on art and music and words. *Les Fleurs du mal*, which touches heart and mind, broke the mould of poetry in France, and changed the course of poetry to come. It remains an exemplar, and unique.

Baudelaire offers more. He moves among the distinguished Frenchmen of his age, concerned with, and reflecting, their achievements, furthering their fame. He was a friend of Gérard de Nerval, Gautier, Leconte de Lisle; he knew, but he disliked, Victor Hugo. He was an eager friend of Flaubert, and he recognised the significance of *Madame Bovary*. From his early years, he also paid homage to Sainte-Beuve, and acknowledged the influence of the *Poésies de Joseph Delorme* on his own poetry. Baudelaire's relations with his literary elders and contemporaries were fruitful, illuminating, sometimes bitter; much could be learned from his influence on the next generation of writers, Mallarmé, Rimbaud and Verlaine. 'Does one not discover in him', asked Gonzague de Reynold, 'a Classic and a Romantic, a Parnassian and a Symbolist? His work may be considered, without exaggeration, as a crossing of the roads down which, in turn, French poetry advanced in the nineteenth century.' In art, he was a discerning critic: a lifelong admirer of Delacroix and Manet, both misunderstood in their time. He discovered Guys, he was among the first to divine the importance of Boudin. In music he was among the earliest, most passionate supporters of Wagner. He is a crucial figure in the history of French culture.

He offers, too, an extraordinary study in psychology. His intense, equivocal devotion to his mother largely explains his failure to form a stable relationship with any other woman. His life was a predictable tragedy. Much of the blame for this rests with his mother, much of it remains with himself, for he was largely the creator of his destiny. In his *Mémoires intérieures*, François Mauriac records that, until the day he died, Baudelaire was both the knife and the wound. 'He had wanted his destiny. He had demanded to have that destiny, and not another. He was his own fatality.' Yet his tragedy became a triumph. As Jacques Crépet wrote: 'The true glory of Baudelaire is that he felt, more intensely than anyone, and splendidly translated, the irremediable misery of the human condition.'

The life of Baudelaire was brief; his work was not extensive. Yet they are so significant in literary history, they have inspired so large a bibliography, that it is hard to do them justice in a single book. Moreover, in six years' research, I have also found substantial new and unfamiliar material. The original draft of this book has therefore been considerably reduced; and, working within limitations, I have sometimes chosen to omit what is familiar in order to include what is new.

I am, of course, indebted to Eugène Crépet, a publisher and acquaintance of Baudelaire, and the founder of Baudelaire studies, and to his son, Jacques Crépet; I have been able to consult not only their published work, but their massive collection of papers. I am grateful to Claude Pichois, for his admirable Pléiade edition of Baudelaire, and for many learned articles; I have gained much from the publications of W. T. Bandy and Jean Ziegler. I appreciate the help I have had from Mme Annie Angremy, Conservateur en chef, Département des Manuscrits, Division des Manuscrits Occidentaux, and from her colleague, M. Pierre Janin, at the Bibliothèque Nationale; I must also express my gratitude to the staff of the Département des Imprimés and the Département des Périodiques. I am glad to thank Mme Françoise Dumas, Conservateur en chef de la Bibliothèque de l'Institut de France, who has allowed me once again to consult the Lovenjoul Collection, and other documents now in her library. I must record my gratitude to Monsieur Jacques Suffel, who reminded me of the whereabouts of André Billy's papers, and to Monsieur Yves Grandfils, of the Bibliothèque municipale de Fontainebleau, who allowed me to use them. I am much obliged to the Conservateur en chef de la Maison de Victor Hugo, who showed me Mme Hugo's correspondence, and to the Mayor of Honfleur, who sent me photocopies of *L'Écho Honfleurais*. I am indebted to M. L. Declerck, First Secretary of the Belgian Embassy, for sending me details of General Aupick's promotion in the Order of Leopold; I gladly acknowledge the kindness of Baron H. J. van Asbeck, who sent me photocopies of documents (including a letter from Aupick) from the State Archives in The Hague. As always, I must record my gratitude to the British Library, especially to Mrs Sally Brown of the Department of Manuscripts, and to the staff of the Newspaper Library at Colindale. I am, once again, indebted to Dr Giles Barber, Mr David Thomas, Miss Gillian Hughes and their colleagues at the Taylor Institution, Oxford. They made available the papers of Féli Gautier, and gave me their expert and ever helpful advice. I greatly value the continuing interest and counsel of Professor Alan Raitt. I owe a constant debt to my literary agent, Michael Shaw, of Curtis Brown, for his understanding, patience and encouragement. To him I gladly dedicate this book.

1987–1993   JOANNA RICHARDSON

PART ONE

The Son of Joseph-François Baudelaire

1821–1828

1

On 7 June 1759, Joseph-François Baudelaire, the son of Claude Baudelaire and his wife Marie-Charlotte, was born at La Neuville-au-Pont, in the canton of Sainte-Menehould, in the Marne. He entered an old Champenois family. His parents and grandparents were vine-growers. His godfather, Joseph Baudelaire, who was also his second cousin, was a cooper by trade. Joseph-François was baptised on the day after his birth.[1]

Despite his humble origins, he had a proper education. Perhaps his parents could afford the schooling of their only child. Perhaps his natural gifts had earned him the interest of a local worthy, who paid for his tuition. More probably he was educated, free, by a seminary with the thought that he would enter the priesthood.

The record of his early life can only be based on occasional documents. Early in September 1775, at the collège de Sainte-Menehould, his name appeared with that of Pierre Pérignon. The friendship between the Pérignons and the Baudelaires was to last long after Joseph-François' death.

In the meanwhile, he was brought up in the Jansenist tradition. From Sainte-Menehould he went to Paris, where he continued his education. He lived in the community of Sainte-Barbe, and he pursued his studies at the Collège du Plessis. From October 1779 to the summer of 1781 he took a course in philosophy at the Sorbonne. On 16 June 1781 he was tonsured. Later that year he became a master of arts, and he began to read theology at the university. In 1782 he took minor orders. Late in 1783, or early the following year, he received the priesthood and the diaconate.[2] In 1783 he was already teaching at the Collège Sainte-Barbe, the famous boys' school in Paris, where Pierre Pérignon was among his colleagues. Late in June or early in July 1785, the abbé Baudelaire left Sainte-Barbe to become the tutor of Félix and Alphonse, the sons of Antoine-César, Comte (and later Duc) de Choiseul-Praslin. His new appointment did not prevent him from demanding a benefice: that of the Benedictine abbey of Saint-Pierre de Ferrières-en-Gatinais, in the diocese of Sens.

He was living in the rue du Bac, but his occupation swept him into a privileged and elegant new world. The Comte de Choiseul-Praslin had recently settled in a palatial *hôtel* in the rue de Bourbon. His art collections enjoyed a European reputation. Joseph-François taught his

pupils in a part of the *hôtel* that faced the Seine, with a noble prospect of
the Tuileries. In summer, they made their stately progress to the château
de Vaux-Praslin. Attended by liveried servants, driven in gleaming
carriages, given an annual allowance of 4,000 francs, Joseph-François led
a resplendent life. He met such familiars of the house as the philosopher
Helvetius, and the philosopher and future politician, the Marquis de
Condorcet. The vinegrowers' son from the Marne delighted in intellectual conversation, luxury and pleasure. He also learned fine manners,
without losing his natural warmth or his original turn of mind.

When the Revolution came, he welcomed it with the enthusiasm of
a liberal, but he recognised his debt to the *ancien régime*. He did not
become a partisan. Indeed, he used his credit on behalf of his
aristocratic friends, and he continued to serve the Comte de Choiseul-
Praslin. On 7 May 1791, he was appointed curé of Dammartin-sous-
Hans, near his birthplace, La Neuville-au-Pont; he refused the appointment on the grounds of his attachment to the Praslin family.[3] He was
indeed attached to them. A few months later, when his father died,
Antoine-César de Choiseul-Praslin succeeded to the dukedom. In 1793,
when the duke was arrested, Joseph-François ensured that he was
released from prison, and he saved some of his property from
confiscation. 'He was heroic, he risked his life twenty times over . . .
He was tireless in his undertakings. He was going round the courts and
prisons day and night.'[4]

He was, for the moment, without an income from the Choiseul-
Praslins, but on 19 November 1793 he resigned his priesthood and the
material benefits it brought him. He gave drawing lessons to earn a
living. Possibly he had never had a vocation for the Church, but he
had always had a taste for painting, and he had artistic ambitions.
Since his days at the Sorbonne, he had sought out the society of artists.
He had met other young men who, like himself, were fresh from the
provinces: men who had nothing but their dreams and letters of
introduction. Claude Ramey, the sculptor, came from Dijon; so did
Jean Naigeon, the artist, sometime a pupil of David. In 1797, Joseph-
François asked 'to be employed in the offices of Public Instruction, . . .
since his tastes had always drawn him to literature and the arts.'[5]

It was, one suspects, not only politics or even the love of art which
had led him to resign his priesthood. He would have found it hard to
accept a celibate existence. His artistic tastes revealed his eighteenth-
century sensuality; his portrait by his friend Jean-Baptiste Regnault
showed a man with dark good looks, and suggested warmth and
unabated vigour. On 9 May 1797, he married Rosalie Janin. He had
met her in an artist's studio. She brought him, in her dowry, some land
at Auteuil, and a farm in the Aisne. On 18 January 1805, at the age of

forty, after nearly eight years of marriage, she gave birth to their son, Claude-Alphonse.

In the meanwhile, Joseph-François had become increasingly involved in politics. The Choiseul-Praslins had not forgotten his devotion; they gave him a modest life annuity, and ensured that he was offered a sinecure. In 1801, according to the *Almanach impérial*, he had been secretary of the commission to administer and control the expenses of the Senate. In 1803 he was appointed head of the offices of the praetorship. In 1811 the *Almanach impérial* mentioned him as head of the Bureaux du Sénat. 'What were the functions of the Secretary in those days?' So his second wife was to wonder, half a century later. 'I don't know. I only know that he had two secretaries under his orders. Then he had other functions as well: he was *Keeper* of the Palace and the gardens, *Inspector* [of accounts], *Comptroller*, with a great number of accounts to keep. It was he who commissioned pictures and statues to decorate the Palace from the artists whom he chose . . . He had a salary of 12,000 francs, and accommodation.'[6] These impressive statements later proved to be incorrect. In 1887, the Senate archivist assured Eugène Crépet that Joseph-François Baudelaire had not been a Keeper, Inspector or Comptroller, and that he had not commissioned artists; nor had his salary been quite so large. 'The records of the Imperial Senate, from 1804 to 1814, revealed that, under the heading *Administration and internal police*, a Monsieur Beaudelaire [*sic*] was head of the department, at a salary of 10,000 francs a year.'[7]

He had, however, been given a house and garden on the edge of the Jardin du Luxembourg. Indeed, he had had his private gate into the public garden; and, on summer evenings, 'after a martial drum had driven out the common taxpayers,'[8] he and Ramey and Naigeon would stroll and talk together under the plane trees. 'As a little girl,' his second wife was to remember, 'I often dined there, with the Pérignons, and it was delightful to run in the Jardin du Luxembourg, when there was nobody about.'[9]

Caroline Archenbaut Defayis was to recall Joseph-François clearly, in later years. 'M. Baudelaire was a most distinguished man, in every way. His manners were exquisite, absolutely aristocratic.'[10] It is through her eyes that one sees him, at the dawn of the nineteenth century:

I knew M. Baudelaire at M. Pérignon's . . . M. Pérignon and M. Baudelaire were old colleagues from Sainte-Barbe, and they had remained very close to each other. He was a friend of the family; they cherished him and fêted him. I was constantly hearing them sing his praises.

This old man (he seemed old to me – I was so young! - with his curly grey hair and his eyebrows black as ebony) pleased me with his very original mind. They often used to say in the family: 'Baudelaire has such a brilliant mind, and he also has the naïveté and the bonhomie of La Fontaine.'

I remember [continued Caroline] how, on state occasions, when there were many guests to dinner at Auteuil, M. Pérignon's country house, I used to see M. Baudelaire arrive in a crested carriage, with a flunkey with powdered hair, with gold braid on every seam, all glittering with gold. The flunkey remained standing behind him, at dinner, to serve him, as it was the custom then to bring a servant with you to serve you at table. M. Baudelaire gave me the impression of a great nobleman. When, later, as his wife, I told him so, he said to me: 'But, child, did it not occur to you that this servant, and the carriage with the arms of the Senate, were put at my disposal for my official visits? When I used them on my own account, I always gave a louis to the coachman, on my return, just as if I had taken a cab.'[11]

These peccadilloes were obligingly overlooked by his superiors. They also allowed him to list his son – then a small child – as an assistant in his office, at a salary of 2,000 francs. It was a kindly means of increasing Joseph-François' income.

He kept his post until the end of the Empire; but his career was tied to that of the Duc de Choiseul-Praslin, and the duke was too inconstant in his politics. On Napoleon's abdication, he turned to Louis XVIII, who generously granted him a peerage. When Napoleon returned from Elba, Choiseul-Praslin protested his devotion to the Bonapartes. After Waterloo, when Louis XVIII was finally restored, he struck the renegade off the list of peers. For the moment, Choiseul-Praslin found himself in disgrace. His protégé, Joseph-François, was invited to resign from his sinecure.

In 1817, he settled at 13, rue Hautefeuille, and devoted his retirement to sketching and painting. He tried his hand at gouaches and pastels.[12] He was, it was said, 'a detestable painter.'[13] He seems to have been drawn to Fragonard, to the *petits maîtres* of the eighteenth century. He had an old painting of St Anthony in the desert, holding a crucifix and tempted by the Devil. He amused himself by producing a profane counterpart, a bacchante holding a thyrsus and surrounded by cupids. The pictures said much about his character.

Joseph-François was now not only retired, he was a widower: his wife had died, prematurely, in 1814. Five years after the death of Rosalie Baudelaire, he found a new wife in the ward of his friend Pierre Pérignon. She had all the domestic virtues. She had no fortune, but she was intelligent, and she was young. He had known Caroline Archenbaut Defayis since she was a child.

*

There is a certain mystery about her origins. The name Archenbaut (or Archimbaut) remains unexplained.[14] However, she had been born in St Pancras, in London, on 27 September 1793, the daughter of two French émigrés. Her father, Charles Defayis, was probably enough of an aristocrat to have needed to escape the Terror. Her mother, the former Louise-Julie Foyot, was the daughter of an advocate, and came from a bourgeois family in Champagne. She had fled to England with Defayis in 1792. Their child was baptised in an Anglican church, St Pancras Parish Church, on the first day of 1794.[15] Since 1791 the Act of Tolerance had given Catholics freedom to worship. St Pancras Church was open to those of the Catholic faith, and Caroline was no doubt baptised by a Catholic priest, perhaps another French émigré.

Little more is known of Charles Defayis, though he is said to have been a soldier, and to have died in the Quiberon affair in the summer of 1795.[16] The very spelling of his name appears to be uncertain – Defayis, Dufays, Dufaÿs, Du Fays, de Fayis – but Jacques Crépet noted that the name was similar to that of several noble English and Norman families which dated back to the time of the Conquest;[17] Crépet wondered if it was here that one should seek the explanation of Baudelaire's reference to 'my ancestors, idiots or maniacs, in solemn apartments, all of them the victims of terrible passions.'[18] Such ancestors may have been the creation of Baudelaire's imagination, part of his attempt to create his legend; they have not yet been identified. Nonetheless, François Porché traced all the anguish of Baudelaire to 'pathological antecedents of congenital origin.'[19]

After 1794 the name of Charles Defayis does not appear on any documents. Julie Defayis could not have survived as an *émigrée*, alone, without regular assistance from the charity committees. These had been set up to help the refugees from France. Every month in 1794 and 1795, she was given £2.13s. 6d. to maintain herself and her child. From 1 January 1796 she was given an additional £1 a month for an English maid; her own ill health made this essential.

For seven years after her daughter's birth, Julie Defayis lingered on in exile. In October 1800, Napoleon signed a decree allowing many *émigrés* to return to France. In mid November, she and her daughter arrived in Paris. A few days later, on 23 November, in a hotel room in the rue de Richelieu, she died. She was thirty-two.[20]

It was due, perhaps, to her ancestry and her unsettled childhood that Caroline Defayis always suffered from poor health, and from a nervous, melancholy disposition. She was hypersensitive, and given to emotional outbursts. She also affirmed her lineage by her natural distinction. Théodore de Banville later suggested that Baudelaire inherited his anachronistic good manners from his mother, 'who was infinitely distinguished and had an exquisite good nature.'[21] She was, he assured Paul Bourget at the end of the century, 'a great lady with perfect manners and a sensitive mind.'[22]

Now, in 1800, she was taken in by a family friend, Pierre Pérignon: the old friend and colleague of Joseph-François Baudelaire. Pérignon could well afford such charity. He had become a celebrated advocate. He had a town house in Paris, 8, rue Neuve-Saint-Augustin, and a country house at Auteuil. Thanks to his professional triumphs, and to the barony which was created for him, he led a magnificent life. Yet he already had four daughters, and his wife was expecting a fifth child; it is hard to explain why he took charge of an orphan who was seven years old. It has been suggested that he was paying a debt of gratitude to her grandfather, Didier-François Foyot, the advocate, who had helped him early in his career; perhaps he felt a deep attachment to the memory of Julie Defayis. Whatever the reason for his decision, Caroline was unusually fortunate in being adopted by the family.

In time she was sent to a boarding-school for young ladies in the Marais; it had been founded by two Irish nuns, the elder of whom, Élisabeth de Mauclerc, was the daughter of Michel Mauclerc, an Irish officer in the French service. Before the Revolution of 1789, she had been an abbess. The younger nun, Marie de Ryan, was her niece, and she had been a canoness. Élisabeth de Mauclerc was on excellent terms with the Pérignons.

Caroline seems to have had a good education, and consolidated her knowledge of English. On her holidays, she returned to the rue Neuve-Saint-Augustin, or to Auteuil; the evenings were spent in needle-work and reading when there was not some splendid dinner or reception. Among the most cherished guests were Joseph-François Baudelaire and his wife. They were both ailing. 'What a sad couple!' wrote Apollonie, one of the Pérignon daughters. 'Poor M. Baudelaire, especially, is very ill.'[23]

It was Mme Baudelaire who died on 22 December 1814; her funeral was held next day at Saint-Sulpice.

Caroline had now become a teacher at the boarding-school in the Marais. She still spent her free time with the Pérignons. The family were kind to her, but she was constantly aware of her own inferior status, and she must have made many painful comparisons. It was clear that only marriage could save her from perpetual dependence. In 1819, she was twenty-five: the fateful age when a French woman was either married or condemned to spinsterhood. She had no fortune of her own, and she could not afford to be too difficult in her choice.

Joseph-François Baudelaire had retired from his official duties, and his health remained indifferent. She was socially superior to him, and she was young enough to be his daughter. To her he was a fatherly figure. The marriage was, at least for her, a *mariage de raison*, but no doubt the Pérignons advised it. On 9 September 1819, she married him at the *mairie* of the eleventh arrondissement. There could be no second marriage in church for a former priest.

The newly married couple settled at 13, rue Hautefeuille. Thanks to the inventory made after Joseph-François' death, we may reconstruct the apartment. From the courtyard the visitor entered the hall, which led into the kitchen and the dining-room. In the dining-room was a faience stove. In the centre of the room stood two round walnut tables and eight straw-bottomed chairs. A dozen gouaches hung on the walls, and a plaster Venus, two busts and six other plaster figures, all on pedestals, recalled that Joseph-François painted after the antique.[24]

The salon was as big as the dining-room, and it contained a billiard table. There were also ten cherrywood chairs, upholstered in black leather, and a small piano. The back wall was hidden by a tall, eight-panelled screen; on either side stood a statue on a pedestal: Apollo on the left, Venus on the right. The remaining walls were almost invisible for gouaches by Joseph-François and his first wife. There were two busts, a statuette of Cleopatra, and one of a hermaphrodite, the latter under a glass bell on the mantelpiece.

The salon led into Alphonse's room, where the walls were covered with engravings and gouaches. There followed a bedroom soon to be used by another child. It contained a small cherrywood bed, a cherrywood table with a white marble top, and a small rosewood chiffonier. Mme Baudelaire's room was furnished with Louis XVI and Restoration pieces, and the mahogany bed and chairs were covered with yellow flowered velvet. A jug and basin in opaline glass, and two Japanese porcelain vases, recalled the occupant's taste for trinkets and especially for antique china. The next-door room was both her husband's bedroom and his library. In the painted wooden bookcase were the *Encyclopédie* of 1772, the works of the Swiss philosopher Lavater, an album of engravings by Piranesi, the works of Voltaire, Crébillon (no doubt Crébillon the elder, the dramatist), and those of Rabelais.

The milieu into which she entered was not one in which the new Mme Baudelaire felt at home. It was elderly, and she was young. Artists came to the rue Hautefeuille, but she took no interest in the arts. Their sensuality offended her. She had not only spent years in the convent in the Marais; like many people who have suffered, she had also taken refuge in religion. As for her husband, the former abbé, he chose to live like an epicurean of the eighteenth century. Age and tastes and attitudes to life: everything appeared to divide them.

On 9 April 1821, at three o'clock in the afternoon, Caroline gave birth to a son. Two days later, Joseph-François took the newborn child to the *mairie* of the eleventh arrondissement. In the presence of the deputy mayor, he recorded the birth, acknowledged his paternity, and announced that he intended to call his son Charles-Pierre.[25] It was a happy but somewhat sober occasion. Joseph-François was sixty-one. His witnesses were Jean Naigeon, now Keeper of the Musée royal du Luxembourg, who was sixty-two, and Claude Ramey, now a member of the Institut de France, aged sixty-five. Baudelaire's birth was attested by the artistic Establishment. It was also evident, even now, that his childhood was to bring its complications.

On 7 June, he was baptised by the abbé Couturier at Saint-Sulpice. His godparents were Pierre Pérignon and his wife.[26]

2

Mon berceau s'adossait à la bibliothèque,
Babel sombre, où roman, science, fabliau,
Tout, la cendre latine et la poussière grecque,
Se mêlaient. J'étais haut comme un in-folio . . .[1]

This poem, 'La Voix', is one of the few places in which Baudelaire recalls his infancy. In his early childhood, he lived among books and pictures, and he was to attest their importance to him. 'Glorify the cult of pictures,' so he was to write, 'my great, unique and primitive passion.'[2] He was, one day, to be parted, brusquely, from this pictorial world which stirred his imagination and aroused his tastes; it was always to be linked to the memory of domestic happiness.

One must largely infer the details of Baudelaire's childhood from scattered comments in letters and in his *Journaux intimes*. He later recorded a lasting affection, since childhood days, for all performing arts.[3] No doubt his mother indulged his affection.

Yesterday I was taken to a theatre [so a child announced in the *Petits Poèmes en prose*]. In great melancholy palaces, behind which you can see the sky and sea, there are men and women, also grave and sad, but much more beautiful, much better dressed than the ones we see every day, and they speak in singing voices. They threaten one another, plead, become distressed, and they often rest their hand on a dagger stuck into their belt. Oh, it's wonderful! . . . It frightens you, you want to cry, and yet you are happy . . . And the strangest thing is that it makes you want to be dressed like that, to say and do the same things, and to speak that way . . .[4]

Perhaps, too, on some public holiday, Mme Baudelaire took her young son to a fair. In his prose poems, which reflect so much of his life, Baudelaire was to record his love of fairgrounds, where strong men strutted in their tights, and dancers leapt and capered in the lantern-light, which filled their skirts with stars.[5]

He wanted to go on stage himself: 'I sometimes wanted to be a Pope, but a martial Pope, and sometimes to be an actor.'[6] He found delight in imitating both. Like all children, he created company in his imagination. 'From my childhood, tendency towards the mystical. My conversations with God.'[7] He seems to have felt the loneliness of an only child, and to have felt, even then, that he stood apart: 'A sense of *solitude* from my childhood. In spite of my family – and among friends, especially – a sense of an eternally solitary destiny.'[8] Yet, despite this sense of isolation, this brooding melancholy, he had a fervent love of life and pleasure. He seems to have inherited his mother's nervous disposition, her fluctuating moods. As a small child, so he maintained, he already 'felt two contradictory feelings in his heart, the horror of life and the ecstasy of life.'[9] There were, it seems, no children's books in the rue Hautefeuille to create the essential childhood world. It was in his father's library that, on his own admission, he first became aware of the conflict between reality and dreams.

> Deux voix me parlaient. L'une, insidieuse et ferme,
> Disait: 'La Terre est un gâteau plein de douceur;
> Je puis (et ton plaisir serait alors sans terme!)
> Te faire un appétit d'une égale grosseur.'
> Et l'autre: 'Viens! oh! viens voyager dans les rêves,
> Au-delà du possible, au-delà du connu!'
> Et celle-là chantait comme le vent des grèves,
> Fantôme vagissant, on ne sait d'où venu,
> Qui caresse l'oreille et cependant l'effraie.
> Je te répondis: 'Oui, douce voix!' C'est d'alors
> Que date ce qu'on peut, hélas! nommer ma plaie
> Et ma fatalité . . .'[10]

Ernest Prarond, who was close to him in the early 1840s, recalled how, on their wanderings through Paris, he had learned about the poet's childhood,

... the family setting in which he grew up, from the little that he said about them. His father was, in his recollections, an old man who was already very old, with long white hair ... He was very learned, and he had already undertaken to educate his son, by walking with him, hand in hand, through the Jardin du Luxembourg. He was very choleric, and he threatened with his stick those dogs which showed a lack of respect for him. Baudelaire spoke about his father like a devoted son.[11]

The portrait of Joseph-François, by Jean-Baptiste Regnault, was to remain with Baudelaire for most of his nomadic life. He was one day to hang in his room his father's painting of the bacchante and the counterpart which showed the temptation of St Anthony. The spiritual legacy of Joseph-François was to be evident. He had taught his son about art, as they admired the prints and pastels in the rue Haute-feuille, the statues in the Jardin du Luxembourg. He had no doubt taught him history, as one who had lived it. He had roused his interest in music: there was a piano in the rue Hautefeuille, and there were a number of musical scores, including works by Gluck and Piccini.[12] With the help of a primer which he had illustrated himself, Joseph-François had taught his son the rudiments of Latin. 'If *le père Baudelaire* had seen his son grow up,' Caroline maintained in later years, 'he would certainly not have opposed his vocation as a man of letters, for he himself was passionately interested in literature, and he had such pure taste! ... He would have been very proud to see him embark on this career, in spite of all the disappointments and tortures that it brings.'[13] Joseph-François had himself written numerous pieces of verse – whether in French or in Latin we do not know. It was from him that Baudelaire inherited his love of literature and art, his patrician manners, his style and sensuality; father and son had a natural affinity which went beyond ties of blood. It was an irreplaceable relationship.

Since Joseph-François still remained in indifferent health, and Charles was very young, the Baudelaires did not often leave the rue Hautefeuille. However, in the summer of 1823, they spent their holidays in the north of France, and no doubt they visited their relations in the Marne, especially Mme Foyot, in Sézanne. Caroline's grandmother was now seventy-two, and perhaps she was already ill. She was to die the following summer, and to make Caroline her residuary legatee.[14]

In Paris, Joseph-François continued to see his local friends. In 1823–4, he still had his complimentary tickets to the Odéon. The theatre had come under the jurisdiction of the palais du Luxembourg, and, after the fire of 1807, he had been involved in rebuilding it. For several years he had also been a member of the reading committee.[15]

Joseph-François had many pleasures; above all, he had his domestic satisfactions: his second wife and second son, and his happy relationship with his elder son, who still lived at the rue Hautefeuille. Alphonse had studied law; and, in 1824, he dedicated his thesis for his master's degree

À mon Père
Faible témoignage
d'Amour et de Reconnaissance.[16]

On 19 January 1825, he was appointed an advocate at the Cour royale de Paris.[17]

Joseph-François was not to see him finish his term of probation. On 10 February 1827, at the age of sixty-eight, he died, so his widow was to write, 'of a horrible convulsion caused by the pain of an ulcer in the bladder. The doctors weren't aware of it, and it burst. They were treating him for other things, gout and gravel.'[18]

On 12 February, his death was recorded at the *mairie* of the eleventh arrondissement. There was no service at Saint-Sulpice, which was his parish church, and, that same day, with curious haste, he was buried at the cimetière Montparnasse.[19] He was buried in a temporary grave, and the concession lasted for five years. In February 1832, when there was a question of a permanent grave, Caroline was to take no action; and, unless Alphonse assumed responsibility, the remains of Joseph-François would have been thrown into a common grave, or into one of the catacombs in the cemetery. Baudelaire cannot have been unaware of the fact. He was well aware of the indignity of the *fosse aux pauvres*.[20]

At the end of her life, Caroline recalled 'M. Baudelaire, of whom I have kept a very sweet memory.'[21] Writing to Alphonse Baudelaire after her second husband had died, she insisted: 'Your father, too, my dear Alphonse, had been *very good, very excellent* to me . . . The filial love, so to speak, which I felt for him has left ineffaceable traces in my heart, and he was constantly the subject of our conversations. The General liked to hear me boast about his character and his great qualities.'[22]

Her second husband had had no reason to feel jealousy. Mme Aupick, so Malassis was one day to observe, 'only spoke about her first husband with complete indifference. It was the General who was her *man*.'[23] It is the most eloquent comment on her marriage to Joseph-François that she did not give him a permanent tomb. No one knows his final resting-place.

3

Immediately after the funeral, a family council assembled to discuss the future of his younger son. Next day the boy's trustees held their first meeting. Among them were Félix de Choiseul-Praslin, the grateful pupil of Joseph-François, and, inevitably, Claude Ramey and Jean Naigeon.

On 9 April, Baudelaire was six. He and his mother spent the summer in a little house – now, alas, demolished – 3, rue de Seine, at Neuilly, near the Bois de Boulogne. In 1827, long before the advent of Baron Haussmann, the Bois de Boulogne was a forest, and Neuilly was a somnolent village. Baudelaire was always to recall those idyllic days.

> Je n'ai pas oublié, voisine de la ville,
> Notre blanche maison, petite mais tranquille;
> Sa Pomone de plâtre et sa vieille Vénus
> Dans un bosquet chétif cachant leurs membres nus,
> Et le soleil, le soir, ruisselant et superbe,
> Qui, derrière la vitre où se brisait sa gerbe,
> Semblait, grand œil ouvert dans le ciel curieux,
> Contempler nos dîners longs et silencieux,
> Répandant largement ses beaux reflets de cierge
> Sur la nappe frugale et les rideaux de serge.[1]

For Baudelaire, said Charles du Bos, 'nothing is profound except the past. It is this alone which communicates, gives the third dimension to everything.'[2] 'For this man, martyrised by time,' wrote Gabriel Bounoure, 'the past is not a lifeless expanse, the past keeps the power of what has been lived.'[3] Yet, as Jean Prévost observed, this poem on Baudelaire's childhood is deceptive in its simplicity. The evocation of Neuilly is strangely reticent. The people to whom Baudelaire refers as *nous* do not appear; the melancholy statues in the straggling grove, the long and silent dinners cast a gloom over the poem, and the unease is intensified by the inquisitive eye of the setting sun. The recollection is clear, and yet the poem is enigmatic. We know, however, that it is addressed to the poet's mother; and it is enough to recall other poems like 'Bénédiction' and 'La Lune offensée' to understand that in time Baudelaire would both love and condemn her. His memories are heavy with reproach. This evocation of a shared existence was to be a hidden reproof to his mother who – he came to believe – had abandoned and betrayed him. The power of this evocation lies in the fact that the central figure is missing.[4]

It was now, after his father's death, that Baudelaire established with his mother the profound and complex relationship which was to determine and dominate his life. Caroline had never been in love with her husband; her devotion to her son had been evident from the first. Now she was a widow, and he was all that she possessed. Baudelaire had learned in his infancy that she would always ultimately do what would please him. They already had a relationship which depended not only on instinctive love, but also on emotional blackmail. They knew how to please and hurt one another deeply, how to cajole and how to compel. Their love was exclusive, and it was jealous. Years later, Baudelaire was to recall his mother's resentment of his old nurse, Mariette, who had earned his lifelong affection.

> La servante au grand cœur dont vous étiez jalouse,
> Et qui dort son sommeil sous une humble pelouse,
> Nous devrions pourtant lui porter quelques fleurs.
> Les morts, les pauvres morts, ont de grandes douleurs,
> Et quand Octobre souffle, émondeur des vieux arbres,
> Son vent mélancolique à l'entour de leurs marbres,
> Certe, ils doivent trouver les vivants bien ingrats,
> À dormir, comme ils font, chaudement dans leurs draps,
> Tandis que, dévorés de noires songeries,
> Sans compagnon de lit, sans bonnes causeries,
> Vieux squelettes gelés travaillés par le ver,
> Ils sentent s'égoutter les neiges de l'hiver
> Et le siècle couler, sans qu'amis ni famille
> Remplacent les lambeaux qui pendent à leur grille.
>
> Lorsque la bûche siffle et chante, si le soir,
> Calme, dans le fauteuil je la voyais s'asseoir,
> Si, par une nuit bleue et froide de décembre,
> Je la trouvais tapie en un coin de ma chambre,
> Grave, et venant du fond de son lit éternel
> Couver l'enfant grandi de son œil maternel,
> Que pourrais-je répondre à cette âme pieuse,
> Voyant tomber des pleurs de sa paupière creuse?[5]

According to Prarond, this poem was written before 1844;[6] but Baudelaire's devotion to Mariette was to last all his life. In his *Journaux intimes* he was to write: 'I commend to you the souls of my father and of Mariette. Give me the strength to do my duty immediately every day and so become a hero and a Saint.'[7] The poem about Mariette begins, again, with a reproach to his mother; and, in the antepenultimate line, the reproach is repeated. Baudelaire implies that Mariette had been his true mother, more concerned and more attentive than his natural mother. She alone would have the right to return and to watch over him.

Baudelaire was profoundly affectionate by nature; and if, in his early childhood, his mother was sometimes jealous of Mariette, he himself

demanded and delighted in his mother's single-minded devotion. He
was also a sensuous child, and he revelled in her world of silk and
satin, furs and fine linen. 'The precocious liking for women. I confused
the smell of fur with the smell of woman. I remember ... In fact,
I loved my mother for her elegance. I was a precocious dandy.'[8]
Baudelaire was always to have an acute sense of smell, and a fragrance
would conjure up a world in his imagination. Yet one wonders, still,
what else he had remembered, what he had hesitated to record.

'I loved you passionately in my childhood,' so he told his mother,
later;[9] and again:

> There was in my childhood a period of passionate love for you; listen,
> and read without fear. I have never told you so much about it. I
> remember a drive in a cab; you were leaving a nursing-home where you
> had been staying, and, to prove to me that you had been thinking of
> your son, you showed me some pen drawings which you had done for
> me. Do you think I have a terrible memory? Later, the place Saint-
> André-des-Arts and Neuilly. Long walks, constant affection. I remember
> the quais, which were so melancholy at night. Oh, that was the good
> time of maternal affection for me. Forgive me for calling it *a good time*,
> for it was a bad one for you. But I was still living in you; you were
> entirely mine. You were both an idol and a friend. Perhaps you will be
> surprised that I can talk with passion about a time which is so distant.
> I'm surprised at it myself.[10]

In later years, he was not only surprised by the passion of his
recollections; he also felt acute, implicit guilt. In *Le Tombeau de
Baudelaire*, Pierre-Jean Jouve observed that

> Baudelaire's great drama ... is performed with his mother. It is the
> drama that we cannot touch, absolutely secret, rooted far away in early
> childhood, and reactivated in a surprising way by the mother's remar-
> riage after the father's death. Baudelaire and Mme Aupick are a couple,
> and the life of this terrible couple witnessed every kind of affection and
> love, weariness and renewal ... Certain letters reveal a formidable
> emotional state ...[11]

Baudelaire was dominated by his relationship with his mother. In
L'Échec de Baudelaire, Dr René Laforgue was to examine his behaviour
in the light of this relationship. Avoiding life, he wrote, often means
remaining a child; nostalgia for the paradise lost is only nostalgia for
a childhood lost.[12] 'In order to keep the infantile situation, Baudelaire
made woman into a mother, in whose presence man was just a child.'[13]
This relationship, added Laforgue, is supremely important if we are to
understand Baudelaire's masochism. 'We shall therefore not be surprised to see Baudelaire's libido dominated, above all, by devices for

self-punishment.'[14] For him, there was to be a malediction in desire, a damnation in the eternal thirst for pleasure. Deep down, Laforgue suggested, Baudelaire was aware that his love of his mother was excessive. 'He remained faithful to that unconscious love, and to it he sacrificed his life, his personal success. And, feeling that he was guilty, he left no stone unturned to make himself chastised, to make it impossible to attain his goal, his ideal . . .'[15]

August and September 1827 had, it seems, been spent at Neuilly. Late in September or early in October he and his mother moved to live with Alphonse Baudelaire at 30, place Saint-André-des-Arts. They later moved to 17, rue du Bac. On 16 October, the contents of the rue Hautefeuille were auctioned. They included 'a hip-bath, copper bath-tub, . . . bolsters, pillows, eiderdowns, feather beds.'[16] One of these was perhaps the cherrywood bed in which Baudelaire had slept. The household effects also included 'a gentleman's wardrobe',[17] for Caroline chose to sell Joseph-François' clothes. She had little time for remembrance. In a second sale that day, the auctioneer sold 'various drawings, loose or framed, gouaches, prints and engravings, . . . several pictures and pastels, some plaster statues, etc, etc, some books, on various subjects.'[18]

The sale brought in 1,505 francs and 60 centimes; on 26 October, the auctioneer took his commission, and paid 'Dame Caroline Dufays, the widow of Monsieur Joseph-François Baudelaire, 1,279 francs and 46 centimes.'[19] Caroline had attended the sale, the destruction of a world, the deletion of her life with Joseph-François. As for her son, he had not merely left the rue Hautefeuille, the idyllic villa at Neuilly, he had left behind a world of tranquillity; for him it was rarely to be found again.

Mme Veuve Baudelaire did not face the prospect of lasting widowhood with equanimity. No doubt she felt that her future was bleak. She was thirty-four; and, if she was to marry again, it would be sensible to marry soon. Prudence and commonsense demanded it; yet, as Fernand Caussy wrote in *La Jeunesse de Baudelaire*, 'her haste reveals to us that she considered her son's feelings to be negligible.'[20]

She might perhaps have made another *mariage de raison* if the unexpected had not occurred. Within a year of her husband's death, she had fallen in love. After years of misery and deprivation, after years of charity and prosaic domesticity, her romantic dreams could now be fulfilled. In this one instance in her life, her sense of the proprieties, her nervousness, her caution, her constant piety were set aside. Early in March 1828, thirteen months after her husband's death,

and a month before her son's seventh birthday, Mme Veuve Baudelaire became pregnant.

4

The origins of Jacques Aupick remain somewhat mysterious. His birth
certificate has not been found; but, if we are to believe an *acte de
notoriété* of 1808, which served him in its stead, he was the presumed
son of Jacques-Joseph Aupick, a captain in the Berwick-Irish Regiment, and of Amélie (or Amelia) Talbot. Pichois maintains that
Jacques-Joseph was an Irish officer in the French service.[1] Georges de
Nouvion records that Amélie was English, and that she was said to
descend 'from the famous general of the Hundred Years War.'[2]

John Talbot, first Earl of Shrewsbury, was one of the most celebrated soldiers of his time, and his courage earned him the name of the
English Achilles.[3] The *Dictionary of National Biography* observes that he
was 'a sort of Hotspur, owing more to dash and daring than to any
true military genius';[4] nonetheless it devotes five pages to his career.
He is thought to have been born in 1388. As Lieutenant of Ireland, he
submitted that country to the rule of Henry V; he also proved himself
to be a formidable opponent of the French. He was killed in a skirmish
at Castellan in 1453, but he left a numerous family. By his first wife,
the daughter of Lord Furnivall, he had had three sons and at least one
daughter; by his second marriage, to the daughter of the Earl of War-
wick, he had had three sons and two daughters. An Italian biographer,
writing of a nineteenth-century Talbot who became the Princess
Borghese, declared that 'few families, in their genealogies, record such
noble and such illustrious names.'[5] If Amélie Talbot did indeed
descend from the Shrewsburys, she had reason to be proud of her
lineage.

Yet her son himself claimed to be 'of Irish origin, through his father
and his mother.'[6] If he was in fact descended from an Irish general,
this was perhaps Richard Talbot, Earl and titular Duke of Tyrconnell.
The *Dictionary of Irish Biography* records that Richard Talbot was born
at Malahide, County Dublin, in 1630. He was the son of Sir William
Talbot, a politician, and he was the brother of Peter Talbot, sometime
Archbishop of Dublin. 'Fighting Dick' fought against Cromwell, fled
to the Continent, and returned to Ireland at the Restoration. On the
accession of James II in 1685 he was given command of the army in

Ireland; two years later he was made Viceroy, and in 1688 he was created a duke. He commanded a regiment of horse at the Battle of the Boyne, and followed the King to France after his defeat. In 1691 he returned to Ireland as Lord Lieutenant, with funds and a promise of French help. He died that year of apoplexy while on active service.[7]

His military exploits and his sympathy for France would no doubt have been recalled by Amélie Talbot, if he was in fact her ancestor; so would his devotion to the Jacobite cause. He had owed all his distinction to King James. According to her son's service records, he had been born in Gravelines on 28 February 1789, and baptised James, a name which was later Frenchified as Jémis, then as Jacques.

If the origins of Aupick remain a matter for speculation, nothing is less certain than the date and place of his birth. The *acte de notoriété* is cautiously worded: 'Since the aforesaid husband and wife died without leaving any information about the place or date of birth of the said child, everything leads one to believe that he was born in some little rural commune, when the aforesaid regiment was passing through.' Since the same document also says that Jémis Aupick 'came to Gravelines in his infancy', towards the middle of 1790, when the Berwick-Irish Regiment was stationed there, the first essentials of Aupick's service records are factitious.[8]

As for his parents, Aupick hardly knew them. In September 1793, his father, Captain Aupick, was killed, or mortally wounded, at Hondschoote. The widowed Mme Aupick was taken into the house of Louis Baudard, a justice of the peace at Gravelines. Soon afterwards she died, and Baudard became virtually a father to her son. Aupick was 'the child of my soul,' so he was to write, 'and the soul of my late wife.'[9] The comment was made in his will, in 1821, in which he left Aupick his house and land, his library and some of his furniture. Aupick chose to share them with Baudard's daughter.[10] He was always to keep the most grateful memory of him.

Aupick was blessed not only with good fortune, but with success, and this constant success was to be evident from the moment he entered the Prytanée national in December 1802. The Prytaneum had been founded two years earlier, at the suggestion of Lucien Bonaparte, Napoleon's brother, to educate the sons of soldiers who had been killed in action or of functionaries who had died in the exercise of their duties. Aupick was trained, from his early youth, in the Napoleonic tradition. At the prizegiving in 1807, he played the title-role in a Napoleonic drama, *Fortunas, ou le Nouveau d'Assas*.

In June 1808, he was sent to Saint-Cyr. On 24 March 1809, he was commissioned as a second lieutenant, and he joined the 105th regiment of the line. The imperial campaigns led him to Austria, Spain and

Saxony. In 1814, he was a captain. During the first Restoration, he was sent to Bourges where, in March 1815, he was decorated by the Duc d'Angoulême. This did not prevent him from rallying to Napoleon during the Hundred Days. Two days before Waterloo, he fought in the Battle of Fleurus, where a bullet lodged in his left femur. It caused the bone to decay, and, for the rest of his life, his leg was to give him intermittent pain. Aupick was looked after devotedly by his adopted father; he was also discharged and put on half-pay for two years.

A few weeks after Waterloo, he asked, despite his wound, to resume his service, this time in the cause of Louis XVIII, and declared that 'among his devoted subjects none will be more faithful, none will deem it a greater honour to live and to die for His Majesty.'[11] However strong his recantation, it had no immediate effect. It was not until 5 August 1817 that Aupick returned to army life, as captain adjutant-major in the third battalion of the Légion du Gers. On 7 April 1818, he asked for permission to live in Paris, where he was called by 'very urgent family matters which will not soon be settled.'[12] No doubt he also wanted to be nearer the political sun. On 3 October he was appointed provisional aide-de-camp to General Durrieu. On 12 December he was admitted into the Corps d'État-Major. He was successively aide-de-camp to Generals Barbanègre, Fririon and Meynadier, under whose orders he served in Spain.

Aupick was always to cultivate authority, and he was always to find a protector. He now earned the approval of the Prince de Hohenlohe, one of those foreign soldiers who considered it an honour to serve under the French colours. A letter from Lieutenant-General the Comte de Meynadier to the Duc d'Angoulême recorded how Hohen-lohe's aide-de-camp had been killed in the Spanish campaign, and Hohenlohe had asked Meynadier to give him his own. Hohenlohe treated Aupick like a son; he later wrote an official report, in which he gave fulsome praise to his aide-de-camp: '*Morals, conduct and principles*. An exemplary model, very devoted, disinterested, noble in his beha-viour, a good husband . . .'[13]

When the report was written, on 24 March 1829, Major Aupick had been married for four months.

It is not known when or how he had met Mme Veuve Baudelaire; but since the end of 1823 he had been living in the rue de l'Abbaye, near the rue Hautefeuille. She could have met him at a neighbour's house; it is also possible that she had kept some Irish friends since her convent days. In *La Jeunesse de Baudelaire*, Fernand Caussy dismissed Jacques Aupick as 'an Irish coxcomb, . . . a corseted, bedizened warrior, who talked unceasingly about his sword, and honour.'[14] Mme Veuve

Baudelaire saw him differently. He was only four years older than herself, and he was still unmarried. He had the self-assurance gained from years of discipline and command. He had the glamour of his uniform. He had robust good looks; and, unlike Joseph-François Baudelaire, he had the élan and confidence of a man in his prime. He was patently a soldier with a future.

It would not be surprising to learn that Mme Veuve Baudelaire determined to become Mme Aupick. Indeed, in *La Famille de Charles Baudelaire*, Georges de Nouvion speaks of her 'decision' to marry Aupick.[15] She may well have lived with him from 1827. Just before he died, in 1857, he spoke of the thirty years they had spent together; she, too, was to speak of thirty years.[16] It was, apparently, early in March 1828 that she conceived his child. On 17 October, Aupick asked the Minister of War for permission to marry. This request was supported by the Prince de Hohenlohe, who made it clear that his aide-de-camp 'wanted to settle this affair immediately.'[17]

The request was urgent, and it was flurried. Aupick mis-spelt the name of his future wife. The date suggests that 'Madᵉ Vᵛᵉ Bodelaire' had been more eager for marriage than he was. It is true that, in law, her widowhood had lasted for a year and six weeks; during that time, she could not have contracted a second marriage. She had, however, determined to ensure it. Her official mourning for Joseph-François had not prevented her from committing herself completely to Aupick; and, when it ended, she was already bearing his child. It is strange that he continued to wait, for more than five months, before he asked for permission to marry her. The fact that he waited until now, when his child was almost due, implies a certain reluctance to commit himself: a wish, perhaps, not to be impeded in his career. If Mme Baudelaire had cast propriety aside, if she had, for once, behaved out of character, Aupick showed, in this one instance, a curious disregard for honour, a remarkable lack of concern for a woman whom he loved. It is possible that pressure was put upon him.

However that may be, on 20 October he was granted permission to marry. On the 31st, there was a second meeting of Baudelaire's trustees, this time including his brother, Alphonse. They noted the projected marriage between Jacques Aupick and Mme Veuve Baudelaire, and they appointed Aupick co-guardian, with her, of the young Charles. Such was the urgency of the marriage that the banns were published only once, by a special dispensation of the Archbishop of Paris.[18] On 8 November, at nine o'clock in the morning, at the mairie of the tenth arrondissement, Commandant Aupick, chevalier de l'ordre militaire et royal de Saint-Louis, officier de l'ordre royal de la Légion-d'honneur, 'aged about 39', married Mme Veuve Baudelaire, then thirty-five years old. Most of the necessary documents had been produced; but the groom could not furnish his birth certificate, and the bride declared on oath that she had been unable to find her parents' death certificates. There was also a marriage service that day at Saint-Thomas d'Aquin.[19]

Three weeks later, on 2 December, in a hamlet in the canton of Creil, Mme Aupick gave birth to a stillborn daughter.

One wonders if this was, perhaps, the time when she left a nursing-home in a cab, with Baudelaire, and showed him some drawings she had done for him. She had felt a need to prove that he was not forgotten. He was not forgotten, but he was irremediably damaged. Illegal pregnancy and stillbirth would have been hard to explain to a child of seven, a child who had been conventionally brought up; but Baudelaire was aware of events. They had inspired him with revulsion for the sexual act, for the animality of love, with contempt for the generality of women. In later life he was to dream of his mother as the madam in a brothel. Not only had Mme Baudelaire become Mme Aupick, she had prostituted herself in her widowhood; not only had she betrayed her first husband, she had betrayed her son, and she had replaced him with a stillborn child. He had lost his mother, his childhood, and a great part of himself.

This sense of betrayal was to express itself in different ways over the years. In Baudelaire's childhood and youth, it was to be reflected in his wild behaviour, his refusal or inability to work; in later years it was also to be reflected in his poetry.[20] When he recalled the little house where they had stayed at Neuilly, he was to recall the old statue of Venus, hiding her nudity behind the trees. When, in 'Lesbos', he spoke of 'Sapho qui mourut le jour de son blasphème,' he was remembering his mother's love-affair, her disappearance as a mother at the moment of her treachery. His correspondence, like his poems, reflects his desperate sense of betrayal. His letters were to reveal the violence of a love which had been disappointed but in no way diminished.[21] His idealization of his mother was to become the basis of his adult sexuality; his disappointment was to make all adult love impossible for him.

Baudelaire had always felt particularly close to his mother. Since his childhood, he had had a sense of isolation and, since his father's death, only his mother had stood between him and a hostile world. He had loved her with passion. She had, as he said, been both his idol and his companion. He was to love her deeply till the end of his days; but now he felt that she had abandoned him. Never again was Baudelaire to trust in a woman, never could he wholly commit himself. Féli Gautier wrote that he never forgave his mother for betraying his father's memory.[22] More importantly, he felt betrayed himself. Nadar wrote briefly in his notes: 'The 2nd marriage – the key.'[23] There was one event which changed the whole of Baudelaire's existence, one event which caused him untold anger, bitterness and grief. This emotional trauma was his mother's second marriage. 'When you have a son [like me],' he was to say, 'you do not re-marry.'[24]

His mother's second marriage was to be a marriage of love. Mme Aupick and her husband were to remain devoted until his death, twenty nine years later. She herself was to speak of 'the golden life which the General brought me, with a very ardent attachment which never failed during the thirty years we spent together.'[25] She cannot be blamed for ensuring her own happiness, for finding a protector for herself and her young son. It was not a dereliction of her maternal duty. Yet it must be said that she re-married with uncommon haste. Borne away by her passion for Aupick, and by her advancing pregnancy, she seems to have shown no concern for her son's feelings. As Raynaud was to write in *Les Parents de Baudelaire*, the day when the wife believed that she had attained felicity, her calvary as a mother began.[26]

Aupick himself was far from hostile to Baudelaire. He understood the hardship of losing his parents; he had learned, from Baudard, how much an adopted father could do for an adopted son. Indeed, he was anxious to treat Baudelaire as if he were a son of his own. The problem was that Aupick was guided by the military virtues of honour and duty, by piety and patriotism, by a bourgeois belief in regular hard work, in the value of paternal authority. Had Baudelaire chosen to enter a profession, Aupick was prepared to use all his influence to help him; but the single-minded, ambitious officer from Saint-Cyr could not understand the artistic temperament. He could not comprehend a boy who showed small regard for discipline, and an early devotion to literature and painting. Baudelaire was patently the son of Joseph-François. Aupick could never give him what Joseph-François would have given him. Aupick's rigid code of behaviour, his lack of sensibility, were to bring Baudelaire much grief in his childhood. In his early manhood, they were to cause an irreparable breach between them. It is ironic that, for all his goodwill and for all his own distinction, Aupick was finally to be remembered by the hatred of the stepson with whom capricious fortune had endowed him.

PART TWO

*The Stepson of
Jacques Aupick*

1829–1857

5

I hasten to tell you, my dear Alphonse, that I have come back from the country, and here I am, settled in Paris at last [so Mme Aupick wrote to her stepson in January 1829]. If your errands sometimes bring you to the rue du Bac, come and chat to us, come and have some soup *en famille*; your little brother is constantly talking about you, and he will be very happy to see you.

Mr Aupick will give you a warm welcome, and I, my dear Alphonse, await you with impatience, I shall always feel like a mother and a friend to you.[1]

Whether or not Alphonse accepted the invitation, he now had other preoccupations. On 30 April, he married Anne-Félicité Ducessois. She was the daughter of Jean-François Ducessois, a retired chief clerk in the administration of the postal services. She was pretty and Parisian, and she was three months short of seventeen. The Aupicks were delighted with the marriage, and a lifelong friendship was to develop between Mme Aupick and the new Mme Baudelaire.[2]

On 31 May, a few weeks after the wedding, Prince Hohenlohe died, and Aupick found himself on the reserve list. He was not a man to tolerate inactivity. He was always anxious to broaden his mind, and since he spoke English, Spanish and German, he no doubt read widely.[3] He also turned his leisure to commercial account.

In 1823, with the assistance of V.-M. Perrot, he had begun to publish the *Nouvel Atlas du royaume de France*.[4] On 15 October 1824 he had been admitted a member of the Société de Géographie.[5] In 1825 the Society's *Bulletin* had accorded gratifying praise to Aupick and to his colleague:

The authors of the *Nouvel Atlas du Royaume de France*, MM. AUPICK and PERROT, continue their difficult enterprise with a speed which is very rare in such a case. Out of the thirty instalments which will make up their collection, twenty-two have already been published. The complete publication will be finished during the course of next year . . . It deserves a place in university departments.[6]

The last instalment was in fact published in 1827, and that year the collection appeared in a handsome album. It was reviewed in *Le Moniteur universel*,[7] accorded a second honourable mention by the

Académie royale des Sciences,[8] and an honourable mention by the Société de Géographie.[9]

Now, in 1829, in his enforced retirement, Aupick returned to his old interests. In 1830, Carpentier-Méricourt published the *Atlas de la cour royale de Paris, acc. de tableaux historiques et statistiques* by Jacques Aupick and A. Perrot.

Such work could not, it seems, be done while there was a child in the house. Aupick had not only moved into his wife's rooms in the rue du Bac; within a year of his marriage, he had decided that he and his wife must live alone. On 1 October 1829, he had announced to General Durrieu: 'We are all well in our little household, Charles is going to boarding-school, and there are two red eyes.'[10] The school was presumably a local school at which he would be prepared for the Collège royal de Charlemagne. It was a harsh decision to make for a child of eight, but Aupick had no time for his stepson's emotions, and, as he said, he 'was not the man to be disregarded.'[11]

He himself was not to remain in reserve for long. In 1830, France embarked on the conquest of Algiers. On 23 March, he was appointed to the general staff of the second division of the African expedition. On 23 June, the expeditionary force landed at Sidi-Ferruch. In three weeks it achieved complete success, and the foundations of the French North African Empire were laid. On 9 July, the news of the victory at Algiers reached Paris. On 2 October, Aupick was promoted lieutenant-colonel.

He did not return to France until July 1831. Luckily he had not needed to take sides once again in politics, or to assure anyone of his fidelity. In July 1830, while he was in Africa, there had been another revolution in Paris. The Bourbons had finally been deposed, and Louis-Philippe, the Citizen King, had come to the throne. Some destinies are blessed by good fortune. Aupick found a new protector in the new King's eldest son, the Duc d'Orléans.

For sixteen months, while his stepfather had been in Africa, Baudelaire had once again enjoyed his mother's whole attention. Predictably, he had done well at school. In July 1831, when Colonel Aupick returned to Paris, Baudelaire was second in his class for composition. On 3 October, he entered the Collège royal de Charlemagne; he was boarded in the rue Payenne with M. Bourdon, who had a reputation for his successes in the entrance examinations to the École normale supérieure, the École polytechnique, and Saint-Cyr.[12]

Late that month, in Lyons, the *canuts*, or silk-weavers, who were almost starving, were granted a slight increase in their wages. Early in

November, the increase was refused by the silk merchants. There was an insurrection, and the workers took over the city. The riots brought bloodshed; under the command of General Comte Roguet, the army withdrew. On 25 November, Aupick was sent to Lyons as chief of staff – or, as Caussy explained, 'to organise the shooting of the silk-weavers who dared to ask for bread.'[13] On 29 November he found himself at Trévoux, with General Roguet, Marshal Soult and the Duc d'Orléans. On 1 December, Government troops occupied the vicinity of Lyons, and on 3 December the Duke made his entrance into the city. There was no resistance. Four days later, Aupick was appointed chief of staff of the seventh military division.

Since it was clear that he would be in Lyons for some time, he summoned his wife and stepson to join him. Baudelaire was taken, after a single term, from the Collège royal de Charlemagne. On 9 January 1832, in the first of his letters to survive, he wrote to Alphonse: 'Since you told me you wanted to come and see us before we left, I have asked mama which day we should be leaving; she doesn't really know, but she said that it might be Friday; in any case, we shall be leaving sooner rather than later, so I think you could come on Tuesday or Wednesday...'[14] Alphonse came to bid farewell; and, shortly afterwards, Mme Aupick and Baudelaire set off for Lyons.[15] They arrived there on 16 or 17 January.

An anonymous guide to Lyons, published in 1844, sang the praises of 'the metropolis of the South of France'[16]: of this city 'with narrow, winding streets, with tall, dark houses, but with verdant hills, justly proud of its peerless situation.'[17] Even this guide suggested that Lyons was forbidding; and an account by a Monsieur Jal, himself a Lyonnais, made this all too plain:

> You stifle and suffocate there [he wrote in 1835]. You are crushed by the dark, tall, ugly houses, seven storeys high, as they hide the sky and the daylight from you. The mud never dries in the streets, where you cannot walk without bruising your feet on sharp paving-stones dredged from the bed of the Rhône. Everything there is dirty, especially the hotels and houses; no comfort at all; the shops are barely lit... No taste in the buildings; fortresses and strongholds for houses; a dreadful sadness everywhere; frequent fogs. One constant thought dominates all the rest: earning money, doing business...[18]

It was an oppressive setting for a young boy from Paris.

It has been said that, with Baudelaire, the infant stage lasted too long, and that it was too roughly destroyed. He had suffered from his father's

death, and from his mother's precipitate second marriage; he had no
doubt suffered from the departure of Mariette. He had been sent to
boarding-school, and to a *pension*. He had been taken away from Paris,
and from school. Now, in Lyons, at the age of ten, he was once again
eliminated from the household. Aupick and his wife had a temporary
apartment near the barracks, at 45, place Henri-IV (the present place
Carnot), but there was no question of his living with them. The
colonel's war-wound made him irritable, and he could not tolerate
noise; he did not intend to have a child in the house. As usual, Mme
Aupick made no effective protest. 'How many rebellious characters',
Baudelaire was one day to write, 'have owed their existence to a cruel
and exacting soldier of the Empire!'[19] Aupick showed a ruthless
unconcern, a dangerous indifference to his needs.

Late in January, within a few days of his arrival in Lyons, Baudelaire
was duly sent to the nearby pension Delorme. The Delormes, a young
couple with two small children, lived in a second-floor apartment on
the corner of the rue Sala and the rue de Boissac. The boys who
boarded with them went to the Collège royal.

> You ask me how many there are in our class [this from Baudelaire to
> Alphonse on 1 April]; there are forty-four to forty-seven in the sixth, and
> take good note of that, because it may excuse me ever so little for the very
> indifferent places I have had. It costs me dearly to say them, but I must
> be brave! In my first composition I was twenty-eighth, and in my second
> I was twenty-first. I don't think you know that it's nearly a week since
> papa went to Grenoble . . .[20]

Aupick had gone there to help disarm the Garde Nationale. He was
still away when, on 9 April, home for the Easter holidays, Baudelaire
celebrated his eleventh birthday. On 25 April, while Mme Aupick was
too busy to put pen to paper, and they were about to move to 4, rue
d'Auvergne, he wrote once again to Alphonse: 'Papa is leaving
Grenoble tomorrow, and he will be in Lyons on Friday. Mama is
preparing some surprises for him; as for me, I've bought two things for
him and I'll let him choose one of them. These two things are, first, an
earpick and toothpick in ivory, a toothpick which cost me 10 sous, and,
secondly, an English pen from Clays in an exotic wooden case . . .'[21] It
was two months since Aupick's birthday. The presents could only have
been a token of affection. Such affection may surprise posterity; yet,
for all the colonel's selfishness, his inexorable discipline, Baudelaire
remained devoted to him.

On 5 August, he took his first communion. He and his mother
also went on an expedition to Charbonnières-les-Bains, where Mme
Aupick, presumably away from her husband, indulged her son with

apricots and pralines. It was at Charbonnières, according to Jules Mouquet, that Baudelaire discovered 'the green paradise of childhood loves' which he was to celebrate in 'Mœsta et errabunda', and to recall in *La Fanfarlo*. He knew 'the artless paradise of timid bliss.'[22] Clément Borgal, in his *Baudelaire*, maintains, more convincingly, that the Lyons idyll had a deeper meaning: it was a symbol of the poet's childhood, which was to leave him, always, with nostalgia for a lost paradise.[23] Alone with his mother, he could no doubt be happy; but his moments of paradise must have been all too rare.

He was more contented, now, since he had left the pension Delorme; but while his mother and stepfather moved to the rue d'Auvergne, they still preferred not to have him with them. Féli Gautier later suggested that Mme Aupick may have felt regrets, and unconscious grudges against her son.[24] This seems improbable, but it is clear that Aupick continued to bring up his stepson according to his own immutable principles, and that Mme Aupick did not challenge him. She had risked her honour, the opprobrium of society, in her determination to marry Aupick; she was now the most submissive of wives. She and the colonel had small time for the boy who had now reached puberty. Féli Gautier described Baudelaire's childhood as 'an apprenticeship in human grief.'[25] There was, alas, much truth in the words. Many years later, after Aupick's death, Baudelaire could still write to his mother: 'You know what an atrocious education your husband wanted to give me; I'm forty, and I don't think without pain about the colleges, or about the fear which my stepfather inspired in me. And yet I loved him, and besides I have wisdom enough today to do him justice. But, when all is said, he was stubbornly clumsy. I want to move on rapidly, because I can see the tears in your eyes.'[26]

Such tears were justified – if they were tears of regret for her ruthless treatment of her son. Baudelaire's life, in his schooldays, was organised to suit the Colonel's wishes. He was given no consistent affection, no outlet for his own deeper feelings. He was a loving child, compelled to know the solitude of the heart. Even in the holidays, when other boys returned to their families, he was not always allowed to live at home.

I am on holiday, but it's just as if I weren't [this to Alphonse on 6 September 1832]. They have had the hateful idea of boarding me out as they do the rest of the year. The worst thing about it is that papa had promised I should travel, and he hasn't got the time . . . But I'm going to be a proper boarder at the Collège [royal], and go into the fifth class, and I hope I shall distinguish myself. I have had two invitations for the country, but mama said she really didn't know if we should go.[27]

No doubt it depended on the Colonel's plans.

On 15 or 16 October, Baudelaire became a boarder at the Collège royal. 'I now wear the uniform of a *collégien*', he reported proudly on 8 November. '. . . I am going to learn English, and I hope I shall soon be in a position to embark on a few conversations.'[28] On 27 December, he recorded that he was doing well, 'and I really mean to work even better in the new year. I have made an arrangement with papa: 5 francs every time I get one of the first six places.'[29]

The new year, 1833, began less happily. He was deprived of leave because his places were disappointing. However, on 12 March he told Alphonse that he had been second in Greek.[30] On 17 May, he announced that he had a fourth place in French; he was also learning to dance. Once again, he was making good resolutions. At the end of the school year, he had two honourable mentions, one of them for composition. That autumn, Aupick presented him with a sort of magic lantern: a phenakisticope. 'The name', said Baudelaire, 'is as bizarre as the invention.'[31]

When the new school year began in October, he was moved up to the fourth class. Aupick was satisfied with his stepson.

'Another year is over [this from Baudelaire to Alphonse on New Year's Day]. In April I shall be thirteen, and two years will have passed far from my brother . . . How bored one is at college, especially in the college in Lyons! The walls are so dark, so dirty and so damp, the classes are so dim.'[32] Edgar Quinet, who had been a pupil for three years, was to keep the same memories of the Collège royal: 'black buildings, shadowy arches, doors bolted and barred, damp chapels, and high walls which hid the sun.'[33] The college seemed a grim prison, set in a forbidding city. Its pupils shared the 'dreadful sadness' of the citizens.

Baudelaire missed Paris; he was weary of 'this city black with coal-smoke.'[34] Years later, he recorded: 'Collège de Lyon, battles with tutors and friends, oppressive periods of melancholy';[35] and, writing of Edgar Allan Poe and his account of his schooldays, he felt, once again, 'a shudder at the grim years of claustration, . . . the unease of wretched and abandoned childhood, the hatred of tyrannical schoolfellows, and the solitude of the heart.'[36] The word 'abandoned' rises from the page; there must have been many times in his childhood when he felt abandoned by the Aupicks. Their unconcern was hard to forgive.

It continued to affect his behaviour and his work at the Collège royal. On 6 February 1834, he was deprived of his exeat. It was not the first occasion on which he had been denied it. 'Mother,' he wrote, ' . . . this is the last time I'll be deprived of leave . . . It really is the last time, I promise, I give you my word of honour.'[37] Soon afterwards, he was once again obliged to explain:

Mama,

You are going to be very surprised to see me deprived of leave again today . . . Since I have long been denied the pleasure of seeing you, I beg papa to have recourse to a very innocent stratagem . . . Let papa tell the vice-principal that you have been in poor health for some days, and I shall be able to hope for special leave.[38]

Colonel Aupick refused to countenance such schoolboy stratagems. Baudelaire was bluntly told that, unless his work improved, his mother would not visit him again. His sense of rejection must have increased with every passing day.[39]

Mme Aupick continued to wound him. She refused to come and see him, refused him any sign of affection. No doubt the Colonel assured her that such neglect would force her son to work. No doubt the Colonel was protecting her; she was far from robust, and she was highly strung. No doubt (perhaps unconsciously) he wanted her entire affection. It would not have been the only occasion on which a man was jealous of his stepson. Whatever the explanation for their behaviour, the Aupicks continued to do untold damage to Baudelaire. On 24 March, he sent Mme Aupick good reports about his work. He asked a question which no son should have needed to ask his mother: 'Have I the right to kiss you, now?'[40]

Two days later, he left the Collège royal for the Easter holidays.

On 6 April, when he returned to school, Lyons was once again disturbed. In February the silk merchants had once again reduced their rate of payment to the weavers. There was a ten-day strike; it failed, and the *canuts* went back to work. The city was peaceful until the Government arrested six leaders of the strike. The trial of the *mutuellistes* – as they were called – was announced for 9 April. That day, Baudelaire's thirteenth birthday, insurrection broke out; the Collège royal, caught between the rebels and the forces of law and order, suffered from the shooting on both sides. The building was nearly set ablaze by a neighbouring fire, which masters and pupils helped to extinguish.

The insurgents demanded – in vain – that the eldest pupils should be allowed to join them. Outside the college, the workers entrenched themselves for the battle. The *collégiens* took refuge in their rooms. On 12 April the insurrection was put down by the army. The college was closed, and the pupils were sent home while the damage to the building was repaired. The college did not re-open for five days.

As for Aupick, he had served Louis-Philippe as zealously as he had served the Bourbons, and Napoleon before them. Before the month was out, he was promoted colonel.

On 30 April, yet again, Baudelaire was deprived of leave. On the evening of 2 May, he wrote to his mother in despair: 'I am fourth, and in *Latin translation*. I beg you to observe to my father that it is in Latin translation. As a reward, I ask you, I beg you, I implore you to forget that I'm deprived of leave and to come and see me when you get this letter, if you aren't ill.'[41] Once again, Mme Aupick seems to have been unmoved. It was perhaps this year that Baudelaire sent her a list of his results at school. He sent them by his 'advocates', some of his fellow-pupils. 'I didn't ask them to come and plead for me,' so he explained. 'They themselves offered to do so, as soon as they saw my anxiety and distress.'[42] His relationship with his mother was pitiful.

In this summer of 1834, leaving Baudelaire to his own devices, she and her husband set off on holiday. They came back at the end of June, to find a letter from Alphonse, congratulating the colonel on his promotion.

My dear Alphonse [this from Mme Aupick on 30 June],
    On our return from our travels in the South of France, we have just found your letter of congratulations to my husband; he is very touched by it, and he asks me to thank you, as he has so little time himself, especially after a brief absence during which the work has accumulated. He doesn't complain of this additional work because he was delighted with our travels, he was as happy as a schoolboy on holiday . . .
    I got through these travels as well as could be; indeed, I acquired such a taste for them that I wanted to go on even further, I wanted to set sail for Italy; I decided to come back only on condition that I was taken on a little excursion every year.
    On our return, we learned with great pleasure that Charles had done wonders: he had always been first or second out of fifty [*sic*]. He is in a good vein; if he chose to go on like this, we should be delighted, he has such abilities that we must demand a great deal. He is very far from being an ordinary child, but he is so thoughtless and so wild, he likes amusements so much! As for the qualities of heart, and nature, he leaves nothing to desire; he is charming company, as good and sensible as he could be, very affectionate. We really have no reproach to make him except that he plays about in class instead of working, and that he has the bad habit of waiting until the last moment to do his work. When you write to him, do say a word to him about this. Tell him how important it is to do *what you have to do* at once, and that *always postponing it* is a fault which brings very serious consequences. This fault in your brother leaves me in despair. I'm doing all I can to cure him of it.[43]

She could write with feeling to Alphonse; she found it hard to show such warmth and understanding to her son. She refused to accept how much he needed her appreciation.

On 31 August, at the prize-giving, Baudelaire received five accessits, including a first accessit for Greek translation and a first for natural history. On 26 September he entered the third class. He did not entirely keep to his good resolutions, and, by the end of the year, he had earned grave reprimands, and he was once again deprived of leave. Late in December, his mother finally consented to see him. Mother and son were both in an emotional state. Her visit ended badly, and she accused him of ingratitude.

> You called me ungrateful – *me*, ungrateful . . . *Me*, ungrateful [he wrote to her on 21 December]! Even if I had not made some excellent resolutions at the beginning of this year, this one word would convert me. I have written you this letter to implore you to come and see me this very day. That will do me much good, and give me much pleasure, because I am very grieved by the wrong that you have done me.
>
> Come and see me, I beg you . . . Ask my father, for me, to forgive me.[44]

He had good marks for the first term of 1835; and one of his schoolfriends, Henri Hignard, left a poignant portrait of him. 'He was much more refined and distinguished than any of our fellow pupils, you could not imagine a more delightful adolescent. We were bound to one another by a warm affection, fostered by shared tastes and sympathies, the precocious love of fine works of literature, the cult of Victor Hugo and Lamartine, whose poems we used to recite to one another . . . We even wrote verse, which, thank God, has not survived.'[45]

Lyons itself was more settled than it had been the previous year; and, writing to a general on the staff of the Duc d'Orléans, Aupick took good care to report the improvement in the situation.[46] While Lyons was more peaceful, and the Colonel discreetly ensured his favour with authority, the year 1835 brought other problems for the family. On 11 April, Dr Choquet, surgeon-major of the First Military Division, operated on Aupick's leg. He removed the bullet which had lodged there at Fleurus, twenty years earlier. That summer, Lyons was threatened by a cholera epidemic; Alphonse invited Mme Aupick and Baudelaire to stay with him at Fontainebleau. Late in August, or early in September, Baudelaire sent him his thanks:

> It is very nice of you, and we are all grateful to you; but, thank God, . . . the cholera hasn't got further than Vienne. There was just one case here, and so we have no worry so far . . .
>
> The moment is approaching, dear brother, when I shall come and embrace you, because mama is quite decided to make me do my *rhétorique*

in Paris. No doubt you will find I have grown a great deal, both in wisdom
and in height.[47]

It was, in fact, on 9 January 1836 that Colonel Aupick, now
commandeur de la Légion-d'honneur, was appointed chief of staff of
the first military division in Paris, under the command of General
Comte Pajol. In mid-February, nearly four years after they had gone
to Lyons, the Aupicks returned to Paris at last.

6

They settled at the staff headquarters of the first military division, at 1,
rue de Lille. On 1 March, Baudelaire duly entered the Lycée Louis-le-
Grand as a boarder. The Colonel himself presented him to the *proviseur*,
M. Jules Pierrot, with the daunting introduction: 'I am giving you a
present, Monsieur. Here is a pupil who will do honour to your college.'[1]
The prophecy was soon fulfilled. On 17 August, Baudelaire received the
first prize for Latin verse, the second prize for Greek translation, the
third accessit for Latin composition, and the third accessit for Greek
composition. At the Concours général, the annual competition between
the senior pupils of French lycées, he had the first accessit for Latin
verse. On 3 October he moved up to the second class.

Such exemplary behaviour did not last. That December his form
master reported 'a great deal of frivolity.'[2] The history master wrote
that he 'worked apathetically', his usher lamented that he 'had no
discipline in his nature.'[3] Émile Deschanel, a fellow-pupil, one day to
be professor at the Collège de France, was to recall 'that, from his
schooldays, he was a poet; and, during the mathematics lessons, we
used to spend our time writing one another rhymed notes.'[4] But
Baudelaire was not simply a feckless schoolboy. He was an unhappy
adolescent who had been deprived of his family. He already showed
certain characteristics which were to become more marked in later life.
Henri Hignard, who had known him in Lyons, remembered: 'I myself
had entered the École normale supérieure, and I went to see him at
his lycée. I found him changed, saddened and sharp...He was
probably suffering, even now, from painful family vexations. They had
a sad effect on his life.'[5]

He spent the Easter holidays of 1837 with his mother and stepfather.
For all their harshness, he still loved them both. Despite Dr Choquet's
ministrations, Aupick continued to suffer from his wound. 'I should like

to have news of papa,' so Baudelaire wrote to his mother when the holidays were over. '[I want to know] if they will soon think of closing the wound, if he is very bored, if he talks to you about me, everything you can tell me . . . One must think about papa above all; and since he is so concerned to make us happy when he is well [*sic*], one must devote oneself to him when he is ill.'[6] Mme Aupick needed no encouragement. 'A slight indisposition from time to time must be a fortunate occurrence in marriage,' so she was to write, years afterwards. 'It gives the loving wife the occasion to display all the love and devotion which fill her heart. And how it delights the man who is the object of such care and affection!'[7]

Early in July, Baudelaire confessed that, once again, he was being detained for his idleness.[8] For the next few weeks, he worked at composition, and set his mind on the Concours général. At last, in mid August, he announced proudly: 'I have the second prize for verse in the concours, and I am therefore reconciled with the principal and the vice-principal. Tell papa, and embrace him for me.'[9] On 16 August, in the presence of the King and many dignitaries, the prizes were awarded to the pupils of the colleges of Paris and Versailles. Baudelaire was among them. Next day, at Louis-le-Grand, he received the second prize for Latin composition, the first prize for Latin verse, a first accessit for Latin translation, and a first accessit for Greek translation. At the Concours général, he had an eighth accessit for Latin translation, and the second prize for Latin verse. Towards the end of the month, the King gave a banquet at Saint-Cloud for seventy of the laureates for the year. Baudelaire was no doubt one of them.

Aupick had had a further operation on his leg, but he had recovered enough to take up a new appointment. He was now chief of staff of the two infantry divisions in camp at Compiègne; he was under the command of the Duc d'Orléans, heir to the throne. His relations with the Duke were those of the *fidus Achates*; they were also those of gratifying friendship. He was well placed to help his stepson, should Baudelaire choose a conventional career.

For the moment, he was well disposed. On 2 November, when Baudelaire had begun his year in the *rhétorique* at Louis-le-Grand, Aupick went riding with him. Baudelaire fell off his horse, remounted, and continued to ride for another three hours. When he reached the rue de Lille, he found that one of his legs could not carry him. 'And here I am now,' he told Alphonse, 'confined to bed, in other words half living, and envying everyone I see who can walk. Mama is disconsolate because I am therefore missing classes . . .'[10] He had badly hurt himself, and he was confined to bed, but there was no question of her keeping him at home. It was from the infirmary at Louis-le-Grand that he told her, five days later: 'The surgeon and the doctor concluded that it had been absurd to let me come back to college; that I was in a pitiful state, and . . . had water on the knee.'[11]

He lingered on in the infirmary. It is not known how often his mother went to see him: only that she did so on 5 December; that day, a month after his accident, he wrote to her: 'Do thank papa for his visit, it gave me enormous pleasure. His visits aren't frequent; but the rarer things are, the more precious they are. I do really love that father of mine. Don't forget to tell him my place.'[12] He had reason to be pleased. He was still in the infirmary, but he had won a second place in Latin.

On 18 December, he returned to his classroom. He had been in the infirmary for six weeks.

Despite the attentions of M. Choquet, Aupick was still unwell; on 10 May he was given leave to take the waters. Towards the end of the month, he and his wife set off for Barèges, the spa in the Pyrenees which had once been patronised by Heine.

While they were away, Baudelaire received repeated visits from one of the Colonel's closest friends. Jean-Louis Émon, a retired artillery captain, had served in the Napoleonic Wars. In *Baudelaire et sa mère* Feuillerat maintains, without evidence, that Émon had been Aupick's aide-de-camp.[13] Perhaps his military career had suffered through the vicissitudes of politics; whatever the reason, he had resigned his commission in 1819. It is not clear if he had had any further occupation. He had, however, two claims to distinction. He was the uncle of the Symbolist painter Gustave Moreau, who became an admirer of Baudelaire and in time painted Mme Aupick's garden at Honfleur. He was also, for some unknown reason, so close a friend of Aupick's that he was in time to be his executor. He and his wife were to exert all too strong an influence on Mme Aupick, and to be intensely hostile to her son.[14]

Now, however, in the summer of 1838, Émon showed the *collégien* only kindness. 'M. Émon is really very good,' Baudelaire reported to his mother on 19 June. 'He comes twice a week, on Tuesdays and Fridays, which should put you to shame.'[15]

Mme Aupick had some cause for shame. In Paris she had rarely gone to see her son at the lycée; and, now that she was in Barèges, she did not even trouble to write to him. 'I am waiting with great impatience for a letter from you,' he told her on 27 June, 'it seems ages now since I had one . . . I beg you, write to me, tell me what you see, and above all give me news of Papa; now that you have doubtless arrived in Barèges, I want to have news all the time, and to follow his cure as if I were with you . . .'[16] Mme Aupick remained silent, and her silence hurt him. Five days later he wrote again: 'My dear, dear mother, you

don't write to me any more. I am bored to death, I love you more
than ever, I think about the holidays more than ever, and above all
I'm afraid of the concours . . . My dear mother, if you only knew how
much I want to enjoy you, and to make you happy before you die!'[17]

There was a brief and unexpected interlude in this depressing life.
On 11 July, King Louis-Philippe invited the lycée to Versailles. Masters
and pupils obeyed the royal command; and next day, for two hours,
they toured the palace and visited the chapel. Then the King himself
appeared, and led them through the Galeries historiques and into the
theatre, where he made a speech to them.

> Papa [Baudelaire announced to Aupick, on 17 July],
> . . . I am sixth in French *discours*, fourth in Latin *discours*, first in Latin
> verse. Now we are thinking of the prize compositions . . . When the day
> comes, I shall give them all my attention. It is only the concours which
> frightens me. I see that mama is so anxious to see me mentioned in the
> concours that, if I wasn't, she would not forgive me; yet nobody is sure
> of anything. However, there, as in college, I will try with all my might.
> A few days ago, the whole college, with all the masters and a school for
> day-boys which adjoins the college, went to Versailles . . .
> I don't know if I'm right, because I know nothing about painting, but
> it seemed to me that the good pictures could be numbered; perhaps I'm
> talking nonsense, but apart from a few pictures by Horace Vernet, two or
> three pictures by Scheffer, and the *Bataille de Taillebourg* by Delacroix, I
> haven't remembered anything, except for one picture by Regnault of
> some or other marriage of the Emperor Joseph; but this picture is
> distinguished in a quite different way. All the pictures of the Empire
> period, which people call very fine, often seem so regular, so cold; the
> figures in them are frequently spaced out like trees, or figurants in opera.
> No doubt it is ridiculous for me to talk like this about the painters of the
> Empire who have been so praised. Perhaps I am speaking thoughtlessly.
> But I am simply giving my impressions. Perhaps this is also the result of
> reading *La Presse*, which praises Delacroix to the skies? . . .
> I don't like to talk to you about your wound. I know that you don't like
> people to show anxiety about you; mama thinks that the progress is very
> slow. If you think it will do you good, stay on, stay where you are until
> next year. I care more about the slightest alleviation for you than I do
> about my holidays . . .
> I adore you.[18]

The words spring from the page: as urgent, as spontaneous as when
they were written. They give the lie to the persistent legend that
Baudelaire hated Aupick from first to last. Now, as a youth, he patently
admired him: his military distinction, his noble principles, even the
wisdom which Aupick was so ready to impart. He admired the courage
of the wounded veteran; it had been, no doubt, in order to impress
him that he had remounted his horse after his fall, and had ridden on,

beside him, for three hours. He was always anxious for Aupick's
hard-earned praise. Whatever he had suffered through Aupick's selfishness, his lack of understanding, his rigid code of behaviour, Baudelaire
continued to love him. Aupick inspired him with fear: a fear that he
was to remember all his life. Yet his letter reveals more than the deference of a schoolboy: it reveals profound affection.

The thought of the Concours général continued to disturb him. 'I can
only tell you that I have no hope except in verse composition,' he warned
his mother on 3 August. 'As for the class, I asked the master, he said that
my verse composition and my Latin dissertation were detestable. So that's
what comes of a year's work, and that's what college triumphs are.'[19]
Three weeks later, he announced: 'Nothing in the Concours. At college,
I had two first prizes, the first prize for Latin verse, and for French
dissertation; the first accessit for Latin translation, and then another
accessit for Latin dissertation which I don't remember.'[20]

It was, in the end, to be a happier summer. Mme Aupick had neglected
her son, apparently for weeks. Perhaps, as usual, her silence had been
a means of forcing him to work, compelling him to earn her approval;
perhaps she had been exclusively concerned with her husband. After
some weeks she had relented, and sent 'charming' letters to her son.
Now, at the Colonel's suggestion, she asked Baudelaire to join them in
Barèges. It was an invitation which any schoolboy might have expected
from his mother, but he was not accustomed to family life. His gratitude
and excitement were pitiful. 'I am burning with impatience,' he told her
on 23 August. 'The trunk is packed. I don't know how long my journey
will take, but in any case it will certainly be too long . . .'[21]

Some five days later, Baudelaire arrived in Barèges. He was to stay
there with the Aupicks for a fortnight, before he set off again in their
company. They made excursions on foot and on horseback to Bagnerres-
de-Bigorre, in the vallée de Campan. There, on the shores of Lac
d'Escoubous, he found the subject of his poem 'Incompatibilité.'[22] He
was seventeen. He had found himself, already, as a poet. He had left
the Concours général, the laurels of the lycée, far behind him.

On 16 October he returned to Louis-le-Grand. He was now in the top
form, the *philosophie*; it was, he told his brother, 'a terrible form, and I
had great difficulty getting in.'[23] He disliked the discipline, and found
it hard to work. The masters were frustrated by his idleness: all the
more, perhaps, because they recognised his quality of mind. They also
resented the contempt which he clearly felt for them: it was a continual
affront to their authority. The sequel was predictable. Early in
December, Baudelaire confessed to his mother:

I am deprived of leave until further notice for bad behaviour in the studio: that is to say that the vice-principal, whom I often ridiculed last year, has seized the first occasion this year to punish me, and, as I was making a noise one day, he said that I had been plaguing him for three years, and that he would ask for an exceptional punishment for me . . . That's what it is to have enemies.[24]

It was, he told Alphonse, no use assuming a thoughtful expression, his mother and stepfather persisted in thinking of him as a child.[25] Yet his intellectual interests showed that he had put away childish things. On 26 February, he sent his stepfather a letter which was remarkable for its seriousness of purpose.

I am writing to make a request which will surprise you very much. You have promised me lessons in fencing and horsemanship; instead of that, I ask you, if you are willing, and if it's possible, if it doesn't inconvenience you, for *a private tutor* . . .

Personally I don't need help to follow the class, properly speaking; what I should ask from a tutor would be additional philosophy, it would be what isn't done in class, learning, *religion* (the study of which does not enter the University programme), and Aesthetics, or the philosophy of the arts, which our professor certainly won't have time to show me.[26]

Baudelaire had already earned distinction for his Greek translations; now he wanted a private tutor to advance his studies.

What I should also ask of him would be Greek – yes, to teach me Greek, which inspires me with great curiosity. Whatever people say today, I believe that it doesn't only bring great delight, it also brings a practical advantage. Why suppress these tastes? Don't they enter into what I want to be? Science, history, philosophy – who knows? Perhaps the study of Greek will facilitate that of German.

I think that a private tutor costs 30 francs a month. The pupil must first have authorization from his father. Then he speaks to the principal and chooses a tutor. Half-an-hour a day, or an hour every other day.

I should choose a very distinguished young master, who has recently left the École normale, and is known at Louis-le-Grand, M. Lasègue. If he could not give me lessons, I would rather do without a tutor . . . [27]

It is not known if Aupick answered. Possibly he refused the request. That would perhaps explain why, on 2 March, M. Carrère, the usher, recorded a deterioration in Baudelaire's behaviour; at the end of the month, his professors noticed that he was working without any visible result. On 18 April, nine days after his eighteenth birthday, he was expelled from Louis-le-Grand.

*

The *proviseur*, M. Jules Pierrot, informed Colonel Aupick of the reasons for his decision. He had asked Baudelaire to hand over a note which had been passed to him by another pupil. Baudelaire had not only refused. He had torn it up, and swallowed the pieces. M. Pierrot had told him that he was exposing his friend to grave suspicions. Baudelaire had burst into laughter. The dignity of the *proviseur*, and therefore of the lycée, had been offended.

On 15 August 1886, Eugène Crépet wrote delicately to Ernest Prarond: 'I shall not ask you why [Baudelaire] left Louis-le-Grand without finishing his studies . . . I think I know the real reason, but I think I should be silent about it, and I know that there is no trace of it in the archives of Louis-le-Grand (at least a letter from the present *proviseur* affirms it).'[28]

The real reason was unlikely to have been a *question de dortoir*. Baudelaire is not known to have had homosexual inclinations. However, he was always quick-tempered. He liked to pose as a hero in front of his schoolfellows. Years later, one of them told Léon Lemonnier: 'He had an exalted character, sometimes full of mysticism, and sometimes full of immorality and cynicism (which were excessive but only verbal).'[29] Perhaps he decided, at eighteen, that a private note was not for official scrutiny, and that he resented the demand. It may well be that, once again, he simply showed his contempt for authority. This incident alone would hardly have justified expulsion, but it was the final gesture in a series of contemptuous gestures. It was, no doubt, the pretext for which the authorities had long been waiting.

Mme Aupick was distraught. That day, from the rue de Lille, Baudelaire drafted a letter to M. Pierrot:

> Monsieur,
> I am home again with my family. When I saw my mother's grief, I understood all my disgrace, and especially hers; and so I want to try to make amends for my offence, if that is possible . . .
> It is not for myself that I ask your forgiveness, but for my mother, who is so distressed to see my career tarnished at its beginning . . .[30]

7

Perhaps this letter was not sent, or perhaps his entreaty was rejected; in either case, Baudelaire was not to return to Louis-le-Grand. Nor was he to live with the Aupicks. Early in June, he was entrusted to the tutor who was to prepare him for his *baccalauréat*. No doubt the Colonel had seen the wisdom of granting his request, for Baudelaire had the tutor he had wanted. Charles Lasègue, then twenty-three, had recently qualified as a *licencié ès lettres*. He was later to turn to medicine, and to become an expert in mental illness. Now, however, he was living with his parents at 24, rue du Vieux-Colombier, and Baudelaire went to lodge with them.

> It is nearly the end of my first week at M. Lasègue's [he wrote to Mme Aupick, a few days later]. I have been welcomed here with all possible grace and kindness. I am absolutely at home. The day is gradually filling up. On Monday I am going to settle down to the *baccalauréat*.
> I don't know what to say to you, and yet I have a multitude of things to say to you – and first of all I must tell you that although M. Lasègue is delightfully kind, although I lack nothing, although I have no right to complain, it seems to me that something is lacking for me! At moments I feel sullen, I think it is you whom I miss. I miss the presence of someone to whom one says all sorts of things, with whom one laughs without any restraint – in fact, although I am very well, materially speaking, I miss you. I should like to see the rest of this year fly like the wind – to see my father cured, and to know what situation we shall be in next year. Yes, it will also be a great delight to see you again.[1]

Everything smiled on Aupick except for his health. In the second half of May he and his wife had left for Bourbonne-les-Bains, where he was, once again, to take a cure.

> I do want to know how long you are going to stay down there [Baudelaire continued, to his mother]. – At first you told me two or three months – and Fanchette [the maid] told me that my father had four months' leave. My God, what a long time that will be! But I shall certainly have to get used to it. I think that the best way to get used to it is to occupy my mind all the time – to work . . .
> I see that the house where I'm going to have my meals is a curious house . . .[2]

It was indeed a curious house. No. 1, rue du Pot-de-Fer Saint-Sulpice (now the rue Bonaparte) was not far from the Lasègues'. It was 'a kind of annexe of the seminary, where the seminary rules virtually continued.'[3] Renan, who stayed there six years later, was to recall: 'One was only accepted there on the recommendation of these gentlemen or of some religious authority. It was the temporary lodging for pupils who were entering the seminary or leaving it, and needed a few free days. Ecclesiastics on their travels, sisters superior of convents who had business in Paris, found it a cheap and convenient retreat.'[4]

Now, however, it offered meals to students with no theological purpose or religious connections; and so it was that the future author of *Les*

Fleurs du mal lived with the Lasègues, but went to dine at the pension which was, one day, to lodge the future historian of *La Vie de Jésus*. His friend Henri Hignard, now a pupil at the École normale, wrote home that Baudelaire 'had become serious, studious and religious.'[5]

He was not too serious to criticise Mlle Céleste Théot, who was in charge of the *pension*.

> She is, so they say, a former servant who has made her fortune through piety [he explained to Mme Aupick] ... When I was presented to Mlle Céleste, the elderly damsel received me with lowered eyes, a false convent air, and a honeyed tone which surprised me ...
>
> You promise to tell me in your letters all you do and think, everything you read. And please give me regular news of our dear father [*sic*].[6]

It was already characteristic of Baudelaire that even his relative happiness was transient. For a young man of eighteen he was still emotionally immature. He had a constant need of his mother. Her prolonged absence weighed upon his spirits. It was only with her – and, for the moment, with his stepfather – that he could be himself; he needed their presence, their constant affection, if he was to bloom. He had begged for tuition from Lasègue. Now, for all his resolutions, he could not concentrate on his work, and he began to resent Lasègue's domestic happiness.

> My dear mother, my good mama [this on 16 July], I don't know what to say to you, and I have all sorts of things to say. To begin with, I feel a great need to see you. How different it is to be with strangers – and it isn't exactly your caresses and our laughter that I regret, it's something indefinable which means that our mother always seems to us the best of women, that her qualities suit us better than the qualities of other women; there is such an understanding between a mother and her son; they live with one another so happily – so that, really, since I have been at M. Lasègue's, I have been ill at ease ... Certainly M. Lasègue, and his mother, too, are endowed with all sorts of qualities. Wisdom, love, good sense: well, it all develops in a form which I don't like. There are trivialities which somewhat repel me. I prefer it to develop more capriciously and more vigorously as it does with you and my friend. In this house there is constant gaiety, and this annoys me.
>
> They are certainly happier than we are. With you I have seen tears, vexations for my father, attacks of nerves for you – well, I *prefer us* like that.[7]

It was, thought René Laforgue, from this period in his life that Baudelaire kept a passion for making his mother cry, for seeing her in tears.[8] It was one way to punish her for mistreating him, one way to prove that she still loved him.

On 12 August, at four o'clock in the afternoon, Baudelaire passed his *baccalauréat*. He was later to tell Charles Asselineau that he was passed out of kindness, thanks to Mlle Théot's intervention with M. Patin, one of the examiners.[9] So it was that he created his legend.

Years later, Théophile Gautier was to embroider on it. Mme Aupick wrote angrily:

> He presents my son as having had little ability in his childhood and youth, never any success at his colleges, never any prizes, and he says that, at his examination for the *baccalauréat ès lettres*, either because he was intimidated, or because he was thinking of something else, he appeared almost an idiot, he was only passed out of kindness. As for that examination, I can't remember how it went, and how Charles behaved on that occasion, but what is quite certain, and I can affirm it, is that, when he was very young, he showed exceptional intelligence, he had enormous success at the colleges which he attended, he always won prizes, in Lyons at first, when my husband was chief of staff there, and then in Paris, at Louis-le-Grand, where he always entered for the *grand concours*, and where he was awarded a prize for Latin verse in 1837. I have in front of me now the medal which was presented to him, and it bears witness to the fact. It is quite possible that Charles, who was never satisfied with himself, might have said that he never worked in his youth, as he should have done.[10]

Meanwhile, on 12 August 1839, the day that Baudelaire passed his *baccalauréat*, *Le Moniteur universel* announced Aupick's promotion to maréchal de camp, a rank which corresponded to that of brigadier-general. He was also put on the reserve list. Next day, Baudelaire addressed himself to the new general:

> I have just seen some good news, and I have some good news to tell you. This morning I read about your appointment in *Le Moniteur*, and, since 4 o'clock yesterday afternoon, I have been a *bachelier*. My examination was pretty indifferent, except for Latin and Greek – very good – that's what saved me.
>
> I am very glad about your appointment – from son to father, these are not banal congratulations like the others you will receive. I'm very glad, because I have seen you often enough to know how much you deserved this; I seem to be playing the man, and congratulating you as if I were your equal or your superior. And so I shall just say this: you know that I am very happy.[11]

Baudelaire had long been conscious of the hierarchy in the household; General Aupick controlled his wife and stepson like the commanding officer he was. Baudelaire did not yet feel hostile to all that Aupick represented, although perhaps he secretly aspired to a comparable level of success; but, from this summer of 1839, their paths were to diverge.

There now remained the serious question of Baudelaire's future, 'and, of all the anxieties which beset me, the greatest', he told his brother, 'is the choice of a profession. That already preoccupies me, and it torments me, especially since I don't feel I have a vocation for anything, and I know I have many different tastes which are all upper-most in turn.[12]

On about 26 August, Mme Aupick returned to Paris from Bour-bonne-les-Bains; a few days later, the General followed her. 'One may conjecture', so Jules Buisson wrote, 'that he would have asked no better than to use his credit for the son of a woman whom he had married purely for love. His one error was to treat Baudelaire as he would have treated his own son, a general's son, an army officer's son. He wanted, with all his heart, to *set* him in the discipline of an official career. But the setting, the cage, horrified the bird.'[13]

Aupick was eager that Baudelaire should prepare for a career in diplomacy; in this he showed a determined ignorance of Baudelaire's true nature. Yet whether Baudelaire became a diplomat, an advocate or a magistrate, he needed further qualifications. On 2 November, no doubt with the warm approval of the Aupicks, and of his brother, he registered at the École de Droit. Meanwhile, the first instalment of his expenses had been paid that summer at the celebrated crammer's, the Pension Lévêque et Bailly, at 11, rue de l'Estrapade.

There, in time, he was drawn, not to law, but to literature. He made acquaintance with the members of the École normande: Ernest Prarond, and Louis-Gustave Le Vavasseur, 'who had his moments of poetry in a youth as verdant as the hedgerows of his native Nor-mandy.'[14] There, too, he met another member of the École normande: Jules Buisson, who 'had a taste for painting in his blood',[15] who modelled and etched in his friends' rooms, and who was one day to be Deputy for Castelnaudary. It was now that Baudelaire came to know Philippe de Chennevières, a future Directeur des Beaux-Arts, and he renewed his acquaintance with Louis de La Gennevraye, who had just left Louis-le-Grand. He met Alexandre Privat d'Anglemont, the nonchalant creole and Bohemian, the ex-medical student who had chosen to live in destitution and to spend his life preparing to write his survey of the poor, *Paris inconnu*. Antonio Watripon was a man of letters, and an impoverished Bohemian. Auguste Dozon, the son of a Deputy, was a linguist and philologist; he was later to become French consul at Larnaca, in Cyprus. Henri Hignard was in lodgings nearby. So was Louis Ménard, the passionate Hellenist, landscape painter, poet and alchemist, the tenant of the famous attic in the place de la

Sorbonne.[16] It was, said Baudelaire, about now that he met the novelist Edmond Ourliac, who had lived in the Romantic heaven of the impasse du Doyenné. He came to know Henri Latouche, translator of Schiller, novelist and poet, and he encountered Gérard de Nerval.[17]

This autumn, at the age of eighteen, innocent and needing experience, Baudelaire also seems to have had his first sexual relationship. He contracted venereal disease.

8

The sexuality of Baudelaire has always been a subject of debate. In his later years, he himself attributed his nature to his tainted heredity.[1] His father had been more than thirty-four years older than his mother; only a freak, said Baudelaire, could have been born to them. His theory was consistent with the teaching of his time; but modern science does not hold that disparity in age could alone account for defects in a couple's offspring. However, his heredity does appear to have been tainted, if not in the manner he supposed. His half-brother, who was said to have had nervous problems, was to suffer a stroke in middle age, and to die of a cerebral haemorrhage with hemiplegia; his mother, who was highly strung, was to die after years of indifferent health, both hemiplegic and aphasic. Little is known of earlier generations, but Baudelaire's heredity may have been tainted on both parents' sides. In *La Maladie de Baudelaire*, Dr Raymond Trial observed: 'Baudelaire, with his unhealthy ancestors, is the typical superior degenerate.' The first symptom of degeneration was, considered Trial, 'the deformation of the sexual instinct.'[2]

The disparity in age between his parents did not wholly explain his physiology. It may, however, partly explain why Caroline had felt no passionate attachment to Joseph-François; and, in her son's early childhood, she appears to have lavished her frustrated affections upon him. In 1861 he sent her a letter which some have considered as evidence of an œdipus complex. 'I loved you passionately in my childhood; later, under the influence of your injustice, I lacked respect for you, as if maternal injustice could justify a lack of filial respect. I have often repented that, since then, although, as is my habit, I did not mention it . . . [Before your second marriage] you were mine alone. You were both an idol and a friend.'[3] There had followed the marriage to Aupick, the years of boarding-school, ordered by Aupick, the

struggles and the black depressions. In his later years, Baudelaire
recalled his mother's second marriage and his subsequent childhood
with bitterness.

Most of his biographers have regarded such recollections as the
inventions of a later day, reflecting the grievances of adulthood, not
childhood. Baudelaire's friends had considered him an ordinary, happy
child, and his youthful correspondence with his mother was undoubtedly affectionate. While René Laforgue, a Freudian, did write of
Baudelaire's Œdipus complex, he thought that his conflicts with Aupick
were the consequence of a neurosis rooted in infancy. His mother's
second marriage had not, he said, caused the trouble, but it had come
as a shock to a child whose Œdipal attachment had not been resolved
in the usual way.[4]

A superficial reading of the letters which Baudelaire wrote in his
youth would indeed imply that he had been a normal and conventional
child. Yet the young Baudelaire was probably not a happy conformist.
What Baudelaire later saw in the schooldays of Edgar Allan Poe says
more about himself than it does about Poe. It reveals his fear of boys
and masters, his sense of being abandoned, and, above all, his
loneliness of heart; it reveals the secret life of the hypersensitive child.
His correspondence with his mother in his later years remains a
constant proof that she was too important in his life, that there was
something equivocal or dishonest in their relationship. Both were
aware that her second marriage had been a catastrophe for him.

In 1856, in a dream, he seems to have identified his mother with the
madam in a brothel. He went to present her with a book, and he
anticipated sexual intercourse with a prostitute. Yet the dream implies
that his virility, supposedly restored through publication, proved un-
equal to the occasion.[5]

The dream discloses the opinion of the Aupick marriage which
Baudelaire professed in his manhood. It also confirms what some critics
have said of his private life. Baudelaire, wrote Léon Daudet, 'is a
man mentally, organically, a man in his courage in facing grief and
death . . . But nature refused him an essential attribute of the *vir*, the
ability to make love effectively to a woman.'[6] Henri Peyre suggests that
Baudelaire suffered from occasional impotence. It was, perhaps, the
result of an excessive dissociation between physical love, which he
associated with prostitutes, and the affection which he associated with
his mother.[7] In *Baudelaire et la mort*, Étienne Bricon speaks of Baudelaire's two passions: 'The taste for death, and the distaste for love, to
which he had been led by his impotence.'[8]

Nadar – who knew him well – bluntly called him 'the Virgin Poet.'[9]
This is curious, since, in his notes, Nadar also wrote: 'Women: Pauline,

Christine – Marcelle, Anna – Delphine, Georgette – much later Mme S., Clésinger's woman with a serpent.'[10] Nadar's public insistence on Baudelaire's virginity is all the more curious since Nadar himself had been the lover of Jeanne Duval, who became – as he knew – the mistress of Baudelaire. Nadar, too, wrote in his notes: 'From the first days of our friendship, Baudelaire's reserve on a certain subject, indeed already his usual chastity, . . . had shown itself in an indifference or an icy coldness towards the slightest freedom of speech. And he did not miss an occasion to cut short any libertine.'[11] Nadar was not the only friend of Baudelaire's to be bewildered about his sexual life. A number of other intimates and acquaintances, including Théodore de Banville (who also shared a mistress with Baudelaire), Émile Deschamps and Louis Ménard, also maintained that Baudelaire died a virgin, despite the evidence of his liaisons, and despite his venereal disease.

Baudelaire himself increased speculation with his statements about bizarre sexual fantasies and desires.[12] Once, an observer was to recall, in the presence of friends in a tavern, Baudelaire told a blonde woman that he wanted to bite her, tie her hands and suspend her by the wrists from the ceiling. This would allow him, on bended knees, to kiss her bare feet. The woman fled.[13]

Some have seen such an incident as proof of Baudelaire's sadism. Cruelty and pleasure were, he maintained, 'identical sensations, like extreme heat and extreme cold.'[14] Yet there remains no evidence that he put such outrageous ideas into practice; and their expression seemed to some merely a sign of his wish to shock conventional society. On the other hand, his idle threat to the woman in the tavern – if it had in fact been made – was hardly proof of sexual normality.

Baudelaire refused, in time, to believe in mutuality in love. He likened love to torture or to a surgical operation. One of the partners, he maintained, must be either torturer or surgeon, and the other victim or patient.

> Even if the two lovers were very much in love, and very full of desire for each other, one of them would still be calmer or less entranced than the other. This one, man or woman, is the surgeon or the torturer; the other one is the patient, the victim. Do you hear those sighs, the preludes to a tragedy of dishonour, those groans, those cries, those rattles in the throat? Who has not uttered them, who has not irresistibly extorted them? . . . These unfocussed sleepwalker's eyes, these limbs whose muscles spring up and stiffen as if attached to a galvanic battery: the wildest effects of drunkenness, delirium and opium will certainly not give you such horrible and curious examples. And the human face, which Ovid thought was created to reflect the stars: there it is, bereft of speech, with an expression of wild ferocity, or slackening in a kind of death. For, certainly, I think it would be sacrilege to apply the word ecstasy to this sort of decomposition.

A hideous game, in which one of the players must lose their self-control.[15]

And Baudelaire added: 'Personally, I think that the unique and supreme delight lies in the certainty of doing *evil* – and men and women know from birth that all pleasure lies in evil.'[16] He felt copulation to be inferior to the poetic act: 'The more a man cultivates the arts, the less randy he becomes . . . Only the brute is good at coupling, and copulation is the lyricism of the masses. To copulate is to enter into another – and the artist never emerges from himself.'[17]

Nobody had more contempt for the generality of women. Baudelaire was to make savage comments in his *Journaux intimes*. 'There are only two places where you have to pay for the right to spend, public lavatories and women.'[18] 'Woman is *natural*, that is to say abominable.'[19] George Sand earned his particular contempt: 'The fact that a few men have managed to be enamoured of this lavatory is a certain proof of the abasement of the men of this century.'[20]

It was, he wrote, significant that Providence had made the means of procreation 'a sign of the original sin. In fact, we can only make love with excremental organs.'[21] Marriage itself was poisonous. 'Unable to suppress love, the Church wanted at least to disinfect it, and it created marriage.'[22] Love was a crime in which man had need of an accomplice. All love was prostitution, and sexual love was patently a sin. In one outrageous statement in his *Journaux intimes*, Baudelaire professed to equate it with bestiality.

> There are, in every man, at every moment, two simultaneous postulations, one towards God, the other towards Satan. The invocation to God, or spirituality, is a wish to be promoted; [the invocation] to Satan, or animality, is a delight in degradation. It is to this latter that one should relate passions for women and intimate conversations with animals, dogs, cats, etc.[23]

Catholicism drove Baudelaire from the thought of physical love; so did the awareness of his genius:

> [There is an] invincible taste for prostitution in the heart of man, from which comes his horror of solitude. He wants to be *two*. The man of genius wants to be *one*, and therefore solitary.
> What is glorious is to remain *one*, and to prostitute oneself in a particular way.
> It is this horror of solitude, the need to lose ones *self* in the external flesh, that man nobly calls *the need to love*.[24]

Contemporaries and later critics failed to understand the religious element, the need for purity which Baudelaire confessed in his journals.

They saw only his public behaviour and his published comments, and they sometimes suspected his virginity or his impotence. At times his public comments indicate sexual repulsion. Nadar wrote that 'Baudelaire seems to have inherited all the Biblical hatred of women, the accomplice of the serpent which ruined man.'[25] Anatole France wrote, with some extravagance, that he 'put twenty centuries of Satanism into a kiss.'[26]

The truth about Baudelaire's sexuality lies somewhere between the extremes of these various interpretations. He was no more the virgin than he was the voluptuary given to all manner of sexual depravities, and the wonder is that the knowledge of his venereal infection and the legend of his virginity could have co-existed for so long. But this is not to deny that his sexual life must have been poor, as one doctor put it, and poor from an early age. Trial maintains that 'there was soon an incompatibility between love and the act of love.'[27] Sartre has asserted that physical possession was too natural to have attracted Baudelaire. One might go further, and argue that his repugnance for physical possession was the key to his aversion for everything natural.[28] 'The woman one loves', he wrote, 'is the one who gets no pleasure from it.'[29] She must, in other words, be frigid; and he cannot, must not give her any satisfaction. There is a line from Musset which, Maurice Barrès was to write, contains all Baudelaire: 'Ces plaisirs sans bonheurs, tout pleins d'un vide immense.'[30]

Like Samuel Cramer, in *La Fanfarlo*, Baudelaire saw love, above all, as the admiration and appetite for beauty. With him, it was not so much the man who sought love, as the poet and the artist.[31] He enjoyed the sensual dream. He was a voyeur rather than a performer. The most intense sensations that Baudelaire experienced were visual. As Charles du Bos wrote in his poignant *Méditation sur la vie de Baudelaire*, the supreme delight for Baudelaire lay in the contemplation of a woman's body.[32] Du Bos spoke of love 'in the only sense that Baudelaire was ever able to conceive and feel it: . . . this contemplative desire which needs only the presence, and only really possesses because it does not possess.'[33] For Baudelaire, there was always a distinction between sexual love and spiritual passion.

> Life [said André Ferran] consists for him in evasions, and love is a means of escape or of flight towards the mystery – infernal or divine. The hours of carnal love are an error in this search for a Happiness enjoyed in the conquest and possession of Perfection . . . [The intoxication of the lover] is an image, but only an image, of that embrace of Beauty which makes Man the equal of God, since it makes him forget the Ennui of limitation and the sadness of the ephemeral.[34]

9

By mid-November, 1839, Baudelaire was suffering from pains and stiffness in the joints, headaches and insomnia. Since he could not turn to his mother or his stepfather, he naturally turned to his brother. Alphonse suggested that he saw his acquaintance Guérin. He also privately arranged that Guérin should give Baudelaire some money on his behalf.

Denis-Alexandre Guérin, now in his early forties, had started his career as a pharmacist in certain Paris hospitals which specialised in the treatment of venereal disease. Thanks to his invention, *opiat balsamique*, he had made a fortune; and, while he still kept rooms in Paris, he had retired to Fontainebleau. On 4 July 1839 he had been elected a municipal councillor. A few years later, he was to be mayor.

On 20 November, Baudelaire called on him in the rue de la Monnaie.

> Thank you very much for the lesson which you got M. Guérin to give me [this to Alphonse later in the day]. I now completely agree with you. This morning, when I read your letter, with the epigraph *errare humanum*, I did indeed vaguely suspect that I should get either advice or money from M. Guérin – I got both. I have taken 50 francs, I confess it's highly probable that I'll take another 50, and I'll be content with that . . .
>
> In the meanwhile, since it is your money that I'm spending, thank you very much.
>
> I have paid for my drugs. I have no more pains or stiffness, and hardly any more headaches, but my digestion is execrable, and I have a constant small discharge, though no pain; with all this I have a splendid complexion, which means that no one suspects the thing.[1]

The 'thing' in question was gonorrhea. Baudelaire had succinctly described the symptoms of a simple gonococcal urethritis. The date of the infection would have been the early autumn of 1839.[2] Guérin was not unduly worried; he does not seem to have referred Baudelaire to a Paris hospital.

In his formative years, Baudelaire had spent little time with his mother and stepfather. He had been a neglected child and, in these crucial early years of manhood, he remained neglected. The Aupicks bore a heavy responsibility, for they had left him to his own devices, and he had developed a taste for squalid sexual encounters. Despite the infection which he caught in 1839, he continued to frequent prostitutes; some say it was in the next three years that he contracted syphilis.[3] Dr Christian Dedet, writing in 1967, maintains that he had probably done so at the time that he contracted gonorrhea. He had been eighteen years and seven months old. When one considers the effect that certain diagnoses can sometimes have on a patient's mind, one will be better able, writes Dedet, to assess the effect that this diagnosis must have had on so young a man. Baudelaire would have understood, early in his manhood, the prospect of degradation, paralysis and madness, the future that might be in store for him.[4]

He did not only suffer, already, from poor health; in 1839 he already suffered from his extravagance. He did not merely assert his independence from the Aupicks, he had begun to show them defiance. He had bought clothes on credit from the General's tailor – and this in spite of the General's instructions. On 8 December, once again, he approached Alphonse:

> I am writing to you for money again; but this is the last time . . .
> This is why I'm asking you again. With the first money you gave me, I paid for some medicines and books, and I spent the rest on entertainments, but I had carelessly forgotten that I owed a small debt to the tailor. When I left college, my father told me explicitly that, whenever I bought something, I should pay cash down. Unfortunately, he goes to the same tailor, and I'm afraid that one fine day he may ask him, casually: 'Does Charles owe you anything, does he pay you promptly?'
> I am going to see if M. Guérin is at home. I am using your permission for the last time, and I shall ask him for 50 francs.
> I say *the last time*, so as not to alarm your generosity, but [also] to impose upon myself the obligation not always to count on someone else's money . . .[5]

Guérin was at Fontainebleau, but Baudelaire saw one of his brother's colleagues, who advanced him the 50 francs Alphonse had offered him. These begging letters to Alphonse were a sad indication of the future.

On 15 January 1840, Baudelaire registered at the École de Droit for the second time. On 18 January, Aupick was appointed commander of the second infantry brigade, which was garrisoned in Paris. Whatever the politics of France, whatever its reigning house, the general's career seemed to flourish.

He kept watch over his stepson's life. On 15 April, a few days after his nineteenth birthday, Baudelaire registered for the third time at the École de Droit. These registrations had doubtless been imposed on him by the Aupicks, who were increasingly anxious to see him enter a profession. They seem to have given little thought to Baudelaire's true nature. Nothing suggests that he would have pursued a conventional career. On 15 July, at the end of the university year, he registered at the École de Droit for the fourth and last time.

In mid-November, he went to stay with Alphonse at Fontainebleau. Alphonse had long ago left the Bar for the Bench. In 1832 he had been appointed an assistant magistrate at Fontainebleau; in 1837 he had been promoted deputy magistrate. On 28 May 1840 he had been elected a municipal councillor in the town where he was to spend all his life. He had now been married for eleven years; and, after the death of an infant son, and a miscarriage, his wife had presented him with a son, Edmond, who was now seven years old. Of all the family, Félicité was to become the most hostile to Baudelaire, and she was to pass on her hostility to her collateral descendants.

There was, it seems, no hostility at Fontainebleau in November 1840. The hospitality was 'splendid.'[6] Baudelaire was still there in December. Perhaps Alphonse saw the visit as a means of keeping him away from bad company.

Whether or not the Aupicks knew of his state of health, they were perhaps aware that he had now found himself a mistress.

I don't remember her name [Ernest Prarond recorded at the end of the century]. Sara, I think. Baudelaire called her Louchette. She lived in the rue Saint-Antoine. One day, Baudelaire had taken me in the direction of the église Saint-Louis, on the pretext of looking, once more, at a *Pietà* by Delacroix. On the way, he asked for Mlle Sara from a concierge whose room opened on to a narrow alleyway. She was out. Baudelaire was infatuated with her when we knew him, but he did not keep a merciful memory of her.[7]

> Je n'ai pas pour maîtresse une lionne illustre;
> La Gueuse de mon âme emprunte tout son lustre.
> Invisible aux regards de l'univers moqueur,
> Sa beauté ne fleurit que dans mon triste cœur –
>
> Pour avoir des souliers elle a vendu son âme;
> Mais le bon Dieu rirait si, près de cette infâme
> Je tranchais du Tartufe, et singeais la hauteur,
> Moi qui vends ma pensée, et qui veux être auteur . . .
>
> Si vous la rencontrez, bizarrement parée,
> Se faufilant au coin d'une rue égarée,
> Et la tête et l'œil bas – comme un pigeon blessé –
> Traînant dans les ruisseaux un talon déchaussé,
>
> Messieurs, ne crachez pas de jurons ni d'ordure,
> Au visage fardé de cette pauvre impure
> Que déesse Famine a par un soir d'hiver
> Contrainte à relever ses jupons en plein air.

Cette bohème-là, c'est mon tout, ma richesse,
Ma perle, mon bijou, ma reine, ma duchesse,
Celle qui m'a bercé sur son giron vainqueur,
Et qui dans ses deux mains a réchauffé mon cœur.[8]

It was a savage poem, yet instinct with pity; it already had the mark of Baudelaire. He was moving towards a poetry in which *le mal* provided the fundamental insights and themes. He understood the depth of his fall, he already felt disgust at sexual practices and needs, he was conscious of the crude animality of love, a love which could be shared and bought and sold. Nonetheless, he was grateful for the chance to lose sight, for a moment, of the world, to feel a warmth which he had not yet known.

It was characteristic of Baudelaire that, even now, a handsome youth on the verge of adult life, he chose a mistress whom most men would have rejected. Perhaps he did so out of defiance, perhaps he did so because he was conscious of his venereal disease, and of his sexual inadequacy. More probably he was drawn to this woman of the streets as he was always to be drawn to the poor; he felt that she would understand his own sense of rejection. Sara the prostitute understood him, satisfied his physical needs, gave him a transient sense of being loved; and, above all, she released his imagination. Like other mistresses to come, she was the essential instrument on which he played his music, she enabled him to pursue his dreams. She was the necessary human figure whom he could transform and transcend.[9]

In December 1840, Baudelaire was once again in Paris. On 31 December, he sent his new year wishes to Alphonse, and announced: 'I have deferred a general reform in my behaviour until the year 1841.'[10]

10

There was need for reform. Baudelaire had abandoned the École de Droit; and, for all his promises to Alphonse, he continued to run up debts. He needed once again to be extricated from a situation which he could easily have avoided. Psychiatrists might say that, unconsciously, he was punishing his mother for betraying him, punishing himself for his excessive devotion to her. He was already bent on self-destruction. Alphonse demanded a complete list of his debts. On 20 January Baudelaire duly sent it, and confessed that the total was much greater

than he had thought. He owed substantial sums to his tailor and
shoemaker, to his hatter, shirtmaker and glover (he was already
something of a dandy). He also owed money to friends, including Louis
de La Gennevraye, whom he had known at the Pension Bailly. La
Gennevraye, he announced, defiantly, had lent him 200 francs 'to dress
a prostitute – taken from a BROTHEL.'[1]

Baudelaire calculated that his debts came to 2,140 francs. Alphonse
found that in fact he owed 3,270 francs, and he reproached him
severely. He offered to help. Not surprisingly, he also took the occasion
to give him a lesson.[2]

> You have written me a harsh and humiliating letter [this from Baudelaire
> on 1 February]. – *I mean to pay myself* what I owe my friends.
> As for the tradesmen, as I can't get through it all by myself, I *beg* you
> to pay two of them, two very pressing ones – a shirtmaker, and an old
> tailor to whom I still owe 200 francs and who *must* have them by
> tomorrow, Tuesday. I owe the same amount to the shirtmaker. If you get
> me out of these, I shall get out of the rest, without papa and mama
> knowing of it. If you don't get me out of it, I shall get it very badly in the
> neck tomorrow.[3]

Next day, the creditors arrived. It was an uncomfortable visit, for
Alphonse had not yet received Baudelaire's request for assistance. This
came on 3 February, and Alphonse drafted an immediate answer:

> My dear Charles,
> ... I told you, and I repeat it now, give me the names and addressess
> of your creditors and of your friends which nobody can know. I undertake
> to confess your stupidities to the General, to serve as a lightning-
> conductor for his justified anger, and then ... to assemble your creditors
> and to reach an agreement with them which allows them to be paid in
> due course.
> Think about this, and decide whether it is better to repent of having
> wildly squandered your money than to continue to run through your
> inheritance in advance.[4]

While Baudelaire struggled with his financial problems, the General
pursued his increasingly distinguished career. In January he had refused
the appointment of commandant of the École de Saint-Cyr. On 1
March he became commandant of the École d'application d'état-
major, and moved to 135, rue de Grenelle-Saint-Germain.

Whether or not Alphonse had spoken to him, he now knew enough
about his stepson's life to conclude that it was time for action. On 19
April, ten days after Baudelaire's twentieth birthday, he wrote to
Alphonse:

The moment has come when something must be done to save your brother from absolute perdition. I am at last more or less acquainted with his position, his behaviour and his habits. The danger is great. Perhaps there is a remedy; but I must see you, I must talk to you about what I am doing, so that you may learn the state of depravation of mind, not to mention [degradation of] body, that Charles has reached. I should like to have a discussion with you, Paul Pérignon, Labie [Jean Labie, the former notary at Neuilly], and Edmond Blanc, who is so good for your brother: a discussion unknown to Charles, in which we should all say what we know, so that we can be fully informed and consider what might be done.[5]

It is surprising to see Aupick mention Edmond Blanc, secretary-general to the Ministère du Commerce et des Travaux publics. It was he, in 1844, who was to introduce Baudelaire to the *Revue de Paris*; but it is not known how he had already been 'so good' for him.

I want this discussion to be unknown to Charles [continued Aupick], so as not to put him on his guard. When the situation is known and clarified, and a decision has been taken, there would be a meeting next day at my house, and Charles would appear. And there these devoted friends would explain to him the errors of his ways, the errors into which he is straying, and they would bring him to accept what is proposed to him.

As I see it, and as Paul and Labie see it, there is an urgent need to tear him away from the slippery streets of Paris. It has been suggested to me that he should make a long sea voyage, to India, in the hope that, being out of his element like this, removed from his detestable connections, and in the presence of everything that he would have to study, he might come back to the right path and return to us perhaps a poet, but a poet who had drawn his inspiration from better sources than the Paris sewers. Think this over. If we meet with this idea, I am prepared to find the means to carry it out.[6]

Aupick was not only aware of his stepson's debts and of his unhealthy way of life. According to Maxime du Camp, who maintained that he had the recollection from Baudelaire, there was now an unforgettable scene. Baudelaire erred, perhaps, by excess of imagination; Maxime du Camp was not the most accurate writer of memoirs, and his account should be read with caution. There was, however, an incident which precipitated events.

One day [recorded Du Camp], Colonel Aupick [*sic*] was giving an official dinner; he had gathered some magistrates, senior officers and important functionaries at his table. Baudelaire, who was then seventeen [*sic*], was present. I don't know exactly what followed. Baudelaire made some ridiculous joke, and no doubt Colonel Aupick put him down smartly. Baudelaire listened to the reprimand. Then he rose and went up to his stepfather, and said to him: 'You are trying to humiliate me in front of

your set. They are pretending to take your stupid talk as wit, and, out of
politeness, they think they ought to laugh at your jokes. You forget that
I have a name which your wife was wrong to abandon, a name which it
is my duty to make respected. You have failed me badly; that deserves
punishment, and I'm going to have the honour of strangling you.' He
threw himself on Colonel Aupick and seized him by the throat; the colonel
freed himself and slapped him twice in the face. Baudelaire had a nervous
attack. Some servants took him away. He was shut up in his room . . . The
solitary confinement lasted for a fortnight.[7]

Du Camp maintains that he was then escorted to Bordeaux, and
put on board a ship which was about to sail for India.[8] In fact he was
first sent to Creil, to stay with a friend of Aupick's, General Dufour.
On 27 April, still unaware of his brother's part in the arrangements,
he told Alphonse that he was setting out on a voyage.[9] On 30 April,
with the pompousness of an elder brother and a magistrate, Alphonse
replied:

My dear Charles,
   I have received your note, in which you tell me that you are leaving
soon. You tell me that they found you were leading a bad life in Paris.
   I have indeed few compliments to pay you on this part of your life. You
left college with the appearance of an accomplished young man. Our
dearest hopes, those of seeing you become a distinguished man, and of
seeing you get on well, began to be fulfilled . . . You have changed that
child full of hopes into an overexcited young man, living only for the day,
not thinking of the morrow, breaking every social bond. You have
discarded morals and customs, and you have turned hostile to people who
are older than you, and therefore could not see your way of life from the
same point of view as yourself.
   Today you recognise your mistake. You understand that your mother,
and the General, and your brother, love you, and that for them your
behaviour must be a cause of affliction. You are going to change it. By
isolating yourself from those who were leading you to your ruin, you are
going to win not new claims to our affection – you have always had that in
spite of your bad habits – but new claims to the esteem of men. You are
going to shake off the filth that was around you, and, free from the
obsessions of every day, trusting in our real affection, you will change
these causes for grief into causes for pleasure. Think how proud your
mother was of your successes at college, how well your prizes on a shelf
bore witness to your powers. As for you, you scorned your college
successes, and you sold your prizes. In your place I should want to
cast this past behaviour far away, . . . cast off this past which has degraded
you . . . .
   Dear Charles, remember that, whatever the career you choose, my
good wishes will always be with you . . . Never forget that your mother,
the General and your brother have only a single thought, a single wish:
to make a man of you.[10]

On 4 May, with military precision, the General wrote again to Alphonse:

My dear Monsieur Baudelaire,

The voyage overseas demands an expenditure of 4,000 francs (3,000 for the journey there and back as a passenger, about 1,000 francs for essential small expenses and travelling to Bordeaux and back to Paris). The destination will be Calcutta. The duration of the voyage, about a year. The captain seems to be the man we need.

I wrote to you that I had borrowed 3,000 francs to pay Charles's debts. You can understand that I should not want to commit myself for a larger sum. These 3,000 francs will remain my responsibility, I can't do more. And so it is absolutely essential to have recourse to a loan against Charles's estate. The family council will therefore be summoned as soon as possible. As you know, it consists of our friends. We have an interest in not telling M. de Praslin about Charles's follies and aberrations. My wife would therefore like to replace him, and MM. Naigeon, Julliot and Ramey by MM. Labie, Olivier, Zédé and Ed. Blanc. Leaving the premises is arranged for the 15th of this month. So try to come with a leave of absence for some days. We will make Charles come on the 7th or 8th and send him off on his travels on the 11th. We have no time to lose. I am producing the 4,000 francs, persuaded as I am that the family council will share our opinion on the need to send Charles out of his element. We shall regularise the loss against Charles's estate after he has left. It would be impossible before: we haven't enough time.

My wife is very eager that Charles should not know about this meeting of the family council. So don't say anything about it.

That is how things stand. Our two characters have conflicted with each other.[11]

Here, for the first time, almost accidentally, Aupick admitted that he was not merely concerned with his stepson's welfare; he confessed his own anger and hostility.

He was anxious, too, about his wife, and the misery she felt at Baudelaire's behaviour.

What violently disturbed me [he explained to another correspondent, early in June], *were new aberrations of my stepson's. These aberrations had caused cruel anguish to his poor mother, and she was all the more unhappy since she struggled to hide them.* Finally, with determination and energy, I gained my ends. Charles was no longer exposed to the perdition of the streets of Paris.

He accepted my reasons. He left for Bordeaux, and on the 10th of this month he boards a ship which is bound for Calcutta. It is a voyage of 12–15 months. By a fortunate and unhoped-for circumstance, Captain Saliz, a former officer of the imperial navy, has been kind enough to take charge of my young man. He tells us that he will treat him as he is treating his own son, who is sailing with him.[12]

Baudelaire had entrusted Le Vavasseur with the manuscripts of his poems. He left for Bordeaux at the end of May. When Henri Hignard returned to Paris after his holidays, he found that Baudelaire had gone.

Unhappy rumours gathered from mutual friends dissuaded me from making my appearance at General Aupick's. People spoke of violent scenes which had broken out between my friend and his stepfather. It had already been easy to see that their relationship was anything but affectionate, and that the son had grievances against his mother's husband. He never spoke to me about them, and deliberately warded off the allusions which sometimes came to my lips. I thought I understood that his mother had been taken from a modest widowhood by the love of a man who was rich and titled [*sic*], a man who was marked out for a brilliant future. She no longer found in this second marriage the respect and consideration which were her due. Those are wrongs which a son finds it hard to bear. It was soon evident that General Aupick brought into his home the overbearing severity of the commanding officer. He cruelly broke any impulse of resistance which the poor boy had been able to show. On his paternal authority, he embarked him on a ship which was about to sail for India.[13]

Mme Aupick remained in anguish: not only at her son's behaviour, but also at the thought of his long absence and of all the dangers that might beset him. At times she wondered whether she would see him again. On 9 June, as the *Paquebot des mers du sud* (296 tons) finally made its way out of harbour, for Réunion and Calcutta, he wrote to her:

My dear and beloved mama, forgive me for the incoherence of my letter – I am taken unawares. We have such a wind that within an hour we shall be on the open sea, and the pilot is about to leave us . . .

The captain is wonderful. Kind, a character, and knowledgeable . . .

I won't have you writing me letters like the last. They must be cheerful. I want you to eat well and be happy, and to think that I am happy. Because it's true. Or almost.

At the next opportunity, I shall write to the General [Aupick was now far from being the *papa* of earlier years]. As I've told you, I am taken unawares. We are already pitching quite violently.

There may be things that I'm forgetting to tell you, but you can say a good many of them in a big embrace, and I give you that with all my heart.[14]

The General approved of this farewell letter from his stepson. 'It is', he wrote, 'a first guarantee of the good effects which we expect from this harsh experience.'[15]

It was indeed to be a harsh experience. Aupick had spoken of 'the perdition of the streets of Paris.'[16] As Hérisson was to observe, if Baudelaire had already contracted syphilis, the family could hardly now have been unaware of his condition. It is, continues Hérisson, 'permissible to think that, if they had been told, they considered this so-called shameful illness as a dishonour which should be carefully concealed. But to send the sick son to India was a cruel and unreasonable measure. It would do no honour to the good sense of the General and of his wife.'[17]

> My husband, General Aupick, adored Charles [so Mme Aupick would herself explain]. When he was a child, he had taken great personal trouble with his education. He had encountered such a fine intelligence, so enquiring and so studious a mind, that it absolutely astonished him, and he grew more attached to it with every day.
>
> After the triumphs at Louis-le-Grand, when college days were over, he had golden dreams of a brilliant future for Charles. He wanted to see him reach a high position in society, and this was not unattainable, since he himself was a friend of the Duc d'Orléans. But how stupefied we were, when Charles refused everything that we wanted to do for him, and wanted to fly with his own wings, and to be an author! What disenchantment in our domestic life, which had until then been so happy! Oh, what grief! It was then that we thought of giving another direction to his ideas, and, above all, of breaking some harmful relationships, by sending him on a sea voyage.
>
> The General came from a sea port, [Gravelines], and he loved the sea with passion; at Charles's age, he would have been enchanted to set sail. He thought that a sea voyage would be better than a journey by land. He could have been mistaken, but he was full of the best intentions for my son.[18]

'Mme Aupick wrote to me that ... they hoped by this voyage *to change the course of his ideas*, and to cure him of his wish to be an *author*.'[19] So Assclincau later told Théophile Gautier. In fact, Mme Aupick had had little say in deciding on the voyage. The General had been responsible. It was the General who had 'gained his ends.'[20] For Baudelaire, the voyage was a humiliating exile. It was an enforced attempt to repair a situation which had now become irreparable.

11

Baudelaire later gave Jules Buisson a dramatised account of the voyage. It owed more to invention and to innuendo, so one surmises, than it did to fact.

He had been embarked, as a pilot's apprentice [Buisson recorded], on board a merchant ship which was bound for India. He spoke with horror about the ill treatment that he had suffered. We used to shudder as we listened to him. And when one thinks what that elegant, frail, almost feminine adolescent must have been in the hands of the sailors, it is more than probable that he was right.[1]

Many legends were, in time, to grow about this voyage – some of them no doubt fostered by Baudelaire himself.

Throughout the voyage [*La Chronique de Paris* recalled, after his death], he distinguished himself by the most eccentric behaviour, and established a relationship with an ayah (the Indian name for a children's nurse), a beautiful and ardent negress who had accompanied a creole family to France, and was going home.

This liaison was the cause of curious scenes on board, and the negress pursued Baudelaire with an affection so ardent that, with the captain's agreement, they consigned the woman to her tiny cabin throughout the voyage.

Among other eccentricities, Baudelaire believed that he had a stomach ailment, and, in order to cure himself, he used to lie in a [jolly-]boat suspended from the handrail, his breast bare in the tropical sun. He claimed that this was the only way in which he got relief, but you can imagine the state of his skin.

Baudelaire showed a great deal of composure in some terrible circumstances. As it sailed round the Cape of Good Hope, the ship was assailed by a fearful storm. The hurricane and lightning had swept away the sails and snapped the masts, and the ship, turned over on one side, completely *engaged*, as sailors say, was only saved by a skilful manoeuvre in which Baudelaire took part. In the midst of the waves which went over the ship – which was little more, now, than a wreck – he helped the second officer to unroll a tarpaulin . . . Thrown by the violence of the wind against what remained of the taut shrouds, it righted the ship as if by miracle.[2]

On 1 September, the *Paquebot des mers du sud* was forced to dock at Port-Louis, the capital of Mauritius, where the most urgent repairs were made.

It was in September, in Mauritius, that Baudelaire made the acquaintance of an advocate, Gustave-Adolphe Autard de Bragard, and his young creole wife.[3] He spent his days at their house in the rue des Tribunaux in Port-Louis, or on their estate in the quartier des Pamplemousses, where Bernardin de Saint-Pierre had set the action of *Paul et Virginie*. He talked literature to his heart's content. It was a delight to him after weeks of isolation. Emmelina de Bragard was known for her beauty; she was only three years older than himself. He loved her with a schoolboy's love; for all his cynicism, and for all his sordid experience, Baudelaire remained an innocent.

On 18 September the *Paquebot des mers du sud* left Port-Louis for Saint-Denis, in Réunion (then the île Bourbon); it arrived there the following day. Baudelaire asked Captain Saliz to let him go home.

At last, on 14 October, after nearly a month in port, and no doubt after long discussion, Saliz was obliged to confess his failure:

General,

I am writing with regret to say that I cannot make your stepson, M. Charles Beaudelaire [*sic*], finish the journey which you had planned for him on the ship under my command. I owe it to the trust which you have been good enough to place in me to give you an explanation . . .

As soon as we left France, every one of us on board could see that it was too late to hope to turn M. Beaudelaire either from his exclusive taste for literature such as it is understood today, or from his determination not to devote himself to any other occupation. This exclusive taste made every conversation which was unrelated to it irrelevant to him, and it kept him out of the conversations which were generally held between us sailors and the other military or commercial passengers. I must also tell you, although I am afraid that it will pain you, of his ideas and his cutting expressions about all the social bonds. These were contrary to the ideas that we were accustomed to respect from our childhood. They were painful to hear from the lips of a young man of twenty, and dangerous for the other young men whom we had on board, and they restricted his social relationships even further . . . In short, his life on board . . . put him into a state of isolation which, I believe, only intensified his literary tastes and pursuits. An event at sea such as I had never known in my long life as a sailor, in which we almost touched death with our fingertips, did not demoralise him any more than it did us; but it increased his dislike of a voyage which, he thought, was purposeless for him, and, although he still remained well, he had moments of sadness. Despite the work involved in sailing a dismasted ship, I did what I could to distract him since I was afraid of the consequences. Contrary to my expectations, and to my great astonishment, our arrival at Mauritius only increased his sadness, . . . and his mind was set on the wish to return to Paris as soon as possible. He wanted to leave on the first ship for France. I felt obliged to refuse, and to keep to the instructions which you had given me.

I recognised that I had no power of constraint to force him to follow me, a mission which in any case I shouldn't have accepted, but I made him see that I had no right to hand over the money you had given me. To this he replied that he would try to do without it, that he would stay in Mauritius, where he hoped he would soon earn enough to pay for his passage, and he said all this with signs of affection for me. On the other hand, from what I saw in our frequent meetings, and from the opinion of a passenger who had all my esteem and remained with him, I was afraid that he might be affected by Homesickness, that cruel illness whose terrible effects I have seen on my travels – that illness whose consequences might have been disastrous for him and would have left a burden of responsibility on me which I should have kept all my life.

And so, at the moment when he alone kept me in Mauritius, I had to draw him on board by giving him the hope that I would do what he wanted, if he still insisted on it.

His lines of argument about the way in which you would take his return, on his partial achievement, it is true, of leaving Paris for some time, helped to win me over, and I thought that I was acting according to your instructions and in your interests by bringing him here, from where he will come straight back to you, instead of leaving him in a country where his inexperience and his mistaken ideas would have exposed him to the most dangerous influences ... I had to agree to his embarking on a Bordeaux ship – he liked the ship and had chosen it himself: *L'Alcide*, Captain Judet de Beauséjour. Unfortunately this ship does not leave until after I do, but I am taking measures to see that everything is carried out properly ...

I commended him in the strongest terms to the captain, whom I know, and I hope that he will return without mishap. It remains for me, General, to record how grieved I am that I have been unable to carry out your plans, but I am convinced that I had no other course to take ...

I have the honour to be,
   General,
      Your devoted servant,

P. SALIZ[4]

On 19 October, after the repairs had been completed, the *Paquebot des mers du sud* sailed for Bengal. Next day, from Réunion, Baudelaire wrote to Adolphe Autard de Bragard:

You asked me, in Mauritius, for some verses for your wife, and I have not forgotten you. As it is decent, right and proper that verses which are addressed to a lady by a young man should pass through her husband's hands before they reach her, I am sending them to you, so that you don't show them to her unless you choose.

Since I left you, I have often thought of you ...

If I did not love Paris and miss it so much, I should like to stay with you as long as possible, and I should compel you to like me and find me a little less *baroque* than I seem.

It is very unlikely that I shall return to Mauritius, unless the ship on which I am leaving for Bordeaux goes there in search of passengers ...

And so I shall await you in France.[5]

Sixteen years later, on her way to France, Emmelina Autard de Bragard died at sea. That week, by historical coincidence, *Les Fleurs du mal* was published. In it was the sonnet 'À une dame créole': a version of the poem which Baudelaire now sent her:

   Au pays parfumé que le soleil caresse,
   J'ai connu, sous un dais d'arbres tout empourprés

Et de palmiers d'où pleut sur les yeux la paresse,
Une dame créole aux charmes ignorés.

Son teint est pâle et chaud; la brune enchanteresse
A dans le cou des airs noblement maniérés;
Grande et svelte en marchant comme une chasseresse,
Son sourire est tranquille et ses yeux assurés.

Si vous alliez, Madame, au vrai pays de gloire,
Sur les bords de la Seine ou de la verte Loire,
Belle digne d'orner les antiques manoirs,

Vous feries, à l'abri des ombreuses retraites,
Germer mille sonnets dans le cœur des poètes,
Que vos grands yeux rendraient plus soumis que vos noirs.[6]

Already, in 1841, the first three lines of the sonnet contain aromas, warmth and indolence, three tropical themes which were often to recur in the poetry of Baudelaire. Already, too, he was haunted by exotic women. He had acquired a commitment to the primitive which, to some extent, remained with him to the end of his life. Meanwhile, on 4 November 1841, on the battered three-master, the *Alcide*, he sailed from Réunion for Bordeaux. On 4 December they put into port at Cape Town.

According to Hérisson, who made a study of the episode,[7] the ship remained in port for four days. Baudelaire was to refer only vaguely to the Cape, and posterity may therefore lose itself in conjecture. Yet – unlike Leconte de Lisle, who had been there, briefly, in 1837 – Baudelaire knew a little English; and he probably had enough money to stay in a family pension. It was probable, too, that he took some of the 'promenades heureuses' which he recorded in his *Notices bio-bibliographiques*.[8] If he did so, if he took a carriage to Constantia and saw the vineyards which produced the celebrated wine, the *constance* he was to mention in 'Sed non satiata', he left no details of his excursions.[9] Yet, twenty years and more later, when he made his notes for a book on Belgium, Baudelaire set down a kind of olfactory geography, and noted that 'the Cape smells of sheep.'[10] This was certainly true, because wool and sheepskin were then the colony's chief exports; the entrails of the dead animals were thrown into the sea, and half-wild dogs would come at night to eat the detritus on the sea-shore. Leconte de Lisle was to recall them in his poem 'Les Hurleurs' – a poem which Baudelaire much admired.

There was another reference to the Cape in his notes on Belgium. It occurred in the passage where he recalled the architecture of Antwerp. 'Mixture of Renaissance and restrained rococo. Style of Cape

Town.'[11] Baudelaire had been struck by the Flemish style of the South
African houses, the Dutch colonial style which still remained despite
the British colonization. Perhaps the artistic landscape of 'L'Invitation
au voyage' was suggested in some degree by his visit to the Cape. It
was the only place with a partly Dutch atmosphere which he had
visited when he wrote the poem. Besides, for more than a century and
a half, Cape Town had been a port of call for Dutch ships on their
way to Batavia, and there was a small Muslim community, descended
from slaves and from political prisoners brought from Java in the
seventeenth and eighteenth centuries by the Dutch East India Company. The half-castes added an exotic note. The interiors and the
furniture of some of the houses still kept this dual tonality, Dutch and
Oriental. Perhaps the duality remained with Baudelaire. In his prose
poem, *Any Where out of the World*, he suggested that his restless soul
might flee to Batavia, to find 'the European spirit wedded to tropical
beauty.'[12]

This visit to the Cape was to be his only visit to Africa; but he
created an Africa in the image of his desires, and in creating it he
revealed himself. As Joseph Nnadi observed, in *Visions de l'Afrique dans
l'œuvre de Baudelaire*: 'The great features of "Africa" as Baudelaire
conceived it are found in his critical works as well as his poetry ... The
works of the artists whom he studies only serve him as a pretext for
revealing his ideal of man.'[13] In 1859, discussing the paintings of the
young Eugène Fromentin, he was to write:

> One must presume that I myself am somewhat affected by a nostalgia
> which draws me towards the sun; because, for me, from these luminous
> canvases, there arises a heady vapour, a vapour which soon condenses
> into desires and regrets. I catch myself envying these men who are lying,
> outstretched, under these blue shadows: these men whose eyes, which are
> neither awake nor asleep, express, if they express anything, only the love
> of rest and the sense of happiness inspired by boundless light.[14]

On 8 December the *Alcide* sailed from Cape Town for Bordeaux.
When the provisions of fresh meat and vegetables and fruit, and the
rations of fresh water, had been exhausted, the diet was reduced to the
preserved food on which travellers were forced to depend; and no
doubt, as the voyage neared its end, food was scarce, and some of it
had grown uneatable.

Proust was later to maintain that Leconte de Lisle showed a deeper
understanding of the tropics than Baudelaire. 'Baudelaire well remembered this tropical nature ... But one feels that he had only seen it
from a ship. Leconte de Lisle had lived in it, and relished every hour.'[15]

Leconte de Lisle had indeed been born in Réunion, and he had spent years in the tropics; but, if Baudelaire's recollections were fewer, they were nonetheless more intense, and this Eastern voyage, the only voyage he made in his lifetime, was to have a formative influence on him and on his poetry. 'While he was still young,' Yriarte was to write, 'Baudelaire went to India [sic], . . . and the impression of this violent nature was never effaced in him . . . The recollection of this nature was revealed in all his tastes, he loved brilliance and violent colours, the enormous and the monstrous . . . There was in him something of the fakir and the dervish, he was contemplative like an Oriental.'[16]

Baudelaire created a legend: the legend that he had been to India. After his death, Asselineau explained to Théophile Gautier: 'Baudelaire himself often spoke to me as if he had been to Madagascar, Malabar and Calcutta [sic] . . .'[17] Gautier adopted the legend: 'Although he loved Paris as Balzac loved it, . . . his recurring thoughts often took him back towards India, his youthful Paradise . . . And, as in fairytales, through a mist of azure and gold, one perceives palm-trees swaying under a warm, balsamic wind, brown faces with white smiles attempting to distract the master's melancholy.'[18] Banville embroidered on this fiction; Asselineau went further, and declared that, 'from his voyage to India, Baudelaire had brought back a very adequate knowledge of the English language.'[19] (Baudelaire had learned English at school, and from his mother.) Jules Levallois, in *Mémoires d'un critique*, remembered: 'I have heard him say that he had hardly arrived in Calcutta before he re-embarked.'[20] Maxime du Camp enlarged on the Indian legend: 'He stopped at Réunion, at Mauritius, and landed in India . . . He supplied cattle for the British Army, he lived I know not where, I know not how; his mother secretly sent money to her son, who rode on elephants and wrote poetry.'[21]

In 1886, in a letter to Eugène Crépet, Ernest Prarond wrote more reliably:

> The real truth is that Baudelaire, who embarked against his wishes, gave the slip to India . . . as soon as he could do so . . . Perhaps Baudelaire obligingly left the general public these rumours of long peregrinations in legendary lands, because he drew from them, with mysterious colours, the appearance of coming back from afar. In any case, he never talked to us about these voyages. He hardly breathed a word to us, on his return, of a brief stay in Mauritius or Réunion. Did he pursue his voyage further? I don't think so.[22]

He had not been, as he later claimed, to Malabar, Ceylon or Hindustan. Captain Saliz' letter proves that he had not been to India; so did the *jugement d'avant faire droit*, which was to be the grounds for

Baudelaire's *conseil judiciaire*. As Hérisson was to observe in *Le Voyage de Baudelaire dans l'Inde*,

> ... he did not tell the truth to friends when he spoke of travels in that country, or to himself when he wrote the autobiographical notes in *Mon Cœur mis à nu*, or to Ancelle in his letter of 1864. Why? Because he had a mental tendency which induced him to alter the truth ... He remained faithful to the falsehood of his youth, through auto-suggestion, or when his memory began to fail him.[23]

On 15 February 1842, with a cargo of sugar and coffee and after more than three months at sea, the *Alcide* docked at Bordeaux. Baudelaire was met by Pierre Zédé: one of the *conseil de famille* who had agreed to send him on his voyage.

As Hérisson notes,[24] Baudelaire was anxious to return to Paris; in April, only two months later, he was to come of age, and to gain his inheritance and his independence. Yet he had cut short the voyage which the General had imposed on him, and he must have been apprehensive of the reception that he would be given. Besides, he was almost certainly aware that, on 2 or 3 March, there would be the drawing of lots for conscription. The best means of avoiding conscription seemed to be not to appear in Paris until matters were settled.

There has been some debate about his movements between 16 February and 2 or 3 March.[25] All doubts and explanations are dismissed by Pichois. On 16 February, according to Pichois, Baudelaire wrote to his mother:

> Dear sweet mama, in two or three days I'm going to embrace you. I have had two vile crossings – but since we shall talk and laugh together again, the good Lord is not entirely bad ...
> They tell me that, apart from your anxiety, you are well. So much the better. When I was at sea, I did nothing but think of your poor dear health.
> Now you can set your mind at rest. Coaches are less easily lost than ships.[26]

Late in February, according to Pichois, Baudelaire returned to Paris. On 3 March, at the Palais de Justice, he took his place in drawing lots for conscription.[27] A few weeks later, he learned that he did not have to enlist. He lived with the Aupicks at the École d'application, 135, rue de Grenelle-Saint-Germain. 'When I questioned him about his voyage,' his mother later said, 'I saw that he did not want to talk about it.'[28]

He brought back with him, Prarond maintained, the only poem he was known to have written on his voyage. 'It is certain that 'L'Albatros' was suggested to him by an incident on the crossing. He recited it to us on his return. Apart from this poem and the recollection of a negress or Malabaraise . . . whom he had seen whipped in Mauritius, the whole journal of his maritime penance seemed a blank page.'[29]

Prarond was inaccurate: no doubt Baudelaire had brought back his poem 'À une dame créole'. In his illuminating book, *Dans les chemins de Baudelaire*, Jean Pommier maintained that 'L'Albatros' was unlikely to have been composed on the voyage; Asselineau, to whom Baudelaire later read his poems, found it a revelation in 1859.[30] It is probable that both critics were right, and that it was an early version of the poem that Baudelaire recited to Prarond. This would not have been the only occasion on which a poem matured in his mind, and was constantly perfected, before he chose to set down the final version.[31] Whatever poems he brought back from his 'maritime penance', the experience was to make Baudelaire a superb maritime poet; and he kept, from his Oriental odyssey, a vision which would never leave his eyes.

In Baudelaire's memory, the sea was nearly always to be calm and sunlit; only in his dreams would it be stormy. Like everyone who sailed, he knew the powerful impression made by the roll of the ship; he knew how the sailor identified himself with the vessel, especially in heavy weather. This recollection was to inspire the lilting allegory of 'La Musique'.[32] This was no doubt among the poems which Dr Alison Fairlie had in mind when she observed that Baudelaire was 'specially original in evoking sensations . . . related to basic muscular or nervous tensions and fundamental rhythms in the human being.'[33] Yet Baudelaire, who was fascinated by fluidity and by geometrical shapes in movement, was to prefer the sight of a ship in port to life at sea. More than once, in his poetry and in his prose, he would record his delight at seeing ships at anchor. He loved the motionless; the rocking of a ship was one of the rare kinds of movement that gave him pleasure.

In his future work, themes or images suggested by the voyage were to fill ten times the space of all the memories of his first twenty years. His voyage was to be almost the only source in his work of the open air, of light and happiness. It was to enrich his sensibility, to free him for ever from social conventions and literary constraints. It was to make him one of the first of French exotic poets, to make him think and write like a man. This unique voyage balances nearly all the rest of his experience – and its absence would have been an irreparable loss for his work. Swinburne was to write of Baudelaire's 'tropical homesickness.'[34] Countless memories of the voyage filled his hungry soul: negresses with shadowy hair, the smell of musk and tar, brilliant colours, curious rhythms, correspondences between the senses. To him 'a scent was to mean more than a sunset, a perfume more than a flower, the tempting demons more than the unseductive angels.'[35] There was to be, as Arthur Symons wrote,

... something Oriental in Baudelaire's genius: a nostalgia that never left him after he had seen the East ... For only the East, when one has lived in it, can excite ones vision to a point of ardent ecstasy ... He is before all things the artist, always sure of his form. And his rarified imagination aided him enormously: not only in the perfecting of his verse and prose, but in making him create the criticism of modern art.[36]

Baudelaire had set out on his voyage as a youth, drawn to the vocation of a poet; he returned with his imagination on fire, and more determined than ever to persevere in the career which he had chosen. Posterity owes General Aupick a debt of gratitude which he had never sought to incur.

12

'How stupefied we were,' Mme Aupick was to remember, 'when Charles refused everything that we wanted to do for him, wanted to fly with his own wings and to be an author! Oh, what disenchantment in our domestic life, which had until then been so happy! Oh, what grief!'[1] She was always to regret that her son had wings of his own. 'If Charles had let himself be guided by his stepfather, his career would have been very different.' So she explained after his death. 'He would not have left a name in literature, it is true, but we should have been happier, all three of us.'[2] Her observations showed her respect for bourgeois behaviour, and her absolute failure to understand her son. 'She knew him less than anyone,' Malassis assured Asselineau at the end of Baudelaire's brief life. 'I imagine that she could easily have lived with him for several thousand years without understanding him in the least.'[3]

Even after his return from his Eastern voyage, Mme Aupick did not lose the hope that he might choose a socially acceptable way of life. Maxime du Camp observed (though again his words should be taken with caution) that she tried to create useful relationships for her son. 'She took him to the official *salons*, and Baudelaire was sometimes more original than was appropriate ... He preferred the taverns where he found himself in touch with a generation of great men to be – poets, writers, artists, sculptors and composers. In these taverns he recited his unpublished poems and became intoxicated with the praise which was lavished upon him.'[4]

For Baudelaire it was a time for friendships. His friendship with Ernest Prarond deepened. Prarond, who came from Abbeville, was five weeks younger than Baudelaire. He was an excellent classical scholar, and he had come to Paris to study law.[5]

> We used to roam around a great deal together [he recalled], and go to dinner at Duval's, the bistro on the corner of the rue Voltaire and the place de l'Odéon, sometimes at the Tour d'Argent, not far from the bridge which leads to the quai de Béthune, very often beyond the barrier, in the direction of Plaisance. Sometimes we went further afield, to a good tavern way beyond the Faubourg Saint-Jacques, at the Moulin de Mont-souris, in a part of the world which in those days was almost waste land . . . On one side, we had a view as far as the fort at Charenton, and on the other a view right over Paris. It was a good place to philosophise.
>
> And so, about five o'clock in summer, we used to set out in search of a place which was scorned by the bourgeois and convenient for conversations . . . There were days when the Chaussée du Maine and the rue de la Tombe-Issoire heard propositions and declarations of principle which would have made the Institut collapse.[6]

Late in March or early in April, as he approached his twenty-first birthday, Baudelaire found lodgings at 10, quai de Béthune, on the île Saint-Louis.[7] On 9 April, he came of age. Five days later, Narcisse Ancelle, the notary at Neuilly, showed him a draft account of his trusteeship, from which he learned that, 'wanting to prove to him, once again, the affection that they feel for him, M. and Mme Aupick here declare that it is their intention to assume personally and completely the expenses of the voyage which they made him undertake with the aim of completing his education.'[8] On 28 April, the account of the trusteeship was signed by the General and Mme Aupick; two days later, Baudelaire approved it. He had inherited his patrimony. He had a fortune of 100,050 francs, a substantial sum for the time. He had 18,000 francs, inherited from his father, at his disposal. He also owned four pieces of land at Neuilly. He had an annual income of 1,800 francs.

That month, he moved to the quai de Béthune. Here, remembered Charles Cousin,

> . . . he installed his chests, his old table with the twisted legs, his Venetian mirror, his very few books (Ronsard and his pleiad; Régnier did not come until later), his cats, and a certain dark oak bed, without legs or columns, a kind of sculpted coffin in which I suppose that he sometimes slept.
>
> We rarely went to hunt him out on his island. We were sure to see him arrive when he had put the finishing touch to 'some new thing or other.'[9]

The 'new thing' was a poem which was, perhaps, one day to be included in *Les Fleurs du mal*. In Louis Ménard's *grenier*, in the place de la Sorbonne, Baudelaire (added Cousin) 'recited, or rather chanted his poems to us, in a voice which was monotonous but imperious, and he compelled the attention of the profane.'[10] It was in this *grenier*, known to the future novelist Octave Feuillet, to Leconte de Lisle, the chansonnier Pierre Dupont, and the Romantic actor Bocage, that Cousin rediscovered 'the clearest picture of the Baudelaire that I knew best: Baudelaire at twenty years old, seeking his way between Villon and Ronsard, mad about old sonnets and young artists, refined, paradoxical, bohemian and a dandy.'[11]

Sometimes Baudelaire came to the *grenier* for a more contentious purpose; as Cousin recorded: 'We arranged to meet one winter day, Baudelaire and I, to taste, in company with L.M., our host at the *grenier*, the delights of hashish.'[12]

Critics have written much nonsense about Baudelaire and his use of excitants. Baudelaire, said Anthony North Peat, 'used to swallow sufficient laudanum to poison five persons. One hundred and twenty drops, however, of that narcotic sufficed to make him talkative and gay, and to inspire him with the power to write.'[13]

Other friends and acquaintances countered such a view. 'Not only did Baudelaire not take hashish or opium, as he boasted that he did,' wrote Levallois, 'but he even avoided spirits . . . He drank nothing but unadulterated wine.'[14] Troubat recalled: 'He drank wine like an epicure, not like a ploughman.'[15] 'He was sober by nature,' remembered Le Vavasseur. 'We used to drink together; I never saw him drunk.'[16] 'He was not in the least a drinker,' Champfleury confirmed, 'but avid for aesthetic discussions over a bottle of porter.'[17] Only at crises in his later life, in despair and misery, did Baudelaire turn to drink for consolation. Now, in the 1840s, if he frequented cafés and brasseries, he did so in order to talk and to observe. If he drank, he did so in moderation; if he took hashish, he did so likewise in moderation. 'The author of the *Paradis artificiels* had certainly tried hashish,' wrote the journalist Maxime Rude, 'but to claim that he sometimes had *déjeuner* off it is only an abominable joke, at best good for stunning innocent bourgeois.'[18] It was a joke that Baudelaire himself would have made, in the days of the île Saint-Louis; it was part of his pose as a dandy, part of his attempt to create his legend.

> Baudelaire was sober like all writers [Gautier recalled], and, while he admitted that the inclination to create oneself an *artificial paradise* by means of some or other excitant, opium, hashish, wine, spirits or tobacco, seems to be part of the very nature of man, . . . he saw in it a proof of original perversity, an impious attempt to escape from *necessary* suffering, a pure satanic suggestion to usurp, here and now, the happiness reserved later as a reward for resignation, determination, virtue, the persistent striving towards the beautiful and the good.[19]

13

On 28 May 1842, Auguste Dozon called on Baudelaire and wrote him a poem. It was an indifferent poem, but it should be remembered because it almost certainly described Jeanne Duval.

> Ô jeune homme ennuyé, tu tiens sur tes genoux
> Ce corps brun et luisant, d'où sort une étincelle,
> Qui, cachée à tes yeux, te pénètre et harcèle,
> Et sans frémissement des fibres de ton cœur,
> Te fait verser pour rien ta bouillante vigueur ... [1]

It was not the only warning of the dangers of loving Jeanne. Dozon already recognised her greed and her stupidity, and the degradation of her nature. Such warnings were always given in vain. Some time between his twenty-first birthday and 28 May, Baudelaire had begun the longest and the most needed liaison of his life.

> Je t'adore à l'égal de la voûte nocturne,
> Ô vase de tristesse, ô grande taciturne,
> Et t'aime d'autant plus, belle, que tu me fuis,
> Et que tu me parais, ornement de mes nuits,
> Plus ironiquement accumuler les lieues
> Qui séparent mes bras des immensités bleues.
>
> Je m'avance à l'attaque, et je grimpe aux assauts,
> Comme après un cadavre un chœur de vermisseaux,
> Et je chéris, ô bête implacable et cruelle!
> Jusqu'à cette froideur par où tu m'es plus belle! [2]

Maxime du Camp maintained that Baudelaire had brought his mistress home from the Cape: 'a negress or a quadroon who, for many years, gravitated round him.'[3] The statement was untrue. Jeanne Duval came later into his life. In 1898, Jacques Crépet examined the records of the hospital to which she was admitted in 1859. Her place of birth was given as San Domingo.[4] Years later, in *Propos sur Baudelaire*, Crépet gave a different account of her origins. He had come to believe that she was the daughter of Jeanne Lemaire, who had herself been born on 25 July 1789, the illegitimate child of a prostitute in Nantes, Jeanne-Marie-Marthe Duval. This ancestry would help to explain why Baudelaire's mistress sometimes assumed the name of Jeanne Duval, sometimes that of Jeanne Lemer or Lemaire. In the eighteenth century, the port of Nantes had had a constant link with Guinea and the West Indies, and it had often seen the arrival of negro slaves who had not found a buyer in the ports. Such details would, as Crépet said, 'help to explain how a little black blood had come to colour the shoulders of [*la Vénus noire*].'[5]

As for her age, it is still more uncertain than her ancestry. In 1859 the hospital records gave it as thirty-two;[6] this was almost certainly understated, and probably by as much as ten years. If in fact she was thirty-two in 1859, she had presumably been born in 1827. Yet she seems to have taken small parts at the Théâtre de la Porte-Saint-Antoine in 1838-9. It was then, apparently, that she became the mistress of Nadar. She could hardly have been eleven at the time.

Besides, Nadar did not record a nymphet, but a woman in her maturity. She had, he said, a special beauty,

> ... a special piquancy for the refined. Under the wild abundance of her frizzled, ink-black shock of hair, her eyes, as big as soup-tureens, seemed blacker still. Her nose was small and delicate, the wings and nostrils exquisitely defined; her mouth was somewhat Egyptian, although from the West Indies ... Her whole expression was serious, proud, and even slightly disdainful. The top half of her figure was long, well-shaped, undulating like a snake, and particularly remarkable for the exuberant, improbable development of the bosom, and this exorbitance, which was not ungraceful, gave the whole the drooping appearance of a branch weighed down with fruit ... Her voice was sympathetic, well toned ...[7]

In July 1842, in his poem 'Le Divan', Banville, in turn, evoked her likeness. In his *Souvenirs*, which appeared towards the end of the century, he affirmed that Baudelaire

> ... only ever loved one woman, that Jeanne whom he always and so splendidly celebrated. She was a coloured girl, very tall, who held her head well: that innocent, superb brown head, crowned with wildly curly hair; and her gait, which was that of a queen, full of a fierce grace, had about it something both divine and bestial ...
>
> And sometimes this contemplator made Jeanne sit in front of him in a big armchair; he looked at her lovingly and admired her for a long while, or recited poems to her in a tongue which she did not understand.[8]

It is as well not to be misled by Banville, for he always tended to exaggerate. The picture of Jeanne which is given by others is – as Féli Gautier was to write – that of a prostitute: 'Pavement prostitute, extra at a *café-chantant*, exotic menial: it is impossible to be quite sure.'[9] It is a prostitute whom we see in certain drawings of Jeanne which were done by Baudelaire himself. Rioux de Maillou was to recall, in *Souvenirs des autres*:

> The dusky Jeanne did not restrict herself to the society of Baudelaire. She had even been seen to dance with a stranger at a dance hall, and to leave

the said dance hall, also on the arm of a stranger.

The fact had been reported to her lover, who had contented himself by observing, with a sigh:

'Poor girl! It's her profession. She does have to live.'[10]

One evening, Baudelaire confessed, he went to his mistress's lodgings. As he was putting the key in the lock, he heard two voices: 'One of them I knew, for it was hers, and the other was a man's . . . Jeanne was with someone. Do you understand? With someone . . . Well, I had the courage to go away.'[11]

With Jeanne Duval, said Marcel Ruff, misfortune entered Baudelaire's life.[12] She installed herself, wrote Gonzague de Reynold, like a bird of prey in a deserted nest.[13] 'The Black Venus tortured him in every way. Oh, if you knew!' wrote Mme Aupick, when her son had died. 'And how much of his money she devoured! In her letters, and I have a mass of them, I never see a word of love. If she had loved him, I should forgive her, perhaps I should love her; but these are [just] incessant demands for money.'[14] *La Vénus noire* had neither mind nor heart; she had the skills and instincts appropriate to a woman of the streets. She would easily have recognised Baudelaire's true needs, and known how to satisfy them, and she would thereby have assured herself of the money that was her only concern. She caused him untold suffering, not only through her infidelity, but also through her addiction to drugs and drink. Marcel Ruff maintains that she loved him, that he had found her a responsive and an understanding companion. Yet one feels that she did not, could not love him, much less understand him. She was the necessary catalyst, her sexuality combined with his recollections of the distant countries he had seen. He needed her for his poetic creation. Jeanne Duval took her beauty from the halo with which Baudelaire was pleased to crown her. She was the mirror in which there appeared, more beautiful, enhanced, all the ghosts and visions of earlier years.

Féli Gautier maintains that Baudelaire 'never gave himself to her, if it is true that, in love, the communion of flesh, without the close communion of soul, is simply a lie to dull human grief.'[15] She held him in the trap of his sexual needs, and she also served as his cover. Far from being the cynical voluptuary of legend, he was tormented, and he was frustrated. He believed himself to be damned. His condition was not her fault. She merely knew how to exploit it, and he knew of no other way to satisfy his appetites. Some men need punishment, and one may recall an observation which Baudelaire was to make in later years: 'The strange thing about woman – her pre-ordained fate – is that she is *simultaneously* the sin and the Hell that punishes it.'[16]

As Michel Butor remarked, there is enough evidence of her coldness and his impotence to suggest that, 'in the hell of their bed, the sexes were reversed.'[17] Perhaps, indeed, she had a Lesbian element in her nature. Nadar, in a cryptic note (but Nadar is not always reliable), mentioned 'relations with her mother + a woman.'[18] Porché was to speak of a maid, Louise, whom Jeanne was to treat as a confidante and companion.[19] Sometimes, continues Porché, if some physical impotence prevented Baudelaire from performing the act of love, 'he would, in his imagination, find exhausting pleasure in seeing it. Witness his taste for licentious engravings, his understanding with Lesbos: Delphine and Hippolyte [in *Les Fleurs du mal*]; Louise and Jeanne.'[20] Such comments were perhaps unjust. Jean Prévost observes that Baudelaire sometimes distances love, in order to give more freedom to poetic contemplation.[21] The love of women for each other was a love which he could witness with a sympathy which was at once sensual and disinterested. The poem 'Femmes damnées' was not so much voluptuous as pensive.

There are no poems in the French language more sensual in inspiration than certain poems in *Les Fleurs du mal*. Yet perhaps Baudelaire had sought in imagination what his senses had refused him. It may be that he only sought the role of a voyeur. What Baudelaire avoided, what he averted and distanced in his poems, was what, for other men, would have been fulfilment in love. It fell to Jeanne Duval to inspire some of the eternal poems in French literature – of which she had no understanding, and for which she felt no respect.

> Bizarre déité, brune comme les nuits,
> Au parfum mélangé de musc et de havane,
> Œuvre de quelque obi, le Faust de la savane,
> Sorcière au flanc d'ébène, enfant des noirs minuits,
>
> Je préfère au constance, à l'opium, au nuits,
> L'élixir de ta bouche où l'amour se pavane;
> Quand vers toi mes désirs partent en caravane,
> Tes yeux sont la citerne où boivent mes ennuis.
>
> Par ces deux grands yeux noirs, soupiraux de ton âme,
> Ô démon sans pitié! verse-moi moins de flamme;
> Je ne suis pas le Styx pour t'embrasser neuf fois,
>
> Hélas! et je ne puis, Mégère libertine,
> Pour briser ton courage et te mettre aux abois,
> Dans l'enfer de ton lit devenir Proserpine![22]

14

Whether or not Mme Aupick knew of her son's liaison with Jeanne Duval, she continued to be anxious about his way of life. He was obliged to ask her not to send him medicines or syrups, not to worry needlessly about him.[1] It was characteristic of Baudelaire that, despite his financial problems, he still bought a picture for her.[2] The General was more severe. On 12 July, excusing himself from dining with his mother, Baudelaire wrote: 'You talk of making your house agreeable to me; but the simplest way is to invite me when you are alone.'[3]

The gap between Aupick and his stepson widened even further. Baudelaire was lost in Bohemia, the General remained triumphant in spite of all political vicissitudes. Next day, 13 July, his friend the Duc d'Orléans, the heir to the throne, was killed in a carriage accident. It was a death which the General himself had nearly shared. Before the Duke left Paris for the military camp at Saint-Omer, he had decided to go to Neuilly to take leave of his parents. Aupick was to accompany him, but a messenger arrived with some urgent letters, and the Duke asked Aupick to attend to them; this delay kept him at the Tuileries. The Duc d'Orléans left alone for Neuilly. There, in the route de la Révolte, his carriage overturned, and he died of his injuries. He was thirty-two.

The tragedy caused Aupick lasting grief. It also revealed some unpleasant aspects of his character. He had recently found himself on military service with the Duc d'Orléans in Luxemburg; they had received a visit from the Grand Duke of Luxemburg, King William I of The Netherlands. Apparently, to mark the occasion, the King had proposed to decorate Aupick; and Aupick was not, now, too shocked or saddened by bereavement to reflect that his patron's death might lessen his hopes of the decoration. On 20 July, a week to the day after the tragedy, he wrote to a Dutch acquaintance, General Baron Fagel, to ensure that he received the honour.

Monsieur le Général,

The dreadful misfortune which has just deprived France of a prince whose remarkable qualities were her guarantee of a happy and glorious future, makes it my duty to delay no longer in calling on your kind intervention to obtain the official letter which confers upon me the Order of the Lion of The Netherlands. An unknown soldier, Monsieur le Général, I had no reason to expect that H. M. the King of The Netherlands would honour me with this signal favour. I feel that I owe it to the benevolence of the August Prince whom we mourn: this Prince who, in calling me to honourable duties beside him, thus placed me, by this fact alone, high in public esteem. It is a blessing to add to those which he lavished upon me, and it is a reason the more why I attach the greatest value to it. I must therefore beg you, Monsieur le Général, to inform His Excellency the Minister of the kindness of His Majesty the King of The Netherlands, and to take the necessary steps so that I am sent an official entitlement which allows me to request permission to wear the insignia of the Order which I owe to the King's generosity.

I shall always keep, Monsieur le Général, a profound recollection [*sic*] of the benevolence which His Majesty and his August Son showed me in Luxemburg. I consider it the most honourable reward for my constant endeavours to pursue as a man of feeling and virtue the noble career to which I have dedicated myself.[4]

A copy of this letter remains in the Dutch State Archives. It reveals more than Aupick's pomposity. It suggests his vanity, his intense ambition, his blatant cultivation of authority. It shows him to be an egotist and a ruthless opportunist. The letter does much to explain why he was often in conflict with Baudelaire.

On 8 October, Aupick was duly appointed Commander of the Order of the Lion of The Netherlands. The death of the Duc d'Orléans did not end the favour which he enjoyed from the reigning dynasty in France: the Duc de Nemours was to pay him the same benevolent attention which his elder brother had shown him. On 11 November he was appointed, by Marshal Soult, to command the department of the Seine, and the Paris garrison.

On his prestigious new appointment, he and his wife moved to 7, place Vendôme: to the splendid early eighteenth-century hôtel de Créqui. Baudelaire could not call on his mother for want of proper clothes, but – extravagant as ever – he sent her a pair of ear-rings to wear in her new and princely setting. It was a gift which would have been more appropriate from a husband or a lover than from a son. The gesture may have been one of those which Mauriac had in mind when he wrote: 'The Œdipus complex is quivering here to the naked eye.'[5] While the General was occupied with military affairs, Baudelaire invited his mother to the quai de Béthune. On 4 December, he announced: 'On the evening of Tuesday, 6th, there will be an elegant dinner here for you. I embrace you with all my heart.'[6] He wrote in a tone of loving complicity.

The year which had seen the beginning of Baudelaire's liaison with Jeanne Duval had also been a year for deepening friendships. It was, it seems, in August 1842 that Privat d'Anglemont had introduced Banville to him. They had met in the Jardin du Luxembourg, and walked through the Paris streets, where Baudelaire had dazzled Banville with his conversation. Then they had sat down to supper in some little tavern, and Baudelaire had talked about cooking:

In India, in Réunion, in Mauritius, he had learned some extraordinary recipes, and he explained them with irresistible charm. Somewhere or other in Africa, staying with a family to whom his parents had recommended him, he had soon been bored by the trivial minds of his hosts; and he had gone off to live alone on a mountain with a very young, very big coloured girl who knew no French. She cooked him strangely spiced ragouts in a big polished copper cauldron, round which there yelled and danced some naked little negro children. Oh, those ragouts, how well he described them, and how eagerly one would have eaten them![7]

Baudelaire had subjugated Banville, and he had enmeshed him in his legend.

They were to spend many evenings with the *chansonnier* Pierre Dupont and the artist Émile Deroy in the little room which Banville occupied at his parents' house in the rue Monsieur-le-Prince. In time they gathered at his small apartment in the place de l'Odéon; Auguste Vitu, the journalist, was to recall Deroy smoking his pipe, and Baudelaire, 'a strange and grandiose poet,' with his elbows on his knees, his head in his hands, adjusting the rhymes of a sonnet.[8] Baudelaire and Banville also met at the Café Tabourey. It was here that Baudelaire encountered Champfleury. Years later, in his *Souvenirs et portraits de jeunesse*, the novelist and art historian set down his early recollections of the friendship:

> One day, Baudelaire appeared with a volume of Swedenborg under his arm; nothing in any literature could, he said, compare with Swedenborg. On our visits to the Louvre, he assured me that *Bronzino*, an affected master, was the greatest artist of any school.
> Another day, you would meet the poet with a big algebra book. Literature no longer existed, it was algebra you had to study . . . A woman with a masculine appearance became the most perfect being in creation, and a thousand other singularities . . .
> Nonetheless Baudelaire's conversations were a fruitful source of learning for me, because I listened attentively to the man who had read much and sought much, and, thanks to the intellectual appetite of a youth of twenty, I did not find it hard to digest these singular fruits . . .[9]

Champfleury recalled these conversations with the respect of youth for maturity. It is strange to record that he and Baudelaire had been born in the same year. Yet Baudelaire was already setting himself apart. By now, said Prarond, he had written 'Don Juan aux Enfers', inspired by the painting by Delacroix. Philippe de Chennevières recalled: 'On the sofa at Le Vavasseur and Buisson's apartment, at 31, rue de Beaune, he often recited us sonnets sharp and vigorous in tone, strange and powerful, the verse of an aristocratic poet, a peerless colourist and descriptive writer . . ."[10] Baudelaire was prepared to read but not yet to publish; he did not yet consider himself the master of his art. Prarond and Le Vavasseur were about to bring out a book of collected poems, and he was invited to contribute to it. He sent his 'scribbled-on paper' to Prarond, and urged him 'always to be very hard on the childish style.'[11] However, he soon showed the pride of the creative artist; perhaps, even now, he was aware of his potential worth. When Le Vavasseur suggested alterations, Baudelaire withdrew his poetry.[12] He could not restrict himself to the École normande; he had seen and dreamed too much, and he was too eager for independence and experience. In 1843, at the Tour d'Argent – a bargemen's restaurant – or in the île Saint-Louis, Baudelaire and the École normande ate and drank together, and found that life was well worth the living. Gradually, however, they grew apart. After 1848, Le Vavasseur returned to his native Normandy; Prarond (who had taken a doctorate in law) was to go home to Abbeville, and to devote himself to local history. Jules Buisson was to enter politics.

Meanwhile, in 1843, Baudelaire bided his time, and he continued to lead an unsettled life. On 30 March he was obliged to borrow 7,500 francs, with a mortgage on his land at Neuilly. By 19 April, he had been obliged to leave the quai de Béthune, and he was living in the rue Vaneau. It was from here that he warned Prarond: 'There is going to be some *upheaval* in my life. It may even be that circumstances suddenly oblige me, reluctantly, to go back to my island.'[14]

The island was the île Saint-Louis. Soon afterwards, he installed himself at 15, quai d'Anjou. On 22 May he asked his mother: 'Would you be good enough to come and see me tomorrow evening, to help me a little in arranging my new lodgings?'[15]

In some ways, the new lodgings were to be disastrous for him. In another note, he told Mme Aupick that he had paid the upholsterer's bill, and that he had no more money.[16] On 11 June, he told her that he had sold his land at Neuilly for 70,000 francs; the sale had been made that morning by Maître Labie, a lawyer at Neuilly.[17] Baudelaire was leaving the profit from the sale, 31,000 francs, in the hands of Me Labie, at an interest of 5 per cent. By 27 June he had 9,500 francs' worth of debts, very nearly twice his annual income. He arranged for his mother to be his representative, and to have his income paid to him. She was also to help invest a sum of 24,150 francs, in agreement with him and with Ancelle. On 31 August, Baudelaire told her that his financial problems had prevented him from dining with her.[18] Perhaps his finances also explained his decision to move again. It was, it seems, at the end of October that he wrote to her:

I shall send someone today to tell you which domicile I have chosen. I can certainly make shift with the conditions which you have made for me. You must come yourself and tell the master of the house. Only there will be no question of a *conseil judiciaire*. If I found that you had set it up without my knowledge, I should escape at once, and this time you wouldn't see me again, because I should go and live with Jeanne.[19]

It was the first time, in his surviving letters, that Baudelaire had mentioned Jeanne to his mother; despite his financial problems, he had set her up at 6, rue de la Femme-sans-Tête (now rue Le Regrattier). It was very near his new lodgings at the hôtel Pimodan, 17, quai d'Anjou. At the hôtel Pimodan itself, there was another cause of temptation. On the ground floor was an antique shop, where Antoine-Marie-Jean Arondel – a Balzacian figure – dealt in curios and old pictures; he was to sell Baudelaire pictures of doubtful authenticity and, from 5 November, to haunt his life by lending him money.[20] Years later, in the margin of a note for Arondel, Ancelle observed that 'the mania for pictures led M. Beaudelaire [*sic*], who was then very young and easy to exploit, to buy worthless canvases. This was the main reason for the establishment of the *conseil judiciaire*.'[21]

15

The hôtel Pimodan had been built in the seventeenth century by the architect Le Vau for Charles Gruyn, Sieur des Bordes. In 1682 it passed into the hands of the Duc de Lauzun, the lover of la Grande Mademoiselle, and in 1779 it belonged to the Marquis de Pimodan. By the early 1840s, however, it had fallen from its ancient glory, and it had come to be known as the hôtel des Teinturiers, because there was a dye-works on the ground floor. It was now that Roger de Beauvoir, the novelist and socialite, grew enamoured of the old *hôtel* on the île Saint-Louis; and it became a Bohemian palace which almost rivalled, in brilliance, the Bohemia of the Impasse du Doyenné.[1]

Roger de Beauvoir was haunted by the deserted courtyard, by the stone lions guarding the main door, by the birdless silence. He admired the ante-room ceiling, on which an assembly of symbolic figures, said to be by the artist Lafosse, represented *The Triumph of Truth*. In the salon, the ceiling was painted by Lesueur. In the bedroom was a secret door, said to have been used by Lauzun when he was pursued by his jealous mistress. 'Despite its shadows and its dust,' wrote Beauvoir, in

Les Mystères de l'île Saint-Louis, 'I was drawn to this old Venetian palace on the banks of the Seine . . . Here the last sounds of the capital died away, for here the heart of Paris ceased to beat.'[2] In the spring of 1844 he moved into the suite of rooms on the *piano nobile*. The silence of the hôtel Pimodan was shattered.

Roger de Beauvoir was not the only culprit. Mme Paul de Molènes, the novelist's wife, was later to record how, one day, the landlord, Baron Jérôme Pichon, rebuked Baudelaire for making so much noise. 'I give you my word', said Baudelaire, 'that nothing extraordinary happens here. I chop wood in the salon, I drag my mistress along the floor by her hair. That is common practice, and you have no right to interfere.'[3]

There was much about the hôtel Pimodan to shock the conventional. From April 1845, after Roger de Beauvoir had departed, his rooms were occupied by Fernand Boissard de Boisdenier and his mistress, the courtesan Marix. Boissard, too, was a young man of means, and, perhaps, of too many talents. Had he needed to work, he might have been an accomplished historical painter, but as it was he flitted from painting to poetry, and from poetry to the violin, and in the intervals he entertained his friends.

The entertainments were so remarkable that, twenty years later, the Goncourts put Boissard and his *hôtel* into *Manette Salomon*, their novel of artistic life in Paris. Boissard's guests were not only drunk with punch. It was in his salon, round a clavichord painted by Watteau, that le Club des Haschischins held the monthly meetings which Théophile Gautier recorded. Years later, Mme Aupick insisted that 'Charles didn't know [hashish] when he was very young and living at the hôtel Pimodan.'[4] He had in fact tried it before he lived there, and once, at least, he was to see Gautier and Balzac taking hashish at the quai d'Anjou. Henri Hignard went further: he maintained that Baudelaire 'belonged to the famous Club des Haschischins.'[5]

It was in the summer of 1843 that the author of *Mademoiselle de Maupin* first encountered Baudelaire. It was, remembered Gautier, at the hôtel Pimodan.

Charles Baudelaire was still an unpublished talent, preparing himself in shadow for the light, with that fierce determination which, with him, doubled inspiration; but his name was already beginning to spread among poets and artists with a quiver of expectation . . .

His appearance was striking. His jet black hair was close-cropped, and, coming to regular points on his dazzling white forehead, it covered his head like a kind of Saracen helmet. His eyes, the colour of Spanish tobacco, had a deep, intelligent look, perhaps a little too searching; as for his mouth, . . . a slight, silky moustache concealed its contour, but allowed one to perceive the mobile, voluptuous ironic curves like those of the mouths once painted by Leonardo da Vinci. His fine, delicate nose, slightly rounded, with quivering nostrils, seemed to scent some vague and far-off fragrance . . .

He was wearing a coat of some shiny black material, drab-coloured trousers, white socks and patent leather pumps, all of it meticulously clean and correct . . . One might say that he was a dandy who had strayed into Bohemia, but kept his rank and manners and that cult of self which is typical of the man imbued with the principles of Brummell . . .

Soon after this meeting, Baudelaire came to see us, to bring us a book of poetry, on behalf of two absent friends . . . From this moment onwards, a friendship was formed between us.[6]

It was also, no doubt, in the days of the hôtel Pimodan that Baudelaire first encountered Balzac. Prarond described their first meeting, although he did not date it.

I can tell you [this to Eugène Crépet] how Baudelaire introduced himself directly to Balzac. He told me about it himself, on the day after their meeting. Balzac and Baudelaire were walking along a *quai*, in opposite directions. Baudelaire stopped in front of Balzac, and began to laugh as if he had known him for ten years. Balzac also stopped, and answered with wholehearted laughter, as if he had re-discovered an old friend. And, having recognised each other at a glance, and greeted each other, these two spirits went on their way together, chatting, discussing, enchanting one another, never able to astound each other.[7]

Charles Asselineau, who was to be the first biographer of Baudelaire, left a graphic account of the hôtel Pimodan in the poet's day:

The *hôtel* was sanctified by the presence of several celebrities, literary and artistic . . . Baudelaire lived in an apartment at the top of the *hôtel* which he rented for 350 francs a year. It consisted, I remember quite well, of two rooms and a lavatory. I can still see the principal room. It served as a bedroom and study, the walls and ceiling were papered in red and black stripes; it was lit by a single window, all the panes of which were frosted except the top row. 'So that I can see the sky,' he used to say.[8]

Banville, always lyrical, was to paint a more detailed picture of Baudelaire's setting:

a small, three-room apartment, which, in its bizarre and personal elegance, was exactly like him. The floor was covered with a warm, thick carpet; all the walls were hung with a glazed paper with an enormous flower pattern in red and black [*sic*] . . . High, square armchairs, upholstered by an excellent craftsman, and very comfortable, were simply made of plain wood and covered in plain linen . . . The main room, which had

an alcove, looked over the river. The centre of the room was taken up by
a huge table, in solid walnut, a rare eighteenth-century masterpiece . . .
There was no library; but, as I came in, I saw some thirty books in an
open cupboard: valuable old editions, clad in irreproachable bindings . . .
On other shelves, there gleamed handsome decanters, a bottle of Rhenish
wine, and green cut glasses . . .[9]

On the red-and-black wall there hung, in time, the portrait of the
tenant of the apartment, painted by his friend Émile Deroy. It showed
Baudelaire the dandy, bearded, and dressed in black, with immaculate
white linen. 'Add patent shoes, pale gloves, and a dandy's hat,'
continued Asselineau, 'and you will have Baudelaire exactly as he was
then, as people used to see him walking round the île Saint-Louis.'[10]

He was a great dandy [confirmed Charles Cousin, in *Voyage dans un grenier*],
and a great theorist of elegance. Not a fold in his coat which was not
intentional. And so what a marvel it was, that black apparel, always the
same, at any time, and in every season. That frock-coat, of such graceful
amplitude, . . . that cravat, so prettily knotted; that long waistcoat, with
the first of its twelve buttons done up very high, and casually half-opening
over an exquisite shirt, with pleated cuffs; those trousers, 'spiralling' down
on shoes of irreproachable lustre. How many cabriolets their brilliance
cost me![11]

Asselineau and Cousin wrote as friends. Others were bewildered,
sometimes irritated, by Baudelaire's alternate poses as dandy and
Bohemian. Champfleury said that his changing moods used to astound
the neighbourhood. 'One morning he appeared with a smile, holding
a large bunch of flowers . . . Two days later, his head was bowed, and
his shoulders hunched, he looked like a Carthusian monk about to dig
his grave.'[12] In his *Portraits cosmopolites*, Charles Yriarte noted: 'For a
long while Baudelaire used to carry a carved dagger; it was to help
him to die with elegance. Of course I know that it was then the fashion
to be doomed to some horrible fate, to aspire to the peace of the tomb;
but that unquiet, deeply troubled spirit was genuinely preoccupied with
the great unknown. All his harmless fads, his thirst for eccentricity, . . .
degenerated into a habit and became second nature to him.'[13]

All these accounts were written after Baudelaire had died; one must
make some allowance for the legend which had long arisen round the
poet of *Les Fleurs du mal*. One must also remember that Baudelaire was
twenty-two when he came to the hôtel Pimodan: little older than a
student at the Sorbonne.

His bohemianism, his *bousingot* truculence, were calculated to astound
the bourgeois; but Charles Yriarte was later to confirm: 'The greatest
debaucheries, the dreams of Capri, and the sadistic orgies of the poet

of *Les Fleurs du mal* existed only in his imagination. Deep down, he was quite conventional.'[14] His dandyism, like his Bohemian eccentricities, was a protest against vulgarity. Whatever his pose might be, it was always a means of distancing himself from other men. It was a means of protection against the world. It was also, perhaps, a means of feigning an assurance which he did not possess.

16

He posed, too, in his attitude towards Catholicism. He often indulged in cynical comments about religion. He did not attend church services; he resented attempts to make him observe Catholic rites. Yet he could not shake off his Catholic dualism, his consciousness of warring flesh and spirit. Christ the Redeemer was to be absent from his work, which tilted the postulates on the side of sin; but, from his childhood, his religious training had made him look upon man and the world through the doctrine of the Fall. Despite his occasional blasphemy, his refusal to conform, he remained among the most profoundly Catholic of poets. Barrès declared that, in Baudelaire, he recognised 'an eternal character, the sinful priest.'[1]

In his more outrageous moods, Baudelaire sometimes claimed to be the son of a priest and a nun.[2] The claim was not entirely untrue. His father had been a priest for some nine years, before he had abandoned the priesthood. His mother had gone to a convent school. She remained intensely devout, and she had brought up her son to share her religious views. She was to be profoundly shocked by some of his poems, but she remained convinced that he was pious at heart. Here, at least, she seems to have understood him. Le Vavasseur, who knew him well, also maintained that Baudelaire was a true Christian.[3] If, at moments, he could not accept Catholicism, he still wanted to do so. His troubled spirit longed 'to turn back towards the fortifying chant of the bells, towards the consoling twilight of the Church, towards the family, towards the mother – the mother, that bosom always waiting for the *failure*, the prodigal and the foolishly ambitious.'[4]

Baudelaire's attitude to life was profoundly Catholic. Sometimes he chose to be outrageous.[5] Yet, as Jean Prévost was to observe: 'Baudelaire only blasphemes as a Christian.'[6] Pierre-Jean Jouve was to record: 'Baudelaire, *vir christianissimus*, . . . as all his written work affirms, demands the absolute and the good, perfection and salvation; and he hides them beneath the splendour of evil. He worships God, and he mentions Satan.'[7] 'Like the Satan of Dante and the Scriptures,' decided Robert de Bonnières, 'Baudelaire had faith without love. And there lies all the greatness of his poetry.'[8]

Jacques Crépet wrote, convincingly, that Baudelaire was Catholic by birth, by upbringing, by study, and by inclination. He had lost faith early in life; but always, even in revolt, he had kept the memory of the religious ecstasies of his first youth.[9] Repeatedly, in his *Journaux intimes*, Baudelaire himself records his respect and his need for religion. 'Even if God did not exist, Religion would still be Holy and Divine.'[10] 'There is a magical effect in prayer. Prayer is one of the great forces in intellectual dynamism.'[11] And again: 'God is the eternal confidant in this tragedy of which every man is the hero.'[12]

17

At the end of 1843, Baudelaire collaborated with Prarond in writing a verse drama, *Idéolus*. It was the first of four theatrical projects which he conceived over the years, and none of them was to be completed. Like many of his literary contemporaries, he had ambitions to be a dramatist, but he did not think like a man of the theatre. He still had the confidence of youth, believed in himself and in his versatility. He was already living too much on hopes and promises.

He was not only concerned with the theatre, or with journalism. Before the end of the year, said Prarond, this feckless youth of twenty-two had already written many of the poems which were to appear in *Les Fleurs du mal*; he recited a number of others which were not to appear in the book.[1]

> The original idea or impression of a number of poems, which we saw born, from 1841 to 1848, go back [recorded Buisson] to that fatal voyage, so terrible for the man, but in more than one way profitable for the poet. He recited these poems to us, sometimes before they were finished, sometimes in our rooms, late at night, with great charm of voice and diction, sometimes out of doors, as he walked along with us, or nestled in the grass in the Bois de Boulogne.[2]

'He read like people officiate,' remembered Charles Yriarte, 'a little pompously, but with rare perfection, and it was a delight to hear him read his sonnets.'[3]

It was in 1843 or 1844 that Baudelaire first met Félix Tournachon, better known as Nadar. Nadar was a Bohemian who rose far above Bohemia. He had lived in poverty, but he had not made a habit of squalor, or an indulgence of penury. He was remarkably gifted; he also had the dynamism, the tenacity of purpose to succeed. He earned celebrity as a writer and as a caricaturist. He was to be – with the possible exception of Carjat – the most distinguished French photographer of the nineteenth century.

Another friendship dates from these years. In 1842, said Jean Ziegler, when he had moved to the quai de Béthune, Baudelaire had become an intimate of the artist Émile Deroy. Their friendship was to last until the artist's early death. Deroy, a year older than Baudelaire, was much influenced by English painters. It was, perhaps, from him that Baudelaire drew his admiration for Sir Thomas Lawrence, and for English art. He was to meet Delacroix too late for Delacroix to have been his adviser when he came to write his *Salon de 1845*. His adviser, so Ziegler maintains, was the young Deroy.[5]

In 1844, in four sittings, by lamplight, at the hôtel Pimodan, after dinner at the Tour d'Argent, Deroy painted Baudelaire's portrait. The young face, with its penetrating, wide-set eyes, its gentle mouth, its slight moustache and beard, is the face of the Romantic *par excellence*. It is also the face of the dandy; and to be a dandy, as Baudelaire understood it, was to aspire to the sublime. The doctrine of dandyism, as Baudelaire conceived it, was a spiritual doctrine. Beauty alone was its law. 'Oh, rare example', exclaimed Banville, 'of a face truly divine, uniting every elegance, every one of the most irresistible powers and enchantments!'[6] The sharp intelligence, the sensibility, the melancholy are already present; the despair and savageness have yet to appear. There is a quality reflected only in this portrait, and in an early photograph by Nadar: it is a kind of youthful gentleness.

Baudelaire grew tired, in time, of Deroy's dandyish portrait – 'that daub,' he called it – and gave it to a friend.[7] Asselineau recognised it as a page of history: 'It resurrects a whole past of poetic and aspiring youth.'[8]

It also resurrected an attitude to life: a denial of maturity. The son who was so deeply attached to his mother regretted that he was no longer with her, and he appeased his regrets by his extravagance. The dandy painted by Deroy continued to show an ostentatious disregard for money. On 5 January 1844 he explained to Mme Aupick:

> You know that I have a new tailor – I needed one – and that, the first time you employ such people, you must give them money. He will mistrust me, and look sour, if I give him a promissory note. I need you to advance

me 300 francs at once – which makes 25 francs more than *the month of February* . . .

I talked to you about leaving a [new year] card on the General, because I thought it was appropriate, and because I thought that this attention would please you. Since you believe that he would be offended, instead of understanding the real reason, there is nothing more to be done, and nothing that I can do. These dreams of conciliation are painful. All I can promise you, as I have told you, is a year of work and good sense – nothing more.

There is a male pride which you, as a woman, and as his wife, cannot understand. Why do you oblige me to be so hard, and why do you delude yourself like this?[9]

For a year and more, the General and his stepson had ignored one another; their characters continued to conflict. Mme Aupick hoped, in vain, for reconciliation.

'I can promise you,' added Baudelaire, 'that, when I have done one or two novels, *I know where to sell them* – two months' work is enough.'[10] The novels were not to be written. In the meanwhile, the debts accumulated. He owed a restaurateur 190 francs. On 29 February he received a bill (probably for 300 francs he owed Arondel); he sent it to his mother immediately.

I really apologise for not having been to visit you [he added, on 3 March]. The month had twenty-nine days, which confused my calculations, and the bill only arrived on the 29th.

Besides – and this is a feeling which will displease you very much – I don't know how to describe to you the unhappy and violent effect produced on me by that big, cold, empty house, where I know nobody except my mother [*sic*]. I only go in warily, I only come out furtively. It has become unbearable to me. Forgive me a little, and leave me to my solitude, until a book emerges from it.

I need my 425 francs. And then I think that, according to the conditions you made for me, you ought to send me money for my expenses in March.[11]

As the year continued, his troubles were not only financial. He had been exempted from conscription in the army, but he had still been obliged to serve in the Garde Nationale. On 28 June, the disciplinary board of the 4th battalion of the 9th Legion condemned le sieur Baudelaire, man of letters, and rifleman in the 4th battalion, to 72 hours' imprisonment, because he had disregarded his duties. On 14 July he was jailed in the prison of the Garde Nationale – vulgarly called the Hôtel des Haricots. Next day he turned, as usual, to his mother:

You must get me out of a fearful trap. I have been in prison since yesterday morning . . .

I absolutely must get out tomorrow − I have business in the country. Once I am out of here, I shall apply myself to settling matters with the *garde nationale*. I have therefore just sent a letter to the general at headquarters in which I have told him that *I am summoned imperiously to my lawyer's by matters of importance − a signature, money, etc*, and that *I should promise to come of my own accord* another day, to serve the rest of my sentence. Now that will have a very good effect − if you go yourself to declare the same untruth, and insist that [the lawyer] absolutely must see me tomorrow . . . The headquarters of the *garde nationale* is in the place du Carrousel − the general is M. Carbonel.[12]

Baudelaire's behaviour was baffling. He could hardly have thought that General Carbonel would accept such an obvious untruth, or bend the rules to suit a prisoner's convenience. He could not have believed that his mother, the wife of the commanding officer of the Paris garrison, would have abetted him in a lie. Presumably she did not call on General Carbonel; and presumably Carbonel himself ignored his prisoner's extraordinary letter. It was on 17 July, after three days in jail, that Baudelaire was released.

18

Another, much more serious judgment was to be passed upon him. Mme Aupick and her husband had become increasingly concerned about his inability to work. He had long since abandoned the École de Droit and, with it, all pretence that he would enter a profession. He was bent on literature, but he had no books to his name, not even regular work as a journalist. He already lived beyond his means, spent money on women, on antiques, on paintings of doubtful authenticity, on rare books and on presents for his mother.

Sometimes, it must be said, his extravagance owed much to his imagination. One day he offered *déjeuner* to Henry Murger's friend, the Bohemian Alexandre Schanne. Schanne had been a pupil of the historical painter Léon Cogniet; he now scraped a living together by selling pictures to junk-shops, giving piano lessons, and even playing the trombone at the Élysée-Montmartre. He was a regular patron of the Café Momus. No doubt he expected to make amends for his pitiful diet when Baudelaire invited him to a tavern in the faubourg Saint-Honoré. Baudelaire ordered a piece of brie, and two bottles of bordeaux. He often ate like this, he said, and persuaded himself that there had been many previous dishes equal to the cheese and wine.[1] No doubt,

said Troubat, quoting the story in his *Souvenirs*, Schanne had told it with
his own style and wit; but, with Baudelaire, one always had to make
allowance for preciosity and the mania for shocking even his friends.[2]

One had to make allowance, too, for his poverty. Now, in the
summer of 1844, he was eating on credit in restaurants, buying clothes
on credit, running up substantial interest. Sometimes he begged:

> He used to go to Mme Prévost's, in the Palais-Royal, and ask her for a
> bouquet, a very beautiful one.
> 'But, Madame,' he used to say, 'I warn you that I shan't pay for it . . .
> I am the poet Baudelaire . . . I need a bouquet, and I don't have the
> means to pay for it . . .'
> 'Well, you shall have it all the same.'
> And he had his bouquet.[3]

He did not only beg; at times he sold his belongings. Louis Ménard,
browsing in a bookseller's 5-sou box, found the copy of his own first
work, *Prométhée délivré*, recently inscribed to Baudelaire;[4] but Baudelaire
was desperate for money. Ultimately, he relied on his mother to ensure
his financial security. In the last two years, he had spent over 44,000
francs of his inheritance. He had sold his land at Neuilly. It was clear
that what remained of his patrimony had to be invested, and that the
capital must be kept intact. He must learn to live within his means, he
must be protected from himself.

This decision may have owed something to what Buisson called 'the
General's abhorred authority'[5]; but, finally, it depended on Mme
Aupick. Some time before 10 August, she asked for a preliminary
judgment from the Tribunal Civil de Première Instance de la Seine.
She made many complaints about her son. His extravagant tastes and
his undesirable way of life had, she said, led her and her husband to
send him to India. Baudelaire had not gone to India; he had returned
from Réunion without permission. The land at Neuilly had been sold
at auction; he owed 13,500 francs. She herself was being sued for five
to six thousand francs. Baudelaire was probably resorting to money-
lenders; he owed 900 francs to a restaurateur. He had bought two
pictures for 400 francs, and sold them for 18 francs.[6]

On 10 August the Tribunal ordered that Baudelaire's family council
should be convened. On 24 August, the family council met once again.
They considered Baudelaire's extravagance in the last years of his
minority; they noted that all attempts to control it had failed. They
observed that,

> . . . once he had reached his majority and become the master of his
> fortune, Monsieur Baudelaire had abandoned himself to the wildest
> excesses; that in the space of eighteen months he had squandered nearly

half his inheritance, which reached a total of about 100,000 francs, and that his most recent behaviour gave cause to fear that the rest of his inheritance would be completely dissipated if there were to be the slightest delay in providing him, a spendthrift, with a *conseil judiciaire* . . .

For these reasons [continued their report], the family council agree unanimously that a *conseil judiciaire* should be given to him, . . . and that the tribunal's choice should fall upon someone other than his mother, . . . because of her state of health and because of a mother's weakness for her children.[7]

On 21 September, the Tribunal decreed that Narcisse-Désiré Ancelle should be Baudelaire's *conseil judiciaire*.

When Ancelle assumed his task in September 1844, he was within a few days of his forty-third birthday. He had been born in Plessis-de-Roye, an *arrondissement* of Compiègne, on 29 September 1801. He had become a notary's clerk at Neuilly, under Maître Guibert, and then under Maître Labie, whom he had succeeded in 1832. That year he had married Louise-Julie Blondel; the marriage was to bring him five children, and a happy domesticity which was to last for more than fifty years. When he was appointed Baudelaire's *conseil judiciaire*, he had just resigned as a municipal councillor in Neuilly (where, in time, a street was to bear his name). He was, however, an assistant justice of the peace, a post which he was to keep for thirty-five years.[8]

Perhaps he undertook too much. Mme Aupick wrote that he was 'full of goodwill, but he is slow and timorous.'[9] Years later, Asselineau, one of Baudelaire's closest friends, was to write: 'Monsieur Ancelle is unfindable, unpunctual, always late, and the difficulty in finding him doesn't hasten matters.'[10] Despite such failings, he possessed the necessary credentials for an adviser.

Ancelle was to need all his acumen and all his patience for the task that was now entrusted to him. Baudelaire fiercely resented this infringement of his liberty; yet, in a sense, he himself had asked for this decision to be made. As Michel Quesnel observes in his perceptive study: 'Through Ancelle, Baudelaire found himself once more at the frontiers of childhood, secretly glad to be there again.'[11] He was dependent on Ancelle as a father figure; he was, still, dependent on his mother. Henceforth, the power of decision did not lie with him; henceforward, like a child, again, he had to conform. In bringing this humiliation on himself he was, unconsciously, taking revenge on his mother for her second marriage; he was also returning to the days when she was Mme Veuve Baudelaire, and she had been entirely his: when she had been both his idol and his friend.

This self-destructive behaviour was not new to Baudelaire. Even in his days at school, he had persistently failed to work, he had repeatedly been punished for indolence and provocative conduct. He had lived on repentance and promises; but the repentance had been brief, the promises had not always been kept. He had wilfully damaged his prospects at Louis-le-Grand, he had not attended the École de Droit, he had already suffered from his casual sexual encounters. Now, at the age of twenty-three, he was rapidly approaching financial ruin.

The establishment of Baudelaire's *conseil judiciaire* was a sensible decision; it was also to be a disaster. Though Baudelaire had patently brought it upon himself, though in certain ways he wanted it, though perhaps he had chosen it as a means of prolonging his dependence on his mother, it left him with a lifelong sense of humiliation. It gave him a sense of permanent immaturity and impotence. Through all his days he was to be tied, like a child, to apron strings, obliged to plead with Ancelle, to beg for his mother's intervention, to be an adult who was not allowed to lead his life as he chose. The *conseil judiciaire* not only inflicted profound humiliation upon him, but a life of unremitting frustration. He was addicted to extravagance as a consolation for unhappiness. Now the drug had been withdrawn from him. His monthly allowance of 200 francs from Ancelle was to make him bitter, compel him to borrow, accumulate interest, and fend off a crowd of creditors for the rest of his life. He was constantly to be short of money, constantly exhausted by financial worries and by the repeated need to change his seedy lodgings, by the chronic disease of poverty. Baudelaire had brought the *conseil judiciaire* upon himself; but it was to darken his existence. It was to turn his life into a burden, and to create conditions which were so inimical to writing that one must feel a certain surprise that his finest work was written at all.

The suffering of Baudelaire, so Jouve was to observe, offers, more or less continually, the spectacle of a labyrinth with no way out.[12] Through the *conseil judiciaire*, Mme Aupick was to torture Baudelaire all his life, and he in turn was to torment her.[13]

19

Ancelle now established Baudelaire's financial situation. In April 1842, at the time he came of age, Baudelaire had a fortune of 100,050 francs; now, in September 1844, there remained only 55,550 francs, which would produce an income of 2,629 francs a year. On 7 December, Baudelaire signed Ancelle's statement.

Despite the establishment of the *conseil judiciaire*, the new year, 1845, opened in an atmosphere of anxiety. It was, it seems, early this year that Baudelaire announced to his mother:

M. Ancelle will come and see you this very day . . . He will talk to you about the matter that I have discussed with you, the matter which so concerns me, since I have an absolute need of rest, and I cannot work without rest.

Since my great failure on New Year's Day [to place my work], I have contracted some verbal engagements, which can bring me in a good deal of money in a month, if I settle down to the task at once.

I beg you, dearest mother, help me in this case, as always. This way of life absolutely has to end, and since M. Ancelle is quite disposed to repay this loan for me, don't be an obstacle to it.

Would you also do me the pleasure of not mentioning your 20 francs to him? He gave me a little money yesterday to carry me up to the end of the month, and he might find it strange that I hadn't mentioned it to him.[1]

The situation soon deteriorated even further. Ancelle kept strictly to the rules which had been laid down, and he refused to give him money.

All I need is twelve days to finish something and sell it [Baudelaire explained to his mother]. If for a sacrifice of *60 francs, which represents a fortnight's peace*, you obtain the pleasure of seeing me at the end of the month give you the proofs of *three books sold*, which represents at least *1,500* francs, and thank you profoundly, will you regret them? . . .

60 francs! Is it really possible, and must I give up finding this last kindness, even from my mother?

I don't want to go and see you again, I suffer too much there; and yet I should like to see you from time to time . . .

The service which I ask of you is meant not only to fulfil the task I've mentioned to you, but to convince me, too, of the need to love you for ever.[2]

Already, in these early days of the *conseil judiciaire*, Baudelaire set the tone for his correspondence with his mother; he was in debt, he had no money, no certainty of money, he was living on hopes and depending on her kindness. He was already circumventing Ancelle, asking her for funds, making her feel guilty about her second marriage, reminding her of his increasing hostility to Aupick, causing, perhaps, dissension between her and her husband, showing alternate brutality and devotion. He was already a victim of life, a victim of his own psychological condition. He had already learned the use of emotional blackmail.

As a *collégien* of seventeen, Baudelaire had told his mother that modern literature was distasteful to him. 'Only the dramas and poems of Victor

Hugo, and a book by S[ain]te-Beuve [*Volupté*] have amused me [*sic*].'[3]
It has been suggested that Prarond had already presented Baudelaire
to Sainte-Beuve.[4] It was probably now, in February 1845, when Hugo
received Sainte-Beuve into the Académie-Française, that Baudelaire
addressed himself to the author of *Volupté*, and sent him a poem he had
written for him.[5] It was a bitter account of his schooldays and the
malaise which he had known as an adolescent, the sympathy which he
had felt when he read the novel – the history of a priest who was a
prey to melancholy and frustration, whose sensuality had been at war
with his spiritual and intellectual nature. Since his schooldays, Baudelaire had frequently returned to *Volupté*; he had found in it, again and
again, an understanding of his own condition.[6] Sainte-Beuve's reply to
this tribute does not survive; but there is every reason to believe that
it established their relationship.

'Sainte-Beuve is at the origin of the art of Baudelaire,' wrote Maurice
Barrès. 'He has that sad, cold, sullen materialism, weary from debauchery. A mixture of the mystic and the sensual.'[7] It was not only
Sainte-Beuve the novelist, but Sainte-Beuve the poet who had an
influence on Baudelaire. In 1829, he had published *Vie, Poésies et Pensées
de Joseph Delorme*; the book consisted mostly of poems, said to be the
work of a friend of his who had died young. They were in fact the work
of Sainte-Beuve himself. Maxime Rude declared that 'over Baudelaire
rises the shadow of *Joseph Delorme*, of that poet too forgotten or too little
read: too effaced, in any case, by his glory as a critic: Sainte-Beuve.
L'Oncle Beuve, as Baudelaire used to say, recognising that he was at least
his nephew. And Sainte-Beuve, for his part, was the last, as one can
imagine, to be mistaken about this relationship.'[8] He was not mistaken.
'You are right,' he told Baudelaire. 'My poetry was like your own; I
had tasted the same bitter fruit, deep down full of ashes. Hence your
very kind, very faithful sympathy for me. I return it to you, dear
friend.'[9]

Sainte-Beuve enjoyed the admiration of the younger man; he
responded to his affection, an affection which went as far as complicity.
Yet, in the crises of Baudelaire's life, Sainte-Beuve was always to
disappoint his 'nephew' – or, as he preferred to call him, his *cher fils*.[10]

There were other friendships, now, which were less distinguished but
more rewarding.

> On his île Saint-Louis [Prarond remembered], Baudelaire also formed or
> strengthened his friendships with artists, Boissard, Feuchères and others . . .
> From this time (1845–1846), Baudelaire was concerned with painting as
> much as poetry. I sometimes followed him to the Louvre – he rarely
> passed it without going in . . . Baudelaire had crazes, he was very drawn

by a Theotocupuli [El Greco], went into the museum for two or three pictures, and left.

He was beginning to discuss the moderns. I need not say how much he admired Delacroix. Among the draughtsmen, as he sometimes took sides violently, he adored Daumier and abominated Gavarni.[11]

He was in fact absorbed in modern art. His critical work seems to have been hardly less important to him than his poetry. As Margaret Gilman observes, through the twenty years of his literary activity the two ran parallel.[12] Early in April 1845, he asked his mother for some money. 'Have there been more *scandals in the house* about the creditors?' he continued. 'My book will definitely appear on the 9th, my birthday.'[13]

The book in question was his first signed work, his *Salon de 1845*, but it was not to go on sale until after 10 May; the introduction was to be dated two days earlier. No doubt Baudelaire was simply anxious to reassure his mother about the progress of his work. In mid April, he was forced to entreat her once again: 'Do me the pleasure, I beg you *as a favour*, of sending me a little money, *30*, if you can, less if you want, even less than that. I am in such a flurry of corrections, posters and slip-proofs, that it is impossible for me to go out, to go in search of money . . .'[14]

Some time in the second half of May, Jules Labitte published the *Salon de 1845*. The book appeared as the work of Baudelaire Dufaÿs. Perhaps the name was intended to suggest patrician lineage, or – as a version of his mother's maiden name – perhaps it was intended to remind Mme Aupick that she had a son.

20

The *Salon de 1845* is written with the brio and the self-assurance of youth, the passion appropriate to its author's age. 'M. Delacroix', he begins, 'is certainly the most original painter of ancient and modern times. That's how it is, what can one do about it? None of M. Delacroix's friends, even the most enthusiastic, has dared to say this simply, crudely, impudently, as we do.'[1] Already, in the first pages of the first of his *Salons*, Baudelaire proclaims his allegiance. It was, it seems, this year that he met Delacroix – possibly through Jules Buisson, who frequented the artist's studio, probably with Fernand Boissard, at the hôtel Pimodan.[2] In his *Salon*, he praises him at a time when he was still more criticised than praised; and his admiration was to endure. It would not be an exaggeration to say that the greater part of Baudelaire's art criticism was to be a glorification of Delacroix.

As Jean Prévost was to observe in his study of Baudelaire, it is almost impossible to exaggerate the influence which Delacroix had upon him.[3] Apart from the influence of certain pictures, there was the influence of the man's prestige, his conversation, his aesthetic ideas, and the example which he set. This influence already dominated the *Salon de 1845*. For Baudelaire, what was supremely important was the spiritual energy of man, whatever direction it might take; he celebrated this energy in his own poetry, and in his criticism. He sought for intensity, energy and fervour. What Baudelaire admired in Delacroix was a man as passionate as himself, but a man who controlled his passions and made them the servants of his work.

We know Baudelaire's taste for engravings, and for long contemplation: a revival, perhaps, of the happy days of his childhood, when he was surrounded by pictures. To substitute them for reality was the action of a man who preferred pictures to living men, a man who often preferred art to nature: a man who had seen Delacroix grow excited about work in the presence of the countless sketches from life which he disdainfully called his dictionary. Why should the artist's work not become, in turn, the poet's museum, his dictionary, his substitute for nature? Delacroix showed Baudelaire how he could organise tumultuous dreams into an artistic destiny. From 1844, the pictures and drawings of Delacroix lived in Baudelaire's imagination; they were to reappear in the images of his poetry. Here and there – as in 'Don Juan aux Enfers' – he was to create a Delacroix in words.[4]

'We only know two men, in Paris, who draw as well as M. Delacroix, one in a similar manner, the other in a different way.' So Baudelaire continued, in his *Salon de 1845*. 'One is M. Daumier, the caricaturist; the other is M. Ingres, the great artist.'[5] Baudelaire respected Ingres, although he was never wholly in sympathy with him. For Daumier he was to feel a lifelong admiration. In later years, he wanted to establish a *catalogue raisonné* of Daumier's work, and he was only deterred by the wealth of material.[6] He was to send him an inscribed copy of *Les Fleurs du mal*.[7] His admiration for Daumier was warmly reciprocated. Daumier kept some of Baudelaire's drawings, including a self-portrait, which he compared for clarity and wit to the sixteenth-century French portraits in the Louvre. He said more than once that if Baudelaire had applied his gifts to painting, he would have been as great an artist as he was a poet.[8]

It is curious that, for Baudelaire, the most important painting in the Salon, after those of Delacroix, was *La Fontaine de Jouvence*, by an artist who was virtually unknown. William Haussoullier was a pupil of Paul

Delaroche, and he was much influenced by Ingres. He has been described as a French Pre-Raphaelite, and there was indeed a Pre-Raphaelite sentiment about this picture, in which the old and frail had drunk from the miraculous fountain and regained their youth. 'The feeling in this picture is exquisite,' wrote Baudelaire. 'In this painting people love and drink, . . . but they love and drink in a way which is very grave and almost melancholy. This is not fiery, restless youth, it is second youth which knows the value of life and enjoys it with serenity.'[9] For Baudelaire, the painting had elegance and absolute assurance, it even recalled some early masters of the Venetian school.

This was to be the only painting by Haussoullier which Baudelaire was to discuss; possibly he came to regret how he had acclaimed the artist's 'sudden, unexpected, brilliant arrival.'[10] Haussoullier was to exhibit at the Salon of 1859, but Baudelaire was not to mention him. Yet now, in 1845, he was moved by *La Fontaine de Jouvence*. He was anxious to defend an artist who had been derided by other critics; and, discussing the work of Louis Matout, he wrote: 'Let M. Matout think of M. Haussoullier, and let him see all that is gained on earth in art, in literature, in politics, by being radical and absolute, and by never making concessions.'[11]

Baudelaire had misjudged the stature of Haussoullier: otherwise his comments were more sure. He was generous to artists of the second rank, but he was well aware of the rank to which they belonged. He felt obliged to deplore the fact that the jury had rejected an allegorical painting by Fernand Boissard; he had no doubt seen it at the hôtel Pimodan. He felt constrained to pay a few considered compliments to Arondel, another denizen of the *hôtel*, who had his ambitions as an artist. Yet if there were concessions to friends and to less desirable acquaintances, there was no attempt to give them an undeserved artistic reputation. Nor was there any false enthusiasm about Meissonier or Horace Vernet, about Dubufe the elder or Hippolyte Flandrin, so fashionable in their portrait painting. 'If M. Dubufe is a very long way from Sir Thomas Lawrence,' wrote Baudelaire, 'at least it is not without a certain justice that he has inherited his graceful popularity . . . M. Dubufe has a son who has chosen not to follow in his father's footsteps, and has strayed into serious painting.'[12] The criticism is fair, and the reference to the English artist has its interest. One wonders when and where Baudelaire had seen his portraits. Lawrence had paid his last visit to France in 1825, when Baudelaire was four; he had died in 1830, and few of his paintings were likely to have been in French hands. Perhaps Baudelaire had discovered Lawrence through his friend Émile Deroy, who was known for his enthusiasm about English art. It

is possible that he had seen *Sir Thomas Lawrence's cabinet of gems*, some
reproductions of pen-and-wash drawings which had appeared in
London in 1837. The only French work on the artist published before
1845 was Feuillet de Conches' *Notice historique sur Sir Thomas Lawrence*
(1842).[13]

Théophile Gautier's criticism was often a transposition of art; it was
brilliant, but sometimes superficial. Perhaps the most striking quality
of Baudelaire's first *Salon* is its penetration, its broad pleasure in the
visual arts. Baudelaire knows, already, how to insinuate himself into an
artist's soul. It is clear that he has long attended exhibitions, visited
studios, examined lithographs and engravings and illustrated books; he
has long been concerned with the properties of paint, with the
inferences of line, with the differences between technique and taste and
inspiration. He has watched the progress of individual artists, and he
has already thought about the correspondences between the arts. He
has, in fact, both an instinctive passion for the arts and a well-informed,
analytical mind. His comments have remarkable authority. He also
shows himself a man of vision:

> Everyone paints better and better [so he ends], which seems to us
> distressing; but as for invention, ideas, temperament, there is no more
> than there was before. No one listens to the wind which will blow upon
> us tomorrow; and yet the heroism of *modern life* surrounds us and presses
> in upon us . . . The *artist*, the true artist, will be the one who can extract
> what is epic from modern life, and make us see and understand, with
> colour or line, how great and how poetic we are with our neckties and
> our patent shoes. May the true seekers give us next year the unique delight
> of celebrating the advent of the new![14]

The poetry of modern life, the search for something new, were to
be recurrent themes in his prose and in his poetry.

Almost as soon as the Salon opened at the Louvre, Baudelaire had met
a man who was to be one of his closest and most loyal friends.

Charles-François-Alexandre Asselineau, who was a year his senior,
had been a fellow-pupil of Nadar's at the Lycée Condorcet. Nadar
records that he was a doctor's son, and he was to study medicine.[15] He
turned instead to literature; he had a passion for poetry, and he was
to give Baudelaire much sympathy and intelligent criticism, without
any thought of a return. A permanent bachelor, Asselineau spent more
than half his income on Romantic first editions (he was reported to
own all the first editions of Balzac). His literary criticism was to be
highly regarded, and he contributed to *L'Artiste*.[16] Charles de Ricault
d'Héricault recorded that he was

... the very flower of the cultivated bourgeois...

Bourgeois through his family, in his appearance, in most of his instincts, he was constantly concerned not to be bourgeois...

For Asselineau, literature, like life, was dominated by this fear of being bourgeois.[17]

It was at the Louvre, on about 15 March, that Asselineau had first set eyes on Baudelaire. Émile Deroy had introduced them to one another, and they had all gone to a bistro in the rue du Carrousel, where Baudelaire had ordered white wine, biscuits, and pipes. They had drawn up a list of the artists whom they would discuss, for Asselineau, like Baudelaire, was writing on the Salon. Next day, it seems, Baudelaire and Asselineau had met once again at the Salon, and they had gone to the café Lemblin for more white wine. Baudelaire had given Asselineau his address. Now, in the summer of 1845, in an interval at the Théâtre de l'Odéon, he encountered him yet again; he took him back to the hôtel Pimodan, where he recited some of his poetry.

Asselineau had a reputation for his devotion to his friends. He was to grow increasingly close to Baudelaire.

> On voit le doux Asselineau
> Près du farouche Baudelaire...,

Banville was to write in his *Odes funambulesques*.[18] Asselineau accepted all Baudelaire's inconsiderate and at times outrageous behaviour. Baudelaire, he often repeated, 'was one of the rare men with whom I was never bored. I seriously believe that he was the only one. With him, there were no gaps in the conversation. His love of conversation constantly revived it. It was just that the discussion sometimes lasted from noon until eleven o'clock at night.'[19] Asselineau bore not only with endless conversation, but with endless demands on his time. For a long while, he recalled, Baudelaire 'had the habit of going to ask his friends for hospitality, for a night, a day, two days, more or less. There were various reasons for this: first, the horror of his lodgings, which were often inadequate and inconvenient, the domestic troubles he often had, when he shared his home, the vexations of creditors, etc, and then the incessant need for conversation...'[20]

Asselineau was undeterred by such demands. He supported Baudelaire in his literary ventures, and helped him in his constant financial problems. He paid tribute to him at his funeral, wrote the first biography of him, and, with Banville, edited the first *Œuvres complètes*. With Poulet-Malassis, the poet's publisher, he was to be one of Baudelaire's true friends.

21

Now, in 1845, Baudelaire was twenty-four. He was already distinguished as a critic of art. Perhaps he already understood his potential as a poet. Yet the shadow side of his life seemed to dominate. He was also anxious about the progress of his syphilis, about his relationship with Jeanne, and, above all, about his unhappy relationship with his mother. He was constantly frustrated by his penury and by his debts. He was, in some ways, an eighteenth-century figure like his father; he needed an unassailable income and freedom from responsibility, he needed to lead an elegant life and to satisfy his expensive tastes. He lived, instead, in the nineteenth century: the most demanding, competitive and mercenary age. He had a minimal income which was paid to him, in instalments, by a *conseil judiciaire*. He was so despondent, so uncertain of himself, so fraught by the demands of Jeanne and the disapproval of his mother, that he wondered if his life should continue. As Clément Borgal wrote in *Baudelaire*, his reaction to society was not so much the revolt of a misanthropist as the result of a fundamental inability to adapt to life.[1] 'The most terrible form of his originality lies', repeated Charles du Bos, 'in a hatred of life which stretches far beyond all its contingencies – this hatred purely of the mind which comes from absolute incompatibility.'[2]

On 29 June, in conversation with Ancelle, Baudelaire discussed what would happen to his inheritance if he should die. Next day, he decided to commit suicide. He made notes about his manuscripts for Banville, and he sent Jeanne – Jeanne Lemer, he called her – to visit Ancelle. She took with her a sealed letter which named her as his residuary legatee.

When Mlle Jeanne Lemer hands you this letter [this to Ancelle], I shall be dead. She does not know this. You know my will. Except for the part reserved for my mother, Mlle *Lemer* should inherit all I leave, when you have paid certain debts – a list of which I attach.

I am dying in dreadful anxiety. Remember our conversation of yesterday. I want, indeed demand, that my wishes are punctiliously carried out. Two people can contest my will: my mother and my brother – and they can only contest it on the pretext of mental derangement. My suicide, added to the various disorders of my life, can only help them to deprive Mlle Lemer of what I mean to leave her. I must therefore explain my *suicide* to you, and my behaviour as regards Mlle *Lemer* – in such a way that this letter, which is addressed to you, and which you will take care to read to her, may serve in her defence, should my will be contested by the people I have mentioned.

I am *killing* myself – without *grief*. I do not feel any of those disturbances which men call *grief*. My debts have never been a *grief*. Nothing is easier than to rise above such things. I am killing myself because I cannot live any more, because the fatigue of falling asleep and the fatigue of waking are unbearable. I am *killing* myself because I am useless to other people – *and a danger to myself.* I am *killing* myself because I believe that I am immortal, and because *I hope.* At the time I write these lines, I am so well endowed with lucidity, that I am setting down *further* notes for *M. Théodore de Banville,* and I have all the strength I need to concern myself with my manuscripts.

I give and bequeath all that I possess to Mlle Lemer, even my few pieces of furniture and my portrait – because she is the only person in whom I have found some rest. Can anyone blame me for wanting to repay the rare pleasures I have found on this dreadful earth?

I *hardly* know my brother – he has not lived *in me or with me* – he does not need me.

My mother, who has so often, and always involuntarily, poisoned my life, does not need this money either. She has her *husband*; she possesses a *human being,* an affection, *a friendship.*

I myself have only *Jeanne Lemer.* I have found no rest except in her . . .

Jeanne Lemer is the only woman I have loved – and she has nothing. And it is you, Monsieur Ancelle, one of the rare men I have met who is endowed with a gentle, noble spirit, whom I entrust with my last instructions about her . . .

You see clearly now that this will is not bluster, or defiance of social and family ideas, but simply the expression of what humanity remains in me – love, and the honest wish to serve a creature who has sometimes been my joy and my repose.[3]

The letter was a clear reflection of his loneliness, his absolute, eternal despair; and yet one may still question his determination. Perhaps he really intended to take his own life, and failed in his attempt. Perhaps – as in other matters – he weakened in his professed resolve. More probably, his letter to Ancelle should be read as a cry for help. He tried, it seems, to stab himself; but when Privat d'Anglemont burst into the *grenier* in the place de la Sorbonne, and told Cousin about the attempted suicide, Cousin did not believe in it; he thought that Baudelaire's knife-thrust 'was meant to touch a heart other than his own.'[4]

That heart was surely his mother's heart. In spite of Jeanne, in spite of his friends, his mother remained the only human being whose presence he needed, whose every sign of love he awaited. Jeanne was his instrument of revenge against his mother. She was, he had said repeatedly, the only woman whom he had loved, the only one who had given him peace. Such statements, made to Ancelle, were intended for Mme Aupick. She was meant to feel responsible for his death. He was killing himself in revenge for the *conseil judiciaire* and, above all, in revenge for her second marriage. She had poisoned his life. If

Baudelaire chose to wound himself only superficially, that was because
he had to enjoy the effect of his suicidal gesture. His wound was not
so serious that he could not stay with Jeanne in the rue de la
Femme-sans-Tête. It was another way to humiliate his mother. The
doctor, who paid occasional visits, seemed to think that rest – and
perhaps the company of Jeanne – was all he needed.

Mme Aupick was horrified by her son's attempted suicide, and,
perhaps, by what Ancelle had told her. Yet she did not go to see
him. Perhaps the General had forbidden her to do so, and to give
herself more cause for anxiety. Perhaps she was afraid of more emotional blackmail. It may be that she disapproved too violently of Jeanne
to set foot in her pitiful lodgings. There was a world between the
General's wife in the place Vendôme, and the kept mulatto woman in
the rue de la Femme-sans-Tête. Whatever the reason, Baudelaire was
told that he could not see her; when he wrote to her, she did not reply.
It was, it seems, early in July, ten days and more after his attempted
suicide, that he explained to her:

> Just as I wanted to get dressed to go in search of you, I found the doors
> locked. Apparently the doctor won't let me budge.
>   And so I can't go and see you. When I write to you, it is M. Ancelle
> who answers, and forbids me to go and see you. And they also lock me up.
>   Do you then take my suffering as a joke? And are you brave enough to
> deprive me of your presence? Let me tell you that I need you, that I want
> to see you and talk to you. So come, then, *come at once* – no prudishness.
> I am with a woman, but I am ill, and I cannot move . . .
>   I must tell you that, if you don't come, that can only occasion more
> misfortunes.
>   You must come *alone*.[5]

Presumably some sort of relationship was restored between mother
and son. In mid-July, Baudelaire left the rue de la Femme-sans-Tête
to settle temporarily in the place Vendôme. He had no doubt agreed
to accept certain conditions – or what he called *la Règle*. One of these
conditions was that he resumed his studies, and he duly registered at
the École des Chartes to study history and palaeography. (It was, as
might be expected, a mere gesture; he never followed a course of
studies, and his file in the archives is empty.)[6] Soon afterwards, Louis
Ménard encountered Baudelaire in the street:

> Baudelaire assumed his most dignified air.
>   'My stepfather and I have been reconciled. We have both cast a veil
> over the past, we have chosen to forget.'
>   'But your poor mother's feelings?'
>   'Mother? She is copying out my poems.'[7]

Such concord could not last. There were soon predictable differences with Aupick. The General was rigidly conventional, he liked an ordered pattern to his days. He found his stepson's way of life intolerable. In a note to his mother, which was apparently written this July, Baudelaire announced that he had gone out of Paris for the day, and that he would not be back for dinner. 'Do not reproach me', he added, 'for this breach of the *Rule*, considering that it is the first.'[8] It was not, presumably, the last. The next, undated note in his correspondence is also a refusal to return for dinner at five o'clock. The letter which follows is his letter of farewell.

I am leaving, and I shan't appear again except in a more appropriate state of mind and finances. I am leaving for various reasons. To begin with, I have fallen into a fearful indolence and torpor, and I need a great deal of solitude to restore myself a little, and to recover strength. In the second place, it is impossible for me to make myself the sort of person your husband would wish me to be; and so it would be robbing him to live any longer in his house. And finally I don't think it is *decent* that I should be treated by him as he seems to want to treat me from now on. I shall probably be obliged to live roughly, but I shall be better. Today or tomorrow I'll send you a letter to tell you which of my possessions I shall need, and where they must be sent. My decision is firm, final and considered; and so you must not complain, but understand it.[9]

It was an extraordinary letter for a son to send to his mother. It implied not only profound resentment of her way of life, but, now, incurable antipathy to Aupick. The stepfather who had been 'papa', 'my father', and 'my bosom friend', had become 'your husband'.

General Aupick was a good man [Maxime du Camp remembered], and open to the things of the mind; but discipline, inflexible discipline, seemed to him the only form of education which one could apply to children or to men. He was a soldier. When he said: 'Right file!', you did not choose to file from the left. He described himself, completely, quite unwittingly, in the coat-of-arms he had designed for himself: azure, with a sword, or pale, and the device: 'All through this.' A sword and a uniform rule to bring up Baudelaire, were not the way to do the trick. This dreamy, defiant, rebellious nature needed a great deal of tenderness . . . One could soften it, but not bend it. Between the stepfather and the stepson, the struggle grew unending.[10]

Aupick had no doubt become more authoritative with the years, Mme Aupick had become still more submissive to him. Baudelaire was no longer a child who could be coaxed with promises of visits and holidays. He was no longer an admiring *collégien* who wanted to impress his stepfather with his physical courage and his excellent results in examinations. Baudelaire now understood, more clearly than ever, that his mother set her husband first, that her chief concern was to ensure his happiness and comfort. He understood that his mother and the General both deplored his personal relationships, his endless financial problems, his social fecklessness, his refusal to commit himself to a conventional career. The General was neither philistine nor averse to literature; but he appreciated, more than most, the importance of discipline and work, the significance of sound relationships, the need for financial security. He had been devoted to his stepson, and no doubt, even now, some of that affection remained. He could – and would – have done much to help him, if Baudelaire had chosen to conform. As it was, he felt anger and despair, sometimes contempt, at the young man's way of life. No doubt he despised him, now, for his attempted suicide. His anger intensified when he saw his wife's anxiety. If Mme Aupick was unhappy, nervous and interfering, the General could only behave in the military way that was natural to him. Some years later, when a young diplomat misbehaved, he wrote: 'I had to give him a lesson. I had long been accustomed to serious matters, and to command... The lesson was given.'[11] It was given now. The General did not know how to coax or to persuade, he simply gave orders. Baudelaire did not intend to take them.

His stay at 7, place Vendôme had been a disaster. His letter to his mother marked the end of any understanding with Aupick. Trial says that the General had shown Baudelaire the door, and forbidden any mention of his name.[12] Never again was Baudelaire to stay under his stepfather's roof; never again, one surmises, did they meet.

Whatever his own misery at his mother's second marriage, however deep his sense of betrayal, Baudelaire had not detested his stepfather from the first. Despite the emotional turmoil, despite his relegation to second place in his mother's affections, despite the rigours of his education, the imposition of the Eastern voyage, the *conseil judiciaire*, he had felt deep affection for Aupick, and he had wanted affection in return. He had admired him, and he had wanted his admiration. Now, in 1845, perhaps for the first time, he understood all that he had suffered through the Aupick marriage. Aupick had taken his mother from him and made his youth a penance. Aupick was trying to ordain his future. The General, his *ami de cœur*, had come to represent all that he detested: self-importance and self-righteousness, bourgeois wisdom, rhetoric, and, perhaps, political opportunism. Three years later, in the February Revolution, Baudelaire was to urge the mob to shoot General Aupick.

Even after this, he was still to be torn between hate and affection. In 1853, he thought of sending Aupick his translation of Edgar Allan Poe, 'as a proof of my esteem, and a proof that I should like his own.'[13]

The General's esteem could not be given. In 1854, he assured his mother: 'Yes, this reconciliation will take place, and honourably, if your husband only has some understanding.'[14] The General could not understand. Ultimately, as Baudelaire wrote: 'I know quite well that any exchange of affection between him and me is impossible.'[15] As Claude Pichois rightly said, Baudelaire had described the most irremediable of dramas, the one which is written deep in people's natures. Montaigne, defining his closest friendship, could only explain: 'Parce que c'était lui, parce que c'était moi.' This formula, which sums up a friendship, can also explain both hatred and incomprehension.[16]

'My decision is firm, final, and considered; and so you must not complain, but understand it.' Baudelaire's farewell letter to his mother was that of a young man who was fiercely aggressive and emotionally insecure. He had no home, no wife or children, and no safe career. Henceforward he was truly in limbo.

The days of the hôtel Pimodan were over. He seems to have wandered for some time round Paris: staying, perhaps, with friends. Sometimes he found himself without a bed. One day he told Louis Ménard why he had left his mother's house. 'It couldn't last: with her you only drink bordeaux, and I only like burgundy. I left. And, for the moment, I'm homeless. When night falls, I stretch out on a bench.'[17] Finally he told Mme Aupick: 'You must send me at once, to *M. Baudelaire-Dufaÿs, hôtel de Dunkerque, 32, rue Laffitte*, the small trunk which contains all my linen – plus some shoes and slippers – and the two black cravats – *plus all my books* . . . You must not send me any letter of reproach or any invitation to come back – I shan't come back. All I can assure you is that you will be glad of this in a little while.'[18]

Mme Aupick seems to have sent him what he needed, and some money. It was not to be the last time that she added, privately, to his meagre allowance from Ancelle. She even seems to have paid his hotel bill.

> Today is the 16th [went his next letter to her]. I am sending you a bill from the hotel. When you give your 45 francs, would you do me the pleasure of not sending any questions or remarks, as you did last time? . . .
> If you could send me a little extra money for myself by the same person, that would make me happy, because I am very noticeably destitute.[19]

He signed 'Baudelaire Dufaÿs', using his mother's maiden name. He was angry with her; but he needed more than her financial support. He wanted, once again, to remind her of their attachment. She vexed him, she enraged him, she made him wretchedly unhappy, but he needed her, just as she needed him — and, sometimes, needed him to be dependent. 'My mother is incredible,' he was to write in his *Journaux intimes*. 'One must fear her and please her.'[20] He behaved, at times, with childish petulance.

> Apparently you don't want to see me [went his next note]. You don't love me even enough for that. But I need to see you myself, I'm going to get dressed; if I don't find you at home between noon and 2 o'clock – *you won't see me again.*
> Is that clear?[21]

The emptiness of such a threat was clear to both of them.

22

On 16 November 1845, *Le Moniteur universel* announced that General Aupick had been promoted Grand-officier de la Légion-d'honneur. His career seemed to move in a curious counterpoint to that of his stepson. Four days later, Baudelaire – whose allowance was 200 francs a month – was due to pay Arondel 6,500 francs. On 24 November, in *Le Corsaire-Satan*, he published an article appropriately entitled *Comment on paie ses dettes quand on a du génie*. It was an anecdote of Balzac, written with a light, ironic touch which belied its author's misery. It was intended, said Baudelaire, to show that the greatest man of the nineteenth century 'could settle a debt as easily as he could tie up the ends of the most mysterious, most complicated novel.'[1] It was not, alas, a gift that he himself possessed.

It was, apparently, early in 1846 that he took a room at 24, rue de Provence. It cost 30 francs a month, and the landlord demanded at least a fortnight's rent in advance. On about 20 February, Baudelaire turned yet again to his mother: 'I *absolutely* must have 30 francs or so no later than today . . . These 30 francs are indispensable. The only thing I'm afraid of is not having them before noon . . . You can hand the money to the bearer of this letter.'[2] Mme Aupick compromised, and sent him ten francs. Presumably she said that they must talk about his finances. Within the next few days, he wrote again:

> I should be very glad if you came to see me tomorrow morning in order to reach an understanding on the use of my money this year, and so that I may point out the important debts to you. As I think that I can now

live on what I earn, I might devote everything or nearly everything to the payment of my debts. As you know, I have had a novella in *L'Esprit public* in the last few days.[3]

Baudelaire was less than honest. As W. T. Bandy has shown, the novella was not original.[4] It was a somewhat unskilled translation of *The Young Enchanter*, a tale which had appeared in an English keepsake, *The Forget-me-not*, in 1836. (Professor Bandy suggests that the tale had been written by the Rev. George Croly.) However, there was no law of copyright in 1846, and while one might deplore Baudelaire's lack of candour, it is illuminating to record that, two years before he published his first version of Poe, he had begun his career as a translator.

Meanwhile, on 3 March 1846, in *Le Corsaire-Satan*, he published his *Choix de Maximes consolantes sur l'amour*. He had written the article, it seems, with his decorous sister-in-law in mind; he pretended to be infatuated by her, which he knew would much embarrass her. It would also embarrass Alphonse, who was well aware of Baudelaire's venereal disease. Baudelaire had not forgiven him for supporting the Eastern voyage and the establishment of the *conseil judiciaire*. He now sent a copy of his article to Félicité, and promised that he would soon send her his *Catéchisme de la femme aimée*, so that she could make her comments. 'Be good enough, Madame,' he ended, 'to be my Providence in the career which is opening to me through *the channel of love*... I almost said through the influence of women.'[5] It was a strangely formal style in which to address his brother's wife; but the phrase he emphasised, *le canal de l'amour*, could have had its sexual implications.

The *Catéchisme* was to be announced on the cover of Baudelaire's next book, but – like many of his other works – it was to remain unwritten. Félicité's comments on his *Maximes* have not, alas, survived. No doubt the article and the letter flustered her and her husband, as Baudelaire had intended. One catches an echo of the affair years later, when he writes to his mother about Alphonse: 'There is nothing more precious in the world than the *poetic spirit*, and *a sense of chivalry*. His political and intellectual nullity, his cynical opinions about women, to whom one must at least show gallantry, if not passion: everything, absolutely everything makes him alien to me.'[6]

Baudelaire had sent his mother *Le Jeune Enchanteur*, and, for the moment, relations between them were restored. It was no doubt to please her that, late in 1845 or early in 1846, he registered for the second time at the École des Chartes. Had he pursued his studies there, he might have earned a comfortable living as a librarian; but, predictably, he could not accept the discipline.[7] Once again, Mme Aupick was obliged to acknowledge defeat.

'She was also forced to conceal any meetings with him from her husband. Baudelaire rejoiced in her visits and, no doubt, in her continuing deception. Some time in the second half of March, she called on him, but he was out.

> Thank you [he wrote] for the good, kind letter which you left for me.
> I should like it if you came to see me *tomorrow morning*. I want to talk to you about *money*. Don't be frightened in the least – it's not a question of borrowing from you, but of a particular arrangement, which is easier to explain than to write.
> I find myself, by a series of steps, both fortunate and inopportune – in the way of earning a lot in a short time – but *tied by the debts you know about*, which become more shameful every day. I have five articles to write for *L'Esprit public, asked for* – two for *L'Époque*, two for *La Presse*, an article for *La Revue nouvelle*. All this adds up to an enormous sum. I have never been endowed with such clear hopes. But at the same time I have my *Salon* on my hands . . .[8]

Perhaps Baudelaire was deliberately deluding his mother; perhaps his confidence was simply misplaced. In April *L'Esprit public* was to publish his *Conseils aux jeunes littérateurs*; but there is no record of his contributions to *L'Époque*, *La Presse*, or *La Revue nouvelle*.

He continued to lead a disturbed existence. It was clear that he could never live on the monthly allowance from Ancelle. He depended too often on hopes and promises, pawning belongings in despair, accumulating debts and interest. His way of life created enervating stress, and made the act of writing still more difficult. It also created unremitting problems with his mother. In April he was twenty-five, but he was still obliged to plead with her like an unhappy child; he was still compelled to ask for help, though once again he begged her not to moralise.[9]

The names of creditors continued to punctuate his letters. They were also heard in the place Vendôme. Early in May, he instructed his mother:

> If someone comes today or tomorrow, to touch a [promissory] note from me, . . . you must simply say that I'm away, and that I shall be back in two days. I shall go and arrange this myself, since I should receive some considerable sums *a few days hence.*
> It may be that I shall ask for my furniture in a few days' time.
> Can you send me this morning the rest of what you promised me, or at least half?
> Don't come and see me until my book has appeared, that is to say in two or three days. I am in a turmoil of proofs and posters.[10]

On 1 May he had written the introduction to his *Salon de 1846*. On 7 May, the book was published by Michel Lévy. It was a marked advance on his earlier *Salon*, and it established him as a critic. He did not write as a journalist, or even as a man of taste, but as a conscientious interpreter who had grown familiar, through study and meditation, with the secrets of art.

23

Enjoyment was a science, wrote Baudelaire, and the exercise of the five senses demanded a particular initiation. True criticism should be partial, impassioned and political, in other words it should be made from an exclusive point of view, but from the point of view which opened the most horizons. Indeed, the critic, like the artist, should be endowed with an artistic temperament. He should be a kind of secondary poet, reflecting and translating the work of art. Every century and every nation had expressed its beauty and its morality; and if Romanticism was accepted as the most recent and the most modern expression of beauty, the great artist would be the one who united the necessary candour and as much Romanticism as possible.[1]

For Baudelaire, Romanticism did not lie in the choice of subject, but in the manner of feeling; it could only come from within. For him, Romanticism was the most contemporary expression of beauty. Romanticism meant modern art: intimacy, spirituality, colour, the aspiration towards infinity, expressed by every means available to the arts. How novel the effect would be, and how divine Romanticism would become, if a powerful artist were to express, with appropriate colour, the dearest dreams and feelings of the age![2]

Baudelaire's reflections on colour were remarkable for their technical knowledge but, above all, for his concern with the correspondences between the arts. This intuition of correspondences, the summit of Baudelairean aesthetics, was explored here for the first time.

I don't know [he wrote] if some analyst has established a complete scale of colours and feelings, but I remember a passage in Hoffmann which expresses my idea perfectly . . . 'It is not only in dreams, and in the slight delirium which comes before sleep, it is also when I am awake, when I am listening to music, that I find an analogy and a close connection between colours, sounds and scents. It seems to me that all these things have been engendered by a single ray of light, and that they should join together in wondrous concert. The smell of red and brown marigolds, especially, has a magical effect on my person. It makes me fall into deep reverie, and then I hear, as it were in the distance, the deep and solemn sounds of the oboe.'[3]

This theory of correspondences was one to which Baudelaire was often to return, in his prose and in his poetry. We shall discuss it at some length when we come to consider *Les Fleurs du mal*.[4] It was a theory which much concerned men of letters, artists and composers in nineteenth-century Europe. Lewis Shanks maintains, in his *Baudelaire: Flesh and Spirit*, that, out of that passage in the *Salon de 1846*, grew Baudelaire's symbolism and the whole school of poetry which he originated.[5]

Romanticism and colour led Baudelaire inescapably, now, to Delacroix. Once again, he wrote with passion and audacity,

> ... for if my definition of Romanticism (intimacy, spirituality, etc) sets Delacroix at the head of Romanticism, it naturally excludes M. Victor Hugo from this position ...
>
> I certainly have no wish to depreciate the nobility and the majesty of M. Victor Hugo, but he is a craftsman who is much more correct than creative. Delacroix is sometimes clumsy, but he is essentially creative ...
>
> One begins with the detail, the other with the intimate understanding of the subject; and so it happens that the former only takes the skin, and that the other tears out the entrails. M. Victor Hugo has become a painter in poetry; Delacroix, always respectful of his ideal, is sometimes, unwittingly, a poet in painting.[6]

It was an astute appreciation. Baudelaire was never an uncritical admirer of Victor Hugo. In Delacroix, in his passion and his search for perfection, his candour and his sense of grief in a sad and unbelieving century, Baudelaire had found a fellow spirit.

> To end this analysis [he wrote], it remains for me to note one final quality in Delacroix, the most remarkable of all, and the one which makes him the true painter of the nineteenth century: it is that singular, persistent melancholy which emanates from all his works, and expresses itself in the choice of subjects, and in the expression of the face, and by gesture, and the style of colouring. Delacroix has a liking for Dante and Shakespeare, two other great painters of human grief; he knows them thoroughly, and he knows how to translate them freely. As one contemplates his series of pictures, one seems to be attending the celebration of some grievous mystery ... It is not only grief that he knows best how to express, it is above all – a prodigious mystery of his painting – grief of spirit. This grave and lofty melancholy shines with a dull light, ... plaintive and profound like a melody by Weber.[7]

In the final chapter of his *Salon*, Baudelaire returned to the theme which he had approached in his *Salon de 1845*. For modern times, so he maintained, were no less fecund than ancient times in the sublime; since every century and every nation had their beauty, modern times must inevitably have their own.

> Does it not have its natural beauty and charm, this much victimised suit? Is it not the necessary suit for our age, this suffering age which even bears on its dark and narrow shoulders the symbol of perpetual mourning? Note well that the black suit and the overcoat possess not only their political beauty, which is the expression of universal equality, but also their poetic beauty, which is the expression of the public soul . . .
>
> Parisian life is rich in wondrous and poetic themes. The wonderful envelops us and overwhelms us like the atmosphere; but we do not see it . . .
>
> The heroes of the *Iliad* do not hold a candle to you, oh Vautrin, oh Rastignac, oh Birotteau, . . . and you, Honoré de Balzac, you the most heroic, the most singular, the most romantic and the most poetic of all the characters whom you have drawn out of your own entrails.[8]

In the *Salon de 1846*, Baudelaire established the importance of modernity. As a critic was to write: 'He is our chief Accuser of the modern world, yet he is also its most patriotic citizen.'[9]

The main themes of Baudelaire's aesthetics had been contained, in embryo, in the *Salon de 1845*; but it was the *Salon de 1846* which marked his real début as a critic. The difference between the two essays is evident from the first. The *Salon de 1845* consists of commentaries on the artists represented at the exhibition; the *Salon de 1846* reveals above all the attempt to elaborate coherent aesthetics of his own.

24

The year 1846 brought Baudelaire new acquaintances and friends. It was now that he came to know Leconte de Lisle, who had recently arrived in Paris to embark on his literary career. It was to be some years before Leconte de Lisle published his first collections of poetry; but his legal training and his social convictions were accompanied by a love of the classics and an uncompromising love of literature. He later told Maurice Barrès that, the day he first met Baudelaire and Ménard, Baudelaire recited them 'Don Juan aux Enfers'. 'I think I discerned', wrote Barrès, 'that Leconte de Lisle had a low opinion of Baudelaire. The desire to produce an effect made the young Baudelaire unbearable.'[1]

Pichois, like Barrès, maintained that Leconte de Lisle suppressed a
certain animosity.[2] The truth was that the relationship was sometimes
difficult; but, as his biographer, Fernand Calmettes, observed, there
were friendly periods, when Baudelaire would invite himself to *déjeuner*.
'Baudelaire's presence was often marked by lively conversation. Baudelaire did feel a family relationship with the intensely imaginative, and
he struggled to redeem his lack of superiority in inspiration [*sic*] by the
mastery of his art.'[3]

Leconte de Lisle, so it appears, questioned his mastery. In some
private notes, he reproached Baudelaire for technical blunders. 'Very
intelligent and original,' so he decided, 'but restricted in his imagination, lacking inspiration. His art is too often clumsy.'[4]

> If this criticism is fair [continued Calmettes], it is not because Baudelaire
> had not made every effort not to deserve it . . . People have often repeated
> the comparison which Baudelaire was accustomed to make: 'Words must
> adapt themselves to the idea, like leather gloves to the hand.' When he
> launched out on his subject, he developed it with a picturesque verve
> beyond compare; and it was the subject of endless conversations between
> Leconte de Lisle and himself.[5]

Neither Leconte de Lisle nor Baudelaire ever doubted that literature
was the first of the arts, and the noblest in expressive power.

> On this sovereignty of literature [added Calmettes], Leconte de Lisle
> was certain to share the doctrine of Baudelaire, and when the discus-
> sion of some point of detail became too heated, he would divert it on
> to the more solid ground of theory . . . He could not avoid all the
> clashes, but he was all the more anxious to avoid them as Baudelaire
> was one of the rare men of letters who gave him any sort of companion-
> ship.[6]

In 1846, an old problem had recurred. That spring, Baudelaire had
been to see J.-A. d'Oroszko, a Polish doctor in the rue Lepelletier who
specialised in the treatment of venereal disease. His mother was,
presumably, aware of his condition. It was, it seems, in October that
he wrote to her:

> Would you have the kindness to write at once to M. Ancelle and ask him
> to advance me 60 or 70 francs at the most in addition to my usual
> amount? . . . It is already some days since I went to see him. I needed
> books and I felt ill – my ulcers in the throat have come back again. He
> didn't give me enough, and between the doctor, the chemist and the
> books, I chose the books. Today the pain is getting worse, and I have
> presumed that you would kindly send him a word so that there isn't any
> difficulty.[7]

Once again there was an element of emotional blackmail in his letter. Mme Aupick must have been disturbed by his recurrent illness and by his buying books rather than medicine. She must also have been touched by his devotion.

> After I moved from the place Vendôme I couldn't find your portrait among my drawings and portraits. In spite of our dissensions and all the bitter things which have divided us, rest assured that I attach great importance to that portrait. Tell *Julien* [your factotum] about it, and let him keep it at my disposal. I shall send for it in the next few days, because on the 15th of next month I am going to furnish a small apartment.[8]

It is difficult to judge where the small apartment may have been. The next of his published letters – or, rather, a bill payable to order – is written from 7, rue de Tournon; but this is the only mention of the address. The bill is dated 7 December – the month in which, apparently, he asked the Société des Gens de Lettres – to which he had belonged since June – to advance him 200 francs on the strength of his novella, *La Fanfarlo*, and of a novel to appear in *L'Époque* (a novel which, again, remained unwritten). There was, he said, a further novella, *Le Prétendant Malgache*, which he held at the Society's disposal.[9]

La Fanfarlo appeared in January 1847 in the *Bulletin de la Société des Gens de Lettres*. It is a cynical, ebullient novella, full of verve and wit; had it been more visual, more lyrical, it might have been the work of the young Théophile Gautier. It bears a certain likeness to *Fortunio* and to *Mademoiselle de Maupin*. The hero, Samuel Cramer, contains much of Baudelaire himself. Asselineau said that he was an exact likeness of the author, the sitter for Deroy's romantic portrait.[10] A poet and a man of letters, a dandy and a gourmet, Cramer, too, found love, 'above all, the admiration and appetite for beauty; he considered procreation as a vice of love, and pregnancy as a spider's malady. He wrote somewhere: "The angels are hermaphrodites and sterile." '[11] For want of a heart, Samuel Cramer 'had a noble intelligence, and, instead of ingratitude, pleasure had engendered in him that delicious contentment, that sensual reverie, which is perhaps worth more than love as ordinary people understand it.'[12] Everything, as Borgal wrote, was already in *La Fanfarlo*.[13]

If Samuel Cramer owed much to Baudelaire himself, Mme de Cosmelly, the heroine, is said to owe something to Félicité, the wife of Alphonse Baudelaire. It was to her, early in March 1846, that Baudelaire had sent his *Maximes consolantes sur l'amour*; it was her opinion that he had solicited. She was less agreeable than Mme de Cosmelly; but she, too, was conscious of decorum. She, too, although she came from Paris, behaved like a bourgeoise from the provinces.

Mme de Cosmelly suffers from her husband's liaison with the dancer La Fanfarlo; Samuel Cramer promises to take La Fanfarlo away from him, and he hopes to be duly rewarded by the grateful wife. Predictably, he himself falls in love with La Fanfarlo. Husband and wife are reunited, but the courtesan understands Cramer's calculations, and she resolves to make him pay for them. 'As for him, he was punished in the way in which he had sinned. He had often aped passion; he was obliged to know it; but it was not the peaceful love, serene and strong, inspired by honest women, it was the terrible, desolating, shameful love, the unhealthy love of courtesans. Samuel knew all the tortures of jealousy, and the degradations into which we are thrown by the awareness of an incurable and constitutional illness – in short, all the horrors of that vicious marriage which is called concubinage.'[14] Baudelaire did not know jealousy, but he knew, all too well, the unhealthy love of courtesans.

25

It was about now that he sat to Courbet for his portrait. *L'Homme à la pipe* was later to be used in the painting *L'Atelier de Courbet*. Baudelaire much admired it, although in time he professed contempt for Courbet and for his school.[1]

Courbet had found it hard to catch a likeness of Baudelaire. 'I don't know', he had confessed, 'how to get down to Baudelaire's portrait. Every day he changes his face.'[2] Champfleury, repeating the comment in his *Souvenirs*, confirmed: 'It is true that Baudelaire had the art of transforming his physiognomy like a convict on the run.'[3]

He changed not only his facial expression, but his hair. Champfleury maintained that he had met him 'leaning on the balustrade of the Pont des Arts, looking at the reflections of a pretty perruque with sky-blue curls. It replaced the elegant hair which, the previous day, had been shaved off down to the skin.'[4] Heredia enlarged on legend. Baudelaire, he said, 'used to dye his hair green, and was very disappointed if people didn't notice it.'[5] 'He was really shocking at first sight,' Champfleury continued, 'so much did the commonplace inspire him with horror. Every kind of order revolted him . . . He had been hurt in his youth, so they said, by contact with a high-ranking army officer.'[6]

Champfleury had, perhaps, touched a deeper truth than he knew. Baudelaire did not merely distinguish himself by his appearance. His resentment of Aupick, his bitterness at his mother's second marriage, had led him to cultivate a persona which would at once embarrass and enrage the conventional, and create a shell for his own vulnerable nature. This persona – as we have seen – was not a simple means of publicity, it was a means of keeping at a distance a world which had constantly offended him.

> If there has been a Baudelaire legend, and on the whole a hardly favourable legend, you may rest assured [said the critic Jules Levallois] that no one contributed to its creation more than he did himself . . .
> At what point did the truth end with him, and the lie begin? That's what one found it hard to know, what perhaps he did not know himself: what he knew less and less.[7]

Baudelaire needed an audience, but he respected people who refused to be astonished by him. Nestor Roqueplan, director of the Opéra, was the last man to let himself be astounded. Baudelaire once showed him a book that was bound, so he maintained, in human skin. 'Human skin?' said Roqueplan. 'But, my dear fellow, that's the only thing they use nowadays. When you come to see me, I'll show you some riding-breeches which I had made from my father's skin. I only wear them on special occasions.'[8]

Others were more impressed by the legend that Baudelaire created. Maxime Rude recorded one of his attempts to alarm the bourgeois.

> One evening, in a restaurant where he was well known, Baudelaire asked for a fillet steak, well cooked, but, above all, tender. When the steak was served, the manager, a family man, came to see if his customer was satisfied.
> 'It's just the fillet I wanted,' answered Baudelaire. 'It's as tender as babies' brains.'
> 'As brains . . .?'
> 'As babies' brains,' replied the mystifier, looking up with his sharpest and most staring gaze.
> The restaurant-keeper rushed downstairs to protect his children.[9]

Baudelaire, continued Rude, did not like children.[10] On the other hand, he had a passion for cats. It was a passion which was not exempt from cruelty. 'He liked to wake them up,' confirmed Rude, 'and, rather unpleasantly for them, by stroking them against the nap. On one occasion I was obliged to intervene, to get him out of a very lively struggle with a big ginger cat in the avenue de Clichy.'[11] Adrien Marx was to record a more offensive habit (although no doubt the story is apocryphal):

> I dined with him regularly, in a tavern in the rue Bréda, which was inhabited by a black cat. How often Baudelaire . . . contented himself with

taking a dozen oysters and making the tom cat eat them, with fatherly concern . . .! It was not unusual for him, after the treat, to seize the animal by the tail, lift it up in the air, and pull out the hairs of its moustache with a joy that bordered on delirium.[12]

Baudelaire continued to shock and to pose. Levallois remembered: 'He rarely took part in our rustic pleasures, he found the green of the trees too insipid. As he used to say, with his poker-faced expression: "I should like the fields tinged with red, the rivers yellow, and the trees painted blue. Nature has no imagination." . . . Everything in him,' continued Levallois, 'was artificial and premeditated, it was all playing to the gallery, even if that only consisted of one person.'[13]

'He was obsessed', recalled Catulle Mendès, 'by the need to astonish and even terrify people; although, in everyday life, he palliated this somewhat childish taste by the noble grace of a gentleman, by a most delicate, most subtle reserve, . . . and although, in art, he redeemed this taste by clarity of thought, the exactness of the image, and what one might call the classic perfection of form.'[14] Maurice Barrès confided in his *Cahiers*: 'It has to be said, and clearly recognised, that there are two Baudelaires: a mystifier, and, underneath, a noble soul.'[15]

Baudelaire confessed, himself, that he was intoxicated by 'the aristocratic pleasure of displeasing.'[16] He did not only want to displease; he wanted, once again, to protect his extraordinary sensibility. Under his mask of imperviousness, defying all emotion, his sensibility, said Nadar, quivered with every vibration.[17] Baudelaire was never to be the superman or the dandy he had dreamed of, because he was always to lack self-control in the conduct of his life. He could not be impassible, and so, for many people, he passed for an intolerable *poseur*. His pose was a carapace. His dandyism was an attempt to distance himself from the vulgar profane, from the bourgeois world of the Citizen King. It was part of his search for beauty. It was related to the cult of the poet as hero.

26

On 13 March 1847, Baudelaire thanked his mother, once again, for money, and promised her that he would make good use of it. For all his explanations, so he told her, she might not understand the importance of the service which she had done him.[1] Laforgue observed, perceptively, that Mme Aupick owed this money to her husband, and that perhaps, for Baudelaire, it symbolised the General pure and simple. His constant demands had more than financial implications.[2]

Nineteen years after her second marriage, Mme Aupick was still torn between her triumphant husband and her wayward son. Aupick's career continued its brilliant ascent. In 1846, he had been promoted lieutenant-general (the equivalent of the modern general of division). In April 1847, the Bey of Tunis had conferred upon him the Order of Nichan, first class. Three months later, on 10 July, the King of the Belgians had created him Grand Officier de l'Ordre de Léopold. Now, on 28 November, he was appointed to command the École polytechnique. There remained a bitter contrast between the stepfather and the stepson. On 29 November, when he had searched in vain for money for two or three days, and found himself hungry, anxious and exhausted, Baudelaire sought refuge at the first *hôtel garni* to hand, at 36, rue de Babylone. Soon afterwards, still in need of money, he went to see Ancelle at Neuilly. Ancelle refused to help him without permission from Mme Aupick. Baudelaire drove to the place Vendôme, and sent up a demand by the factotum. It was – unless letters have been destroyed – his first communication with his mother for eight months.

> It is only when I am reduced to the last extremity, that is to say *when I am very hungry*, that I come to you [he told her], it makes me feel such loathing and vexation ... I am not coming up to see you, because I know *the insults, the affronts and humiliations with which I should pay for what I need.* I am going back to Neuilly *at once* to take your authorization. I am waiting downstairs in a carriage for this answer.
> Destroy this note, *because it would be shameful for you if it were found.*[3]

Mme Aupick kept the note. It is not clear if she authorized her son to approach Ancelle. She seems to have sent him 15 francs by her factotum, and a reply which deeply wounded him. On 4 December, still from the rue de Babylone, Baudelaire wrote to her again:

> In spite of the cruel letter with which you answered my last request, I felt it was permissible to approach you once more. I know perfectly well what anger this will cause you, and what difficulty I shall have in making you understand the legitimacy of this demand; but I feel such a deep conviction that this can be infinitely and definitively useful to me, that I hope to make you share it ...
> Now this is what I ask of you, *on my knees*, I feel so strongly that I am reaching the final limits, not only of other people's patience, but also of my own. *Send me, even if it costs you a thousand griefs, and even if you do not believe in the usefulness of this final service, not only the sum in question, but enough to live on for three weeks or so.* You will arrange things as you see fit. I believe so completely in the use of time and in the power of my will, that I am *absolutely sure* that if I could manage to live a regular life for a fortnight or

three weeks, *my mind would be saved.* This is a last attempt: *it's a gamble.*
Gamble on the unknown, dearest mother, I beg you . . . It has happened
to me to spend three days in bed, sometimes for lack of linen, sometimes
for lack of wood. Honestly, laudanum and wine are poor resources against
grief. They make the time pass, but they do not re-create life. And then
one needs money to make a beast of oneself. The last time you were kind
enough to give me 15 francs, I hadn't eaten for *two days* – forty-eight hours.
I was constantly on the road to Neuilly, I didn't dare confess my wrongs
to M. A[ncelle], and I only kept awake and erect thanks to the brandy
someone had given me – and I detest spirits, and they twist up my stomach.
May such confessions – for your sake and mine – never be known to living
men or to posterity! For I still believe that posterity concerns me.[4]

He was, he said, enduring a misery which was beyond her comprehension. He wanted, one last time, to see if her financial aid would help him.
He had appealed to her heart, by telling her how he could not always
afford to eat; he had appealed to her pride, by making her ashamed
that a son of hers should be in such distress. He knew, he said, that
any mistress of a house, like herself, would deplore irregular expenses,
but, if she did not help him, he would have to emigrate to Mauritius.[5]
Perhaps Baudelaire had remembered the Autard de Bragards; perhaps
he had thought – as his father had once thought – of being a tutor to
young children. 'I shall do it', he told his mother, 'as a punishment
and atonement for my pride, if I fail in my final resolutions.'[6]

It was now eight months, so he explained, since he had been asked to
write two substantial articles on the history of caricature and the history
of sculpture. He had still not written them, but he could do so easily.
They would bring him in 600 francs, though the sum would only cover
urgent needs. However, he had made a resolution for the new year: he
would write works of pure imagination. He would write novels – and, he
assured his mother, it was just a question of diligence. Mme Aupick had
often reminded him of his age, of the increasing need to be established.
'Time is flying,' he himself reminded her, now, 'and a few more days of
idleness can kill me. As I've told you, I have so abused my strength that
I have reached the final limits of my own patience, and I am incapable
of a great effort without a little help.'[7] He had determined, so he said, not
to see Ancelle again; he had had two unpleasant meetings with him. He
would like the pleasure of receiving this final favour from his mother.

One more word. For a long time you have tried to exclude me completely
from your presence. No doubt you hope that this exclusion will bring an
end to my problems . . . Do you think that my soul is strong enough to
endure this perpetual solitude? *I promise you not to come and see you the first
time unless it is to bring you good news.* But from then on I ask to see you, and
to be well received, and indeed in such a way that your demeanour, looks
and words protect me against everyone in your house.[8]

It was a transparent reference to the new commandant of the École polytechnique.

Baudelaire was, as usual, suffering from his own self-destructive nature. Pichois maintains that, in 1847, 'seven years after the primary syphilitic infection, another pathogenic factor came to worsen the clinical picture. *Alcoholic intoxication* appeared ... with associated *opiomania*. Alcoholic abuses (wine and brandy) seem to be the principal cause of the painful *gastritis*, then of the *gastro-enteritis* which Baudelaire treated with laudanum.'[9] It was, in fact, eight years since he had contracted gonorrhea and, probably, syphilis. Whether or not, in 1847, he was addicted to laudanum, there seems to be no record of alcoholism: indeed, his friends observed that he drank wine in moderation, and he himself had told his mother that he detested spirits. There has so far been no adequate appraisal of his psychological condition; but he suffered more, one may surmise, in mind than in body. He could not bring himself to work, even when editors invited him, even when he needed the payment that they promised him. He despised himself for his idleness, and yet he seemed unable or unwilling to overcome it. The conflict between his wealth of ideas and his inability to express them caused him deep depression and exhaustion. He was aware of passing time, and aware, too, of his powers. He was, as he said, concerned with posterity. His failure seemed to him a sin; and, as a Catholic, he spoke of doing penance.

He knew, no doubt, that he was already losing the goodwill of his editors; he had angered the patient and affectionate Ancelle. There remained only his mother; and, this time, she acted swiftly. He had written to her on 4 December; next day he wrote again – this time a heartfelt letter of thanks.[10]

The Aupicks were about to move to temporary lodgings at 66, rue de Clichy, and then to the commandant's quarters at the École polytechnique; but – whatever the General's hostility – mother and son were now reconciled. It remained a question of meeting when Aupick was absent. On 16 December, Baudelaire asked his mother to meet him later that day at the Louvre.

> ... I have a horror of everything in your house, and especially of your servants. I ask you to be *at the Louvre today, at the Museum, in the big Salon carré*, at whatever time you give me, but as soon as you can ...
> I shall take care to be there first. Thank you for your last letter, you had lost that tone for a long while. It was that letter which induced me to ask you for this meeting.[11]

27

His own tone, too, was different. He had promised to pay her a new year visit (no doubt when his stepfather was absent).

> My dear mother [this on 2 January], . . . you can be absolutely sure that I don't forget anything I promised you. If I don't come and see you immediately, it is because I am very anxious to be able to assure you, with absolute certainty, that my affairs are going better; and, in the second place, for a reason that will make you laugh, you will think it so trifling, it is that I don't think I'm well enough dressed to visit you. *I will see you* in two or three days.[1]

He was well enough dressed to see Champfleury, the novelist and art historian, whose *Contes* he reviewed in *Le Corsaire-Satan*. Indeed, Champfleury claimed that, from 1848, he spent twelve to fifteen hours a day in his company.[2]

It was not, however, with Champfleury but with Gustave Courbet, Charles Toubin and Alphonse Promayet, that Baudelaire was strolling round Paris on the afternoon of 22 February. Toubin was one of the editors of *Le Corsaire-Satan*. Promayet, a composer of waltzes and of sacred music, was a childhood friend of Courbet, who painted him several times, notably in *Un enterrement à Ornans*. He had possibly met Baudelaire at the Brasserie Andler-Keller, where he was one of the habitués. He made only a brief appearance in his life.[3]

It was yet again a time of revolution in Paris. Louis-Philippe and his government had prohibited a series of banquets to be held by the parliamentary opposition; one of them had been arranged for that day. There was general dissatisfaction with the government; and on 22 February, instead of the cancelled banquet, there was a protest in the Paris streets. In the place de la Concorde, Baudelaire and his friends saw a protester killed by a *garde municipal*. Baudelaire and Courbet went to the offices of *La Presse* to speak to its editor, Émile de Girardin, and to condemn this act of barbarity. The next afternoon, with Toubin, Promayet and Champfleury, Baudelaire went to the café de la Rotonde, near the École de Médecine; here they learned that there was fighting in the quartier Saint-Denis, and that the National Guard had been called out. They crossed the river; and, from the place du Châtelet, they heard the shooting. They reached the boulevard du Temple to learn that hostilities were over.

They were in fact far from over.

> It was nearly nine o'clock [recalled Toubin] when we returned to the Left Bank. Baudelaire proposed – to use his favourite expression – to keep me

company while I had dinner, he was enchanted by what he had seen in the last two days . . . I had never seen him so cheerful, so lively, so tireless, and he was not accustomed to walking. His eyes were sparkling. After dinner we went to the Rotonde, and in this café, which had been so animated on all the previous evenings, we found Courbet absolutely alone in the presence of a glass of beer and in company with his pipe. The night was horribly dark, and a lugubrious silence reigned throughout the quartier. Suddenly the tocsin began to sound: first from Saint-Séverin, then from Saint-Étienne-du-Mont and Saint-Sulpice. Somebody ran past, and shouted in a voice that froze us with fear: 'To arms! They are murdering our brothers . . .' We rushed into the street, there was no one to tell us anything, but Saint-Sulpice continued and we ran in that direction at the risk of breaking our necks in the darkness. The bell stopped, and, just as we reached the square in front of the church, a hail of bullets struck the wall of a house above our heads, and we beat retreat, faster than we had come . . .

Driven back on this side, we went down to the Pont-Neuf. It was occupied by a battalion of the line, which permitted people to pass from the Right Bank to the Left, but not from the Left Bank to the Right. From time to time, terrified people arrived from the Right Bank to tell us about the incident in the boulevard des Capucines, the corpses carried by torchlight, and the barricades rising up on every side.

It was the incident in the boulevard des Capucines which had turned a riot into a revolution. A witness wrote:

I had seen the crowds start singing cheerfully down the boulevards, and at first they went on their way peacefully and without resistance . . . But in the boulevard des Capucines a body of troops, both infantry and cavalry, was massed on the two pavements and across the road, guarding the Ministry of Foreign Affairs and its unpopular Minister, M. Guizot. Faced with this impassable obstacle, the leader of the column of people tried to stop and turn aside; but the irresistible pressure of the huge crowd weighed on the front ranks. At that moment a shot rang out, from which side is not known. Panic followed, and then a volley. Eighty dead or wounded remained on the spot. There arose a universal cry of horror and fury: Revenge! . . . And, a few hours later, Paris was covered with barricades.[5]

Next morning, 24 February, Toubin met Baudelaire and Armand Barthet at the carrefour de Buci. They were armed with sporting-guns, and prepared to fight behind a barricade which only protected them up to the waist. According to Jules Buisson, who professed to have seen them there that evening, Baudelaire had also found the occasion to express his deepest personal hostility.

How often [reflected Buisson] he must have cursed the General for the salutary checks which restrained him! With the violence common in weak men, in childlike souls, he dreamed of nothing but revolts, encounters and occurrences in which, in imagination, he killed the poor General, like a rabbit.

One knows what scorn and hatred he felt for the republicans ... However, in 1848, on the evening of 24 February [sic], I met him at the carrefour de Buci, in the middle of a crowd which had just pillaged a gunsmith's shop. He was carrying a brand-new, gleaming, double-barrelled rifle, and a superb yellow leather ammunition pouch, which was equally immaculate. I hailed him, he came up to me feigning great animation: 'I have just fired a rifle!' he said. I smiled, and looked at his gleaming new artillery. 'Not for the Republic, I'm sure!' He did not answer, but he shouted a lot, and always with this refrain: they must go and shoot General Aupick.[6]

Buisson had come to feel contempt for Baudelaire's hostility to Aupick. In Baudelaire 'entre Dieu et Satan', Jean Massin found it moving. 'If there can be extenuating circumstances for detesting a stepfather, we may, in strict justice, grant them to Baudelaire ... This detested stepfather here assumes the symbolic grandeur of a whole ignoble world ... In a word, it is everything that is basely mediocre and believes itself to be wonderfully just, that Baudelaire wants to bring down.'[7]

While Baudelaire was taking part in the insurrection, Aupick himself was struggling to control his cadets at the École polytechnique.

He had only been there for a few months, and he had succeeded General Rostolan, whose severity in all matters of discipline had hardly softened in his latter days [so Pinet recorded in his Histoire de l'École Polytechnique]. General Aupick, aide-de-camp of the Duc de Nemours, had established himself by taking the most benevolent measures, and he had already earned the devotion of his pupils. A former adjutant at Leipzig, he had witnessed atrocious scenes in the great battle between the nations, and several times, with real emotion, he had told them about the memories of his youth. They loved the old soldier of the First Empire as much as the commandant full of gentleness and kindness, a commandant who could be firm if need be, but appreciated the work, the age and the character of the young men whom he had just been called upon to command.[8]

It is a touching portrait, drawn by a former pupil of the École polytechnique: it is an unexpected and illuminating likeness of the stepfather of Baudelaire. It is confirmed by another pupil, Charles de Freycinet, who had been nineteen at the time, and was one day to be a colleague of Aupick's in the Senate. General Aupick, he wrote in his Souvenirs, 'was not an ordinary commandant. He combined great firmness with kindness and with a rare wisdom.'[9] Aupick understood cadets, although he could not understand a poet.

However, on 23 February 1848, even Aupick found it hard to control the young men under his command. They had gathered to discuss what part they should take in the insurrection.

As the General entered the lecture-hall [Pinet continued], people were shouting: 'We must go out! We must go out! At once!' . . . The General spoke: 'I urge you not to go out,' he said. 'Paris is rather disturbed, some crowds have collected in the rue Saint-Denis and the rue Saint-Martin, but it's nothing serious. I am not ordering you to stay here, but I advise you to do so in the interest of the School.' It was wise advice; very few pupils followed it. At two o'clock most of them went out . . .

Throughout the morning of the 24th, the pupils' agitation increased from one minute to the next. At eight o'clock they rushed to the recreation rooms to lay their heads together, to deliberate, to determine what action to take. The General . . . decided to summon them to the lecture-hall again. He wanted to repeat the advice and the exhortations which he had given them the previous day, but his attitude seemed irresolute, his advice embarrassed. 'Keep your trust in me,' he told them, 'be calm and patient.' 'But suppose we all wanted to go out at once?' the pupils replied . . . The General was opposed to their doing so. 'I have no power at all', he said, 'to prevent you going out. I shall open the gates, but if you go out you will pass over my body.'[10]

The scene recalled his performance in the title-role of *Fortunas*, as a youth of eighteen at the Prytaneum, but it was wholly in Aupick's character. Heroics were not, now, enough. Devoted though they were to him, his cadets ignored his appeal, and once again went out into the streets to stand between the army and the people.

Later that day, there was a violent incident outside the main gates of the École polytechnique. As Pinet recorded:

Two or three hundred men armed with knives and spears [sic] tried to force their way into the courtyard so that they could seize some weapons. A company of infantry, patrolling in the quartier, drew up in front of the gates, there was rifle fire, the crowds retaliated, several soldiers fell. At the sound of rifle fire, General Aupick rushed to the scene. He was now alone with the staff officers, the chief physician and the various employees, and he gave shelter to the soldiers. He was surrounded by the crowd, threatened with death, and a workman was taking aim at him. He was struggling fiercely to free himself. As they were tearing off his epaulettes, two Polytechniciens appeared. 'Villains!' they shouted. 'Get away, it's our General!', and they literally covered him with their bodies.[11]

Charles de Freycinet gave a more sober account of events. 'During the day, an armed gang took possession of the guard-house, and they would have killed the General if two cadets had not rushed up in time to protect him.'[12] Baudelaire's wish had nearly been fulfilled.

*

That day, 24 February 1848, Louis-Philippe abdicated in favour of his grandson, the son of the late Duc d'Orléans. It soon became clear that only a republican government would satisfy the masses. Louis-Philippe escaped to exile in England, and a provisional government was set up, under the leadership of the Romantic poet Alphonse de Lamartine. On 25 February, the Second Republic was proclaimed, and the country proceeded to elect an Assemblée constituante.

'After the revolution of February 1848,' so Julien Lemer was to remember, 'the elegant and fashionable Baudelaire was seized by a fit of ardent democracy; he frequented the popular Societies . . .'[13] Late in February he attended the second meeting of the Société Républicaine Centrale; it was presided over by Auguste Blanqui, the socialist revolutionary. On 27 February there appeared the first issue of *Le Salut public*, to which Baudelaire contributed. The paper had been established with 80 francs which belonged to Toubin and his brother. The first issue had been planned at the café Turlot, on the corner of the rue Hautefeuille, where – nearly twenty-seven years earlier – Baudelaire had been born. It is said that he himself, clad in a white smock, sold the second issue on the streets. There was not enough money left to produce a third issue of the paper.[14]

On 1 March, *Le Moniteur universel* announced that Aupick was among the army officers who had rallied to the provisional government. One word, it has been said, seems to characterize his life, and that word is service. 'To serve France, certainly, under and beyond different régimes, but also to serve in the absolute sense, to exercise a function for which one has been created, to be the instrument of a superior force, Power. Specialists in military psychology are well aware of the existence of this kind of senior officer whose political ideas are non-existent, or virtually so, whose minds . . . have been broken in, very early, to obedience. Power always finds them happy to "serve", and always loyal, provided that it remains Power.'[15] Aupick had not only been trained for military service, he had also inherited this apolitical sense of obedience. He was his father's son; and his father's regiment, one of the last in the Irish Brigade in France, had finally marched behind a banner which bore both an Irish harp and fleurs-de-lys.[16] On 3 March 1848, the provisional government announced that Aupick would remain the commandant of the École polytechnique.

However, it had now become an untenable appointment for him. Soon afterwards, recorded Pinet, he was retired because of his ties with the Orléans family.[17]

Aupick was now fifty-nine, but he was still favoured by good fortune. He was offered a brilliant new career. Lamartine, who had a formal acquaintance with him, was now the Minister of Foreign Affairs, and he was re-organising the Corps diplomatique. It was a somewhat delicate task. As soon as he was assured that certain foreign governments were favourable towards the Republic, he chose his ambassadors and ministers.

On 8 April, the provisional government appointed Aupick envoy extraordinary and minister plenipotentiary to Turkey. There were varying opinions of the appointment. On 12 April Baroness Bonde, the wife of a Swedish diplomat, wrote to her friend Mrs Ashburnham: 'It may interest you to know that the minister at Constantinople is to be General Aupick . . . I presume he is *gênant* here, for he has no diplomatic antecedents, and if he were useful he would not be sent somewhere else.'[18] However, on 13 April (strangely enough, after the appointment had been made), Lamartine asked Jean-Baptiste-Adolphe Charras, the under-secretary for war, to put Aupick at his disposal. Two days later, Charras agreed.

> General Aupick [recorded Lamartine] . . . had been attached to the princes for a long time, but the members of the Government and the Minister of the Interior confidently chose him to represent the Republic in one of the most important posts abroad. His first loyalty was to his country. Great military capacity and a thoughtful and unerring mind marked General Aupick out for a post in which the diplomacies of the world might clash. Only his aptitudes were questioned [*sic*], we were certain of his conscientiousness.[19]

The Orléans family did not resent his rallying to the Republic (and, later, to the Second Empire), although they had done so much to promote him. There is no record that Baudelaire sent his congratulations to Aupick; and there was no question of their meeting.

Late in April or early in May, Baudelaire explained to his mother:

> For three days I have tried to find a way to see you and talk to you, which is indispensable; because it is a question of your authorization for me with M. Ancelle. I suffer greatly at the thought of meeting your Husband; and so you must deign to fix a time when I shan't meet him at your house. This visit is all the more indispensable because it may well be that I shall leave before you.[20]

The journey he had in mind was perhaps the journey to Château-roux which he was finally to make later in the year. It was, presumably, early in May that he wrote to his mother once again: 'I shall come tomorrow. Take care that I am well received and not disturbed. In the first place I have to say my farewells to you, and then there is a word

from you which is absolutely essential to me.'[21] The word might have
been about his financial situation; it is much more probable that, on
the eve of her departure, when she was about to go abroad, and leave
him, perhaps, for years, Baudelaire wanted to be assured of his
mother's affection.

Mme Aupick was unwell, and she was overwrought. She was devoted
to her husband, proud of his achievements, excited by the prospect of
a legation. She was grievously disturbed by the rift between her husband and her son. She was well aware of her son's emotional dependence upon her. She was apprehensive at leaving him to his financial
problems, his literary crises, his bouts of depression and ill-health, and,
above all, to the predatory Jeanne. No doubt she allowed herself to
make some unwelcome observations. As for Baudelaire, resentful and
unhappy at her departure, he allowed himself – one must surmise – to
express his antipathy to the General, and his bitter sense of rejection.
He spoke with vehemence about Jeanne. He seems to have asked his
mother for money for her. Mme Aupick refused it angrily. The farewell
visit was a disaster.

By 12 May, the Aupicks were at Marseilles; a few days later, on the
Mouette, they set sail for Turkey. On 19 June, Édouard Thouvenel, who
was then the chargé-d'affaires, wrote home from the legation in
Athens: 'We have had a passing visit from General Aupick . . . If our
[other] ambassadors are like him, diplomacy will not have lost by the
change.'[22]

28

The advent of the Second Republic had not brought tranquillity to
France. From the beginning, the new Assemblée nationale had been
obsessed with political dogma. The left-wing leaders of Paris, frustrated
by the elections, carried on an increasingly bitter agitation in the Press
and in the popular clubs. On 15 May – perhaps the day that the
Aupicks sailed – the club leaders tried to overthrow the Assemblée
nationale. Baudelaire was to mention the date in *Mon Cœur mis à nu*,
and to recall the 'taste for destruction' which this day had left in him.[1]

The only result of the insurrection was that nearly all the left-wing
agitators disappeared from the political scene, either in flight abroad
or into prison. They therefore cannot be held responsible for the
popular rising in June.

The hope of salvation, with which the unemployed and starving masses had poured on to the streets in February, had given place to disillusionment. Under the Republic, conditions had become worse instead of better. After the February Revolution, the provisional government had established the *ateliers nationaux*. These national workshops were little more than a system of registering the Paris unemployed for the payment of a miserable dole. This charity proved to be ineffective. On 22 June it was therefore decreed that all the unmarried workers in the *ateliers* should join the army, and that the rest should go to the provinces, on penalty of losing their payments. The distress and disappointment caused by this decision brought a new and violent insurrection in Paris. At first it was not resisted, because there were no troops. This was due to the problems of provisioning them in Paris and to the lack of barracks. However, once the regular troops had been brought into action, the end of the insurrection was assured. In four days of hard fighting, the rebel quarters were taken street by street.

Baudelaire declared that he had fought with the insurgents. Le Vavasseur found him in the streets, exalted, with the smell of gunpowder on his hands. On 5 July, in *Le Représentant du peuple*, P.-J. Proudhon demanded the repeal of the decree of deportation drawn up against the rebels; in August, he advised the supporters of the Republic not to be violent, and not to give the monarchists any pretext for repression. On 21 August, Baudelaire tried to enter the Chamber, to hand Proudhon a letter of support; innocent as ever, he asked him for an interview, and declared that he shared his ideas. Proudhon does not seem to have answered.[2]

It is strange that this political activity did not represent a serious concern with politics. Baudelaire had welcomed any opportunities to express emotions, but these emotions had been personal. In *Mon Cœur mis à nu*, he was to write: 'I have no convictions, as they are understood by the men of my century, because I have no ambition . . . However, I have some convictions, in a nobler sense, which cannot be understood by the men of my time.'[3]

After the coup-d'État of December 1851, he was to take no active part in politics, and he did not even trouble to vote.

In the meanwhile, in October 1848, Baudelaire went to Châteauroux on one of the strangest errands of his life. Insurgent and republican, he was to be the editor of a new paper, *Le Représentant de l'Indre*, which was conservative in its views. He owed his appointment, so it seems, to Arthur Ponroy, whom he had known at *Le Corsaire-Satan*. Years later, Firmin Boissin explained:

Arthur Ponroy's father, [Jean-Sylvain Ponroy], an advocate in the Indre, had just founded a daily paper at Châteauroux to defend conservative interests.

The post of editor-in-chief was vacant. Ponroy offered it to Baudelaire, who accepted it, and set off.

As soon as he arrived, a great banquet was given in honour of the new editor-in-chief. There were the principal shareholders in the paper: rich, honest, bourgeois, a little *prudhommesques*. Baudelaire did not utter a word. At dessert, one of the guests expressed his surprise at this silence.

'But, Monsieur Baudelaire, you aren't saying anything?'

The mystifier answered:

'Gentlemen, I have nothing to say. Haven't I come here to be the servant of your minds?'[4]

According to R. H. Sherard, the English journalist, Baudelaire's reply was even stronger. 'You have brought me down here to be the lackey of your intelligence. I am not paid to talk to you.'[5]

The first issue of the paper appeared on 20 October. The subscribers were scandalised by Baudelaire's first article. His editorship lasted only a week.

Some forty years later, Firmin Boissin assured Eugène Crépet:

As for the episode of Baudelaire the journalist at Châteauroux, I had it, verbatim, from M. Arthur Ponroy himself. He told me the details at the café Tabourey, near the Odéon, in the presence of two witnesses who are, alas, now dead: the late Édouard Fournier, and one of my best friends, Constant Thérion – the former being the same man who gave Alphonse Daudet one of his heroes in *Les Rois en exil*, the preceptor of the boy king of Illyria, Élysée Mérault . . . [6]

There was a final, unexpected twist to the story of Baudelaire's visit to Châteauroux. On 6 December, he learned from Ancelle that his mother had paid for his journey.

I must confess [he wrote to her, on 8 December], that this disclosure of M. Ancelle's, about this remittance, greatly surprised me, no less than his concern to conceal it in the first instance. I was, I admit, very greatly surprised that, over there [in Constantinople], you deigned to continue to think of me, and to concern yourself about my eternal financial vexations, especially after the very unfeeling manner in which you received me a few days before you left.

With that nervous stubbornness, that violence which is peculiar to you, you abused me, solely because of a poor woman, *whom I have loved for a long while simply out of duty*, that's all. It is curious that you who have so often, and for so long, talked to me of spiritual feelings, and of duty, should not have understood this singular liaison, in which I have nothing to gain, and in which atonement, and the wish to repay devotion, play the greater part . . . Now, at the age of twenty-eight all but four months, with an immense poetic ambition, separated for ever and ever from the *honourable world* by my tastes and principles, what does it matter if, building my literary dreams, I also fulfil *a duty*, or what I believe to be a duty, to the great detriment of the vulgar ideas of honour, money, and prosperity? Please note that I do not in the least implore consent; it is simply the admission that I might well be right . . .

The only thing which really interests me about you is to know how your voyage went, if you are all right over there, and if your health is better than it was here.

As for me, although literature is less in favour than ever, I am still the same, that is to say that I am absolutely convinced that my debts will be paid, and that my destiny will be gloriously fulfilled.[7]

For all the daily, unremitting miseries of his life, Baudelaire was sure of his future.

29

Little is known of Baudelaire in 1849. Only one dated letter in his hand survives, and one which is presumed to have been written that December.[1] On 5 February, however, Delacroix recorded that Baudelaire had called on him, and that his ideas seemed 'as modern as can be.' They had talked of Daumier, whom Baudelaire admired. Baudelaire had said that Daumier found it difficult to finish his drawings.[2]

He, too, found it hard to finish his work. His collection of poems, at present called *Les Limbes*, was due to appear on 24 February, but it remained unpublished. His financial situation was as desperate as ever. By October, he had spent all his income for the year. Soon afterwards, however, with his usual extravagance, he commissioned Palis, the calligrapher, to make a fair copy of his poems. He made a payment on account of 11 or 12 francs; he still owed some 28 francs for the work when, on 3 December, he left, alone, for Dijon.

The purpose of this visit seems obscure; it is only clear that he went to Dijon in the hope of earning money. Although there is no trace of his collaboration in the socialist paper, *Le Travail*, it is possible that he worked for its new editor, Jules Viard. Apparently he expected to stay in Dijon for some time, because he thought of renting a small apartment. Before he left Paris, he saw Ancelle, and asked him for the extra money to pay for his new lodgings. Ancelle could not afford to be liberal. He was obliged to pay Palis for his work on Baudelaire's poems. He gave Baudelaire the customary sum.

Baudelaire's troubles were not only financial. He had been ill, or so it seems, before he left Paris. Almost as soon as he reached Dijon, he had secondary complications of the syphilis which he had contracted a few years earlier. On 9 January, after a difficult meeting with Ancelle, Jeanne arrived in Dijon to join him.

> I have been quite seriously ill, as you know [he told Ancelle next day, in a long, aggressive letter]. My stomach is somewhat unsettled by the laudanum; but this isn't the first time, and it's strong enough to recover.
>   Jeanne arrived yesterday morning, and told me at some length about her meeting with you. Everything has been a calamity for me for a long time. And so I wasn't surprised to hear things which prove that you understand absolutely nothing about my life . . .[3]

Palis had grossly overcharged Ancelle for his work; if Ancelle were brave enough, added Baudelaire, he should claim a refund of 12 francs. Ancelle had not understood that it would be cheaper to live in a small apartment in Dijon than to stay at a hotel; he still failed to appreciate that extra money was urgently needed.

> *Besides* [continued Baudelaire], *the proprietress of the hotel has just told me that she needs some money for the 15th. So you see that there is not a moment to lose, since you will receive this letter on the 12th.*
>   *If you immediately send me 400 or 500 francs, that is to say January and February, I shall leave thé hotel at once,* and two days later I shall be settled in a place of my own. In that case, I should not ask you for money again until 1 March. That would certainly be much more sensible; it would be a great advantage to me, and you would gain the certainty that I was better and I was spending less . . .
>   One word more . . .
>   You behave like a child. However, I have reproached you often enough for your sentimentality, and shown you the futility of your affection where my mother is concerned. Put that aside once and for all, and, if I have something broken in my spirit on that score, pity me and leave me in peace. And Jeanne as well. There are still many other things, but let's forget them. Only I beg you, if by chance you have some occasion later to see Mlle Lemer, don't make game of her, don't talk so much again, and be more serious . . .
>   Allow me, before I end this letter, to add a few words which bear small relation to what precedes, but I am taking advantage of the occasion to tell you everything which is in my heart . . .
>   The situation which you are in, as regards myself, is strange. It is not only legal, it is also, so to speak, one of sentiment. It is impossible that you should not know it. As for me, I am very unsentimental, and I have not been able to escape this truth. The sombre solitude which I have created around myself *has only bound me closer to Jeanne*. It has also accustomed me to consider you as something important in my life. This

brings me to the point. If this is, inevitably, your situation, as regards myself, what does it generally mean, this singular lack of understanding of my interests? *What does it mean, this bias in favour of my mother, whom you know to be guilty?* What do they mean, your tiresome repetitions, your egotistical maxims, your brutalities, your insolence? It is quite true that I have returned as good as I have got, but this is all nonsense. Our relationship must improve.[4]

It was Baudelaire who should have shown common civility and understanding. Ancelle was twenty years his senior. He discharged his duties with unwavering patience. He resolutely chose to ignore the outbursts of anger and contempt with which Baudelaire assailed him.

If Baudelaire had indeed gone to Dijon to work on *Le Travail*, his visit lost its purpose in the spring. On 20 March, after a series of condemnations and fines, the paper ceased publication. It is not known exactly when he returned to Paris, but Asselineau said that in 1850 he had called on him in lodgings near the boulevard Poissonnière. It was then that Baudelaire showed him 'the manuscript of his poems, splendidly copied out by a calligrapher. It formed two quarto volumes, bound and gilt-[edged]. This was the manuscript that was used for the printing of *Les Fleurs du mal*.'[5] No doubt Asselineau paid this visit before 10 May, when Baudelaire was living at 95, avenue de la République, at Neuilly.

The address is given in a letter to Gérard de Nerval. The letter contains the first mention of the man who was going to be 'the first publisher of poets, the John the Baptist of Alphonse Lemerre.'[6] He was, more importantly, to be the publisher of Baudelaire, and one of his most intimate friends.

Paul-Emmanuel-Auguste Poulet-Malassis had been born on 16 March 1825. He was the last descendant of a family of printers and publishers in Alençon, the first of whom went back at least to 1539.[7] The family were to be commemorated by the naming of a square in the town. As Monselet was to observe, the young man's only grief in the world 'was to be called Poulet-Malassis. You can imagine the jokes there were about that ridiculous name.'[8] (Baudelaire was to call him Coco mal perché.)[9] Malassis, like his father before him, had gone to the lycée in Alençon; it was no doubt intended that he should also follow him in his career, and become the printer to the prefecture. Intellect and imagination decided otherwise. Almost as soon as he left school, he showed his love of literature. Almost at once he wrote his first article and published his first reprint. He collaborated with Léon de la Sicotière on a handsome volume of local history: *Le Département de l'Orne archéologique et pittoresque.*

On 28 August 1847, he was accepted as a *bachelier* by the Faculté des
Lettres in Paris. That December, he entered the École des Chartes,
the institution founded to train archivists and librarians. The École des
Chartes brought him Paris with all its temptations, and he soon
contracted venereal disease. From his first day in Paris, he also went
to political extremes. In June 1848, he and some friends had founded
L'Aimable Faubourien, Journal de la Canaille. The publication had ceased
after the fifth issue; but, on 23 June, Malassis – who was a keen shot
– had been arrested with the insurgents, rifle in hand. He had been
jailed in the fortress at Ivry, then taken to the galleys at Brest, where
they imprisoned the survivors of the insurrection. Only the intervention
of a friend, Oudinot de La Faverie, saved him, it is said, from
execution. That December, on the intervention of the Deputy for the
Orne, he was released, and he resumed his studies in Paris.

It was, it seems, on about 9 May 1850 that Malassis first met
Baudelaire, in the company of Champfleury. Their sympathy for each
other was immediate. The friendship was confirmed that summer when,
according to Delvau, Baudelaire frequented La Laiterie du paradoxe,
a tavern in the rue Saint-André-des-Arts.[10] Lemercier de Neuville, the
puppeteer, recorded Baudelaire and Malassis at the Cabaret Dinochau,
in the quartier Bréda.

> Among the occasional habitués, I must not [he wrote] forget Baudelaire,
> Poulet-Malassis and Hippolyte Babou. They generally met at Poulet-
> Malassis', [at 27, rue Neuve-Bréda, now rue Clauzel], since he preferred
> his cooking to Dinochau's.
>   For Malassis was a great gourmet. He used to give delectable dinners
> to a very small number of friends: dinners washed down with fine wines,
> and served on valuable plates. Rare faience and distinguished pictures
> adorned his dining-room, and delighted the eyes, while the mind was busy
> with the sparkling conversation of the guests.[11]

Alphonse Daudet saw Malassis, again with Baudelaire, at the Brasserie
des Martyrs: 'A publisher such as one rarely sees, Malassis: witty and
curiously well-read, he went royally through a handsome fortune, publishing the people he liked . . . And it is not without emotion that I
recall that sly, pale face, elongated by the two points of a red beard,
a Mephistopheles of the time of the Valois.'[12]

Maxime Rude took a different historical perspective: 'With his
red-gold hair, slim, well-built, a little stiff but elegant, Malassis recalled
Velasquez' Philip II . . . It is true that this gallant man was as republican as Saint-Just.'[13] In his *Confidences d'un journaliste*, Rude paid him a
further tribute: 'Malassis had a prodigious belief, a belief in literature
and poetry . . . He sought out those who were mad about the pen, as

others have been about the cross [of the Légion-d'honneur]. He belonged to the generation of 1848, he tended its flowering.'[14]

Malassis did not pursue his studies at the École des Chartes, but he earned higher qualifications. He won the deep affection of Baudelaire, and his own place in literary history.[15]

As for his mother, Baudelaire had tried in vain, for months, to write to her; but he could not forget their last meeting, when she had abused him for his relationship with Jeanne, and he could not ever forgive her for her second marriage, or forget that she had imposed the *conseil judiciaire* upon him. She herself, it seems, had decided – no doubt at her husband's insistence – that she would not write to her son. As long as she was abroad, however many years her husband's Turkish mission might continue, she would only communicate with him through Ancelle. It was a ruthless decision, but mother and son were divided, now, by distance as well as their past history; and, as long as Mme Aupick stayed in Constantinople, there remained small chance of reconciliation.

While Baudelaire was living in squalor and uncertainty, the General was leading a life which not only satisfied his sense of duty, but seemed a princely reward for public service. Had it been the last appointment of his career, it would still have been reward enough.

> Providence, which has never failed me, from my most tender infancy, would thus have crowned my career of 44 years devoted to the service of my country. You will agree [this to Thouvenel] that it would be impossible for me to enter the last phase of life under more honourable auspices. [I am speaking of] retirement, the state which allows you to relive the past, and only to concern yourself with the future out of attachment to those you love, and out of filial devotion to your native land.[16]

On 25 April 1850, he had told the same correspondent: 'I feel my shoulders light and my heart full of joy.'[17]

It was little wonder. In their winter palace in Pera, in their summer palace in Therapia, he and his wife delighted in an existence which was a world away from their early married life in the rue du Bac. Years later, in *L'Italie et Constantinople*, Charles Asselineau was to recall Therapia, on the European bank of the Bosphorus.

> The presence of the British and French ambassadors, who have set up their summer residences here, gives Therapia a particular importance ... The gardens of the palace of the French Ambassador, very fine and very extensive, cover the whole hillside, and crown it with a double row of parasol pines which one can make out from the sea ... Even if the summer palace of the French Ambassador were not a gift made by a recent sultan to the French Government, our ambassadors would have found reason enough in the beauty of the place to determine their choice. Therapia, which stretches

out into the sea, commands the Bosphorus on both sides . . . From the
terrace of the French palace, the view extends as far as the Black Sea,
beyond the estuary of the river, and embraces the whole Asian coast . . .[18]

It was here, on 3 July 1850, that Lamartine, on a visit to Turkey,
came to dine with Aupick and the staff of the Legation.[19] It was here,
on 27 November, after a courtesy visit in Constantinople, that Flaubert
arrived on his Eastern travels, with Maxime du Camp. 'The General
in a dressing-gown with velvet collar and trimmings,' he recorded;[20]
and again: 'The good General disregards diplomatic behaviour; in
private he punched Maxime hard in the back several times, and called
him a damned scoundrel.'[21] Relations with Aupick were so congenial
that, on 6 December, Flaubert and Du Camp dined with him at the
Legation in Constantinople.[22]

However happy her marriage, however grand her circumstances, the
General's wife remained in an impossible position. This was evident to
Du Camp.

One evening, in Constantinople, in the palace of the French Legation,
General Aupick, who was then Ambassador [*sic*], asked me after dinner:
'Has literature made some good recruits since you left Paris?' I mentioned
La Vie de Bohème, by Henry Murger, which had been produced, with
success, at the Théâtre des Variétés. 'A few days ago,' I added, 'I had a
letter from Louis de Cormenin. He told me: "At Théophile Gautier's I
recently met a certain Baudelaire, who is going to make himself a name;
his originality is a little too deliberate, but his poetry is powerful. He has
a poet's temperament, which is something rare in our age." ' As soon as
I mentioned Baudelaire, Mme Aupick bowed her head, the General
glared at me as if he had received a challenge, and Colonel [de] Margadel
tapped me on the foot to warn me that I was entering dangerous territory.
I remained somewhat embarrassed, knowing that I had made a blunder,
and not understanding what it was. Ten minutes later, the General and
Flaubert were arguing, without listening to each other, and both talking
at once, about some or other book by Proudhon. Mme Aupick came up
to me, and whispered: 'He's got talent, hasn't he?' 'Who's that?' 'The
young man whom M. de Cormenin praised to you.' I nodded, silently,
because I understood less and less.

 Colonel [de] Margadel left at the same time as we did, and took us to
his apartment in the palace, to show us his fine collection of lepidoptera.
'My God!' he said to me, 'you nearly set everything ablaze when you
mentioned Charles Baudelaire. He is Mme Aupick's son . . . The General
will not have his name mentioned in his presence.' . . . Colonel [de]
Margadel told us that Baudelaire and General Aupick had quarrelled, and
would never see each other again.[23]

Aupick himself forgave the *faux pas*. On 14 December, the eve of
their departure, Flaubert and Du Camp dined again at the Legation.[24]

30

They were to be among the last of the Aupicks' guests. Some three years after he had been appointed Minister to Turkey, the General's mission was about to end. On 20 February 1851 – apparently without consultation – he was appointed Ambassador to the Court of St James's. It was extraordinary promotion for a man who was not a diplomat by profession. On 14 March, in a letter to the Foreign Minister, he acknowledged his flattering appointment. 'I am deeply touched by this testimony of great confidence, and I ask you to assure M. le Président that I shall strive to justify it.'[1] He made his arrangements to leave Turkey. On 25 March, he confessed that 'Mme Aupick is not leaving Pera, and especially Therapia, without regret. As for me, tired as I am by all I see and all that I foresee, I long for some rest, and, when the occasion arises, I shall probably seize it.'[2] On 26 April he was received by the Sultan in farewell audience. Four days later, he and his wife embarked on the dispatch-boat *La Vedette*.

Aupick was weary after three years burdened with official cares. Mme Aupick was not only sad at leaving Turkey, she was unwell, and she was an indifferent sailor. Aupick described their voyage home in a letter to Édouard Thouvenel. Since they had met in Athens in 1848, the two men had established an excellent official relationship; there was also a firm friendship between Aupick and the man who was now Minister in Athens, and would one day be Minister of Foreign Affairs.

> We had a delightful voyage [this from Aupick on 26 June]. The breaks in it had become essential, because of my wife's health. Her sufferings at sea were only half cured on land, which slightly spoilt what we were doing. However, we turned to quite good account the time which I thought I had at my disposal.
>
> Nor shall we forget the welcome which we received in Athens, . . . or Messina, where a dreadful threat of a storm made us drop anchor. We shall not forget Naples, or Rome, or finally Lyons, where I stopped for four days to judge for myself what had become of that redoubtable stronghold (I saw them begin to fortify it in 1831). From the military point of view, it has become a most wonderful achievement.[3]

Mme Aupick delighted in the prospect of England. ('When shall we be able to murder the Queen's English together?' she once enquired of a friend. 'In the meanwhile, *I am quite yours, my dear*.')[4] She had been born in London. Aupick, who had Irish and perhaps English blood, admired British patriotism. 'It is a proud nation, the British nation,' he had told Thouvenel, 'and we should certainly learn from them a little of what is called national feeling.'[5] In London, his appointment was welcomed. A senior civil servant wrote to M. Brenier, the new Minister

of Foreign Affairs, in Paris: 'I have been instructed to state to Your
Excellency, that the selection for this post of a Person who, in the
honourable and important mission which he has lately found at the
Porte, has so justly acquired the highest consideration and esteem,
cannot fail to be extremely gratifying to The Queen and to Her
Majesty's Government.'[6]

Yet although Aupick had accepted the Embassy in London like the
obedient soldier that he was, he had no intention of taking up 'the
great and noble mission.'[7] It was to be the only occasion in his life
when he would refuse to obey an order. He kept his resolution entirely
to himself. On the night of 3 June, he arrived in Paris. Next day he
was received by the Prince-President, Louis-Napoleon.

> An hour later, I left him [he explained to Thouvenel], relieved of the
> immeasurable honour which he had been good enough to do me . . . It
> was splendid, it was very honourable for me. But they should have known
> that I could not possibly accept it . . . So I remained silent in Pera, in
> Athens, everywhere, even with my wife, who was dreaming of England.
> And I remained silent till the 4th. I told the President my reasons. He
> attempted to oppose them. I expressed myself in such a way that he saw
> that it was really a foregone conclusion . . . You know the reasons for my
> refusal to go to London. I could not accept the role that my position would
> create for me in the presence of the Orléans family. Call it what you will:
> it will always be a role of distinguished espionage. I cannot accept it . . .
> I am the last of my race, I shall go as an honourable soldier to my final
> rest.[8]

An ambassador is always to some extent a spy in regard to the previous
dynasty, if it shows the slightest wish to regain the throne. The Orléans,
who had done so much to further his career, were in exile, now, in
England. He could not bring himself to betray them.

As for the Orléans in Spain – the Duc de Montpensier and his wife,
the brother-in-law and sister of Queen Isabella – Aupick simply
considered them as Spaniards. He neither sought nor refused contact
with them. On 18 June, quite happily, he accepted the Embassy in
Madrid.

On 7 June, Ancelle told Baudelaire that, after three years' absence, his
mother was back in Paris. She was staying at the hôtel du Danube, rue
Richepanse. Baudelaire wrote to her at once:

> M. Ancelle told me today that you had arrived in Paris. He also told me
> that you wanted to see me. That gave me great pleasure, and I confess
> that, if you hadn't shown the wish to do so, I had decided to go ahead
> and ask you for permission to see you [*sic*].

But M. Ancelle, who is a good man, was wrong to promise that I should go and see you. He was foolish to do so. I wish I could express myself in a way which did not wound your affections, but after all you can guess why my dignity forbade me to set foot in your house.

On the other hand, the respect I owe you does not allow me to receive you at the house of someone you hate. And so I expect of your affection, that you will be kind enough to come to *Neuilly*, to a lodging *where I am alone*. I shall stay in for these two days, Sunday and Monday . . . If, in this letter, some unsatisfactory phrase has slipped in, despite me, don't reproach me, you know how awkward I am in writing.[9]

It was a pitiful letter for a mother to receive from her son. His hatred of her husband gave her conflicting loyalties. She was still obliged to have an almost clandestine relationship with her own child. She was disappointed, angry and apprehensive.

As for Baudelaire, he had parted from her, three years earlier, with bitterness and rage. He could not bear the presence of Aupick. He not only resented him, he resented the behaviour which Aupick had imposed on his mother. It was the General who had sent him on his Eastern voyage; it was the General, no doubt, who had persuaded her to appoint a *conseil judiciaire*. If Baudelaire often found himself near penury, beset by creditors, too troubled to sleep or to write, if he was constantly obliged to move from one seedy lodging to another, it was – in his mind – the Aupicks who were responsible. They did not understand his gifts or appreciate his needs. They violently disapproved of Jeanne – and, for all her faults, she remained, in the words of Jacques Crépet, 'the redeeming vampire'. She was the only person who gave him peace.[10]

During the last three years, while the Aupicks lived in ministerial splendour, Baudelaire had done little to establish himself in literature. The chasm between them had widened.

Mme Aupick, so it seems, did not immediately go to Neuilly; but she sent a letter which was loving enough to change the emotional climate. On 12 June, he wrote again: 'My dear mother, I should be glad to see you on MONDAY the 16th . . . *If you can't come*, warn me by letter, because, without this precaution, *I should wait for you indefinitely*.'[11]

The reconciliation with his mother had brought a new tone in his letters. In the last few years, especially since she had left for Turkey, he had doubted her affection for him. He had had good reason to do so. In her three long years abroad, it seems, she had not written to him once; she had communicated through Ancelle. No doubt her behaviour had been dictated largely by her husband; but perhaps it had also been her own mistaken means of persuading her son to change his ways. She had not ceased to care for him; she found the silence painful, but she felt that she was acting for the best. She had no doubt of her own importance to him; but she had shown no understanding of him. Baudelaire did not respond to anger or compulsion, and he always abhorred authority. It was not her prolonged pretence of indifference which moved him, it was her unchanged affection.

Mme Aupick found her son in pitiful financial straits. He was thirty, now, but in July she felt obliged to buy him clothes. His threadbare coats and his frayed shirts offended her innate elegance, her increasing sense of dignity, and the sight of them stirred her maternal heart. Years later, she lamented to Asselineau:

> Wasn't my poor child the martyr of his lofty mind? How he must have suffered, knowing his own worth, when he was begging for work and he was harshly refused by publishers who were worth less than himself, on the pretext that what he wrote was too eccentric! When I came to spend two months in Paris, between our two embassies in Constantinople and Madrid, what a cruel situation I found him in! And I, his mother, had so much love in my heart, so much goodwill for him, and I couldn't get him out of it![12]

Before she left for Spain, she asked him to promise to mend his ways. On 9 July he sent her the written undertaking which she needed.[13] She sent him, in answer, a letter which delighted him. Next day, 10 July, she set out with her husband for Madrid. Although her health had often been a problem in the past, Aupick travelled in the summer heat. The journey was exhausting, and it was made still more so by the numerous ceremonies which greeted him across the Pyrenees. 'Escorts were ordered to accompany me; I refused them,' he reported to Baroche, now Minister of Foreign Affairs. 'On the outskirts of towns, detachments of cavalry had been sent to meet me. At Burgos the chief military and civic authorities came to call on me, a guard of honour was drawn up under my window, and a military band gave me a serenade.'[14] On 28 July, after eighteen days of travelling, he and his wife arrived in Madrid.

31

In mid-July, Baudelaire had moved with Jeanne Duval to 25, rue des Marais-du-Temple. On 28 August he received his September allowance, and spent it all on clothes and furniture.

He had now lived for six weeks with Jeanne, and found that living with her did not bring him the peace which he had expected. On 30 August, less than two months after he had sent her his written understanding, he confessed to Mme Aupick:

When you left, you thanked me, in a charming letter, for the promises I made you. And here I am, beginning by failing in them. Now that my position is regulated with M. Ancelle, I had *almost forbidden* you to send me some money; and now I myself come to appeal to your eternal kindness . . . If 200 francs exceed possibility, let it be 150; if 150 are too much, let it be 100, IN SHORT IT DOESN'T MATTER HOW MUCH, and if through you I cannot reach the end of the month or even the end of the first fortnight in peace, let me at least have a few days' respite so that I know how to manage . . .

I am very troubled and very sad. One must admit it, man is a very weak animal, since habit plays so great a part in virtue. *I have had all the trouble in the world to set to work again.* And I should still delete the AGAIN, because I think that I've never set about it . . .

I am really very sad . . . And then, what can I show? My book of poetry? I know that, a few years ago, it would have been enough for a man's reputation. It would have created a diabolical sensation. But today, conditions and circumstances have changed. And, if my book *hangs fire*, what then? Drama, the novel, even history, perhaps. But you don't know what the days of doubt are like.[1]

He himself was well aware how few people would appreciate his work. That was one reason why he had waited years for publication. He had, it seems, discarded many poems which he had found too facile or too immature.

It is not clear whether, now, in the summer of 1851, Mme Aupick sent money to her son in answer to his latest demand; it is only clear that, in 1851, she advanced him a total of 1,000 francs. His literary crisis continued. Yet if Baudelaire was not, for the moment, in poetic vein, his critical faculties remained alert. On 15 October, writing to an unidentified bookseller, he showed his serious interest in an American writer for whom he felt an instinctive and extraordinary sympathy.[2]

32

Baudelaire drew nothing from Edgar Allan Poe that was not already in himself. His most valuable gain was confidence in his own aesthetic

principles, and the courage to cultivate what he considered his true
genius. Yet, for Baudelaire, the American seemed like a long-lost
brother: he found in him extraordinary affinities. Poe – who had died
in 1849 – had similar complexities in his private life, he felt the same
bitterness towards the world. He, too, understood the search for an
artificial paradise. He had the same interest in the macabre and the
supernatural. In the life and work of Poe, Baudelaire immediately
recognised a new yet strangely familiar world. Camille Mauclair was
to write of the imaginative perversion with which Baudelaire 'assimil-
ated Poe's life to his own. He discovered him, he admired him; he
immediately imagined that the man for whom he felt fraternal
sympathies was also the fatal model, the inevitable precursor of his own
destiny, and he forced the apparent analogies so as not to disturb this
arrangement, the romanticism of which attracted him.'[1] Mauclair
considered that 'the emotional wound and the irreparable damage had
been real for Poe. Baudelaire imagined his own . . . '[2] Such comments
were exaggerated; and yet, as Lewis Shanks suggests, Baudelaire may
have magnified the influence of his heredity. 'He wished to see himself
as a martyr to his exceptional nature and to his education, a monster,
yet a victim. Poe provided his restless ego with a satisfying mirror: he
tried to be "his heir in all things." '[3]

As Asselineau was to write, Baudelaire became possessed by Poe. He
searched the taverns and ordinaries of Paris to find an English sailor
who could explain navigational terms to him.

> One day [continued Asselineau], I went with him to a hotel in the
> boulevard des Capucines, where they had informed him of the arrival of
> an American man of letters, who should have known Poe. We found him
> in shirt and underpants, in the middle of a flotilla of shoes of all kinds
> which he was trying on with the help of a shoemaker. But Baudelaire did
> not spare him. Whether he wanted to or not, he had to undergo
> interrogation, between a pair of half-boots and a pair of pumps. Our
> host's opinion was not favourable . . . In particular I remember that he
> told us that Poe was a bizarre character, and that his conversation was
> not at all *consecutive* [*sic*]. As we went downstairs, Baudelaire rammed his
> hat on violently, and said to me: 'He's only a Yankee!'[4]

Baudelaire now called several times, in vain, on Amédée Pichot, a
leading anglicist and the editor of the *Revue britannique*, who had long
ago translated *The Gold Bug*. (He was in fact to publish the *Nouvelles
choisies d'Edgar Poe* in 1853, with Hachette.)[5] Since Pichot was not in
Paris, Baudelaire asked a bookseller to order him the works of Poe
from London, 'the edition with the obituary, if there is one.'[6] Perhaps
he had heard of the Redfield edition of Poe, which contained such a
notice, from his friend Albert de La Fizelière, who had recently

published translations of *The Black Cat* and *The Fall of the House of Usher*. For Baudelaire was not alone among Frenchmen in discovering the American author. As Léon Lemonnier recalled, in *Les Traducteurs d'Edgar Poe en France*, Émile Forgues had made Poe known to French men of letters, and Mme Meunier had spread his name among the general public.[7] Yet if Baudelaire was not the only French admirer of Poe, he still remained among the first; and this month, October 1851, introducing the re-established *Revue de Paris*, Théophile Gautier announced: 'Scrupulous translations of Heinrich Heine, . . . of Edgar Poe and Emerson, . . . will keep the readers of the *Revue* acquainted with the intellectual movement in the old world and the new.'[8]

On about 3 February 1852, Baudelaire discussed with Champfleury and Armand Baschet, the editor-in-chief of *La Semaine Théâtrale*, the founding of a new periodical, which would be called *Le Hibou philosophique*. He drew up a plan for Champfleury, in which he suggested articles on Gautier and Sainte-Beuve, and an article on the literary schools of the day, which would bear on various poets, including Hugo, Banville, and, surprisingly, since Baudelaire felt contempt for him, Alfred de Musset. He listed the publishers who might be useful to them. On a rough sketch for the periodical, Champfleury noted an article by Baudelaire: *De la Caricature*.[9]

Le Hibou philosophique was to be stillborn; but, in the *Revue de Paris*, a much more significant project was to come to life. On about 19 February, Maxime du Camp announced that the proofs of Baudelaire's article on Poe would soon be ready for correction.[10] On 21 February, at Du Camp's request, Baudelaire went to the printers' to correct them. Next day he sent a note to the proof-reader, pointing out two omissions to be rectified. After Baudelaire had died, Charles Yriarte, the journalist, was to recall his remarkable literary conscience:

> He re-read what he had written twenty times over, let it mature in a drawer, took it out and again re-read it, [altered it] until it was perfect. A printer's error, or a misprint, drove him to despair . . . These infinitely small details have their importance, and they are characteristic, because it is this sense of mathematical precision and exactitude which drew Baudelaire to Edgar Poe, and gave French literature the *Histoires extraordinaires* and the adventures of Gordon Pym.[11]

In 1852, Baudelaire's financial position remained so precarious that, on 23 February, he wrote to the President of the Société des Gens de Lettres, and boldly asked him for 60 francs. He pointed out that he owed the Society 42 francs, and that he was sending him a novella. He hoped, he said, that the novella would appear in the *Bulletin* and acquit his debt; he hoped that the 60 francs would be repaid on the probable publication of some articles in *Le Pays*.[12]

The 'very curious novella', which Baudelaire submitted 'with absolute confidence,' seems to have disappeared without trace.[13] As for the study of laughter and the caricaturists, which would 'probably' appear in *Le Pays*, it was not in fact to be published there. Baudelaire, as usual, lived on speculations, on disappointments and on hopes deferred. However, on receipt of his letter, Francis Wey, vice-president of the Society, recommended that he should be given 50 francs.[14]

On 1 March, the first part of *Edgar Allan Poe, sa Vie et ses Ouvrages* appeared in the new *Revue de Paris*, to which Baudelaire had been introduced by Gautier. It was the first instalment of the first important study of Poe to appear in France.

> One could not analyse this genius more delicately [Gautier was to write]: this genius which sometimes seems to border on madness, this genius whose basis is a pitiless logic taking the consequences of an idea to the very end. This mixture of passion and coldness, of intoxication and mathematical processes, this strident mockery shot through with lyrical effusions of the highest poetry, were wonderfully understood by Baudelaire. He had been filled with the liveliest sympathy for this noble and bizarre character who so greatly shocked American *cant*, . . . and the assiduous frequentation of this dizzying spirit exercised a great influence upon him.[15]

Four days after the first instalment appeared, Baudelaire told Ancelle, in despair: 'I am obliged to take from you tomorrow (*either early in the morning, or at the time of déjeuner or dinner*), the money which I should only take on the 15th, in nine days, 200 francs. I shall live till the 15th of next month on the money from this piece which is in course of publication . . . You know that for me this month is *the great month, the separation*. I need a great deal of money; I have only my pen *and my mother*. Because, as for you, you don't count.'[16]

It was a gratuitous and savage gibe; but next day he called on Ancelle at 11, rue de la Révolte, and the long-suffering mayor of Neuilly gave him his monthly allowance, 200 francs, nine days before the date which had been agreed.

The separation which Baudelaire had mentioned in his letter was his separation from Jeanne. She confiscated his correspondence; she drank, she was unfaithful to him, and she constantly demanded money. The previous autumn, the tension between them had grown so acute that he had struck her on the head with a console table. One day he was to recall

. . . the quarrels, the atrocious scenes: . . . Jeanne throwing crude insults in his face, confessing infidelities; he himself seizing her by the shoulders, shaking her violently, and then, more and more enraged, hurling her down, grasping her by the hair and spinning her round like a sling which he was about to throw, until the black creature's feet banged against the furniture and her cries brought in the neighbours. After which came total exhaustion.[17]

Edmond Richard, recording this in his *Notes sur la Présidente*, suggested that Baudelaire probably exaggerated.[18] Whatever the facts, he was now determined to leave Jeanne. On 27 March, after an interval of seven months, he wrote once again to his mother. He did so 'from a café opposite the main post-office, in the midst of the noise, the backgammon and the billiards, so as to have some peace and facility for reflection.'[19]

33

Baudelaire frequented a number of the cafés where men of letters and journalists, poets and artists, used to meet. He did so not only in order to write, for he found the ambience distracting; he did so in order to listen, to talk and to observe. The memoirs of his contemporaries offer a series of verbal photographs of Baudelaire in Second-Empire cafés: caustic, aloof, patrician, delighting in serious conversation, sometimes calculating his outrageous comments. Yet, whichever café he frequented, whoever his companions might be, whatever his passing mood, he remained patently a man apart.

In *Un Café de journalistes sous Napoléon III*, Philibert Audebrand recorded him in the café de Robespierre, in the rue Neuve-des-Petits-Champs. Baudelaire, said Audebrand,

. . . looked less like a poet of bitter delights than a priest from Saint-Sulpice. Since he had lost nothing of the habit of playing the misanthropist, he sat down by himself at a small round table. He ordered a tankard of beer, and a pipe, which he filled with tobacco, lit, and smoked to the end without uttering a word all the evening. But, as he already had admirers, . . . it sometimes happened that a neophyte came in search of him with great ceremony, either to pay court to him, or to read his poems to him. Invariably the smoker remained as imperturbable as an oriental, . . . and went on drinking and smoking until he had kept his petitioner waiting a long while. On one occasion one of them thought that they would please

him, and came up, smiling, with a copy of that day's *Figaro*, in which he
was mentioned.

'Well, monsieur!' cried Baudelaire, with every sign of disdain, 'who
asked you for this paper? I never cast my eyes on such obscenities.'

And he returned to his smoking.[1]

Baudelaire was also seen in the Brasserie des Martyrs.[2] The Brasserie
stood in the rue des Martyrs, fifty yards from Notre-Dame-de-Lorette,
and more than one writer observed the ironic aptness of the name. It
was known simply as 'the Brasserie', just as ancient Rome had been
known as *urbs*, The City; and if, declared the Bohemian writer Alfred
Delvau, 'if, by some whim of providence, Paris should vanish, if
nothing were left standing but two or three houses which deserved to
be saved, including the great hostelry of intellect called the Brasserie
de la rue des Martyrs, one could build a new and interesting city with
the human material one found there.'[3] It was in the Brasserie that the
Bohemians assembled. 'Eugène Vermersch had just ordered a glass of
beer, ten feet away from us,' Audebrand continued. 'He was sitting
next to Baudelaire, who was looking down on him, rather like a
magnificent Newfoundland dog might do on a little lap-dog. Moreover,
the newcomer seemed to be content with this smile: the alms which
his illustrious colleague . . . deigned to offer him.'[4]

Lofty companionship was not found in the cafés and brasseries, but
Baudelaire needed a different stimulus. Sometimes he simply wanted
an audience. 'How many times,' recalled Nadar, 'I was overcome by
surprise, almost by anger, to find him seated in a café, elbows on the
table, with a perfect imbecile! He would spend a whole evening
developing his most abstract theories in front of a void . . .'[5] Baudelaire,
on occasion, bore with the company of fools; he sometimes enjoyed
the society of the eccentric and the extravagant. Sometimes he
contented himself with the undistinguished. In the Andler-Keller
brasserie in the rue Hautefeuille, he 'tried the effect of his Edgar Poe
on his companions, who served him as dynamometers, and sometimes',
remembered Alfred Delvau, 'he scored a thousand for terror.'[6]

In *La Cité des intellectuels*, Firmin Maillard remembered Baudelaire at
the Divan Lepelletier.[7] Baudelaire also went to the cabaret Dinochau,
in the heart of the quartier Bréda, where Édouard Dinochau was
generous with credit.[8] He patronised an English tavern in the rue de
Rivoli, where he enjoyed Bass, and consulted the publican, Gough,
about his translations, and to Austin's, in the rue d'Amsterdam, where
the beer was so good that he later recommended it to Vigny.[9] Maurice
Dreyfous observed him in the café de Madrid. He used to arrive there
about five o'clock, 'always solemn, dressed all in black, and usually
accompanied by the bibliophile Charles Asselineau . . . Asselineau

looked like Baudelaire, he had adopted the same white cravat, which increased his air of resemblance even more.'[10]

Baudelaire could also be seen in the café de Bade, in the boulevard des Italiens, where Félix Régamey drew his portrait, and in Hill's Tavern, in the boulevard des Capucines, a few yards from Nadar's photographic studio; Parisians thronged here to enjoy York ham 'et des pintes de pale ale.'[11] He went to the café de Foy, in the Galerie Montpensier in the Palais-Royal. He sometimes joined Barbey d'Aurevilly – 'that old itinerant paradox'[12] – at the café Tabourey, in the rue de Vaugirard.

Of all these cafés – and there were others – it was the café Lemblin, in the Palais-Royal, which deserves to be remembered.[13] It was in the café Lemblin, late in 1854 or early in 1855, among the billiard players, the whist and chess enthusiasts, and perhaps over a cup of the establishment's excellent coffee, that Hippolyte Babou, the critic and short-story writer, was, after long discussions, to suggest the final title for Baudelaire's book of poems. Monselet confirmed: 'This title, *Les Fleurs du mal*, was found by M. Hippolyte Babou and proposed by him to Baudelaire, in my presence.'[14]

34

Meanwhile, on 27 March 1852, in his long, belated letter to his mother, Baudelaire complained of the difficulty of escaping Jeanne, and of the difficulty of writing in cafés. 'The result', he told her, 'is a perpetual state of anger inside me. It is certainly not the way to write long works. I had forgotten a great deal of English, which made the business still more difficult. But *now, I know it very well.* Indeed I think that I have brought matters *to a happy conclusion.*'[1]

He was pleased with his translation, but he was intensely unhappy with Jeanne. He asked his mother to write to him at Mme Olivier's, and not at his own address.[2] The Oliviers were old friends of the family. Théodore Olivier was one of the founders of the École centrale des arts et manufactures; his wife, Marguerite-Aline, was the daughter of the sculptor Claude Ramey, who had been a friend of Joseph-François Baudelaire.

Now Baudelaire himself had need of friends, and need of privacy. As he told his mother: 'Apart from the fact that Jeanne knows your writing – *I don't have a single drawer that I can lock!* [this phrase was underlined by Mme Aupick] – do I ever know what wind will blow upon my mind, and where I shall sleep? It has sometimes happened that I have escaped my lodgings for a fortnight, so as to refresh my mind a little . . .'³

He had been inspired by Jeanne, he was accustomed to her, he would always feel indebted to her, but it was now unbearable to live with her. In an outburst of misery, he confessed to his mother:

Jeanne has become an obstacle not only to my happiness, that would be no great matter; I too can sacrifice my pleasures, and I have proved it; but [she is also an obstacle] to the perfecting of my mind. The nine months which have just passed have been a decisive experience. Never can the great duties which I have to accomplish, the payment of my debts, the *conquest* of my claims to fortune, the gaining of celebrity, the solace for the griefs that I have caused you, be accomplished in such conditions. *Once she had certain qualities*, but she has *lost* them, and I myself have gained in perspicacity. TO LIVE WITH A PERSON who is never grateful to you for your efforts, who counteracts them with a permanent clumsiness or malice, who only considers you as her servant and her property, with whom it is impossible to exchange a word on politics or literature, a creature who *will not learn anything*, although you have suggested giving her lessons yourself, a creature WHO DOES NOT ADMIRE ME, and who is not even interested in my studies, who would throw my manuscripts into the fire if that brought her more money than letting them be published, who turns out my cat, which was my only distraction in the lodgings, and who brings in *dogs, because* the sight of dogs makes me ill, who doesn't know, or won't understand, *that to be very miserly, just for ONE month*, would let me, thanks to this momentary respite, finish a big book – well, is this possible? Is it possible? I have tears of shame and rage in my eyes as I write this to you; and, really, I am delighted that there is no weapon in my lodgings; I think of the times when I cannot possibly listen to reason, and of the terrible night when I cut her head open with a console table. This is what I have found where, ten months ago, I thought I should find comfort and rest. To resume all my thoughts in a single thought, and to give you an idea of all my reflexions, I believe *for ever and ever* that the woman who has suffered and borne a child is the only one who is the equal of men. To give birth is the only thing which gives a woman spiritual understanding. As for young women with no status and no children, they are just coquetry, ruthlessness and elegant debauchery.⁴

It was a remarkable statement; it seemed to contradict Baudelaire's hatred of the natural. Yet, as Porché observes, one must always return to the son's letters to his mother, when one wants to find 'what remains of the normal person, *the gentleman*, in this depraved man.'⁵ Baudelaire's admiration for motherhood is not a denial of his anti-naturalism; it reveals the dual nature which is the essential truth of his character. This duality of Good and Evil in Creation, this struggle between the two empires, is not only the foundation of Baudelairean poetry, but that of Baudelaire himself: troubled by debauchery but, at the same time, thirsty for pure love, for soothing words, maternal caresses; and here, once again, we find the ineffaceable traces of his childhood passion. The passion that would finally triumph over all other feelings had already had its influence on certain sensual tendencies: in the perfumes which enthralled him, perhaps he always sought the perfume of his mother's silks and furs. From his early childhood, he had kept an unappeased hunger for pure affection. There were to be many women from whom, without confessing it, he sought the satisfaction of this need.

> However [he explained to his mother, now, in March 1852], one must come to a decision. I've been thinking of it, now, for four months . . .
>
> This is what I have decided. I shall begin at the beginning: that is to say, by leaving. I cannot offer [Jeanne] a substantial sum, and so I shall still give her money several times, which is easy for me, since *I earn it quite easily* [*sic*], and since if I work diligently I can earn more. BUT I SHALL NEVER SEE HER. She can do what she likes. Let her go to Hell, if she wants to go there. I have spent ten years of my life in this struggle. All the illusions of my youth have vanished. All that remains is a bitterness which is perhaps eternal.
>
> And what is to become of me? I don't want to set up a small apartment for myself, because, even now, although I have greatly changed, it would run too many dangers. Furnished lodgings horrify me. While I wait for something better, I have decided to take refuge with a doctor friend of mine. For 150 francs, instead of the 240 which he asks from other people, he is offering me a good room, a beautiful garden, an excellent table, and a cold bath and two showers a day. It is a German treatment which is very suitable for the feverish state which I am in.
>
> So I mean to take advantage of the quarter-day, and of moving out on 7 April – *our apartment is already let to our successors* – in order to escape. But I don't have a sou. *I have done several things which will be printed next month.* BUT AFTER THE 8th. Now do you understand? What's to be done?[6]

Once again, Baudelaire was living on hopes to be unfulfilled. The second part of his study of Poe appeared in the *Revue de Paris* on 1 April. His translation of *Berenice* appeared in *L'Illustration* on 17 April; it seems to have been his only other publication that month.

On 7 April, two days before his thirty-first birthday, Baudelaire broke with Jeanne Duval. He went, it is thought, to a hydrotherapy clinic. There were several of them in Paris and in the suburbs, including those of Dr Fleury at Bellevue and of Dr Pigeaire at Neuilly. Banville was to go to the first of these for treatment in 1857; Champfleury was to have treatment at the second in May 1852. Considering the close relationship between Baudelaire and Champfleury at this time, it is probable that Baudelaire went to Dr Pigeaire's clinic in the rue Saint-James, at Neuilly.

All these arrangements called for money. In the second week of April, he received his mother's authority to be given 1,100 francs, 500 francs of which were with Ancelle. He collected the latter sum. On 17 April he called on the Oliviers, to collect the remainder of the money. They took the occasion to lecture him about his financial problems. They also refused to give him the 600 francs, on the pretext that he had already received 500 francs from Ancelle. The Oliviers duly returned the 600 francs to Mme Aupick, in Madrid.[7]

Their behaviour was grossly unjust. Baudelaire brooded on the injustice. Next day he wrote a fierce letter to Olivier.[8] He appeased his anger, but did not send the letter. The following day he felt obliged to apologise to Champfleury for the 'abominable' expense to which he had put him for his dinner; he explained that his money had been sent back to his mother.[9]

Whatever his vow not to see Jeanne again, it was not strictly kept; in the spring of 1852, he went to see her two or three times a month, to take her money. From May to July his address was 11, boulevard Bonne-Nouvelle. There is no indication in his comments to his mother that he had postponed his separation, or that he was living with Jeanne again. Yet on the back of a letter to Du Camp, dated 9 May, is a note, presumably addressed to her, instructing her to have *déjeuner* ready when he returned at 11 o'clock.[10] There must have been some good in her which neither his mother nor his friends could perceive; what he felt for her, now, must have been something deeper than passion, something warmer than human pity.

Moreover, Baudelaire was incapable of living without women. He may have professed to despise them, but he could not do without them. He needed a feminine atmosphere more than physical possession. He could never find such domesticity. Nadar observed that 'the man who has wedded the Ideal no longer has a right to the Family';[11] yet, as Tamara Bassim wrote, in *La Femme dans l'Œuvre de Baudelaire*: 'In spite of everything, Woman remains for him a primitive need which nothing can fill; the suffering which this causes him and makes him inflict determines all his activity, whether in matters of love or of the spirit.'[12]

35

It was now, in May 1852, that Maxime du Camp, the journalist and man of letters (and the friend of Flaubert) came to know him.

I was living [Du Camp recalled] in a little country house at Neuilly which I had rented for the season. Baudelaire came to see me there . . .

'I am thirsty, monsieur,' he said to me. I offered him beer, tea or toddy. He answered: 'Thank you, monsieur, but I only drink wine.' I offered him either bordeaux or burgundy. 'Monsieur, I will drink some of both, if I may.' They brought two bottles, a glass, and a carafe of water. 'Monsieur,' he said, 'would you have this carafe removed? I don't like to see the water.' During the hour our conversation lasted, he drank both bottles of wine, in large gulps, slowly, like a ploughman. I remained all the more impassible since, every time he emptied his glass, I saw him look out of the corner of his eye to see the impression which he might be making.

He had great originality, but it was often diminished by the pains he took to emphasise it . . .

Such puerilities did not prevent us from being good friends, and we were always glad to see each other, in spite of the often prolonged intervals which his irregular life imposed on our relationship. I only ever knew him impoverished, lodging in furnished rooms, renewing his bills payable to order and trying to throw his creditors off the scent: creditors who were numerous, for he only ever borrowed small sums at a time . . .[1]

Du Camp could be malicious. He could also be kind. This summer, he lent Baudelaire 200 francs. Baudelaire's financial problems continued, nonetheless, and they brought other problems in their train. In July, he left the boulevard Bonne-Nouvelle. Perhaps he was attempting to throw more creditors off the scent; perhaps he hoped to avoid his bills or, at least, defer them by his abrupt departure. However, since he had failed to warn his landlady that he was leaving, she naturally continued to charge him rent. She determined to keep his books and papers until he paid the rent for the lodgings which he did not use.

His troubles were largely self-inflicted, and his pitiful condition did not change. Late in August, he gave a novella to the Société des Gens de Lettres. He also sent a request for 60 francs.[2] It seems unlikely that he was given money. The novella did not appear in print.

His misfortunes continued. In September, under the title of *L'Aéro-naute hollandais*, the *Revue britannique* published Amédée Pichot's translation of *Unparalleled Adventures of One Hans Pfall*. Baudelaire had, it seems, expected to see them publish his own translation, and he felt that the *Revue* had cheated him. No doubt he felt even more aggrieved when the *Panteon*, in St Petersburg, published a Russian version of his *Edgar Allan Poe. Sa Vie et ses ouvrages*, without a fee or an acknowledgment.[3]

He himself remained intent on translating Poe; he worked with the precision and the dedication of a scholar. He had, it is said, spent four years perfecting his English before he embarked on the translation. He was determined that his version should be definitive. As Monselet was to observe, he studied Poe 'with a rare power of assimilation, and translated him with terrifying passion.'[4] In literature, from the first, he transcended his predecessor. Poe wrote with vulgar smartness; Baudelaire translated him into classic French.

On 1 October, *Le Puits et la pendule* appeared in the *Revue de Paris*, with two of Baudelaire's poems: 'L'Homme et la mer', and, more importantly, 'Le Reniement de Saint Pierre'. Baudelaire thought that the publication of this poem was politically dangerous, and he was afraid that there might be legal proceedings. The *Revue de Paris* was indeed to die a sudden death, but not as a result of this poem. In 1858, after Orsini's attempt to assassinate Napoleon III, the government saw fit to suppress certain publications which were hostile to the Empire. However, as Du Camp observed, 'had the *Revue de Paris* only served for the first publication of... Baudelaire, Gustave Flaubert and Eugène Fromentin, it would have justified its existence.'[5]

The publisher Victor Lecou was now anxious to bring out Baudelaire's translation of the collected *Histoires extraordinaires*. Baudelaire continued to work on them. In December 1852, in his study *De quelques Écrivains nouveaux*, Ernest Prarond lamented that he had abandoned poetry; he expressed the hope that he would become a poet once again.[6] Baudelaire had not ceased to be one. On 9 December, he wrote a letter to Mme Sabatier, La Présidente; he sent her anonymously, in a carefully disguised hand, a poem, 'À une femme trop gaie', which he dedicated to her.[7]

36

La Présidente, as Gautier christened her, and as posterity calls her, was born in Mézières, in the Ardennes, on 7 April 1822.[1] She was the daughter of the Vicomte Harmand d'Abancourt, Prefect of the Ardennes, and Léa-Marguerite Martin, a young sempstress. Through the good offices of the Prefect, Léa-Marguerite was married to André Savatier, a sergeant in the 47th Infantry Regiment; Sergeant Savatier agreed to recognise the child, and to give her his name. She was duly baptised as Aglaé-Joséphine Savatier; the name Apollonie had been given her (so she would always say), but the registrar of births refused to use it, as it did not appear among those of the saints. The moment she gained her independence, she adopted it, and changed her surname to the less plebeian Sabatier.

When she was three, her nominal father left the army, and the family settled in Paris, in the quartier de la Monnaie. They later returned to Mme Savatier's old family home in the faubourg du Pont-de-Pierre, in Mézières; and here, where she had given birth to Aglaé and two sons, Mme Savatier gave birth to a second daughter, Irma-Adelina, known in literary history as Bébé, then as Adèle Sabatier. The child was born on 6 September 1832; three weeks later, Sergeant Savatier died, leaving a widow and four children. The family must have understood the meaning of poverty.

Marguerite Savatier was in time to marry another old soldier, Mathieu Cizelet; it was, perhaps, this second marriage which brought her back to Paris. She settled in the village of Les Batignolles, and took in sewing. As for Aglaé, she showed promise, already, of becoming a soprano; and the principal of a local *pensionnat* was so impressed by her voice that she took her in at a special fee. It soon became clear that she was also endowed with uncommon beauty. When she was fifteen or sixteen, Auguste Blanchard and Charles Jalabert, two young pupils of Paul Delaroche, collaborated in painting her portrait. She was wearing a black velvet bodice, a scarlet skirt, and a broad-brimmed hat draped in black lace. In this fancy dress, which she had worn at a carnival ball, she made her first appearance in the world of the arts. In about 1840, she was taken to Italy by Ernest Meissonier. He painted her many times, and taught her both the rudiments of drawing and those of love.[2] It is also said that she posed for the sculptor Jean-Baptiste Clésinger – generally known as Auguste – and that in 1844, perhaps rather earlier, she became his mistress. Jean Ziegler suggests that she lived with Clésinger until 1846.[3]

She herself was a gifted painter of miniatures (she was in time to exhibit at the Salon de la Société des Amis des Arts, and eventually at the Salon itself).[4] Yet she still seemed destined to be a singer; she had singing lessons from Mme Damoreau-Cinti, who had turned to teaching since she had retired from the stage. No doubt she might have been a concert artiste or sung in opera if, at a charity concert, she had not been introduced to one of the organisers. Alfred Mosselman determined her future.

François-Alfred Mosselman, born in 1810, came of an old bourgeois family in Brussels, and he had arrived in Paris after the Revolution of 1830, with his brother-in-law, Comte Le Hon.[5] Fanny Mosselman, Mme Le Hon, was to be the mistress of the Duc de Morny.[6] Charles Le Hon was Belgian Minister at the Court of Louis-Philippe, and, for some years, Mosselman had been an attaché at the Belgian Legation. In 1835 he had married Eugénie Gazzani, daughter of the receiver-general of finances in the Eure; there were to be four children of the marriage. In 1836, he had left the diplomatic service; and from 1837 he had devoted himself to the family business, the Société des Mines et Fonderies de zinc de la Vieille-Montagne. Mosselman had, undoubtedly, a coarse streak in his nature. ('How much will your church really cost?' he asked an architect. 'All complete, WAFER IN MOUTH?')[7] Yet he was a friend of Alfred de Musset; he became a patron of the arts, and he showed a taste for Romantic painting and for what was to be known as the Barbizon School.[8]

Mosselman fell in love with Aglaé – or Lili, as he called her. She herself was dazzled by the prestige of an unknown world. In 1846, she allowed him to instal her in an apartment at 4, rue Frochot. The rue Frochot was in what was known as the quartier Bréda – or, as the dandies called it, Breda Street. It was the *quartier* of the kept woman.

Since Alfred Mosselman was married, he sometimes needed a confidant and go-between; he found one in Fernand Boissard, who lived at the hôtel Pimodan, on the île Saint-Louis. Boissard was later to be the lover of Bébé, and the father of her daughter, born in 1849 in the rue Frochot.[9]

It was at the hôtel Pimodan, in the summer of 1843, that Gautier had first met Baudelaire. He was not the only person to impress himself, that day, on Gautier's receptive inward eye. There for the first time, at the quai d'Anjou, Gautier had seen Aglaé Sabatier. She sat near the window,

> ... and, having cast off her little black lace shawl, and the most delicious little green bonnet that Lucy Hoquet or Mme Baudrand had ever trimmed, she was shaking out her red-brown hair, which was still wet, because she had come from the École de Natation; and her whole person, draped in muslin, exhaled, like a naiad's, the freshness of the bathe. With glance and smile she encouraged the verbal tourney, and from time to time threw in a word of her own, sometimes bantering, sometimes approving, and the battle raged harder than ever.[10]

In one swift impression, Gautier caught Apollonie, as he called her, with all the grace and freshness of her twenty-one years. In his sketch one seems to catch the essence of her nature: her ease, vitality and radiant health. She is elegant, happy, assured, and already presiding over her brilliant Bohemia.

Mosselman, too, was determined to have her likeness in perpetuity. He asked Clésinger to make a cast of her body. The commission suggests a boastful owner, not a devoted lover, or a connoisseur of the arts, and at first she rejected the idea. One regrets that she agreed, at last, to the humiliation: that she countenanced Mosselman's vulgarity. Clésinger made a single cast of her *Rêve d'amour*.

However, since it failed to fulfil Mosselman's expectations, he asked him to sculpt a bust of Apollonie, and a marble statue, based on the cast. Long before the Salon opened in 1847, the statue was the talk of the Paris studios. Clésinger's exhibits this year included the bust of Mme A. S. and (No. 2047) *La Femme piquée par un serpent*. Courbet's portrait of Baudelaire, *L'Homme à la pipe*, had been rejected by the Salon jury; but the crowds collected round the figure of Apollonie which, though it was marble, writhed in an ecstasy of pain on a bed of tinted flowers.

Gustave Planche, who was renowned for the acerbity of his criticism, condemned the statue dourly in the *Revue des Deux Mondes*:

> To begin with, this woman stung by a serpent is not expressing pain in the least; the serpent is clearly an extra, it has quite obviously been added later. If one really had to define the expression on this face, if one had to say what it means, what emotion it reveals, certainly no honest man endowed with commonsense would call it pain. It is impossible, in fact, to see anything here except the convulsions of pleasure.[11]

Delacroix dismissed the statue as 'a daguerreotype in sculpture';[12] Achille Devéria, the lithographer and book-illustrator, agreed that the statue appealed to sensuality rather than taste, 'and this is a bad tendency which must not be encouraged.'[13] In a poem in *L'Artiste*, on 25 April, Henry Egmont declared that the sight of La Présidente herself had made the statue seem a sacrilege, 'livrant à tous les secrets de mon cœur.'[14] Gautier, a lover of the sensual, praised the realism of the statue; in *Le Poème de la femme: Marbre de Paros*, published two years later, he still dreamed of the living marble figure.[15]

The casting of *Rêve d'amour* and the sculpting of *La Femme piquée par un serpent* were not alone in suggesting the permissive atmosphere of 4, rue Frochot. The Goncourts found Apollonie 'a real Bacchante with a casual grace, an abandoned nonchalance in her movements, an enveloping voluptuousness.'[16] Edmond recorded tartly: 'Spent the evening with the famous Présidente . . . A rather pretentious character, with a vulgar warmth, a rather common courtesan. This fine woman in the classical style, slightly coarse, suggests to me a sutler of fauns.'[17] Years later, Apollonie's last lover, Edmond Richard, wrote in his puritan, provincial style: 'Too casual in the cultivation of her mind, too complaisant, too free-and-easy, she had stripped herself of modesty. She left the door open to daring liberties, because she had not shown herself to be scandalised by the first.'[18] One suspects that the licence in her salon was largely verbal; it is reflected, here and there, in the heavy gallantry of Flaubert's letters, the obscenities of Maxime du

Camp's correspondence. It is seen, above all, in the famous letter which Gautier sent to her from Rome, in the autumn of 1850.[19]

Yet one should not be over-serious about the tone of conversation in the quartier Bréda. The woman who makes it her profession to please men can hardly be prudish; and the liberty which allowed Gautier to write his *Lettre à la Présidente* allowed him, also, to address her a delicately sensual poem in *Émaux et Camées*. 'À une Robe rose' is his homage to a splendidly desirable woman. He presents Apollonie in perpetuity: her rose-pink dress revealing her superbly sculpted lines, and caressing her with all the warmth of his own desires.[20]

Whatever the tone of conversation in the rue Frochot, Apollonie created a haven for a brilliant circle of habitués. Richard – who had never known it – recorded dully that 'they came, urged on by a certain pleasure in fine food, to take a rest from their work and their current vexations, and to refresh their eyes with the sight of a beautiful woman, who had equally intellectual friends around her, and the services of a good cook.'[21] Meissonier observed, more gratefully, that Apollonie was buoyant, 'delicate and good, attractive and intelligent, wonderfully organised, capable of everything. She adored light and gaiety and sunshine. And these were in her nature, too. For the weary man, it was a rest and an exquisite relaxation to find her always the same, always unchanged, a real means to forget the cares of life, of which she delightfully relieved you.'[22] He addressed her, fondly, as Madame de Saint-Frochot.[23] Every Sunday, she gathered round her table a constellation of admirers. She gave them such understanding and such happiness that when, after five months' absence in Russia, Théophile Gautier returned to Paris, he remembered only that it was Sunday, and took a cab at once to the rue Frochot.[24]

It was Gautier's daughter, Judith, who recalled the visits of La Présidente to Neuilly, when, on Thursdays, her parents received at the rue de Longchamp. It was she who, in *Le Second Rang du Collier*, the second volume of her autobiography, recalled her visits to 'the famous *amphitryone*, who had for so long gathered all the artists of the age around her table.'[25]

> I had known her since I was a child [Judith remembered], and I was very fond of her. When I was very small, she had wanted to do my portrait, for she painted pretty miniatures, with a very delicate art which she had been taught by Meissonier himself. So I had to go and sit, and I spent whole afternoons with her. She lived in the rue Frochot, in an apartment on the first or second floor, I can't remember which [it was the second] . . .

The hall, which was just a sort of corridor, seemed gay and cheerful. A big window, which overlooked some gardens, lit it up brightly through some light blinds painted with flowering branches. In a birdcage, full of parakeets, bullfinches and bengalis, out-chattering and out-singing one another, the wings were fluttering in the light, and the mischievous barking of two little griffons, which had rushed up to the door, added to the happy din which greeted you on the threshold.

The dining-room was just opposite the front door, and this famous room, where wit and verve were spent so extravagantly every week, was neither very vast nor very sumptuous. The walls were covered with dark red material, symmetrically hung with delftware and pictures. The massive, square oak table must have been drawn out to the walls for the Sunday feasts.

On the right of the dining-room, a suite of three rooms led into one another, the boudoir, the bedroom, and, right at the end, the lavatory. It was prettily quilted, velvety, comfortable and fresh.

There were no windows. The whole of one wall was glazed in, and lit up the rooms; under the foliage of the blind which covered them, the interior looked like a greenhouse.

The drawing-room, square and spacious, was to the left of the dining-room. Its windows opened on to the street. There were divans, comfortable armchairs, poufs and cushions, and distinguished paintings on the walls – among them the lifesize *Polichinelle* by Meissonier, and, in the centre of a panel, the superb portrait of the mistress of the house, with her little griffon on her lap, painted by Ricard.

La Présidente arrived from the far end of the apartment, and announced herself with a trill, which turned into a silvery laugh.

Three graces radiated from her the moment you set eyes on her: beauty, goodness and happiness . . .

She was quite tall, and handsomely built, with the most delicate wrists and ankles, and charming hands. Her hair was very silky, golden chestnut in colour, and fell as if of its own accord in heavy waves, touched with occasional lights. She had a clear, smooth complexion, and regular features, with something mischievous and witty about her expression, and a small, smiling mouth. Her air of triumph seemed to shed light and happiness around her.

Her clothes were full of imagination and taste. She hardly conformed to fashion, she created a quite special one of her own. Great artists, among her Sunday guests, gave her advice and designed dresses for her . . .

For the sitting, we installed ourselves in the dining-room. It was very bright because of the glass wall which bulged out at the corner of the house, enlarging the room like a half-tower, and containing flowers in *jardinières*.

La Présidente brought up a small easel, and brushes as fine as needles, and took up her palette, and I tried to keep still. She chatted to me, and told me stories, and the miniature made slow progress.

Sometimes she kept me to dinner, and, at about 8 o'clock, Marianne [the servant] would come and fetch me.[26]

La Présidente: the very title endowed Apollonie with an aura of the eighteenth century, conferred upon her a sort of elegant preciosity. Flaubert is said to have drawn on her for the character of La Maréchale in *L'Éducation sentimentale*.[27] Edmond About, as a student, had been overwhelmed by the portrait of Mme Sabatier, in Venetian dress, which established Gustave Ricard's reputation at the Salon of 1851. It was, he wrote later, 'one of those challenging works which catch the eye and compel our admiration. I remember when it was first exhibited, I was at the École normale, and I escaped with some of my friends from Saint-Marc Girardin's lectures to go and see Mme Sabatier, with her little dog on her lap. Then we rushed back as fast as we could to the great hall of the Sorbonne, happy to keep, in our mind's eye, the memory of such a radiant beauty.'[28]

Baudelaire had worshipped La Présidente in secret. He had met her first, it seems, at the hôtel Pimodan; and apparently he had loved her from the beginning. He had met her since (surmises Porché) at the café Momus, perhaps at a theatre or a concert.[29] He had walked home, alone with her, at night:

> Une fois, une seule, aimable et douce femme,
>   À mon bras votre bras poli
> S'appuya (sur le fond ténébreux de mon âme
>   Ce souvenir n'est point pâli) . . .[30]

Since 1851 he had been a frequent visitor to the rue Frochot.

La Présidente greeted him on a Sunday evening as she greeted any other guest; and, moving in the same room, seated at the same table, she remained an unattainable ideal. She was cut off from him by Mosselman, by her health and happiness, by the fact that she did not need him. Her gaiety and her radiant health had sometimes made him bitter, in his jealous and resentful moods, but he was enthralled by the goodness of her nature. With Jeanne Duval, his *Vénus noire*, he had known the torments and some at least of the pleasures of physical love; but Apollonie was his *Vénus blanche*. She was more: she was *la Muse et la Madone*. He knew that she was a Bacchante, more than a Madonna, and that, perhaps, was why he sent her poems without signatures. He did not want to risk the destruction of his essential dream.

With brutal honesty, wrote Edmond Richard, he told her about Jeanne Duval, 'that woman of the streets who excited in him attraction and hatred, anger and pity, jealousy and the desire for tenderness. Often, in the albums of La Présidente, he drew the profile of this wicked black Venus who was neither intelligent nor beautiful.'[31] He did not do so to arouse her jealousy; he intended no comparison. He needed La Présidente in another sphere. In the squalor of his life, he needed someone in whom to believe, in order to be able to know that beauty and goodness still existed. All he asked of La Présidente was to allow him to preserve this faith. In his imagination she became perfection. Some saw this as a sign of his Platonism.[32] Poetry, he wrote, 'is what is most real, it is what is only completely true in *another world*.'[33] 'In the presence of Mme Sabatier,' a critic would maintain, 'we can estimate the poet's power all the better from the images he draws from her.' In his heart it was a platonic romance.[34] Nadar, in his notes, confirmed: 'Chastity – Baudelaire's platonic romance with Mme S.'[35]

Mme Aupick had been in Turkey, and she was now in Spain. She had been away for more than four years. She remained his one true love, and she had determined the nature of all the other loves in his life. Baudelaire needed to replace his mother by a madonna, an image of perfect, pure maternity.[36] Suddenly, in the rue Frochot, he recognised his goddess. Mme Sabatier was the idol of the Romantic myth. She was to play the same part in the life of Baudelaire as Jenny Colon in the life of Gérard de Nerval, or Élisa Schlesinger in the life of Flaubert. His old, respectful love of Mme Sabatier was transformed into spiritual devotion, and his religion was founded.

37

On 10 January 1853, Baudelaire called on Victor Lecou, and delivered the manuscript of *Histoires extraordinaires*. He was duly paid, but he was so dissatisfied with the text that he wanted to revise it completely. He asked for the printing to be stopped, and he agreed to pay the printing costs already incurred. Thanks to Baudelaire's perfectionism, Lecou missed the winter publishing season. It was to be some months before he and his translator were reconciled.

Baudelaire could hardly afford to repay the costs. In February he was obliged to borrow 300 francs from the leader of a claque at the Théâtre de l'Odéon. The publication of more translations in the new daily paper, *Paris*, and in *L'Artiste*, did little to alleviate his misery. His unsettled life and his state of mind prevented him from writing a libretto for the Opéra, and a drama for the Théâtre du Boulevard. He suffered both from his poverty and from his inability to work. Besides, Jeanne was ill, and, as usual, she needed money. He never ceased to feel a duty to her.

In Madrid, the Aupicks continued to enjoy the rewards of years of conformity. For all his professions of loyalty to the House of Orléans, the General had not wavered in his allegiance to the Bonapartes. When the Prince-President had become Emperor of the French, he had affirmed his allegiance once again.[1] In August 1852, on the Fête Napoléon, a national holiday under the Second Empire, he had 'lit up the Embassy with the cross of the Légion[-d'honneur], a cypher, coloured lights, etc. I think,' he announced to Thouvenel, 'I did what was best.'[2] Now, on 29 January 1853, he celebrated the marriage of Napoleon III and Eugénie de Montijo by giving a grand ball. 'More than 500 people filled my reception rooms from midnight until two in the morning,' so he told his usual correspondent. 'The last polka-dancers left the floor at 6 o'clock.'[3] Aupick was simple in his tastes, but he was splendid in his embassies.

Such public displays of patriotism were appreciated in Paris as no doubt they were in Madrid. So were his proven wisdom and diplomacy. There was now a threat of war in the Crimea, and Aupick was invited to return to his former mission – since dignified as an embassy – in Constantinople. 'My old wound is the only reason for my refusal [this to Thouvenel]. The wound has been open since 1837, and it has got worse. Splinters have been coming out of it for the past few months, and other splinters have to be removed.'[4] He suffered not only from his wound, but also from recurrences of a serious but unidentified illness – possibly dysentery – which he had contracted some twenty years earlier, in Algeria. He was now sixty-four, but he had aged beyond his years.

His days as a diplomat were over, but his wisdom was still needed. On 8 March he was appointed a Senator.[5] On 5 April, Isabella II – with whom he had once danced a quadrille – conferred on him the Grand Cross of the Order of Charles III. On 21 April he left for France.[6] He and his wife were eventually to settle in Honfleur, but to keep a pied-à-terre in Paris, at 91, rue du Cherche-Midi.[7]

Some time in the second half of March, passing through Paris, Mme Aupick had seen her son, and she had shown him 'wonderful indulgence'.[8] On 26 March, from 60, rue Pigalle, no doubt encouraged by her kindness and by the thought of her constant charities in Madrid, he wrote to her in desperation.[9] The letter gave such a picture of his state of mind, and of the bitter complexities of his life, that it needs to be quoted at some length.

> I am beginning [he told his mother] with the harshest and most painful thing. I am writing to you with my last two logs on the fire, and my fingers frozen. I am going to be sued for a payment which I should have made yesterday. I shall be sued for another at the end of the month. This

year, that is to say from the end of last April until now, has been a real disaster for me, although I have possessed the means of making it quite different . . .

Why, you ask, didn't I write before? But you don't know shame. And, besides, what prevented me from doing so was the promise I had made to myself never to write to you unless it was to announce good news. And also the promise never to ask you for a sou. Today, that isn't possible.

After I received your money, *a year ago*, . . . I paid the year's deficit, and I lived alone. This is where misfortune begins again. I was living in a house where the landlady made me suffer so much, through her cunning, her wrangling and cheating, and I was so unhappy, that I left, as is my habit, without saying a word. *I didn't owe her anything*, but I was stupid enough to let the rent run on, although I wasn't living there – and so the money I owe her represents the rent for a lodging which I haven't lived in. I knew that this vile creature had had the audacity to write to you. Now, imagining that I could soon send for them, I had left with her *all my books, all my manuscripts, some finished, others begun, cardboard boxes full of papers, LETTERS, DRAWINGS, EVERYTHING, in fact, everything that is most precious to me: papers.* In the meanwhile, a publisher – a rich and friendly publisher [Victor Lecou], had gone mad about me, and asked me for a book. Some of the necessary manuscripts were there. I tried to begin again, I re-purchased some books, and I continued not to write to you. On 10 January, my contract obliged me to deliver the book, I received the money, and I delivered to the printer a manuscript which was so imperfect that, after the first few pages, I saw that the *corrections* and the *alterations* to be made were so considerable that it was better to discard *the printing*, and *to re-compose* . . . The printer didn't get corrected proofs, and he grew angry; the publisher thought I was mad, and he was furious! And he had told me so clearly: *Don't worry about anything. You have been looking for a publisher for some years: I'll look after you, and I'll publish everything you write.* Poor man, I made him miss the winter season, it is now three months since I dared to write to him, or see him. The book is still on my table, *unfinished.* I've paid half the printing costs . . . Really, I'm going mad. This book was the starting-point of a new life.

That isn't all. The Opéra, the director of the Opéra [Nestor Roque-plan], asked me for a new style of libretto, to be set to music by a new composer of repute. I even think that they might have had it done by *Meyerbeer.* It was a stroke of luck, perhaps an income for life. There are people of fifty, of established reputation, who have never obtained such a favour. But poverty and disorder created such atony, such melancholy, that I missed all the meetings. *Fortunately*, I haven't received a sou.

That isn't all. The partner of a director of the Théâtre du Boulevard asked me for a drama. It was to be read this month. *It hasn't been written.* Out of deference to my connection with this gentleman, the leader of a claque has lent me 300 francs which were intended to ward off another disaster last month. If the drama were written, it wouldn't matter . . . But the drama isn't written; there are scraps of it *with the woman at the hotel I mentioned*, and the payment falls due in six days, at the end of the month. What will become of me? What is going to happen to me?

There are moments when the desire comes over me to sleep without end; but I cannot sleep, because I am always thinking . . .

I have something else to tell you. I know that you are so good and understanding that I make it my duty to tell you everything . . .

A year ago, I separated from Jeanne, as I had told you . . . For some months, I went to see her two or three times a month, to take her a little money.

And now she is seriously ill, and in the most absolute poverty. I never talk about this to *M. Ancelle*; the wretched man would be too delighted. Obviously a small part of what you send me will be given to her. I am now vexed that I've told you that, because, in your clumsy maternal arrangements, you are capable of sending her money, without warning me, through M. Ancelle. It would be extremely improper. You don't want to hurt me again, do you? This idea is going to grow, and to take root in my mind, and torment me. Finally, I am going to explain to you what I am suffering in that direction. She has made me suffer greatly, hasn't she? How often – and, indeed, to you, not long ago – a year ago – how often I've complained! But in the presence of such a wreck, a melancholy so profound, I feel my eyes full of tears – and, in a word, my heart full of self-reproach. I have taken away her jewels and her furniture twice over, I have made her run up debts for me, sign promissory notes, I have struck her on the head, and, finally, instead of showing her how a man like me behaves, I have always given her an example of debauchery and an unsettled life. She suffers – and she is silent. Isn't there reason there for remorse? And am I not guilty here as I am in everything?

To you, I should in your old age have given the delight which my talent should make you hope for – and I haven't done so.

I am guilty towards myself; this disproportion between determination and ability is something unintelligible to me. Why, when I have such a right and clear idea of usefulness and duty, do I always do the opposite?

Some time ago, that idiot Ancelle told me that he had written to you that I was well. The imbecile doesn't understand or know a thing about it, or about anything else. I don't want to worry you, there's no need. Besides, my health is so robust that it can rise above everything. But this abominable existence and the brandy – which I'm going to stop – have damaged my stomach for some months, and besides I have unbearable nervous troubles – exactly like women. Anyway, it was inevitable.

Do you now understand why, in the midst of the dreadful solitude which surrounds me, I have understood the genius of Edgar Poe so well, and why I have written his abominable life so well?

Talking of this, I must tell you that this damned book, and my publisher's loss of confidence, and the delays and accidents I'm afraid of, . . . in fact this affair which was definite three months ago, is growing more vague and uncertain every day . . .

Poor dear mother, there is very little room for affection in this abominable letter. If I told you that ten times I have planned to procure myself some money to rush to *Madrid*, simply to clasp your hand, you wouldn't believe me, would you? If I told you that, when I am deep in my fearful melancholy moods, I often talk in a whisper to you, you would not believe me. You would think that these were the inventions of filial politeness. I have such a strange soul that I don't understand it myself.

And then, I shall no doubt see you soon; just as one dresses up for special occasions, I shall try to dress up my poor mind, to receive you with dignity. I have often asked people how you were – they have always said: *well*. Is it true?

One word more. Send me the maximum money, that is to say as much as you can, without inconvenience to yourself, for after all it is quite right that I should suffer. And if you don't have money, authorize me to get some from M. Ancelle, even if you haven't sent him any since April.

Don't be too harsh on me; when this painful crisis is over, I shall recover. I embrace you, and I clasp your hands.[10]

It was a tormented letter; and though Mme Aupick seems to have helped him, and returned, ahead of her husband, to Paris, Baudelaire's financial troubles continued. He was now vexed by his landlady in the rue Pigalle, as well as his former landlady at Neuilly. They quarrelled bitterly over payments and receipts, and she gave him notice to quit for 9 May.[11]

It was not only these termagants who exerted pressure upon him; Baudelaire had other creditors. It was, it seems, later in April, when they sent *gardes commerciaux* to lie in wait for him in the rue Pigalle, that he took refuge in a sleazy and obscure hotel.

I have been obliged to leave my room to-night [he explained to his mother], and to sleep – no doubt for two days, until someone has arranged matters for me – *in a squalid, small, unfindable hotel*, because I was surrounded and spied on where I was, in such a way that I couldn't go out any longer. I left without money, for the very simple reason that there wasn't any. This letter asks you for 10 francs, to get through these two days, until the 15th. I'm still in bed, and I'm waiting anxiously.[12]

38

Baudelaire was to find a more attractive refuge. Since his visit as a *collégien*, in the days of Louis-Philippe, he had always been drawn to Versailles. He had admired the formal gardens on a visit with his mother; and Maxime Rude recorded spending a day at Versailles with Baudelaire and Hippolyte Babou. Baudelaire clearly knew it well. 'He knew the busts concealed in the very depths of the thickets.'[1] Asselineau recorded that Philoxène Boyer, that pitiful Bohemian writer,[2] once kept Baudelaire in Versailles for a month. They stayed at an inn, where

they were given credit; they were constantly setting off for Paris to
get money, but they never brought it back. Asselineau kept 'several
lamentable letters' from Baudelaire, 'begging me to go and rescue
him.'[3]

In *Vieux Souvenirs d'un Étudiant de 1852*, Émile Geidan gave his version
of the episode.[4] Towards the end of 1852, a group of young law
students had rented an apartment at 60, rue de Seine. Into this circle,
Philoxène Boyer introduced Banville, Murger and Baudelaire. In April
1853, while the students were preparing for examinations, the apartment was closed to visitors. One day, nonetheless, Philoxène Boyer
arrived to announce that he and Baudelaire were going to Versailles
to work on a history of Louis XIV. It was, he said, to be based on the
lives of the various people whose portraits adorned the palace galleries.
A fortnight later, he re-appeared.

> 'We have', he said, 'been guilty of a grave indiscretion. We settled in a
> big hotel in Versailles, and our resources were soon exhausted. We left
> the night before last, driven out by the owner, with our pockets empty.
> We left our modest luggage in his hands as a guarantee of our debt. Then
> Baudelaire advised me that we should take refuge in a brothel. He is still
> there as a hostage. I have come to beg all our friends to get us out of this
> scrape.'
> We were disgusted by the story. The strings of our half-full purses were
> scarcely loosened.
> Philo left. We were extremely surprised to see him re-appear, three days
> later.
> 'I went back to Versailles without enough money,' so he confessed. 'I
> had an angry reception from Baudelaire. "You stay here," he said to me,
> "I'll be back this evening." Well, he didn't come back, and my hosts threw
> me out as if I were a thief. I have come back from Versailles on foot,
> exhausted and dying of hunger.'
> We gave him a small subsidy, and that was the last we heard of the two
> Bohemians.[5]

Baudelaire's visit to the brothel may, perhaps, explain the 'excessively
strange' letter which he wrote on 9 May 1853.[6] It is no doubt one of
the 'lamentable letters' which he addressed to Asselineau; it has since
been listed in a catalogue as 'too strange to print in its entirety,'[7] and
it is not even included in the Pléiade edition of Baudelaire's correspondence. If Baudelaire was indeed taking refuge in a brothel, it would
explain why, in May, he sent another poem to Mme Sabatier, with the
comment, in English: 'After a night of pleasure and desolation, all my
soul belongs to you.'[8]

> Quand chez les débauchés l'aube blanche et vermeille
> Entre en société de l'Idéal rongeur,

Par l'opération d'un mystère vengeur
Dans la brute assoupie un ange se réveille.

Des Cieux Spirituels l'inaccessible azur,
Pour l'homme terrassé qui rêve encore et souffre,
S'ouvre et s'enfonce avec l'attirance du gouffre.
Ainsi, chère Déesse, Être lucide et pur,

Sous les débris fumeux des stupides orgies
Ton souvenir plus clair, plus rose, plus charmant,
À mes yeux agrandis voltige incessamment.

Le soleil a noirci la flamme des bougies;
Ainsi, toujours vainqueur, ton fantôme est pareil,
Âme resplendissante, à l'immortel soleil![9]

Apollonie Sabatier was much in his thoughts in these early summer days at Versailles. On 3 May, in a hand which, as usual, he disguised, he had sent her a further poem: 'Ange plein de gaieté, connaissez-vous l'angoisse . . .?'[10] On 9 May, he sent her yet another poem, 'Confession'.[11]

Baudelaire had, it seems, returned to Paris by mid-June. His landlady had presumably chosen to overlook their old disagreements, for he returned to live in the rue Pigalle. As usual, he lived on expedients, and on goodwill, which he constantly exhausted. His mother was about to leave with her husband for Barèges. Aupick had to take his annual cure. On 27 June, Baudelaire confessed:

> I feel so sad this morning, so ill at ease and discontented, that I do not have the courage to pay you a farewell visit. I assure you that this is the only reason. You know that I have sudden inexplicable whims. Besides, a visit to you always makes me uneasy . . . Couldn't you send me . . . a letter to suggest somewhere or other where we could talk for an hour or two?
>
> It would be very gracious if this were a dinner, or *déjeuner*, or a walk. But this is a luxury which is not indispensable.[12]

It is not clear whether Mme Aupick arranged a farewell meeting; but she sent her son a handsome sum of money. 'I was very vaguely expecting a little surprise,' he acknowledged, on 1 July, 'but I did not believe it would be so fine. Frankly, I am quite delighted, and I imagine that, in two or three days, having all the means to make amends for six months of idleness, I shall hardly have any excuses.'[13]

39

The Aupicks left to spend three months in the Pyrenees. Baudelaire's financial state grew more critical than ever. In August, he allowed himself to become indebted, yet again, to Arondel. On 18 September he wrote desperately to Nadar: '*Try, try* to contrive that, when I come to see you tomorrow, you've found me a small sum of money, even the most trifling. You know I lead the most exhausting life. Forgive me for worrying you so frequently.'[1] Even if Nadar gave him money, it was not enough. That autumn, Baudelaire spent 120 francs on some clothes. He borrowed 40 francs against his purchase. Late in September, Mme Aupick and her husband returned to Paris. On the last day of October, Baudelaire begged her, once again, for money.[2]

He also settled down in his furnished room to finish his work on Poe. On 13 November, the first part of his translation, *Le Chat noir*, appeared in *Paris*. The daily newspaper had been founded by the Comte de Villedeuil, and it bore the name of *Paris Lundi, Paris Mardi*, etc, according to which day it appeared. It was a not undistinguished paper: the Goncourts, Murger and Banville were among Baudelaire's fellow contributors. On 14 November, the second part of *Le Chat noir* was published, and the first part of *Morella*. On 15 November there followed the second part of *Morella*. That day, Baudelaire's financial plans were thrown into sudden disarray: Jeanne Duval's mother died in Belleville.

Not for the first time, Jeanne became the instrument of Baudelaire's revenge. He had not forgotten how his mother had failed to give his father decent burial. In his study of Baudelaire's hidden motives, Michel Quesnel suggests that, now, he took his revenge by making her pay for the burial of Mme Lemer.[3] The General's wife was to pay for the mother of a prostitute; the unfeeling widow of Joseph-François Baudelaire was now to pay for a stranger. Perhaps Baudelaire was unaware of his deeper motives when he approached Mme Aupick; but Quesnel's suggestion remains convincing.

My dear mother [this from Baudelaire on 18 November], the day before yesterday [*sic*] I had someone to bury. I gave all I had, but the expenses amounted to 140 francs, of which I still owe 60 francs, and I have undertaken to pay these in two days, that's to say this morning. You can well imagine that I have thought of everyone before approaching you. Nothing in the world would make me go to M. Ancelle before the end of the month. I beg you, don't write me sentences like these: *Really, Charles, you distress me*, etc – or else: *When one is an orderly man, one always has enough money available to pay these things* . . . REFUSE ME FLAT, OR SEND ME THE MONEY.[4]

Mme Aupick promptly sent it. 'I thought you could only send me 50 francs,' he answered. 'However, on re-reading your letter, I noticed that you thought you'd sent me 60. I beg you to post me 10 francs at once, *at once* . . .'[5]

Flurried and short-sighted, she sent him 20 francs. 'Thank you with all my heart,' he answered. 'This is what I did yesterday morning. I immediately sent the 50 francs I had in hand to the Mayor of Belleville, who had *stood surety* for me, and told him that I should send him the missing 10 francs today. As for the addition of an extra 10 francs, that is a very nice idea of yours; they will allow me to live shut up in my room for three days.'[6]

They allowed him little peace. On 1 December he sent a messenger to his mother to collect his rent; he had promised to pay his landlady at noon. He was, he added, reconciled with his publisher, Victor Lecou; and, any day, Mme Aupick would see 'a series of very substantial pieces' in *Le Moniteur universel*. These, he maintained, would bring him in five hundred to seven hundred francs.[7]

He was less fortunate than he hoped to be. A few days later, *Paris* was suppressed by the courts; he had lost a home for his translations and a source of revenue. Victor Lecou, who had offered, once, to publish all he wrote, was not to publish the tales of Poe; he sold his stock in trade to Hachette. As for *Le Moniteur universel*, it contained nothing by Baudelaire that month. *Le guignon* continued to pursue him.

Besides, as usual, he frustrated his own good intentions. He had meant to pay his rent promptly. It was, perhaps, with the thought of Jeanne that he behaved with wild extravagance, and took a second lodging in the rue Pigalle; it remained empty, but it cost him 60 francs a month. On 10 December, yet again, he appealed to his mother.[8]

She sent him such a letter that its effect remained with him for days. She herself was frugal by nature, she believed in order and economy, she was exhausted and disturbed by his demands for money: demands which he had made incessantly for the past ten years. She was worried by his dependence on her: a dependence which she wanted and yet resented. She was troubled by an extravagance that often seemed insane, by his chronic inability to work. She was troubled, too, by the need to hide her maternal generosity from Aupick. Baudelaire now owed her 110 francs, and she reminded him of his debt. In despair, he turned to another source. On 16 December, he wrote to Malassis, now living in Alençon.[9] He was already in debt to him; and it is not clear if Malassis complied with his request.

For nine days, over Christmas, Baudelaire remained in his room at 60, rue Pigalle, confined there by financial necessity. He could not afford to spend, or to meet his creditors. Yet this solitary confinement gave him back a taste for work, and a setting which he felt to be his own. He did not want to be disturbed. On Christmas Eve, when a letter arrived from his mother, he chose not to open it for two days.

On 26 December, by messenger, he sent her his answer. What he had to say was, once again, in revenge for her past; and, once again, it was a means of criticising her present behaviour. It was not enough that she had paid for the burial of Mme Lemer. It was not enough that she had sent him money.

If I had a quite substantial sum today, 100 francs, for example [so he told her], I shouldn't buy shoes, or shirts, I shouldn't go to a tailor or a pawnbroker. Yesterday was the last moment allowed for the accomplishment of an act which I consider an *essential* Duty, that is to say the exhumation and reburial of a woman who gave me all the money that remained to her, without a murmur, without a sigh, *and above all without giving me advice.* I have to write to a mayor, and then to the Prefect of Police. The plot will cost me 86 francs, it's clear that there will also be some or other tip, some gravedigger's swindle. THAT will come before the shoes; besides, I am so accustomed to physical sufferings, I know so well how to put on two shirts under a torn coat and trousers which are pierced by the wind; I am so adept at fitting straw soles or even paper soles into shoes with holes in them, that almost all I feel is pain of spirit. However, I must confess that I have reached the point where I no longer dare to make sudden movements or even walk too much for fear that I shall tear my clothes still further.

I WILL NOT PAY A SOU OF MY DEBTS. I shall fend off my creditors until my book is finished. I have reason to believe that I find the same goodwill at *Le Moniteur* as when I went there three months ago; my life is so confused that I can't remember the exact date any more. What I mean is this: to be able not to freeze, to be able to walk without watching all my movements, to keep enough money to work *without interruption or respite* for at least sixteen days – that is my fixed idea, and has been so for a long time. Now – even supposing that my clothes are sold [against my debts], and that I have to buy others, 150 francs would be enough to solve *all these problems . . .*

I need a word from you to avoid three hours of conversation with Ancelle.[10]

Mme Aupick was disturbed by the tone of this letter. She sent a note in answer immediately. 'Really, my dear mother,' he wrote, 'I am most distressed that I have grieved you. How can you take brutal expressions so much to heart?'[11]

On 27 December she authorised Ancelle to give her son 150 francs. Baudelaire had already sent him a receipt for 250 francs. Ancelle sent him only what Mme Aupick had permitted; he also sent him a kind of letter of credit for his own tailor. Baudelaire was reluctant to appear in rags before Ancelle's tailor. On 30 December he went out to redeem

three items of clothing which he had pawned, but he found that two
of them had been sold. He sent to redeem the remaining clothes, a
pair of trousers, for 20 francs. While he was out that evening, Ancelle
called to summon him to Neuilly next day.

> What the devil does he want to tell me [Baudelaire asked his mother]?
> Some painful news? Some old affair with a creditor? But how does he
> expect me to go – not counting the loss of the day – and spend 10 or 12
> francs on carriages – or drag myself through the mud and snow? . . .
>   Let me tell you that M. Ancelle causes me such embarrassment and
> such apprehension, that when, on three or four occasions, he has called
> on me, I have wanted to move in order to hide my address from him. It
> occurs to me that he is compromising me, and that he is gossiping with
> the inferior creatures by whom one is obliged to be surrounded . . .[12]

He did not visit Ancelle. At noon he wrote to his mother, yet again:
'Let me get out of this difficulty and work for four or five days . . .
Whatever happens, I need intensive work, like a cauterization of old
wounds.'[13]

40

The financial problems continued into the new year. On 3 January he
asked Mme Aupick to pay his rent.[1] 'Rest assured', he added, 'that I
shan't ask you for anything more from now onwards, or at least not
for a very long time . . . I shan't write to you until I have paid another
visit to the editor of *Le Moniteur*, who must think me a *humbug* – and
until my mind is at rest about the future of my articles.'[2]

Julien Turgan, a tough ex-medical student, was co-editor, with Paul
Dalloz, of *Le Moniteur universel*. Baudelaire, in his *Carnet*, was to list him
among his 'Vilaines Canailles.'[3] He hesitated to publish the translations
of Poe. However, Baudelaire had another enterprise in mind. Recently,
at a dinner at Philoxène Boyer's, he had been moved to recite his poem
'Le Vin de l'assassin'. Hippolyte Tisserant, the leading actor at the
Théâtre de l'Odéon, had suggested that Baudelaire should turn it into
a two-act play, and had said that he himself would gladly play the main
part. In mid-January, he sent Baudelaire a flattering letter, and urged
him, once again, to write his drama, *L'Ivrogne*. On 28 January Baudelaire replied, and, almost unbelievably, asked him for money.[4] Tisserant proved to be an obliging friend.[5]

On 31 January Baudelaire triumphantly announced his theatrical plans to his mother:

> Something fortunate has happened to me, which could soon have very important consequences . . . Let me tell you in two words what it's about. It's about a great five-act drama [*sic*] for *the Odéon* on poverty, drunkenness and crime. To be honest, I haven't read my *scenario* to the directors; but the leading actor of the theatre has demanded, so to speak, that I should do this for him, and the truth is that I have managed the construction of this big plot with a skill which I didn't know I possessed . . .
>
> I beg you, don't keep my messenger . . . I am waiting for this man to send him to a newspaper with an article; and then I must go to Neuilly. Purely and simply give him the 40 francs [my monthly rent].[6]

It is hard to know what the article was (if indeed it existed). Baudelaire was not to publish any article in a Paris newspaper until 25 July. As for *L'Ivrogne*, 'one mustn't delude oneself,' he had explained to his mother. 'I must now *write the play*.'[7] As so often with Baudelaire, there was an unbridgeable chasm between the conception and the finished work. He wrote in his head; he found it extremely hard to fix his thoughts on paper. *L'Ivrogne* was not to be written. All that exists is the plan, in the form of a letter to Tisserant.

Mme Aupick lived on fading hopes and, no doubt, on regrets. She lived, too, with the abiding certainty that her son would exploit her affection. She must have known that there would be no respite from his demands.

The next demand was not long in coming. On 6 February he wrote to her in desperation: 'My dear mother, *no discussion*. Whatever happens – whatever happens – *do you understand that? Whatever happens* – I must have the sum of *two hundred francs this very day*; I have just asked M. Ancelle for it . . . He is afraid and hesitant; with a word from you he will not hesitate. So give me a word for him, and make haste, and don't send me lamentations . . .'[8]

There seemed to be no end to the squalid pressures of everyday life. On about 15 February he left the rue Pigalle for 61, rue Sainte-Anne, where he tried to hide from his creditors at the hôtel d'York. Rarely can there have been such a contrast between the misery of a man's existence and the splendour of his vision. It does not matter that the dream did not correspond with the reality, that the goddess was a fallible woman. It only matters that, for Baudelaire, especially at moments of anguish, the goddess and madonna existed. He sent a poem to La Présidente, and sought relief in his continuing dream.[9]

> I do not know [he wrote to her] if I shall ever be allowed the supreme delight of telling you myself about the power which you have acquired

over me, and about the perpetual radiance which your image creates in my mind. I am simply glad, for the present moment, to swear to you again that never was love more disinterested, more imbued with respect than the love I cherish secretly for you, the love that I shall always hide with the care which this loving respect demands.[10]

41

On 23 February, Baudelaire sent his mother a demand for 40 francs, with which to pay the rent on 8 March.[1] The demand was suspect, since it came a fortnight in advance; but he said that he was anxious not to go back to his room without a sou. It would, he explained, be easy for him, next month, to pay for his room from the money he collected at Neuilly.[2] Baudelaire often lived in a world of dreams and speculations, but there followed a confession which must have made his mother anxious about his state of mind. 'Let me explain to you, in two words, what often created my problem with the rent: it is that, for several months, it was not 40 francs that I had to pay, but 100. I had a second apartment in the house, which remained empty. I had taken it up in anticipation of a sudden improvement in my affairs. In the end I gave it up, and now I am even.'[3]

He needed more than financial help. He was nearly thirty-three, but he urgently needed his mother. 'I can never see you,' he continued. 'I can't go and visit you, and you *don't want* to come . . . Look, be very nice, what prevents you from coming to see me today at the *hôtel d'York, rue Sainte-Anne?* . . . Refuse me the money, come and scold me, even revile me, but at least come; and don't refuse me both things at once.'[4] It is unlikely that Mme Aupick went to the rue Sainte-Anne; but, presumably, she sent her son 40 francs. That day, he returned to the rue Pigalle.

The forty francs soon disappeared. On 8 March he sent her *The Poetical Works of Edgar Allan Poe,* and he was once again in distress.

Tomorrow morning [he told her] I am going to Neuilly to ask M. Ancelle for the money *which is due to me for April.* As I don't want to struggle or argue against his timidity and his HONEST PARSIMONY, and as your handwriting is all-powerful, I should like to find this evening when I come home – 60, rue Pigalle – I had the courage to come back on Shrove Tuesday – as I say, I should like to find a word from you, addressed to him, enclosed in an envelope addressed to me. It is possible that I may make no use of it; if he complied without a struggle, I should have no need of the letter; but, if he argues, what can I do? When he feels carried away, he still has a mania for giving me *one or two louis at a time, with which I clearly can't do anything.* Now since my overcoat isn't holding together any more – it held for two and a half months longer than I expected – I absolutely must go and find something to replace it . . . In the second place – although my rent of 100 francs is now reduced to 40, I want to make peace with my landlady tomorrow. And finally, I want to have something left so that I can work for a few days. It is impossible that all this doesn't come to 150 francs . . .[5]

The humiliation continued. Next morning, he went to Neuilly to collect his April money. Ancelle gave him an instalment of 75 francs. Baudelaire's immediate problems were only made more acute.

There seemed to be no solution to them. *Le Moniteur universel* remained reluctant to take his translations of Poe's stories. On about 10 March, he wrote to Sainte-Beuve, and asked him to intervene with the editors.[6] Sainte-Beuve dictated his answer to a secretary. He no longer intervened, he said, unless his intervention directly concerned his own work.[7]

Even before Sainte-Beuve replied, Baudelaire's financial troubles grew still worse. On about 11 March René Lurois, one of his creditors, presented himself to Mme Aupick, and demanded money from her. She told Baudelaire. 'I am going off', he answered, 'to silence that wretched *Lurois*; I won't have him plaguing you . . . *When you have finished reading the English poems which I lent you, don't send them back to me* – as I have copies of many of the pieces – but *send them instead,* ON MY BEHALF, to M. CAPÉ, *bookbinder to the Empress, rue Dauphine.*'[8]

Mme Aupick was alarmed, and she was apprehensive. Her devotion remained, her anxiety to do what was best, but the *conseil judiciaire* was still a leitmotiv in her existence, as it was in that of her son. It appeared to have created more problems than it had solved. She had entrusted Ancelle with the administration of her son's finances; but she was constantly being asked to intervene with him, to sanction further advances, to give Baudelaire substantial and additional sums to cover his increasing deficit and to fulfil his desperate needs. All this she had to do, presumably, without her husband's knowledge; she had to do it for a son who was not on speaking terms with him, a son who would not come to their house. She was still obliged to meet him *en cachette.*

It was not surprising that she dreaded seeing his accounts. He could not shake off his earlier debts; he was constantly acquiring new ones. Poverty-stricken as he was, he still chose to have his books bound by Capé, bookbinder to the Empress. When it was a question of clothing his books or himself, Baudelaire rejected mediocrity. His taste, his dignity, his respect for excellence remained. There was a heartrending contrast between the man and his situation, between the way of life that he preferred and the way of life in which he was now lost. He was aware that his financial problems were largely of his own creation, and yet he continued to' create them. His urge for self-destruction remained. He felt imprisoned by his circumstances. He was in fact often imprisoned by his character, his own attitude of mind.

On 9 April he was thirty-three. There was, it seems, no letter from his mother. Four days later, he asked her: 'Did you think of me on 9 April: that fatal day which so cruelly calls me to order . . . ? I wanted to write you a fine letter on the subject, but [what could I say]? You must be so tired of hopes.'[9]

42

He himself continued to worship La Présidente in secret. On 8 May he sent her a letter, once again unsigned; and with it he sent the most exalted and the most poignant poem that he wrote for her.

It is a very long time, Madame, a very long time since I wrote these lines. Still the same deplorable habit, reverie and anonymity. Is it the shame of this ridiculous anonymity, is it the fear that these lines may be bad, and that the competence does not match the loftiness of feeling, that have made me so hesitant and so timid this time? I know nothing at all about that. I am so afraid of you that I have always concealed my name from you, believing that a nameless adoration – clearly ridiculous for all the crude and sensual women of the world whom we might consult on the subject – was, when all is said, almost innocent – and could not disturb anything, trouble anything, and was, morally speaking, infinitely superior to a foolish and vainglorious pursuit, a direct attack against a woman who has settled her affections – and perhaps her obligations. Are you not – and I say this with a little pride – not only one of the most loved – but also the most deeply respected of all creatures? . . . To cut it short, to explain to you my silences and ardours, ardours which are almost religious, let me tell you that, when my being is wrapped in the darkness of its natural wickedness and stupidity, it dreams profoundly of you. From this exciting, purifying dream some happy chance is generally born. You are for me not only the most charming of women – of all women – but also the dearest and the most precious of superstitions . . . How happy I should be if I could be certain that these lofty conceptions of love had some chance of being well received in a secret corner of your adorable mind! I shall never know.

À la très chère, à la très belle
Qui remplit mon cœur de clarté,
À l'ange, à l'idole immortelle,
Salut en l'immortalité!

Elle se répand dans ma vie
Comme un air imprégné de sel,
Et dans mon âme inassouvie
Verse le goût de l'éternel.

Sachet toujours frais qui parfume
L'atmosphère d'un cher réduit,
Encensoir oublié qui fume
En secret à travers la nuit,

Comment, amour incorruptible,
T'exprimer avec vérité?
Grain de musc qui gis, invisible,
Au fond de mon éternité!

À la très bonne, à la très belle,
Qui fait ma joie et ma santé,
À l'ange, à l'idole immortelle,
Salut en l'immortalité!

Forgive me, that is all I ask of you.[1]

His love for her was, in his own words, incorruptible. He knew that
she had 'settled her affections'. He had no intention of disturbing them.
In some ways she appeared to him an almost maternal figure, showing
him the constant sympathy which his mother had so often failed to do.
She remained his guardian angel. He genuinely loved her, but, above
all, he loved the necessary image which he had created of her. He
needed to worship at the shrine; the very respect which he felt for her
made a commonplace liaison impossible. He remained in love with 'the
dearest and the most precious of superstitions'.[2] He preferred this
nameless adoration.

    Nonetheless, he could not content himself with platonic love; despite
his devotion to Apollonie, despite his quixotic loyalty to Jeanne, he
needed a terrestrial mistress. Intensely complex as he was, he was
already drawn to the actress who is known to students of Baudelaire
as *la Belle aux cheveux d'or*.

She had been born Marie Mardel at Saint-Jean-des-Vignes (Saône-et-
Loire) on 30 September 1827: the daughter of Aimé Bruneau, a
stonecutter, and Bénoîte Mardel, a working woman. By her parents'

marriage on 13 April 1828, she had been legitimised as Marie Bruneau (sometimes spelt Brunod).[3] In the theatre she was known as Marie Daubrun. She had made her début at the Théâtre Montmartre in the autumn of 1845, and appeared at the Vaudeville the following year. In *The Theatres of Paris*, Charles Hervey noted condescendingly:

> Made a very modest *début* July 13, 1846, as *Mlle Lange* in the piece of that name. Mlle Daubrun's figure is short but symmetrical, and her face, though not positively pretty, is far from plain. Her movements are as yet deficient in grace, and her style of acting is rather too characteristic of the *banlieue*; but she possesses a germ of natural talent which only stands in need of cultivation. Her worst defect is a husky voice, which, though it might escape notice in drama, will always be a stumbling block in her way at a vaudeville theatre.[4]

She needed not only cultivation but also a stroke of good fortune. A few days after her appearance in *Mademoiselle Lange*, she took over the part of Mlle Hermance de Ligny, which had been given to Mme Doche, in the vaudeville *Les Fleurs animées*. *Le Tintamarre* declared that the part 'is infinitely better played by Mlle Daubrun than it was by her predecessor, Mme Doche – even though she had created it with all the poetry of her person.'[5] In 1847, at the Porte-Saint-Martin, she had played Princess Rosalinde in *La Belle aux cheveux d'or*, and had earned the praise of *Le Tintamarre* for her golden hair, and an ironic dismissal from the *Mercure des Théâtres*: 'Mlle Daubrun – *la Belle aux cheveux d'or* – has come straight from Montmartre with a little branching off to the Vaudeville. She is nearly always pretty on stage; but she seems to us to have the ambition to follow Mlle Georges.'[6]

It is doubtful whether she saw herself as a tragic actress; but, as a critic wrote when she died: 'She passed through nearly all the theatres in Paris, adorning them with her talent.'[7] She adorned them, too, with her statuesque person, and men recalled not only the splendour of her hair, but the mystery of her green eyes. Among her admirers was Théodore de Banville who, in 1852, became her lover.

In an engaging and useful study, Albert Feuillerat traced her complex emotional life. Baudelaire, he maintained, had seen her as early as 1846, in *Les Fleurs animées*; he had seen her again in *La Belle aux cheveux d'or*, the elaborate *féerie* in which she appeared like a vision of purity and innocence.[8] Feuillerat maintains that Baudelaire had courted her in vain.[9] Whether or not this was so, she had remained inaccessible. In 1853, when he was closely linked with Banville, it seems (according to Feuillerat) that he met her once again.[10] Perhaps, for the moment, she had tired of Banville; certainly Baudelaire was drawn to her. This interest in Marie Daubrun might help to explain the irregularity of his letters to La Présidente. 'Each of his epistolary explosions', Feuillerat observes, 'closely followed an absence of Marie Daubrun.'[11] While Marie was on tour, Baudelaire looked towards the rue Frochot; when she returned, La Présidente was, for the moment, forgotten.

> These coincidences [writes Feuillerat] recur too regularly to be accidental, and they allow us a glimpse of what occurred in 1853 and at the beginning of 1854. These intermissions of the heart, as Proust would have called them, suggest the curve of Baudelaire's hopes when he returned to his passion for *la Belle aux cheveux d'or*. The poet saw the actress again and vaguely began to pay court to her once more. But he had not progressed enough for the relationship which had been established to withstand the effects of absence. And this state of indecision, with its intermissions and its new beginnings, apparently lasted until May 1854. That month, the prelude to the long eclipse of Mme Sabatier, would mark the moment when Marie Daubrun finally yielded to the poet's supplications.[12]

Pichois records that Baudelaire came into her life between April 1854 and January 1855.[13] Poggenburg maintains that Baudelaire became her lover some time before 21 July 1854.[14] Whatever its actual date, the brief and turbulent liaison was to inspire one of the finest cycles of poems in *Les Fleurs du mal*: among them 'Le Beau Navire' and 'L'Invitation au voyage'.[15]

On about 10 May 1854, Baudelaire finally left his ground-floor room at 60, rue Pigalle. He settled at the hôtel du Maroc, 57, rue de Seine.

The move did not solve his financial problems. On 16 May, he asked one of the proprietors of *Le Constitutionnel* for 1,000 francs as an advance on the publication of his writing.[16] It was refused because of the unfinished state of his manuscripts. That day he was due to give 300 francs to Jeanne Duval, but he could not do so.

The future of his drama, *L'Ivrogne*, was also in question. On 18 May, Marie Daubrun left the Odéon for the Théâtre de la Gaîté. Baudelaire then abandoned the idea of giving the title role to Tisserant. He chose Philibert Rouvière, of the Gaîté, as his leading actor. There were other problems. After much hesitation, *Le Moniteur universel* had finally refused to publish his translations of Poe. Some time before 3 June, Barbey d'Aurevilly recommended the translations to *Le Pays*.

It was, it seems, in 1852 or 1853 that Baudelaire had first invited himself to call on Barbey.[17] Only two of his letters to Barbey are known, and only a few of Barbey's letters to him have survived; yet it is clear that, despite the difference in age (Barbey was thirteen years older than Baudelaire), they enjoyed a long and lively friendship. It was based on esteem and on genuine affection. Barbey was a novelist, a critic, a writer of verse and of prose poems. He was the author of a book on Brummell. He was already a legend: not only for his wit and outrageous dress – a scarlet tabard, a Papal cap, trousers with silver stripes – but also, it was said, for such feats as 'eating raw lamb with the appetite of a cannibal.'[18] Early in the twentieth century, Baron de Bouglon was to tell Féli Gautier: 'I know that the great critic had the highest esteem for the gifts of Baudelaire, whom I saw 40 years ago at the rue Rousselet. At this distance, my recollections are of the vaguest – except for this: that – at a time when men wore moustaches and beards – Baudelaire was clean-shaven, and that Raymond Brucker jokingly called him *clericus Baldelarius*,'[19] Firmin Boissin kept a clearer recollection. He had, he said, met Baudelaire 'three or four times in the company of Barbey d'Aurevilly . . . Indeed [he told Eugène Crépet], I have a distant recollection of a quite astonishing conversation which took place between these two writers of genius about the dogma of the Immaculate Conception. It made one wonder if, in their youth, they had not, both of them, pursued theological studies in some or other seminary.'[20]

Now, on 3 June 1854, at Barbey's instigation, Baudelaire wrote to Armand Dutacq, the manager of *Le Pays*, and asked for his support with the editor. He described himself, not without pride, as 'the initiator' of Poe.[21] M. Lefranc, the reader at *Le Pays*, remained undecided about the publication: he wondered if Poe's tales were perhaps 'too eccentric' for his conservative readership.[22] In the meanwhile, Baudelaire remained in poverty; this summer, he borrowed a further 200 francs from Maxime du Camp.[23] He had always been fastidious in his choice of clothes, he had been renowned as a dandy; but now, in June 1854, when his future biographer Eugène Crépet first encountered him, he was wearing a winter overcoat and a garish red and yellow muffler, perhaps to conceal the absence of a shirt.[24] He could not afford summer clothes, let alone elegance.

On 25 June, once again, he turned to Mme Aupick: hoping, no doubt, that she would send him money.

> And my affairs? My affairs? you're going to say. They have gone through yet more phases. They are like the Eastern Question: they are finally settled. But at what a cost, my God! I am losing 1,300 francs. In other words the need to publish very quickly has made me accept 700 francs for something which is worth 2,000. I shall probably sign my contract tomorrow with *Le Pays, Journal de l'Empire*, and then I shall go like a madman and borrow money on the strength of it. The complete work will appear in A MONTH.[25]

On 15 July, *Le Pays* announced the forthcoming publication of the *Histoires extraordinaires*. On 25 July, the paper began to publish

Baudelaire's translation. The publication was to continue, with some interruptions, until April 1855.

No doubt Mme Aupick had announced this success to her husband; and no doubt he had shown his approval. This might explain why she now determined that her husband and son should be reconciled. She wrote a long letter to Baudelaire. On 28 July he answered:

> Yes, of course, it will all come right; yes, this reconciliation will take place, and honourably, if your husband only has some understanding. Yes, I know all that I have made you suffer.
>
> At the moment, I am very flurried. There are a mass of sluggards and reprobates who make me lose my days through their visits – I am hoping to seal myself up hermetically. In the evening I'm at the printer's – I can't lose any more time, because the printing would overtake me, it goes so fast . . .
>
> Despite the unbearable fatigue of this translation, I am quite determined to find time to do my drama scenarios.
>
> Ah! That reminds me! The 40 francs! Is it possible today? They will go to the proprietor of the hotel as a small payment on account.[26]

43

In the meanwhile he was reduced, as so often, to expedients. That day, since he was penniless, he approached the Société des Gens de Lettres, and once again demanded an advance.[1] Ancelle considered a more solid source of income: he thought of finding him a sinecure at the Hôtel de Ville. Ancelle was not without his influence. Since 1851 he had been mayor of Neuilly, an office which he was to hold for seventeen years.

> One must give up the Hôtel de Ville [Baudelaire announced to him, on 1 August]; from today, I am obliged to return to my busy life. I don't know if *between now and the 5th I shall find a few hundred francs to escape Arondel*; but in any case I can't remain like a bankrupt gambler . . .
>
> I have just had an interminable letter from my mother, who has left without coming to see me.[2]

Perhaps she had gone with her husband in search of the retreat which they now sought, far from the pressures and demands of Paris: the retreat in which, as Aupick mournfully observed, he could lose himself in recollection and prepare himself for 'the great sleep'.[3]

Perhaps they had already found the little house on the cliffs at Honfleur. It stood on a spur of the Côte de Grâce, between the road to Trouville and the sea. From the *maison joujou*, as Baudelaire was to call it, there was a view of the Seine estuary, which recalled the view of the Bosphorus from Therapia (indeed, the terrace in the garden was one day to be christened Le Bosphore). The contract of purchase was to be signed in March 1855. The General signed it on the advice of his friend, Jean-Louis Émon, who spent his summers next door at Honfleur.

The little house, said Jean-Aubry,

> ... was surrounded by a garden which was small, but planted with extremely fine trees. In order to enjoy the view from the villa more conveniently, the General added verandas to it, and his taste for rare plants led him to build a conservatory, and to plant his garden with exotic species which were allowed by the mildness of the climate. The following year, he acquired part of the garden which belonged to the neighbouring hospital ...
>
> The house had only one storey, with attics; the ground floor was slightly raised, the kitchen in the basement ... On the east side of the house, that is to say the one which looked towards Honfleur, there was a big veranda, which the General had christened the *Mirador*: you entered it by a flight of steps straight from the garden; this veranda formed a sort of hall adorned with green plants, and people preferred to sit there, because of the view that they enjoyed ...[4]

Mme Aupick later described 'the little drawing-room, ... the little room which leads into the Mirador, the room where there are views of Constantinople.'[5] Pichois maintains, inexplicably, that the Mirador was a rustic kiosk, with windows of coloured glass, on the cliff edge.[6] Wherever it was, from the Mirador one could easily follow the coming and going of ships and fishing-boats which entered or left the harbour.

Meanwhile, in 1854, wherever she and her husband had gone, Mme Aupick chose to show her displeasure with her son, and with his financial arrangements. As usual, when she disapproved, she left Baudelaire in solitude, so that he would feel the burden of her absence.

His problems continued to beset him. On 5 August, the day when he was due to pay Arondel several hundred francs, *Le Pays* suspended publication of his translations of Poe. It was only a temporary break in publication, but it caused him anxiety. As for Arondel, he did not simply call on Ancelle. He acquired the oppressive habit of waking Baudelaire himself with a visit every morning. On 13 August, Baudelaire had a curious letter from him. He sent it to his mother, who was now back in Paris.

> When one receives such letters point-blank, how is it possible [he asked] to write poems, articles on painting, plans for dramas, or even translations?

I received this curious letter yesterday morning, and I still preferred it to this cruel visit [from Arondel] which interrupts my sleep at 8 o'clock every morning. The meeting between him and M. Ancelle was very tough, and *I am the one who will be afflicted by it.* Send this letter (his letter) at once to M. Ancelle, whom moreover I shall go and see on my return from Marly, on my way back to Paris . . .

I have carefully read all you write to me about your embarrassments and hardships. However I have reckoned that *without being angry* you could send me about twenty (20) francs today, out of which I shall keep 5 to go to Marly, a money matter; *but I swear to you that I'm not putting myself to this trouble for Arondel.* As for the other 15, I can tell you what it is . . . Today is Marie [Daubrun]'s birthday . . . I am not rich enough to give presents, but a few flowers sent this evening would be proof enough of sympathy. I don't want your 40 francs any more, *they are no use to me.*[7]

By 22 August, when Baudelaire next wrote to Mme Aupick, he had decided, after all, to accept her 40 francs. He had, it seems, kept his room at the hôtel du Maroc, but he was regularly having supper with Marie Daubrun.

Dear sweet mother, give the messenger the 20 francs that make up the 40 francs for the end of the month. It goes without saying that I shan't ask you for anything on the first. I am not living here any more, I'm not spending anything here any more, which obliges me always to have some money in my pocket. Anyway, it's better . . .

This necessity of living outside makes me lose time, and sometimes work in the reading-room or even in the café – because, in the middle of all this, *I am working.* When shall I have a valet and a cook – and a household?[8]

Baudelaire used the word *ménage*, which could also mean a family; but he used the word with bitterness. He longed for calm and comfort; but he had long known that he could not enjoy the married state. His constant poverty, his lack of conventional prospects, his uncertain state of health, his distaste for the act of love: all precluded him from marriage. So did his angry independence, his cultivated eccentricities. He had been drawn to Jeanne, to Apollonie Sabatier, to Marie Daubrun: to actresses and courtesans. He could not be attracted by a bourgeois alliance. Mme Aupick must have recognised the fact long ago, and perhaps she did not entirely regret it. There would be no wife or child to intrude upon her relationship with her son.

In mid-September *Le Pays* resumed publication of the *Histoires extraordinaires* – only to interrupt it a fortnight later, after a number of complaints from readers. On 26 September, needing a powerful ally in his cause, Baudelaire called on Gautier at Neuilly. Gautier was out; and, as Baudelaire explained that evening, somewhat tactlessly, to the critic Paul de Saint-Victor: 'I went to *Théophile's* this morning, and, not finding him at home, I have thrown myself on you.'[9] Saint-Victor, who wrote for *Le Pays*, answered generously: 'I am enthralled by the truly *extraordinary* tales which you are translating in etchings, so to speak. I am constantly demanding their regular publication in the paper, and I am as indignant as you about the demands of the four or five imbeciles who have protested. In such circumstances, and when one is sure of offering genius to the public, my advice is that one should go on, and continue to cast pearls before the swine, in spite of their grunting.'[10]

Baudelaire was concerned not only with the *Histoires extraordinaires*, but with the future of Marie Daubrun. On 13 October, he asked Gautier to write a favourable notice of Marie, who was about to make her début in *Les Oiseaux de proie*, at the Gaîté.[11] Next day he wrote again to Saint-Victor: 'I wish with all my heart that you would find a felicitous phrase for *Mlle Daubrun*.'[12] The first performance of *Les Oiseaux de proie* took place on 16 October. Saint-Victor amicably wrote: 'Don't let us forget Mlle Daubrun, so touching and so proud in the part of the Duchesse de Guérande; one cannot be more nobly and more naturally a great lady from top to toe.'[13]

Baudelaire continued to struggle with his penury. On 17 October he asked Nadar, who had recently married, if he could lend him a little money. 'I don't know', he wrote, 'if it is quite decent for me to come and disturb you in your new life . . .'[14] It was hardly decent; and it is not known if Nadar helped him.

Other friends were anxious to do so. Adolphe Le Maréchal, who was known for his love of the theatre, introduced him to Hippolyte Hostein, director of the Théâtre de la Gaîté. They talked for a long while about *L'Ivrogne*. Hostein promised Baudelaire that he would stage it. On 8 November, Baudelaire reminded him of the drama.[15] He was desperate for money. On 14 November, although he already owed them 80 francs, he once again approached the Société des Gens de Lettres.[16] This time he asked them for some 60 francs and promised, in return, to send them an article within the week. The President, Francis Wey, decided to wait for the manuscript before he sent him money. The article was not delivered.

On 4 December, Baudelaire turned to his mother in despair:

> You know my strange life, and you know that every day brings its contingent of rages, quarrels, difficulties, errands and work . . .
> Today it is a question of exactly the same needs as the other month. YES OR NO, can I buy some clothes? I don't say: can I walk in the street without being looked at, I don't care about that – but must I resign myself to going to bed, and to staying in bed, for want of clothes? . . .

In fact, it's absolutely absurd always to buy new things, when one can procure better ones for the same amount. For me it's just a question of a payment on account to my tailor, and of redeeming the things already made.

Out of the sum that I should like to take from M. Ancelle, the same as the other month (350 francs), I shall also give a payment on account to [Mme Lepage], the manageress of my hotel . . . All the money that I receive from *Le Pays*, either on account this month, or as a final payment on New Year's Day, will obviously go on that; because this woman has given me notice for 9 January, and I have vowed that, from that date, I shall not put myself in the claws of a hotel proprietor again.

I shall go back to concubinage, and if on 9 January I am not installed at Mlle Lemer's, I shall be at *the other's* [Marie Daubrun's]. Whatever happens, I must have *a family*: it is the only way to work and to spend less . . .

I am very worried.

I now remember something which struck me at our last meeting – that is a certain anxiety you showed about the approach which you thought I could make to the civil tribunal. In fact, I am capable of making it – but not stupid enough to do so without having *some claims to success*. And, unfortunately, I am obliged to admit that there would not now be *any chance at all*. In short, I think that my life was *damned* from the beginning, and that it is so *for ever*.[17]

It was not the only time that Baudelaire thought of asking for the removal of the *conseil judiciaire*. He was thirty-three; but the tribunal would hardly have granted him his request. Had they done so, he would doubtless have spent his remaining capital, and lost his regular income for ever. He was constantly humiliated by the *conseil judiciaire*, but it represented his only financial security.

On 8 December, Mme Aupick authorised him to ask Ancelle for 300 francs; next day, at Neuilly, Baudelaire received them. Later that month, one future prospect was decided for him. Marie Daubrun was a capricious actress. In the past eight years she had worked for nearly all the theatres in Paris. She seems to have been impatient, ambitious and quarrelsome. Now, in mid-season, while she was playing the Duchesse de Guérande, in *Les Oiseaux de proie*, she broke her contract with the Gaîté. Hostein, the director, threatened to sue any other theatre which employed her. Marie Daubrun, now banned in Paris, set off on a tour in Italy.

44

As the new year, 1855, began, Baudelaire lost himself in his work on Poe. Every day he translated an instalment of the *Histoires extraordi-*

naires.[1] He also began to write *Fusées*: the random thoughts on love, philosophy, religion and literature which were both a *déversoir* and the basis for a confession. It was this year that Nadar photographed him in a Louis XIII chair. He looked some twenty years older than his age. His hair had receded; heavy lines ran from his nose to the corners of his tightlipped mouth. His eyes were penetrating, and full of distress.

On 7 January, Baudelaire asked Armand Dutacq, the administrator of *Le Pays*, to give the 250 francs which were due to him to his landlady, Mme Lepage.[2] He had expected to leave the hôtel du Maroc two days later, but his dreams of concubinage had vanished: Marie Daubrun had gone to Italy, and he was not to settle with her or with Jeanne. On 18 January, still from his hotel, he wrote to Félix Solar, the businessman and bibliophile, asking for an immediate loan of 20 francs (he already owed him 40).[3] That day he also wrote to Émile Montégut, whom he had often met at the café Tabourey. Montégut was a regular contributor to the *Revue des Deux Mondes*. He was, moreover, on excellent terms with the editor, François Buloz. Baudelaire wanted him to ensure the publication of a substantial number of his poems.[4]

Le Pays continued to publish his translations of Poe; he hoped that they would be published in book form by the Société générale de librairie. In February he sent a list of them to Armand Dutacq of *Le Pays*, who had founded the publishing firm, and added an anxious comment on his financial affairs.[5] As usual, they remained distressing. Soon after 3 March he finally left the hôtel du Maroc. During the next month he was to change his hotel room six times. On 5 April he turned to his usual correspondent:

A few days ago, unable to bear the horrible life I live any longer, I asked M. Ancelle to lend me 1,000 francs to fit up a suitable lodging. He appeared to consent, and then he changed his mind. I therefore gave it up, and proposed to pay for part of the furniture myself out of the money for my book [*Histoires extraordinaires*]. But this morning, I asked him to advance me the commonplace sum of 350 francs and gave him the surest means of recouping them. I am evidently obliged to find a temporary lodging. In the last MONTH I have been obliged to move SIX times, living in the damp, sleeping among fleas – my letters (the most important) refused – tossed about from hotel to hotel. I had taken a big decision: I lived and worked at the printers', because I could no longer work at home. How I managed to continue my book, how I am not ill, I really do not know. But I can go no further, especially as the work has to begin again, very intensively; it is impossible to conceive a longer series of misadventures. And the publisher and I are in a hurry. The business in *Le Pays* [the translations of Poe] ends in three days, and I have to begin again elsewhere; and I have no home – because I cannot give the name to an unfurnished hovel where my books are *on the floor*. Besides, while I am waiting for my final lodging, I must be *comparatively* very well and very calm; because my head cannot contain so many ignoble and vulgar vexations, as well as constant concern for a work which must be well done. And so I asked *him* for 350 francs (in fact, according to his *little* habits, he gave me 100 of them this morning, but that is absolutely *useless* to me) . . .

And, most ridiculous of all, in the midst of these unbearable, exhausting upheavals, I MUST write poetry, which I find the most tiring occupation in the world.[6]

On 7 April, Baudelaire told Victor de Mars, the secretary of the *Revue des Deux Mondes*, that he was preparing an epilogue for *Les Fleurs du mal*.[7] Next day, the eve of his thirty-fourth birthday, he finished his work for *Le Pays*. On 30 May he called, unannounced, on François Buloz. Fraught with hopes and disappointments, he had quarrelled with Dutacq, and he wanted Buloz' help in his affairs.[8]

On 1 June, introduced by a prudent note said to have been by Émile Montégut, a note intended to allay Buloz' anxieties, the *Revue des Deux Mondes*, that stronghold of conservative Romanticism, published eighteen poems by Baudelaire. Their publication was a signal honour. They appeared, for the first time, under the title of *Les Fleurs du mal*.

Maxime du Camp long remembered the effect of their publication:

It caused amazement, and it was a triumph. People admired the expert composition, the metallic strength of the verse, but more than one reader was shocked by the acridity of thought. They were accustomed to seeing French poetry cover only sweet, tender or melancholy themes; the jeremiad of the poets was lost in a cloud of undefined suffering . . . With *Les Fleurs du mal*, it was not like that any more; the author dissected himself.[9]

> Ma jeunesse ne fut qu'un ténébreux orage,
> Traversé çà et là par de brillants soleils;
> La tonnerre et la pluie ont fait un tel ravage,
> Qu'il reste en mon jardin bien peu de fruits vermeils.
>
> Voilà que j'ai touché l'automne des idées,
> Et qu'il faut employer la pelle et les râteaux
> Pour rassembler à neuf les terres inondées,
> Où l'eau creuse des trous grands comme des tombeaux.
>
> Et qui sait si les fleurs nouvelles que je rêve
> Trouveront dans ce sol lavé comme une grève
> Le mystique aliment qui ferait leur vigueur?
>
> – Ô douleur! ô douleur! Le Temps mange la vie,
> Et l'obscur Ennemi qui nous ronge le cœur
> Du sang que nous perdons croît et se fortifie![10]

André Gide was later to maintain that Baudelaire owed his survival to perfection of form: not a simple, logical perfection like that of Heredia in his sonnets, but a secret, musical perfection.[11] Baudelaire, he said, was the first to have made this secret perfection, quite deliberately, the purpose and the reason for his poems; and this was why, after *Les Fleurs du mal*, European poetry could no longer be the same. Musical perfection was not here a mere question of verbal sonority, it was also a certain choice of expression, no longer dictated only by logic, an expression which went beyond logic, through which the poet-musician fixed, as precisely as a definition, the essentially indefinable emotion:

> Mais le vert paradis des amours enfantines,
> Les courses, les chansons, les baisers, les bouquets,
> Les violons vibrant derrière les collines,
> Avec les brocs de vin, le soir, dans les bosquets,
> – Mais le vert paradis des amours enfantines,
>
> L'innocent paradis, plein de plaisirs furtifs,
> Est-il déjà plus loin que l'Inde et que la Chine?
> Peut-on le rappeler avec des cris plaintifs,
> Et l'animer encor d'une voix argentine,
> L'innocent paradis plein de plaisirs furtifs?[12]

As Baudelaire wrote in *Richard Wagner et TANNHÄUSER à Paris*: 'In music and in painting and even in the written word, although it is the most positive of the arts, there is always a lacuna filled by the listener's imagination.'[13] It was certain, continued Gide, that the poetry of Baudelaire – and this was exactly where its power lay – demanded a sort of connivance from the reader, and it invited him to collaborate. The apparent impropriety of terms, which was to vex certain critics so much, the expert vagueness which Verlaine was to make one of the conditions of poetry, this space between the imagination and the idea, between the word and the object, was exactly the place which poetry was to inhabit. And if nothing was more compromising than this permission not to speak clearly any more, that was because the true poet was the only one who could take advantage of it.[14]

45

In May 1855 Baudelaire had written three articles on the fine arts at the International Exhibition in Paris. The first of them, a discussion of critical principles, appeared in *Le Pays* on 25 May.[1] What, he enquired, would a modern archaeologist make of some curious Chinese artefact? It was an example of universal beauty; but, in order to appreciate it, the critic must learn to understand the unknown milieu which had produced this unforeseen creation. Few men completely possessed the divine grace of cosmopolitanism, but all of them, to some degree, might acquire it. Those who were most gifted in this regard were those for whom no academic veil had spoiled their vision of the complex truth. In a passage which clearly referred to his own Eastern voyage, Baudelaire expressed his conviction that if a civilised man were set down in some distant land, his feeling for it would in time create a new world of ideas in him,

> . . . a world which would become an integral part of himself, and would stay with him, in the form of memories, until he died. These build-ings, whose shapes would at first vex his academic eye, . . . this flora which disturbed a memory laden with native recollections, these men and women whose muscles did not vibrate in the classic way of his own country, whose gait was not in harmony with the usual rhythm, whose glance was not cast with the same magnetism, these aromas which were no longer those of the maternal boudoir, these mysterious flowers whose deep colour forced itself upon the eyes, while their shape tormented the gaze: . . . all this world of new harmonies would slowly enter him . . .; all this unknown vitality would increase his own vitality; several thousand ideas and sensations would enrich his own human dictionary . . .[2]

It was a transparent statement of Baudelaire's own condition: not only of the influence of his Eastern voyage, but of his mother's influence, which was far more profound.

Now, in *Le Pays*, in this discussion of critical principles, he professed contempt for the academic critic. He pleaded for a touch of the bizarre; he proposed to speak in the name of feeling, ethics and pleasure. He hoped in time – so he recorded – to publish an appreciation of the exhibition of English art, 'a glorification of our neighbours'.[3]

It was a task with which Baudelaire was much in sympathy. Ten years earlier, in his *Salon de 1845*, he had recorded his admiration for Sir Thomas Lawrence.[4] In his *Salon de 1846*, he had acclaimed Reynolds and Lawrence as leaders of the Romantic school of portrait-ure.[5] Now, in 1855, he visited the exhibition in the avenue Montaigne, but he postponed his appreciation until he had studied English art more closely. He also read the ten articles which Théophile Gautier devoted to English artists in *Le Moniteur universel*.[6]

Four years later, when he discussed the Salon of 1859, Baudelaire was to use his earlier impressions. He refreshed his memory by re-reading Gautier.[7] Now, in 1855, while he prepared his glorification of English art, he turned to the chief masters of the French school.

On 3 June, his appreciation of Delacroix appeared in *Le Pays*.[8] 'No one', he wrote, 'since Shakespeare excels like Delacroix in fusing drama and reverie in a mysterious unity.'[9] Victor Hugo, he had heard, had derided the ugliness of Delacroix's women, 'but M. Victor Hugo is a great sculptural poet whose eyes are closed to spirituality.'[10] To Baudelaire, Victor Hugo had his limitations. Delacroix had a deeper vision, an awareness of modernity. He seemed the artist best equipped to present modern woman. As for his sense of colour, Baudelaire wrote with inspiration:

> Seen from too great a distance to analyse or even understand the subject, a painting by Delacroix has already produced an effect of richness, happiness or melancholy on the soul. One would say that, like magicians or hypnotists, this painting projects its thoughts from a distance. This singular phenomenon is due to the power of the colourist, to the perfect accord of the tones, and to the harmony (already established in the artist's mind) between the colouring and the subject. If I may be forgiven these linguistic subterfuges to express the most subtle of ideas, it seems to me that this colour thinks by itself, independently of the objects it may clothe. Then these wonderful concurrences of colour often make one dream of harmony and melody, and the impression which one takes away from his pictures is often almost magical . . .'[11]

There were days when man became aware of the correspondences between the senses: days when the sky seemed more transparent, when sounds rang musically, when colours spoke, when perfumes recounted whole worlds of thought. To Baudelaire, the painting of Delacroix seemed to translate those fine days of the spirit.

He sent a copy of his appreciation to Delacroix himself; and, on 10 June, the artist sent his thanks. 'May the good public see through my eyes, but especially through yours.'[12]

The letter was grateful, but it lacked the warmth which might have been expected. Towards the end of the century, Jules Buisson tried to explain Delacroix's reserve towards his censer-bearer:

> Delacroix thanked him warmly. But I know that, in private, he complained about the critic who had found cause to praise something disordered in his work, the lack of health, the stubborn melancholy, the livid hue of fever, the dim, bizarre, abnormal light of illness. 'In fact he bores me,' he used to say, for . . . the taste for decadence, which is fashionable today, was not at all to his taste – to Delacroix's taste.'[13]

There was reserve, to say the least. One need only read the dismissive phrase with which, six months after publication, he was to thank

Baudelaire for *Les Fleurs du mal*: for a copy inscribed to him 'with eternal admiration.'[14] 'I owe you many thanks for *Les Fleurs du mal*. I have talked to you a little about it, but it deserves much more than that.'[15] Delacroix was more than twenty-one years older than Baudelaire, and a generation divided them. Delacroix was a well-born bourgeois, and he was patrician in his sensibilities. To him, Baudelaire was a young Bohemian, and, after 1857, a condemned and compromising Bohemian. After 1857 there was an evident cooling in the tone of Delacroix's letters. As if to emphasise the incompleteness of the relationship, none of Baudelaire's letters to Delacroix has yet been found. Baudelaire later spoke, in public, of Delacroix's affection, but he knew that no affection had existed.[16]

However, in June 1855, Delacroix duly thanked him for his appreciation; he asked to see the other articles which appeared in *Le Pays*.[17] Unfortunately the paper rejected Baudelaire's assessment of Ingres, perhaps because it was too critical of a figure of national renown. Indeed, *Le Pays* refused to publish any more of his contributions. The fault lay largely with Baudelaire. The editor had wanted a series of articles which would serve as a guide to the exhibition. Baudelaire had written monographs better suited to a review. Distinguished though they were, they remained a challenge to authority. Not for the first time, it seemed as if he had invited rejection.

He compounded his errors. On 30 May, the day when he had quarrelled with Dutacq, the administrator of *Le Pays*, he had called, uninvited, on François Buloz. For twenty-four years, Buloz had edited the *Revue des Deux Mondes*, and he had given it exceptional literary standing. He was also at one time editor of the *Revue de Paris* and Administrator-General of the Comédie-Française. He was now fifty-two and an honoured member of the Establishment. Such a conventional figure could hardly have welcomed Baudelaire's impulsive visit, his desperate request that Buloz should use his influence on various publishers, and concern himself with Baudelaire's career. Buloz seems to have made it plain that the visit was inopportune, and all the more so as the *Revue* was going to press.

Baudelaire was impervious to Buloz' disapproval. Exactly a fortnight later, on 13 June, though he knew that once again the *Revue* was about to go to the printers', he wrote to Buloz to propose himself as a contributor and to announce that he would call that day.[18]

It was an extraordinary letter to address to an editor of such distinction. Baudelaire was not merely aggressive (as he often was, in seeking favours); he was also arrogant, and he was tactless to the point of being defiant. He demanded special terms, he proposed to visit Buloz for the second time when he knew that he would be hard-pressed. He demanded money. It is said that Buloz had received a warning from authority after his publication of poems from *Les Fleurs du mal*; he had also received protests from his subscribers.[19] He should have been approached with consummate care.

If the interview with Baudelaire did take place that evening, its outcome is unclear. Soon afterwards, Malassis referred to him as a contributor to the *Revue des Deux Mondes*;[20] but the *Revue* contained nothing else by Baudelaire this year.

On 8 July, *Le Portefeuille* published *De l'Essence du rire*. It was the first published version of an essay which Baudelaire seems to have written no later than 1846, and revised in about 1851–3. *Le Portefeuille* announced: 'This article is taken from a book called *Peintres, Statuaires et Caricaturistes*, which will soon be published by Michel Lévy.' The book was not finished; the article seems to have come from a dossier. Baudelaire also took from it the two articles on caricature, which made their first appearance in print in 1857. The dossier has not yet been found; the three articles were finally to appear in the *Curiosités esthétiques*.

As Pichois writes, Baudelaire's ambition was all-embracing.[21] He planned, in his book, to consider a great part of Western art. As it is, by defining the grotesque as an aesthetic category, he was an innovator in France.

De l'Essence du rire was, so he claimed, the work of a philosopher and an artist.[22] Caricatures were not merely ephemera. They excited laughter, but they represented the moral and physical ugliness of man, and, in the eyes of the philosopher, nothing human was frivolous. Laughter and tears were not to be seen in the earthly paradise, in which it seemed that all Creation was good. Laughter and tears appeared because man lacked the strength to repress them. The comical was one of the clearest signs of the Satanic in humankind. Laughter came from the thought of ones own superiority: the sight of someone else's misfortune. Laughter was essentially human and essentially contradictory, it was both a sign of grandeur in relation to animals, and wretchedness in relation to God.

Two years later, in *Le Présent*, Baudelaire was to publish two more pieces from his dossier. In *Quelques caricaturistes français* he sang the praises of Daumier, 'for Daumier has taken his art a long way, he has made it a serious art; he is a great caricaturist. To appreciate him as he deserves, one must analyse him from the artistic and moral points of view. As an artist, what distinguishes Daumier is assurance. He draws like the great masters . . . As for morality, Daumier bears certain likenesses to Molière.'[23] Grandville, as Baudelaire recognised, 'had an unhealthily literary mind, always in search of illegitimate ways of forcing his idea into the realm of the plastic arts.'[24] It was 'for the mad side of his talent that Grandville was important.'[25] Gavarni was a more than interesting artist, but 'the real mission of Gavarni and Daumier was to complete Balzac, who, incidentally, was well aware of it, and valued them as auxiliaries and commentators.'[26] This may perhaps have been true of Gavarni; but Daumier went beyond caricature, he was more than an auxiliary, a commentator on other people's work. He was a powerful and heartrending painter, and in this essay, surprisingly, Baudelaire did not give him his due.

In *Quelques caricaturistes étrangers*, Baudelaire paid tribute to Hogarth and Cruikshank, but, strangely enough, omitted Rowlandson and Gillray. He discussed the element of fantasy which Goya had brought into comedy, and he touched, superficially, on the caricatures of Leonardo da Vinci and Brueghel.

Now, in the summer of 1855, when he published *De l'Essence du rire*, his life remained a permanent storm. He often dreamed of the *maison joujou*, 'the diminutive Zion at the mouth of the Seine.'[27] He could not cross the threshold in the lifetime of General Aupick; but it was, it seems, this summer that he assured his mother: 'Not a day passes without my eyes turning towards your cottage . . . What a void around me! What spiritual gloom, and what fears of the future!'[28]

He was living now – and would live until December – in a furnished room at 27, rue de Seine; he was waiting until he could furnish a lodging of his own. At last, on 3 August, he signed a contract with Michel Lévy for the *Histoires extraordinaires* and the *Nouvelles histoires extraordinaires*. He was to receive one twelfth of the catalogue price for the two books. There was to be a first printing of 1,500 copies. Baudelaire pasted a piece of paper on to the contract, to record advances received and to come.[29]

46

August brought a disturbing element into his life. In the early days of the month, after an Italian tour which had lasted all the winter, Marie Daubrun returned to Nice, unsure of her future. She could not find work in Paris, since Hostein remained unappeased, and still threatened to sue any boulevard theatre which engaged her. She asked Baudelaire to rescue her from this impasse. The Odéon was soon to stage *Maître Favilla*, by George Sand; the role of Marianne, Favilla's wife, would suit her perfectly. Hostein, she thought, would hesitate to sue the Odéon, which was the second theatre of France. This seemed to her to be the way to return to Paris with honour.

To Baudelaire it also seemed the way to rediscover his mistress. On about 7 August he wrote to Philibert Rouvière, the actor, and asked him to intercede for her with Gustave Vaëz, one of the directors of the Odéon.[1] On 13 August, he himself assured Vaëz that Marie would be delighted to perform in George Sand's play.[2] The suggestion was reasonable, for George Sand had admired 'the beautiful Madame Daubrun, with the musical voice', when she had performed in her *Claudie* at the Porte-Saint-Martin.[3] All might have ended well, had Baudelaire not chosen to announce that Marie Daubrun would like an increase in her salary. It was this ill-timed request which destroyed her prospects. A few hours later, he learned from Narrey, another director of the Odéon, that there was no point in negotiation.

Next day, with prudent, if excessive, flattery, Baudelaire asked George Sand to intervene.[4] George Sand assured him that she would do so, and she wrote twice to Vaëz.[5] On 15 September, *Maître Favilla* opened at the Odéon, but it was Mme Laurent, not Marie Daubrun, who performed in it. Baudelaire did not forgive George Sand for her failure.[6]

It was a failure which affected Marie's career; it also ended his own hopes of a continuing relationship. It has been said that Marie Daubrun loved money more than she loved men. It might be more true to say that her theatrical ambitions were more important to her than financial advantage. As Feuillerat observed, she wanted the tinsel of glory from those writers on whom she bestowed her favours.[7] Baudelaire had brought her no theatrical renown. When she returned from Nice to Paris, Banville once again became the genius whom she felt called upon to inspire. In the autumn of 1855, Banville was working on his *Histoire d'une comédienne*, and this novella, published at the beginning of November, was 'written on the corner of the hospitable table of Mlle Marie Daubrun'.[8] She had taken Banville to live with her – a Banville who was far from well, a poet who needed all her sympathy.

She and Banville made no attempt to conceal their liaison. Baudelaire forgave them: indeed, in September 1856 he asked Daumier to draw a frontispiece for Banville's *Odes funambulesques*.[9] Early in 1858, in reply to a note which has not survived, Banville wrote to him: 'Your letter made me very happy. It showed me once again an affection and a sympathy which I have never ceased to count on, and I reciprocate them most sincerely, in spite of the circumstances which have separated us.'[10] In 1861, Baudelaire published a generous appreciation of Banville in *La Revue fantaisiste*.[11]

One of the curious traits in Baudelaire's character was, so Feuillerat observes, his inability to feel jealousy.[12] This comment is not entirely true: he remained bitterly jealous of his mother's relationship with Aupick; he was to be afraid of feeling jealous of La Présidente's other admirers. Yet it is true that he endured the infidelities of Jeanne Duval, and that he felt affection for Mosselman, the protector of La Présidente. It may be that, as Feuillerat remarks, what he most loved about love was the intellectual intoxication which it gave him.[13]

Yet he was no doubt wounded by Marie's rejection: not so much, perhaps, by her cruelty as by the destruction of an illusion. He was all the more saddened since, with her – another of his hopeless dreams – he had glimpsed the prospect of a settled existence.

It was not only Marie who had now abandoned him. His mother, too, had once again refused to have direct relations with him. Perhaps she had allowed herself to be guided by her husband. Perhaps she was too concerned about her own health, and about that of Aupick, to accept the burden of her son. Perhaps she could no longer bear his emotional blackmail and his financial demands. Whatever the reason, she had once again decided only to speak to him through Ancelle.

On 4 October, Baudelaire wrote to her in despair:

My dear mother, I don't know your address [*sic*], I am obliged to entrust Ancelle with forwarding this letter. The letter which I attach to it, and which I should be much obliged if you would return to Ancelle, will serve to explain and substantiate my own. This month, like the third month of every quarter, is really terrible, but all the more terrible since I have to settle in a new lodging, AND THAT ON THE 8th. Despite Ancelle's refusal to advance me money, I was almost able to sleep in peace, because the most urgent expenses were, I thought, to be paid with the money which I still have to receive from *Michel Lévy*. *Michel* has bought two books from me, he has almost entirely paid for them in advance. All that remains is *300 francs* which I expected to get from him on the *6th*. But the day before yesterday I found a letter from him complaining of my delays, of my way of working, and of my numerous corrections, which caused much expense at the printers', and finally he threatened to make me pay these expenses. In these conditions, it seems to me impossible to take this money from him on the *7th*. [*sic*], since he talks of keeping it as security against the expenses which are caused by my method of work. He is also *determined*, and he is right, that the *two* volumes should appear in *November* – that's the good season – and he sends an employee to me sometimes *twice* a day to collect either proofs or manuscripts. It is clear that, by this terrible process, I shall be ready in time. However, I still cannot find myself on the street on the 7th, over head and ears in difficulties, with my books on my hands, and a furious publisher. The most unpleasant thing is that the necessity of making these two books appear on time prevents me from earning money, since I haven't got time to concern myself with anything else. Otherwise it would be quite easy for me to do something for the *Revue des Deux Mondes*, on which I shall work quite regularly, as soon as I have completed this unavoidable task. The *Revue des Deux Mondes* has the beginning of a work of mine, and it can make me live decently. Just live. Because, as for the debts, I am not thinking about them yet. As for the debts, it's the Theatre which will pay them . . . I should be glad if, before the 8th, Ancelle could advance me not the large sum I need, it is too large, but just 300 francs; even 200 would be enough to remedy the first difficulties, and to let me work fast enough to soothe the soul of an anxious publisher. Although you no longer want to have direct relations with me, you will find it quite natural that I should send you the first volume, as soon as it appears. One of my friends has made me a present of some superb paper on which I shall have a few library copies printed. It is very hard and very painful to work with such cruel and such trivial anxieties. And Ancelle should certainly have given me this small advance, of his own accord. It is not that writing to you is something painful for me. What is painful for me, is never to have an answer in your own hand.

Allow me to embrace you.

CHARLES

Michel Lévy will also publish (but when?) my book of Poems, and my critical articles.

The *Revue des Deux Mondes* will probably publish a novel of mine in December.[14]

The letter revealed Mme Aupick's devastating behaviour to her son. It was a tragic letter, not only on account of present anxieties; it was also, as so often, a record of hopes deferred and disappointed. Michel Lévy had already twice announced the publication of *Les Limbes* – the original title of *Les Fleurs du mal*; henceforward the fate of the critical articles was to be tied to that of the poems. As for the splendid library copies of Poe, they were not to be printed. For all Baudelaire's hopes, the *Revue des Deux Mondes* was not to publish him again.

One reason for their refusal was perhaps an article which had appeared in *Le Figaro* on 4 November. Five months after Buloz had published some of *Les Fleurs du mal*, Louis Goudall had chosen to make a savage attack on them, and on their author. 'M. Baudelaire', he concluded, 'will henceforth only be quoted among the *failures* of modern poetry.'[15]

47

In Honfleur, in their *maison joujou*, the Aupicks delighted in their retreat.[1]

> My wife is as happy as a child with the new house [the General had written], the chief beauty of which is provided by nature. From her drawing-room, and dressing-room, and from her garden, she has a marvellous view, which is not to be despised, even if one has lived for three years on the Bosphorus. As for me, I just laze away the time, reclining in a green and shady bower on the edge of the cliff, with a few books open beside me in case I need them, and I dream to the murmur, or crash, of the waves – as the case may be – on the shingle below. To this enchantment is added a new one in the song of the warblers which I protect in my office as king and master of the place.[2]

As king and master, he took pleasure in the marble bust of himself, one day to be bequeathed to the town of Gravelines – which duly named a street in his honour. The other rooms in the house were hung, as his wife desired, with toile de Jouy; but his study walls, reported Goncourt, were hung with sailcloth, like a tent:[3] a reminder of his Algerian campaigns. On his desk stood a miniature of the Duc d'Orléans, by Mme Mirbel. An ornate black frame, with the initials FO, and the date of the sender's tragic death, contained three letters from the Duc d'Orléans to his chief of staff. Beside these relics lay a brace of pistols which had once belonged to the heir to the throne; in accordance with his will, his widow had presented them to Aupick. On the mantelpiece, in a small black marble frame, was the bullet taken from Aupick's femur in 1837.

In a larger frame, the gift of his friend Émon, were his decorations. Presumably these were only his French decorations: the cross of chevalier de l'Ordre de Saint-Louis, the increasingly ornate crosses, the rosettes and ribbons and stars which marked his unremitting promotion in the Légion-d'honneur. It would have taken several frames to display his constellation of foreign Orders. There were the insignia of Grand Officier de l'Ordre de Léopold, accorded him by Belgium in 1847, and those of Grand Cross of the Order of the Oak Crown of Luxemburg (1849), and Grand Cross of the Order of the Lion of The Netherlands (1850). There was the Order of Nichani Iftikhar, first class, awarded to him by Tunis in 1847; there was the Order of Nichani Iftikhar, in brilliants, presented to him by the Sultan of Turkey on 19 June 1850, when he was Minister to Constantinople. There were the insignia of Grand Cross of the Order of the Redeemer, awarded by Greece in 1850, and the Grand Cross of the Order of Gregory the

Great, bestowed by Rome in 1851. There was the humble Order of St
Ferdinand of Spain (2nd class), which he had received, as a young
aide-de-camp, in 1823; there was also the Grand Cordon of the Order
of Charles III, presented to him in 1853 as ambassador to Madrid.
Even this collection was not yet complete: the Medjidie, first class, was
to be accorded him by Turkey on 13 June 1856. The *maison joujou* was
adorned with likenesses of Aupick; it was also a monument to his
career, a constant, irrefutable proof of a lifetime of success. It was a
gratifying ambience.[4]

Yet now, in 1855, the picture grew less roseate. 'My wife suffered
greatly during the 4 months of the summer,' the General reported to
Thouvenel. 'A sluggish stomach, rebelling against everything, refusing
everything . . . She grew extremely emaciated, and I was very anxious.
In the end they found a suitable diet, and the trouble was put right.'[5]
On 24 October he wrote again to Thouvenel, now Ambassador in
Constantinople:

> Our health is not as good as we should like. My poor knee is becoming
> more and more troublesome. In the end it will pin me down here completely.
> And so I consider that I'm fortunate to have created myself this retreat.
> It lets me enjoy, *from my armchair*, one of the most splendid views that it is
> possible, I won't say to find, but even to imagine. As for my wife, she is
> recovering from a persistent indisposition which has worried me a great
> deal. She was so weak that she could not set one foot in front of the other.
> Her strength is coming back. God preserve us for one another![6]

In his medical study of Baudelaire, Dr Raymond Trial was to give
a sad picture of Mme Aupick's condition:

> Her natural piety was intensified by her misfortunes, and, in her latter
> years, it turned into a mysticism tainted with neurosis. Her mental health
> was never very strong, and from time to time she had nervous crises of
> an ill-defined kind. Her son often referred to them, and reproached her
> for a sort of instability . . .
> Her body, like her soul, was afflicted, and, in the days of her prosperity,
> she haunted the spas, not for imaginary ailments, but to treat quite clear
> organic lesions: sensorial optical troubles, which threatened her with blind-
> ness; spinal pains, and especially trouble in moving her legs, which
> developed to the point of paraplegia.[7]

Despite his ailments and his wife's poor health, Aupick continued to
pursue his lifelong interests. He was still concerned with the Société de
Géographie. Towards the end of his career, as the president observed,
'he wanted to associate himself with our work.'[8] In 1850 he had written
from Pera to the secretary-general, recommending a dragoman from
his Legation as the Society's Turkish correspondent.[9] On 27 April 1855

he was elected a vice-president of the Society;[10] and on 21 December that year, in the absence of the president, he took the chair at the annual general meeting.[11]

He also continued his career in the public service. On 8 February 1854, he had finally been put on the army reserve list; but he was now a member of the municipal council at Honfleur, and he represented Gravelines on the Conseil général du département du Nord. He divided his time between Honfleur and Paris, where he attended meetings of the Senate. He attended regularly – as might be expected – and he regularly voted for the Government. On 7 September 1854 he was appointed, with Prosper Mérimée, to the commission which was to publish Napoleon's correspondence. 'Here, as always, the good general performed the greatest service, and soon became one of the most useful members of the commission.'[12]

Among his colleagues in the Senate, there were some who felt a particular affinity with him. They, too, had fought for France, and for liberty, before they served their country at the Palais du Luxembourg. Baron de Lacrosse had fought his way from Elba to Paris, lost three fingers at the battle of Craone, and acted as aide-de-camp to General Vandamme at Waterloo. Vice-Admiral Baron Hugon, as a young sea captain, had asked to fight in the Greek War of Independence, the cause in which Lord Byron had died; he had sunk a Turkish frigate at Navarino.[13] All Aupick's fellow Senators had survived decades of turbulent politics to become pillars of the Establishment. They were now elderly and conventional. In age, and in beliefs, they were a world away from Baudelaire.

There had been a time when Baudelaire spoke of reconciliation with Aupick. Now, in 1855, he expressed only his hatred. That December, hearing a false rumour that Delacroix might become a Senator, he observed to Ancelle, ironically: 'There's M. Aupick condemned to sit with a very obscure man.'[14] Aupick, the opportunist, represented all the values that he scorned, the values that were meaningless beside those of great art.

Aupick did not only rouse his permanent hostility. He was also a barrier to his happiness. It was clear that there could be no lasting reconciliation between Baudelaire and his mother as long as the Senator remained alive.

Since Mme Aupick still refused to have direct relations with her son, it was from Ancelle's, on 20 December, that he wrote to her again:

> My dear mother, I have a great deal to say to you, and M. Ancelle, who will forward this letter to you, knows all about it . . .

Above all things, I want to see you. For over a year, now, you have refused this, and I really believe that your legitimate anger should have been appeased. There is in my relationship with you something absolutely abnormal, absolutely humiliating for me, which you cannot really want to maintain. If this entreaty is not enough to satisfy you, do at least perform an act of generosity. I am not positively old, but I can soon become so. It seems to me impossible that you should want to maintain this situation ... Because my mind is made in a certain way, which obviously seems eccentric to you, you should not conclude that I take an unhealthy pleasure in this absolute solitude and in this remoteness of my mother's. I told you, I think, a moment ago, that I can grow old; but there is worse. One of us can die, and really it is painful to think that we run the risk of dying without seeing one another ... For a long time, already, I have been quite ill, in body and soul, and I want at one stroke, at a single stroke, a complete rejuvenation, an immediate satisfaction of body and soul. The years accumulate without one or the other, and really it is hard.

Ancelle will tell you of my wish, I should go further: of my firm resolution to settle down at last in a lodging which I chose two months ago. And so, almost as I move in, I shall have some rent to pay, as the lodging has been rented for the last two and a half months, and I haven't been able to live there, for want of money

I am absolutely weary of a life of seedy restaurants and furnished lodgings; it is killing me and poisoning me. I don't know how I have borne it.

I am weary of colds and headaches, and temperatures, and above all of the need to go out twice a day, and the snow, and the mud, and the rain. I say this to [Ancelle] unceasingly; but he wants your authority before he grants my wish.

I don't have anything, and so it is a question of a bigger sacrifice or a bigger advance than usual. But I shall also gain immense benefit from it, and that almost immediately. Above all, no more waste of time. That is my plague, my great plague; because there is a condition which is even more serious than physical pain. It is the fear of seeing it weaken and go to ruin, and disappear, in this horrible existence full of shocks: the wonderful poetic faculty, the clarity of ideas, and the power of hope which really constitute my capital.

My dear mother, you are so unaware of the nature of a poet's life, that no doubt you will not understand much of that argument; yet it is there that my main fear lies. I do not want to die obscurely, I do not want to see old age approach without having a regular life, I shall NEVER resign myself to that; and I think that I am very precious, I don't say more precious than other people, but precious enough to myself.

To come back to my establishment, I lack everything: furniture, linen, clothes, even saucepans, mattresses, and my books, which have gone astray with several binders; I need everything, everything, at once. Ancelle cannot undertake such complicated things, as I have made him understand. Besides, all these expenses are dependent on each other. My establishment depends on the possibility of leaving the place that I am in. My peace depends on the completeness of this establishment. Several of these things have been ordered. In three days it will be done. As it's tomorrow that I have to leave the rue de Seine, or else I leave all my possessions there (and the book I'm working on? – and the printer! and the publisher!); supposing I had the money today, I should sleep on the floor for two or three days, and I should work where I could; because I cannot stop.

I have chosen this lodging in the quartier of the boulevard du Temple, *18, rue d'Angoulême*; the house is handsome and above all peaceful; and so I shall be installed like a gentleman; at last! – that, as I told you, will be a real rejuvenation, I need an absolutely private life, and a life of complete chastity and sobriety.

My two volumes [of Poe] are going to appear at last; and, during the new year, through the *Revue des Deux Mondes*, and through Ancelle, I shall be able to live decently. I am not worried about that. I shall at last have a place of my own. Henceforward you will not have to suffer such importunities. There will be no further reason to do so. I have taken every precaution to ensure that this new establishment is completely protected against all misfortune.

Oh, my God! I was forgetting the sum. With 1,500 francs, everything will be settled in three days. Frankly, a poet's life is worth that.[15]

Mme Aupick was shocked.

I am [she told Ancelle] much distressed by Charles's condition. You could, to set his mind at rest, write to inform him that I agree to this further sacrifice of fifteen hundred francs of capital. That's his main concern. Don't promise anything else. He has hurt me so bitterly, and his attitude is so far from being what it should be, that I don't feel at all disposed to renew our relations. I've never gone to see him that I didn't come back displeased with him. My advice only irritates him, and then he's insolent to me. As you can readily imagine, I can't tolerate that. All the same, in spite of the coolness on my part, I am very much perturbed by his state of neglect and distress, and there's nothing I wouldn't do to alleviate his condition. Unfortunately, what can I do? Save on my allowance, that's all. But it makes no difference whatsoever, nothing alters his horrible life. It's all very discouraging.[16]

It was small wonder that she felt discouraged. She was well aware of the contrast between her Senatorial standard of life and the squalid existence of her son; she understood the contrast between her own contented domesticity and the solitude of Baudelaire. She suffered from her son's distress, from the permanent hostility between him and her husband. She suffered from the financial demands which he unremittingly made of her, from his fierce, aggressive behaviour.

On 22 December, Baudelaire duly settled at 18, rue d'Angoulême. He was to live there with Jeanne Duval (or, as she now called herself, Mme Lemer).

48

In the rue d'Angoulême, he continued to work on the introduction to the *Histoires extraordinaires*. On 25 February – since his quarrel with the paper was not final – part of it appeared in *Le Pays*, with his translation of Poe's poem 'To my Mother'. That month, in *Le Journal amusant*, Nadar declared that this introduction was as interesting as the book.[1] In March, in the *Revue française*, Auguste de Belloy maintained that it was more remarkable than the tales themselves.[2]

It was remarkable, above all, because in the American author Baudelaire recognised so much of his own philosophy, so many parallels with his own life. In the literature of every country, so he began, there were men who bore the word *guignon*, or bad luck, upon their brows. The life of Poe had been a tragedy; Americans would admit that he had been a man of genius, but they did not forget his disorderly life, they had no pity for a poet who could have been driven mad by his grief and isolation. They were only concerned with time and money.

Poe's parents had died in destitution when he was still a child. He, like Baudelaire, had known what it was to lose his father; he had known in a different way — what it meant to be deprived of his mother. Poe had been adopted by a rich merchant in Virginia, and taken to a boarding-school in England. The five years that he spent there had not been unhappy, and yet they recalled to Baudelaire his own sense of imprisonment, his isolation and his fears in Lyons and at Louis-le-Grand. Poe had returned to America, and – like Baudelaire – he had been defeated in the battle of life. His writing had been so ill paid that he had found himself in poverty; an admirer recorded him skeletally thin, wearing a threadbare coat and ragged trousers, 'and, with all this, a proud air, grand manners, and eyes which were shining with intelligence.'[3] It was a portrait of Baudelaire himself. Poe's literary life had improved, he had married, and he had continued his journalism, but it had not been enough to save him from disaster. His wife had died; he himself had suffered from *delirium tremens*. He had died in 1849, at the age of forty.

Baudelaire recognised in Poe many of his own inherent strengths and weaknesses and fears. He followed the life of Poe with fascination. Implicitly, in one respect, he envied him. For Poe, who had lost his mother, had found maternal love. He had owed his moments of sobriety and happiness 'to a wonderful maternal protection. This enveloped the sombre man of letters, and with the weapons of the angels it fought off the evil demon born of his blood and his earlier misery.'[4] Baudelaire dedicated his translation to Poe's mother-in-law,

Maria Clemm. 'I owed this public tribute', so he told her, 'to a mother whose greatness and goodness do as much honour to the World of Letters as the wonderful works of her son.'[5] The tribute suggested all that he had needed, and still needed, from Mme Aupick: all that he had failed to receive.

Years later, in a letter to Asselineau, Mme Aupick herself attempted to explain her behaviour:

> I do not need to reproach myself, like some parents whose children go astray because they have refused to be guided by them . . . I once fought hard against his vocation; but, the moment he had published something, I changed my tone – perhaps I even, unwittingly, changed my opinion; I always stimulated and encouraged him as much as I could. But did he need this?
>
> Apart from a very few moments of weakness, I always found him strong [*sic*]; I never saw him allow himself to be cast down in the midst of his greatest misfortunes [*sic*] – for your friend was very unhappy, unhappier than you can imagine.[6]

The letter shows the chasm that lay between Mme Aupick and her son, her pathetic inability ever to understand him.

On 12 March 1856, Michel Lévy published *Histoires extraordinaires*. It was the first of Baudelaire's books, it pushed back the frontiers of literary geography, and it was to bring him the only substantial money that he earned. His translations, so Gautier was to write, were 'so excellent that they seemed original works . . . Thanks to Baudelaire we had that most rare surprise: a literary savour which was totally unknown.'[7]

At five o'clock on the morning of 13 March, the day after publication, Baudelaire himself wrote to Asselineau, to tell him of a dream from which Jeanne had just awoken him.[8] It was the only dream which he felt impelled to record immediately on waking. The fact that he did so, and that he sent this account to a trusted friend, suggests that he was aware of its significance. It was the dream which Michel Butor analysed a century later in *Histoire extraordinaire. Essai sur un rêve de Baudelaire.*

It had been, in Baudelaire's dream, two or three o'clock in the morning, and he had been wandering in the streets. He had met Hippolyte Castille, the novelist and publicist, who had taken him in his carriage to a well-known brothel. Baudelaire had considered it his duty to give the madam of this brothel a copy of his book, which had just appeared. As Butor wrote, the madam was Baudelaire's mother (this was his opinion of her second marriage), and by giving her the book he had avenged himself for the *conseil judiciaire*, and he had regained his manhood and his independence. The publication had alone made him adult and free.[9] In his dream it was an obscene publication, a necessary excuse to enter the bordello.

The moment he had entered, he noticed that he was exposing himself, and he reflected that it was indecent to appear like this. He also found himself barefoot, and saw that he had stepped into a puddle. He went upstairs and, from that moment, there was no further question of the book. He found himself in a series of vast galleries, where prostitutes were talking to men, some *collégiens* among them. The walls of the galleries were hung with drawings of every kind, some of them obscene. The bordello as picture gallery is another striking feature of the dream, as the dreamer was an art critic; but the equation may well have meant the gallery or museum as a secret meeting-place. He had sometimes arranged to meet his mother in the Louvre, to avoid encounters with Aupick.

In his dream, in this curious museum, there were not only pictures: there was also a live exhibit, a monster which had been born in the house, and now remained forever on a pedestal, crouching in a contorted, bizarre position. He and Baudelaire were deep in conversation when Baudelaire awoke, exhausted. He had, he thought, been sleeping in the same position as the monster. Baudelaire claimed to be ignorant of the hieroglyphic nature of his dream; he indicated otherwise by identifying his posture with that of the monster on its pedestal. He himself was the monster born in his mother's house – *le monstre rabougri*, the rejected poet of 'Bénédiction'. Alive, he was condemned to the sterile existence of the museum – neither to life nor to death, but to limbo.

In *L'Échec de Baudelaire*, his thoughtful and provocative psychoanalytical study, Dr René Laforgue went further:

> We should be tempted to wonder if the history of the foetus, the idea of anatomical relics in a museum which are expressed in his dream are not related to the memory of a miscarriage or something like it that had struck him and fascinated him in his early childhood. Add to this his obsession with blood, with death and with sensual pleasure, and we may wonder if it was not an event of this sort which, in his case, very early turned his tastes in this direction. However that may be, until we are better informed about his early childhood, it is impossible to understand in a satisfactory manner the reason for his real rancour against his mother, whom he always more or less reproached with being the cause of his misery.[10]

Dr Laforgue published his study in 1931: before it was known that, in 1828, Mme Aupick had given birth to a stillborn daughter.

Her continued ruthlessness, her repeated rejection of her son remained unforgivable. In the spring of 1856 she still refused, resolutely, to see him or even to write to him. On 15 March, he left a copy of *Histoires extraordinaires* with Ancelle, to be forwarded to her.

That day he asked Barbey d'Aurevilly to write a word in favour of his book.[11] On 18 March, he sent two copies to Maxime du Camp.[12] Next day, he addressed himself to Sainte-Beuve:

> Here, my dear protector, is a kind of literature which may not inspire you with as much enthusiasm as it does me, but it will undoubtedly interest you. *Edgar Poe*, who is not much in America, must be, I mean I want him to be, a great man for *France*; I know how courageous you are, and how you love what is new, and so I have boldly promised your help to *Michel Lévy*.
>
> Could you write me a note to tell me if you will do something in the *Athenæum français* or elsewhere?[13]

'My dear friend,' replied Sainte-Beuve, 'I am all prepared. I certainly owe that to Poe and to you, to your old friendship for me. If they like, I will do something quite short for the *Athenæum*, I have an idea for it; it can't be a study of Poe, but some considerations about your translation. You are a fine translator.'[14] Sainte-Beuve was always willing to commit himself in private, but he did not write the article he promised.

On 1 April, the *Revue des Deux Mondes* published a note on *Histoires extraordinaires*. That day, the *Revue de Paris* praised the 'important' study of Poe, and observed that, 'with his fiery and somewhat incoherent talent, M. Charles Baudelaire was better suited than anyone to translate the terrible Tales.'[15] On 6 April Delacroix, to whom Baudelaire had sent a copy, noted in his journal: 'For the past few days I have been reading Baudelaire's translation of Edgar Poe with great interest. In these really *extraordinary*, that is to say *extra̲human* conceptions, there is a charming fantasy which . . . is absolutely denied to our French natures.'[16] On 23 April, *Le Figaro* praised Baudelaire, 'that spirit clear and shining and as cutting as a sword, at once exact and philosophical', a spirit which 'had all the necessary qualities to revive that of Poe.'[17] After Goudall's article of the previous November, this was reparation. Philarète Chasles, the anglicist, who was fond of Baudelaire, and admired him, published a panegyric in the *Journal des Débats*.[18]

Such publicity encouraged *Le Pays* to offer a new contract to their once discarded contributor. On 8 May, Baudelaire announced to Ancelle:

> I have at last found a means of procuring for myself the several hundred francs which I need. Once again, I am beginning a long work for *Le Pays*: *Les Aventures d'Arthur Gordon Pym*. It will be paid for in advance; but they

won't give me anything until at least half is done. *Mirès*, the owner of *Le Pays*, will be here in a few days. I must leave several instalments at the paper for the moment of his arrival.

With 150 francs, I can work for a fortnight, *and to refuse them to me is to deprive me of the 1,500 francs which I need.*[19]

49

His penury was now so acute that, on 6 June, despite her continuing and ruthless silence, he asked his mother, yet again, for money. 'My heart is heavy, heavy with a thousand things,' he told her. 'This is the fourth time that I beg you to let me embrace you. I don't understand why you persist in refusing me . . . I ask you that as a weary, wounded man asks for a pleasure, a cordial, a consolation.'[1]

She relentlessly refused him a sign of her affection. She seems to have sent him the money he demanded, but one suspects that she sent it enclosed in a blank sheet of her notepaper. It was on a sheet with the monogram 'CA' that he wrote to her, later in the day: 'You have caused me great sorrow – very great sorrow. I'm not talking about the *humiliation* of not receiving a word from you. I mean that I really wanted to embrace you.'[2]

On 9 June, he moved to the hôtel Voltaire, 19, quai Voltaire, a few doors away from the offices of *Le Moniteur universel*, and from those of the *Revue européenne*. He was to stay there for more than two years. His repeated moves reveal his constant poverty, his situation as a hunted man. Baudelaire dreamed of a home of his own; but he could no longer have his own furniture without risk of seizure. Mme Aupick's charity had only served to throw a few grains of millet to the clamorous flock of creditors. Baudelaire once said that he would have had more peace of mind if he had spent his whole fortune in his youth.

Six weeks after he had settled at the hôtel Voltaire, he wrote, once again, to his mother, and, predictably, asked her for money.[3] It is not clear whether Mme Aupick authorised the loan, or whether she sent her son a hundred francs. There was still no question of her seeing him. She sent him a vehement letter of reproach.

Baudelaire was in torment: so disturbed that he himself provoked a series of quarrels with Jeanne Duval. On about 27 August, after a fortnight of angry scenes, they separated once again. After fourteen years, on her insistence, the liaison was broken. On 11 September, Baudelaire turned to his mother, now in Honfleur:

I beg you not to answer me with a letter like the last one that you sent me. In the last few days I have been through too many torments, humiliations, and even sorrows, to need you to add your quota. Some days ago – about ten days ago – I wanted to write to you. Since Ancelle was away and travelling about in the South of France, I wanted to ask you to send me a little money, it didn't matter how much, to let me leave Paris, divert myself, kill time; but I should have had to give you an explanation, and I shall tell you in a moment why I didn't do so. Only, since time has passed, and the event which befell me has sapped my strength to the point where I cannot work, it is now no longer a question of pleasure, or of distraction, but of need, and of an urgent need. I have gone back to work to try to forget things. But you know how exhausted one is by squabbling and arguing with brutal people; now Ancelle may not be here for another week or ten days, and this man (the man in whose hotel I am living) is plaguing me beyond all measure on account of a trifle of two hundred francs or so.[4]

Such was his misery, such were the emotional and professional pressures upon him, that Baudelaire could not even correct the proofs of work already done.

Michel Lévy [he continued] is making me wait from day to day for the signature of our third contract; my table is laden with uncorrected proofs, and so it's a bad moment to borrow money from him. This man [my hotel-keeper] wants his money tomorrow. Mind you, I could pacify him with 100 or 150 francs; but I have got the notion into my head of using the rest to go and see you [at Honfleur], not for long, for a day or two, and not in your house, don't worry. I should just go to the hotel; you would come and embrace me, and I'd leave again. Besides, I have to work intensively, and I don't think of staying away for long . . .
    As I told you a moment ago, I didn't write to you, although I desperately wanted to, and at the time I thought you were still in Paris, because the explanations that I should have had to give you would obviously have given you pleasure, a sort of maternal pleasure that I couldn't have borne. My condition must have been very plain, because, when Michel Lévy saw me in that condition, sometimes dejected, sometimes furious, he asked no questions, left me in peace, and didn't even ask me to write any more. My liaison with Jeanne, a liaison of fourteen years, is broken. I did all that was humanly possible to ensure that this break did not occur. This heartrending parting, this struggle, lasted a fortnight. Jeanne maintained imperturbably, all the time, that I had an intractable character, and that, besides, one day, I should thank her myself for this decision. There you see the crude bourgeois wisdom of women. Personally I know that, whatever good fortune, whatever pleasure, money or distinction may come to me, I shall always regret this woman. You may not really understand my grief, and it may appear too childish to you. Let me confess, then, that I had set all my hopes upon this head, like a gambler; this woman was my sole distraction, my only pleasure, my

only friend. In spite of all the emotional tremors of a tempestuous liaison, never did the thought of an irreparable separation clearly enter my mind. Even now, and yet I am absolutely calm – I find myself thinking, when I see some or other beautiful thing, a lovely landscape, anything that pleases me: why isn't she here with me, to admire this with me?[5]

They were almost the terms in which, as a youth of seventeen, Baudelaire had regretted his mother's absence.[6]

You see [he continued, now], that I don't disguise my wounds. The shock was so violent that I needed a long time, I assure you, to understand that work might have its pleasures, and that, after all, I had duties to fulfil. In my mind I felt eternally 'what is the use?' – not to mention a sort of obscure veil before my eyes and an eternal ringing in my ears. That lasted quite a long while, but it has finally gone. When I understood clearly that it was really *irreparable*, then I was seized with a nameless rage; for ten days I did not sleep, I vomited, and I was obliged to hide, because I was constantly weeping. My fixed idea was also an egotistic idea: I saw before me an endless number of years without a family, without friends, without a mistress, always years of solitude and hazards – and nothing for the heart. I could not even draw my consolation from my pride. Because it was my fault that all this had happened; I had used and abused, I had diverted myself by tormenting, and I had been tormented in my turn. Then I was seized by a superstitious terror. I imagined that you were ill. I sent a messenger to you [in the rue du Cherche-Midi]; I learned that you were away, and that you were well; at least they told me so, but repeat it to me in your letter.

What is the use of continuing this account, which to you may merely seem bizarre? I should never have believed that emotional anguish would engender such physical tortures, and that, a fortnight later, one could attend to ones business like any other man. Here I am alone, completely alone, and most probably for ever. For I can no longer, *on the emotional side*, put my trust in human beings, *any more than in myself*, and I have henceforward simply to concern myself with my interests, my finances and my vanity, and with no delight but literature . . .

Answer me soon; because you know very well that I haven't just written to you about a vulgar question of money, however worrying that may be . . . I still only work inattentively, and I am mortally weary. There are still moments when everything seems empty to me.

I embrace you with all my heart.[7]

It was this appeal which finally stirred Mme Aupick's maternal feelings. She knew, above all, that, now that Jeanne had gone, she herself remained supremely important to her distressed and vulnerable son. She wrote him a long and unusually affectionate letter, and she sent him money immediately. 'I thank you with all my heart', he answered, 'not so much for the money, although it has saved me from great difficulties, . . . as for the feelings which you have expressed . . . Let me say again, I did not expect such comfort from you.'[8]

50

Mme Aupick left Honfleur on 14 September. She went with her husband to Bourbonne-les-Bains, where he was once again to take a cure. Aupick was sixty-seven, now, and he was failing. On 9 October, back at Honfleur, he explained to Thouvenel:

> When you are suffering, and suffering greatly, you lack the courage to write to your friends; it is almost a new token of friendship, because in this way you avoid telling them about your miseries. Well, that is what has happened to me. I went to Bourbonne. I found nothing there but pain, and, besides, I suffered from the sight of the serried ranks of the glorious wounded from the Crimea. In general, however, they felt better for the effect of the waters, and, apart from the distress I felt at the sight of their mutilations, I felt real admiration in the presence of their manly and martial figures. They were the true models of what we called *les vieux de la vieille*, to whom I eagerly paid homage at the beginning of my career. As for me, disabled long ago, I dragged myself round among them as best I could. The attempt doesn't seem to me to have been successful . . . I came back, with my wife, to our hermitage in a sorry state, hardly able to walk and therefore only going out in a carriage. The shortest walk caused me cruel attacks, and it does so still. Nothing dangerous so far, but this inability to move is very painful for an old foot-slogger. I am resigned, and, to spare myself useless regrets, I consider myself as a permanent cripple without hope of cure. If there should be an improvement, it will be all the more appreciated. Nonetheless, I am continuing with that part of the work which has devolved on me in the collection they are making of the correspondence and writings of Napoleon I. That is what made me go to Paris at the end of last month for the collation of numerous documents which I had sent to be copied. I also had business interests there.[1]

The visit had, however, been brief. He had returned as soon as possible to Honfleur, where he meant to stay as long as he could.

> Very probably, [he added, on 24 October], I shall spend my winter beside the fire, only going out in a carriage to take the air. If my condition doesn't improve, I shall just appear in the Senate on crutches, so that people know that I haven't yet gone west. I shall bid farewell to the commissions, and give up any part in the work. If it is to be worth

anything, it must be the result of careful discussions, and these are impossible for people who cannot seek information. In the meanwhile, I am thoroughly enjoying the wonderful late autumn. Heaven is giving it to us to compensate for a wretched September, which was nothing but squalls and tempests.[2]

On 21 October, Baudelaire had signed a contract with Michel Lévy for *Les Aventures d'Arthur Gordon Pym*. He had sold his work long before he had finished it, and long before *Le Moniteur universel* published it in serial form.

Early in November, he had a stern letter from his mother. On 4 November, the saint's day which they shared, he wrote to her:

I cannot let this day go by without showing you, in a few lines, that I never forget you. Only a few lines – because you know my periods of idleness, which later corner me into hurried work. This is the position in which I now find myself. However, I believe that you can now have absolute confidence in my destiny. The fears that you have expressed are vain. If the money matters are difficult to disentangle, the spiritual health, which is most important, is excellent. The misfortune which, at first, had so cast me down, the misfortune which was so puerile for people without imagination, but so fearful for me, has since given me an immoderate love of life. I am in process of writing the second preface, that is to say the introduction to the *Nouvelles Histoires extraordinaires*, which you will receive in a few days. As for the third vol[ume], you will read it day by day, since you take *Le Moniteur.*

Will you allow me to laugh a little, just a little, about this wish which you constantly express to see me *like everyone else*, and to see me worthy of your old friends, whom you obligingly mention to me? Alas! You know quite well that I shan't be like that, and that my destiny will be accomplished otherwise. Why don't you talk a little about marriage, like all mothers?

To be quite honest with you, the thought of that woman [Jeanne Duval] has never left me, but I have had such complete experience of the business of life, which is only lies and empty promises, that I feel myself incapable of falling again into the same inextricable snares of the heart. The poor girl is ill, now, and I have refused to go and see her. For a long time she avoided me like the plague, because she knows my fearful temperament, which is all cunning and violence. I know that she has to leave Paris, and I am glad of that; although, I admit, I was overcome by sadness to think that she could go and die far away from me.[3]

The letter was full of contradictions and unanswered questions. He had, he said, refused to visit Jeanne. Had she therefore sent for him? Did she already regret her impulsive behaviour? He supposed so, because she had long attempted to escape him. Was she really ill? She was, in fact, to survive him by years. Was she indeed to leave Paris?

Had she not told him so in order to gauge his feelings and measure how much power she still had over him? His first reaction to the thought of her departure from Paris had been relief; his second had been regret, when he reflected that she might die far away from him. What emerged from all these contradictions was that he had overcome the crisis, and that he remained divided between regret and satisfaction. It was the sense of deliverance that was uppermost, because he ended his letter: 'To sum up briefly, I have a diabolical thirst for pleasure, glory and power. This, I have to say, is often shot through, not often enough – don't you agree, dear mother? – by the wish to please you.'[4] Mme Aupick was not pleased by his confessions. She sent him a harsh letter, and told him that it was time that he was worldly wise.

Whatever his transient relief about his private life, Baudelaire remained in a permanent state of anxiety about his finances. On 12 November, he wrote yet again to Louis-Stanislas Godefroy, of the Société des Gens de Lettres; he asked for a loan of 250 francs, to enable him to finish the preface to the *Nouvelles Histoires extraordinaires*. Michel Lévy, so he said, refused to pay him for the third volume until the second volume had appeared, but he would in time repay Godefroy for the loan. Baudelaire already owed him 50 francs.[5] It is not clear whether Godefroy sent him money.

Nouvelles Histoires extraordinaires was not to appear until the following year. There were, however, serious problems with Michel Lévy. The publisher, who had left him in peace during his crisis, remained aware of the table 'laden with uncorrected proofs',[6] and he was now predictably angry about the delays in publication. On 4 December, Baudelaire confessed to Malassis that he was '*on the worst possible terms with Michel*'.[7]

Malassis' answer has not survived; but Malassis, it seems, undertook to publish *Les Fleurs du mal* (on which Lévy had taken an option long ago), and a volume of Baudelaire's criticism. Such behaviour was tempting providence. However, despite contractual problems, Malassis agreed to be Baudelaire's publisher. On 9 December, Baudelaire announced: 'I can now confess all the pleasure that your letter gave me . . . I had got myself into a damnable situation. One day, in a moment of anger with Michel, I had boasted to him that I could depend on you.'[8]

He could indeed depend on him. Malassis had gone into partnership with his brother-in-law, Eugène de Broise. The two men had chosen *Concordiæ fructus* as the motto of their publishing house.

The concord was not absolute. Timid and solemn, De Broise remained the antithesis of Malassis. He was, considered Malassis, 'a very good sort', but 'his learning and his taste in art rival those of M.

Prudhomme.'[9] However, in 1855, the firm Poulet-Malassis and De Broise had established itself at 4, rue de Buci. It was the golden age of the publishing house which was to revive the typographer's art and to publish Baudelaire, Gautier, Banville and Leconte de Lisle.

Even before they had signed their first contract, Baudelaire and Malassis had begun to exchange orders to pay, which they could anticipate. They did so with increasing difficulty, because these orders did not relate to commercial transactions; they were like cheques without guarantees. However, the process gave much relief to Baudelaire. On 11 December, he posted Malassis his receipt for the 200 francs which had been sent to him; these were an advance on the 500 francs which had been agreed as the advance for 1000 copies of *Les Fleurs du mal* and 1000 copies of his book of criticism.[10]

On 30 December, he and Malassis signed a contract for two books. The first, *Bric-à-brac esthétique*, was intended to be a collection of art criticism. Baudelaire had cherished the idea since 1853. The collection was due to be delivered at the end of February. In fact the project was to be realised only after his death, under the title *Curiosités esthétiques*.

The other book, to be delivered on 20 January, was *Les Fleurs du mal*.[11]

51

It was not, of course, delivered then. On 29 January, Baudelaire explained to his publisher: 'You might have guessed I was dawdling a little. That was in order to have absolute peace for a work which I want to do with care.'[1] That evening, he sent Malassis the dedication of *Les Fleurs du mal*: his tribute to Théophile Gautier.

Baudelaire had, it seems, first met Gautier in the summer of 1843, at the hôtel Pimodan.[2] Prarond believed that he had been drawn to Gautier by his concern for the arts.[3] The few surviving letters to Gautier suggest a certain closeness: indeed, Baudelaire always uses the intimate form of address, which is unusual for him, especially as he is writing to a man ten years his senior. Baudelaire's friendship with Gautier was always evident. He had often been to Gautier's Thursdays in the rue de Longchamp; he had met him frequently on Sunday evenings in the rue Frochot. He appreciated Gautier's warmth, his humour and generosity, his coruscating conversation. He felt in sympathy with the man whose Bohemian instincts, whose sometimes outrageous wit, whose love of the visual arts, whose concern for literature he shared. Yet Baudelaire, so Gautier said, later, 'always wanted to keep the attitude of a favourite disciple in the presence of a sympathetic master ... Never, in the greatest familiarity, did he fail in that deference, which we found excessive, and from which we would gladly have dispensed him.'[4]

Baudelaire was not mistaken in choosing Gautier as his master.[5] Faced with *La Comédie de la mort*, he divined a sombre man, haunted, like himself, by the idea of destruction, of nothingness, and he saw him consoled by art, provided with a pleasure of which nothing could deprive him. Baudelaire professed to find art superior to nature; he was disillusioned and embittered by his deeper human relationships. Gautier's example taught him that the plastic arts were rich enough in images, indeed in ideas, to take the place of nature and to feed the poet's inspiration.

As for the dedication of *Les Fleurs du mal*, which Baudelaire discussed and agreed with the recipient, it was, perhaps, fair to call Gautier the 'impeccable poet'; but the words *parfait magicien* were to provoke considerable comment. Gide was to wonder whether the dedication was not one of Baudelaire's most ingenious paradoxes.[6] Henri de Régnier considered that the dedication was a protest against the expansive Romanticism represented by Victor Hugo.[7] To Ernest Raynaud, everything suggested that it was only a disguised appeal to Gautier to use his influence in his favour; it repeated the phrase in Baudelaire's letter to him: 'Protège-moi ferme!'[8]

Raynaud was surely mistaken. Baudelaire had loved Gautier's poems in his early manhood; he had admired him as a critic who spoke of the arts as a painter and a draughtsman and as a poet. He believed, like Gautier, in Art for Art's Sake. He believed, like Gautier, in the theory of *correspondances*. He did, more than once, express conflicting or changing opinions about poets, but he had long been fond of Gautier the man. He also had enough integrity, enough awareness of his own distinction, not to sell the dedication of *Les Fleurs du mal* for literary patronage.

On 4 February 1857, Baudelaire gave the manuscript of his book to Mme Dupuy, Malassis' representative in Paris.[9]

On 8 February, still from 19, quai Voltaire, he announced to his mother that he had finished ten of the eighteen instalments of *Arthur Gordon Pym*; his translations were to follow the current serial in *Le Moniteur universel*. He expected publication any day.

> Tomorrow, Monday, I shall ask for a first payment of 500 francs on account. They will probably refuse me. I should like Ancelle to lend me

[the amount] for a week. Next week, I shall receive *1,000 francs* of it, and I shall return him his *500* at once . . .

You understand that, *if I cannot wait even a week for 500 francs*, that means that I am in serious trouble . . .'[10]

Mme Aupick had other anxieties. Late in December, when they came to Paris from their hermitage, her husband had been confined to his chair, and finally to bed. On 8 January, he had told Thouvenel:

Now that I have talked to you about my miseries, let me tell you, in compensation, that my wife is well, that she happily spent the summer and even the autumn on her clifftop, absorbed by her flowers and their scents, enjoying the wonderful view of the estuary of the Seine. She had hardly arrived here before she was already counting the days which she still has to spend in Paris before she returns to what she calls her sweetmeat box . . . We shall spend the winter and part of the spring like hermits beside the fire. I cannot walk, or stand, if I am to avoid the return of the inflammation which gives me such cruel pain.'[11]

Mme Aupick, understandably concerned about her husband, had less sympathy to show her son. She sent him 50 francs and some handkerchiefs. She instantly refused his request to borrow 500 francs from Ancelle.

My dear mother [he replied, on 9 February],

. . . To begin with, I expected an absolute refusal on your part to have a hand in it, and so I was not too disconcerted. God may give me an inspiration to find tomorrow morning the 500 francs which I needed this morning . . .

I will not see Ancelle. All our affairs will be settled by letter. And so you have no need to brace him, since he won't be attacked.

I embrace you with all my heart, and ask you to let me know which day you will come and see me.

The 50 francs (!) are maternal, but the handkerchiefs are a stroke of genius.'[12]

52

It was in these oppressive circumstances that Baudelaire turned to the publication of *Les Fleurs du mal*. Next day he wrote to Malassis about the printing of the book: the typeface, the spacing, and the dedication.[1] Gautier himself admired his literary conscience.[2] Baudelaire was constrained by his own demands for perfection; that is, perhaps, one reason why he was to publish so little poetry.

As for his determination not to see Ancelle, it was shortlived. On 20 February, at the desperate hour of six o'clock in the morning, he scribbled him a note:

> My dear friend, I shall come this evening to collect the rest [of my March allowance] from you. I have been obliged to plunge into work. I am exceedingly hard pressed by *Le Moniteur* . . .
> This time, 5 o'clock in the evening, is very inconvenient, because I have to be at the newspaper offices at the same time, but with a carriage I shall manage it. I just beg you to be indulgent, and not to keep me for too long . . .[3]

Baudelaire spoke of his own convenience. He rarely considered the convenience of his *conseil judiciaire*. Yet this year the local directory listed Ancelle not only as mayor of Neuilly, but as chairman of the board of charity, senior deputy to the justice of the peace, administrator of the savings bank, and vice-president of the cantonal commission for primary education.[4] Ancelle had many demands on his time beside those of his family and of an aggressive, demanding poet.

On 25 February, at last, *Le Moniteur universel* began to serialise *Les Aventures d'Arthur Gordon Pym*. The serial was to continue, erratically, until 10 April. Even now, the work brought its problems. Julien Turgan, one of the editors of *Le Moniteur*, sent Baudelaire a letter of reproach: Baudelaire had not, he said, produced the fifteen columns which he had wanted.[5]

Nouvelles Histoires extraordinaires were to be published in book form on 8 March, by Michel Lévy. Baudelaire sent a copy, sumptuously bound, to La Présidente. His thoughts remained with *Les Fleurs du mal*, and he was aware, already, that they might offend authority. On 7 March, he explained to Malassis:

> Tomorrow, Sunday, Théophile comes to *Le Moniteur*; I want to show him the dedication before I send it to you . . .
> I have spoken to Turgan of the event that I and one of my friends should need to be protected. He said to me: Get acquainted with Mérimée. He is all-powerful in such matters.[6]

Next day, he and Gautier duly discussed the dedication of *Les Fleurs du mal*. On 9 March, he sent the patient Malassis '*the new dedication*, discussed, agreed and authorised by the magician, who explained to me very clearly that a dedication should not be a profession of faith – which also had the fault of drawing attention to the dangerous side of the work.'[7]

The correspondence with Malassis, working in Alençon, continued for the greater part of March. Late that month, Malassis threatened to print without Baudelaire's approval, should there be any further delays.[8] 'Your letter is as undeserved as it is mad,' answered Baudelaire on 30 March. 'And if, on Wednesday, through some postal delay, the [fourth] sheet hasn't reached you, and if you were to print at once, as you have threatened, you would simply oblige me to reimburse you for all your expenses.'[9] The gesture, as they both knew, was ridiculous.

Malassis' patience was severely tested, but the correspondence continued. 'Forgive me a million times', wrote Baudelaire on 4 April, 'for calling your attention once more to the need to correct the proofs . . . I know how hateful one makes oneself with this pestering; but I've taken your establishment very seriously, and you yourself once confessed to me that you believed, as I do, that, in every kind of production, nothing was permissible except perfection.'[10]

53

While Baudelaire and Malassis discussed the presentation of *Les Fleurs du mal*, the background of Baudelaire's life had been changing. For some months, General Aupick had been a confirmed invalid. On 23 January, he had written his final letter to Thouvenel. He had not expressed discouragement – the feeling was unknown to him – but he had expressed his disillusionment. He recalled the idealism which had inspired him since his youth; and, sadly, he recalled *Fortunas, ou le Nouveau d'Assas*, the drama in which he had performed at the Prytaneum, half a century ago.

> My excellent friend [he told Thouvenel], self-denial, absolute devotion to ones country, the happiness of serving this country, of sacrificing oneself without reserve, are very rare, and rarer in the upper classes than they are in the lowest ranks. D'Assas was just a captain; it was an ordinary grenadier who *obeyed* every order that Guibert gave him, and each of these orders was almost a death warrant. Pride, self-love and egotism seem to increase mathematically in proportion as a man rises in the social scale.[1]

It was a sad conclusion after a lifetime of public service.

Aupick was dying, so a fellow Senator, Baron de Lacrosse, was to write, 'as the result of an honourable wound'.[2] It was the bullet wound in his femur which he had received at Fleurus, forty-two years earlier. It had pained him all his life; now he was dying

> . . . of the indescribable agony caused by the decay of the bones. The skill of the foremost doctors in Paris was powerless to hold back a life which was ready to depart; but at least the progress of the illness was slowed down by the wonderful care of a devoted wife, who made him find a charm in living, even in the midst of incessant torture.
>
> Our colleague watched the approach of death with calm: that calm which is the recompense for a life in which all the duties of the citizen and the soldier have been loyally fulfilled.[3]

On 2 April, conscious, no doubt, that his end was near, Aupick made his will. He did so in a florid style, and yet this final testament revealed his piety, his affectionate nature, and an unexpected humility.

> I am a Christian, and I die in the bosom of our Holy Catholic, Apostolic and Roman Church.
>
> I pray that my Creator, in His infinite mercy, will gather in my poor tainted soul.
>
> I am an imperfect creature, and I have sinned. I ask forgiveness from God and from mankind.
>
> I ask those whom I may have wounded knowingly or otherwise in their concerns or their affections to forgive me as I forgive, from the depths of my soul, those who may have been my enemies.
>
> I was born in the humblest station in life, and Providence has accorded me a brilliant career. I have followed it without letting myself be dazzled. Now that I have reached the end of this career, my honest hope is to end it humbly, as I began it. I therefore now express the formal wish that no civil or military honours should be paid to me. I also ask my friend M. É[mon] to insist strongly on this point if it is necessary.
>
> There will be a funeral service appropriate to my parish. After the service, my body will be taken to the cemetery. If some friend – and I think I have left trustworthy and devoted friends – intended to scatter a few words of regret over the still open grave, I thank him from the depths of my heart, and I beg him all the same not to do so.
>
> I take with me the regret that I have not been able to give my fellow citizens of Gravelines effective proof of my affection for them; one of my last wishes is for their prosperity.
>
> I commend to the care of my friends my beloved wife, whom, for thirty years, I have always found affectionate and devoted at my side. She has done so much to make the exercise of high office easier for me, especially abroad, where her grace of mind, together with the kindness of her manner, gave her *salon* a charm which everyone was pleased to recognise.
>
> I give her my last thought, and I seek refuge in the bosom of my Creator.[4]

General Aupick had, so to speak, mentioned his wife in despatches, and there was no doubt that she had been an exemplary wife. He was anxious to ensure her future comfort. On 25 April, he wrote a letter to the Emperor. 'It is not for me', recorded Baron de Lacrosse, 'to recall the words in which he revealed his fears about the future of his wife; but I saw the letter written by a hand which was still firm, because the dying man was strengthened by a trust that was not to be disappointed.'[5]

On 27 April, when he had received the last rites, Aupick died at home in Paris, at 91, rue du Cherche-Midi. 'At 11 o'clock that night, he ceased to breathe, in other words to suffer.' He was sixty-eight. He had, declared Lacrosse, led 'a blameless life'.[6]

He had never directly mentioned his stepson in his letters to Thouvenel. He had not mentioned him in his will, and he had made it clear by the omission that there could have been no sympathy between them. In his career he had been prepared to serve different régimes; in his private life he had refused to compromise. This dismissal of his stepson went further still: in the *faire-part* of his death, which was sent out by his widow and by Jean-Louis Émon, his executor, there was no mention of Baudelaire. On the day after his death, distraught with grief and full of memories, Mme Aupick told her son that he dishonoured her, and she forbade him ever to contemplate living with her.[7]

On 29 April, *Le Moniteur universel* announced the General's death 'with regret'. In Honfleur, where he had been a member of the municipal council, *L'Écho Honfleurais* reported: 'This death caused a feeling of grief among our population, who saw in it the disappearance of one of the men best placed to maintain the interests of our town and port.'[8] The paper later published a two-column obituary, taken from *Le Moniteur de l'Armée*:

> This brief account of General Aupick's most distinguished and numerous services can [it concluded] give only an imperfect idea of this untiring military and political career, a career in which he showed the energy of a well tempered soul, the lofty intelligence of an enlightened mind, the exactitude of a practical man, and the affable manners which he could not conceal behind an exterior which was naturally cold and severe.
>
> General Aupick was only sixty-seven [*sic*]. He might still have brought to our councils, for many years, the fruits of his long experience of events and men.[9]

On 30 April, at half-past ten, his funeral procession set out from the rue du Cherche-Midi.[10] He had expressed the wish that no civil or military honours should be paid to him; but the Emperor sent his representative, and a constellation of Senators, Generals and diplomats showed the respect in which he had been held. *Le Moniteur universel*, the official paper of the Second Empire, published an account of a funeral which was hardly the humble one he had requested.

> The funeral of Senator and General of Division Aupick took place this morning, with the greatest simplicity, according to the last wishes of the honourable departed.
>
> However, a multitude of colleagues and companions-in-arms assembled round the coffin of the man who is sorely missed by the Senate and the army. The example was set by His Excellency Marshal the Duc de Malakoff [a hero of the Crimean War, soon to be Ambassador in London]. Notwithstanding the dignity with which he is invested, he chose to show his personal feelings for General Aupick by being one of the pallbearers.
>
> The other pallbearers were M. Mimerel (from Roubaix), Senator, and member (as the General had been) of the Conseil général du département du Nord; General of Division the Marquis de Castelbajac, Senator and former Ambassador to St Petersburg; General of Division Comte Dessales, Senator.
>
> Apart from the deputation which included the Vicomte de Barral and M. Herman, there were a great many members of the Senate in the funeral procession, among them MM. F. Barrot, de Beaumont, Comte Boulay de la Meurthe, comte de Casabianca, de Chapuys-Montlaville, General Carrelet, Doret, Baron Dupin, Vice-Admiral Baron Hugon, Baron de Lacrosse, General Comte Regnaud de Saint-Jean-d'Angély, General Baron Piat, Thayer, Tourangin, etc.
>
> His Majesty the Emperor was represented by one of his chamberlains, the Comte d'Arjuzon.
>
> Their Excellencies Marshal Comte Vaillant [Minister for War] and Admiral de Parseval-Deschênes attended the ceremony, as well as several counsellors from the Ottoman Embassy in Paris.
>
> General Foltz led a deputation from the École d'état-major, of which General Aupick had once been commandant.
>
> It would be difficult to draw up a list of the distinguished personages who paid a final tribute to General Aupick: we observed Generals d'Aigremont, de la Rue, Lheureux, Oudinot, Duc de Reggio, Mengin, Comte d'Oraison, Trochu, Rohault de Fleury, Levaillant, Legendre, Morin.
>
> A modest grave had been prepared in the cimetière Montparnasse. The General's body was laid there when the religious rites had been performed, but no eulogy was delivered. This was also his express wish.[11]

There was no mention of Mme Aupick, or of Baudelaire, who was, ironically, the chief mourner.

A plain stone slab, surrounded by a plain iron railing, marks Aupick's grave. Upon it stands a memorial stone, engraved with his name and titles, and, in a laurel-wreath, the General's crest: a hand with a sword, and the motto: 'All by this'.

On 1 May, at a meeting of the Société de Géographie, the president, M. Daussy, announced the grievous loss that it had suffered in the

death of General Aupick, and he paid tribute to his memory.[12] Later
that year, M. Alfred Maury, the secretary-general of the central
committee, recalled him as one of the most esteemed members of the
society: 'A general who had learned in the hard profession of war how
to handle matters of politics: a general who, in difficult times, represented France at Constantinople, with the same steadfastness with
which he had defended it at Waterloo.'[13] The General, wounded at
Fleurus, had not fought at Waterloo, but he had defended France,
nonetheless.

Early in May, while *Le Moniteur universel* described the General's
funeral, and the Senate expressed its 'deep regrets' at its 'grievous
loss',[14] Baudelaire corrected the proofs of *Les Fleurs du mal*. On 10 May,
apparently through the influence of Gautier, *L'Artiste* published three
of the poems which were to appear in the book.

On 17 May, through the good offices of Malassis, the *Journal d'Alençon*
published 'Le Balcon': a poem which, as Pichois writes, had no need
of Debussy to be pure music. It was one of the finest poems of recollection in the French language.[15] The poem, as Quesnel observes,
had its autobiographical importance. Whether or not Baudelaire was
conscious of it, the mother of memories, *mère des souvenirs*, was Mme
Aupick; she was also the *maîtresse des maîtresses*, the woman whom
Baudelaire felt to be the rival of Jeanne. 'Le Balcon' referred to both
women: the woman who was permitted to him and the woman who
was forbidden him. Mme Aupick, *maîtresse des maîtresses*, had determined
his loves; they were indissolubly linked to her, bound to her in a
common destiny.[16]

> Mère des souvenirs, maîtresse des maîtresses,
> Ô toi, tous mes plaisirs! ô toi, tous mes devoirs!
> Tu te rappelleras la beauté des caresses,
> La douceur du foyer et le charme des soirs,
> Mère des souvenirs, maîtresse des maîtresses! . . .[17]

There was no mention in Baudelaire's letters of the death of Aupick;
but, on 19 May, he called on his mother.

> I found you a little impatient to have a mourner's prayer-book [he wrote
> to her next day]; so, while you are waiting for yours to be restored (at
> least three weeks), I am sending you this one. It isn't beautiful, but it's
> almost respectable.
> All the pages of the other one will be cleaned; all the stains will
> disappear, even the grease marks. As for the torn pages, they will be
> repaired as soon as possible.
> I shall see you this evening.[18]

Now that the General had gone, Baudelaire could visit the rue du Cherche-Midi, and prove his devotion to his mother.

Despite the high positions he had occupied, so Georges de Nouvion was to explain,

> General Aupick left no fortune when he died, as he had hesitated to save on the salaries which he had received. Outward display had seemed to him a duty, in the accomplishment of which he had deeply appreciated the qualities of mind, the grace, the elegance and the social sense of his wife. By a decree of 25 May 1857, his wife, now a widow, was provided with a pension of 6,000 francs, to which she had been entitled as the widow of a general. With the income of 2,000 francs which came to her through the liberality of her first husband, this was about all that remained to her of 'the golden life' which she had known.[19]

On 25 May, the *Bulletin des lois* announced that she had been granted her pension; soon afterwards, she wrote to Achille Fould, the Minister of State, to thank him for his generosity.[20] There was no reason, now, for her to keep a *pied-à-terre* in Paris, and she wanted to live in her *bonbonnière* in Honfleur. She decided to sell all the furniture in the rue du Cherche-Midi, and to auction the horses and carriages. She returned to Honfleur and left Valère, her factotum, in Paris to supervise affairs. She asked her son to report the details to her.

> Valère finally came this morning [he told her, on 3 June]. All the furniture has been sold for 25,000 francs; Valère says that the total (that is to say including the horses, the harness and the carriages) should come to 32,000 francs. I imagined that that was a good sum, almost exactly what you wanted, and enough to rid your mind of all these ignoble and unbearable material details. Tell me exactly how it is, and if you feel absolutely relieved.[21]

She should indeed have felt relieved. She was able to invest some 30,000 francs. With her pension, and the annuities recorded in her two marriage contracts, she now enjoyed an annual income of some 11,000 francs. In 1857, she could live in comfort.[22]

The death of Aupick – the great intruder, as Pichois called him[23] – had raised both the question of her future and that of the future of Baudelaire. The *maison joujou* had been intended simply as a summer house, where Caroline and her husband would spend three months of the year. It was, in her own words, 'just a tiny, tiny little dolls' house.'[24] It was only suitable for a husband and wife; it was now a shrine to Aupick's memory. Even if she had urged her son to make his home with her, it would have been disastrous for Baudelaire to commit himself to life at Honfleur, or to permanent, inescapable proximity to his mother. Nor would it have satisfied this widow, now approaching sixty-five, uncertain of her health, and anxious to conform to convention. 'I am much loved in this town, of course,' she would write, one day, 'I am too unfortunate not to excite a great deal of sympathy.'[25] Mme Aupick was concerned with her small provincial circle, and she was influenced by their opinion. She was especially concerned with that of her confessor, the abbé Jean-Baptiste Cardine, the senior priest of the parish of Sainte-Catherine – 'that accursed curé,' said Baudelaire.[26] She was also concerned with that of the Émons, who were to play an increasing part in her life. Émon had been a close friend of the General's, and he was now his executor. He and his wife lived in Paris, in the rue des Martyrs; but they spent every summer at Honfleur, where they lived next door to her. Émon was, a neighbour said, 'a slave to his loyalty to General Aupick and to his widow.'[27] Now, in the early days of her widowhood, he and his wife were with her constantly. On 16 June she confessed to Alphonse Baudelaire:

> The presence of the Émons is a great consolation to me. They are wonderful to me. The husband gives me enormous help with my affairs. The wife is the most charming, the most lovable person in the world, but she is very cheerful [*sic*]. However, she is most affectionate, and she is very understanding. When she sees me weep and moan, she sympathises with me in my grief, and weeps with me, but her native disposition soon gets the better of her, and her gaiety returns immediately. And so I restrain myself a little in front of her, because I don't want to impose the sight of endless tears upon her in exchange for her kindnesses.[28]

Mme Émon was sympathetic, but she was firm. She would not let Mme Aupick indulge in grief. She and her husband were also determined that she should not be disturbed by her son. Their influence upon her was extraordinary. In a postscript to this letter, addressed to Félicité Baudelaire, Mme Aupick added: 'Tell Alphonse that I am pleased with his brother, at least as far as feelings are concerned; as for order, I don't know if he'll ever change. I am much afraid that he won't. When the Émons leave to go and see their daughter, I shall take advantage of that moment, when I shall be entirely alone, to induce Charles to come and spend some time with me.'[29]

She showed astonishing deference to the Émons' wishes. While the Émons lived next door, it became increasingly difficult for her son to visit her. It was no doubt on their advice that she finally told him that she would not have him at Honfleur. Baudelaire replied that he had had no intention of coming.[30]

He was, in time, to visit Honfleur and, on one occasion, to live there for some months. He was to tell his mother that living at Honfleur was his dearest dream. Yet the Émons' wishes still prevailed. Besides, René Laforgue maintains that Baudelaire still felt guilty about his love for his mother; and, even after Aupick's death, he needed a punishment for his wholly imaginary sin. He needed a barrier between his mother and himself. 'Aupick had died, but the barrier still existed, as it had probably already existed before him.'[31]

For many years, perhaps since his schooldays at the Collège royal de Lyon, when he had first become aware of himself, Baudelaire had shown his resentment of the Aupick marriage. His mother had considered him largely as the General's stepson; he himself had constantly emphasised his difference from Aupick, exaggerated his faults, tried to disgrace himself. Since he could not be the man whom his mother loved, the person whom – so he believed – she preferred to himself, he had determined – perhaps unconsciously – to be his opposite. By doing so, he was certain to keep her in suspense, to be her constant preoccupation, and to make her feel guilty. Aupick had represented order, respect and hierarchy. Baudelaire had represented disorder, insolence and licence.

Now that the General had gone, he felt a filial concern, a sense of responsibility, and a deep relief that, once again, he and his mother were not divided.

> Not long ago [he told her], you paid me the most outrageous compliment on the change in my behaviour to you, which proves that, although you are my mother, you don't entirely know me. The sale, your (momentary) debts, your health, your solitude, they all concern me; whether things are important and significant, or whether they are commonplace and trivial, I assure you that I'm concerned about them: not out of filial duty, but passionately.
>
> I want to give you, in two lines, the reason for my behaviour and my feelings since my stepfather's death; in these two lines you will find the explanation of my attitude in this great sorrow, and at the same time [the explanation] of my future conduct. This event has been, to me, a solemn thing, like a call to order. I have sometimes been very hard and very rude to you, my poor mother; but, after all, I could consider that someone else had taken charge of your happiness, – and the first thought that struck me at the time of his death was that, henceforward, it was I who was naturally responsible for it. All that I have allowed myself, heedlessness, egoism, violent rudeness, as there always are in a disturbed and isolated life, all that is forbidden me.[32]

He was still as heedless, as self-centred, as ever. He was only aware of her advancing age, and aware that he depended on her. He added, with a lack of tact, an egoism which were quite remarkable:

Everything which is humanly possible to create you a new and special happiness for the latter part of your life, *will be done*. It isn't so difficult, after all, since you attach such importance to the success of all my plans. In working for myself, I shall work for you.

As for my wretched debts – and my celebrity, so indolently sought until now, and henceforth so painful to achieve, *don't worry too much about them*. Provided that every day one does a little of what one has to do, all human passions are naturally resolved. I ask you only one thing (*for myself*), that is to endeavour to keep well and to live for a long while, as long as you can . . .

Goodbye, dear mother, answer me *meticulously*, and believe that I belong to you absolutely, and that I belong only to you.[33]

The final sentence was perhaps the most significant that Baudelaire was ever to write. If he literally meant what he said, it would explain the fundamental disaster of his life: his inability to accept his mother's second marriage, his inability to form any permanent relationship with another woman, and, in a sense, his refusal ever to admit his manhood, and to put away childish things. There seems no doubt that, perhaps unconsciously, this was what his mother had wanted. By her single-minded devotion, by her later alternate affection and neglect, she had kept him in a state of permanent subjection. There can be no doubt about her maternal love; but she alone had largely destroyed him. Now, at the age of thirty-six, he 'belonged to her absolutely, and he belonged only to her.'[34] It was a devastating indictment of his mother's failure.

Early in June, according to her instructions, he went to the cimetière Montparnasse. He learned that Aupick's body had been transferred to a new grave. He found the General's new grave, and he laid flowers on it.[35]

PART THREE

The Author of
Les Fleurs du mal

1857

54

On 13 June, Baudelaire sent Eugène de Broise the list of those who were to receive copies of *Les Fleurs du mal*.[1] Among them were three English writers: De Quincey, who was to have such an influence on *Les Paradis artificiels*, Browning and Tennyson. Tennyson, writes his grandson, was troubled by 'the state of French art and thought, and its great influence on the world . . . Yet he read Baudelaire's *Fleurs du mal*, and admitted that, in spite of the shocking nature of its subjects, the French poet was a moralist in his way.'[2]

On about 15 June, at the printer's, Baudelaire inscribed the complimentary copies. On the half-title of Gautier's copy he confessed: 'My very dear Théophile, the dedication printed on the first page is only a very pale shadow of the friendship and the real admiration that I have always felt for you. You know this. Ch. Baudelaire.'[3]

He sent Sainte-Beuve a copy with his 'filial friendship.'[4] On 20 June, Sainte-Beuve replied:

I have received your pretty book [*sic*], and first of all I must thank you for the kind words you sent with it; you have long accustomed me to your good and faithful friendship. I knew some of your poems through having read them in various collections; gathered together, now, they have a quite different effect. To tell you that this general effect is sad could not surprise you; that is what you wanted. To tell you that, in gathering your *Fleurs* together, you have not recoiled from any kind of image or colour, however alarming and afflicting it might be, is something that you know better than I do; that again was what you wanted. You are indeed a poet of the school of art, and, if we were speaking to each other, there would be many observations to make about this book. You, too, are one of those who seek poetry in everything; and as, before you, others had sought it in regions quite open and quite different: as they had left you little room; as the terrestrial and celestial fields were nearly all harvested and, for more than thirty years, the lyricists of every kind have been at work, – you, who have come so late, and arrived the last, have said to yourself – I imagine: *Well, I shall still find some poetry, and I shall find it where no one has considered gathering and expressing it.* And you have chosen Hell, you have made yourself a devil. You have tried to tear their secrets from the demons of the night. In doing that with subtlety, with refinement, with a rare talent and an almost *precious* abandon in expression, by *perfecting* detail, by making yourself the Petrarch of the horrible, you appear to have amused yourself; and yet you have suffered, you have grieved as you paraded your vexations, your nightmares, your spiritual tortures; you must

have suffered greatly, my dear child. That particular sadness which rises
from your pages and in which I recognise the last symptom of a sick
generation, whose elders are well known to us, is also what will be
esteemed in you.[5]

Such comments might have served Baudelaire, had they been
published in *Le Moniteur universel*. Coming, as they did, in a private
letter from a professional critic, they only underlined Sainte-Beuve's
intention not to commit himself.

'Au Lecteur', the first poem in the collection, may not deserve the title
of a preface, for it does not embrace all the cardinal themes of the
book. It is, however, typical of the poet's tone. Baudelaire lists the vices
of man, he insists on the preponderant influence of the Devil; he asserts
that there is complicity between the reader and the poet. The vices he
describes are not those of the poet alone, they are also those of the
reader, who is implicated in advance in all the poet's miseries and sins.

> La sottise, l'erreur, le péché, la lésine,
> Occupent nos esprits et travaillent nos corps,
> Et nous alimentons nos aimables remords,
> Comme les mendiants nourrissent leur vermine.
>
> Nos péchés sont têtus, nos repentirs sont lâches;
> Nous nous faisons payer grassement nos aveux,
> Et nous rentrons gaiement dans le chemin bourbeux,
> Croyant par de vils pleurs laver toutes nos taches...
>
> Si le viol, le poison, le poignard, l'incendie,
> N'ont pas encor brodé de leurs plaisants dessins
> Le canevas banal de nos piteux destins,
> C'est que notre âme, hélas! n'est pas assez hardie.
>
> Mais parmi les chacals, les panthères, les lices,
> Les singes, les scorpions, les vautours, les serpents,
> Les monstres glapissants, hurlants, grognants, rampants,
> Dans la ménagerie infâme de nos vices,
>
> Il en est un plus laid, plus méchant, plus immonde!
> Quoiqu'il ne pousse ni grands gestes ni grands cris,
> Il ferait volontiers de la terre un débris
> Et dans un bâillement avalerait le monde;
>
> C'est l'Ennui! – l'œil chargé d'un pleur involontaire,
> Il rêve d'échafauds en fumant son houka.
> Tu le connais, lecteur, ce monstre délicat,
> – Hypocrite lecteur, – mon semblable, – mon frère![6]

The most repulsive of all vices is, to Baudelaire, *l'ennui*, and by this he does not mean romantic melancholy, but *ennui* in the theological sense: sin accompanied by remorse and despair.

The word *ennui* suggests the significance of the first section of the book. 'Spleen et idéal': the title means not only nostalgia and aspiration, but the dual nature of man. As Baudelaire was to affirm in *Mon Cœur mis à nu*: 'There are in every man, at every moment, two simultaneous longings, one for God and the other for Satan. The invocation to God, or spirituality, is a wish to ascend; the invocation to Satan, or animality, is a delight in degradation.'[7]

The aggressive bitterness of the introductory poem is found again in the first poem of the section 'Spleen et idéal'. In 'Bénédiction', Baudelaire takes up the romantic theme of the poet who is misunderstood, the poet who is cursed by the world.

> Lorsque, par un décret des puissances suprêmes,
> Le Poète apparaît en ce monde ennuyé,
> Sa mère épouvantée et pleine de blasphèmes
> Crispe ses poings vers Dieu, qui la prend en pitié:
>
> – 'Ah! que n'ai-je mis bas tout un nœud de vipères,
> Plutôt que de nourrir cette dérision!
> Maudite soit la nuit aux plaisirs éphémères
> Où mon ventre a conçu mon expiation!' . . .[8]

This curse upon the poet is itself, so Baudelaire insists, the sign of a vocation, and so it is a sign of a blessing. The poet rises above the hostility of the world, and sees his very suffering as a preparation for heaven.

It is difficult not to hear personal echoes in 'Bénédiction': indeed, in this poem Baudelaire sets down his spiritual autobiography, his love of his mother and his bitterness at her betrayal. The poem is unusually rhetorical, and yet there can be no doubt of its sincerity. His feelings for his mother are too bitter and too profound to be made explicit. It is the excess of feeling, not its absence, which obliges him to stylise his emotion.

'Élévation' is linked to 'Bénédiction' by the theme of purity; in ridding itself of the flesh, the spirit rediscovers the purity of childhood. A second theme, intertwined with the first, links the poem to the sonnet which immediately follows; by this purification, the spirit once again becomes worthy to understand 'the language of flowers and of silent things',[9] that is to say *correspondances*.

> La Nature est un temple où de vivants piliers
> Laissent parfois sortir de confuses paroles;

L'homme y passe à travers des forêts de symboles
Qui l'observent avec des regards familiers.

Comme de longs échos qui de loin se confondent
Dans une ténébreuse et profonde unité,
Vaste comme la nuit et comme la clarté,
Les parfums, les couleurs et les sons se répondent.

Il est des parfums frais comme des chairs d'enfants,
Doux comme les hautbois, verts comme les prairies,
– Et d'autres, corrompus, riches et triomphants,

Ayant l'expansion des choses infinies,
Comme l'ambre, le musc, le benjoin et l'encens,
Qui chantent les transports de l'esprit et des sens.[10]

The poet was the translator of the universal analogy. Nature was a dictionary, and the artist – Delacroix, Baudelaire himself – read it, and transformed it in his imagination. In Picon's words, he 'transfigured the actual world with the help of an inner cipher which recomposed it, or rather composed what did not yet exist. The *correspondances* immanent in nature, the *correspondances* which appear as its poetic order, only arise at the call of a soul which seeks a vast spiritual analogy in the universe . . . In his poem 'Correspondances', Baudelaire recognises his artistic doctrine and the key to his poetry.'[11] Baudelaire's sonnet was to become the manifesto of the Symbolist Movement. As Rimbaud wrote: 'To inspect the invisible and to hear the unheard is different from reviving the spirit of dead things. Baudelaire is the first seer, the king of poets. He is *a true God*.'[12]

Baudelaire was only one among French men of letters who was concerned with *correspondances*.[13] It is possible that he owed some of his interest to Balzac. It has been suggested that Baudelaire, and Rimbaud after him, were inspired by *Louis Lambert*, which had appeared in 1832. Balzac's novel speaks of the theories of Swedenborg, the eighteenth-century philosopher and mystic; but it does not speak of *correspondances* as Baudelaire understands them. Another critic sets Balzac aside, and quotes the passage in *Roger* in which Alphonse Karr points out the analogy between impressions produced by Gothic stained-glass windows and the seraphic sounds of the organ. A third quotes a remark attributed to Léon Gozlan: that piety is pale blue, resignation pearl grey, and joy is apple green.[14] In 1853, in *L'Artiste*, Comte Gustave de la Moussaye had discussed the relationship between sight and sound, and presented an harmonic chromatic scale, in which C was red, F was pale green, and G was blue. 'The harmonic laws of the world',

he ended, 'are connected to one another by identical relationships, and
. . . they form a grand homogeneous whole whose rays converge in the
centre of everything, which is God.'[15] He extended the concordance
between colours and sounds to the whole system of the senses.

Baudelaire may have read any or all of these works, and he is known
to have studied the theories of Swedenborg; but a much more constant
influence upon him was that of Théophile Gautier.

The perception of correspondences was, in Gautier, very highly
developed.[16] The correspondences which he recorded may be found in
his travel books, in his novel *Spirite*, and in his criticism of art and
literature. They are most often found when, his emotions stirred, his
technical knowledge least strong, he writes about music. Gautier was
one of the first to use correspondences freely in his prose, and he began
to use them at least as early as 1836, when, in *La Presse*, on 29 November,
he gave a vivid impression of Rubens' picture of the Assumption: 'This
picture is so fresh, so pink and so flowery that it smells sweet, and it
casts about the church an enchanting aroma of spring.'

It seems, then, that Gautier's account of his hashish dreams in 1843,
in which he heard colours, saw luminous and spiral music, and swam
in an ocean of sonority, was not the first literary expression of a
synopsis of the senses, but the logical development of a theory which
he had long practised, the most extravagant expression of ideas which
had long been natural to him. Though he did not invent either
transposition or correspondences, though he was not the first or the
only writer to use them, Gautier was surely among the first to practise
them easily and naturally in his prose; and in this practice his creative
imagination and his predominantly plastic way of thinking played a
large and evident part.

In 1859, Baudelaire himself was to declare his admiration for
Gautier's 'immense innate understanding of *la correspondance*'.[7] It seems
most probable that he had become aware of *correspondances* through
articles in two popular daily papers written by a poet and critic whom
he much admired; and when Mallarmé later confessed that 'the deep,
underlying treasure of *correspondances*, the intimate accord of the colours, and the recollection of the inner rhythm and the mysterious
science of the word' were stirred within him by Gautier's poetry,[18]
perhaps he, too, may have been prepared by the prose of the journalist.

The theory of *correspondances*, so significant to Baudelaire, was to
continue, and to touch both prose and poetry in nineteenth-century
France. In 1861, Flaubert told the Goncourts: 'When I write a novel,
I have the idea of *translating a colour*, a nuance. For example, in my
Carthaginian novel, I want to do something purple. In *Madame Bovary*,
I only thought of rendering a tone, the mouldy colour of the life of

woodlice.'[19] In 1872, in his *Petit Traité de la poésie française*, Banville declared: 'Poetry is at the same time Music, Sculpture, Painting, Eloquence; it should charm the ear, delight the mind, make objects visible, and excite in us the movements which it chooses to arouse; and so it is the one complete and necessary art, and the one which contains the rest, just as it presupposes all the rest.'[20] Since then, as Ibrovac observed in 1923,

> Arthur Rimbaud's wonderfully clever sally on *Voyelles* has become a theory, the so-called theory of *coloured audition*, M. Charles Henry has established a scientific æsthetic which seeks 'to connect our physiological organism with the conditions and the laws of beauty', and M. René Ghil, in his *Traité du Verbe*, has claimed, according to Helmholz's studies of acoustics, that 'harps are white, violins are blue, brass instruments are red, flutes are yellow, and organs are all black.'[21]

René Ghil had spoken of *l'audition colorée*, 'to which all the arts will unconsciously return to lose themselves in total Communication.'[22]

It is clear that *correspondances* meant, for Baudelaire, not only the relations between the senses, but the Platonic relation between earth and heaven. As Raynaud wrote: 'Baudelaire is a seer. Beneath the form of things, he seeks their significance and the reason for their existence. He seeks the link which joins the ephemeral to the eternal. Between the phenomena [on earth] and those of the beyond he discovers mysterious correspondences.'[23] Borgal confirmed: 'Baudelaire's theory of correspondences rests on metaphysical considerations. He some-times calls them analogies – relationships between things or feelings which guarantee the essential unity of the cosmos. Only a particularly sensitive or developed imagination can perceive them.'[24] Balzac had written in *Séraphita* that 'to know the correspondences between the Word and the heavens, the correspondences which exist between the visible and ponderable things of the terrestrial world, is to have the heavens in ones understanding.'[25] This was the understanding that Baudelaire was seeking. He believed in the Platonic tradition, which considered the union of the soul and the body as a fall; he believed, with Joseph de Maistre, in a previous existence, and in the pre-exist-ence of souls. Deciphering *correspondances* on earth was one of the essential paths to reintegration. Like Wordsworth, he had intimations of immortality. In opiates and wine, in love and art, he tried, in vain, to recall his former life. He knew that only death would bring a return to the soul's true habitation. This, as Borgal wrote, 'is the explanation of Baudelaire's incurable *nostalgia*, which one must understand in the etymological sense of the word, as a malady of the return. Never does the poet envisage life after death in its true aspect as a future life, but as the recovery of a previous condition, away from which he can only feel Ennui.'[26] Art, then, as Daniel Vouga said, 'is born of the absence of paradise, but of the memory of paradise: more precisely, it is both the absence and the memory of paradise, and that is why Baudelaire can find in it the best proof of our immortality – of the immortality of our soul, attested by the *reminiscence*.'[27]

This sense of immortality affirms the Catholic nature of Baudelaire. 'Les Phares' re-affirms another tenet of his Catholicism. In 'Bénédiction' he had recognised his suffering as a preparation for Heaven. In 'Les Phares' he sees great artists, the beacons of the human race, reflect the frustration, the anger and the grief of the world.

> Ces malédictions, ces blasphèmes, ces plaintes,
> Ces extases, ces cris, ces pleurs, ces *Te Deum*,
> Sont un écho redit par mille labyrinthes;
> C'est pour les cœurs mortels un divin opium!
>
> C'est un cri repété par mille sentinelles,
> Un ordre renvoyé par mille porte-voix;
> C'est un phare allumé sur mille citadelles,
> Un appel de chasseurs perdus dans les grands bois!
>
> Car c'est vraiment, Seigneur, le meilleur témoignage
> Que nous puissions donner de notre dignité
> Que cet ardent sanglot qui roule d'âge en âge
> Et vient mourir au bord de votre éternité![28]

Suffering is not only a preparation for heaven, but the clearest sign of the dignity of humankind.

There was no doubt of Baudelaire's own suffering. In 'Le Mauvais Moine', he compared his heart with a tomb; in the next sonnet, 'L'Ennemi', he compared it with a garden desecrated by a storm. It was hard to identify the enemy in question: perhaps it was Time or Death, Satan, or Remorse, or Ennui. Perhaps it had elements of all of them. The title of the sonnet 'Le Guignon' proclaimed the ill fortune which Baudelaire felt had haunted him since birth. In 'L'Homme et la mer', he recognised the unfathomable depths of man and ocean, the resemblance between their pitiless, unending struggles, and their love of death.

'Correspondances' was to have a significant effect on Symbolism. 'La Beauté' has long been considered a tenet of the Parnassian creed:

> Je suis belle, ô mortels! comme un rêve de pierre,
> Et mon sein, où chacun s'est meurtri tour à tour,

Est fait pour inspirer au poète un amour
Éternel et muet ainsi que la matière . . .[29]

It was here that Baudelaire reacted – like Flaubert and Gautier –
against passion; it was here, some said, that he came closest to the
author of *Émaux et Camées*. In 'L'Idéal' and 'La Géante', he proclaimed
his love for the monstrous: for Lady Macbeth, for Night, the daughter
of Michaelangelo, for a young giantess, whose breasts would give him
shade on summer days. The first sonnet has a grandeur, an insatiable
love of the impossible, which are typical of Baudelaire. The second
sonnet represents Baudelaire the mystifier: the truculent *poseur* of the
hôtel Pimodan. With 'Les Bijoux' – a poem reminiscent of some early
paintings by Delacroix – he begins the cycle of Jeanne Duval, and
reveals his poetry in splendour:

La très chère était nue, et, connaissant mon cœur,
Elle n'avait gardé que ses bijoux sonores . . .[30]

There are – as has been said before – no poems in the French
language more sensual than certain poems in *Les Fleurs du mal*. Yet
Léon Daudet understood that what surprised Nadar, who had been
the lover of Jeanne Duval, 'was the small personal experience of the
author of *Les Fleurs du mal*, in contrast with the unequalled splendour
of his love poems. Because the *frisson nouveau* of which Hugo so rightly
spoke, in reference to Baudelaire, consists of intellectual uncertainty as
much as carnal disorder, Banville's opinion about Baudelaire's frigidity
. . . was the same as Nadar's.'[31] These poems to Jeanne do not express
elegant, romantic regrets, or praise the generality of women. They are
addressed to one, unique woman, whose familiar body captivates the
poet, whose movements enthral him, whose aromatic hair stirs his
recollections and his dreams: a woman whose very coldness stimulates
his desires. There is no doubt of Baudelaire's passion. Yet it is also true
that he never speaks of the consummation of love; he has only the
pleasures of a *voyeur*, the delights of his imagination. It seems as if the
lover's only satisfaction is to contemplate; the pleasures which he
celebrates are those of an artist. These poems reflect the tension of
sexual attraction, but never the fulfilment of desire.

They would alone lead one to question Baudelaire's capacity for
making love, while they proclaim, for all time, his capacity for feeling
it. By some transcendent paradox, his inadequacy as a lover led him
to make amends in his imagination, and to record not only the sexual
excitement, the sensual pleasure which his mistress gave him, but a
whole world of poetic dreams:

Quand, les deux yeux fermés, en un soir chaud d'automne,
Je respire l'odeur de ton sein chaleureux,
Je vois se dérouler des rivages heureux
Qu'éblouissent les feux d'un soleil monotone;

Une île paresseuse où la nature donne
Des arbres singuliers et des fruits savoureux;
Des nommes dont le corps est mince et vigoureux,
Et des femmes dont l'œil par sa franchise étonne.

Guidé par ton odeur vers de charmants climats,
Je vois un port rempli de voiles et de mâts
Encor tout fatigués par la vague marine,

Pendant que le parfum des verts tamariniers,
Qui circule dans l'air et m'enfle la narine,
Se mêle dans mon âme au chant des mariniers.[32]

Baudelaire, as François Porché said, did not discover the sense of smell, but he did more: he created it, because he named it. He walked surrounded by aromas which transformed themselves into landscapes, landscapes which echoed in the distance like muffled horns or sang a melancholy song to him; and if, when he spoke of Jeanne, he spoke of a hemisphere in her hair, it was that for him the world of Jeanne was peopled by dreams.[33] No one, said Jean Prévost, had a more illustrious sense of smell than Baudelaire. For him, an aroma was above all a means of recollection. He was the first to express the secret emotions and the intimacy evoked by fragrances.[34] Jeanne, in *Les Fleurs du mal*, is not Jeanne as she was in life. She is stripped, here, of her triviality. She is magnified, and clothed in symbols.

The cycle of Jeanne Duval, *la Vénus noire*, is followed by that of La Présidente, *la Vénus blanche*: or, in the words of Baudelaire, *la Muse et la Madone*. Baudelaire knew that Apollonie Sabatier was no madonna; but for him, undoubtedly, she realised an essential ideal. She was benevolent and beautiful. Her concern for him gave her an almost maternal dignity. She was a beacon in his darkness; her presence soothed his soul and invigorated his spirit. It enabled him to forget himself. He had magnified Jeanne, and clothed her in symbols; now he magnified Apollonie. She incarnated his ideal; but in this ideal − as in that of Jeanne − there was little of her real self.

Que diras-tu ce soir, pauvre âme solitaire,
Que diras-tu, mon cœur, cœur autrejois flétri,
À la très belle, à la très bonne, à la très chère,
Dont le regard divin t'a soudain refleuri?

> – Nous mettrons notre orgueil à chanter ses louanges:
> Rien ne vaut la douceur de son autorité;
> Sa chair spirituelle a le parfum des Anges,
> Et son œil nous revêt d'un habit de clarté.
>
> Que ce soit dans la nuit et dans la solitude,
> Que ce soit dans la rue et dans la multitude,
> Son fantôme dans l'air danse comme un flambeau.
>
> Parfois il parle et dit: 'Je suis belle, et j'ordonne
> Que pour l'amour de moi vous n'aimiez que le Beau;
> Je suis l'Ange gardien, la Muse et la Madone.'[35]

The cycle of Jeanne Duval had been that of carnal love; the cycle of Mme Sabatier had been that of spiritual love. Baudelaire had written anthems in her praise. The cycle of poems inspired by Marie Daubrun is more difficult to define. Ruff defines it, rightly, as the cycle of equivocal love.[36] Gentleness is there, and jealousy. 'Le Poison' emphasises the power of sexual passion. 'Ciel brouillé' indicates the relation between the woman and the landscape: it suggests the mystery in Marie's eyes, which are sometimes overcast, like skies in autumn; Baudelaire wonders if he will take pleasure in their winter. The poem is the work of a man who feels that his emotional life has entered a period of decline.

'Le Beau Navire' suggests the correspondence between the woman and the ship; it recalls the affection for a sister, or for a child, which one finds in 'L'Invitation au voyage'. The richness and maturity of the experience described in this poem correspond to the richness and maturity of 'La Chevelure', but devotion has taken the place of passion.[37]

> Mon enfant, ma sœur,
> Songe à la douceur
> D'aller là-bas vivre ensemble! . . .[38]

The opening lines of 'L'Invitation au voyage' strangely recall a passage in Shelley's 'Epipsychidion':

> . . . Emily,
> A ship is floating in the harbour now,
> A wind is hovering o'er the mountain's brow;
> There is a path on the sea's azure floor,
> No keel has ever ploughed that path before . . .
> Say, my heart's sister, wilt thou sail with me?[39]

Yet Shelley hopes to take his love to an island in the Aegean; and, for all its magic, it is less enchanting than the nameless land to which

Baudelaire aspires. One may also turn – as, probably, Baudelaire had turned – to *De France en Chine*: Dr Melchior Yvan's account of his travels. He, like Baudelaire, had landed at the Cape of Good Hope, where the houses suggested comfort and luxury, and tranquil happiness, where a multitude of ships stood offshore, where everywhere the visitor saw irrigation canals, bordered with poplar trees.[40] Whatever his sources, Baudelaire transcended them. It is the calculated vagueness of his destination that enthrals us. It is at once specific and anonymous. It exercises our imagination and turns an earthly paradise into a symbol of another world.

> ... Vois sur ces canaux
>   Dormir ces vaisseaux
> Dont l'humeur est vagabonde;
>   C'est pour assouvir
>   Ton moindre désir
> Qu'ils viennent du bout du monde.
>   – Les soleils couchants
>   Revêtent les champs,
> Les canaux, la ville entière,
>   D'hyacinthe et d'or;
>   Le monde s'endort
> Dans une chaude lumière.
>
> Là, tout n'est qu'ordre et beauté,
> Luxe, calme et volupté.[41]

'Mœsta et errabunda' contains several Baudelairean themes: the hated city, spleen, escape, the sea, and nostalgia for the lost paradise of childhood, a desolating longing for innocence. It owes much to the elegant sensuality of Watteau, a little to the amorous reveries of Corot; but, whatever debt he owes to French artists, Baudelaire speaks, again, with his own voice:

> Comme vous êtes loin, paradis parfumé,
> Où sous un clair azur tout n'est qu'amour et joie,
> Où tout ce que l'on aime est digne d'être aimé,
> Où dans la volupté pure le cœur se noie!
> Comme vous êtes loin, paradis parfumé!
>
> Mais le vert paradis des amours enfantines,
> Les courses, les chansons, les baisers, les bouquets,
> Les violons vibrant derrière les collines,
> Avec les brocs de vin, le soir, dans les bosquets,
> – Mais le vert paradis des amours enfantines,

L'innocent paradis, plein de plaisirs furtifs,
Est-il déjà plus loin que l'Inde et que la Chine?
Peut-on le rappeler avec des cris plaintifs,
Et l'animer encor d'une voix argentine,
L'innocent paradis plein de plaisirs furtifs?[42]

Baudelaire was to write that music widened heaven. One might say the same of his poetry, at the height of inspiration.

'La Cloche fêlée' comes from his soul: indeed, at the end of the century, Jules Buisson called Baudelaire 'une âme . . . qui s'était fêlée au premier choc de la vie.'[43] Now, in his sonnet, Baudelaire confides that it is bittersweet to recall ones memories to the sound of bells in the winter mist; but his own soul is cracked, and, when it wants to sing out its anguish, it sounds like the death rattle of a man who has been forgotten by the world.

It is a bitterly despondent sonnet for a poet still in his thirties; and the burden of life is again recorded in the poem: 'J'ai plus de souvenirs que si j'avais mille ans . . .' The poet is a vault which holds more dead than a common grave. He is a boudoir full of melancholy pastels and dated fashions. The endless days drag on, and tedium assumes the proportions of eternity. The living world seems nothing, now, but a granite sphinx, vaguely forbidding, forgotten by geographers, and unknown to mankind. There seems a reminiscence, here, of Shelley's sonnet, 'Ozymandias', of the shattered statue of the king of kings, forgotten in the lone and level sands. When Flaubert acknowledged his copy of *Les Fleurs du mal*, he said he was desolated by this poem.[44]

The burden of life is found, once again, in the poem which follows: 'Je suis comme le roi d'un pays pluvieux . . .' Here again the hero is young and yet very old, and there is no pleasure on earth which can rouse him from his lethargy. In the next poem, the heavy sky weighs upon the soul, and the days seem sadder than the night; the very earth becomes a prison cell. Slow funeral processions pass through the soul. Hope is vanquished, and anguish is triumphant.

Baudelaire's poems on spleen were followed by two poems which recalled the distant paradise of his childhood. The section 'Fleurs du mal', which gave the book its title, was among the most controversial in the collection. Three of the poems spoke of Lesbos and of Lesbianism. It was not surprising that they should do so. Jeanne herself has been suspected of having Lesbian inclinations. Baudelaire was drawn towards perverted women by his erotic imagination. Lesbian love also accorded with his distaste for nature and fecundity; Lesbos was the land of the unnatural and the sterile. There was no complacency in these poems. Baudelaire knew that these women were damned. Morality was therefore not in question.

In 'Les Métamorphoses du vampire', the poet's mistress sucks the very marrow from his bones, and turns into a bag of pus and then a skeleton. The theme of metamorphosis was not uncommon in the Romantic period; one recalls the metamorphosis of Véronique, the sorceress, in Gautier's *Albertus*. Philothée O'Neddy had written 'Succube' in his collection of poems, *Feu et Flamme*. Rémy de Gourmont was later to suggest that Baudelaire's poem was an imitation of the dream of Athalie, in Racine's tragedy;[45] and there are indeed certain parallels between them. Both pieces describe the figure which appears, the movement of sympathy towards it, and the simultaneous, macabre transformation of the apparition. However, Racine presented Jezebel in dream, and Baudelaire presented his dream, or hallucination, as if it were real, in order to increase a sense of fear. Racine's picture, wrote Rémy de Gourmont, 'is less picturesque, and superior by its very sobriety ... Baudelaire's picture is of a morality which, although sarcastic, is very striking; it sneers, ... but its sneer is a warning, and one which Baudelaire gives to himself ... When Baudelaire metamorphosed the dream of Athalie, did he do so consciously, or did he obey a reminiscence?'[46] It seems quite probable that he obeyed a distant reminiscence of Racine.

On Baudelaire's own admission, 'Un Voyage à Cythère' echoes two articles in *L'Artiste* in 1844, in which Gérard de Nerval had recalled an incident in his travels round the Eastern Mediterranean. Sailing near the coast of Cythera, he had noticed on the clifftop what he took to be a monument; it had proved to be a gallows, with a corpse hanging from it.[47]

> ... Le ciel était charmant, la mer était unie;
> Pour moi tout était noir et sanglant désormais,
> Hélas! et j'avais, comme en un suaire épais,
> Le cœur enseveli dans cette allégorie.
>
> Dans ton île, ô Vénus! je n'ai trouvé debout
> Qu'un gibet symbolique où pendait mon image ...
> – Ah! Seigneur! donnez-moi la force et le courage
> De contempler mon cœur et mon corps sans dégoût![48]

Maurice Barrès found it strange – despite the poet's syphilis – that Baudelaire 'should have no esteem for himself, for his body, for his soul. Where', he asked, 'can he find support? It is a first stage in Christianity.'[49]

The next group of poems in *Les Fleurs du mal* were to disturb that assumption. In 'Le Reniement de Saint Pierre', Baudelaire took up the familiar theme of God the tyrant, Who rejoices in His creatures' suffering. To this he joined a second theme, that of the empty Heavens, where God is absent or even dead. This theme had been used by Vigny in *Le Mont des Oliviers*, and by Nerval in *Le Christ aux Oliviers*. For them, as for Baudelaire, Christ was indeed only the Son of Man. Baudelaire's originality did not lie in the resumption of these themes, but in the conclusion, when he spoke of remorse. Perhaps the Son of Man regretted that he had deceived mankind. This suggestion of regret gave a quite new meaning to St Peter's denial. The denial was not inspired by cowardice; it was the revenge of a man who was undeceived.[50]

In 'Les Litanies de Satan', Baudelaire echoed Milton's admiration for Satan in *Paradise Lost*, an admiration which Shelley had shared in his *Defence of Poetry*. In these litanies, which recall the litanies of black masses, Baudelaire proclaims his admiration and his compassion for the Devil. He leaves him Prince of the Damned, and he damns himself with him.

A group of poems on wine was followed by three poems on death. In 'La Mort des Pauvres', the poor aspire to death as the consolation for life, the hope of eternal comfort. 'La Mort des Pauvres' is the masterpiece of that art of transfiguration, of changing the values of things, which we call the poetic fiat. It is also the masterpiece of Baudelaire's charity.[51] In 'La Mort des Artistes', the artist aspires to death as the beginning of a new creative life.

On 25 June 1857, *Les Fleurs du mal* was put on sale at three francs a copy. Thirteen hundred copies were printed.

The effect was, as Banville said, 'immense, prodigious, unexpected, mingled with admiration and with some indefinable anxious fear.'[52] A whole side of human nature, until then excluded from the domain of art, was shown for the first time. 'The very title, *Les Fleurs du mal*, is', wrote Léon Daudet, 'a symbol, and it does not mean, as people have believed, the flowerbed of Satan, but the sad and splendid flowering of physical and moral suffering.'[53] *Les Fleurs du mal* was not merely the autobiography of a soul; it was the autobiography of *homo duplex*, divided modern man.

More than a century after its publication, a critic could maintain: 'European poetry is different after 1857. It is not only that this collection has been read and thought about by most of the great European poets who have followed, but also that the very substance of the experience which is formulated in *Les Fleurs du mal* has increasingly revealed itself to be the central experience of modernity.'[54]

55

On 4 July 1857, Monsieur Lanier (his Christian name has not come down to us) wrote to Malassis. He was a partner in Julien, Lanier, Cosnard & Cie, printers and booksellers in the rue de Buci; they specialised in religious works, and acted – somewhat surprisingly – as depositary for the books which were published by Malassis and De Broise. Lanier warned Malassis that a rumour was spreading that *Les Fleurs du mal* would be seized.[1] Next day, on the front page, *Le Figaro* carried an article by Gustave Bourdin, attacking Baudelaire. Bourdin, once a student of architecture, was now an insignificant journalist, but he was a son-in-law of Jean-Hippolyte de Villemessant, who was the editor of the paper.[2] Émile Bergerat, the dramatist and journalist, was one day to remember him kindly: 'Unlike his father-in-law, so surly to those who bore the lyre, the excellent Bourdin, a most cultivated man, was passionately fond of the pastimes of the Pindus . . .'[3] However good the impression which he made in later years, his behaviour now was odious. While he recognised some of the poems as 'masterpieces of passion, art and poetry', he specified others which, in his judgment, merited legal proceedings. Baudelaire believed that Bourdin largely ensured that *Les Fleurs du mal* would be brought to court.[4]

In his comments to Eugène Crépet, Asselineau later wrote:

B. was always convinced that this accusatory note, signed G. Bourdin, had come from the Minister of the Interior. Indeed, one day, when he was at the École de natation, having met [Bourdin] at the café, he was tempted, so he told me, to take advantage of the fact that he, [Bourdin], was naked, and that he, Baudelaire, was dressed and booted, to inflict corporal punishment upon him. One must admit that B's suggestion may be exaggerated, but that it did not lack credibility, because *Le Figaro* was generally considered to be protected by the Minister, and it was, moreover, quite capable of rendering such services.[5]

On 6 July, an anonymous article in the *Journal de Bruxelles*, written in fact by Armand de Pontmartin, defender of the Church and of morality, predicted that there would be a court case about *Les Fleurs du mal*. Leconte de Lisle learned of the seizure of the book, but he waited for five days before he told Oscar de Watteville, of the Ministry of Public Instruction, who in turn informed Baudelaire.[6] On 7 July, the Attorney-General received a letter about the book from the Minister of the Interior. The Director of the Sûreté publique informed the Parquet that the author of *Les Fleurs du mal* had committed an offence against public morals. Next morning, Malassis 'had a letter from père Lanier, informing us that the nature of the books we publish prevents

him henceforward from putting his staff at our disposal for the sale.'[7]
To complicate matters, De Broise was ill, there was much to do at the
printing works, and both he and Malassis were kept in Alençon.

The seizure of *Les Fleurs du mal*, the prospect of its being brought to
court, were not the only reasons for Baudelaire's anxiety. Mme Aupick,
recently widowed, was lost in desolation, overcome by her new solitude,
and constantly concerned about her son. On 9 July he assured her:

> You need have no anxiety at all about me. It is you yourself who cause
> me anxiety, and the most acute anxiety, and certainly the letter you sent
> me, absolutely full of desolation, was not made to soothe me. If you give
> way like this, you will be ill, and that will be the worst of misfortunes and,
> for me, the most unbearable anxiety. I want you not only to look for
> diversions, but to have new pleasures . . .
>
> As for my silence, there is no reason for it, except one of those languors
> which, to my great dishonour, sometimes overcome me, and prevent me
> not only from devoting myself to my work but even from fulfilling the
> simplest duties. Besides, I wanted not just to write to you, but at the same
> time to send you your prayer-book and my book of poetry.
>
> The prayer-book is not quite ready . . .
>
> As for the Poems (which appeared a fortnight ago), I had intended, at
> first, as you know, to show them to you. But, as I thought more about it,
> it seemed to me that, after all, as you would hear people talk about them,
> at least through the reviews that I should send you, modesty on my part
> would be as ridiculous as prudery on yours. I have had sixteen personal
> copies on ordinary paper, and four on laid paper. I have kept one of the
> latter for you, and, if you have not received it yet, that is because I wanted
> to send it to you bound.[8]

Then, with unusual passion, an assurance which he did not often
express, Baudelaire himself set down his creed, assessed *Les Fleurs du
mal*, and defiantly affirmed his status:

> You know that I have always considered that literature and the arts pursue
> an aim independent of morality. Beauty of conception and style is enough
> for me. But this book, whose title: *Fleurs du mal*, – says everything, is clad,
> as you will see, in a cold and sinister beauty. It was created with rage and
> patience. Besides, the proof of its positive worth is in all the ill that they
> speak of it. The book enrages people. Moreover, since I was terrified
> myself of the horror that I should inspire, I cut out a third from the proofs.
> They deny me everything, the spirit of invention and even a knowledge
> of the French language. I don't care a rap about all these imbeciles, and
> I know that this book, with its virtues and its faults, will make its way in
> the memory of the lettered public, beside the best poems of V. Hugo, Th.
> Gautier and even Byron.[9]

His literary creed, his belief in his enduring fame, were unlikely, as he
knew, to be appreciated in Honfleur. 'Just one piece of advice,' he

added. 'Since you live with the Émon family [*sic*], don't let the book be found in Mlle Émon's hands. As for the curé, whom no doubt you receive, you can show it to him. He will think that I am damned, and he won't dare tell you so. They had spread the rumour that I was going to be prosecuted; but this won't happen.'[10]

Two days later, nonetheless, Baudelaire asked Malassis to hide the whole edition of *Les Fleurs du mal*.

> You should have 900 copies in sheets. There were still 100 at Lanier's; these gentlemen seemed quite astonished that I should want to save 50 of them. I have put them in a safe place [no doubt with Asselineau], and I have signed a receipt. So there are 50 left to feed the Cerberus Justice.
>
> That's what comes of sending *copies* to LE FIGARO!!!!
>
> That's what happens when one doesn't want *to launch* a book properly. If you had done all that needed to be done, at least we should have the consolation of having sold the edition in three weeks, and we should just have the glory of a lawsuit, which it is easy to get out of, anyway.
>
> You will receive this letter in time, I hope. It will leave tonight, you will get it at 4 o'clock tomorrow. The seizure has not yet taken place . . .
>
> I am convinced that this misadventure has only occurred as a result of the article in *Le Figaro*, and of idle gossip. The trouble has been caused by fear . . .'[11]

That day, although it was '*the terrible Sunday*' when Gautier wrote his weekly article for *Le Moniteur universel*, Baudelaire begged him for a two-minute audience.[12] He knew of his official connections, and no doubt he wanted his help. On 12 July, he wrote to his mother: 'I am overwhelmed by torments.'[13]

It was not surprising that he felt tormented. That day, once again, *Le Figaro* attacked *Les Fleurs du mal*. 'Everything in it which is not hideous is incomprehensible,' wrote J. Habans, 'everything one understands is putrid . . .'[14] That day, Baudelaire himself sent a note to Alfred Delvau, editor-in-chief of the newly founded paper *Le Rabelais*, and asked him not to publish a review immediately; he was afraid that it might be unfavourable, and attract the seizure of the book.[15] Delvau postponed the publication of his article; it was, in fact, to be highly sympathetic. Baudelaire also addressed himself to Édouard Thierry. A contributor to *Le Moniteur universel*, Thierry was a librarian at the Bibliothèque de l'Arsenal, and, two years later, he was to be appointed Administrator-General of the Comédie-Française.

> A few days ago, by chance, I met Turgan [Baudelaire explained to him, now], and asked him if there would be an article on *Les Fleurs du mal*. He answered: *Yes, of course*.
>
> To begin with, is that definite?

If it is, I address myself to you personally to get this article in as soon
as possible. Would it be possible on Tuesday, that is to say the day after
tomorrow? You would do me a rare favour, I assure you, because I am
slandered beyond all measure. I really need, and need at once, an
intelligent, cultivated man who will say that there are some good lines in
French in *Les Fleurs du mal*.[16]

Asselineau recalled how, on 13 July, he accompanied Baudelaire to *Le
Moniteur universel* and waited there, on the pavement on the quai
Voltaire, until Turgan returned from his call on Achille Fould.[17] The
Minister of State had passed Thierry's review. As Baudelaire had
hoped, it appeared next day. Thierry called *Les Fleurs du mal* 'a
masterpiece of savage realism, a book of the greatest style, and of a
magisterial ferocity'. Baudelaire, he said, 'had created an Eden out of
Hell, where Death walks with her sister, Sensuality . . . He has written
the ultimate truth . . . *Les Fleurs du mal* have a dizzying scent.' Thierry
defended Baudelaire against the accusation of immorality, and he set
Les Fleurs du mal 'under the stern aegis of Dante'.[18]

All that I can offer you [wrote Baudelaire], as a token of my gratitude, is
this *last* copy on fine paper . . .
  Oh, you have avenged me for the rascals! . . .
  Your article is full of understanding and of politics. How grateful I am
to you for insisting on that immeasurable sadness, which is in fact the only
morality of the book!
  Without you, no one might have dared to talk about my literary worth,
and everyone would only have talked about the horror of the themes . . .
  I grasp your hand with all the warmth of a man who knows what he
owes you![19]

There was a more distinguished admirer. Baudelaire had met Flaubert
in the rue Frochot before the summer of 1857; but on 13 July, from
Croisset, Flaubert had sent him the first of his letters which was to
survive:

My dear friend,
  To begin with, I devoured your book from beginning to end, like a cook
devours a serial story; and now, for the last week, I have been re-reading
it, word by word, and, frankly, it delights me.
  You have found the way to rejuvenate Romanticism. You are not like
anyone else (which is the first of all the qualities).
  The originality of the style flows from the conception. The phrase is
stuffed with the idea, full to bursting point.
  I like your sharpness, with its delicacies of language, which set it off like
damascening on a fine blade . . .
  In brief, what pleases me above all in your book, is that Art predom-
inates in it. And then you sing of the flesh without loving it, in a sad,

detached way, which is sympathetic to me. You are as unyielding as marble, and as penetrating as an English mist.[20]

'I do not think,' Charles du Bos observed, many years later, 'that anyone has ever better expressed what makes Baudelaire unique among French poets.'[21]

On 15 July, the *Journal de Bruxelles* published an angry attack on *Les Fleurs du mal*. 'Nothing can give you an idea of the tissue of baseness and obscenity that this book contains . . . Even quotations are impossible for a decent writer.'[22] On 17 July, the Parquet ordered that *Les Fleurs du mal* should be seized. That day, out of curiosity, Baudelaire attended the funeral of Béranger. To Roger de Beauvoir, who observed the black crepe on his hat, he explained: 'Make no mistake. I am in mourning for *Les Fleurs du mal*.'[23]

On about 20 July, he addressed himself to Achille Fould, the Minister of State. It was on Fould that *Le Moniteur universel* depended, as the official newspaper of the Second Empire. 'Monsieur le Ministre,' wrote Baudelaire, '. . . why should I not tell you candidly that I am asking you for your protection, so far as it is possible to obtain it? I ask you because, through your intellect, even more than your position, you find yourself the natural protector of Literature and the Arts.'[24]

On 20 July, Baudelaire sent a note to the absent Malassis: 'I really need to know at once which day you will be in Paris. No seizure *here* – what about the seizure in Alençon?'[25] The book had in fact been seized at the printer's, in Alençon, and at the publisher's in Paris; but, on 13 July, Malassis had sent two hundred copies to be disposed of in Paris, unknown to the authorities.[26] Three Ministers were now involved in the case: Fould, the Minister of State, Abbatucci, Minister of Justice, and Billault, Minister of the Interior.

56

Some time between 24 and 27 July, Baudelaire appeared before the examining magistrate. The magistrate was benevolent, but he questioned him for three hours. Late in July, Barbey d'Aurevilly offered to send Baudelaire his article on *Les Fleurs du mal*. *Le Pays* had refused to publish it; Billault had forbidden them to do so, or even to discuss Baudelaire. Barbey thought that the article might serve in his friend's defence.[1] On 27 July, Baudelaire told his mother: '*I need a woman.*

Perhaps there might be a way of involving Princess Mathilde in this affair; but I am racking my brains in vain to find it . . .'[2]

It was curious that Baudelaire did not think of the *parfait magicien ès lettres françaises*, to whom he had dedicated *Les Fleurs du mal*. Gautier was an assiduous and much loved guest of Notre-Dame-des-Arts. It was still more curious that Baudelaire did not think of Sainte-Beuve. He, above all, might have been an intermediary, for he advised the princess on her patronage. He was, one day, to be outraged at the thought that Catulle Mendès might lose a sinecure because he had been imprisoned for offending public morals.[3]

In some ways, Baudelaire himself understood the significance of his prosecution. He begged his mother 'only to consider this scandal (which is causing a real stir in Paris) as the foundation of my fortune.'[4] It has to be said that Baudelaire was not entirely innocent. He guessed, if he did not know, the risks he ran. He was genuinely shocked by the prosecution, he was angry that there was a legal case, and yet he had no more chosen to avoid it than he had chosen to avoid the *conseil judiciaire*.

Late in July, he sent a signed copy of *Les Fleurs du mal* to Piétri, the Prefect of Police. He also sent a copy to Gustave Chaix d'Est-Ange, who had agreed to be his advocate. Chaix d'Est-Ange seemed a natural choice. His father, Louis-Adolphe Chaix d'Est-Ange, was soon to be Imperial Procurator-General; he himself had recently won Flaubert an acquittal in the case of *Madame Bovary*. Baudelaire urged him to remind the court of the 'monstrosities' which Lamartine had published in *La Chute d'un ange*, and the obscenities in Béranger's *Le Bon Dieu* and *Margot*.[5] It was only a few days since Béranger had died, and he had been accorded a national funeral. 'If you are obliged to defend yourself,' Veuillot had observed to Baudelaire, 'say that when a whole nation enquires about this poor wretch's health, they have no right to prosecute the author of *Les Fleurs du mal*.'[6] It was impressive support from a militant Roman Catholic writer.

On 4 August, in Brussels, *L'Indépendance belge* gave details of the seizure of the book, and of the imminent prosecution; it declared, surprisingly, that Sainte-Beuve had been very active in Baudelaire's defence. On 14 August, from Croisset, Flaubert wrote: 'I have just heard that you are being prosecuted because of your book . . . This is something new: to prosecute a book of poetry! Until now the magistrates left poetry completely in peace. I am greatly shocked.'[7]

Flaubert, more than anyone, understood Baudelaire's position. He had recently been prosecuted for alleged offences against public morals in *Madame Bovary*. He and Baudelaire lived under a régime of lamentable prudery. In a single year, it attempted to condemn the novel and the book of poetry which many now consider among the paramount works in nineteenth-century French literature. The Second Empire was at times a misguided age. 'When you have finished Lord Byron,' so the critic Ximénès Doudan had recently enquired of a correspondent, 'will you read that wretched book they call *Madame Bovary*? It isn't the same kind of literature [*sic*]. I don't know what they're thinking of, the young people of today, who find it beautiful . . . It would have made Racine and Voltaire violently sick.'[8]

On 17 August, Baudelaire saw his advocate. That day, Mme Veuve Dondey-Duprey published *Articles justificatifs pour Charles Baudelaire, auteur des FLEURS DU MAL*; the pamphlet included a note by Baudelaire himself and reviews by Édouard Thierry, Frédéric Dulamon, Barbey d'Aurevilly and Charles Asselineau.[9] Barbey d'Aurevilly asked Baudelaire to send him copies of the articles, which he would give to his friend Raymond Brucker. Brucker, himself a man of letters, would then show them to his friend Ernest Pinard, the advocate for the prosecution, to influence him in the poet's favour.[10]

On 20 July, Baudelaire had had a letter from Sainte-Beuve, offering him some arguments for the preparation of his defence.[11] Chaix d'Est-Ange was anxious for permission to use this letter. 'Oh, dear friend, I have something very serious, very important to ask you,' Baudelaire confessed to the critic on 18 August. '. . . I should really be very glad if you could grant me a brief conversation of three minutes today.'[12] He seems to have gone to the rue Montparnasse. Sainte-Beuve simply handed him some notes on possible lines of argument: *Petits moyens de défense tels que je les conçois.*

'I should have a great deal to write about Baudelaire,' Asselineau confided, later, 'although I have written his Life.'[13] In fact he left some unpublished comments on Sainte-Beuve's behaviour.

Among the guarantees on which B. could depend, the most decisive was that of Sainte-Beuve, who had been his friend for a long time and was very ready to help him [*sic*]. Unfortunately an unlucky precedent prevented him from doing so. A little while earlier, M. Billau[l]t, then Minister of the Interior, had brought *Mad. Bovary* before the courts, and they had acquitted it. When judgment had been given, S.B. had discussed the book, and praised it, in the *Moniteur*. This article had caused a stir even in the Conseil des Ministres. 'What', so M. Billau[l]t said, 'a book that I'd had before the courts, and it is praised in the official newspaper! etc.' S.B. had no trouble in making B. understand that it was difficult to repeat the offence. There remained M. Thierry, entrusted with the literary column, and he could quite well give his opinions before judgment was passed. 'Let M. Thierry write his article,' said Sainte-Beuve. 'He is a poet and he will be very good for you. Then, when the commotion is over,

I shall come back to you in a general article.' Thierry's article therefore became Baudelaire's sheet-anchor.[14]

•

Thierry had published a powerful and perceptive tribute in *Le Moniteur universel*. Sainte-Beuve did not write the article he promised.

No doubt, as an official critic, he was in a delicate position; but he showed extraordinary meanness. He did not authorise Baudelaire to publish his letter. He himself only published it in full when Baudelaire was dead, in a furtive appendix to the *Lundis*.

In *Baudelaire et Sainte-Beuve*, Fernand Vandérem gave a likely explanation of his conduct.[15] In 1829, Sainte-Beuve had published *Vie, Poésies et Pensées de Joseph Delorme*; the following year he had published *Les Consolations*. He had long understood that he had been surpassed as a poet. His fellow Romantics had eclipsed him, and he had missed no opportunities to disparage them. The new generation of writers baffled him. He overlooked Leconte de Lisle, and he was to ignore the young Verlaine. Perhaps he failed to appreciate the importance of Baudelaire. More probably he appreciated his stature all too well.

Maxime Rude recalled how, at the time of the publication of *Les Fleurs du mal*, Baudelaire had chanced to encounter the critic in the Palais-Royal, and he had asked him directly: 'Monsieur Sainte-Beuve, aren't you going to bring yourself to talk about me?' Sainte-Beuve had answered deviously: 'You can understand that I hesitate. I should look as if I were praising myself.'[16] The answer was a reference to the *Poésies de Joseph Delorme*, and to their influence on Baudelaire. It was a characteristic means of evasion. Baudelaire understood this, but he also understood Sainte-Beuve's standing in literature, and he knew that it was wiser not to quarrel with him.

Meanwhile, on 18 August, the day he asked Sainte-Beuve for a moment's conversation, Baudelaire also wrote a letter of much greater significance. That day he sent Mme Sabatier a copy of *Les Fleurs du mal*. It was printed on laid paper, and bound by Lortic in bright green half morocco. Apart from the colour of the binding, the copy was identical to the one which he intended for his mother. On the fly-leaf he had written: 'À la Très belle, à la Très bonne, à la Très Chère.'[17]

No doubt La Présidente had known the identity of her admirer since the summer of 1855, when he had published three of her poems in the *Revue des Deux Mondes*. She may well have known it earlier, thanks to her literary friends, or to the recognition of his writing, or to her own feminine instinct. Both she and Baudelaire had remained silent about the poems, and for years they had maintained a pretence of ignorance. The pretence was tactful, but it had been futile. If Mme Sabatier's younger sister knew that Baudelaire was in love with Apollonie, and knew that his letters to her were 'wonderful', the authorship of the poems had long been *un secret de Polichinelle*. Now, however, on 18 August, for the first time, after five years, he himself discarded his anonymity:

Chère Madame,
   ... This is the first time that I have written to you in my own hand. If I were not overwhelmed by affairs and by correspondence (the hearing is the day after tomorrow), I should take advantage of this occasion to ask your forgiveness for so many follies, so much childishness. But, anyway, haven't you taken enough revenge, especially with your young sister? Oh, the little monster! She struck me dumb one day when we met, and she let out a great burst of laughter in my face, and said to me: '*Are you still in love with my sister, and are you still writing her wonderful letters?*' I understood that, in the first place, when I wanted to conceal myself, I concealed myself very badly, and then that your enchanting face disguised a most uncharitable spirit. Blackguards *fall in love*, but poets *idolize*, and your sister is hardly made, I think, to understand the things which are eternal.
   Allow me, then, at the risk of amusing you, too, to renew those declarations which amused that little madcap so much. Imagine an amalgam of reverie, sympathy, respect, and a thousand childish things full of gravity, and you will have something like this very real feeling which I cannot describe any better.
   To forget you is impossible. They say that there are poets who have lived all their lives with their eyes fixed on a beloved image. I believe, in fact (but I am too biassed), *that fidelity is a sign of genius*.
   You are more than an image loved and dreamed of, you are my *superstition*. When I do something stupid, I say to myself: *My God! If she knew!* When I do something good, I say to myself: *That is something which brings me closer to her — in spirit* ...
   I saw my judges last Thursday. I shan't say that they aren't handsome: they are abominably ugly, and their souls must resemble their faces.
   Flaubert had the Empress in his favour. I need a woman. And, a few days ago, the bizarre thought took hold of me that, perhaps through acquaintances and perhaps through complex channels, you could get a word of sense to reach one of those crude minds.
   The hearing is on Thursday morning, the day after tomorrow.
   The monsters are called:

President	Dupaty
Imperial Procurator	Pinard (formidable)
Judges	Delesvaux
	De Ponton d'Amécourt
	Nacquart

Court 6.
   I want to leave all these trivialities aside.
   Remember that someone is thinking of you, that his thoughts are never trivial at all, and that he slightly begrudges you your mischievous *gaiety*.
   I beg you most ardently to keep henceforward for yourself everything that I may

confide in you. You are my usual Company, and you are my Secret. It is
this intimacy, in which I have given myself the cue for so long, which has
emboldened me to use such a familiar tone.

Farewell, chère Madame, I kiss your hands with all my Devotion.

                                                    CHARLES BAUDELAIRE
All the poems between page 84 and page 105 belong to you.[18]

It is said that, through her old friend Charles Jalabert, then painting
his second portrait of the judge, Mme Sabatier was given an introduction to De Belleyme, the president of the court of first instance. 'This
magistrate, who loved art and artists, received her petition with the
most gracious kindness, but he was obliged to observe that time was
too short to act with any hope. It was the eve of the hearing.'[19] Mme
Sabatier did more than approach De Belleyme. On 19 August, in
answer to Baudelaire's letter, she wrote to him to say that she loved
him.[20]

57

On 20 August, Baudelaire appeared before the sixth court of the
Tribunal de la Seine. The advocate for the prosecution, Ernest Pinard,
was one day to be Minister of the Interior; but his true claim to
remembrance was that he was chosen to condemn two of the master-
works in French literature. On 29 January, he had urged the court to
condemn Flaubert for offending public morality in *Madame Bovary*. On
7 February, just as Baudelaire was delivering the manuscript of *Les
Fleurs du mal* to Malassis, Flaubert was acquitted. 'I maintained that we
should keep to the original judgment,' remembered Pinard, 'censuring
the incriminated passages, without recognising that they constituted an
offence . . . We had to prevent a more resounding acquittal.'[1] Pinard
was no doubt anxious to prevent a still more resounding acquittal of
Baudelaire. In his memoirs, where he gave a confused account of
events, he also made it clear that there were political considerations.
Flaubert was 'an assiduous and welcome guest in the salons of Princess
Mathilde.'[2] Baudelaire had 'many friends in the republican camp.'[3]
The inference was unmistakable.

Yet perhaps the earlier acquittal weakened Pinard's speech for the
prosecution of *Les Fleurs du mal*. As Pierre Dufay would one day write,
his indictment was half-hearted, and he did not seem to feel that he
was on sure ground.[4]

To prosecute a book for offending public morality is always [so Pinard explained] a delicate matter. If the prosecution fails, one creates a triumph, almost a pedestal, for the author; if it succeeds, one has assumed the appearance of a persecutor.

Let me add that, in the present case, the author comes before you protected by writers of distinction, serious critics whose testimony complicates the task of the public prosecutor even further.

And yet, gentlemen, I do not hesitate to fulfil it. It is not the man whom we have to judge, it is his work. It is not the result of the prosecution which concerns me, it is only the question of knowing if it is justified.[5]

Guided by Bourdin's article, M. Pinard then dissected *Les Fleurs du mal*, and indicated the passages which he felt to be immoral. He condemned 'Les Bijoux', 'Le Léthé', 'Lesbos', and 'Les Femmes damnées'.[6] As Pierre Dufay was to observe, M. Pinard could discover obscenity where it did not exist, and where he himself created it.[7] Predictably he also found offences against religion, 'that great Christian morality which is in truth the only basis of our public morals.'[8] He therefore condemned 'Le Reniement de Saint Pierre', as *Le Figaro* had suggested, and, for good measure, 'Abel et Caïn', 'Les Litanies de Satan' and 'Le Vin de l'assassin'. 'An offence to public morality [continued M. Pinard]: this I find incontestably proved . . . in all these poems, the author tries to force each situation as if he were laying a wager to give senses to those who no longer feel. You, gentlemen, who are the judges, only have to choose. The choice is easy, because the offence is almost everywhere.'[9] The court was, in fact, to make its choice, and not to condemn some of the poems which he had suggested to them. 'Be merciful to Baudelaire,' Pinard concluded. 'He is an unquiet and unbalanced soul. Be merciful to the printers, who are taking cover behind the author. But do condemn certain poems in the book, and thereby give a warning which has become essential.'[10]

For Gustave Chaix d'Est-Ange, who defended Baudelaire, the poet was not 'unquiet and unbalanced', but 'a great artist and a deep and impassioned poet', whose gifts had already been officially recognised.[11] 'He is more [insisted Chaix d'Est-Ange]: he is a man of integrity, and that is why he is an artist of conviction . . . Seriously, can his intentions be in question? And can you hesitate for a moment about the aim that he has pursued and about the end that he has chosen?'[12]

Les Fleurs du mal, said Chaix d'Est-Ange, had been intended to inspire a hatred of evil; it castigated sin like a priest. Baudelaire was not original in displaying vice in order to condemn it; Molière had done the same. It was dangerous to judge a whole work by a few isolated poems, by a few expressions taken here and there and skilfully juxtaposed. A passage from *Harmonies poétiques* might be called *Blasphème* or *Malédiction* rather than *Désespoir*; yet who had considered prosecuting Lamartine for offences against religious morality? Chaix d'Est-Ange read passages from Musset and Béranger and, finally, the most explicit passages from *Mademoiselle de Maupin*. Baudelaire's work, he ended, was no more audacious than other work which was printed and reprinted every day. 'I am sure that you would not want to strike this true gentleman, this great artist.'[13]

Pinard was an established lawyer of thirty-five. Chaix d'Est-Ange was twenty-four, and he lacked experience. Though he was concerned with two cases remarkable in literary history, he was not to make his name at the Paris Bar. He was only his father's son, and he was to leave no trace in the *Dictionnaire de biographie française*. Baudelaire's friends seem, nonetheless, to have been unduly harsh about his defence. Malassis considered it 'ridiculous.'[14] Since Baudelaire had to plead not guilty, and he had chosen this means of defending himself, his advocate had been obliged to conform. In *Les Fleurs du mal*, so Baudelaire said later, he had put all his heart, all his affection, all his religion, all his hate;[15] but through them he had sought for truth and beauty. *Les Fleurs du mal* had indeed been written in good faith.

The judges' verdict, so it seems, exceeded even M. Pinard's hopes. The charge of offending religious morality was set aside. Six incriminated poems were suppressed, and, by order, they were not to be republished. Baudelaire was sentenced to a fine of 300 francs, Malassis and De Broise to a fine of 100 francs apiece for offending public morality. The judges found attenuating circumstances, and article 463 of the penal code saved Baudelaire from imprisonment.

The sentence was still excessive; and this condemnation, which he was always to consider as a misunderstanding, affected Baudelaire more than might have been expected. His book was deprived of six of the poems which he most cherished. The architecture of the work was damaged. The condemnation saddened and offended him. Asselineau asked him if he had expected an acquittal. 'I expected', answered Baudelaire, 'that they would make me honourable amends.'[16]

58

The condemnation of *Les Fleurs du mal* caused outrage in the world of literature; yet, as the Marquis de Custine observed to Barbey d'Aurevilly, Baudelaire had been '*condemned but not judged*.'[1] Champfleury wrote that, at this hearing, 'the artist won even the votes of his adversaries. The imperial advocate himself pronounced . . . an indictment which was enthusiastic rather than accusing. The tribunal seemed to understand that it was concerned with a true poet.'[2] Hippolyte Babou was of the same opinion. On 21 August, he had written to Malassis: 'You must have heard of the fatal verdict . . . Your best defender, yours and Baudelaire's, was M. Pinard, the imperial advocate.'[3]

Malassis himself had prudently remained in Alençon. His outspoken comments, and his political past, could only have prejudiced the court against him. He now told Asselineau that he would bury the entire edition of *Les Fleurs du mal* rather than reprint it in accordance with the court's decisions. In fact, two hundred copies, which remained from the print run of a thousand, were modified in accordance with the verdict.[4] Malassis sold off copies in a mutilated form, with blank sheets inserted to replace the poems which had been suppressed, or even stubs of pages left where they had been cut away. Baudelaire begged him not to continue this 'absurd surgical operation'.[5] However, in one form or another, all the copies of the book seem to have been sold in the year that followed. In a catalogue published in August 1858, Malassis announced that it was out of print.[6]

Meanwhile, on 23 August 1857, still unaware of the tribunal's decision, Flaubert wrote to Baudelaire: 'Keep me informed about your affair, if it doesn't bore you too much. I am as interested as if it concerned me, personally. This prosecution is idiotic. It revolts me.'[7]

Baudelaire had had another eminent supporter. In March, he had asked Turgan about the need to be protected, should his book prove to be dangerous. 'Get acquainted with Mérimée,' Turgan had answered. 'He is all-powerful in such matters.'[8] Possibly Baudelaire had written to him. When it became known that he was going to be prosecuted, Mérimée had quietly gone to the Minister of Justice, and had tried, in vain, to persuade him to drop the case. 'I took certain steps on that occasion,' he told Banville years later, 'and the Minister of Justice bullied me a little, but he softened in the end . . .'[9] As Mérimée's biographer writes, he was 'given to acts of disinterested charity, but liked to do them as stealthily as possible, for fear of being thought sentimental. So when Mme de la Rochejaquelein mentioned that she had heard that he had intervened on Baudelaire's behalf, he immediately denigrated *Les Fleurs du mal*, and invented contorted excuses for his own kindness.'[10]

Mérimée's relations with Baudelaire were always to be curious. On two occasions, Baudelaire asked him for advice; no doubt they met, for Mérimée later professed to keep 'a very vivid memory of the originality of his character.'[11] During Baudelaire's last illness, Mérimée supported the petition to give him a Government grant. Yet, in private, he was always dismissive. After Baudelaire's death, he was sent the *Œuvres complètes*, which, he said, enraged him. Baudelaire, he informed a correspondent, had written poems 'which had no merit except that of offending public morals. At the moment, they are making him into a misunderstood man of genius.'[12]

Others were more appreciative. On 30 August, from Hauteville House, in Guernsey, Hugo wrote to Baudelaire: 'Your *fleurs du mal* shine and dazzle like stars . . . I applaud your vigorous spirit with all my might . . . You have just received one of the rare distinctions which the present régime can bestow. What it calls its justice has condemned you in the name of what it calls its morality. That is a crown the more.'[13]

Baudelaire did not only suffer from the emotional strain of prosecution; his monthly allowance of 200 francs, issued to him by Ancelle, made the fine of 300 francs hard to contemplate. Late in August, he went to see Ernest Pinard, the advocate for the prosecution, and Marc-Antoine Vaïsse, procurator-general at the Cour de Paris. To Malassis he wrote: 'I should have been glad to settle with you, this evening, the line of conduct we are going to follow if I don't appeal. If I agree to submit at once, there will be remission of the fine.'[14]

Baudelaire did not appeal. The question of remission continued for some months. On 6 November, no doubt recalling her support of Flaubert in the recent case of *Madame Bovary*, he addressed himself to the Empress.[15] On 20 January 1858, the Minister of Justice reduced the fine from 300 francs to 50 francs.[16]

Nearly a century later, on 11 May 1949, after years of sporadic attempts to reverse the judgment, it was finally quashed, and Baudelaire was officially vindicated; henceforward the six banned poems could legally appear in *Les Fleurs du mal*.[17]

Meanwhile, in the late summer of 1857, Baudelaire had still to experience one of the saddest moments in his life.

PART FOUR

The Widow's Son

1857–1864

59

Mme Sabatier's letter of 19 August, and a second letter she wrote to Baudelaire, have not, alas, survived; nor have the many other letters which she sent him. Their fate is evident from a note by Jacques Crépet, which remains among the Crépet Papers. 'Mme Sabatier's letters to Baudelaire [were] with Ancelle. This is clear from a note from Eugène Crépet to Narc [?]. Dated 11–vi–86. They must have been inadvertently destroyed.'[1] Before they were destroyed, it seems, Eugène Crépet had taken copies; Jacques Crépet found them in his father's dossier and, on 3 March 1902, he published the few extracts that we know. As he explained in *Le Journal*, he had chosen them 'from among many others.'[2] There are today no letters from Mme Sabatier among the Crépet Papers. It is hard to believe that either of the Crépets would have destroyed an archive of such importance; but the copies of the letters, like the originals, have disappeared. Their disappearance is a grievous loss to students of Baudelaire and to admirers of La Présidente. It leaves an episode of deep significance permanently unexplained, a cardinal relationship permanently misunderstood. Moreover, it is now impossible to judge the exact sequence of events; for, while many letters have vanished, the few that we know have been incompletely quoted, and none of them has been dated.

It is, however, clear that, for the first time in her life, Apollonie Sabatier found herself loved by a man who demanded nothing in return. She had known the largely physical love of Mosselman, the vulgarity of the Clésinger sculptures; but though Mosselman had finally lived apart from his wife, and though, for the past year, he had been a widower, there is no record that he thought of marrying his mistress. Now she had inspired devotion of a quite different order. With 'an absolute lack of modesty', she wrote to Baudelaire from her heart. 'It seems to me that I have belonged to you since the first day I saw you. Do what you will about it, I am yours, body, heart and soul.'[3]

If this was the first of her letters to him, it is strange that Baudelaire did not answer her confession in writing. Instead, on the evening of 20 August, the day of the hearing, or, more probably, on 27 August, he called at the rue Frochot. His devotion to her was plain.

Today [she wrote, afterwards], I am more serene. I am more aware of the influence of our Thursday evening. I can tell you, without your accusing me of exaggeration, that I am the happiest of women, that I have never felt more deeply that I love you, that, quite simply, I have never seen you nobler, or more adorable, my divine friend. You can preen yourself, if that flatters you, but don't go and look at yourself [in the mirror], because, whatever you do, you will never manage to give yourself the expression which, for a moment, I saw on your face. Now, whatever happens, I shall always see you like this, it's the Charles I love; you can purse your lips and frown with impunity, I shall take no notice of it, I shall close my eyes and see the other Charles . . .[4]

On 30 August, he called on her again; and, knowing that he was timid, wanting to show her gratitude, she did what to her was most natural, and offered herself to him.

What followed still remains unclear; but, as Camille Mauclair was to write:

The disservice to himself, the imaginative perversion which led Baudelaire to mystify and to suffer from it, are both found, more significantly than anywhere else in his life, in his heartbreaking adventure with Mme Sabatier. There he deceived by deceiving himself, there he knew his great moral bankruptcy, and, finally, both his artificial and his real pride were destroyed, and with them his life in its essential armature.[5]

Perhaps he felt alarmed by the violence of his passion. Perhaps her Rubenesque figure – she was thirty-five – deterred the man who professed to be attracted to thin women. Perhaps he was repelled by the thought of the sexual act – the animal condition; and then, perhaps, as Porché wrote: 'When he had worshipped Mme Sabatier, Baudelaire . . . had transferred to her all the arrears, all the unused homage of filial love. This transfer, now, had no further reason for its existence. Unconsciously, the man was sure to withdraw from the idol the spiritual maternity which he had lent her, in order to return it to his real mother.'[6] Aupick had died. A few weeks earlier, Baudelaire had written to his mother: 'Believe that I belong to you absolutely, and that I belong only to you.'[7]

It is here, perhaps, that one discovers the unspoken explanation of the tragic failure with Mme Sabatier. As Tamara Bassim writes: 'For Baudelaire, only one woman exists: his mother. She will be all women, and all women will be Her.'[8] For Baudelaire the pure and superior form of love had assumed a maternal figure. This complexity of amorous maternity had fixed itself upon La Présidente.[9] As Thibaudet observed:

The fear of love, the horror of passion, the inability to love in the full and usual sense of the word, . . . may perhaps only conceal a deeper emotion . . .
After one unique and cruel experience, he decided that to love the guardian angel, the Muse and the Madonna, to have La Présidente as a

mistress, . . . would be a sort of incest. In the obscure memory of his flesh, in its unconscious continuation while he was a child and an adolescent, all this order of feelings had been expressed in upheavals which were too deep not to make his soul remain fearful and his inner life out of balance.[10]

His physical relationship with La Présidente not only had undertones of incest; it also destroyed the image of the Madonna and the guardian angel. Charles du Bos wrote, perceptively:

It was enough to know Baudelaire to know that this adventure could not admit of a different epilogue. With Baudelaire, indeed, there is not only a split, there is absolute incompatibility between love and possession. The duality is written in the very depths of his nature. What common measure [can there be] between the celebration of the highest cult and the satisfaction of the lowest appetite? Between love, the fount of strength, the spur of genius, and possession, the mere instrument of oblivion?[11]

Michel Quesnel is in accord. 'To worship, as a body, the body of this woman, was to deny the mediator in her, and to return to the temptress. It was to honour in the host, not the living presence of Christ, but the baker's dough.'[12]

Whatever he felt, La Présidente found herself in love with him. She also destroyed, for ever, the aura of the unattainable. For five years, Baudelaire had worshipped her as an ideal; now he saw that she was only a woman. 'Woman', he wrote in his *Journaux intimes*, 'cannot separate the soul from the body. She is simplistic, like the animals.'[13] Apollonie did not understand what dream she had destroyed. She only felt herself to be less attractive than *la Vénus noire*. She kept a drawing of Jeanne Duval which Baudelaire had done, one evening, at the rue Frochot, and she pasted it into her copy of *Les Fleurs du mal*. Under it she wrote: 'Son idéal!'[14]

Whenever he was touched to the quick, Baudelaire showed an implacable rigour, a sarcasm which were peculiar to him. On 31 August, he wrote La Présidente one of the strangest letters which an accepted lover could have written: moving from the intimate form of address to the formal *vous*, moving between affection and cynicism, love and gallantry, with painful unconcern.

I have destroyed the torrent of childish nonsense which was piled up on my table. I haven't found it serious enough for you, dear darling. I am taking up your two letters again [the letters in question have not survived], and I am writing a new answer to them.

I need a certain courage to do so, because I have appalling neuralgia, enough to make me scream, and I woke up with the inexplicable emotional malaise which I brought away from you yesterday evening.

. . . *an absolute lack of modesty.*

That is why you are still more dear to me.

It seems to me that I have belonged to you since the first day I saw you. Do what you will about it, but I am yours, body, heart and soul.

I beg you to hide this letter, hapless woman! – *Do you really know what you are saying?* There are people who imprison those who do not pay their bills of exchange; but no one punishes the violation of vows of friendship and of love.

And so I said to you yesterday: you will forget me; you will betray me; the man who entertains you will bore you. And today I add: the only one to suffer will be the man who is a fool enough to be serious about matters of the soul. You see, my most beautiful darling, that I have *hateful* prejudices about women. In fact, *I have no faith*; you have a fine soul, but, when all is said, it is a woman's soul.[15]

'*In fact, I have no faith.*' In *Le Platonisme de Baudelaire*, Marc Eigeldinger explained:

> Baudelaire discovered that the myth of pure love is a construction of the mind, that the cult of the idolized woman is not a true religion, but a *counter-religion* which conceals the presence of Satan. Between the beloved and the idea which the poet conceives of her, there exists a hiatus, a void which nothing can fill. The awareness of this rupture, this tragic division brings the collapse of the myth, the decristallisation and the failure of the ideal love. This is what happened with Baudelaire, when Mme Sabatier wanted to repay him for his Platonic love. Baudelaire lost the *faith* on which his religion was based ... The myth of the inviolable Goddess cannot survive the collapse of faith; for, deprived of the faith which maintains it, it loses its mysterious, sacred aura, and it soon disintegrates completely ... Nonetheless, this heartrending experience conforms to the Platonic dialectic of love. The poet of *Les Fleurs du mal*, although he failed, had sought in love a path to salvation, a means of rising to the ideal of Beauty. The sublimation of the mistress into the ideal woman had been confirmed as impossible.[16]

> Look how our situation has been utterly changed in a matter of days [Baudelaire continued, to Apollonie]. In the first place, we are both afraid of hurting a good man who has the happiness of still loving you.
>
> And then we are both afraid of our own passion, because we know – at least I do – that there are bonds which are difficult to break.
>
> And then, and then ... A few days ago you were a deity, which is so convenient [*sic*], so noble, so inviolable. And now there you are, a woman. And suppose if, by some misfortune, I should acquire the right to be jealous! Oh, what torture even to think of it! But with someone like you, whose eyes are full of smiles and favours for everyone, it would be martyrdom.[17]

There was an echo of his words in his *Journaux intimes*: 'Love may derive from a generous feeling: the liking for prostitution; but it is soon corrupted by the liking for possession.'[18]

The second letter [he continued] bears a seal of a solemnity which would please me if I were quite sure that you understood it. *Never meet or never part!* That means definitely that it would be much better never to have known one another, but that, when you have known one another, you should not part. On a farewell letter, that would be a most amusing seal.

It will all be settled in the end. I am rather a fatalist. But I do know that I have a horror of passion – because I have experienced it, with all its degradations; – and now the beloved image which presided over all the adventures of life becomes too alluring.

I don't really dare to re-read this letter; perhaps I should be obliged to modify it, because I am much afraid of hurting you. It seems to me that I must have revealed something of the low side of my character.

It seems to me impossible to make you go like this to [the poste-restante office in] that squalid rue J.-J. Rousseau. Because I have many other things to say to you. So you must write to me to suggest a way.

As for our little plan, if it becomes possible, let me know a few days in advance.

Farewell, dear beloved. I am a little vexed with you for being too charming. Know, then, that when I take away the fragrance of your arms and your hair, I also take away the desire to return to them. And then, what an unbearable obsession![19]

The 'little plan' remains a mystery; but it is clear at least that Baudelaire did not intend to leave her. Nonetheless, it seems that she returned the letter to him; she wanted to efface the offence which he had caused her. Some say that he transposed this letter into the poem 'Semper eadem' which was to be published three years later.[20]

> 'D'où vous vient, disiez-vous, cette tristesse étrange,
> Montant comme la mer sur le roc noir et nu?'
> – Quand notre cœur a fait une fois sa vendange,
> Vivre est un mal. C'est un secret de tous connu,
>
> Une douleur très simple et non mystérieuse,
> Et, comme votre joie, éclatante pour tous.
> Cessez donc de chercher, ô belle curieuse!
> Et, bien que votre voix soit douce, taisez-vous!
>
> Taisez-vous, ignorante! âme toujours ravie!
> Bouche au rire enfantin! Plus encore que la Vie,
> La Mort nous tient souvent par des liens subtils.
>
> Laissez, laissez mon cœur s'enivrer d'un *mensonge*,
> Plonger dans vos beaux yeux comme dans un beau songe,
> Et sommeiller longtemps à l'ombre de vos cils![21]

It was not her that he had wanted. It was the lasting dream, the mirage necessary to his heart.

Most women would have been too hurt or too indignant to trouble any further about the relationship. It is a measure of Mme Sabatier's understanding that she used all her tact, her loving understanding, to play the part which she would not have chosen. She determined to be accepted as a friend.

> Listen, dear [she answered], shall I tell you what I think? It is a cruel thought, and one which hurts me very much. I think that you don't love me. That is why you have these fears, why you hesitate to contract a liaison – for in such conditions it would become a source of vexation for you and a continual torment for me. Do I not have the proof in a phrase in your letter? It is so explicit that it makes my blood turn cold. *In fact, I have no faith.* But then you have no love. What can be the answer to that? Isn't it clarity itself? Oh, my God! How I suffer at the thought, and how I want to weep on your breast! I feel that that would relieve me. Whatever has happened, I shall not change anything about our meeting tomorrow. I want to see you, even if it be only to practise my part as a friend. Oh, why did you try to see me again?[22]

It would be difficult to say why Baudelaire had done so. Perhaps he himself did not know the reason. Perhaps he did not dare to break a liaison with such brutality. Perhaps he wanted to be sure that he was right to break it. Apollonie could hardly understand him, for he seemed to seek her and to escape her, to love her and to hate her, to desire her and to reject her. With him, as Trial would observe, 'there is no thesis without antithesis, no hydromel without gall, no truth without a lie.'[23] On 2 September, it seems, they met each other as arranged. On 4 September, Baudelaire called on her, once again, to show that he was still much affected by all that troubled her; he found that she was out, but he stayed to dinner. Two days later, he explained:

> I came to tell you something that you know and do not doubt, which is that I am always dismayed and distressed by everything that distresses you.
>   I expected to dine with you and Mosselman, but it was a dinner from which grace was absent. For you cannot presume that the Russian Gentleman replaced you. At least for me.[24]

On 8 September, he wrote that he could only offer her two balcony seats for the first performance of *Le Roi Lear* at the Théâtre impérial du Cirque, but, if Mosselman chose to accept a balcony seat, she could ask Gautier for hospitality. He would certainly receive a box, as the drama critic of *Le Moniteur universel*. 'I most humbly kiss your royal hands.'[25] On 10 September he sent her the tickets for the performance, which had now been postponed for a day. He would not go, he told her, unless she were going; he wondered if he should fetch Mossel-man.[26] On 13 September, when she was due to give her Sunday dinner, he sent her a note to excuse himself. 'However,' he ended, 'I shall contrive to come and wish you a brief good evening, and the same to our excellent friends. I beg you not to misinterpret my very humble excuses.'[27]

No doubt she knew how to interpret them. She recognised that he was escaping her. He had returned to the prison of his solitude. He longed for love, and yet he lacked the courage to accept it. She loved him still, and showed it in her sensibility, her warmth of feeling, in her comprehension of love, in the reproachful letter that she sent him:

What comedy or rather what drama are we performing? For I don't know what to think, and I must confess that I am deeply troubled. Your behaviour has been so strange, for the last few days, that I don't understand it at all, any more. It's too subtle for a dullard like me. Help me, my dear, I only want to know what mortal cold has blown on that fine flame. Is it just the effect of wise reflection? That's come a little late. Alas! is it my own surpassing fault? I should have been grave and thoughtful when you came to see me. But what can one do? When my lips tremble and my heart beats, my sensible thoughts fly away . . .

Your letter has come. I don't need to tell you that I expected the message. So we shall just have the pleasure of seeing you for a few moments? Very well, then, as you like. I don't generally criticise my friends' behaviour. You seem to be terribly afraid of finding yourself alone with me. But that's what is really necessary! You do what you want about it. When this mood has passed, write to me or come. I am indulgent, and I shall forgive you for the hurt you do to me.

I cannot refrain from saying a few words about our disagreement. I had determined to behave with absolute dignity – but less than a day has passed, and my heart is already weak and yet, Charles, my anger was quite justified! What must I think when I see you fly from my caresses, if not that you are thinking about *her*, whose soul and black face have just set themselves between us? In fact, I feel humiliated and abased. If it weren't for my self-respect, I should abuse you. I'd like to see you suffer. Because I'm burning with jealousy and one cannot possibly reason at times like these. Oh! dear friend, I hope that you will never suffer from it. What a night I've spent, and how I have cursed this cruel love! . . .

I have waited for you all day . . . In case your caprice should urge you towards the house tomorrow, I must warn you that I shall only be in from one till three, or, in the evening, from eight until midnight.

Good morning, my Charles. How is whatever heart remains to you? Mine is calmer, now. I am reasoning hard with it so that I shall not bore you too much with its weaknesses. Have no fear. I shall manage to force it to come down to the temperature you dream of. I shall very certainly suffer, but, to please you, I shall resign myself to every possible pain.[28]

Had she been stronger and more decisive, it has been suggested, she might have kept him. Had he been less tormented, he might at last have escaped a life of anguish.[29] Such speculation is vain. There was no doubt of her devotion; but, practicalities apart, Baudelaire himself was past salvation. He had been so since his early childhood: since he had first become aware that his mother had betrayed him.

A few days later, knowing her affection for trinkets, he sent Apollonie an antique inkwell. He sent it to her anonymously, and wrote to her the next day to excuse himself for his stupidity.[30] On 17 November, he sent her two novels which he wanted her to read; but he had 'absolutely no idea' when he could attend one of her Sundays.[31] As Porché wrote: 'There is a heartrending melancholy in these little gifts. They are like the flowers one lays on tombs, they are the sign that all is dead – except for regret.'[32]

60

On 18 October, very much delayed, Baudelaire's critical study of *Madame Bovary* appeared in *L'Artiste*. It was, he said, an advantage to be published so late; it gave him the freedom simply to concern himself with the love of Beauty and Justice.

The thought of justice recalled not only Flaubert's acquittal on the charge of offences against morality; it also recalled Baudelaire's own condemnation. Indeed, the review of *Madame Bovary* allowed him to take an oblique revenge on the judges of *Les Fleurs du mal*.

> Since I have uttered that splendid and terrible word, Justice, may I be allowed – since it also gives me pleasure – to thank the French magistrature for the shining example of impartiality and good taste which it gave on this occasion [the case of *Madame Bovary*]? . . . In short, one may say that, through its noble poetic sympathy, this verdict was final; that the Muse had won the day, and that every writer, at least all those who are worthy of the name, were acquitted in the person of M. Gustave Flaubert.[1]

Flaubert, as Baudelaire perceived, had come at a time when society was sated and brutalized. He had determined to be dispassionate in his account of passion. All Flaubert had failed to do was to rid himself of his masculinity. For all his zeal, he had been unable not to transfuse a man's blood into the veins of his creation.[2] Emma Bovary had had a masculine energy and ambition. To Baudelaire, 'this bizarre hermaphrodite had kept all the attractions of a virile mind in a charming female body.'[3] She appealed to his taste for the ambivalent. She was truly great, but above all she was pitiful, 'and, despite the systematic rigour of the author, who has tried his utmost to be absent from his work, and to play the part of a showman with his marionnettes, all *intellectual* women will be grateful to him for having raised the female to such a high power, so far from the pure animal and so near the ideal man, and to have made her share this double nature of calculation and reverie which constitutes the perfect being.'[4]

It was audacious for a poet who had been condemned to voice his praise of a novelist who had been acquitted. The gesture was characteristic of Baudelaire. Flaubert himself was delighted with the assessment. 'My dear friend, . . . you have entered into the secrets of this work, as if my mind were yours. It is *completely* understood and felt.'[5]

Baudelaire was working, now, in a regular way of which he rarely found himself to be capable.[6] He was, no doubt, translating and adapting De Quincey's *Confessions of an English Opium-eater*. On 9 December he sent Turgan the first part of his adaptation, and promised to send a further instalment every day. He thought that the work would be finished on the 15th, and might run to ten or eleven instalments.[7] It might have brought him a handsome sum, but Turgan refused to publish it.

Financial problems loomed again. Baudelaire went twice to Neuilly to see Ancelle, and twice Ancelle was out. As Baudelaire planned to go to Alençon and to Honfleur, he had preparations and purchases to make; he took some money from Vincent Blanché, the notary who had succeeded Ancelle in his practice. 'And now, as soon as I return,' he informed Ancelle, 'I shall submit to whatever monthly reduction you may choose.'[8]

He wrote from Alençon, where he was staying with Malassis. For Malassis, as for Baudelaire, it had been a bitter year, not only on account of financial problems and litigation. For the past year and more, he had been in love with Assclincau's niece. That summer, he had begged Asselineau to approach his sister, 'and to ask her if, at the end of the year, if my position is really what I told you, and today it's better, and above all, of course, if I did not have the misfortune of displeasing your niece, she would see no obstacle to a marriage which would fulfil all my hopes.'[9]

It was now the end of the year, and Malassis was rejected.

In December 1857, Baudelaire left his unhappy publisher in Alençon. He had planned to go to Honfleur; but, in fact, he returned to Paris.

Once again, he was overcome by despair at his life, by fear of the work which remained undone. Not for the first time, he was paralysed by his depression. On Christmas Day, alone in Paris, he turned yet again to his mother:

> Since the beginning of this month [he wrote to her], my table has been laden with proofs which I have lacked the courage to set my hand to, and there always comes a moment when, with great pain, one must emerge from the abysses of indolence . . .
> I embrace you, and I beg you to be, henceforward, full of indulgence; for I have the greatest need of it, I assure you. If ever a man were ill, without medicine being concerned, it is surely me.[10]

Medicine should no doubt have been concerned with Baudelaire, but he avoided medical opinion. He was indeed ill. He not only suffered from syphilis, and from his prolonged use of laudanum, he suffered from years of poverty and emotional stress. He had been damaged, in childhood, by his mother's betrayal and neglect. He had been damaged, in his youth and early manhood, by the effects of her second marriage, by her moods of alternate devotion and dismissal. It was thanks to her that he 'knew nothing of love but the phantom of love'.[11] As one medical critic observed, he was 'constitutionally depressed . . . Baudelaire's ailments conditioned his literary work: all that is interesting in his literary and artistic productions is connected, in particular, with his psychic imbalance.'[12] His misery had informed his work, but it had largely destroyed him.

Now, at the end of 1857, his languor and his misery remained; so did his poverty. So did his extravagance, and at times he spent with absolute unconcern for the future – assuming, no doubt, that his mother would always rescue him. That day, Christmas Day, he made some purchases from Maury, the jeweller in the rue d'Aguesseau; among them were an amber necklace, three strings of big pearls with a silver-gilt clasp, and a pair of amber ear-rings.[13] It is not known for whom they were intended. Baudelaire bought the jewels on credit, and he paid the greater part of the bill. Yet the sum – 250 francs – exceeded his monthly allowance. It was a reckless way to prepare for the new year.

His mother wrote to him fondly. ·Her warmth and understanding encouraged him to unburden himself.

> Certainly I have great cause for complaint about myself [he told her, on 30 December], and I am very surprised and alarmed by my condition. Do I need a change of place? I don't know. Is it physical illness which weakens the spirit and the will, or is it spiritual cowardice which tires the body? I don't know. But what I feel is immense discouragement, an

unbearable sense of isolation, a perpetual fear of some vague misfortune, a complete distrust of my strength, a total absence of desires, the impossibility of finding some or other amusement. The bizarre success of my book and the hatreds it aroused interested me for a little while, and after that I had a relapse. You see, my dear mother, that this is a tolerably serious state for a man whose profession is to produce and dress up fictions. I constantly ask myself: What's the use of this? What's the use of that? And that is the real spirit of spleen . . .

I am going to tell you, very briefly, what prevented me, not from going to see you down there (I couldn't do so), but from answering you. I was afraid both of afflicting you and of not being understood. The day after my stepfather's death, you told me that I dishonoured you, and you forbade me (before I had thought of making a request on the subject) ever to contemplate living with you. Then you obliged me to make humiliating overtures of friendship to M. Émon. Do me this justice, dear mother, that I bore that with the humility and meekness which your lamentable situation demanded of me. But then, after writing me letters which contained nothing but reprimands and bitterness, after reproaching me for that cursed book, which, after all, is only a very defendable *work of art*, you invited me to come and see you, and gave me to understand that M. Émon's absence allowed me to stay at Honfleur, *as if M. Émon were entitled to open or close my mother's door to me*, and finally, when you carefully advised me not to run up debts at Honfleur – then, really, I was so bewildered, so surprised that it is presumable that I became unjust. See what a lasting mark that letter has left in my memory. I didn't know what to decide or reply. After I'd read it, I found myself in indescribable agitation, and finally, after a fortnight, not knowing what decision to take, I decided not to take one at all.

I do indeed believe, my dear mother, that you have never understood my intolerable sensibility . . .

Suppose we tried once and for all to make one another happy?[14]

61

On 11 January 1858, Baudelaire wrote again to his mother. He was not only preoccupied with business and financial matters, but he was increasingly unwell.

I am [he told her] overwhelmed with business and vexations. I never talk to you about them because it would distress you needlessly.

Besides, as if to increase my troubles, I can only walk now with the greatest difficulty; my right leg is swollen, rigid and quite unusually painful; some people say it's cramp, and others say it's neuralgia [*sic*].

Thank you very much for your pharmaceutical prescriptions; I have put them carefully on one side, and I shall make use of them. Besides, my stomach is better for the moment, thanks to ether, and the colics have been stopped with opium. But opium has terrible disadvantages.

Come down there at once, you say? But you aren't thinking of all the manuscripts that I have to finish first, and of everything that I have to pay . . .

I have told a few friends about my plan to settle in Honfleur. Everyone tells me it's a stroke of genius. Indeed, in this way I shall put an end to agitation and fruitless journeys, and find the solitude that I love so much. Besides, I must hope that if, in Paris, in the midst of countless torments without name, I earn 5 or 6,000 francs with very little work, I shall earn much more in good and peaceful surroundings.[1]

He was entirely self-absorbed. He did not mention the pleasure he would find in his mother's company. For someone who professed not to talk about his vexations, he talked to her about them very freely. For someone who was anxious to spare her distress, he talked alarmingly about his health.

Baudelaire's concern about his health was not misplaced. The condition of his leg marked a development in his syphilis – though he himself professed to be unaware of the cause. Mosselman thought he recognised Baudelaire in the street, but he found him so changed in appearance that he could not be sure. La Présidente grew anxious, and wrote to him.

Chère amie [he replied], yes, it was me that Mosselman saw, he saw me in a sorry state, looking everywhere for a cab. I had managed to stop the choking fits with ether capsules, and the colics with opium, when a new infirmity befell me. I can only walk with great difficulty; as for coming downstairs by myself, that is an enormous undertaking. The height of misfortune is that I have countless errands and business affairs. I don't need to tell you that the ridiculousness of the pain haunts me more than the pain itself.

I shall come and see you in a few days – but in any case when I don't limp any more and I feel very cheerful. You know my principles . . .

Greetings to Mosselman.

All yours.

CH. BAUDELAIRE[2]

It was, it seems, on 19 January that he had a letter from his mother. She sent him a little money.

My leg is all right now [he assured her]. I don't know what it was; but it was protracted and very painful . . .

Thank you very much indeed for your generosity, and I shall profit from it – as a BEGINNING. But your letter clearly says that you are embarrassed. I beg you to explain to me how and why you are embarrassed. Is it still some old debts? Is it as a result of obligations or charities?[3]

He did not consider – or, more probably, he pretended not to know – that her constant charity was himself.

Baudelaire needed – he had said – to hide nearly all he thought. He did not tell her that he had paid several visits to Antoine Jaquotot. Maître Jaquotot, a notary, was an old friend of hers; he had been a witness at her second marriage, and a member of the family council which had asked for the appointment of the *conseil judiciaire*. Baudelaire was fond of him; he had not seen him for twenty years – except at Aupick's funeral – but he had now called on him five or six times to discuss his financial relationship with his mother. Early in February, he decided to have no further dealings with Ancelle; he reached an understanding with Jaquotot that the notary would represent him to Ancelle and to his mother in all financial matters.

On 20 February he wrote to Jaquotot at length about the plan. At Aupick's funeral, he recalled, Jaquotot had expressed the hope that Baudelaire would now live with his mother. Baudelaire had, he admitted, been expecting an offer from her; but, before he had mentioned the subject, his mother had declared that she would never live with him. She had, at the time, been in such distress that he had borne the humiliation. Quite recently, of her own accord, she had expressed the wish that he should live with her in Honfleur. Both of them were now impatient for him to settle there; Baudelaire wanted Ancelle to release a year of his income so that he might pay some debts and essential expenses and move to Honfleur a few days hence.[4]

Baudelaire was afraid, he said, that he might appear to be exerting emotional blackmail. 'On this point I should like to say this. Although my very real interest demands that I should go to Honfleur and stay there – and that, as soon as possible – it isn't only my interest which urges me to do so. Even if I didn't find any personal advantages, in financial matters, rest and work, I WANT, I assure you, *I want to live with my mother*.'[5] There also remained the question of whether he intended to stay in Honfleur.

My answer is: *I have a horror of Paris and of the cruel life that I have led here for more than sixteen years, which is the unique obstacle to the fulfilment of all my plans. I am so absolutely determined to stay down there, first of all to please my mother, and also in my own interest, that nothing will make me live in Paris again . . .*

Cher Monsieur, there is little to add. I definitely want to lead this life of retirement which is led by one of my friends – whom I shall not name. Through the communal life which he leads with his mother, he [Flaubert] has found sufficient peace of mind to produce – only recently – a very fine work; and he has become famous at one stroke.

My mother has a strong faculty which I laugh at in public, and admire in private. It is ORDER, the sense of order which creates freedom. I have various reasons to think that I shall catch the infection by contact . . .

Allow me, dear Monsieur, [although] I am asking you a favour, to give you a little advice. This letter is written, I think, in a way to be shown to my mother, she will guess from it everything that I haven't had time to put into it. You can therefore add it to the excellent reasons in my favour which you will have because of your excellent mind and your authority as an old family friend. It seems to me that the friendship which you have for my mother impels you to make my plan succeed.

Rest assured of my genuine gratitude, in spite of all the nonsense about me which has no doubt been recited to you . . .[6]

Next day Jaquotot sent Baudelaire's letter to Mme Aupick.[7] She took some time to consider her answer. She was anxious that her son should feel all his obligation to Ancelle. On 23 February she wrote to him, and suggested that he reached an understanding with Ancelle about the loan of 2,500 francs. She also asked Ancelle to enquire what use her son would make of this sum; she was, not unnaturally, afraid that some of the money might go to Jeanne or to some other woman in his life.

Ancelle might have chosen to speak to Baudelaire himself, but their relationship was strained, and he was inquisitive by nature. On 25 February, he visited the hôtel Voltaire. No doubt he persuaded himself that he had good reason for his enquiries. In fact he seems to have been borne away by his curiosity. For a middle-aged man, a mayor, a magistrate and a notary, his behaviour was unpardonable.

For the moment, Baudelaire was unaware of Ancelle's machinations. On 24 February he had received a letter from his mother which had given him boundless pleasure.

At last, at last, I've been understood [he told her]! . . .

Oh, it was high time! I expect everything from this new establishment: peace, work and health. Because *I believe I'm ill*, and an invalid, *even imaginary*, is an invalid. What are these perpetual fears, these attacks of breathlessness, and these palpitations, especially when I am asleep?

Ten days after the money has been put into my hands, I shall be in Honfleur . . .[8]

The letter was written on 26 February. Next morning, Baudelaire received a note from his mother, refusing him the money which he expected.

62

.

She was in fact trying to improve relations between her son and
Ancelle. Jaquotot had, wisely, now withdrawn from the affair, and she
wanted to make Baudelaire feel grateful to his *conseil judiciaire*. She
therefore told him that Ancelle would come and give him funds.
Baudelaire answered with unusual restraint: 'I have had three days of
great delight; that is still a gain, delight is so rare. Whatever happens,
I thank you sincerely for that. But it was only a pleasant dream. I don't
give up going to Honfleur. My longing will increase every day. But I
shall go with my [own] money, and when I have been able to get out
of the difficulty myself.'[1]

Mme Aupick's diplomacy had been remarkably ill-judged; but a
much more serious problem was to come.

> *However dreadful this is* [Baudelaire continued], *it still isn't the worst*. Ancelle,
> to whom no doubt you have already written, is going to come and bore
> me to death with his services, and, when he sees that I refuse his money,
> he will want to do me service in spite of myself. He is going to force
> himself into my company, try to force his way into my affairs, extricate
> an account of my problems from me by force. The very thought of his
> visit turns my suffering to rage . . .
>
> And so I beg you, in your mercy, if you haven't written to him yet, not
> to write anything to him at all. If you have written to him, write to him
> again to tell him that your decision and our agreements should be null
> and void. I want to live, and I will not have that bore of an Ancelle
> stealing my time and my peace. *My peace!*[2]

Baudelaire's apprehension was all too justified. At about noon that
day, he learned of Ancelle's visit to the hôtel Voltaire.

> I am [he told his mother] writing at the dictation of M. Denneval, the
> owner of the house I'm living in.
>
> 'Two days ago, M. Ancelle came to pay me a secret visit, and he
> told me that you wouldn't pay me, that if you told me that you would
> pay me, *you were lying, as you constantly lie to him, that he had person-
> ally given you 500 francs to be handed to me as payment on account.*' (I
> have never, for more than eighteen months, received 500 francs from
> M. Ancelle.)
>
> 'DOESN'T M. BAUDELAIRE RECEIVE WOMEN?' And a mass of
> ignoble questions ('DOES HE COME BACK LATE?' . . . ETC).
>
> And so M. Ancelle is a miserable coward, and while I was writing to
> you this morning to reject any intervention from him, and guessing that
> it would be dangerous, he was already engaged *in his usual business*.
>
> He also declared that he would pay nothing, and that I would pay
> nothing, as is his habit.[3]

No doubt there was much heated conversation between Baudelaire and Denneval. Baudelaire was naturally enraged by Ancelle's gross indiscretion. Yet his reaction went beyond anger. It did not only reveal the frustration and bitterness that he had felt for years. It was so violent that it leads one to question his stability. Two and a half hours later he added a postscript to his letter: 'ANCELLE IS A WRETCH, AND I'M GOING TO SLAP HIM IN THE FACE IN FRONT OF HIS WIFE AND CHILDREN, I'M GOING TO SLAP HIM IN THE FACE *at four o'clock* (it's half-past two), and, if I don't find him in, I shall wait for him. I swear that this will have an end, and a dreadful end.'[4]

It was not the first time, or the last, that Baudelaire weakened in his resolve. Repeatedly, throughout his life, he would make threats or extreme decisions only to renounce them. At four o'clock, the time at which he had determined to attack Ancelle, he was still at the hôtel Voltaire, and writing, yet again, to his mother. It was Denneval, so he maintained, who had persuaded him to change his mind.

> The proprietor of the hotel is terrified by the consequences of his revelation. He has just come up to my room and begged me not to commit any act of violence . . .
> *I shan't go to Neuilly today.*
> I agree to wait before I take my revenge . . .
> If I don't get *handsome reparation*, I shall strike Ancelle, I shall strike his son, and they will see a *conseil judiciaire* suing M. Ch. Baudelaire in court for aggravated assault.[5]

Meanwhile, if he did not take revenge on Ancelle, Baudelaire took protracted revenge on his unhappy mother. An hour later, at five o'clock, he wrote to her again:

> *Honestly*, did you entrust that idiot with coming and playing the spy (*it was the day before yesterday*, and I learned it a moment ago)? Did you ask him to enquire into my morals, whether I stayed out all night, *to come and settle down among servants, at the risk of making himself ridiculous*, to slander me (and I'm thirty-seven, and I have a name, and I should have been happy long ago if a mistake had not stood in the way of all my plans), to come and declare (and you've obviously told him to pay) that I shouldn't pay and that he wouldn't pay, . . . etc . . .?
> I am really distressed at the vexation that I am causing you. I have to work, and now I have to look for seconds should there be an actual dispute between me and Ancelle, or between me and his son . . .
> Poor dear mother, I know your nerves, you are going to suffer. But really, honestly, is it my fault?[6]

Mme Aupick must have suffered, and it was his fault. Twice again, that day, he expressed his fury to her. 'I absolutely must have satisfaction.

My anger won't give me a moment's peace until I have had it.'[7] And again:

> Yet another letter; but since this morning all I have been pleading for is my honour . . .
>
> My God, what sort of difficulty have you put me into? *I absolutely must have a little peace, all I ask is that.* What have I done to be deprived like this of something which anyone has a right to demand?[8]

He was already ill with syphilis. Now he was ill with rage. Next day he was again at his desk.

> Dear mother,
>
> . . . Now I am going to return, with resignation, to a new martyrdom, singularly aggravated by all this, and by lost hope. Who knows if I shall succeed in getting the necessary money – and when?
>
> As soon as I have a moment's peace (comparatively speaking), *I shall think about settling my personal quarrel with him, and it will be serious, I promise you* . . .
>
> Yesterday evening, the day ended with a fever and neuralgia which lasted all night. Finally, this morning, I was relieved by violent and repeated vomiting . . .[9]

Mme Aupick was shaken by this avalanche of letters. On 1 March, she wrote to Ancelle in despair:

> I beg you, for mercy's sake, to stop all this: *it has made me ill.* I have had 4 different letters from Charles by the same post, and they are all marked by such despair that I am really afraid it will drive him mad. His landlord has turned his head with his gossip and his stupid talk. I had written to M. Jaquotot to be kind enough to act as an intermediary between Charles and you. I'm afraid that he hasn't wanted to be involved. As you had mentioned him in a letter to me, as being able to undertake this distribution of the 2,400 francs [*sic*], and as I had refused, not considering then that his intervention was necessary, I also asked him in my letter to reach an understanding with you about it, since Charles is violently prejudiced against you, and, fearing that [you] might speak ill of him to other people as you had done to his landlord, will abandon his journey, and will manage to get through by himself, he says, and he rejects the 2,400 francs, because he thinks you have made this advance. I thought I'd done well in letting him believe it. I wanted to make him feel all the obligation to you. *I was wrong.* I see that mysteries are never any good . . .
>
> Oh, if I could have foreseen all this, I should have said to you in the first place that we had to make the whole, complete sacrifice at our own risk and give him the money. We shouldn't be where we are now. This sum of money isn't worth all the anxieties it causes me. At the present moment, Charles may be ill; he wrote to me that he had a fever, vomitings and neuralgia. I myself am suffering cruelly from my stomach. Can one

digest when one is a prey to cruel anxieties? And I attached so much importance to your getting on well together! When he is here, I shall no doubt calm him, and he will be fond of you again, as he used to be. I hope so, I want this very deeply . . .'[10]

Baudelaire still contrived to believe that he was free of Ancelle. On 5 March, he told his mother that he was not involving himself in the Ancelle-Jaquotot affair, and that he had treated Ancelle kindly, giving him false explanations for his change of notary.[11]

Circumstances demanded that, even now, he continued to deal with him.

I am drunk with shame, with anger and with insults [he told his mother on 8 March]. And yet I should have been hardened to it for twenty years. I finally went back to Neuilly this morning. But yesterday evening, when I went to bed, I had decided to make Ancelle expiate sixteen years of torture.

From Neuilly I went to a stockbroker with a stock certificate. As long as I live I shall remember the horrible tone in which the clerk asked me: 'Are you M. Ch. Baudelaire?' (On the certificate, after my name, it said: *Ancelle, conseil judiciaire.*) It was pointed out to me that if I wanted the money tomorrow evening (tomorrow, the 9th), I needed M. Ancelle's signature today. So there I was, obliged to go back to Neuilly to collect Ancelle. How exhausting! Finally we arrived on time. The stockbroker made an advance, and everything has been paid today. The two receipts are with M. Ancelle.

When we left, I went with him to the café de Foy. There I met Michel Lévy with a former Deputy whom I know. I had to talk to Michel Lévy about an important matter, a big edition of Edgar Poe. Ancelle was very intrigued, and he couldn't bear the thought of not making the acquaintance of this idiotic (but very rich) Jew. He went up to him and greeted him. Michel said that he didn't know him. *On this I took my hat and fled.* He must have announced to Lévy: 'I AM THE MAYOR OF NEUILLY AND M. BAUDELAIRE'S CONSEIL JUDICIAIRE!'

And he is going to go like this and settle down at Gautier's; he is going to settle down at Jeanne's. What the devil will he do at that poor invalid's? On one occasion he saw me at a concert with a woman; he wasn't happy till he had found a means of sitting next to us. Why? I blush when people ask me: 'Who is that man?'

Oh, how I suffer! I should like to take revenge. I have already shown him my contempt in a thousand ways, but he isn't aware of it.[12]

On 6 April, Baudelaire set to work on *Les Paradis artificiels*. At about the same time, since his anger was finally spent, he sent a book to his *conseil judiciaire*. This advance copy of *Les Aventures d'Arthur Gordon Pym* was inscribed: 'To my friend N. Ancelle.'[13]

63

On 27 April, Mme Aupick had attended the special mass on the first anniversary of her husband's death. In her year of widowhood, she had become increasingly aware of her devotion to her son. She tried to believe in his new determination to work, in his determination to pay his debts. She was conscious of his growing fame. She admired his translations of Poe, and, though she was shocked by certain poems in *Les Fleurs du mal*, she began to believe in his poetic powers. When Alphonse Baudelaire sent her his sympathy on the anniversary of Aupick's death, she answered with a new sense of pride:

> Thank you, my dear Alphonse, for your kind remembrance of the 27th. Yes, of course, this day was very cruel for me. The mass affected me very much. There were a lot of people there; I was stronger than I should have expected, I put on a good face. I don't have the Émons yet, nor do I have Charles. Do you know that your brother is beginning to have a great and noble reputation? *These fleurs du mal*, which have caused so great a stir in the literary world, and sometimes, alas, contain horrible and shocking descriptions, are also endowed with great beauties. There are some wonderful stanzas, of a purity of language, a simplicity of form which produce the most splendid poetic effect. He possesses the art of writing to an eminent degree. For all his eccentricities, Charles *has an incontestable gift.* If the *fleurs du mal* were mediocre, they would have passed unnoticed, like so many other works, you can be sure. Isn't it better to have too much fire and too much artistic greatness than barrenness of ideas and commonplace thoughts? As for his translations of Edgar Poe, as a work of style [they] are most remarkable, and indeed astonishing, they are as good as an original. I didn't know that he had such a perfect understanding of English. So here I am at last with a little hope in your brother's future. When I recall the Past, I think it is a great deal to see him now with this love of work carried to the extreme, and the ambition to pay his debts with what he earns; he maintains that he needs two years to do this. If he were to take 4 or 5 years, it would still be very fine. I count a good deal on his stay here in this lovely countryside, and on his contact with me, to give him gentler inspirations. I have let myself talk to you at length about Charles, convinced as I am that you will rejoice in his triumphs – *and he will have them.*[1]

To Baudelaire himself she wrote with affectionate reproach for his continued absence from Honfleur. On 13 May – the day that Michel Lévy published *Les Aventures d'Arthur Gordon Pym* – Baudelaire sat down to answer her.

> I have never seen such a great aptitude for inventing fears! And what an extraordinary idea to preach to me that it is in my interest to go and join you! I know it is; but I am driven by a nobler feeling.

So I have never changed my idea. And so you must not sign your letters: *your poor mother*, or reproach me that I often wrote to you when I was so anxious, and that now I'm no longer anxious I don't write to you any more. All this, dear mother, is equally unfair.

I am still very anxious, and I have never changed my idea...

This Gustave Flaubert, whose work you asked for, attained his glory in a very curious way, at the first stroke, and he is a good friend of mine. We are generally insulted together in the papers, although there is no connection between the two of us. He knows you very well, and he has often talked to me about the charming way he was received at Constantinople.[2]

No doubt he had also talked to Baudelaire about his life at Croisset with his mother. There was no guilt, there were no regrets, in their relationship. Mme Flaubert had long provided the tranquil, ordered setting in which he could commit himself to literature. There was a world between Mme Flaubert, placid, understanding and admiring, and the highly-strung, demanding Mme Aupick. Baudelaire must have known that his mother could not provide a haven such as Flaubert enjoyed.

Now, in the early summer of 1858, he was not only concerned about his payment from *Le Moniteur*; he was also pursued by the *Revue contemporaine*. They had given him an advance of 300 francs for an article on hashish, the article had not yet been delivered, and the paper was constantly sending messengers to the hôtel Voltaire to demand it.[3] The advance was no doubt already spent, and, as usual, he found himself in urgent need of funds. On 14 May he wrote to Malassis, in Alençon, to ask him for money.[4] He expected an answer from him by return of post. Malassis did not reply. On 16 May he wrote again.[5] On 19 May, he asked him for a promissory note for 600 francs, payable at Honfleur.[6] Matters grew still worse. Baudelaire delayed his visit to his mother, and, on 9 June, he warned her: 'They are going to come to you tomorrow to demand 600 francs from me... You must tell whoever comes: *M. Baudelaire is certainly coming here, but no doubt it won't be for three weeks or so. He is now living at* 19, QUAI VOLTAIRE, IN PARIS. And then you must ask *if it is necessary for me to send the money to Honfleur, or if I can pay in Paris.*'[7]

Next day, in spite of his instructions (one wonders how sincerely he had meant them), Mme Aupick settled his debt. She wrote, reproachfully, to tell him so. He replied with irritation, no doubt caused by guilt:

My God! You didn't understand my letter...

Instead of understanding something so simple, you try, for three pages, to persuade me that I have counted on you...

I implore you, do just what I ask, and nothing more...

I am very distressed to have worried you, dear mother. I don't think I have compromised you. In any case, rest assured that I have never thought of making you pay one of my debts.[8]

The assurance carried small conviction.

In this summer of 1858, he suffered not only from financial problems, but from disappointment in his friends. On 14 June, in *Le Moniteur universel*, he read Sainte-Beuve's article on Feydeau's novel, *Fanny*. Ernest Feydeau was an indifferent author; his true distinction was to be, by his second marriage, the father of the playwright Georges Feydeau. Nonetheless, his latest novel had been vastly successful. He and Baudelaire often met in the rue Frochot; they had disliked each other from the first, and Baudelaire, who sensed his own literary powers, was well aware of Feydeau's pretentions. 'That article', he told Sainte-Beuve, 'inspired me with dreadful jealousy . . . Won't you make an excursion into the depths of *Edgar Poe?*'[9] Sainte-Beuve refused to make the excursion. Since April he had been teaching at the École normale supérieure; and, while he did not cease to contribute to *Le Moniteur universel*, he was obliged to restrict his contributions. Yet it is a matter of regret that, for all his protestations of friendship, and even, perhaps, of his admiration and affection, he refused to give Baudelaire the encouragement that only he could give: a critical study over his own signature. Sainte-Beuve, wrote Léon Lemonnier in his *Enquêtes sur Baudelaire*, 'was one of those who want to succeed according to the ways of this world. All his life, he respected people in office, and institutions in repute, because he wanted to obtain official recognition for his gifts. How, then, . . . could he have published a line in favour of a poet found guilty of offending public morals, a poet who had been sentenced like a criminal?'[10]

After the letter of 14 June, Baudelaire did not write to him for two months. It was a measure of his disillusionment. Yet, in a Paris which seemed largely hostile, he still needed the intellectual stimulus, the moral tonic which Sainte-Beuve could give him. On 14 August he wrote again, humbly: 'Is it permissible to come and warm oneself and strengthen oneself a little by contact with you? You know what I think about debilitating and tonic men. If I disturb you, then, you must blame your quality, rather than my own infirmity.'[11]

Flaubert was in Croisset. Gautier was not an intellectual, Alfred de Vigny he had yet to meet. No one in Paris could give Baudelaire such conversation as Sainte-Beuve. As Vandérem was to observe: 'One can understand that, for a poet of this breadth and culture, familiarity with Sainte-Beuve, even if it were ineffectual, must have been the sheet-anchor, the *præsidium* he dreamed of. And one can understand why, in order to keep, it, Baudelaire had endured so many mortifications.'[12]

64

Baudelaire was, however, depressed for a multiplicity of reasons. Twice
this summer he had spoken to his mother about 'a very serious affair'
for which he needed Mérimée's support, 'an idea he had got into his
head.'[1] This was, it seems, the cross of chevalier de la Légion-d'honneur. It was a remarkable ambition for a man who expressed his
contempt for bourgeois values, his disdain for the Establishment, and
the independence of his art. Yet Baudelaire remained complicated.
Although he was frequently unorthodox, he kept a certain concern for
convention; and, in his solitude, especially after the condemnation of
Les Fleurs du mal, he felt an increasing need for recognition. On 15
August, the fête Napoléon, the summer honours list was duly published. Henry Murger, the author of *Scènes de la vie de Bohème*, was appointed
a chevalier de la Légion-d'honneur; Jules Sandeau, part author, with
Émile Augier, of *Le Gendre de Monsieur Poirier*, was created an officier. A
few days later, Baudelaire lamented to his mother:

> There's the fifteenth of August gone, and the decoration hasn't come. I
> don't know if I ever told you that there had already been a question of it
> last year, but that the court case about *Les Fleurs du mal* had made them
> postpone the question until later. Anyway, to be absolutely frank, the
> recent appointments are so unpleasant to me that I am delighted not to
> have been thrown into a batch, and especially into that one.[2]

Baudelaire was never to receive the scarlet ribbon which he coveted.
Years later, in *Mon Cœur mis à nu*, he wrote bitterly: 'There are certain
women who are like the ribbon of the Légion-d'honneur. You don't
want them any more because they have been sullied by certain men.'[3]

On 30 September, *De l'Idéal artificiel – le Haschisch* appeared in the *Revue
contemporaine*. On 4 October, Baudelaire confessed to Alphonse de la
Calonne that he was not sure that he would finish the sequel, *Un
Mangeur d'opium*, that evening. If, he suggested, he had finished it on 6
October, it might perhaps be published on the fifteenth. He proposed
to call on Calonne early next morning. Baudelaire was not merely
unpunctual; he was recklessly demanding. 'If I were a botanist,' he
added, 'I should draw a beautiful flower here, by way of signature: a
forget-me-not. You know what I'm referring to. The lodging [at the
hôtel Voltaire] is rented, and I have also rented the one I'm going to
take [in the rue Beautreillis].'[4] The forget-me-not was eloquent. His
need of money was unrelenting.

On 12 October he signed a contract with Calonne. It has now been
lost to sight; but it seems that he engaged to give the *Revue contemporaine*

enough material for twelve printed sheets a year, for the sum of three thousand francs. If he could bring himself to do regular work, he would be sure of funds. Calonne showed extraordinary patience with him.

For the moment, he remained in financial need. His plans to live in Honfleur were affected. His mother kept *the dear home*, as she called it,[5] in a constant state of readiness, and she expected him from day to day. On 19 October he announced that he was leaving next day for Honfleur, and would be with her on the 21st. 'I am only coming to embrace you and to chat. I am leaving again immediately, and I shall finally come back and settle at the end of the month.'[6]

He was demanding, aggressive, deplorably unfeeling. He himself had told her, after Aupick's death, that he was now responsible for her happiness. In the eighteen months of her widowhood, he had not once been to Honfleur, or shown a real concern for her welfare. He was solely concerned with his own. Now he arrived at the *maison joujou* for the first time, and he left again with the speed of light. On 23 October, once again from Paris, he announced that he was sending her a first parcel of books; at intervals, for the rest of the month, she would receive more consignments of his belongings. The books, he told her, must be unwrapped, and put on his table or his chest-of-drawers, 'not thrown on the floor'.[7]

She accepted all his arrogance and all his impositions, and she behaved 'in a wonderful and charming way'.[8] She sent him 300 francs, and wrote about a new room for him. This was no doubt the small study which she prepared for him next to his attic bedroom. Baudelaire refused to sleep in the General's room; she would have been unhappy had he done so.[9] Her plans for him seem to have been extensive. 'It is all very ingenious,' he told her on 27 October, 'but how long will it take? ... I don't need to tell you how touched I have been by the astonishing activity of mind which you bring to my small needs. It makes me almost ashamed.'[10] She was not merely active, she was agitated, her mind was in a ferment. She did not only hope for pleasure in his company; she also hoped, of course, to reform him. 'You're quite right to hope that the communal life which I'm about to take up with Charles will be beneficial to him,' she told her stepson, Alphonse Baudelaire. 'Heaven only knows how much I hope for that myself! But what tireless and unceasing efforts I shall have to make to succeed in influencing that strange and remarkable character!'[11]

It was not simply a question of reform, it was also a question of diplomacy. Baudelaire could not give up his pipes and cigars; she herself detested the smell of tobacco. 'My dear mother, as I told you,' he wrote, 'I marvel at the concern and activity which you are showing for me. But really don't carry your zeal as far as *an exhaust-valve*. I'm afraid that this modern invention may be deplorable. When you want to rid a room of smoke, you open the window.'[12] The valve was a needless expense, he added, and it might also damage a ceiling.[13] Mme Aupick continued to brood about the exhaust-valve. On 31 October, he wrote:

> Do forget your fantastic idea of a valve. Are you really afraid that I shall blow up, like a steamer? . . .
> As for my hand, which is becoming clumsier every day: no, it isn't rheumatism, because it doesn't hurt.[14]

It was not rheumatism; the increasing disability of his right hand marked the progress of his syphilis.

Baudelaire intended to leave the hôtel Voltaire on 31 October. However, he continued to keep his room from day to day. In November he lived mostly, it seems, with Jeanne Duval at 22, rue Beautreillis, in the working-class district of the faubourg Saint-Antoine. For all his decisions to break with her, he could not discard her.

Mme Aupick, in Honfleur, grew increasingly bewildered and flurried. He sent her three crates of his books. She thought that they were recent purchases. He assured her that they were not. 'Promise me,' he added, 'not to have any more imaginings.'[15]

Her imaginings continued, and her anxiety made him desperate.

> My dear mother [he wrote to her, probably next day], let me tell you simply: *You're tormenting me.*
> No, no, no, no, what you're afraid of will not happen. (You always say *in February*; you mean: *in April*.)
> I am delighted that this chimney is finished, I should like to set out at once . . .
> I embrace you with all my heart, and I beg you not to worry.[16]

Between 12 December and the end of the month, Baudelaire twice visited Alençon, and he spent twelve days with Malassis. He returned to Paris on 28 or 29 December. On his journey, in the buffet at Chartres, he scribbled to his mother: 'I wish *us* a happy new year.'[17]

65

In January, before he finally set out for Honfleur, Baudelaire paid several visits to the Ministry of Public Instruction. There he saw

Auguste de Châtillon. Portrait-painter-in-ordinary to the Hugo family, engraver and songwriter, Châtillon earned his living as a functionary. He and several other friends interceded in Baudelaire's favour with the Minister, Gustave Rouland. Baudelaire hoped to obtain a grant for his translations of Poe. On 22 January he was given 300 francs.

The news appears to have reached him in Honfleur; and it was from Honfleur, on 27 January, that he wrote to Châtillon to thank him for his intervention and for his constant friendship.[1] On 1 February he announced to Malassis: 'Here I am, absolutely settled, and ready to fulfil all my duties; I mean deprived of a pretext for failing to do so.'[2]

There was a new tone in his letters: a tone of confidence and purpose, and – rare in his correspondence – a tone of happiness. Richard Burton was to write of this visit to Honfleur that there was 'a uterine character in this enclosed but liberating space'.[3] If, as Baudelaire maintained in *Le Peintre de la vie moderne*, 'le génie n'est que *l'enfance retrouvée* à volonté,' both he and his mother were going to extraordinary lengths to re-create its conditions. 'Now, for a few brief months, in another "maison petite mais tranquille", that "vert paradis des amours enfantines" was miraculously restored, and, with its restoration, Baudelaire experienced a burst of creativity unique in his lifetime ... He was delivered as though magically of all the barriers which, especially since the disasters of 1857, had held his creativity in check.'[4] On the Baudelairean stage, Pierre Emmanuel maintained, 'one drama is everlastingly repeated ... One might call it the drama of the forbidden return to the womb, or else the return to the forbidden womb.'[5] As Burton boldly wrote, Baudelaire and his mother were 'free to pursue their illicit love-affair: not so much, perhaps, that incestuous mother-son love, ... as the elder sister/younger brother idyll they had shared some thirty years previously in the rue Saint-André-des-Arts and at Neuilly.'[6]

In his *Journaux intimes*, Baudelaire himself recorded: 'Study the great Malady of the horror of a Home. Reasons for the Malady. Progressive development of the Malady.'[7] He needed solitude and he detested it; he condemned marriage, but he needed domesticity. He could not have borne a permanent existence with his mother in the provinces; and yet he was happy, now, as never before or afterwards: 'happy with the happiness that only the unhappy know'.[8] It has been rightly said that this visit to Honfleur was the last contented and peaceful period of his life.

> Ces serments, ces parfums, ces baisers infinis,
> Renaîtront-ils d'un gouffre interdit à nos sondes,
> Comme montent au ciel les soleils rajeunis
> Après s'être lavés au fond des mers profondes?
> – Ô serments! ô parfums! ô baisers infinis![9]

66

At the turn of the century Charles Bréard, a local historian, recorded the house which was known, by then, as *le pavillon Baudelaire*. With a certain disregard for facts, Bréard explained that it had been owned 'by General Baron Aupick, an officer of Irish origin, . . . who was ambassador in London, then in Madrid . . . It was after the death of his stepfather, with whom he was in conflict, that Charles Baudelaire came to stay with his mother, in Honfleur . . . People still remember this strange poet's eccentricities.'[1]

Honfleur had once been a thriving port. The place was quieter, now, and yet Baudelaire's visit, in the early months of 1859, was not to be a simple provincial retreat. It was at Honfleur, in February or March, that he made the acquaintance of a local artist, Eugène Boudin. Jean-Aubry recalls, in his life of Boudin:

> Schanne, the 'Schaunard' of the *Vie de Bohème*, and Courbet, had decided to go to Le Havre to see the sea and to *botanise* on the coast. In a shop window in the rue de Paris, the master of Ornans noticed some conscientious little marine paintings which immediately interested him. He asked for the painter's address, and he was directed to Boudin. The latter, delighted by the meeting, made himself their guide, took them to Honfleur and settled them half way up the hill . . .
>
> One morning in the port, our friends were not a little surprised to meet Baudelaire, who was ruralising at his mother's.[2]

In his memoirs, Schanne himself recorded his surprise. 'We had thought that Baudelaire was busy cultivating his *Fleurs du mal* in a hotel in the rue Mazarine . . .'[3] The account is already open to suspicion: Baudelaire had some thirty addresses in Paris over the years, but the rue Mazarine was not among them.

> Baudelaire [continued Schanne] explained to us that he was forced to stay with his mother, la Générale Aupick, who had a country house near the town, and he added: 'I'm taking you to dinner, and I'm going to introduce you to her.'
>
> We were most embarrassed [remembered Schanne], because we hadn't brought any [suitable] clothes; our travelling reefer-jackets might even have been said to be in a picturesque condition. In any case it was deplorable. But our friend insisted in an almost imperious tone, and so we found it impossible to refuse him.
>
> I still see my friend Courbet, bent double to give his arm to the mistress of the house, who was very small, and followed, as by an aide-de-camp, by my no less grotesque self . . . The dinner, very sumptuously served, was delightful in every way . . .
>
> We had coffee on a verandah full of rare plants, from which one could

see all the stars rise up or sink into the waves.

At about nine o'clock, however, we left this enchanting place. We had to return to Paris overnight.[4]

•

It was at this point that Schanne entered the realms of imagination. Baudelaire, he continued, had gone with them as far as the boat, he had embarked, and caught the train with them at Le Havre in order to escape from his mother. With paradox after paradox, he had entertained them until they arrived, with three francs between them, at the Gare Saint-Lazare.[5]

It is of such stuff that legends are made. As a matter of history, Courbet's painting, *Bouquet d'asters*, now in the museum at Basle, bears the inscription: 'Dédié à mon ami Baudelaire, 1859'.[6] It is, perhaps, a memento of their meeting. Ideology was one day to divide them, but so far their friendship was unbroken.

While he was staying at Honfleur, Baudelaire also went to Boudin's studio, in the rue de l'Homme-de-Bois, in Le Havre, where he saw several hundred studies of sea and sky. His encounter with Boudin did not create any lasting bond between them. The poet's correspondence does not mention Boudin, the artist's published and unpublished letters refer only once to Baudelaire.[7] However, there remained a permanent witness to this meeting in the *Salon de 1859*, in which Baudelaire devoted a lyrical page to the man whom Corot called 'the king of skies'.[8] 'One day, without any doubt,' wrote Baudelaire, 'he will display, in finished paintings, the prodigious enchantments of sky and sea.'[9]

Mme Aupick had given her son two adjoining rooms in the *maison joujou*. The bedroom looked over Honfleur. From the study, Baudelaire, like Boudin, found the enchantments of sky and sea prodigious. 'Le Port', a prose poem, was to be inspired by his recollections of Honfleur.[10] Meanwhile, in his mother's house, in the early weeks of 1859, he was finally working. In the evenings, he studied English with her; during the day, he turned to the adaptation of De Quincey, and he returned to his poetry. In the first days of February, he sent Barbey d'Aurevilly three poems in manuscript: 'L'Albatros', 'Le Voyage', and 'Sisina'. On the back of the manuscript of 'Sisina', he wrote a list of titles, noting the poems he had already done.[11] '*Your poems are magnificent*,' answered Barbey on 4 February. '. . . Your 'Voyage' has a lyrical élan, an opening of *Albatross's* wings, which I didn't know you possessed, blackguard of Genius!'[12]

The poems were the fruit of these fertile, halcyon days. Baudelaire always loved the sea: the sense of peace and vastness that it gave him. Jean-Aubry once remarked that, in all probability, Baudelaire had not

seen the sea between his Eastern voyage in 1841–2 and his rapid visit
to Honfleur in October 1858. After seventeen years, it had stirred his
sympathies and memories. It was now, it seems, in 1859, that he
re-wrote 'L'Albatros', the poem which he was said to have brought
back from his travels; it was now that the vast and changing spectacle
of the sea and sky at Honfleur assured posterity of 'Le Voyage'.[13] In
his study of English influences on Baudelaire, Jean Pommier suggests
that, in *The Ancient Mariner*, he may have found the two themes of the
albatross and the voyage, which might be dissociated and separately
treated; Pommier also suggests a relationship between certain lines in
'Le Voyage' and lines in Tennyson's 'The Lotos-Eaters' about the land
'in which it seemèd always afternoon'.[14] There is no record that
Baudelaire read *The Ancient Mariner*; nor is there any record that he
read Tennyson, although he asked twice for the poet to receive
complimentary copies of his books. Yet one wonders, still, what English
he had studied with his mother on those winter evenings. Perhaps they
had read Byron. Baudelaire himself was to mention 'the systematically
Byronic tone' of 'Le Voyage',[15] and in the lyric 'To Inez', in the first
canto of *Childe Harold's Pilgrimage*, Byron had sung of the ceaseless
journey of the man who was weary of life, but could not escape the
hell of his own heart.[16]

Whatever the literary influences upon Baudelaire, his poetry was his
alone. Le Dantec was one day to emphasise 'the miraculously unique
quality of Baudelaire as a maritime poet ... One can imagine his
intoxication on the day when, at Honfleur, ... the mirage of his
youthful visions suddenly appeared to him and translated itself into the
vast symphony of 'Le Voyage'.'[17] Baudelaire loved the sight of ships
rocking at anchor, the dreams of spiritual adventure that they stirred
in him. 'Those fine, large ships, imperceptibly rocking on the tranquil
sea, those sturdy ships, with an idle and nostalgic look, do they not ask
us in a wordless tongue: When do we set out for happiness?'[18]

In February 1859, Baudelaire had a small pamphlet printed in Honfleur. It contained 'Sisina', 'Le Voyage' and 'L'Albatros'.

On 23 February he sent Maxime du Camp a copy of 'Le Voyage',
and he asked to dedicate it to him.[19]

In an illuminating article, *Baudelaire et Maxime du Camp*, Yoshio Abé
offers some explanations for the dedication.[20] Du Camp, he maintains,
was considered the most committed traveller of his generation, and in
his latest collection of poems he had affirmed his vocation. Perhaps
Baudelaire wanted to show a relationship between 'Le Voyage' and
'Les Convictions', in which Du Camp confessed that, in all his travels,
he had not found the means to comfort himself for his sad dreams.

Another explanation for the dedication was, Abé suggests, a mischievous intention to tease the poet of the useful and the progressive, the believer in democracy, the deist who attacked the Church. There were indeed evident links between 'Le Voyage' and Du Camp's two collections of poems: *Les Chants modernes* (1855) and *Les Convictions* (1858). They emphasise the chasm between genius and talent.

In 'Le Voyage', Baudelaire describes a band of travellers setting out on a voyage round the world. They leave in a mood of elation, but almost at once it changes to a mood of profound discouragement. The underlying theme of 'Le Voyage' is the tragic disproportion between aspiration and reality. The poet begins by recalling the comfortable world of childhood: the world of the rue Hautefeuille, the world of lamplight, maps and prints – a universe in which, for the first time and the last, a man feels secure and satisfied. In the second line we have the sensation of the world expanding to fulfil the child's desires, but this world is artificial like the prints, and like the lamplight which illuminates it. The travellers are constantly buoyed up by fresh hopes which constantly bring fresh disillusionment. The voyage becomes a sad pursuit of an unknown, unattainable ideal. Their experience is in itself a summary of *Les Fleurs du mal*, Baudelaire's final comment on modern civilization. The travellers end exactly where they started, with nothing left to do but to embark on another journey. This time it is the last journey, for 'Le Voyage' is an allegory of man's life from the cradle to the grave. It leaves the travellers disillusioned, battered and exhausted, waiting for death in the hope that this final voyage may bring them something new.

> Ô Mort, vieux capitaine, il est temps! levons l'ancre!
> Ce pays nous ennuie, ô Mort! Appareillons!
> Si le ciel et la mer sont noirs comme de l'encre,
> Nos cœurs que tu connais sont remplis de rayons!
>
> Verse-nous ton poison pour qu'il nous réconforte!
> Nous voulons, tant ce feu nous brûle le cerveau,
> Plonger au fond du gouffre, Enfer ou Ciel, qu'importe?
> Au fond de l'Inconnu pour trouver du *nouveau!*[21]

On this one unique occasion, so Prévost was to write, the poet was to resume all the diverse people he had been. This man for whom nature was so narrow, so monotonous, this man who had seen the world through art rather than in its natural state, would no longer be his own shadow or his own reflection on things. It was, in short, for death to give him a new sensation; and so 'Le Voyage' deserves to be the final poem in *Les Fleurs du mal*, the one which marks the successive stages of the poet's life – memoirs which are the memoirs of us all. One hope alone will restore to the poet the elation of his first departure. The wind from the open sea remains the only chance of freshness; death is the only certainty which remains to man, and the poet tries to make it the only hope.[22]

'Le Voyage' is remarkable for its range and variety of tone, for its sardonic, astringent humour, and for its poise and sophistication. The main theme is also the main theme of *Les Fleurs du mal*. Baudelaire's poetry is filled with voyages and plans for voyages. The sea is a symbol of liberation in his poetry, but it is also a symbol of ceaseless, exhausting movement which brings no rest and no relief. Desires revolve in circles, rising and falling, shifting and changing, until at last emotions destroy themselves by their own internal friction. *Les Fleurs du mal* is a tour of the modern world which begins with 'Bénédiction' and ends with 'Le Voyage'. In the course of his tour, Baudelaire examines the spiritual problems of his age. Its problems remain our problems today.

67

Early in March, Baudelaire returned from Honfleur to Paris. He lodged, once again, in the rue Beautreillis, with Jeanne Duval. He plunged at once into Parisian life. He sent two poems to Sainte-Beuve ('Danse macabre' and, perhaps, 'Le Voyage').[1] On 5 March, ungener- ous as ever, Sainte-Beuve replied:

> My dear Friend,
>   I am unwell. I have throat trouble, which forbids me conversation of any length.
>   I have received your 'Danse' and your 'Océan' [*sic*], you are following your vein. I shall only be able to express my praise and my reservations in a chat . . .
>   I hope, however, that if you stay here a few weeks, I shall be able to see you and to talk . . .[2]

On 13 March, while Baudelaire awaited a summons to the rue Montparnasse, and Gautier himself remained in Russia, *Théophile Gautier* appeared in *L'Artiste*. It was a generous appreciation of the *magicien ès lettres françaises*, the man who had 'the majestic modesty of the true man of letters'.[3] It was, observed Baudelaire, a paradox that, for many years, Gautier had filled Paris and the provinces with the renown of his journalism, but that no one had found time to read 'Albertus', 'La Comédie de la mort', or 'España'. Gautier had not deigned to be a popular poet, and, as Baudelaire observed, 'aristocracy isolates us.'[4]

Mademoiselle de Maupin, that hymn to Beauty, that dream pursued with the obstinacy of an artist, had finally established the essential condition for works of art: the changeless and exclusive love of Beauty. If the word *writer* was applied only to those who created works of the imagination, Gautier – said Baudelaire – was the writer *par excellence*, because the love of Beauty was his guide. This innate love of perfection made him a critic apart. No one had better expressed the happiness given to the imagination by the sight of a fine work of art. Gautier had not only a love of Beauty, a cosmopolitan love of art, but technical brilliance. He also had 'an immense innate understanding of universal *correspondence* and symbolism . . . To use a language cleverly is to practise a sort of evocative magic. It is then that colour speaks, like a deep and resonant voice, . . . that perfume stirs the complementary thought and recollection . . .'[5] Baudelaire himself, enthralled by the theory of *correspondances*, was well aware how often, in his prose and poetry, Gautier had used them. Gautier, he wrote, was a model for future generations. He was indeed a perfect man of letters.

Despite all the superlatives that Baudelaire employs, indeed because of such excessive praise, one detects a lack of inspiration. Almost exclusively, in this article, Baudelaire refers to Gautier's early work; only once does he mention *Émaux et Camées*, his most celebrated book of poems, the model for the school of Art for Art's Sake, which had appeared in 1852. Baudelaire spends much time on generalities. His article is perceptive, and it is affectionate, and yet it hardly explains the warmth of the dedication of *Les Fleurs du mal*. Baudelaire's opinion of Gautier had always fluctuated, and would always do so. In 1845, he had implied that Gautier was a literary hack; in 1846 he had dismissed him as 'a stringer of words'.[6] In the autumn of 1859, he was to denigrate him to Victor Hugo.[7] In 1863 he was to criticise him sharply in *L'Œuvre et la vie d'Eugène Delacroix*.[8] It is curious that he should show such malice and hypocrisy towards the friend to whom he had paid the most splendid tribute of his life.

At Baudelaire's request, his article on Gautier had now been sent, in proof, to Victor Hugo in Guernsey. Baudelaire thought of having it separately published as a pamphlet. Malassis prepared to publish it.

Baudelaire had received 100 francs for his article, but he was still in grave financial straits. We do not know the nature of the 'painful accident' which kept him in Paris; indeed, we do not know if it occurred. However, on 26 March, he felt constrained to write, once again, to the President of the Société des Gens de Lettres: 'A painful accident keeps me in Paris and prevents me from going home. I need some money to mitigate this unexpected misfortune. I have been bold enough to believe that a demand for 300 francs would not be rejected by you and by my friends on the Committee.'[9] A scribbled note on the letter reads: '150 francs.'[10] Baudelaire still needed money. On 1 April, in aggressive mood, he approached Jean Morel, the director of the *Revue française*. He had promised him some copy; he needed money from him, when he was about to leave for Honfleur.[11]

He expected to set out within the next few days; but, dramatically, his plans were changed. On 5 April, Jeanne Duval suffered a stroke. That day she entered the Maison municipale de santé, 200, faubourg Saint-Denis.[12]

There were happier events. On 10 April the *Revue française* published 'Sisina', 'Le Voyage', and 'L'Albatros'. Baudelaire had already sent copies of the poems to Flaubert.[12]

> I was both touched and delighted [Flaubert answered].
> Your three poems have made me dream endlessly. From time to time I re-read them. They remain on my table like luxuries, which one likes to look at; 'L'Albatros' seems to me a pure diamond . . .
> I grasp your hand with much affection.[13]

His warmth belied the comments which his niece, Mme Franklin Grout, was one day to make to Féli Gautier: 'My uncle always spoke of Baudelaire with admiration, but I don't think that he was among his intimates.'[14]

By 21 April, Baudelaire was back at Honfleur. It was from his mother's house that, eight days later, he sent Malassis instructions for printing his study of Gautier.

> And now [he wrote] something serious as a postscript; I have come back here to work fast and to make up for the time I lost in Paris through a great misfortune.
> You will receive this letter and the third order to pay on Saturday 30 [April]. On 3 May I have to pay 120 francs at the Maison de santé, plus 20 francs to the nurse. I cannot go back to Paris. Take advantage of the Saturday [tomorrow] to cash this order . . ., and, *on Sunday*, send 150 francs (a note for 100 and one for 50 or a money-order) to M. le directeur de la Maison municipale de santé, 200, faubourg Saint-Denis. You will say in your letter that you are sending this on behalf of M. Baudelaire for the board and lodging of Mlle Jeanne Duval . . .
> Even if all this is a great bother to you, I count on your friendship. I will not have them turning my paralytic out.[15]

Baudelaire's brutal tone disguised genuine concern.

Malassis did as he was asked, but matters were not so simply settled. On 3 May, Jeanne herself dictated a letter to Baudelaire, to tell him that the money had not arrived. Next day he turned, again, to Malassis. 'I beg you, my dear friend, to write immediately to the director of the Maison municipale de santé . . . You should also write to the manager of the railway to complain.'[16] He was all the more anxious since the doctors had decided that Jeanne was in no condition to leave hospital. As usual, he himself was destitute. Mme Aupick, naturally hostile to Jeanne, refused to lend him another 150 francs for her upkeep, and there followed an appalling scene. Four days later, on 8 May, Baudelaire wrote once more to Malassis:

> Mon cher, I apologise profoundly for my stupid demand. I was deceived by a letter from that terrible woman (not written by herself, because she couldn't write), telling me that nothing had been received. In her wretched mind, made stupid by illness, she had found this ingenious means of procuring the money twice over, without thinking how easy it was to verify. I wanted to borrow 150 francs immediately, from my mother . . . She had an abominable row with me, and I retaliated. It has made my mother ill. And, since the 4th, I have been in bed myself, with my stomach and intestines seized up, and a neuralgia which moves around with every change of wind, and gives me such sharp twinges of pain that I cannot sleep.
>
> Such are the results of anger and anxiety. This predicament must end, for work and money and time are all one.[17]

In mid-May, so Baudelaire told Nadar, his mother went away, briefly, and left him at Honfleur. Perhaps she did take a holiday; she needed a respite. Yet a doubt persists. While Baudelaire himself was far from well, she would hardly have left him alone in the villa in the rue de Neubourg. Perhaps he was telling a diplomatic lie when, on 14 May, he wrote:

> My dear Nadar, I am like a soul in torment. I have been thoughtless enough to let my mother set off on a short journey without asking her for money, and I am here, alone, not lacking butcher's meat or bread, etc, but absolutely without a sou, and exposed to a mass of inconveniences, as a result of this calamity. I thought that, if it wasn't a complete embarrassment for you, you would have the charity to send me (immediately, alas!) a postal-order for 20 francs, which I shall repay you on the 1st of the month, if you agree not to laugh too much at this promise. In fact I have to go to Paris then. I can have your reply in the morning the day after tomorrow, if you do me the favour of thinking of me before 5 o'clock. *Ch. Baudelaire, Honfleur, Calvados.* This address is quite enough.
>
> To give you an idea of my difficulty, which alone can excuse such a

ridiculous request, imagine that I *need* to go and spend a few hours at Le
Havre (at least don't imagine that this is with the thought of debauchery),
and that I cannot do so, for want of the thing in question.[18]

It has been suggested by Pichois, in his edition of the letters, that
Baudelaire was in need of opium. This seems more than probable.
Baudelaire had once needed laudanum, the medicinal form of opium,
to soothe his stomach pains, the result of the progress of his syphilis.
Now it had become an essential drug. He probably used laudanum as
an anti-depressant, as De Quincey had originally done.[19] In February,
from Honfleur, he had lamented to Malassis: 'I am very depressed, my
dear friend, and I have no money to pay my chemist in Paris.'[20] He
was no doubt wary of the chemist in Honfleur (who, by a quirk of
history, was the father of the humorist Alphonse Allais).

Years later, Mme Allais gave her recollections to Léon Lemonnier,
who was writing his *Enquêtes sur Baudelaire*:

> 'I hardly saw General Aupick,' she said . . . 'I knew Mme Aupick better.
> She was a small and very distinguished woman dressed in old-fashioned
> clothes, wearing splendid jewels and lace which she had brought back
> from Constantinople . . .
>
> Did I often see *la générale*? Yes, of course, she came to the pharmacy
> nearly every day, and she used to give my husband a prescription, and
> say to him: "It isn't urgent: Mme Allais can bring it to me."
>
> She lived in an elegant house full of curious furniture . . .
>
> What struck me most was that, when she was widowed, Mme Au-
> pick never sat down at table without her husband's place being laid
> opposite, even when her son was there. And yet he and the General had
> fallen out . . .
>
> I often saw the poet at the pharmacy. He looked old, but he was very
> agreeable and distinguished in his manners . . . He had acquired the
> opium habit, and he used to beg my husband to supply him with some.
> But M. Allais never gave him more than a conscientious pharmacist
> could do.'[21]

Perhaps, in May 1859, Baudelaire needed to go further afield.
Whatever Nadar suspected, he remained a loyal friend. On 16 May,
Baudelaire duly thanked him, 'not only for the 20 francs, but especially
for *an excellent and delightful phrase in your letter*. That is a real and solid
declaration of friendship. I am unaccustomed to affection.'[22]

There remained an unbelievable contrast between the squalor of the
life and the splendour of the poetry. Marcel Proust was one day to
observe how foreign the superficial, everyday self, which begged for
help and struggled against debts, remained to the inner self, to the
author of *Les Fleurs du mal*.[23] As for Jeanne Duval, as Arthur Symons

said, she was simply a silent instrument that Baudelaire awakened to a music that was all his own.[24]

> Ô toison, moutonnant jusque sur l'encolure!
> Ô boucles! Ô parfum chargé de nonchaloir!
> Extase! Pour peupler ce soir l'alcôve obscure
> Des souvenirs dormant dans cette chevelure,
> Je la veux agiter dans l'air comme un mouchoir!
>
> La langoureuse Asie et la brûlante Afrique,
> Tout un monde lointain, absent, presque défunt,
> Vit dans tes profondeurs, forêt aromatique!
> Comme d'autres esprits voguent sur la musique,
> Le mien, ô mon amour! nage sur ton parfum.
>
> J'irai là-bas où l'arbre et l'homme, pleins de sève,
> Se pâment longuement sous l'ardeur des climats;
> Fortes tresses, soyez la houle qui m'enlève!
> Tu contiens, mer d'ébène, un éblouissant rêve
> De voiles, de rameurs, de flammes et de mâts:
>
> Un port retentissant où mon âme peut boire
> À grands flots le parfum, le son et la couleur;
> Où les vaisseaux, glissant dans l'or et dans la moire,
> Ouvrent leurs vastes bras pour embrasser la gloire
> D'un ciel pur où frémit l'éternelle chaleur . . .[25]

On 19 May, partly paralysed, Jeanne Duval left the Maison municipale de santé in the faubourg Saint-Denis. Next day, in the *Revue française*, there appeared 'La Chevelure': one of the glorious cycle of poems which Baudelaire had written for her.

68

When Baudelaire was invited by Jean Morel to discuss the Salon of 1859, he had been asked to describe a philosophical stroll among the paintings. This suited his conception of reviewing a Salon; it was also the only way to consider the current exhibition. There was not an abundance of talent; there were, in his opinion, no new artists of true distinction. It had been announced that English artists would be exhibiting their work, and Baudelaire had rejoiced in the thought of renewing his acquaintance with the artists whose work he had admired four years earlier, at the International Exhibition of

1855. He had an uncommon knowledge of the English school, a remarkable sympathy with their work. They were not, alas, to show their canvases, and he was obliged to restrict himself to the work of French artists. He would, he said, have liked to enthuse about his compatriots, but he was compelled to admit that, in general, they were mediocre.

Such mediocrity only served to emphasise the brilliance of Delacroix, the painter of sensibility and intense imagination, the painter constantly in search of technical perfection. There was no doubt of Baudelaire's hero among modern artists. He despised literary painting, the canvas that told a story or attempted to moralise; he loved the paintings which, like poetry, created atmosphere, and left room for the imagination. While Delacroix was the chief exemplar of the artist-poet, Baudelaire found another in the young Eugène Fromentin. Perhaps, indeed, he found in him a reflection of himself: a recollection of his own, now distant, voyage to the East:

> If I said of him that he was a teller of travellers' tales, I should not say enough; because there are many travellers who lack poetry or a soul, and his soul is one of the most poetic and precious that I know. His painting, properly speaking, sensible, powerful, well controlled, clearly originates from Eugène Delacroix. With him, too, one rediscovers that expert, natural understanding of colour which is so rare among us. But light and warmth, which cast a kind of tropical fever over certain minds, stir an insatiable fury in them, and drive them into dances yet unknown, cast only a gentle, peaceful contemplation into his soul . . .[1]

Baudelaire discussed the art of the portrait, and he paid tribute to Gustave Ricard (who had memorably painted La Présidente). He wrote of landscapes, and deplored the self-consciousness of Millet's peasants, the restraint of Corot; he turned to Boudin, whose studio he had recently visited.[2] From Boudin's studies one could already guess the season, the time of day and the direction of the wind. His seascapes inspired Baudelaire with a prose poem. So, too, did the landscapes in Meryon's engravings. Baudelaire had 'rarely seen the natural solemnity of a city represented with more poetry.'[3]

Baudelaire had sought imagination in the Salon; and, having rarely found it, he had had to confine himself to the work of a few men; but he had spoken of the artists who have come down to posterity.

On 10 June, the first part of the *Salon de 1859* appeared in *La Revue française*. On 20 June, the second instalment was published, and he sent both articles to Delacroix.

> How can I thank you properly for this new proof of your friendship [Delacroix replied]? You come to my aid when I find myself mauled and

vilified by a good number of serious or so-called serious critics ... You treat me as one only treats the *great dead*; you make me blush, and at the same time you please me very much ...

Goodbye, cher Monsieur; publish something more often. You put yourself into everything you do, and those who admire your talent only complain of the rarity of your appearances.[4]

69

On his return to Paris in the second half of June, Baudelaire had plunged once again into his life of trouble and uncertainty. Before the month was over, he was exhausted with fatigue, and he had already moved twice.[1]

Late in June or early in July, he took a room at the hôtel de Dieppe, 22, rue d'Amsterdam. It was on the fifth floor, it was seedy, and there was constant noise from the street below. However, it was near the Gare de l'Ouest, which was convenient when and if he chose to visit Honfleur. He was desperate, as ever, for ready money. He sent an apologetic note to Paul Meurice, the dramatist, and the faithful factotum of Victor Hugo, asking to borrow '50 francs or even less for *four or five days*'.[2]

He paid a brief visit to Alençon, where his publisher was doubtless glad to see him. Malassis was working 'like a day-labourer', and he found the provinces 'malaria to the willpower and the mind'.[3] On 20 July, the *Revue française* published the third and last instalment of Baudelaire's *Salon de 1859*. It was the final issue of the periodical.

That day, at the offices of the *Revue*, he found two letters from Mme Aupick.

My affairs are almost going well [he answered], but for the terrible question of expenses ... If I had not been really compelled to come to Paris, I should not have come here. It is not only the expenses which distress me, but something which is more serious, the impossibility of being clearsighted and concentrating my thoughts. I am dazed, addle-headed, stupid; you know that I had acquired the habit of slow and patient thought, the habit of happier days ...

I am staying until the end of the month at the *hôtel de Dieppe, rue d'Amsterdam*, where I am as badly off as I can be.[4]

He expected to return to Honfleur early in August; but the letters which he wrote that month are all dated from Paris. In his noisy room

in the rue d'Amsterdam, he was translating Poe's *Eureka*. Whatever his
complaints about the hôtel de Dieppe, he was to stay there, with one
short break, for the next five years.[5]

On 15 September, *La Revue contemporaine* published 'Les Sept Vieillards'
and 'Les Petites Vieilles', which Baudelaire was later to dedicate to
Victor Hugo. On 23 September he sent the poems to Hugo, and asked
him for his literary protection. He wanted Hugo to write a letter which
could be published with his brochure on Théophile Gautier.

It was in company with Édouard Ourliac, through whom he also
knew Pétrus Borel and Gérard de Nerval, that Baudelaire had first
been presented to Victor Hugo. It had been in about 1840, in his last
months at the pension Bailly. Hugo was then thirty-eight, and he was
living at 6, place Royale (now place des Vosges). Perhaps Baudelaire
had joined the flood of visitors at the evening receptions. If so, it was
surprising that, on his return from his eastern voyage, he had not
re-appeared in the place Royale.[6] Perhaps, already, he had felt
antipathy towards the man and his coterie of acolytes. The letter which
he sent him, now, showed some of Baudelaire's most disagreeable
qualities. Its cynical bravado was distasteful, its humility was calculated, its encomiums were patently insincere.

He had, he said, the greatest need of Hugo, and he appealed to his
kindness. He had recently asked for a copy of his article on Gautier to
be sent to Hugo in Guernsey, but he did not know if Hugo had
received it. He had, however, learned from Paul Meurice that Hugo
had written to him, and the letter seemed to have gone astray. Whether
or not the letter was related to the article, he had much regretted it:
'A letter from you, Monsieur, whom none of us has seen for so long:
from you, whom I have seen only twice and that nearly twenty years
ago, is something so agreeable and so precious!'[7]

Even Hugo could not have been deceived by such flattery; and even
he may have felt offended by what followed. Baudelaire – as we have
seen – often professed two judgments on his friends: the ones he reached
as a reflective man, and the ones he reached in a bad humour. It was
a continuing necessity for his spirit, for *homo duplex*, to feel affection and
dislike, admiration and contempt, for the same person. Two years
earlier, Baudelaire had dedicated *Les Fleurs du mal* to Gautier. Now, in
private, he expressed contempt for him. Whether he did so in order to
emphasise Hugo's majesty, or whether he genuinely felt that Gautier
was inferior, his comments were both disloyal and unnecessary.

> As for the writer who is the subject of this article [he explained], the writer
> whose name has served as a pretext for my critical considerations, I may admit
> to you *in confidence* that I know the deficiencies in his remarkable mind. Often,

when I have thought of him, I have been distressed to see that God refused to be completely generous. I haven't lied, I have eluded, and I have dissembled. If I were called to testify in court, and if my testimony, absolutely true, would harm a person favoured by Nature and dear to my Heart, I swear to you that I should lie with pride; for laws are less important than feeling, and friendship is, by its nature, infallible and ungovernable. But, where you are concerned, it seems to me absolutely useless to lie.

I need you. I need a voice more powerful than my own, more powerful than that of Théophile Gautier. I need your imperious voice. I want to be protected. I shall humbly print what you deign to write to me. I beg you, don't restrain yourself. If, in these proofs [of the brochure on Gautier], you find something to criticise, rest assured that I will dutifully publish your criticism, but I will do so without too much shame. A criticism from you: is it not a favour, since it is an honour?

The poems I attach to this letter have been stirring in my mind for a long while. The second piece was done *in order to imitate you* (laugh at my impertinence, I laugh at it myself), after re-reading some poems in your collections, in which such splendid charity mingles with such touching familiarity . . . When *Les Fleurs du mal* appears again, enlarged by three times more material than justice suppressed, I shall have the pleasure of inscribing above these poems the name of the poet whose works have taught me so much, and gave such delight to my youth.[8]

While he awaited Hugo's answer, Baudelaire continued to translate *Eureka* for *La Revue internationale*. The Geneva monthly was concerned with morals and with politics. As Jacques Crépet was to observe, many years later, it published literature on sufferance.[9] It was an unlikely publication to give sanctuary to Baudelaire and Poe. However, in October it began to serialise *Eureka*. Michel Lévy refused to discuss *Eureka*'s publication as a book until it had appeared in the Swiss periodical; but Baudelaire quarrelled with the editor, Carlos de Rode, and, having published instalments in November and December, and in January 1860, the *Revue* refused to continue.[10] Baron Félix Platel, who wrote the literary chronicle for the paper, dismissed *Eureka* as 'that gigantic charade by one of the two great men of America (the other is Washington), translated by the man who is the first poet of the new France.'[11] It was a handsome tribute to Baudelaire, and a condemnation of his work.

Meanwhile, in the last days of September 1859, both Baudelaire and Malassis grew anxious about the expected letter from Victor Hugo, which they hoped to publish as a foreword to *Théophile Gautier*. 'This is all I can tell you,' wrote Baudelaire on 1 October. 'Victor Hugo, I know, does his correspondence on Sundays . . . But even if the worst comes to the worst, and supposing he only had my packet on Monday, he is going to answer me tomorrow. You understand that this letter, if it is important, can help the sale of the brochure.'[12]

At last, on 6 October, the oracular answer came from Hauteville House:

Your article òn Théophile Gautier is one of those pieces which powerfully provoke our thoughts. It is a rare merit, to stimulate thought; it is only the gift of the elect . . . I have never said art for art's sake, I have always said: art for the sake of progress. Fundamentally, it is the same thing, and your mind is too penetrating not to feel it. Forward! That is the word of progress; it is also the cry of art. All the speech of poetry is there. *Ite.*

What are you doing when you write those striking poems, 'Les Sept Vieillards' and 'Les Petites Vieilles', which you dedicate to me, and for which I thank you? What are you doing? You are advancing. You endow the heaven of art with some indefinable, macabre ray of light. You create a new emotion, *un frisson nouveau.*[13]

The final comment was to be one of the most perceptive ever to be made on Baudelaire; it was certainly the most celebrated.

Baudelaire copied out the letter for Malassis, who was in Alençon. He himself, it is said, had hoped to leave Paris on 10 October;[14] but, if there had been any thoughts of returning to Honfleur, they were brushed aside. Mme Aupick wrote to him in tones of fierce reproach.

This is a very harsh letter [he answered]. How can you suppose that I should abandon some sensible plans – and that I don't want to come back to you, and other lunacies? . . .

You always imagine that I am ungrateful – absurd! – and then you forget that, having been an idler and a libertine for a long while, I am now obliged (which is very grievously comical) to play the part of father and guardian. It is not just a question of expenses, it's a question of thinking for an enfeebled mind.[15]

He was a child with his mother, but he felt a father with Jeanne. Her helplessness gave him a sense of adult responsibility; he was moved, besides, by gratitude for a distant past, by the feeling that he must atone for his wrongdoing to her.

70

Since Marie Daubrun had taken Banville under her wing, appointed herself his sick-nurse and his muse, Banville's condition had worsened.

In the spring of 1857, he had entered Dr Fleury's clinic at Bellevue; and, for the moment, the ménage had been broken.[1] Marie Daubrun disappeared from sight. Lyonnet, in his *Dictionnaire des comédiens français*, records that, from 1857 to 1859, she played duennas' parts in Marseilles;[2] Feuillerat found no evidence that she had done so, or that she had acted in Paris, where presumably – thanks to her quarrel with Hostein, the director of the Gaîté – she still remained banned from the theatre.[3] Only in the summer of 1859 did she re-appear on a Parisian stage. On 5 August, at the Gaîté, she made amends for her turbulent departure, and played Hélène Morales in *Les Pirates de la Savane*.[4]

Once again, it seems, despite her infidelity, she turned to Baudelaire for support; once again, he allowed himself to become ensnared. On 30 October, in the *Revue contemporaine*, there appeared 'Chant d'automne'. It was dedicated to 'M.D.', and Pichois considers that it had only recently been written.[5] It spoke of the imminence of winter, the thud of logs unloaded in courtyards; at every thud the poet shuddered, and it seemed to him that somewhere a coffin was hurriedly nailed down. The sound seemed to herald a departure: the second ending of a hopeless dream; and, in his fear of a second desertion, Baudelaire begged Marie Daubrun not to take her love from him. It did not matter, now, whether she was mistress, mother or sister, provided that she loved him, for she was the last ray of sunlight to illuminate a life in its decline.

> J'aime de vos longs yeux la lumière verdâtre,
> Douce beauté, mais tout aujourd'hui m'est amer,
> Et rien, ni votre amour, ni le boudoir, ni l'âtre,
> Ne me vaut le soleil rayonnant sur la mer.
>
> Et pourtant aimez-moi, tendre cœur! soyez mère,
> Même pour un ingrat, même pour un méchant;
> Amante ou sœur, soyez la douceur éphémère
> D'un glorieux automne ou d'un soleil couchant.
>
> Courte tâche! La tombe attend; elle est avide!
> Ah! laissez-moi, mon front posé sur vos genoux,
> Goûter, en regrettant l'été blanc et torride
> De l'arrière-saison le rayon jaune et doux![6]

There are moments, as Martin Turnell has said, when, in reading Baudelaire, we suddenly become aware that we are listening to the voice of a civilization.[7] So it is, here; 'for this is the voice of a man who seems indeed to have traversed the whole range of human experience, and to feel at the end of it only an immense lassitude. It is because the voice speaks for what Paul Bourget called "une civilisation vieillissante" that Baudelaire's "De l'arrière-saison le rayon jaune et doux"

has a wider reference than Macbeth's "the sear, the yellow leaf".'[8]
The poem is universal; it is also intensely personal. Baudelaire is
seeking, above all, for maternal love. Death will come; and, in its
name, the weary lover seeks for rest in love – not in the love that other
men desire, but in maternal consolation.

Baudelaire had not only shown his love for Marie Daubrun; he had
proclaimed himself to be her defender. She was to perform at the Gaîté
until 1 November. As her engagement neared its end, he approached
Ponson du Terrail. The prolific novelist was a friend of Anicet Bourgeois,
one of the most productive dramatists of the period. Baudelaire's letter
does not survive, but, on 6 November, Ponson du Terrail answered: 'I
shall see M. Anicet, and rest assured that I shall do all I can to please
Madame Daubrun. Only the *impossible* would stop me.'[9]

It proved to be impossible to find Marie a part. Some three weeks
later, she signed a contract with the Thibaud company, which was
about to set out for Nice. She took with her not Baudelaire, but
Banville, who was now gravely ill; once again she played the part of
his sick-nurse and muse.[10]

Early in December, Baudelaire expressed his anger at her second
betrayal. For him, in spite of everything, she had remained the princess
of *La Belle aux cheveux d'or*. In the poem 'À une Madone', he identified
her with one of those Virgins of the Seven Sorrows whom the mediaeval
mystics had sometimes represented with their hearts pierced through
by seven swords. It was not now the seven blessed sorrows of the
Virgin, it was the seven capital sins which Baudelaire proposed to plant
in the heart of his madonna. In this poem, he prostrated himself at the
feet of this fickle creature as an enraged supplicant, but also as an
admirer. It was difficult to say which triumphed, the enchantment or
the furious revolt; but, as Trial was to write, certain poems in *Les Fleurs
du mal* may be considered as cerebral equivalents to an act of sadism.[11]

> ... Enfin, pour compléter ton rôle de Marie,
> Et pour mêler l'amour avec la barbarie,
> Volupté noire! des sept Péchés capitaux,
> Bourreau plein de remords, je ferai sept Couteaux
> Bien affilés, et, comme un jongleur insensible,
> Prenant le plus profond de ton amour pour cible,
> Je les planterai tous dans ton Cœur pantelant,
> Dans ton Cœur sanglotant, dans ton Cœur ruisselant![12]

From this moment, Marie Daubrun virtually disappeared from the life
of Baudelaire. She prolonged her engagement in Nice until June 1860,
living openly with Banville; and with her departure Baudelaire reached

the end of the useless quest for ideal love. The double betrayal of Marie Daubrun had finally destroyed for him the possibility of salvation through a woman's devotion. He could no longer found on love the permanence of the state of spiritual grace.[13] Marie Daubrun was to bear much responsibility for the growing misery which weighed upon the last years of his life – a life deprived henceforward of the only hope which maintained him in his struggle against despair.

> Vous êtes un beau ciel d'automne, clair et rose!
> Mais la tristesse en moi monte comme la mer,
> Et laisse, en refluant, sur ma lèvre morose
> Le souvenir cuisant de son limon amer.
>
> – Ta main se glisse en vain sur mon sein qui se pâme;
> Ce qu'elle cherche, amie, est un lieu saccagé
> Par la griffe et la dent féroce de la femme.
> Ne cherchez plus mon cœur; les bêtes l'ont mangé.
>
> Mon cœur est un palais flétri par la cohue;
> On s'y soûle, on s'y tue, on s'y prend aux cheveux!
> – Un parfum nage autour de votre gorge nue! . . .
>
> Ô Beauté, dur fléau des âmes, tu le veux!
> Avec tes yeux de feu, brillants comme des fêtes,
> Calcine ces lambeaux qu'ont épargnés les bêtes![14]

It is doubtful whether Marie Daubrun ever felt any love for the man who had entrusted her with what was best in himself. It is doubtful, too, if she ever understood the beauty of the dream which she had aroused. Yet, by playing the consoling mistress, she had given Baudelaire a few months of illusory happiness.

She herself continued her theatrical career until the turn of the century. Lyonnet records that in 1889, after thirty-seven years on the boards, 'she obtained a pension of 500 francs from the Société des Artistes dramatiques. A former actress from the Opéra-Comique, Mlle Lemercier, gave her a pension of 700 francs and paid her rent. A friend gave her 15 francs a month. And so the old actress managed to rub along. She died in her humble lodgings, at 29, quai Valmy, [on 7] February 1901.'[15] She was seventy-four.

Her funeral service was held on 9 February, at Saint-Martin-du-Marais. Coquelin *aîné*, the actor, paid most of her funeral expenses. Her furniture was sent for auction. Her papers and photographs, which filled a trunk, were burnt by her concierge, who had heard her say that she would not like them to be seen. No doubt that is why there are no letters to her from Baudelaire – with one still questionable exception.

In time Maurice Goudeket, the third husband of Colette, acquired
two books which had belonged to Marie Daubrun. One was the *Poésies*
of Banville, triumphantly inscribed by the requited lover to his mistress;
the other was the second edition of *Les Fleurs du mal* with the
melancholy inscription:

> À Marie Daubrun
> Témoignage de vieille affection
> C. B.

The inscription was, presumably, written in 1861: a sober record of the
past, not a sign of hope or desire. Marie Daubrun had had the books
identically bound.[16]

71

In the first week of November 1859, *Théophile Gautier* was put on sale.
Baudelaire sent signed copies of his brochure to his mother and to a
number of friends, including La Présidente.[1] On 24 November, Hugo
instructed Meurice: 'If you see Baudelaire, I have received his charming little book on Gautier. Thank him for me.'[2] The imperious message
was no doubt delivered. On 7 December, Baudelaire sent Hugo a new
poem, 'Le Cygne', 'as a very inadequate token of the sympathy and
admiration which your genius inspires in me.'[3]

The sympathy was erratic, like the admiration. The modesty was
civil but misplaced. In its depths and in its echoes 'Le Cygne' was
among the finest of Baudelaire's poems. There are echoes in it of the
albatross, of the Eastern voyage, of his own remembrance of a paradise
lost. In this poem, instinct with compassion and regret, Baudelaire
paints himself to the life.

'Like everything you do, your 'Cygne' is an idea,' Hugo assured him.
'Like all real ideas, it has depths . . . One has a glimpse of these abysses
in your poem, which is also full of quivering and tremors . . .'[4] 'Le
Cygne' was to be one of three poems dedicated to Hugo in the new
edition of *Les Fleurs du mal*.

Mme Aupick had always been of a nervous disposition, and widowhood
and advancing age had not made her more serene. All that remained
to her was her son, and he seemed to do his utmost to disturb her.

Early in November, she was utterly perplexed and dismayed. The local bank had asked her to accept a promissory note on his behalf. She wrote to him, and told him of her agitation.

What an extraordinary imagination you have [answered Baudelaire]! . . .
What a singular idea to expect the Bank to show delicacy of feeling and to guess that it would agitate you by asking you for a signature in my absence!
As for supposing that someone or other should draw a bill on me and advise the banker to demand your acceptance, that is a fantasy, pure madness . . .[5]

It was neither fantasy nor madness. As Malassis confirmed, she had signed a promissory note for 1000 francs.[6]

In the meanwhile, Baudelaire continued to hector her, to denigrate her and to disturb her. He explained that he had not sent her instalments of *Eureka*, as they would have been beyond her understanding. He was, he said, worried about the way she had disturbed his two rooms at Honfleur, but he would soon see them for himself.[7] Apprehensive and unhappy, she was still unsure when he would return to live with her. When she asked him, he responded bitterly. When she expressed her anxiety about his finances, he accused her of callousness.[8] Early in December, he took the extraordinary step of writing to Troussel, a bailiff at Honfleur, to ask him to calm her.[9] If Troussel called on her, she can only have been disturbed by his visit, and still more disturbed by her son's state of mind.

In mid-December, after an interval of five months, he himself paid a rapid visit to Honfleur. The magic of the place remained, the delight of seeing his mother, the pleasure of the ordered life which she created round her. After his death, Mme Aupick was to feel close to her son at Honfleur. 'How I love and miss him here!' she wrote to Asselineau. '. . . I'll show you the place where he stretched out his arms to the sky and sea, and said to me many, many times: "Oh, if I had no debts, how happy I should be here!" '[10]

As for his life, in the closing days of 1859, it remained irremediable. On 19 December, he was back in Paris. He invited Malassis to discuss the contract for four volumes, which they were soon to sign. On 21 December, Malassis called at the hôtel de Dieppe; they agreed on the publication of a volume a month, as from February. Baudelaire asked Paul Meurice to return the 'fearful' drawings of prostitutes by Guys which he had lent him; he wanted to show them to Calonne and to Malassis to give them an idea of the article which he had in mind.[11]

On 28 December, he wrote to his mother. Recalling her years at the French Legation in Constantinople, the picture of Constantinople in her drawing-room, he had sent her a Turkish drawing by Guys; he was anxious to know whether she admired it.

> Though you haven't written to me at all, I presume that you are satisfied with your New Year present. You are the first person to whom I have been able to fulfil this duty, this year. And this drawing [*La Femme turque au parasol*, by Guys] is the only Oriental piece which I have been able to extract from this extraordinary man, on whom I am going to write a long article (the last of the pieces which will make up the *Curiosités esthétiques*).[12]

It is strange that Mme Aupick had not acknowledged the present from her son; he had chosen it with taste and care. Perhaps her silence was partly explained by the fact that she did not like it. After his death, she was to give it to Barbey d'Aurevilly.[13]

Meanwhile, on 28 December, Baudelaire told her of his anxieties and plans.

> Here [he added] is a year less stupidly occupied than the rest, but it's only a quarter of what I mean to do during the year about to begin. Suppose I were to become infirm, or to feel my mind decaying before I had done all that it seems to me that I should and can do!
>
> I beg you, tell me that you are well, that you really love me, and that you believe in my destiny.[14]

72

On 1 January 1860, Baudelaire signed a new contract with Malassis for the second edition of *Les Fleurs du mal*, and for *Opium et Haschich*, *Curiosités esthétiques*, and *Opinions littéraires* (these last were to be included in the posthumous volume *L'Art romantique*). He was to receive 150 francs on delivery of each manuscript volume, and a further 150 francs when each of them was ready for the press.[1]

He intended to leave for Honfleur on 9 January; but even now there was room for misunderstanding. On 7 January he wrote to Mme Aupick: 'You can imagine what sadness I've endured since I had your letter this morning, telling me that you were scanning the boats from Le Havre.'[2] Passengers from Le Havre had to come by boat across the estuary to Honfleur. Despite his plans, it was to be a long while before he came.

He was not only worried about his work, and, as usual, about his penury. On 13 January he received an ominous reminder of his physical condition. It was, he told his mother, a curious attack:

> I was away from my lodgings; I had an almost empty stomach. I think I had something like a cerebral congestion. A kind old woman got me through it by some strange means or other. But, when I had recovered from it, I had another attack. Vomitings, and such weakness, and dizzy spells, that I couldn't climb one step of the stairs without thinking that I was about to faint. After a few hours it was all over. I came back to my lodgings yesterday evening; I am perfectly well, but I am as tired as if I had made a long journey . . .
>
> A rather comical detail of my sad adventure . . . is that I didn't for a moment lose my reason. I was afraid that people might think that I was drunk.[3]

These seizures were probably an indication that the tension of Baudelaire's existence was becoming more than he could bear; and yet, as François Porché remarks, he does not seem to have had a doctor in Paris.[4] Since his attempted suicide in 1845, there had been no suggestion that a doctor came to visit him. In 1846, he had been to see d'Oroszko, a specialist in venereal disease, but he had not followed his prescriptions. It seems unlikely that Baudelaire could have paid a doctor's fees – but, for him, that was hardly a reason for not seeking medical advice. No doubt he was afraid that a doctor would prescribe a way of life that would disturb his habits. The opium which he took to cure his colics was perhaps itself the cause of his colics; the ether capsules which he used to cure his choking fits could well create another addiction. Even now, when his condition dramatically declined, Baudelaire preferred not to see a doctor. It seemed a deliberate challenge to his future.

It was, perhaps, precisely that. As Pichois concluded: 'Baudelaire knows more about it than the doctors of his time; he sees further than they do. The derangement of the senses was something he instigated before Rimbaud. Despite his flashes of hope, he had the certainty that he had been promised to the night, that he would be struck to the heart of his wonderful faculties. Poetry is bought at this price.'[5]

Mme Aupick had 'a simple, devoted, loving heart, a trusting, grateful soul'.[6] On 17 January she settled a substantial order to pay at Honfleur. She told Baudelaire that she had done so, and, as usual, she took the occasion to give him some advice.

> What can I send you except my thanks [he answered], and – as you can imagine – a genuine expression of regret for all the trouble and disturbance that I cause?

But I must point out to you that it is the first time that such a thing has happened [*sic*], and that, moreover, I have already paid several thousands of francs' worth of promissory notes at Honfleur.

As regards the promise that you demand, I ask no better than to make it and to keep it. But I can only fulfil this promise as from today. There are still orders to pay. *I shall always be a week in advance.* You strive to show me that your health should be precious to me. Oh, my God! I know it all too well! Sometimes I shudder with terror when I think of the isolation into which I shall be plunged one day. Even if glory has come, there will be no compensation for the absence of that life of regular domestic affection which I have so longed for and have never known . . .

You are completely wrong in what you tell me about the regimen which is indispensable for me. It's not a question of indigestion. It was my mind that was affected. Although I only understand it all in a confused way, I am persuaded that one day some misfortune will befall me through the spleen, or through the heart.[7]

In *La Maladie de Baudelaire*, Trial maintained that Baudelaire was now in irreversible decline. He also affirmed that his creative faculty was henceforth to diminish.[8] This theory is hardly in accordance with the facts. But Nature showed him, now, no sympathy; he was burdened by the weight of time. On about 10 February, he sent Malassis a new poem, 'Obsession', for the second edition of *Les Fleurs du mal*.

> Grands bois, vous m'effrayez comme des cathédrales;
> Vous hurlez comme l'orgue; et dans nos cœurs maudits,
> Chambres d'éternel deuil où vibrent de vieux râles,
> Répondent les échos de vos *De profundis*.
>
> Je te hais, Océan! tes bonds et tes tumultes,
> Mon esprit les retrouve en lui; ce rire amer
> De l'homme vaincu, plein de sanglots et d'insultes,
> Je l'entends dans le rire énorme de la mer.
>
> Comme tu me plairais, ô nuit! sans ces étoiles
> Dont la lumière parle un langage connu!
> Car je cherche le vide, et le noir, et le nu!
>
> Mais les ténèbres sont elles-mêmes des toiles
> Où vivent, jaillissant de mon œil par milliers,
> Des êtres disparus aux regards familiers.[9]

Baudelaire sent the sonnet with the contract he had recently signed, and 2000 francs, in part payment of his debt, to Malassis. Such was the complexity of his finances, that he also asked him for 970 francs. He added: 'If you had been in Paris in the last few days, you would have heard the sublime music of Wagner. It has been an event in my life.'[10]

In the autumn of 1859 Wagner had settled with his wife, Minna, near the Champs-Élysées. Early in 1860 three Wagner concerts were given in Paris. The first had been given at the Théâtre des Italiens on 25 January; the second had followed on 1 February; the third a week later. Some conservative French critics already dismissed this 'music of the future'. Baudelaire found it a revelation. On 16 February, he confessed to Malassis: 'I don't dare talk about Wagner any more. That music was, indeed, one of the great delights of my life; it is certainly fifteen years since I felt so carried away.'[11] It was fifteen years since he had written his *Salon de 1845*, and had praised the majesty of Delacroix. Instinctively, in the tones of an equal, Baudelaire recognised the precursors, the future leaders of schools, of his time. His knowledge of music seems to have been negligible, and his experience had been confined to a general sensitivity to the beauty of sound, until Wagner gave it meaning for him.

Whatever his reluctance to discuss Wagner with his friends, Baudelaire remained among his first and most fervent admirers in Paris. Next day, 17 February, he wrote to him:

Monsieur,
    . . . I owe you *the greatest musical delight that I have ever known* . . .
You conquered me at once. What I felt is indescribable, and, if you deign not to laugh, I will try to translate it for you. At first it seemed to me that I knew this music, and later, on reflection, I understood where this delusion came from; it seemed to me that this music was *my own*, and I recognised it as every man recognises the things that he is destined to love . . .
    And then the character which mainly struck me was the grandeur. It represents the grand, and it urges one towards greatness. Throughout your works, I have found the solemnity of great sounds, of the grand aspects of Nature, and the solemnity of the grand passions of man. One feels immediately borne away and subjugated . . . And another thing: I often had a feeling of a rather curious kind, that is the pride and delight in understanding, in letting myself be penetrated, invaded, a truly sensual delight, which is like the pleasure of rising in the air or riding on the waves. Usually these deep harmonies seem to me like those excitants which quicken the pulse of the imagination. Finally I also felt, and I beg you not to laugh, some sensations which probably derive from my cast of mind and my frequent preoccupations. There is everywhere something spirited, something excessive and superlative. For example, to use comparisons borrowed from painting, I imagine a vast expanse of dark red before my eyes. If this red represents passion, I see it coming gradually, through all the transitions of red and pink, to the incandescence of the furnace. It would seem difficult, even impossible, to attain something

more ardent; and yet a final rocket comes and traces a whiter track on the white which serves as its background. This is, if you like, the supreme cry of the soul which has risen to its paroxysm.[12]

Here, with his taste for transpositions, Baudelaire reveals his own concern with the correspondences between the arts.

When Wagner read this appreciation, he recognised the presence of 'an extraordinary spirit'.[13] He kept the letter. After the First World War, when German inflation was as its worst, Cosima Wagner gave it – no doubt as payment – to the Parisian couturier, Jacques Doucet.[14] In the meanwhile, with Gounod, Gustave Doré, the Émile Olliviers and a host of others, Baudelaire was to become a familiar figure at the composer's Wednesdays.[15]

73

At times he could admire wholeheartedly; at times he found it hard to disguise his professional distaste and his personal antipathy. Two days after he wrote to Wagner, Baudelaire found himself obliged to thank Ernest Feydeau for a copy of his latest novel. He was, he said, extremely busy, but he would find time to read *Catherine d'Overmeire*.[1] His reluctance to do so was evident, his dislike of Feydeau was plain. It was, indeed, so intense that it even kept him, now, from the rue Frochot. On 4 March he asked La Présidente to excuse him from the weekly dinner. It was not the first time that he had done so. 'Last Sunday (don't laugh, and keep to yourself what I'm whispering to you), it was through a dreadful fear of being obliged to talk to Feydeau about his latest novel.'[2]

It was nearly three years since La Présidente had declared her love for Baudelaire, and destroyed his essential dream of the Madonna and the Muse. Yet a deep affection still remained. 'I embrace you *as a very old friend* whom I shall always love,' he had written to her. 'The word *friend* is a lie; it is too vulgar, and it isn't loving enough.'[3] Now, on 4 March 1860, he assured her with a touch of gallantry:

If you imagine that I never think of you, you would be very much mistaken. And I should tell you so more often if you hadn't chosen to look at me with such wicked eyes. Yesterday, I wanted to bring you an album which I have had put aside for you; but I have decided to wait a little, and ask for other proofs. *I didn't find them fine enough.*[4]

1. The *maison joujou* at Honfleur. The figure seated on the steps is presumably Mme Aupick (1793–1871). This is the only known surviving likeness of her.

2. Joseph-François Baudelaire (1759–1827), first husband of Mme Aupick, and father of the poet. From the portrait by Jean-Baptiste Regnault.

3. 'The man is superb in his decorative, commanding appearance.' General Jacques Aupick (1789–1857), stepfather of Baudelaire. This lithograph by Léon Noël after the portrait by Gorotwoth shows the General when he was French Ambassador to Madrid.

4. 'I now wear the uniform of a *collégien.*' Baudelaire in his schooldays, probably at the Collège royal de Lyon.

5. Baudelaire in the days of the hôtel Pimodan. From the portrait by Émile Deroy, 1844.

6. Narcisse–Désiré Ancelle (1801–88).
Notary, Mayor of Neuilly, and *conseil
judiciaire* of Baudelaire.

7. *La Maîtresse de Baudelaire* (1862). Jeanne Duval, *la Vénus noire*, from the portrait by
Édouard Manet, now in Budapest.

8. Paul-Emmanuel-Auguste Poulet-Malassis (1825–78) came from a dynasty of printers in Alençon. He published *Les Fleurs du mal*, and won the lasting affection of its author. Baudelair was to him 'like a chosen brother'. This undated photograph was taken by Paul Nadar.

9. 'The very flower of the cultivated bourgeois': Charles-François Asselineau (1820–74).
Bibliophile and man of letters, and the first of Baudelaire's biographers, he was one of the
poet's true friends. This photograph by Nadar was taken in about 1857.

10. *La Vénus blanche*. Apollonie-Aglaé Sabatier (1822–90) inspired a cycle of poems in *Les Fleurs du mal*. This portrait of her, in Venetian dress, established the reputation of the artist Gustave Ricard at the Salon of 1851.

11. *La Belle aux cheveux d'or*: the actress Marie Daubrun (1827–1901). Her liaison with Baudelaire inspired a number of poems, including 'Le Beau Navire' and 'L'Invitation au voyage'. This undated photograph was taken by Carjat.

12. Baudelaire. From a photograph by Nadar, 1855.

13. Baudelaire. From a photograph by Nadar, 1862.

14. Théophile Gautier (1811–72): *le poète impeccable*, to whom Baudelaire dedicated *Les Fleurs du mal*. This photograph of him, by Nadar, was taken in about 1856.

15. 'M. Delacroix is certainly the most original painter of ancient and modern times.' So Baudelaire wrote in his *Salon de 1845*. This photograph of Eugène Delacroix (1798–1863) was taken by Nadar in 1858.

16. Charles-Augustin Sainte-Beuve (1804–69) was arguably the most influential French critic of his day, but – for all his protestations of affection – he refused to give Baudelaire any public appreciation. This photograph of him in later life was taken by L. Pierson.

17. 'It seems to me very difficult not to admire his character as much as his gifts.' So Baudelaire wrote of Édouard Manet (1832–83). This photograph of the artist was taken by Nadar in about 1865.

18. Three sketches by Baudelaire.
Top: Champfleury (1821–89),
novelist and art historian. The
miniature self-portrait of the poet
was drawn by way of signature.
Circa 1850. *Bottom*: Charles
François Asselineau. *Right*: Self-
portrait, the first of a series of
three, *c.* 1859.

19. Baudelaire. From a photograph by Carjat, *c.* 1861–2.

20. Baudelaire, aged about forty-three. This photograph was taken in Brussels by Charles Neyt, *c.* 1864.

He had once given his mother and Mme Sabatier copies of *Les Fleurs du mal*, identically bound except for the colour. Now he wanted to give them both copies of an album of Meryon's engravings. La Présidente remained a comforting and maternal presence. 'I am so unhappy and weary,' he explained to her, 'that I am avoiding all distractions. Indeed, though I long to know him, I have very recently refused a charming invitation from Wagner. I'll tell you later what all this means.'[5]

La Présidente was anxious, and she answered him by messenger. Her letter has not survived; but, later that day, Baudelaire replied:

> If I told you that I have enormous vexations; that I have never known such a storm; that I have need of solitude, you would not believe me. But if I tell you that my nose is swollen, big and red like an apple, and that in such cases I don't even go to see men (let alone women), I am sure that you will believe me.
>
> The great difficulty was removed. Because I met Feydeau, who did not miss such a fine occasion to hear someone talk, and to talk, about himself. Fortunately I had foreseen this case, and I had quietly prepared for it. I summoned up all my audacity, and I said to him: 'Your work is sublime, etc; but, etc.' He made it perfectly clear that with him the *buts* are ill received. Do you really know, and I'm being honest, that he embarrasses me more than V. Hugo himself? . . .
>
> You see that, with you, I like scandal. If it is true that one should always be careful of ones accomplices, I should like to be excessively scandalous about everyone with you, *so that I could never leave you again.*[6]

It was the last of his letters to her which has survived. Indeed, she was not to stay much longer in the rue Frochot. That summer, after a liaison of thirteen years, she and Mosselman were to separate. Mosselman was drawn to Laurentine Bernage, the future Mme Camille Lelong, who was eighteen years younger than his mistress. Apollonie refused an annuity of 6,000 francs, and she sold many of her possessions, including the bust of herself by Clésinger and a painting by Boissard, who had so often welcomed her at the hôtel Pimodan. There, she said, she had spent 'the most fruitful, the happiest, and the most carefree hours of her artistic life.'[7]

Mosselman died, still a widower, in 1867. In 1861, Apollonie herself moved to a small apartment at 10, rue de la Faisanderie. Judith Gautier recorded that,

> . . . with the remains of her past luxury, she arranged a little ground-floor apartment which was still a delightful nest. She did her own cooking, and sang as she did it, with turquoises on her beautiful hands . . . I much admired her courage and her strength of character. She was still *la très-chère, la très-belle,* and *la très-bonne,* she to whom the author of *Les Fleurs du mal* had vowed so secret, so ideal a love . . .[8]

However, by the end of 1861, Apollonie Sabatier seems to have been engaged in a new liaison. Her protector was, in all probability, an old acquaintance of hers, Richard Wallace, the natural son of the Marquess of Hertford. They travelled together, sometimes to the Isle of Wight or the Italian lakes, sometimes to visit museums in Holland or Belgium. Wallace promised Apollonie that, if ever he became rich, he would remember her; and in 1870 he inherited a fortune from his father: sixty million, the château of Bagatelle on the edge of the Bois de Boulogne, and all the art collections in Lord Hertford's *hôtel* in the boulevard des Italiens. That September, he settled a handsome sum on La Présidente (Flaubert said it was fifty thousand livres);[9] and every month thereafter she received her income. After the Franco-Prussian War, she decided to resume the Sunday dinners, to re-create the brilliance of the rue Frochot.

However, some conjunctions of the stars do not repeat themselves; and time had changed both Apollonie and her friends. Baudelaire was dead, and Gautier had not long to live; Flaubert drifted out of her existence. She herself had long since lost her physical perfection. Edmond de Goncourt, always a misogynist, had recorded: 'She is getting fat, her smooth shoulders are becoming blotchy. Age is re-creating this Rubens goddess in the style of Jordaens.'[10] In 1874 she moved to the avenue d'Eylau; but the dinners in Passy were pale reflections of the dinners in the quartier Bréda.

In 1873 she had met Edmond Richard. By his own account, he had come to Paris from the provinces, impelled by curiosity rather than ambition. He had found a minor post in the administration of the railways. During the Siege of Paris, he had mounted guard on the ramparts with a Dr Zabé, who chanced to be related to La Présidente, and in time the doctor introduced the awkward young provincial to the woman who had known Baudelaire. Edmond Richard was, it seems, the last of her lovers; after she died, he recorded her in his *Notes sur La Présidente*.

In the melancholy hours of the last period of her life, when conversation brought the name of Baudelaire back to her lips, La Présidente liked to recall the details and the incidents which did honour to the qualities of the man. [She spoke of] his concern with the cleanliness of his clothes which suggested long usage, with his hands, even with his linen which was frayed but impeccably white; his delicacy in responding with special presents for the attention which had been shown to him. With a fond smile, she recalled a walk she had taken with him in the Tuileries, on the terrace at the edge of the water: an unforgettable walk, she used to say, and one which had given the poet the subject of his short poem 'La Confession' . . .[11]

La Présidente spent her last years at Neuilly. In 1889 Augustin-Thierry, then a pupil at the Lycée Louis-le-Grand, was taken by a schoolfriend to visit this relic of an age that seemed long past. At the age of sixty-seven, flaccid, lined, grey-haired, bereft of her fine complexion, she disillusioned him; but he went again to see her, and, discussing a recent article by Ferdinand Brunetière, a harsh criticism of *Les Fleurs du mal*, she came to talk, at last, about Baudelaire.

It was now more than thirty years since *la Vénus blanche* had ceased to be the poet's madonna. She was shocked by Brunetière's criticism. 'It isn't true,' she protested, 'poor Charles was a religious man. His blasphemies were only a pretence. And then he was extremely proud, like all timid people – he was a dreamer, melancholy, perpetually troubled. I knew him very well, I think, better than this man who slanders him.' La Présidente broke off; and then, as if she had plumbed the depths of her past, she murmured: 'Perhaps it was I who had no faith.'[12]

On the entreaties of Paul de St Victor [recorded Edmond Richard], and knowing that she was helping to establish the fame of the author of *Les Fleurs du mal*, La Présidente opened the little dossier of papers (letters and poems received from 1852 to 1860) which Monsieur Tourneux published [after her death] in *Le Livre moderne*. People then learned of the destruction [sic] of 'these ardent, almost religious poems, imbued with romantic melancholy, with unassuaged desires and with imaginary realizations'. . . . But people did not know that the woman, the Muse, the Madonna, the object of this pure, fierce and reverent adoration, had herself been moved by passion, and that, one day, despite the protests of reason, . . . she had opened her arms. Her own letters, found among the papers of Charles Baudelaire, . . . allow one suspicion to remain. It is only a suspicion, but an almost ferocious suspicion, and that is that the man she loved, the man who felt the pleasures of love with such poetry, had never envisaged the happy chance that he might be loved. And so, when this happiness was offered him, when the dream changed to reality, he rejected it, with a horror of passion . . . Yet, although this woman was stunned, she still remained under the spell of the ardent poetry . . . Under her rancour she found the ultimate pity . . .

The heart of the woman who is truly in love is illimitable.

As far as we know, La Présidente never told anyone at all, even ambiguously, about her cruel disappointment.[13]

She died on 3 January 1890. She was buried in the old cemetery at Neuilly.[14] 'Family included,' recalled Augustin-Thierry, 'fewer than ten of us followed her coffin. And so she set out on her last journey, departed unescorted and alone, *la très belle, la très chère*, who had known so many friends: whom a great poet, one of the greatest among the great, her lover for a day, had glorified.'[15] The plaster mould, from

which Clésinger had once cast *Rêve d'amour*, 'was broken and destroyed,
. . . on the orders and in the presence of her sister.'[16] That year, at the
Hôtel Drouot, her possessions were auctioned. Among the drawings
and engravings was *Le Sommeil de Vénus*, which had been attributed to
Boucher. Among the paintings was Meissonier's portrait of La
Présidente, in a cream silk Louis XV dress adorned with lace and blue
ribbons. *La Dame au chien*, by Ricard, which had once hung in the rue
Frochot, was now sold for 15,000 francs.[17] Crépet notes that the heirs
of La Présidente 'parted amicably with the greater part of her papers,
and with volumes adorned with precious dedications.'[18]

74

In his *Salon de* 1859, Baudelaire had paid tribute to Charles Meryon.
He was one of his rare admirers. Meryon, a former naval officer, had
abandoned a career at sea to devote himself to his art; since 1850, he
had exhibited drawings and engravings of the principal views of Paris.
He was a master etcher, but his compatriots paid him small attention,
and he suffered both from neglect and from mental illness. In the
spring of 1858 he had been committed to Charenton. When he left the
asylum in 1859, his friends had recognised that his condition was
incurable. He was imprisoned in his atrocious life, which was to end
at Charenton in 1868.

Baudelaire, with his sure instinct, had acknowledged Meryon's
artistic stature. Meryon had shown his gratitude. On 23 February 1860,
he had sent him an album, *Eaux-Fortes sur Paris*. It was, he wrote, 'a
poor way to thank you for the devotion which you have shown me.'[1]

It was strange that Baudelaire did not keep this thank-offering from
an artist whom he much admired. Perhaps he felt that it might fall to
the bailiffs or the pawnbrokers, and that it was safer at Honfleur. Five
days later, he posted the album to his mother – who, alas, had not
appreciated Guys.

> This album has been meant for you for a long while [he explained], and
> I hope it will please you more than the Turkish woman . . .
>   I had vowed not to write to you, in spite of my anxiety, until I was
> triumphant. But, the day after tomorrow, 1 March, an order to pay will
> arrive in Honfleur, and this time, as I am absolutely determined that you
> should not suffer from my ventures, you must say: *My son is going to be away
> very much longer than I'd thought* (that's a lie: I'm going to come back), *get
> yourself paid at 22, rue d'Amsterdam.*[2]

Mme Aupick predictably settled the order to pay at Honfleur. She did not even rebuke her son, though she would have been justified in doing so.

She was not only patient, she was generous. She did not only settle his orders to pay; she sent him a valuable shawl, no doubt a relic of ambassadorial days, for him to sell. It was a poignant gesture of love. Baudelaire was touched, and could not bring himself to sell it. He pawned it in the hope of redeeming it later, and with the money he received (250 francs) he completely clothed himself.[3]

Whatever criticism may be made of Mme Aupick, she suffered sorely, now, for the misjudgments of the past. Her nervous state brought on stomach pains and insomnia. Alone, in her villa on the coast of Normandy, she was beset by demands from her ruthless son. He was prepared – as he had always been – to resort to emotional blackmail to gain his ends. On 1 March she had settled an order to pay which should not have been sent to Honfleur. On 26 March, Baudelaire explained:

> My dear mother, I must distress you again. Tomorrow, 27 [March], and on 1 April, two new orders to pay will arrive at Honfleur. (THE LAST. Since you forbade me, I haven't signed any others.) I WILL NOT have you making heavy sacrifices for me, even if you should wish to. This is *an absolutely honest request* that I am making you [*sic*]. *I will not*, I cannot, without a shudder, think of what you wrote to me recently: *Charles, although you are good and you can earn money, I am afraid that you will ruin me* ...
>
> I implore you most ardently, be indulgent, remember that I am suffering great anguish, and that my mind is sick ... Don't send me one of those torrents of reproaches which do me so much harm ...[4]

On 2 April, he announced that he would come and see her in a few days.[5] The visit was of course deferred. In the meanwhile, Mme Aupick sent him 100 francs, and offered to pay 200 francs on an order to pay which would fall due on 12 April.

75

On 9 April, Baudelaire was to be thirty-nine. His anxieties appeared to be unending. *La Revue internationale* had not only broken off the serial publication of *Eureka*, and refused to print the rest of the manuscript; they had also refused to pay Baudelaire the 400 francs which they owed him. He thought he might need to sue them for payment.[1] There was another problem. Eugène Crépet, the first of the dynasty of

Baudelaireans, was preparing his anthology *Les Poètes français*. The fourth and final volume was to be devoted to modern poets. He had asked Gautier to write an appreciation of Baudelaire; he had invited Baudelaire to contribute a number of studies, including one of Gautier. Crépet was to earn the gratitude of scholars for his work on the posthumous fame of Baudelaire, but his relationship with the living poet was to be difficult. Baudelaire chose to see him sometimes as a bourgeois tyrant, sometimes as a timorous philistine; he wrote to him with extraordinary arrogance, and he listed him in his *Carnet* among the 'vilaines canailles'.[2] Crépet was an affable, disinterested man, and he was to show him a tolerance which verged on nobility.[3]

However, in the spring of 1860, Crépet demanded alterations to the literary studies, and threatened to make them himself if Baudelaire did not do so before he left for Honfleur.[4] Baudelaire threatened to withdraw his contributions and to repay his advance.[5]

There proved to be no need for withdrawal or for repayment; but his financial state remained desperate. On 14 April, he announced to Michel Lévy:

> I absolutely must have 200 francs at once. Perhaps I am entitled to ask you for them . . .
> If I am not entitled to ask for them, I ask you for them all the same, knowing how obliging you are.
> I shall come and see you tomorrow morning Sunday or Monday . . .
> *Eureka* is completely finished.[6]

It was finished; it was not, however, polished, and it was not to be published for three years.

On 19 April, Baudelaire warned Malassis that he would have to go to Honfleur to fetch the manuscripts of six poems; but he would not leave, he said, until he had honoured some orders to pay which would fall due on 10 May. He was also having trouble with Cousinet, the restaurateur in the rue du Bac, who had presented a promissory note for payment at Honfleur.[7] Mme Aupick had sent her son a stern rebuke. 'You overwhelm me with reproaches which I find very painful,' Baudelaire told her. 'Do remember that I live in a kind of dreadful nightmare, with never any respite.'[8]

For Mme Aupick there·was now another source of distress. Alphonse Baudelaire had recently suffered a severe stroke. 'I will do what you want about Alphonse,' Baudelaire assured her.[9] Perhaps, at her suggestion, he wrote to him, or to his wife, but he did not go to Fontainebleau to see him.[10] He had virtually ignored him for years.

His behaviour was to earn him the intense hostility of Félicité and her collateral descendants. When Baudelaire, his mother and Félicité had died, the Ducessois family inherited a mass of his correspondence. Philippe Auserve recorded that Marie-Anne Ducessois, the niece of Félicité,

> . . . had most of Baudelaire's letters to his family in her hands. She could not bear to have the poet discussed in front of her. She had remained a spinster, and, deeply devout, she lived in the quartier of Saint-Sulpice. When her young nephews wanted to tease her, they knew quite well what to say: 'Aunt, tell us about cousin Baudelaire.' And the poor woman would cover her face with her hands, and make a gesture as if to repel some sort of monster, and murmur: 'Horrible! Horrible!' Finally, in her own words, since she had no wish to keep the Devil with her, she burned a great number of letters which she did not consider *proper*, and decided to give the remainder to Jacques Crépet, who published them.[11]

One file, however, had escaped her censorship. It contained nearly a hundred early letters, and it had been hidden, for reasons unknown. By a series of miracles it survived the prudery of Mlle Ducessois and the ravages of the Second World War. On Marie-Anne's death, the documents that had belonged to her came into the possession of her nephew, Raphaël Ducessois, who had been a minor functionary at the French consulate in Florence.[12] He was living in retirement nearby, in a house at Signa. During the war, Auserve continued, the house was bombed, 'the library ceiling collapsed, and it was followed by part of the roof. The débris covered the books and archives; it was thought that everything was lost. Ten years later, some masons who were repairing the wall brought out a small packet carefully wrapped in oilcloth. Under a half-rotten floorboard, they had found a hundred letters from Baudelaire.'[13] Auserve published them in 1966, in *Charles Baudelaire: Lettres inédites aux siens.*

As for Mme Aupick's letters to her son, they have not yet come to light. Perhaps they are still hidden. Perhaps, on his death, she herself destroyed them. If the letters still survived on Mme Aupick's death, it was Félicité who came to inherit them; it was probably Félicité or Marie-Anne Ducessois who, protectively, consigned them to the flames.

76

On 29 April 1860, Hugo wrote to thank Baudelaire for his appreciation of his drawings in his *Salon de 1859*. 'You have in you, dear thinker, all the strings of art! Once again you prove the rule that, in an artist, the critic is always equal to the poet.'[1]

This idea of the symbiosis of the poet and the critic whom he bore within him was to be taken up again in Baudelaire's study of Wagner. Meanwhile, early in May, he set to work on a study of Hugo himself. 'Now send me all the Hugo you have on your shelves,' he told Eugène Crépet, with whom he was again on friendly terms. 'I must saturate myself with it for twenty-four hours.'[2] It was hardly time enough in which to consider Hugo's work, but Baudelaire had promised to finish the article within the week. As usual, he failed to keep his promise. In mid-May, in a note which shows signs of the confusion in which it was written, he announced to Crépet: 'I have been ill since yesterday, and I cannot move. I *want* to bring you this study myself.'[3]

He was, however, concerned above all with *Les Paradis artificiels*, which were at last about to appear. 'I have a horrible fear of making a *fiasco* with my book,' he told his mother on 18 May. 'And to think that there must be another four this year!'[4] Late in May, Malassis finally wrote from Alençon to Ernest Daudet, brother of Alphonse: 'I have just published [a little book] by Baudelaire: *Les Paradis artificiels*. *Opium et hachisch*. It is a very curious study of the effects of these excitants, written as one might expect by the translator of Edgar Poe. It appeared only a week ago.'[5]

In the first part of the book, *Le Poème du hachisch*, Baudelaire gave a precise account of the various kinds of hashish, and their modes of preparation. Hashish, he observed, should be taken in a happy frame of mind, in agreeable surroundings, perhaps to the sound of music. There were three phases of intoxication. The first was one of strange and uncontrollable hilarity; then came a momentary lull, and then a sensation of extreme cold in the hands and feet.[6] Then came the height of the experience,

> ... an extraordinary acuteness of all the senses. Smell, sight, hearing, touch: all have an equal part in this progress. The eyes gaze at infinity. The ears perceive sounds which are almost indiscernible ... [It is then that] the hallucinations begin. External things assume curious appearances ... They grow distorted, and transform themselves ... Then come the most curious ambiguities, and the transpositions of ideas. Sounds assume colours, and colours contain music.[7]

It was the experience which Gautier had described after a hashish session at the hôtel Pimodan;[8] it touched, once again, on the theory of *correspondances* which was dear to him and to Baudelaire.

Sometimes, continued Baudelaire, the personality vanished, and the hashish-eater forgot his own existence; the sense of time and place had disappeared. Then followed physical exhaustion, overwhelming languor. 'It is the punishment for the impious prodigality with which you have spent your nervous energy. You have scattered your personality to the four corners of the earth, and what a labour it is, now, to gather it together and to concentrate it again!'[9]

Baudelaire then described the dangers of eating hashish. Poisonous excitants seemed to him 'one of the most terrible, one of the surest ways in which the Spirit of Darkness can enlist and enslave the lamentable human race.'[10] Indeed, 'it was forbidden to man, on pain of decay and intellectual death, to disturb the primordial conditions of his existence, and to destroy the balance of his faculties with the surroundings in which they are meant to move: in a word, to interfere with his destiny and to substitute a new kind of fate.'[11]

Baudelaire was well aware of the perils of drugs, of the indignities which they could cause. When Armand Fraisse prepared to review *Les Paradis artificiels*, and asked him 'for information about opium and hashish, he urged me', Fraisse remembered, 'not to try them at all.'[12] Man sometimes needed to exalt his personality, to seek a state of grace; but man, wrote Baudelaire, 'is not so abandoned, so deprived of honest means to reach heaven, that he is obliged to call upon pharmacy and magic. He does not need to sell his soul to pay for the friendship, the intoxicating caresses of the houris. What is a paradise that one buys at the cost of ones eternal salvation?'[13]

Le Poème du hachisch is, patently, not written by an addict. It is an almost clinical assessment of the stuff of dreams, a scientific appraisal of the drug. 'Like the doctor who pricks himself with a Javanese arrow so that he can see an antidote, it was as a *scholar*', Champfleury said, 'that Baudelaire studied the poisons.'[14] It was also as a Catholic. *Le Poème du hachisch* was a plea for the health and dignity of man. As Gautier wrote, perceptively: 'He blames the man who wants to escape the fatality of grief.'[15]

The second part of *Les Paradis artificiels* reinforces this belief. It is largely an adaptation of De Quincey's *Confessions of an English Opium-Eater*. Baudelaire is passionately drawn to this book, to its melancholy and intense romanticism. In the life of De Quincey, as in the life of Poe, he sees certain similarities with his own. De Quincey's childhood reminds him that 'the precocious taste for the feminine *world*, ... for all this flowing, sparkling, scented paraphernalia, is the making of superior genius.'[16] It is a recollection of the rue Hautefeuille. He writes with urgency about De Quincey's poverty and solitude, for he, too, has known poverty and solitude. He writes with passion about De Quincey's addiction to opium, and his fierce, persistent struggle to break it, because he himself has long been dependent on laudanum, as a cure for colic, as an anti-depressant, as a means of seeking oblivion. It is this identification with his subject which gives life to the second part of *Les Paradis artificiels*. Baudelaire recognises in De Quincey the agonising fate of a man of letters who has destroyed his capacity for thought, his ability to write. He keeps all his moral aspirations, but he can no longer fulfil them.

77

On about 19 June, on a visit to Victor Hugo in Guernsey, Pierre-Jules Hetzel, the publisher, gave him a copy of *Les Paradis artificiels*.[1] Baudelaire's gift was not disinterested; with the book there came a letter asking Hugo for permission to reprint some poems in Crépet's anthology, *Les Poètes français*. Hugo responded to admiration, even when it was insincere.

> If it is just a question of including a few short poems, I might, I think, grant permission . . . What enchants me about this, is that my name would be mentioned by you and encrusted in one of those profound and beautiful pages which you know how to write.
>
> And, talking of this, what a powerful book it is, your *Paradis artificiels*! It is sparkling mystery. *Poème du hachisch* is a surprising study, true and fantastic, absolutely full of the words and the brilliance of the unknown. The chapter *Morale* is magnificent. Thanks to you, I have at last read that famous *mangeur d'opium*. You bring the work to life again, vividly. To analyse like this is to create . . .[2]

Meanwhile, on 25 June, with his usual generosity, Flaubert acknowledged his copy of the book. 'I can't tell you strongly enough how excellent I have found your work from beginning to end, it is very noble, very powerful, and very searching in style . . . You have found the means to be classic, whilst you remain the transcendent romantic whom we love.'[3]

On 26 June, Baudelaire wrote to Paul Dalloz, one of the editors of *Le Moniteur universel*. 'It goes without saying that if Sainte-Beuve agreed to concern himself with this book, which I think worthy of his attention, all would be for the best . . .'[4] Dalloz replied that he considered the *Paradis* worthy of Sainte-Beuve. He advised Baudelaire to ask him for a review.[5]

Baudelaire never understood – perhaps he did not want to understand – the deviousness and the selfishness of Sainte-Beuve. Even after the court case of *Les Fleurs du mal*, he was persuaded that Sainte-Beuve might help him. There was little doubt of the primacy of Sainte-Beuve as a critic: a primacy only challenged, perhaps, by Théophile Gautier. Sainte-Beuve, in his weekly column in *Le Moniteur universel*, could make and unmake reputations. Baudelaire approached him, now, with humility, and with undeserved affection.[6] Sainte-Beuve remained as evasive as ever. He was teaching, so he told Baudelaire, at the École normale supérieure, and he had at least five articles to write; but in a month's time, if Baudelaire was still in Paris, he would like a long conversation 'about this very intelligent, very ingenious, very subtle book.'[7]

78

On 12 July, from the hôtel de Dieppe, Baudelaire announced to Malassis:

> I am leaving on the 16th or 17th, having done a good many things, having settled matters with *Le Constitutionnel*, which has really behaved very well; I have delivered a tolerable amount of copy, and I have received 1,000 francs. I shall receive something more at the time of my departure, and I shall work on the *Wagner*, and on my drama, at my mother's. I am going to make a series of brief stays in the country: at *my brother's* (he has just had a stroke: Providence would have done better to cure someone else who concerns me more); *at Flaubert's* (he is clamouring for me); *at my mother's*, and *with you*; then I go back to Honfleur.[1]

Fontainebleau was not far away; but Baudelaire was not to pay a visit to Alphonse. He had not seen him for eighteen years,[2] but the news of his stroke did not arouse even a momentary sympathy. Two days later, Baudelaire asked Malassis to postpone his departure for Granville until 31 July, insisting that he would be with him on the 29th. They could, he said, 'arrange the *Fleurs* together, on the last two days of the month.'[3] Such was his poverty that he spent a day trying, in vain, to procure a free rail ticket to Alençon. He was obliged to postpone the meeting.[4]

It was not his most serious offence. Early in August, Baudelaire confessed to his mother that he had misappropriated 1,620 francs which belonged to his publisher. He would now have to find this sum

in order to pay one of Malassis' debts. Once again – as with the bailiff
– he had shown disquieting lack of judgment. In order to avoid the
shock that this news would cause her, he had taken an extraordinary
precaution: he had written to the abbé Cardine, her curé at Honfleur,
so that he could come and comfort her.

When he had done so, even he was concerned about the effects of
his action. On 4 August, he wrote to her again,

> . . . just to tell you, to repeat to you, how anxious I am about the effect
> that my letter will have on you. The more I think about it, the more afraid
> I am that I have hurt you. This anxiety is now as great as the anxiety that
> I shall not be able to make amends for the harm I've done, and that I
> shall therefore pass for the most dishonest of men.
>
> Perhaps you will find that the idea of asking that excellent curé in
> advance to help you in your grief is indiscreet or even ridiculous. But what
> can I say, except that I lost my head and that, knowing the fluctuations
> of your health so well, I only thought of finding some or other way to
> assuage your grief? Really, this idea sprang from the most natural and the
> most filial intention.
>
> My stomach and my sleep are still in an abominable state.[5]

So was his mind. His behaviour to Malassis had been unpardonable;
his approach to the abbé Cardine had been both indiscreet and
ill-conceived. Once again, he manipulated his mother shamefully. He
had presented her with a massive debt, and assumed that she would
settle it. He knew that, when she was tried beyond endurance, she
could resort to protracted silence. As usual, when he was desperate, he
resorted to emotional blackmail: to a vague threat calculated to disturb
her. Next day he warned her: 'In my terror, in fear of a refusal from
you, I may perhaps very soon take a step at which the whole of my
nature recoils.'[6]

His letter was cruelly perverse. He loved her, but he wanted to hurt
her; he depended on her, but he seemed to do his utmost to damage
her. Mme Aupick understood; she, too, knew the power of emotional
blackmail. She reminded him that she had 'a predisposition to
irremediable attacks.'[7] However, she also asked Ancelle to give him
1,620 francs to settle the order to pay on 9 August.

In her *maison joujou* at Honfleur, she had much to disturb her. An
unwelcome visitor was due to arrive from Paris; and, more alarmingly,
the cliff beside her house in the rue de Neubourg was steadily
crumbling. (The street, which runs parallel to the cliff edge, now ends
in a cul-de-sac. There remains only a section of the rue de Fresnes,
now rue Charles Baudelaire.) The erosion of the cliff left her in
constant apprehension, and the expense of shoring up her garden was

a cause of perpetual anxiety. Now that she had authorised Ancelle to give him money, she would have welcomed a respite from her son.

On 7 August, he wrote yet again: 'Dear mother, there are certainly a good many worries and vexations, one after the other. As for the lady you mention to me, that is a temporary annoyance from which you will still perhaps get some pleasure . . . As for the crumbling of the cliff, that is more serious. I have eaten up a mass of your money in the last two and a half years, and it would be really distressing if these accidents recurred whenever the weather was bad enough to cause havoc . . .'[8] Concern for his mother was followed by acute concern for himself.

> As for me [he continued], you mustn't be anxious, *except about the thing you know about*. Of course I am horribly dissatisfied with my health. But the body would be well, if the soul were well. The soul will never be well . . .
>
> Once again I repeat all my gratitude and all my regrets. But you mustn't exaggerate what I've done; as a thoughtless act it was monstrous, *but I'd done it several times without mischance*, and it did not occur to me for a moment to misuse this money, and to abandon myself to chance for the means of repaying it.[9]

The final phrase said more, perhaps, than Baudelaire intended.

He ended his letter at five o'clock. At eleven o'clock that night he added: 'Oh, how weary I am, how weary I've been for many years already, of this need to live twenty-four hours every day! When shall I live with pleasure?'[10]

He might well ask the question. Late in August he confessed to his mother: 'For several months I have been ill, with an illness which one cannot cure, faintheartedness and debilitation. Physically this is complicated by sleeping badly and by violent pains. Sometimes by fear, sometimes by anger.'[11]

Repeatedly, in his correspondence, he mentioned that he was going to visit his mother. He does not seem to have gone to Honfleur. He preferred the dream to the reality. It was from Paris, late in August, that he wrote again to Malassis about *Les Fleurs du mal*.[12] It was still from the hôtel de Dieppe, rue d'Amsterdam, that, on 27 September, he sent him the account of what he owed him: the considerable sum of 5,611 francs. Baudelaire sent orders to pay for 2,920 francs, and asked him to settle a loan of 920 francs. 'The purpose of this is to rid me of the hotel in the first days of October, and to let me go and live in the lodgings where I had *my* furniture taken, two months ago.'[13] This was a small apartment at 4, rue Louis-Philippe, at Neuilly. He had rented it, extravagantly, since early in July. Jeanne was already living there. He was not to move there until December.

79

Mme Aupick had her own continuing anxieties. There had been much rain in August and September, and part of her garden, near the cliff edge, had now fallen away. Baudelaire, to whom she wrote, was scarcely concerned with her troubles. He answered her letter with accusations, and with praise of Jeanne, with thoughts of suicide and sudden death, and with disturbing talk of her own demise. He was ruthless to the point of sadism. Mme Aupick had referred to his debts.

You rack your brains [Baudelaire replied], you try a thousand times to understand, instead of simply saying to yourself: the *Conseil Judiciaire!* That appalling error which has ruined my life, blighted all my days and given all my thoughts the hue of hatred and despair. *But you don't understand me.*

Now I am going to talk, seriously, without undue emphasis, about some very melancholy thoughts. In spite of that diabolical courage which has so often sustained me, I can die before you. What has held me back [from suicide], for eighteen months, is Jeanne. (How would she live after my death, since you would have to pay all I owe with what I have left?) There are other reasons, too: leaving you alone! And leaving you the horrible difficulty of sorting out a chaos which I alone can understand.

The mere idea of some preparatory work to facilitate the understanding of my affairs, is enough to make me constantly postpone the accomplishment of an act which I consider to be the most rational act in life. I must be honest, I have a pride which sustains me, and a savage hatred of all mankind . . .

I embrace you, very sadly. I love you with all my heart. You have never known it. There is this difference between you and me, that I know you by heart, and that you have never been able to understand my miserable character.

CHARLES

I have carefully read all you told me about the crumbling of the garden. It is very sad. Poor little house! If I have the health and strength to survive all my torments, I vow not only never to sell it, but even never to mortgage it.[1]

Such a promise must have seemed empty, coming from Baudelaire; but there was no doubt that he was fond of the *maison joujou.* He felt that it belonged to him as much as it did to his mother. Three days later, he added:

My dear mother,

I shall be at Le Havre at noon tomorrow, Monday. Only I don't know when I shall be able to cross the river.

I am not coming to torment you, or to make you weep. I am coming to discuss my affairs and to try to make myself well understood . . .[2]

Next day, 15 October, as he set off for Honfleur, eleven of his poems appeared in *L'Artiste*.

> La Maladie et la Mort font des cendres
> De tout le feu qui pour nous flamboya.
> De ces grands yeux si fervents et si tendres,
> De cette bouche où mon cœur se noya,
>
> De ces baisers puissante comme un dictame,
> De ces transports plus vifs que des rayons,
> Que reste-t-il? C'est affreux, ô mon âme!
> Rien qu'un dessin fort pâle, aux trois crayons,
>
> Qui, comme moi, meurt dans la solitude,
> Et que le Temps, injurieux vieillard,
> Chaque jour frotte avec son aile rude . . .
>
> Noir assassin de la Vie et de l'Art,
> Tu ne tueras jamais dans ma mémoire
> Celle qui fut mon plaisir et ma gloire![3]

Some saw in 'Un Fantôme' the apotheosis of the woman who had been Jeanne Duval and, in 1860, was only her ghost.

Baudelaire had promised that he was not coming to Honfleur to torment his mother, but simply to discuss his affairs. His main reason for the visit was, of course, that he hoped for money from her. He already owed her more than he was likely to repay, and she found herself financially hard-pressed. On 18 October, he explained in dudgeon to Malassis: 'My dear friend: Nothing. The reason is the financial difficulty caused by the great collapse [of the cliff]. And then I've verified that I owed my mother 23,000 francs. So I return to my inferno – with 400 francs. I was counting on 3,000, of which 1,000 were intended for you.'[4]

80

Malassis would have welcomed the sum. He had recently conceived an audacious plan to retrieve his fortunes. He would save the middleman's profit. Instead of travelling constantly to and from Alençon, he had decided to establish new offices in Paris. That month, the *Revue anecdotique* announced that he had rented a shop on the corner of the passage Mirès (later the passage des Princes) and the rue de Richelieu.

'There is', it explained, 'much talk about the decoration of this new bookshop. The realist painters are to paint ceilings and frescoes; there is talk of Courbet, Amand Gautier and others. People will come there, as they do to the Librairie Nouvelle, to leaf through and read the latest publications. It will be a meeting-place, where people will learn the literary news of the day.'[1]

In 1861 and 1862, with Charles Asselineau and Pierre Jannet, the publisher of the Bibliothèque elzévirienne, Malassis was to direct the *Revue anecdotique*. It was, in a sense, to be the official gazette of Poulet-Malassis and De Broise. In due course it announced:

> The establishment of the publishers Malassis and De Broise in the passage Mirès has fulfilled the artistic promises which we mentioned. Already, over the elegant oak bookcase, there stands out a series of medallions painted as a fresco on a brown background and representing some of the authors published by the house: Monselet, Hugo, Th. Gautier, Champfleury, Th. de Banville, Baudelaire, Babou, Asselineau, etc.
>
> Several of these portraits, the work of MM. Bonvin, Soupplet, Lafond and Legros, are striking likenesses.[2]

Baudelaire's portrait, by Alexandre Lafond, was an all too eloquent likeness of the poet of *Les Fleurs du mal* at forty.

> The terrifying face [noted Edmond Deman] is that of a tragic actor and, at the same time, that of a priest who celebrates black masses. The lofty expression is intensified by the way the lips turn down at the corners, in deep furrows, and by the wide-eyed, ironic, searching gaze.
>
> The head, which is almost lifesize, is set against a greenish background [*sic*] which emphasises its impressive sadness.[3]

When, in time, Malassis moved from the passage Mirès, this was the one medallion he kept.

Comte Gérard de Contades (writing as Un Bibliophile ornais) observed that Malassis made his shop 'a real intellectual club, in which the most delicate, but also the least prudent men of letters used to vie with each other to demand his elegant vignettes and his pretty red fleurons for their verse or prose.'[4] He had more taste than commercial sense. Malassis, said Jules Troubat in his *Souvenirs*, 'so loved his publications that it hurt him to see them disposed of; he preferred to keep them and to damage his own trade. He was too artistic to manage his business well. He was distinguished and excessively generous by nature.'[5]

His literary venture could not last; but, while it did, it delighted his contemporaries. Like Renduel among the Romantics, Lemerre among the Parnassians, and Vanier among the Symbolists, Poulet-Malassis and De Broise was one of the most distinguished imprints in nineteenth-century France.

Near Malassis' shop, in the passage Mirès itself, there was soon to be an office which would also be familiar to Baudelaire: the office of *La Revue fantaisiste*. The review, which first appeared on 15 February 1861, was founded by the young poet Catulle Mendès, who described his office as a 'passably extraordinary' place.

> It was there that, every afternoon, at about 3 o'clock, there came Théodore de Banville; . . . Charles Asselineau, with the sleek, long hair, already grey, and that ironic, tender smile which only Nodier had had before him; . . . and Charles Baudelaire, slim and elegant, slightly furtive, almost frightening, because of his vaguely frightened attitude, haughty, moreover, but with grace. He had . . . the air of a very fastidious bishop, slightly damned, who had put on exquisite secular clothes for a journey – His Eminence Monseigneur Brummell.[6]

It was in the offices of *La Revue fantaisiste* that Baudelaire met the prolific man of letters Jules Claretie. 'When I knew him, at the *Revue fantaisiste* of our dear Catulle Mendès, passage des Princes, and at the weekly *Figaro*, to which he brought his articles on Guys, Baudelaire', recalled Claretie, 'was already over forty . . . He seemed very much older. A sort of ancestor. He was extraordinarily reserved and polite. With Hugo and with Baudelaire, politeness was part of the genius.'[7]

Claretie was more fortunate than some in his relations with Baudelaire. It was, no doubt, in the offices of *La Revue fantaisiste* that Baudelaire encountered José-Maria de Heredia: the young Parnassian poet, half Spanish and half French, who in 1861 came to live in Paris. Heredia much admired *Les Fleurs du mal*; he often read them aloud, 'and he eloquently praised their bold conciseness and their refined subtlety.'[8] Such appreciation did not, it seems, ensure the friendship of their author. Heredia described, somewhat bitterly, his famous introduction to Baudelaire: 'As I was expressing my respectful admiration, the poet of *Les Fleurs du mal* stared at me coldly . . . Interrupting me brusquely, he said: "Monsieur, I don't like young men." He said no more, and turned his back on me.'[9]

81

Meanwhile, on 18 October 1860, Baudelaire himself, in Honfleur, wrote to Grandguillot, the editor of *Le Constitutionnel*:

Dear Sir,

I came here in search of money, and I have found none. I am coming back to Hell on Sunday. Very probably I shall come and see you on Tuesday or Wednesday, and we shall examine the end of the *Guys* together.

I beg you, earnestly, do all you can to help me with 500 francs.[1]

On 21 October, having spent six days with his mother, Baudelaire left Honfleur for Paris. He delivered the manuscript of his *Guys* to *Le Constitutionnel*. Silence followed. Later that month, or in November, he explained to Houssaye:

M. Grandguillot is one of the causes of my current problems. Having crammed me full of offers and promises, he has now vanished into thin air. I cannot therefore get money from him, and the worst of it is that I am even anxious about the manuscript which I delivered. If it's refused, and if I can recover it, would it suit you? It is the analysis of the gifts of an *unknown* man, a man *full of genius*, a hundred of whose drawings I possess.[2]

There seemed, for a while, to be a chance of more serious money. On 20 November, perhaps through an introduction from Malassis, Baudelaire met the composer Robert August Stoepel. German by birth, and French by naturalisation, Stoepel had emigrated to America, where he had composed a number of operettas. He had recently written an oratorio based on Longfellow's poem *The Song of Hiawatha*; it had been performed in Boston and in New York, and he hoped to see it performed in Europe. Now, in Paris, Stoepel turned to the translator of Edgar Allan Poe. Baudelaire anticipated a fee of 1,500 francs and performances at the Théâtre-Italien, and he set to work immediately. It was not only a matter of translation; he had to reduce eight hundred lines of English verse to a mere three hundred in French. It was one of the most ungrateful tasks that he ever undertook. When Stoepel changed his mind, and demanded a prose translation, Baudelaire patiently embarked on it. However, by 5 December, Stoepel suddenly left for London, owing his translator 400 francs. Baudelaire continued his work, still hoping to be paid. Then he sought help from the Société des Gens de Lettres; Stoepel did not answer their letters. Finally he consulted a lawyer, Maître Hippolyte Marin, who started an action against Stoepel; but the matter was never to be settled.[3]

In the meanwhile, on 15 December 1860, Baudelaire moved to Neuilly, to be with the hemiplegic Jeanne Duval. It proved, from the first, to be a disastrous decision.

My dear mother [this on 1 January 1861],

...I have been installed here (4, rue Louis-Philippe, Neuilly) for a fortnight, and, as usual with me, I am very unhappy. Take the word in a spiritual rather than a physical sense.

And so I've come back to my old idea, which is to settle finally in Honfleur, except for a week a month (I cannot cut Paris out, because of business), and then to pay my expenses day by day. For reasons which I may perhaps explain to you, I shall probably not return to Neuilly...

And so (provided, however, that things sort themselves out as they do in my mind), I shall be able to prepare to leave between the 15th and the 20th. In spite of your absurd New Year prohibition, I shall bring you your New Year present.

Les Fleurs du mal are finished. They are busy doing the cover and the portrait. There are thirty-five new poems, and all the old poems have been radically altered.

For the first time in my life, I am almost satisfied. The book is *almost good*, and it will remain a witness to my loathing and my hatred of everything.[4]

That day, in the *Revue européenne*, there appeared 'Recueillement': a poem that remains a witness to his unremitting misery.

In Honfleur, and in Paris, the misery continued into the new year. Only in his letters to his mother did Baudelaire confess the reasons for his deep unhappiness. On about 5 January, he took up his pen once again:

My dear good mother,

...You know that I came to Neuilly with the aim of spending less money and also of being agreeable to a sick woman.

Now you are going to see what has happened, and, first and foremost, remember that I've controlled my temper for a whole fortnight.

When you have lived for nineteen years with and for a woman, you have something to say to her every day. Now here I found a brother who had re-appeared, a year ago, and he remained in Jeanne's room from 8 o'clock in the morning until 11 o'clock at night. Not a second for confidences. Since I wanted to treat her carefully, in her present state, I contained myself for a long time; finally, one evening, at midnight, I told her, with all possible tact, that I had come here for her sake, that I had no right to drive her brother out, but that, since I was excluded, I was going to go home to my mother, as she, too, had need of me. I told her that I did not in the least intend to deprive her of her money, but that since her brother occupied her entirely, to my detriment, it was right that he, who earned more than a man of letters, and did not have 50,000 francs' worth of debts, increasing with interest, should come to the aid of his invalid sister and should henceforward pay his share, two-thirds or a half, of the expenses necessary to her. I expected an explosion of bad temper. Not at all, but a great many tears. She told me that she knew my devotion, my torments, my agonies, *that what I said was perfectly right*, that she was going to urge her brother to go back to work, but that she was much afraid that my demand would be ill received...

In fact, the next day she broached the subject . . .

You would never guess the reply, so stupid and so inhuman that if it had been made directly to me I should have slashed the man's face with a cane. 'That I ought to be accustomed to hardship and difficulties – that, when one took responsibility for a woman, it was because one knew that one could take it – that, as for him, he had never saved money – and that, even for the future, one must not count on him.'

I asked Jeanne *what she thought of such an answer*. Personally, I imagined that there might be something behind it, that perhaps she had incurred some heavy debt to her brother, so that he felt entitled not to stint himself. I questioned her gently on the subject. 'How much have you borrowed from your brother *for the past year*, while I was living at the hotel?'

'He only gave me 200 francs.' That was her reply. That means, in plain French, that, finding a ready-made life at his sister's, he was in no way eager to return to work. It is not surprising that she is so badly dressed and that she hasn't the money to pay her doctors.

I was touched by the flowing tears on this aged face [*sic*], all this indecision in an enfeebled creature. My anger was appeased. But I am in a state of constant irritation which my external worries are not designed to diminish.

(To give you an idea of these, I need 4,000 francs on the 10th, and I have 1,860.)

That's how things stand.

When Jeanne needs to see me, she comes to my room. This gentleman does not leave her room – and, if I decide to leave Paris, he will not help his invalid sister.

I have very often and rightly accused myself of monstrous egotism. But, my God! mine has never gone as far as that.[5]

The letter showed an innocence which was extraordinary for a man of forty. After nineteen years with Jeanne, only a quixotic innocent could still have accepted this man as her brother. Jeanne herself had long ceased to be an object of desire; but her past had been tumultuous and, in her enfeebled state, she would have been an easy prey for some ruthless former lover who chose to live at the expense of her protector.

Mme Aupick marked the letter 'answered'; but her answer does not survive. She had always disapproved, intensely, of the woman whom she called *la Vénus noire*; she had always resented Baudelaire's devotion to Jeanne, and his financial commitment. The thought that – with her own assistance – he was also keeping this louche man from his mistress's past must have angered her and disturbed her deeply. She can only have urged her son to leave Neuilly. It had been his last attempt to share his life with Jeanne. Only one woman now remained to him.

On 10 or 11 January, less than four weeks after his departure, Baudelaire returned to the hôtel de Dieppe.

In the first week of February, the second edition of *Les Fleurs du mal* was published, at 3 francs a copy.

82

More than thirty poems which had not appeared in 1857 were published in this new edition. The first of them was 'L'Albatros', which – said Ernest Prarond – Baudelaire had brought back from his voyage to the East. Prarond claimed that Baudelaire had recited it to friends soon after he came home.[1] Henri Hignard, who had known Baudelaire in Lyons and at Louis-le-Grand, and had also seen him in 1843–6, recorded that his friend had recited the poem to him at that time, and that it had been 'composed on the bridge of the ship on the high seas.'[2] Yet Baudelaire had had the poem printed at Honfleur in 1859, with 'Le Voyage' and 'Sisina', and he had sent the brochure to friends as poetry which was recently composed. The apparent contradiction may be resolved. It seems quite probable that the first version of 'L'Albatros' dated from the voyage of 1841–2, and that this had been taken up again in 1859, and perhaps in a different form.[3]

This explanation is supported by some remarkable evidence. In 1855, as Pichois records, Dr Melchior Yvan had published *De France en Chine*, an account of his voyage in 1844, when he had landed at Réunion. He had seen petrels and albatrosses follow the ship, and he recalled how the sailors had lured an albatross on board. 'When it was drawn on to the bridge, the albatross did not try to escape; it looked, with surprise, at the enemies which surrounded it, and it stumbled on the hard and solid ground.'[4] Yvan's impressions bore a strong likeness to those of Baudelaire. It is not too fanciful to suggest that Baudelaire had read them.

The influence of Dr Yvan may, I think, be found in more than one of Baudelaire's poems, and I have discussed it in detail elsewhere.[5] One may, however, recall that, in Réunion, the doctor had seen a beautiful mulatto woman, walking barefoot, under a red parasol: the precursor of la belle Dorothée, in Baudelaire's prose poem.[6] Dr Yvan had also landed at Cape Town, where the houses had 'une apparence de confort et de bonheur calme qui fait plaisir à voir . . .'[7] There seems an anticipation, here, of the refrain of 'L'Invitation au voyage':

> Là, tout n'est qu'ordre et beauté,
> Luxe, calme et volupté.[8]

There follows an even closer link between *De France en Chine* and *Les Fleurs du mal*.

> Je préfère au constance, à l'opium, au nuits,
> L'élixir de ta bouche où l'amour se pavane . . .[9]

In her notes on 'Sed non satiata', Enid Starkie suggests that the local wine at Cape Town 'must have made a deep impression on Baudelaire, since he links it with burgundy – his favourite wine – and opium, which he calls *les clefs du paradis*.'[10] Three years after Baudelaire's visit, Dr Yvan was equally impressed. He wrote three pages about the four varieties of constantia. An hospitable local resident gave the doctor 'so generous a taste of his heavenly wines that we were on the point of forgetting earthly things.'[11] It would not have been surprising if Baudelaire had read this popular book which enhanced his own recollections.

In the second edition of *Les Fleurs du mal*, his inspirations were manifold. 'Le Masque', dedicated to the sculptor Ernest Christophe, had been suggested by a statue which Baudelaire had seen in his studio: the figure of a voluptuous woman whose smiling face was only a mask. Behind the mask was her real face, which expressed not joy, but the agony of life, and of life to come. 'Hymne à la beauté' emphasises that, for Baudelaire, beauty was a temptation, a *fleur du mal*. 'La Chevelure' was one of the great poems which belonged to 1858–9, and no doubt it was inspired by Jeanne. It repeated the theme of 'Parfum exotique', in which the fragrance of her breasts had recalled exotic memories. Now the aroma of her hair evoked a distant world; the sonata had become a symphony.[12] The series of four poems, 'Un Fantôme', was again inspired by Jeanne: but, now, by the 'poor invalid',[13] half paralysed, which she had become. Only memory remained.[14]

'Semper eadem' has the tone of the poems which were addressed to Mme Sabatier, and it was possibly inspired by her; but we should be wise to see it simply as a transition from the cycle of carnal love to that of spiritual love. 'Chant d'automne' and 'À une Madone' belong to the cycle of Marie Daubrun. 'Chant d'automne' shows a familiar defencelessness against a hostile world. The poet feels the imminence of an inner winter, a winter of the spirit rather than a threat of wind and snow. Yet it is not a question here of judging Baudelaire's nervous condition; the marvel is that from this excessive sensibility he has drawn a poem of unquestioned beauty, in which we all of us recognise our moments of despair.[15] In *Baudelaire 'entre Dieu et Satan'*, Massin rightly observes that when, at last, the poet 'gives himself over, . . . then our consent is borne away, the consent of our whole being . . . Baudelaire is here the equal of the most divine, of Michaelangelo, Beethoven . . . or Keats; he breaks down the doors of our soul.'[16]

'Chanson d'après-midi' belongs to one of the casual encounters in the poet's 'dark Siberia',[17] perhaps to the mysterious Élisa Nieri (or Neri, or Guerri), whose real identity remains unknown. She was a friend of Mme Sabatier and, it seems, of La Castiglione; she was something of an adventuress, and she was, perhaps, a spy in the service of Piedmont. She inspired Baudelaire with a sonnet, 'Sisina'.[18] Yet, as Jean Prévost remarks, the career of Baudelaire, as a poet of love, reveals less and less, as the years go by, of the countenance and person of the beloved. In the love of a woman, the poet only seeks and only finds his own desire for peace, his own anxieties, his personal grief. In love he celebrates a new form of solitude.[19]

The edition of 1861 contains two of Baudelaire's most despairing poems. In 'Obsession', the forests echo the lamentations of man, and the sea echoes the bitter laughter of the defeated. In 'Le Goût du Néant', hope and love are swallowed up by time, and the human spirit is vanquished. 'L'Horloge' returns to the melancholy thought of the passing hours; it ends the section 'Spleen et Idéal' by harshly emphasising its pessimism.

The section which follows, 'Tableaux parisiens', was created for the edition of 1861, and it emphasises its modernity. Eight of the eighteen poems had appeared in the section 'Spleen et Idéal' in 1857. Among the new poems was 'Le Cygne'. Brombert has shown it to be the microcosm of all that is most modern in Baudelairean thought.[20] Crossing the new Carrousel, in a Paris changed beyond recognition by Haussmann, the poet sees a swan that has escaped from its cage on the site of an old menagerie. Bewildered by the absence of water, it seems to reproach the Almighty for lack of rain. The second part of the poem is on a different plane. It is an orchestration of a simple theme. It has all the urgency and power with which Baudelaire could write about despair. It is a lamentation of misfortune; it echoes the loneliness and the bewilderment of the albatross, the fall of Andromache, the exile of the negress, regretting the palm-trees of her native Africa. It comes from the poet's depths, and it sympathises with everyone who has lost the irrevocable, with the captive and the vanquished, the misery of humankind.

> ...Je pense à mon grand cygne, avec ses gestes fous,
> Comme les exilés, ridicule et sublime,
> Et rongé d'un désir sans trêve! et puis à vous,
>
> Andromaque, des bras d'un grand époux tombée,
> Vil bétail, sous la main du superbe Pyrrhus,
> Auprès d'un tombeau vide en extase courbée;
> Veuve d'Hector, hélas! et femme d'Hélénus!
>
> Je pense à la négresse, amaigrie et phtisique,
> Piétinant dans la boue, et cherchant, l'œil hagard,
> Les cocotiers absents de la superbe Afrique
> Derrière la muraille immense du brouillard;

À quiconque a perdu ce qui ne se retrouve
Jamais, jamais! à ceux qui s'abreuvent de pleurs
Et tètent la Douleur comme une bonne louve!
Aux maigres orphelins séchant comme des fleurs!

Ainsi dans la forêt où mon esprit s'exile
Un vieux Souvenir sonne à plein souffle du cor!
Je pense aux matelots oubliés dans une île,
Aux captifs, aux vaincus! . . . à bien d'autres encor![21]

There follow 'Les Sept Vieillards' and 'Les Petites Vieilles', both dedicated, likewise, to Victor Hugo. They, too, describe misfortune and despair. In the first of them, in a Paris filled with dank yellow mist, the poet sees an aged beggar tramping the streets. The broken, hostile old man is followed by another, then yet another. Seven identical beggars pass, and, before an eighth appears, the poet hurries home, disturbed by the absurdity and mystery.[22] Some critics have wondered if the seven beggars represent the seven capital sins, or the seven days of the week; but the poem is a hallucination, not an allegory, and in the first and last stanzas Pichois has seen the origins of Rimbaud's 'Le Bateau ivre'.[23] In this hallucination, city and sea merge inextricably: Paris and Honfleur, where Baudelaire is maturing and writing his poetry.

'Les Petites Vieilles' was, so Baudelaire told Hugo, 'written in order to imitate you.'[24] What he copies is the tone of charity, mingled with familiarity, which produces the touching grandeur of Hugo's work. In Paris, Baudelaire watches the pathetic old women in the streets, and he reflects on the souls concealed under the ragged clothes, in the crippled bodies. He is moved by the old women's disabilities and by their stoicism; he is led to speculate about their past and their uncertain future.

Ruines! ma famille! ô cerveaux congénères!
Je vous fais chaque soir un solennel adieu!
Où serez-vous demain, Èves octogénaires,
Sur qui pèse la griffe effroyable de Dieu?[25]

In Paris, Baudelaire finds more cause for despair than for delight. 'Les Aveugles' may well have been suggested by a chance encounter in the streets. The blind men feel their way through the endless darkness, and become symbols of desperate mankind:

Ils traversent ainsi le noir illimité,
Ce frère du silence éternel. Ô cité!
Pendant qu'autour de nous tu chantes, ris et beugles,

> Éprise du plaisir jusqu'à l'atrocité,
> Vois! je me traîne aussi! mais, plus qu'eux hébété,
> Je dis: Que cherchent-ils au Ciel, tous ces aveugles?[26]
> •

Baudelaire doubts the very existence of light. As he wrote to his mother: 'I long with all my heart (and how sincerely, none can understand but myself!) to believe that some external and invisible being is concerned with my fate; but what can I do to believe it?'[27]

For Baudelaire, as Hiddleston has rightly observed, 'poetry should not be a collection of separate poems, it should represent a spiritual adventure.'[28] Baudelaire himself was convinced of his morality, and of his own spiritual purpose. He understood the alchemy of poetry.

> Anges revêtus d'or, de pourpre et d'hyacinthe,
> Ô vous! soyez témoins que j'ai fait mon devoir
> Comme un parfait chimiste et comme une âme sainte.
>   Car j'ai de chaque chose extrait la quintessence,
> Tu m'as donné ta boue et j'en ai fait de l'or.[29]

83

On 18 or 19 February, Baudelaire wrote to Calonne about the 1,300 francs which he now owed him. He hoped to settle his debts with manuscripts. 'There would be no point in bringing me a manuscript,' Calonne replied. 'You've postponed it for too long. There's no way to settle matters now. You have always put me off for the past year and more, and today conditions are quite different. So come and see me and tell me what you have done, and what you expect to do.'[1] The meeting, according to Baudelaire, was even more unpleasant than the letter. He sent the letter to Armand du Mesnil, who posted it to Auguste Lacaussade. The former secretary of Sainte-Beuve was now the editor of the *Revue européenne*. Du Mesnil urged Lacaussade to take Baudelaire as a contributor.[2] Lacaussade recalled, years later: 'I facilitated his access here, and it was here that he published . . . one or two articles on Wagner . . . These pages by Baudelaire were the first, or among the first, to be devoted to Wagner in Parisian reviews.'[3]

Meanwhile, in 1861, matters became still more bitter and more complicated. Baudelaire hoped to pay his debts to the *Revue contemporaine* with his earnings from the *Revue européenne*. However, on 28

February, the *Revue contemporaine* published two poems which he had
hoped to give to its rival. Early in March, he lamented to Lacaussade:

> Alas, the poems have appeared. I learned it this morning.
>
> My copyist is copying [*sic*] the end of the *Guys*. I shall see you this
> evening or tomorrow evening, at 5 o'clock.
>
> When I told M. de Calonne that I'd publish pieces *here*, in order to pay
> *his* debt by instalments, he declared that from now on it was no use
> bringing him anything whatever, and that he was going *to countermand two
> articles about books of mine.*
>
> It's mad. I don't understand it at all.
>
> I have seen *Tannhäuser* yet again; I think I am sure of myself for the
> 18th.[4]

Wagner had already invited Baudelaire to the dress-rehearsal of
Lohengrin on 19 February.[5] On the morning of 10 March, Baudelaire
called on him; that evening they met again, at Tortoni's, the fashionable restaurant in the boulevard des Italiens. Baudelaire attended one
of the dress-rehearsals for the Wagner concerts at the Opéra.[6] The first
performance of *Tannhäuser* took place on 13 March; it was given a
turbulent reception. Two days later, the *Revue contemporaine* insisted:
'Never have we seen in Paris a poorer, more ridiculous libretto than
that of *Tannhäuser*, the very name of which jars on our ears ... In
France, we want something more than a drama without interest and a
score without a melody.'[7] On 18 March, *Tannhäuser* was performed
again, and Paul de Saint-Victor published a violent attack on Wagner
in *La Presse*.

While Wagner and his music of the future suffered from Parisian
hostility, Baudelaire was suffering from his usual penury. Malassis had
undertaken to publish two volumes of his criticism; but, for some
months, as he himself was in difficulties, he had thought of ceding them
to another publisher, P.-J. Hetzel. Baudelaire had recognised the
proposition as possible salvation for them both. He called on Hetzel,
who again was worried about money, but – so Baudelaire told
Malassis: 'He said that, in a few months' time, with your agreement,
he would willingly take charge of *Réflexions sur quelques-uns de mes
contemporains*. As for the *Curiosités*, he urges us strongly to change the
title.'[8]

The news came in a letter which Baudelaire wrote to Malassis, in
Alençon, on about 20 March; he was now being sued for 1,900 francs.

> I want to add a few words [he continued], the sort of words I can say
> only to you ... I am not, as you know, a sniveller or a liar. In the last two
> months, especially, I have fallen into an alarming debility and despair. I

have felt myself attacked by a kind of illness *à la Gérard*, namely the fear of being unable to think any more, or to write a line. It was only four or five days ago that I managed to verify that he didn't die because of that. It is an important point.[9]

Gérard de Nerval had spent his latter years on or over the verge of insanity; in 1855 he had committed suicide. Baudelaire was haunted by the thought of him. The reference to Nerval here is all the more interesting since he had expressed his fear of intellectual death in letters at the end of his life, but he had never expressed it in his published works. There seems to have been a deeper friendship between him and Baudelaire than Baudelaire's two surviving notes suggest.

I have the greatest desire to see you here [Baudelaire continued, to Malassis]. It's not a question of the delights of friendship, it's a question of you, and of your interests. Add to that the uselessness of the excellent De Broise, and consider the future . . . Sainte-Beuve said to me the other day: 'Where is Malassis?' 'In Alençon.' *'But he's mad!'*[10]

Malassis, like Baudelaire, was harassed, now, by creditors. Though he had recently established his bookshop in Paris, he stayed on in Alençon to save his printing works. 'No one', he answered, 'can be more unfortunate than we are for credit. I don't think they'd give us cash for bars of gold.'[11]

Baudelaire, in Paris, lost himself in work. For three days, from 20 to 22 March, from ten o'clock in the morning till ten o'clock at night, he stayed at Pancoucke's, the printer's, going through 'an enormous quantity of tobacco',[12] and 'improvising' his study of Wagner. The work was intellectually exhausting, but it gave him a sense of purpose. He was encouraged by a note from Wagner himself, inviting him to call.[13] On 24 March, the third performance of *Tannhäuser* was given at the Opéra; and, harassed by the criticism which he found in Paris, Wagner withdrew his work.

On 1 April, *La Revue européenne* published *Richard Wagner et TANNHÄUSER à Paris*. Next day Baudelaire met Dentu, the editor of the review, who was to publish his article as a brochure. He promised to give him the text two days hence, with an addition on which he was still working.[14] The booklet was to appear early in May. 'He was a fanatic from the first,' Judith Gautier recalled. 'So it was that he saved honour.'[15]

For Baudelaire, his appreciation of Wagner was more than a matter of national honour. He had recognised that Wagner's music revealed a new art, an art analagous to his own, an art which, despite its vagueness, suggested to different listeners the same general effects of light and colour and even the same visual images. Baudelaire had been haunted by the work of Poe and Delacroix. Now, once again, he had found a master whose work corresponded with his own instincts, emotions and beliefs. Wagner had revealed a universal soul. The overture to *Lohengrin*, and Wagner's *Lettre sur la musique*, showed Baudelaire that he had done in poetry what Wagner was doing in music. He had done the same thing unconsciously in *Les Fleurs du mal*. In an unfinished preface to the second edition of his poems, he had written that he had planned to show 'how poetry touches music through a prosody whose roots plunge deeper into the human soul than any classicist theory indicates.'[16] It has been said that Baudelaire, alone in his time, was capable of instantly understanding Wagner's genius.[17]

84

On 1 April, the day on which his article on Wagner appeared in the *Revue européenne*, Baudelaire answered a letter from his mother. He had gradually come to accept the harsh truth. He finally doubted, indeed despaired of his creative powers. He would not be able to write those works of pure imagination which he had dreamed about for so long. He felt impotent in work, as in life.[1]

Mme Aupick, too, felt impotent, and deeply depressed. She suffered from four years of widowhood, from her provincial isolation, from her poor health and her nervousness, and, above all, from the behaviour of her son. She was troubled by his physical and emotional condition, by his unremitting debts and, now, by the new edition of his poems. She herself was devout, and she had been shocked by his blasphemy and his invocation to Satan, by his conviction for offences against public morals. She was disturbed when her confessor, the abbé Cardine, criticised her son, and, having asked persistently for a copy of *Les Fleurs du mal*, received one from Baudelaire, and informed her that he had burnt it. In a moment of particular anguish, she told Baudelaire that she wished that she were dead.

From 1861, his own depressive state remained unending. On 1 April, when he wrote to her, his misery remained acute.

I have [he told her] fallen into a sort of perpetual nervous terror; dreadful sleep, dreadful awakening, the impossibility of doing anything. My copies [of *Les Fleurs du mal*] remained on my table for a month before I could find the courage to wrap them up ... In this horrible state of mind, powerlessness and hypochondria, the idea of suicide returned. I can say so, now that it has passed. At every moment of the day, this idea tormented me. I saw absolute deliverance from everything. At the same time, and *for three months*, by a contradiction which was singular, but only apparent, I *constantly* prayed (to whom? what particular being? I have absolutely no idea) to obtain two things: for me, the strength to live; and, for you, many, many years. Let me say, by the way, that your wish to die is quite absurd and hardly charitable, since for me your death would mean the final blow, and the absolute impossibility of happiness.

The fixed idea [of suicide] vanished in the end, driven out by some intense and unavoidable work . . . Since then, I have fallen ill again with languor, horror and fear. Physically, I have been quite ill two or three times; but one of the things which I find particularly unbearable is that, when I go to sleep, and even when I am asleep, I hear voices very clearly, whole sentences, but very banal, very trivial, and completely unrelated to my affairs.

Your letters have come; they are not of a kind to comfort me. You are always ready to stone me with the crowd. [All this] dates from my childhood, as you know. How, then, do you manage always to be the opposite of a *friend* to your son, except in financial affairs? . . .

As for M. Cardine, it is a serious matter, but in a completely different sense to the one that you imagine. In the midst of all my griefs, I will not have a priest coming to struggle against me in the mind of my old mother, and I'll put a stop to that, if I have the strength.[2]

Michelet, too, in *Du Prêtre, de la Femme, de la Famille*, had deplored the influence of spiritual directors in women's lives. It was significant that Michelet had wanted to keep confessors from wives, while Baudelaire was thinking of his mother. Yet, as Tamara Bassim wrote in *La Femme dans l'œuvre de Baudelaire*: 'For Baudelaire, only one woman exists: his mother. She will be all women, and all women will be Her.'[3]

For the moment, the thought of M. Cardine continued to occupy him.

This man's behaviour is monstrous and inexplicable [he continued]. As for burning books, no one does it nowadays, except madmen who like to see paper blazing up. And I had stupidly deprived myself of a precious copy, to please him and to give him something which he had been demanding for three years! And I have no copies, even for my friends! You have always had to humiliate me in front of somebody. It happened with M. Émon [at my stepfather's funeral]. Remember. Now it's with a priest who doesn't even have the delicacy to keep a hurtful thought from you. And finally he didn't even understand that the book was Catholic in its conception! But that is a consideration of another order . . .

About the *conseil judiciaire* . . . That accursed device! It was the maternal device of a mind which is too concerned with money. It was a device which has dishonoured me, driven me into recurrent debts, and has killed all kindness in me. It has even thwarted my education as an artist and a man of letters, which has remained incomplete. Blindness creates greater calamities than malice . . .[4]

Baudelaire asked his mother for 200 francs; although it was the beginning of the month, he had no money. He was being sued for 2,000 francs' worth of promissory notes. Mme Aupick promptly sent him 300 francs. 'For today, thank you, thank you', he wrote to her on 3 April. '. . . Your letter demands a long reply. It distressed me. I assure you that I am lost, absolutely lost. Suppose I do live, I see a long prospect of years, without pleasure, without rest, and *without work*.'[5] His pessimism remained – especially in his letters to his mother. He was bitterly aware that, on 9 April, he would be forty, and enter middle age. Looking at a Nadar photograph of Baudelaire, the gaunt, lined face, the desperate eyes, Gaëtan Picon was to write that, at forty, Baudelaire was a centenarian bowed beneath his memories.[6] He despaired of the present and of the future.

Nonetheless, in the spring of 1861 he had some immediate reason for satisfaction. On 15 April, Wagner expressed the solace and delight which he had found in Baudelaire's article. 'It gives me', he wrote, 'more honour and encouragement than anything that has ever been said about my poor talent . . . I am very proud to call you a friend.'[7]

There is little information about the relations between Baudelaire and Wagner; the occasional mentions in Baudelaire's correspondence lead us to presume that these were only ephemeral. Yet Baudelaire was among the first Frenchmen to praise Wagner as he deserved.

85

Late in April, at the price of one franc, Dentu published *Richard Wagner et TANNHÄUSER à Paris*, in the form of a brochure. It was Baudelaire's one attempt at music criticism. It was not the work of a professional musician or, indeed, of a musicologist; it was the work of the author of *Les Fleurs du mal*, among the most personal essays that he wrote.

Music was allusive and formal, discreet and universally relevant. As J. A. Hiddleston observes, it was a basic element of the Baudelairean world.[1] Thoughts that were dear to Baudelaire's mind and to his imagination appeared here with a force that revealed the catalysing power which Wagner exercised upon him. When he first heard the overture to *Lohengrin*, he had felt swept out of the world; and 'what would be really surprising,' he wrote, 'would be that sound *could not* suggest colour, that colours *could not* give the idea of a melody, and that sound and colour were not fit to translate ideas; for things have always been expressed by a reciprocal analogy, since the day when God created the world as a complex and indivisible whole.'[2]

Wagner led Baudelaire to the system of *correspondances*, that central theory in his poetry; he led him also to consider the relation between music and space, between the visions due to music and those that were released by drugs:

> No musician excels, like Wagner, in *painting* space and depth, material and spiritual . . . He has the art of translating, by subtle gradations, everything that is excessive, immense, ambitious, in the spirit and nature of man. Listening to this ardent and despotic music, it sometimes seems that, in the shadowy background, torn by dreams, one rediscovers the dizzying conceptions of opium.[3]

Wagner led Baudelaire, again, to the theory of the symbiosis of the creator and the critic. 'It would be phenomenal if a critic became a poet, and it is impossible for a poet not to contain a critic . . . People who reproach Wagner, the composer, for having written books on the philosophy of his art, and drawn from them the suspicion that his music is not natural and spontaneous, should also deny that Vinci, Hogarth and Reynolds could have done good paintings, simply because they deduced and analysed the principles of their art.'[4]

As for *Tannhäuser*, it represented the profound concern of Baudelaire as a Catholic poet: the struggle between the two elements which had chosen the human heart as their battlefield: that is to say the flesh and the spirit, Hell and Heaven, Satan and God. *Tannhäuser* represented, too, the savageness of love.[5] The Baudelairean universe is reflected, here, just after it had been reflected in the second edition of *Les Fleurs du mal*.[6] Baudelaire had not taken Wagner as a pretext for expressing his own theories, but in Wagner's work he had discovered a mirror-image of himself.

The brochure on Wagner was not to sell. Five years later, it was to be remaindered at half price. Nadar sent a copy to Mme de Metternich, one of Wagner's supporters; she eventually returned it to him, with a note of thanks. The pages were uncut.[7]

On 6 May, Baudelaire himself turned once again to his mother. The letter that he sent her was unusually long, and yet it should be quoted at some length. Few of his letters, even to her, revealed so much about his health, his state of mind, and his relationship with her: the intense, profound, uneasy relationship which dominated his life.

> If you really have the maternal instinct and if you're not yet weary, come to Paris [he urged her], come and see me, and even fetch me. For a thousand terrible reasons I cannot come to Honfleur myself, to seek what

I should like so much, a little courage and a few caresses. At the end of March I wrote to you: *Shall we ever see each other again?* I was in one of those crises in which one sees the dreadful truth. God knows what I should give to spend a few days with you – with you, the only being to whom my life is attached: a week, three days, a few hours.

You don't read my letters carefully enough, you think I'm lying, or at least that I'm exaggerating when I talk about my griefs, my health, my horror of life. I tell you that I should like to see you, and that I cannot hasten to Honfleur. Your letters are full of errors and false ideas which conversation might rectify, and which volumes of writing would not destroy.

Whenever I take up my pen to explain my situation to you, I'm afraid: I'm afraid of killing you, of destroying your frail body. And as for me, though you do not know it, I am constantly on the verge of suicide. I believe that you love me passionately: you have a blind spirit, but so great a character. As for me, I loved you passionately in my childhood: later, under the pressure of your injustices, I lacked respect for you, as if maternal injustice could authorise a lack of filial respect; I have often regretted it, although, according to my habit, I have said nothing about it. I am no longer the ungrateful, violent child. Long meditations on my destiny and on your character have helped me to understand all my faults and all your generosity. But, in short, the harm is done, done by your imprudent acts and by my errors. We are evidently destined to love one another, to live for one another, to end our lives as properly and smoothly as possible. And yet, in the terrible circumstances in which I am placed, I am convinced that one of us will kill the other, and that finally we shall kill one another. After my death, you will cease to live, that is obvious. I am the only thing that makes you live. After your death, especially if you died from a shock which I had caused, I should kill myself, no question about that. You often talk about your death with too much resignation. It would not set anything right in my situation; the *conseil judiciaire* would be kept (why shouldn't it be?), nothing would be paid, and, in addition to my griefs, I should have *the horrible feeling of absolute isolation*. It's absurd for me to kill myself, isn't it? 'So you're going to leave your old mother all alone,' you will say. Really, if I'm not strictly entitled to do so, I think that the amount of griefs which I have suffered for *nearly thirty years* would make me pardonable . . .

Every minute proves to me that I no longer have a taste for life. You committed a great indiscretion in my youth. Your indiscretion and *my old errors* weigh upon me, and envelop me.[8]

It is unlikely that Baudelaire referred to his mother's second marriage. It is much more probable that he was thinking, once again, about the *conseil judiciaire* which had been imposed on him. As for his 'old errors', he was no doubt recalling his early extravagance, and the venereal disease which he had contracted in his youth.

My situation is atrocious [he continued, now]. There are people who pay me compliments, people who pay court to me, there may perhaps be some who envy me. My literary situation is more than good, I can do what I want. It will all be printed [*sic*]. As I have an unpopular sort of mind, I shan't earn much money, but I shall have great fame, this I know – provided that I have the courage to live. But my spiritual health is wretched – perhaps destroyed. I still have plans: *Mon Cœur mis à nu, some novels*, two *dramas*, one of them for the Théâtre-Français. Will all this ever be done? *I don't think so any more.* As regards respectability, my situation is dreadful – and that is a great misfortune. Never any rest. Inconceivable insults, outrages, affronts, which corrupt and paralyse the imagination . . .

In a moment I shall come to positive, in other words present matters. Because I really need to be saved, and you alone can save me. I want to say everything today. I am alone, without friends, without a mistress, without a dog, and without a cat, to whom I can complain. All I have is the portrait of my father, which is always silent.

I am in that horrible state that I went through in the autumn of 1844. A resignation worse than fury.

But my physical health, which I need for you, for me, for my duties, that is another question! I must talk to you about it, although you pay very little attention to it. I don't want to talk about those nervous diseases which are destroying me day by day, and annul my courage: [I mean my] vomitings, insomnia, nightmares and fainting fits. I have talked to you about them too often. But it is no use being shy with you. You know that when I was very young I had a syphilitic infection, which I later thought completely cured. In Dijon, after 1848, it broke out again. Once again it was palliated. Now it has come back, and in a new form, patches on the skin, extraordinary fatigue in all the joints. You can believe me: *I know what I'm talking about.* Perhaps, in the misery in which I'm sunk, my terror worsens the disease. But I must have a strict way of life, and I can't give myself over to this in the existence which I lead.[9]

René Laforgue maintains that Baudelaire was affected by cerebral syphilis, and suffered from it from about 1861.[10]

I leave all this aside [Baudelaire continued, to his mother], and I want to resume my dreams; before I come to the plan I want to reveal to you, I take a real pleasure in it! Who knows if I shall be able, once again, to open my whole soul to you, that soul *which you have never appreciated or understood*! I write this without hesitation, I know so well that it is true.

There was in my childhood a period of passionate love for you . . . You were entirely mine. You were both an idol and a friend. Perhaps you will be surprised that I can't talk with passion about a time which is so distant. I'm surprised at it myself. It is perhaps because I have conceived, once again, the desire to die, that the old things appear so vividly in my mind.

Later on, you know what an atrocious education your husband wanted to give me; I'm forty, and I don't think about the colleges without pain. [Nor do I think without pain] about the fear which my stepfather inspired in me. And yet I loved him, and besides I have wisdom enough today to do him justice. But, when all is said, he was stubbornly clumsy. I want to move on rapidly, because I can see tears in your eyes.

Finally, I escaped, and from that time forward I was absolutely abandoned.[11]

The phrase is ambiguous, but Baudelaire was abandoned by the Aupicks, and abandoned in his way of life.

I was only in love with pleasure, and with perpetual excitement [so he explained]; with travels, fine furniture, pictures, prostitutes, etc. I bear the punishment for that too cruelly today. As for the *conseil judiciaire*, I have only one thing to say: I now know the enormous value of money, and I understand the seriousness of everything that relates to money; I know that you could have believed that you were wise, that you were working for my good; but there is still a question, a question which has always haunted me: how can it be that this idea never crossed your mind? 'Perhaps my son may never know how to behave, to the same degree as I do; but perhaps he may also become a remarkable man in other respects. In that case, what shall I do? Shall I condemn him to a double and contradictory life, a life which is honoured on the one hand, odious and despised on the other? Shall I condemn him to drag a deplorable stigma into his old age: a stigma which harms him, a reason for impotence and grief?' It is clear that if this *conseil judiciaire* had not been set up, everything would have been spent. I should really have had to acquire the taste for work. The *conseil judiciaire* was set up, *everything is spent, and I am old* [he was forty], *and I am unhappy.*

Is it possible to recover? That is the whole question.

All this return to the past was intended only to show that I have some excuse to offer, if not an absolute justification. If you feel some reproaches in what I'm writing, do at least understand that this does not in any way alter my admiration for your great heart, my gratitude for your devotion. You have only the genius of sacrifice. Not so much reason as charity. I ask you for more. I ask you for advice, support, complete understanding between you and me, to get me through this. I implore you to come, come. I am at the end of my nervous strength, my courage and my hope . . .

I ask you for your happiness, and I ask you for [mine], in so far as we can still know *that.*[12]

His happiness depended largely on financial security: a security which, in adult life, he had never known. He recognised the extravagance of his early youth; he had long ago become aware of the all-pervasive misery of poverty. His poverty increased his inability to work, it drove him to expedients which he found humiliating and, no doubt, contemptible. He felt increasingly unable to save himself by his own exertions. Once again, he turned to his mother.

You have let me propose a plan to you, here it is: I ask for a half-measure. The transfer of a substantial sum limited to 10,000 [francs] for example,

2,000 to free me immediately; 2,000 in your hands to remedy foreseen or unforeseen necessities, necessities of life, clothes, etc . . . for a year (Jeanne will go into a home where the strict essentials will be paid) . . . Finally, 6,000 francs in the hands of Ancelle or Marin, which will be spent slowly, franc by franc, prudently, so as to pay perhaps more than 10,000, and prevent any shock or scandal at Honfleur.

There is a year's tranquillity. I should be a very great fool and a very great rogue, if I didn't take advantage of this to renew myself . . .

If you adopted this plan of blessedness, I should like to be reinstalled at the end of the month, perhaps immediately. I authorise you to come and fetch me. Of course you understand that there are a mass of details which cannot be put in a letter. In a word, I should like it if every sum were only paid after you had agreed, after careful discussion between you and me: in other words, that you should be my real *Conseil judiciaire* . . .

I beg of you, give me peace, work, and a little love.

It is clear that, in my present affairs, there are some things which are horribly urgent, and so, in the inevitable jobbery with banks, I have once again committed the offence of misappropriating, for my personal debts, several hundred francs which did not belong to me. *I was absolutely compelled to do so.* It goes without saying that I thought I could redress the wrong at once . . . Today I have had *the terrible courage* to write and confess my sin to the person concerned. What scene is there going to be? I have no idea at all. But I wanted to clear my conscience. I hope that out of consideration for my name and my gifts they will not create a scandal, and that they will agree to wait.[13]

Next day, he duly reported: 'I have seen the person whose visit I dreaded. What a humiliation!'[14]

It was indeed a humiliation. Once again he had cheated his publisher; this time he had misappropriated 800 francs which belonged to him, in order to pay his personal debts; it was a dastardly way to behave, especially to a loyal friend who had grave financial problems of his own. All Baudelaire could do for the moment was to give Malassis a letter for Auguste Lacaussade, the editor of the *Revue européenne*, to say that Malassis was entitled to the payment for his two articles. The first of these articles, *Peintres philosophes*, had not yet been delivered; the second, *Dandysme littéraire*, was 'still very muddled'.[15] Malassis had much to forgive.

So, indeed, had Mme Aupick; but, in her generosity, she sent her son a further 500 francs. He wrote to thank her, and to describe his meeting with Malassis.

I have finally had the meeting which I dreaded so much. It was more than mild. The friend in question came to see me, suspecting that I was in a very sad state of mind. He told me that he thought that what I had done was almost natural and inevitable; that he was even surprised that such events had not occurred more often to me in the horrible crises in which he had seen me for so long. All this was said without irony. Personally, I felt humiliated by this kindness. 'However,' he added, 'as I have the most urgent need of my money, tell me when and how you can make amends for this.' As I did not yet count on you, I answered that the *Revue européenne* had promised to pay me in advance for everything that I delivered, and that I should hand over to him the fee for the two forthcoming pieces, which will almost cover the amount. Unfortunately, he has the greatest need of his money *before the 25th*. So I must work without respite. Now, this morning, when I read your letters, my first thought was *to resist* this indolence and idleness which always follow a momentary relief; because, in this case, one forgets the problems of the future; *in fact it is one of the reasons why I personally should not want my conseil judiciaire to be removed*, or all my debts paid at once. *Beatitude would create idleness.* To my mind, this *conseil judiciaire* should only be abolished when I have – or you have – the moral certainty that I can always work, continually, and even when there is *no need*.

And so I am going to behave as if I did not have the hope of being rescued by you.[16]

Baudelaire had made an illuminating confession. For all the years of resentment of his *conseil judiciaire*, for all his savage comments to his mother and Ancelle, he recognised the need for the arrangement. Indeed, at moments he was grateful for it.

86

Mme Aupick did not come to Paris to see him, or to take him back to Honfleur; she did, however, make him offers and promises. She also suggested that he should approach Ancelle. It was not the first time that the notary caused problems. On 21 May, Baudelaire wrote to her in despair:

It's you who told me that Ancelle might *perhaps* do something. He himself came to explain *at great length* that there was nothing to be done, and that he could not do anything . . .

The evening he came, it was too late for him to go home and dine with his family; I took him out to dinner at a restaurant. Thanks to his horrible awkwardness, it was *impossible to dine*. He got on my nerves so much that I quarrelled with the tavern-keeper.[1]

Baudelaire had no need of Ancelle in order to quarrel with tavern-keepers. Asselineau records that he used to harass them with questions about the freshness of their butter and the quality of their wine.[2] Nonetheless, it had been an unfortunate evening.

On 24 May, Baudelaire signed a contract with Malassis, giving him the exclusive right to publish all his work, both past and future, until he had recovered the 5,000 francs which Baudelaire owed him.[3] Next day Baudelaire wrote cheerfully to his mother about the progress of his affairs.[4] On 27 May he confessed that he had asked Ancelle for 500 francs, which were to be given to Malassis; he also announced that he had just appeared before the committee of the Société des Gens de Lettres, to explain the Stoepel affair. Stoepel still refused to pay him for his translation of Longfellow. He hoped that the Society would sue Stoepel on his behalf.[5]

Another offensive acquaintance was about to turn to him. On 1 June, the *Bibliographie de la France* announced the publication of Ernest Feydeau's novel, *Sylvie*.

In *Théophile Gautier. Souvenirs intimes*, Feydeau was later to record how he had introduced himself to La Présidente. He had been asked to her Sunday dinners, 'at which she did the honours with as much urbanity as kindness . . . I do not cease to marvel', he wrote, 'at the absolute coolness of some of the guests and at the exquisite tolerance of the mistress of the house. One really had to have the sweetest nature to tolerate all Baudelaire's mystifications.'[6]

As he listened to the outrageous conversations at the rue Frochot, Feydeau could not, so he explained, deny himself the pleasure of turning them to account, 'and the novel of mine entitled *Sylvie* was born of the eccentricities which were uttered at La Présidente's table.'[7] Feydeau's novella ends with the marriage of his heroine, Sylvie, and his hero, Anselme Schanfara. Yet one may still recognise in this *étude*, as Feydeau pretentiously called it, certain elements of the real romance.

Anselme Schanfara is, for the purposes of fiction, twenty-two, while Baudelaire had been in his thirties when he wrote poems for La Présidente. However, Anselme is a poet; and his conversation is precisely the conversation which had angered Feydeau at the rue Frochot: 'Like those satiated gourmets who can no longer live except on truffles, caviare and red pepper, Anselme preferred China to France, Bohemia to society, hashish to lemonade, . . . and women who traded in their beauty to angelic young girls.'[8]

Anselme Schanfara did not merely repeat Baudelaire's conversation. His physical appearance was largely modelled on that of the author of *Les Fleurs du mal*. It is hard, too, not to see a certain resemblance between the 'fictional' heroine and the woman whom Feydeau knew, and also admired, as he records, in Gustave Ricard's portrait. Sylvie has the sensuous mouth that Ricard had painted; she has, 'over all her features, some indefinable sovereign air of repose and mystery, an expression of disdain and strength, an indescribable mixture of guile and goodness'.[9] Goodness, *la bonté*, was a quality observed by Baudelaire and by every admirer of La Présidente.

87

On 15 June, *La Revue fantaisiste* published Baudelaire's study of Victor Hugo: the first and one of the most perceptive of the series *Réflexions sur quelques-uns de mes contemporains*.

It has been said that Baudelaire was the only French poet of his time who was not indebted to Victor Hugo.[1] It is also clear, from comments in his letters and in his *Journaux intimes*, that Baudelaire felt small sympathy for the man himself, and for his uncritical clan of admirers.[2] Yet he still remained aware of his stature. If, in time, he recognised the flaws in Hugo's novels, and felt embarrassed by the *Chansons des rues et des bois*, he still recognised the significance of his earlier poetry. In 1861, Hugo had left his first Romantic lyrics far behind him. The death of his elder daughter, and years of exile in the Channel Islands, had made him the poet of *Les Contemplations* and, most recently, *La Légende des siècles*. He had turned to religion and philosophy and, now, to history. As Baudelaire wrote, 'the colours of his dreams are tinged with solemnity, and his voice has deepened in its rivalry with that of the Ocean.'[3]

Hugo had created a movement in literature which still continued in the 1860s; he had been a providential spirit. He had, from the first, said Baudelaire, been the man most clearly elected to express in poetry the mystery of existence. No artist was more universal, more fitted to establish contact with the forces of universal life. Hugo understood the most fugitive and complex sensations transmitted by living things and by so-called inanimate nature. Swedenborg had revealed the meaning of correspondences. Lavater had shown the meaning of the contour and dimension of the human head. If one continued the demonstration, one arrived at the truth that all God's creation was hieroglyphic. Hugo was aware of this mystery, and his awareness inspired his poetry. This sense of mystery, of what Delacroix had called his dictionary, this awareness of correspondences which Baudelaire had found in Gautier and in Wagner's music, was what drew him now to Victor Hugo.

Hugo did not only have grandeur, Baudelaire continued, he was 'a genius without frontiers'.[4] He was an artist as well as a poet, he was a powerful draughtsman and painter. He worked in every field of literature, he wrote of love and war and domesticity, the misery of the poor and the splendour of national glories. He was the poet of the excessive and the immense. In *La Légende des siècles*, he had created the only epic poem which could be created by a man of his time for readers of his time. He was one of those rare mortals, rare above all in literature, who increased in strength with passing years.

For all his personal dislike of Victor Hugo, Baudelaire acknowledged his significance.

He was well aware of his own. It was in a letter to his mother, on 10 July, that he announced one of his most extraordinary projects. Eugène Scribe, the popular dramatist, had recently died, and his chair was vacant at the Académie-Française. 'Several people', wrote Baudelaire, 'urge me to take advantage of the present vacancy, or of the imminent probable vacancies, to stand for election to the Académie.'[5]

88

No true friend would have done so. It is probable that the idea was Baudelaire's alone. Time after time, throughout his life, he revealed a curious desire to cause his own failure or to invite certain punishment. Constantly unsure of himself, he wanted official recognition, public proof of his distinction. He wanted to impress and please his mother. He needed rehabilitation after his conviction. Yet now, in the summer of 1861, after the court case of *Les Fleurs du mal*, after some twenty years of controversy, he could hardly have thought that he would be elected to that bastion of conservatism and tradition, the Académie-Française. He could not even have believed that he would be seriously considered as a candidate. Nadar spoke of Baudelaire's 'stupefying naïveté'.[1] Baudelaire's decision to stand was not so much naïve as masochistic. He had found a new occasion to suffer public humiliation.

Mme Aupick sensibly attempted to deter him. Her letter has not survived; but, on 25 July, when he asked her to lend him 250 francs, Baudelaire returned to the subject.

To belong to the Académie is, to my mind, the only honour which a true man of letters may solicit without shame. As for the Academicians whom you have criticised or ridiculed, and whose vote you are certain not to get, you take care to call on them when you're sure to find them out. But your reply to my letter is wrong on two points: (1) I didn't tell you that I wanted to stand immediately. I told you that I wanted to stand *very soon*. M. Scribe's chair is vacant; perhaps there are others. I'm not sure. (2) You have to resign yourself to being refused two or three times. You have to [find your] rank. The number of votes I obtain the first time will serve to show if I have a real chance for the future.[2]

Mme Aupick sent him money at once. On 27 July he thanked her, and expressed his relief that one crate of his belongings would already be at Honfleur, and out of reach of his creditors. A second crate was on its way.[3]

In Paris, the bills continued to fall due, and his fame continued to grow. On 15 August, *La Revue fantaisiste* published his studies of Pierre Dupont and Leconte de Lisle: the last of his *Réflexions sur quelques-uns de mes contemporains*.

In his comments on Dupont one hears, above all, the tone of affection. Baudelaire elected to sing the praises of the *chansonnier*, the writer of patriotic verse who had made himself the poet of the poor and the deprived. He recalled how, years ago, on one of their strolls through Paris, Dupont had mentioned a lyric which he had just written. He had been unsure of its worth. It was *Le Chant des ouvriers*; he had recited it to Baudelaire, who had been much moved. 'I know', wrote Baudelaire, 'that the works of Pierre Dupont are not finished and in exquisite taste; but he has the instinct, if not the reasoned sense of perfect beauty.'[4] He belonged to the natural aristocracy of those spirits which owed more to nature than they did to art.

Baudelaire's appreciation of Leconte de Lisle was surprisingly brief, but he made it clear that, in the author of *Poèmes antiques*, soon to publish *Poèmes barbares*, he had found a man to admire. He admired his ardent but impartial curiosity about religions, his universal love: not for mankind itself, but for the different forms in which, in different ages and different climates, man had clothed beauty and truth. He shared his cosmopolitanism, his love of the exotic, his scholarly concern with Greece and Rome; he respected his technical perfection, his powers of evocation and, perhaps above all, the patrician intellect which marked his poetry. Like Baudelaire, Leconte de Lisle felt serene disdain for anything that was not superior.

Baudelaire, the critic, was himself to be criticised. On 14 August, in the *Revue des Deux Mondes*, Armand de Pontmartin discussed the state of poetry in 1861; and, having assessed some more conventional poets, he deplored Baudelaire's sick and overexcited imagination.[5] Poetry, he said, was alien to Baudelaire: 'Poetry turns sour in his mind, like those excellent wines which cannot bear certain places or atmospheres.'[6] What sort of society, he asked, 'what sort of literature would accept M. Charles Baudelaire as their poet?'[7]

Later this year, in the *Revue européenne*, Leconte de Lisle was to answer Pontmartin and, at the same time, to reply to Baudelaire. He was to make his public comments on *Les Fleurs du mal*.

> It is [he concluded] not a work of art which one can understand without initiation. We are here no longer in the world of universal banality. The poet's eyes plunge deeply into circles of Hell not until now explored, and what he sees and what he hears there in no way recalls the ballads in fashion. There come forth maledictions and lamentations, songs of ecstasy, blasphemies, cries of anguish and of grief. The tortures of passion, the ferocity and cowardice of society, the bitter tears of despair, irony and disdain: all merge with power and harmony in this Dantesque nightmare pierced here and there with luminous outlets through which the spirit flies to ideal peace and joy . . .
>
> Finally, if one records that the author of these original poems easily carries into his prose, with a new intensity of refinement and perspicacity, most of the qualities which he displays in his use of the poetic tongue, one will recognise that many excessive things should be forgiven him, because he has exclusively loved Beauty, such as he conceives it, and he expresses it like a master.[8]

This was all the public homage that Leconte de Lisle could pay to *Les Fleurs du mal*. As his private papers have since emphasised, this vague, evasive, florid piece of prose was not dictated by real sympathy. Few contemporary critics even surmised the rank which posterity was to accord to Baudelaire. Yet it is sad that a poet of the stature of Leconte de Lisle did not show more perception.

On 1 September, Baudelaire wrote, once again, to his mother: 'Tomorrow, or the day after, I shall pack up a box of pictures and drawings (there will be a fourth), and then I shall come and spend four or five days with you . . . This journey has no purpose, no definite purpose – except *to embrace you* (the anxiety had come to be unbearable) and then *to refresh my spirit* . . .'[9]

There is no evidence that he paid a visit to Honfleur in September; after 2 September, there is a gap of two months in the surviving correspondence. Early in November, his mother accused him of neglecting her. 'You make me very unhappy', he answered, 'by always supposing that I don't love you . . . I am very busy. Money, unfinished works, preparing my return to Honfleur, the Académie, etc.'[10] The Academic campaign was, for him, another reason for not choosing a regular life at his mother's side.

89

Baudelaire had not abandoned his Academic dream. His friends had accused him of making an alliance with the Philistines because he had thought of standing for the chair of Eugène Scribe. Maxime du Camp, who was to be elected in 1880, told him that he dishonoured himself by his candidature.[1] A few days after Baudelaire wrote to his mother, there occurred one of the 'imminent probable vacancies' which he had mentioned to her. On 21 November came the death of Père Lacordaire, the Dominican priest who was renowned for his teaching and his oratory. There was a second vacant chair among the Immortals. On 11 December, advised by the feline and this time unforgivable Sainte-Beuve, Baudelaire drafted a letter to Abel Villemain, the permanent secretary of the Académie-Française. He asked to be registered as an Academic candidate.[2]

It was, it seems, that month that he asked Asselineau if he could safely present himself to Émile Augier (whom he had once ridiculed in print).[3] So it was that he embarked upon the traditional visits to the Immortals, to solicit their votes. On about 15 December, he called on Henri Patin, the elderly professor of Latin literature at the Sorbonne. Patin – who had examined him for his *baccalauréat* – received him kindly. He also told him that Alfred de Vigny was in better health.[4] (The improvement was to be only temporary. Two years later, he was to die of cancer.) Baudelaire asked Vigny if he might call on him. 'I beg you earnestly,' he ended, 'dismiss me at once, and without ceremony, if you are afraid that a visit, however brief, would tire you.'[5]

The visit to Vigny was hardly brief. Vigny recorded:

> I receive Baudelaire's visit, conversation from 2 o'clock till 4. He is very erudite, knows English well, lived in and saw much of the East Indies at the age of seventeen [*sic*]. He knows, summarises and explains Edgar Poe very well. From a literary point of view, he seems to exist only as a translator of this philosophical novelist. He has the distinguished, ailing appearance of the studious and hardworking man. I tell him that he has been ill-advised, he has been mistaken in already writing the official letter in which one declares ones candidature . . .
>
> But since he's begun, it is a good thing for him to continue these visits round the Académie. *He is certain*, I told him, *not to be elected*, but he will gain thirty occasions for very curious observations about these pensioners of literature.[6]

Baudelaire was moved and delighted by Vigny's sympathy. There was a generation between them, but they were both patrician, pessimistic, stoic, both in need of religious belief, both devoted to their art. In this anglophile to whom he could talk of his translations, this aristocrat who understood the dandy as hero, this poet who saw the emptiness and the grandeur of modern life, Baudelaire seems to have found a fellow spirit. Baudelaire, who often had a public and a private opinion: who could, in honesty, both condemn and praise, had only praise for Alfred de Vigny. After this first meeting, he sent him copies of his books and brochures. 'Monsieur, thank you again', he wrote, 'for the charming way in which you received me. However great the idea that I had formed of you, I had not expected it.'[7]

Some time after 16 December, Baudelaire paid the statutory visit to Alphonse de Lamartine. There was an impassable literary divide between the Romantic poet, now in his seventies, and the author of *Les Fleurs du mal*. No doubt Lamartine received Baudelaire as the son of Mme Aupick; it was he who, long ago, in his days as a statesman, had appointed Aupick Minister to Constantinople. He now told Baudelaire that he was too young to expose himself to an affront, and he tried to dissuade him from standing for election. When he learned that Baudelaire was already officially listed, Lamartine advised him to pursue his candidature to the end, since the harm had already been done.[8]

Baudelaire was ruffled by Lamartine; but he was enraged by the reception which he was given by Abel Villemain, 'a fool, a vulgar fellow, a pompous monkey',[9] and the permanent secretary of the Académie-Française. Lemercier de Neuville reported the beginning of their conversation.

'You are standing for the Académie, monsieur,' said Villemain. 'Well, how many votes have you got?'

'The permanent secretary knows as well as I do that the rules forbid the Academicians to promise their votes,' answered Baudelaire. 'And so I shan't have any votes until the day when, doubtless, nobody will vote for me.'

'I've never been original, myself,' said M. Villemain.

'Monsieur, how do you know?' asked Baudelaire, mildly.[10]

On about 20 December, Baudelaire told Arsène Houssaye: 'The rumour has got back to me that, since my candidature was an *outrage* to the Académie, several of these gentlemen have decided that they would not be at home to me. But that's too fantastic to be possible.'[11] It was not too fantastic. Baudelaire thought that Mérimée avoided receiving him because he had an imperialist candidate in view.[12] Mérimée had no candidate at the time.[13]

In the meanwhile, Baudelaire continued to solicit votes. On 23 December, he wrote despairingly to the poet Victor de Laprade, in

Lyons. He listed his qualifications, including 'my deplorable *Fleurs du mal*.'[14] He declared himself grossly insulted by Villemain. 'Forgive me, Monsieur,' he ended, 'for writing to you at such length, but I am relieving myself with someone whom I do not know, and in whom I divine a certain sympathy, for the fatigue which my first visits have caused me . . . I beg you to accept this letter as the equivalent of an official visit.'[15] The 'virtuous and pedantic Laprade', as Baudelaire had once called him,[16] was exasperated by such flippancy.[17] In *Le Siècle*, Edmond Texier, the journalist, declared that Baudelaire's election would shatter the windows of the palais Mazarin into a thousand pieces.[18]

90

In mid December, it appears, Mme Aupick had paid a visit to Paris. It was the first that she had made since her husband's death; it must have been brief, for she did not see her son. Whatever the purpose of her journey, the excitement of Paris had left her weary of her solitude, and understandably bored with provincial life.

Poor dear mother, so abandoned [this from Baudelaire on Christmas Day]! Your last letter distressed me very much . . . What! This miserable little visit to Paris had such an effect on you that now you are bored – you who were never bored! I was most surprised by your letter . . .

If you ask me how I can have the cruelty to leave you for so long without news and without consolation, I who am everything to you and have no way to thank you and entertain you except by talking to you about myself [*sic*], I shall answer first that I have been ill several times, and then (and this is the main and deplorable reason) that, when I have the misfortune to neglect a duty, this duty is more difficult to fulfil next day, that it then becomes more difficult, from day to day, until finally it seems to me something impossible to perform. This is due to the state of anguish and nervous terror in which I constantly live, and my observation applies to all possible duties, even to the very sweet and natural one of writing to my mother. I never get out of situations except by an explosion; but what I suffer in living, you see, is indescribable! Finally, in November, two catastrophes befell me one after the other. And now, as if I didn't have enough accumulated difficulties, I have just added a new one, that of my candidature. Oh, if I'd known! What torture! What exhaustion! You couldn't imagine how many vexations, how many letters, how many applications this curious fantasy demands. I have only seen a few Academicians; my nerves are already shattered. Yet there is something fortunate in this tiring episode, and that is that I'm interested in it. Now, one can't live without a mania, a *fad*. And I still see suicide before me as the unique and above all the easiest solution to all the horrible complications that I have been condemned to endure for so many years . . .

I am saying things pell-mell; I have so many things to say. Believe me if you will; I swear to you that if I have committed this rash act [of standing for the Académie], it is above all because of you. The only thing which interests me personally is the pitiful emoluments attached to the office, and I don't even know the exact figure. Because you can well imagine that I do not, in my conscience, feel the need for the approval *of all those old fools*. (I am using the term which even some Academicians use to describe the others.) But I said to myself that you attached immense importance to public honours, and that if, *by miracle*, that's the word, I should succeed, it would give you immense delight. It is true that I also said to myself: if by some extraordinary chance I were to succeed, my mother might perhaps understand at last that I cannot remain in a situation which dishonours me. Perhaps, then, we might discover a solution . . . That accursed *conseil judiciaire* has always made me timid and clumsy. It seems to me that I am bearing some shameful stigma on my body, and that everyone can see it. Judge what I have endured for seventeen years . . .

I shall write to you again to tell you about the phases in my ridiculous attempt (the *Académie* again) . . . Vigny, whom I had never met, was wonderful . . . As for me, I am too unfortunate to move in the direction of kindness, and, if I live, I think that I shall end by writing some atrocious book which will make them drive me out of this vile country . . .[1]

As Camille Mauclair was to write, Baudelaire 'flogged himself into making his existence something exceptional, monstrous, solemnly complicated.'[2]

He had not only his needless Academic concerns, but his unremitting financial anxieties. *La Revue fantaisiste* had ceased publication, so had *La Revue européenne*, and two sources of income were now denied him.

I am *without a paper*, threatened by *an enormous crisis* on New Year's Day [Baudelaire continued to his mother], obliged to live, and overwhelmed by exhaustion as a result of what I call *my rash act*, that is to say my accursed candidature, not to mention the exhaustion caused by a woman who is still unwell, who must be supported and consoled, and to whom I could not easily give money except by not living in Paris any more. However, *I have sworn* to endeavour not to fall into one of those horrible depressions which you have so often seen me in, and to try to face all these things at once. But I don't know how.[3]

One means of salvation was to earn some money; and that day, Christmas Day, Baudelaire also addressed himself to Arsène Houssaye, the editor of *La Presse* and of *L'Artiste*. Houssaye had already written some prose poems, and an entertaining *Histoire du quarante et unième fauteuil de l'Académie française* (the number of Academicians is limited to forty). Baudelaire asked him to mention his Academic candidature in *La Presse* and in *L'Artiste*. He also sent him a prose poem, announced that he was writing a number of others, and that he intended to dedicate them to him.[4]

91

On 1 January 1862, the *Revue anecdotique* announced that 'the somewhat Dominican profile of M. Baudelaire continues to shake all the chairs at the Académie [*sic*].'[1] On 5 January, in *Le Boulevard*, Charles Bataille, a Bohemian writer ten years younger than Baudelaire, recognised his gifts, but declared that he was too young for election.[2] Baudelaire's Academic ambition continued to occupy the Press. On 19 January, in *Diogène*, Jules Claretie predicted that Baudelaire would not be elected to the Académie, though he now inspired a literary school.[3]

Next day, Sainte-Beuve entertained the readers of *Le Constitutionnel* with *Des prochaines élections à l'Académie*. The article appeared almost exactly eighteen years after Sainte-Beuve himself had been received among the Forty. It was an open letter to his colleagues, a waspish and absolute dismissal of Baudelaire as a candidate.

> People wondered [wrote Sainte-Beuve] if, by standing, Baudelaire wanted to play a trick on the Académie... More than one member of the Académie had to be taught how to spell M. Baudelaire's name, because he was completely unaware of his existence. It is not as easy as one would think to prove to Academicians who are politicians and statesmen that there are some poems in *Les Fleurs du mal* which are truly remarkable for their inspiration and their art; to explain to them that, among the author's little prose poems, *Le Vieux Saltimbanque* and *Les Veuves* are jewels, and that in short M. Baudelaire has found the means of building himself, at the end of a peninsula which is said to be uninhabitable, and beyond the bounds of known romanticism, a bizarre kiosk, very ornate, very over-done, but elegant and mysterious: a kiosk in which one grows drunk on abominable drugs in cups of exquisite porcelain. This singular kiosk, made of marquetry, of a deliberate and composite originality, which, for some time, has drawn people's eyes to the furthermost extremity of the romantic Kamschatka: this is what I call *the Baudelaire folly*. The author is content to have done something impossible, in a place where no one thought that anyone could go. Does this mean, now, when everything has been explained

to rather astonished colleagues, that all these curiosities, these relishes and refinements seem to them to be titles to the Académie, and has the actual author been able to persuade himself that this is so? What is certain, is that M. Baudelaire gains from being seen, and that where one would expect to see the entry of a strange, eccentric man, one finds oneself in the presence of a candidate who is polite, respectful, exemplary: a nice young man who is eloquent in speech and absolutely classic in his manners.[4]

It was a devious, malicious commentary by the paramount critic of the day in a paper which the Establishment would be sure to read. It was an unforgivable way for *l'oncle Beuve* to behave to his admirer; and Sainte-Beuve did not regret his duplicity: indeed, he reprinted the article in his *Nouveaux lundis* in 1863.

This gratuitous public malice would have been reason enough for Baudelaire to have ended the relationship. Sainte-Beuve had failed to review the *Histoires extraordinaires*, he had refused all public praise of *Les Fleurs du mal*, all public comment on *Les Paradis artificiels*. He had not only refrained from giving Baudelaire acclaim; he had now indulged in open condemnation. His behaviour suggested an uncommon meanness of character. It showed the critic's love of power, the feline games in which he delighted, and, above all, it showed his jealousy. Baudelaire was seventeen years younger than himself. As Vandérem was to observe:

> Once and for all he had determined his position with his 'young friend'. Account closed, credit stopped. He would never speak of Baudelaire again . . .
> As long as Baudelaire remains obscure, he omits him or diminishes him, and he fails to appreciate his worth. As soon as the glory of his 'young friend' dawns, he is silent, for fear of helping him.
> With Baudelaire, he begins with incompetence and he ends with envy.[5]

Two phrases in his *Portraits littéraires* seem to confirm that Vandérem was right. Sainte-Beuve declared that, 'the disciple was the prey and the leprosy of the great man.' He added that, 'in poetry and art, one is excused from liking ones heirs presumptive.'[6]

Sainte-Beuve's behaviour was contemptible. Baudelaire's behaviour was extraordinary. He was grateful for the alms of such publicity. 'Yet another favour that I owe you! When will this end? – and how can I thank you?'[7] He was not only grateful for Sainte-Beuve's 'encouragement', he still asked him for advice on his candidature. He still considered him his presiding spirit.

> Promise me, I beg you [he continued], to find a few moments to answer what follows . . .

I think it is politically wise to opt for Lacordaire's chair. In this case, there will not be any men of letters. This was originally my plan, and, if I haven't followed it, it was *so as not to disobey you*, and so as not to seem too eccentric. If you think my idea is good, I shall write a letter to M. Villemain before Wednesday, in which I shall briefly say that it seems to me that a candidate's choice should not simply be determined by the wish to succeed, but should also be a sympathetic tribute to the memory of a dead man. Indeed, Lacordaire is a *romantic* priest, and I love him. Perhaps I shall slip the word *Romanticism* into the letter . . .

Despite my tonsure and my white hair, I want to talk to you like a small boy. My mother, who is very bored, constantly asks me for *something new*. I have sent her your article. I know what maternal pleasure she will get from it. Thank you for me and for her.[8]

Mme Aupick, too, was sure of Sainte-Beuve's benevolence. 'I was so happy and so proud about that praise,' she wrote to him, years later, 'especially since it came from you, Monsieur! How is it that I did not thank you then? I want to repair this omission now, and to send you all the affection and gratitude which my heart has given to those who have appreciated and who love my son.'[9]

In the meanwhile, *l'oncle Beuve* answered Baudelaire:

My dear child,

I am delighted by your thanks. Indeed, I was a little anxious, I must admit, because, if you titillate, you are never sure not to scratch too much. I don't advise you to set out this *Lacordaire antithesis* in a letter. I think it would be better to leave things as they are, without writing any more. But this deliberate choice of Lacordaire, the *Romantic-Catholic*, would appear excessive and shocking, which you wouldn't wish, with your discretion as a candidate.[10]

The Académie-Française was only one of Baudelaire's preoccupations. In the first weeks of 1862 he was far from well. To Sainte-Beuve he spoke of 'an old wound' – a euphemism for syphilis.[11] There was now a sign of much more serious illness. Pichois suggests that laudanum and alcohol, and the effects of venereal disease, predisposed him to cerebral attacks.[12] On 23 January, in his *Journaux intimes*, Baudelaire confided:

Morally and physically, I have always had the sense of the abyss, not only the abyss of sleep, but the abyss of action, of the dream, of memory, desire, regret, remorse, beauty, number, etc.

I have cultivated my hysteria with pleasure and with terror. Now I am perpetually dizzy, and today, 23 January 1862, I have been given a singular warning, I have felt *the wind of the wing of imbecility pass over me.*[13]

For the rest of his life he was to live with the fear of insanity; and, from that moment, his health deteriorated.

On 24 January, the day after his singular warning, he turned to Flaubert for help in the Academic election. 'I'm told that you are a close friend of [Jules] Sandeau's . . . I should be immensely obliged if you would write and tell him what you think of me.'[4] Flaubert wrote at once to Sandeau – an Academician who was most renowned as the collaborator of more famous authors, George Sand and Émile Augier.[15] 'I have a great respect for M. Baudelaire,' answered Sandeau, 'and for his gifts; I consider him a poet and a true gentleman. It would not displease me to give him a sign of appreciation; I should also like to do something which would give you pleasure.'[16] Finally Baudelaire saw Sandeau:

> My dear friend [this to Flaubert],
> M. Sandeau was charming, his wife was charming, and I really think that I was as charming as they were, since we all performed a concert of praise in your honour . . .
> As for my affair, Sandeau reproached me for taking him unawares. However, he will speak on my behalf to some of his friends at the Académie . . .[17]

The one undoubted benefit of Baudelaire's decision to stand for the Académie-Française had been his encounter with Vigny. On 26 January, he wrote to him again, in a tone of grateful affection; he asked him whether he should stand for the chair of Père Lacordaire. 'I shall', he wrote, 'take no decision before I have had your advice.'[18] Vigny answered next day:

> Since 30 December, Monsieur, I have been very ill again, and almost always in bed. There I have read and re-read you, and I must tell you how many of these *fleurs du mal* are, for me, *fleurs du bien*, and delight me . . .
> If your health permits you to come and see how I set about concealing my own wounds, come on Wednesday (29th), at 4 o'clock in the afternoon. You will know, and read, and sense, how much I've read you, but you won't know with what pleasure I read to others, to Poets, the real beauties of your poems, which are still too little appreciated, and too lightly judged.
> You had told me that your official Academic letter had been sent. In my eyes, that was a mistake and I told you so, but it was irreparable, and I resigned myself to seeing you go astray in the Labyrinth. But now you tell me that it was only a plan [*sic*], I advise you frankly not to take another step in these circuitous ways which are familiar to me, and not to write a word which is intended to get you listed as a candidate for any of the vacant chairs . . .[19]

Vigny had misunderstood Baudelaire's decision to stand. Baudelaire had only asked him – as he had asked Sainte-Beuve – whether he should apply for the vacant chair of Lacordaire. It was an extraordinary question from a poet who had nearly been condemned for offences against religious morality. On 3 February, Baudelaire announced to Sainte-Beuve: 'I haven't written a word, as you advised; but I am patiently continuing my visits, to make it well understood that, as regards the election to replace le père Lacordaire, I want to pick up a few votes from _Men of Letters_.'[20]

On 9 February, Sainte-Beuve replied. He warned Baudelaire to make no further visits. He advised him, brusquely, to withdraw from the election.[21] It was, it seems, this uncompromising letter which led Baudelaire to withdraw his candidature.[22]

It was to be his only attempt to become an Academician. He had stood for election partly in a spirit of bravado, knowing that his court case and his legend were against him, knowing that his reckless honesty, his bitterness and mockery, his constant debts and poverty would not help his case. It is virtually certain that he would not have been elected to the chair of Eugène Scribe. He had invited instant rejection when he had chosen to stand for the chair of Père Lacordaire. Posterity cannot doubt that he was a profoundly Catholic poet; but it would have been as difficult for the Académie to elect him as it would have been, in later years, for them to elect his disciple, Verlaine.

Yet Baudelaire had also stood because he recognised his worth. He had once aspired (perhaps he still aspired) to the Légion-d'honneur. He had considered the Académie-Française as the only insitution whose benediction was worth possessing, whose ultimate approval was worth soliciting. Like Gautier, to whom he had dedicated _Les Fleurs du mal_, like Verlaine and Rimbaud, like Flaubert, Maupassant and Proust, he was not to sit among the Forty. His failure to be elected was the failure of the Académie itself.

On 20 February, Albert, Prince de Broglie, grandson of Mme de Staël and son of the Academician, Victor, Duc de Broglie, was elected to the chair of Père Lacordaire. On 3 April, Octave Feuillet, novelist and dramatist, and contemporary of Baudelaire at Louis-le-Grand, was elected to the chair of Scribe. Between these two elections, on 1 March, _L'Artiste_ published 'Le Gouffre'. Baudelaire had already earned the suffrage of posterity.

> Pascal avait son gouffre, avec lui se mouvant.
> – Hélas! tout est abîme, – action, désir, rêve,
> Parole! et sur mon poil qui tout droit se relève
> Mainte fois de la Peur je sens passer le vent.

En haut, en bas, partout, la profondeur, la grève,
Le silence, l'espace affreux et captivant . . .
Sur le fond de mes nuits Dieu de son doigt savant
Dessine un cauchemar multiforme et sans trêve.

J'ai peur du sommeil comme on a peur d'un grand trou,
Tout plein de vague horreur, menant on ne sait où;
Je ne vois qu'infini par toutes les fenêtres,

Et mon esprit, toujours du vertige hanté,
Jalouse du néant de l'insensibilité.
– Ah! ne jamais sortir des Nombres et des Êtres![23]

92

In March 1862, however, Baudelaire had a more demanding personal problem than that of his Academic ambition. It was the continuing problem of Jeanne. There is a gap of five weeks in his letters to his mother, and none of her letters seems to have survived; but it is clear that they had quarrelled over Jeanne and her demands for money. On 17 March Baudelaire asked bitterly: 'What have I done, for seventeen years, if not forgive? (I admit that, since the woman was beautiful, people may suspect that my indulgence was very interested.) But when she was struck by illness and [premature] old age, what did I do for three years? I did what the egoism of men does not generally do. I even brought to charity the enthusiasm of pride.'[1] Now he learned that Jeanne had approached Malassis, and had also demanded money from Mme Aupick.

> The beginning of your letter [Baudelaire continued] leads me to believe that you were almost deceived, you claim to be more generous than I am. At the moment when I signified to Jeanne that she must count on anyone but me, I had just given her all that I possessed, trusting in my genius and in my star to get what I needed . . .
> You can see quite well that I am not a wild animal.[2]

He was, however, savage in his letters to his mother; he could still not forgive her for the past. All his adult life he had used her shamefully. He was – perhaps unconsciously – taking his revenge.

> Your candour [so he told her], your aptitude for being deceived, your innocence, your sensibility make me laugh. Do you really believe that, if

I wanted, I couldn't ruin you and throw you into poverty in your old age? Don't you know that I am cunning and eloquent enough to do it? But I restrain myself, and, at every new crisis. I say to myself: 'No. My mother is old and poor, I must leave her in peace. I must work hard enough to manage to get through it.' . . .

Forgive me for playing the pedant and the misanthropist with you. I am sure of everything that I affirm. I had a terrible education, and it is perhaps *too late* for me to be able to save myself.[3]

His moods changed constantly; but, threatening or sad, he never ceased to make demands of his mother. On 29 March, once again, he asked her, urgently, for money. 'I have promised my landlord 300 francs for the day after tomorrow (*above all, I must have peace here*). I intended to give him 375 francs which I am due to receive from *La Presse*. (*L'Esprit de M. Villemain*, three articles commissioned, finished and delivered.)'[4] The articles were not in fact finished or delivered. The satirical study only exists in the form of notes. It is also quite possible that *La Presse* had not commissioned it from Baudelaire, in spite of his good relations with the editor, Arsène Houssaye.

I assure you [so he told his mother] that there is no disorder in my life [*sic*]. It becomes more orderly with every day. I am sad, resigned to everything, even to suffering to the end of my life, resigned to the *conseil judiciaire*, and determined simply to do all I can to have it destroyed. I am going to have four volumes to publish this year. I should wager that these four volumes will pass *unnoticed*. People don't do me justice. As soon as I have agreed to contracts for these volumes [one was already sold to Malassis], and as soon as I've placed the articles – some finished, some not yet finished – which complete them, I shall come back to you . . .

And so I shall come back soon, not to save money (as you brutally insinuate), but *for the pleasure of being with you* and of living in *good society*. I must tell you that, the longer I live, the more all society and all conversation grow tiring and importunate to me.[5]

Mme Aupick's answer does not survive; but next day she sent her son the money which he had demanded. She refused Chateaubriand's *Mémoires d'outre-tombe* and the Chinese blinds which he had offered her; no doubt she was afraid that she would have to pay for them. She reproached Baudelaire for his improvidence. On 31 March he told her, brutally: 'Your letter is very confused, my dear mother. I understand that you don't want blinds because you're afraid of being obliged to pay for them . . . I was thinking of the Mirador. But why refuse the Chateaubriand, which you had wanted? . . . And what do you mean by: "Il *me* faut *me* prendre si à court"?'[6] Baudelaire was playing the aggressive pedant. He knew exactly what his mother meant.

Years later, in conversation with Edmond de Goncourt, Mme Sichel, the antique-dealer's wife, recalled Mme Aupick at Honfleur:

... small, delicate, slightly hunchbacked, with big, gnarled hands which could hold six dominoes, and so blind, moreover, that she had to hold her sewing up to her nose.

Then [continued Goncourt] she described her house to me: her house at the top of the cliff, at the end of the Côte de Grâce, chosen by the General ... in a place which reminded him of the entrance to the Golden Horn ... The stables contained two imposing carriages, whose owner had been obliged to sell her horses, when she had been reduced to living on her widow's pension. The maids used to bring out these carriages and give them an airing for an hour, every Saturday, in the paved courtyard.

It seemed to the young girl which Mme Sichel was at the time that the old lady had a high opinion of her son's intelligence, but that she did not dare to show it, because of the authority which was exercised over her by a M. Hémon [*sic*]. He considered her son a scoundrel, who always talked about coming to see his mother, never came, and only wrote to her to ask for money ...

Several times, in her romantic way, the old lady said to Mme Sichel, whose name is Laura: 'I'm sorry my son doesn't want to get married. I should be so delighted if he were your Petrarch.'[7]

Mme Aupick still contrived to live in a romantic world. She needed some escape from reality. She was agitated by her son's incessant demands for money. She found it hard to refuse him; she feared, now, for her own security. Her inheritance and her pension could ensure her a comfortable future. Baudelaire's demands could destroy it. Émon's contempt for Baudelaire was largely justified.

93

In the last twenty-one years, Baudelaire had chosen to forget his elder brother. He had once cherished and respected him, sought his advice. All fraternal affection, all trust and all respect had long since gone. In 1841 Alphonse had sent him 'a harsh and humiliating letter' about his debts;[1] he had perhaps reported them to Aupick. He had supported Aupick in arranging the Indian voyage; he had supported the establishment of the *conseil judiciaire*. To Baudelaire this had been betrayal. He had come to detest him. In 1846, with a certain flippancy, and perhaps with the hope of making mischief, he had paid verbal court to his brother's wife. No doubt Alphonse had reacted angrily, and no doubt Baudelaire had chosen to feel contempt.

> My brother deeply wounded me on two occasions [he had explained to his mother in 1856] ... My brother's crime is called stupidity, that's all – but it is a lot ... I prefer *wicked* people, who know what they're doing, to *good stupid people*. My repulsion where my brother is concerned is so acute that I don't like people asking me if I have a brother. There is nothing more precious in the world than the *poetic spirit*, and *a sense of chivalry*. His political and intellectual nullity, his cynical opinions about women, to whom one must at least show gallantry, if not passion: everything, absolutely everything makes him alien to me.[2]

As Pichois observed in his essay *Alphonse Baudelaire, ou le magistrat imprudent*, Alphonse – like his brother – had had certain flaws in his character which had made him a failure in life;[3] but, while Baudelaire earned immortality, the failure of Alphonse had been complete. If it owed much to nature, it also owed much to injustice and to misfortune. In 1846 he had become an examining magistrate at Fontainebleau; but, five years later, he had aroused some criticism. There were observations about his professional inadequacy, and about his personal weaknesses. There were irrelevant comments on his financial problems, and insinuations about his political sympathies. On 15 October 1851, a report had been sent to the Garde des Sceaux, who was responsible for the judiciary.

> M. Baudelaire, now aged 47, has spent his whole career as a magistrate at Fontainebleau ... He is a good man; he is a strictly correct and diligent magistrate, but he has no order or method, and he lacks judgment and firmness of character. His examinations bear the mark of this lack of sense and judgment, and some people have seen in them – wrongly, I believe – an indication of bad political opinions. He is, besides, too often led to show excessive and inappropriate leniency to some of the accused ...
>
> As a member of the Conseil municipal, M. Baudelaire exaggerates his role and his importance, and again, in this kind of work, he displays a zeal which is ardent rather than practical.
>
> Finally, M. Baudelaire's financial situation is bad ... The cause of this hardship seems to be related to some sacrifices which M. Baudelaire imposed upon himself in 1848, to support one of his brothers-in-law; but, however honourable the reason may be, this situation is nonetheless regrettable, and, up to a certain point, it is harmful to the magistrate's authority. 'What does most harm to M. Baudelaire,' said one of the magistrates whom I consulted, 'is his character. No one takes him seriously, and people ask how functions as serious and important as those of an examining magistrate can be entrusted to a man who is undoubtedly honest, but a man who has the enormous defect of lacking good sense, as well as judgment and a knowledge of how to behave.'

I could therefore have no hesitation, Monsieur le Garde des Sceaux, in suggesting to you today that M. Baudelaire should resume the functions of an ordinary magistrate.[4]

On 11 November 1851, Alphonse Baudelaire was dispossessed of his functions as examining magistrate, and once again became an ordinary magistrate. It is difficult not to see him as the victim of intrigue.

His fortune had been sacrificed, his career compromised, but a final ordeal still awaited him. On 26 December 1854, his surviving son, Edmond, died of typhoid fever at the age of twenty-one. Baudelaire had received the *faire-part* too late to attend his nephew's funeral; but he had promised to visit his brother soon. At the moment, he explained, he was 'overwhelmed with business'. He added: 'It is many years now since we have seen each other.'[5] There is no record that he went to Fontainebleau.

Aupick, then an ailing elderly Senator, had sent an instant letter of condolence.[6] It was not the only sign of sympathy which he was to show to the magistrate at Fontainebleau. Six months after Aupick died, his colleague at the Senate, General Husson, asked the Minister of Justice to restore Alphonse to his former dignity. This had, he said, been Aupick's wish a few days before his death. The Minister was silent. On 28 February 1859, Husson made a further attempt to have Alphonse reinstated: 'My friend, M. Baudelaire, fulfilled the functions of an examining magistrate at Fontainebleau for some years; but he was the victim of an intrigue which deprived him of them. He ... is very eager to resume them.' Again the Minister turned a deaf ear.[7]

Alphonse was not only unfortunate in his profession and in his private life. He also seems to have suffered from ill-health. Georges de Nouvion says that he was diabetic.[8] Trial maintains that he had nervous problems.[9] Ernest Prarond was, by chance, a witness of his neurotic behaviour.

On 12 January 1856, a circumstance enables me to fix the date exactly, I was leaving the hôtel de l'Aigle Noir at Fontainebleau ... I heard someone shout to the driver of the horse-omnibus: 'To M. Baudelaire's!' The coach stopped outside a handsome house. A man burst into the coach like a hurricane. It was M. Baudelaire, a larger edition of our Baudelaire, taller, more robust, with violent gestures, in fits and starts, a Baudelaire with galvanic gesticulations ... There was, however, a strong likeness between this intemperate Baudelaire and the sober Baudelaire.[10]

Early in 1860 this 'intemperate Baudelaire' had had a stroke. Baudelaire himself appears to have been unmoved. Within the next few weeks, Alphonse had recovered enough to resume his official functions, but he was no longer able to do consistent work, and in 1862 he asked to retire from the Bench. On 25 January, Gerbé de Thoré, the imperial prosecutor at Fontainebleau, reported on his request. He drew a picture of a pathetic man, whose loyalty and uncomplaining work had been ill rewarded.

> Monsieur Baudelaire [he wrote] has always fulfilled his functions with zeal, and indeed with uncommon ardour. His chief concern was to do his duty. Not content to do the work which was regularly delegated to him, he always put his time and labour at the service of those colleagues who were kept from the tribunal by absence or illness.
>
> During the ten years he spent as examining magistrate, he was constantly working in his office.
>
> When he became an ordinary magistrate again, it was he who was always entrusted with taxes and inquests, since the examining magistrate was too busy to keep even a part of this service.
>
> Finally, it was he alone who, almost always, remained at his post during the holidays, fulfilling all the demands of the service.
>
> M. Baudelaire is married. He had a handsome fortune (about 300,000 francs) before 1848. At the time of the revolution, a brother of his wife's, an unfortunate manufacturer, suffered as a result of the general recession. Without hesitation, M. Baudelaire came to his aid, hoping to save everything. The honour of his brother-in-law was saved; but M. Baudelaire saw his 300,000 francs disappear. All that remains to him now as a personal fortune is an income of about 800 francs a year.
>
> Moreover, seven years ago, he lost an only son, who was twenty years old [*sic*].
>
> Loved and esteemed by everyone, M. Baudelaire has a conciliating spirit, indeed he is popular in Fontainebleau. At the time of the municipal elections, he never asks for anything, but he is always appointed a member of the council by a large majority.[11]

He had in fact first been elected on 28 May 1840, and he remained a councillor until his death.[12]

On 18 March 1862, he retired from the Bench. His retirement was to be brief. On 14 April he died at his house, 25, rue des Petits-Champs, at the early age of fifty-one. He had suffered a cerebral haemorrhage, and his left side was paralysed.[13] It was a curious presage of Baudelaire's own fate.

Baudelaire did not attend his brother's funeral. Not until 11 May did he send a letter of condolence to his widow.[14] It was a strangely self-absorbed letter. It was an unconvincing display of family affection. He could have written at any time in the previous four weeks; he could himself have gone to Fontainebleau. As it was, his conduct had been uncaring, even hostile. It was, apparently, next day, 12 May, that he finally arrived in Fontainebleau with his *conseil judiciaire*. Financial affairs could wait no longer.

Despite my sister-in-law's kind reception, my visit was very painful for me [so he complained to his mother]. A whole day with Ancelle! Can you imagine what that's like? A man who is not only stupid but mad!

And then the phantom of the *conseil judiciaire* appeared three times during the day, in the presence of a registrar, a notary, an advocate, and goodness knows who else. Ancelle no doubt rejoiced in the humiliation; he had dragged me down there without warning. I have never been malicious, but I think I am allowed to become so.[15]

His own behaviour had been unforgivable, but one can understand his bitterness; at the age of forty-one, he was still treated as a minor. The settlement of his brother's affairs had emphasised, in public, that Baudelaire could not sign legal documents except in the presence of his *conseil judiciaire*. As for his relationship with Félicité Baudelaire, it had been doomed for years, ever since he had pretended to be enamoured of her. She had not understood his badinage, or his irony. She was embarrassed, petty and pretentious. She vexed him, and she roused his contempt. No doubt she made him feel guilty about his neglect. In August he was obliged to spend a day with her again. It was, he told his mother, 'a dreadful bore'.[16]

The news of his brother's death had reached Baudelaire as he was correcting the proofs of an article. Hugo's latest novel, *Les Misérables*, was to appear in five parts, of two volumes each, the last of them on 5 July. On 20 April, *Le Boulevard* had published Baudelaire's review of the first part of the massive work. It was an apparently generous tribute to the book and to its author. *Les Misérables*, Baudelaire concluded, was 'a book of charity, a deafening call to order to a society which is too enamoured of itself, and too indifferent to the immortal law of fraternity.'[17]

Whatever his published comments on *Les Misérables*, Baudelaire remained cynical. A few months later, he told his mother: 'The book is ignoble and inept. I showed, on this occasion, that I possessed the art of lying. He [Hugo] thanked me in an absolutely ridiculous letter. That proves that a great man can be a fool.'[18] His feelings for Hugo remained ambivalent. 'Certainly, he admired Victor Hugo,' wrote Asselineau, in his unpublished notes on Baudelaire. 'He bore witness to this, publicly, in many articles, especially in the notice for M. Crépet's French poets. He even insisted . . . on reviewing *Les Misérables* itself, and in this he showed all his dexterity, because, at heart, the book, with its moral enormities, its deplorable paradoxes, shocked him deeply. He had a horror of false sensibility, of virtuous criminals and angelic prostitutes.'[19] When the second and third parts of the book were published, in May, Baudelaire confessed: 'I am much afraid that

I shan't have the courage to ask for them. The Hugo family and the disciples make me shudder.'[20]

On 15 May, he was due to find 600 francs for Malassis. That morning, he called on Arsène Houssaye, the editor-in-chief of *La Presse* and an editor of *L'Artiste*, and asked him for some money in the form of accommodation bills. Houssaye lost his temper, and they had a violent argument. Later that day, Baudelaire explained: 'I did not come to ask you for money this morning . . . I came to say to you, do all you can to fill *L'Artiste* and *La Presse* with me for a while. *Guys, Villemain, Mercier, Dandysme littéraire, Peinture didactique*, will be excellent pieces.'[21]

Of all these projects, only one, the essay on Guys, was to be realised.

At the end of May, 1862, Baudelaire gave notice to his hotel. He was paying cash, from day to day. His mother suggested that she should send him 500 francs so that he could buy himself some clothes. She thought that he should buy them ready made; she would ask Ancelle to send the money to him.

> Let me tell you [answered Baudelaire, on 31 May], that not only do I accept, but that I should like a further 100 francs . . .
>   I am having five very busy days, I'm leaving on the 6th, I'm at Le Havre on the 7th, I shall be with you on the 8th, Pentecost.[22]

Mme Aupick sent him the authorization to receive 500 francs from Ancelle; but the prospect of Honfleur receded. Once again, she waited for his visit in vain.

He remained in Paris, where, on 1 July, he signed a new contract with Malassis. He gave him 'the exclusive right, henceforward, to publish his literary works, published and unpublished, in any form.'[23] The contract embraced *Les Fleurs du mal*, *Les Paradis artificiels*, and the translations of Poe; it included all his future books and articles, 'criticism, novels, short stories, history, philosophy, etc'. This assignment was made in consideration of an advance of 5,000 francs, which had already been paid to him; it had been agreed on 24 May 1861, and was simply renewed now that Malassis' partnership with De Broise had ended. However, if Malassis recovered his advance in the next four years, Baudelaire was to resume the rights to his work, and the present sale was to be considered a sale with faculty of redemption. This contract assured Baudelaire the most sympathetic of publishers; it assured Malassis of a chance to recover his money.

On 12 July, *Le Monde illustré* published the first instalment of *Le Joueur d'échecs de Maelzel*, Baudelaire's translation of Poe's story. On 2 August, when the fourth and last instalment appeared, the *Bibliographie de la France* announced that Hachette had just published the fourth volume of *Des Poètes français*. This volume, the only one in the series to enjoy a success, included seven studies by Baudelaire, one of them his study of Gautier. It also included seven of Baudelaire's poems, preceded by a study of him by Gautier himself. 'My dear Théophile,' Baudelaire assured him on 4 August, '. . . it is the first time in my life that I have been praised as I should like to be.'[24]

He was, it seems, working hard this summer. In a letter apparently addressed to Édouard Houssaye, he refused an invitation 'because I have tremendous things to finish while your brother is away, and they must be ready on his return.'[25] They were, presumably, some of his *Petits Poèmes en prose*, and some of the articles which he had mentioned to Arsène.

Late in August, and late in September, a score of his poems were to appear in *La Presse*. However, nearly all the articles were to remain unwritten. The plan to go to Honfleur still remained unfulfilled; Mme Aupick saw her hopes constantly deferred, and Baudelaire grew more frustrated and more bitter than ever.

I expect you're bored, aren't you [he asked his mother on 10 August]? Very bored? I'm going to come. I have already taken my precautions, that is to say that I have made it impossible for myself not to leave at the end of the month . . .

So I shall come, to *our* home, on the 31st, the 1st, 2nd or 3rd. Since you love me so much, and you want to try to be interested in the only things that amuse me, I shall be able to recompense you and prove to you that I know you, that I love you, that I can value and appreciate a maternal heart.

At last, at last! I think that at the end of the month I shall be able to escape the horror of the human face. You wouldn't believe how far the Parisian race is degraded. It is no longer that delightful and agreeable world that I once knew; the artists know nothing, the men of letters know nothing, not even how to spell. All these people have become abject, inferior perhaps to society people. *I am an old man*, a mummy, and they bear me a grudge because I am less ignorant than the rest of men. What decadence! Except for D'Aurevilly, Flaubert, Sainte-Beuve, no one can understand me. Only Th. Gautier can understand me when I talk painting. *I have a horror of life.* I repeat: I am going to escape the human face, but especially the French face . . .

I love you and embrace you. Tell me that you are well (if it's true), and that you will live for a long while yet, for me and just for me. You see that I have the ferocity and the egotism of love.[26]

None of his letters to La Présidente, nor his surviving letters to Marie Daubrun and to Jeanne Duval, was written with the same urgency. Only to his mother did Baudelaire express such ferocity and egotism.

He was forty-one, yet he wrote to her with the fervour of a youth of twenty, with the exclusive need of a child.

He had told her that, within the next three weeks, he would have to make arrangements with various papers, so that some of his debts could be paid in his absence. Two of the papers he mentioned were not, in fact, to publish his work. The third periodical, *Le Monde illustré*, was not to publish any more of his translations until 1863. There remained *La Presse*. On 18 August, he set aside their violent argument, and wrote to its editor-in-chief:

> My dear Houssaye,
>   If you don't come to my assistance today, *I shall this very day find myself without a lodging*, and in such a situation that I shan't have the peace I need to do a little work . . .
>   The sum I need is too substantial for me to be in any way entitled to ask you for it; but 250 francs, which no doubt represent two big *Variétés* articles, which you have, would perhaps allow me to make my man be patient for a few days . . .
>   I shall come and see you today.[27]

Baudelaire referred to the *Petits Poèmes en prose*. It was that day that Hetzel – who later bought the rights to them – assured Houssaye: 'There is no paper which can hesitate to publish this strange classic.'[28] On 26 August, *La Presse* published the first nine *Poèmes en prose*, dedicated to Arsène Houssaye; next day it published a further five. On 31 August, in *Le Boulevard*, Théodore de Banville hailed the publication as 'a real literary event'.[29]

94

> Who is the man among us who has not, on his ambitious days, dreamed of the miracle of a poetic prose, musical without rhyme or rhythm, supple and rough enough to adapt itself to the lyrical movements of the soul, the undulations of reverie, the shocks of perception?
>   It is above all from the frequentation of enormous cities, the crossing of their countless connections, that this obsessive ideal is born . . .'[1]

It was this ideal which led Baudelaire to write his prose poems. In *Les Fleurs du mal* he had touched the bounds of poetry, he had created *un frisson nouveau*; now he pursued his exploration in a different region of literature.

For Baudelaire, as Marcel Ruff explains, the poem, and the work of art in general, is not defined by a certain form, but by the effect which is produced.[2] If *Les Fleurs du mal* had represented romantic poetry, *Le Spleen de Paris* was to represent the poetry of realism. It was occasionally lyrical; but, in general, music was replaced by images, by the associations which derived from them. It was through association that the daily life of Paris, however commonplace, gained its resonance. If *Les Fleurs du mal*, as Baudelaire insisted, had had an architecture of its own, *Le Spleen de Paris* was to have no shape. As he himself told Arsène Houssaye: 'It has neither head nor tail, since everything here . . . is at once both head and tail.'[3] *Le Spleen de Paris* was to be a modern and audacious undertaking.

It was an original enterprise on which Baudelaire embarked only with caution. The idea had come to him as he had read *Gaspard de la Nuit*, the prose poems of Aloysius Bertrand. They had appeared in 1842, a year after Bertrand's death, with a preface by Sainte-Beuve. The work had, however, had less influence on Baudelaire than his published comments suggest. He had come to believe that traditional forms of poetry were superfluous and needlessly restrictive. He was perfectly aware of creating a new literary instrument, and he proclaimed it with that mixture of modesty and pride which was peculiar to him, in the open letter to Houssaye which introduced the first poems of 1862:

> As soon as I had begun to work, I realised that not only did I remain a very long way from my mysterious and brilliant model, but also that I was doing something (if it can be called *something*) singularly different. It is a chance of which anyone but myself would no doubt be proud, but a chance which can only deeply humiliate a spirit which considers it the poet's greatest honour to accomplish *exactly* what he planned to do.[4]

Le Spleen de Paris: the title is misleading. In this collection of vignettes and anecdotes, moralities and meditations, the themes are not exclusively Parisian. They are all, however, marked by a Parisian spirit. Whether they express Romantic spleen, or the longing to escape to distant lands, they reflect a modern and Parisian soul. *Le Spleen de Paris* is a singular work, as Baudelaire had intended. It comes from a laboratory where he performs literary experiments. This laboratory is not the hothouse in which he had cultivated *Les Fleurs du mal*, even though it is connected with it. In fact, *Le Spleen de Paris* runs parallel at times with *Les Fleurs du mal*, parallel but separate, because the prose nearly always seems to be later than the poetry. After 1860, Baudelaire almost entirely abandons the verse form (if one takes account not of the poems that he rediscovers, but of the poems that he composes).

The instrument with which he explores poetic reality is the prose poem. His prose, said Gautier, admiringly, 'was scanned, worked and polished like the most condensed poetry.'[5] His prose showed more than literary distinction. In *Le Spleen de Paris*, Baudelaire spoke with his own voice.

The first prose poem, 'L'Étranger', records the poet's sense of being alien in the world, his sense of solitude; this otherness, this curse of the alien, are, however, the sign that he is blessed, in a society which is hostile to him. His solitude is the solitude which he had felt since childhood, the solitude reflected in 'Bénédiction', in his correspondence and in *Mon Cœur mis à nu*. It is a solitude which, in setting him apart, proclaims his distinction. The stranger has no parents, no brother or sister, and he does not know the meaning of the word 'friend'. He does not know where his native country lies. 'Beauty? I should love it readily, if it were a goddess and immortal.'[6] This love of beauty is a recollection of his love for Mme Sabatier, of his need to worship rather than possess. The stranger loves the passing clouds; it is a passion which recalls that of his Icarus in 'Les Plaintes d'un Icare'. The mysterious stranger, *l'homme énigmatique*, shares some of Baudelaire's deepest beliefs and aspirations.

Time and again *Le Spleen de Paris* reflects the need to escape the dreadful burden of existence. It is an enduring theme of his work. In 'Enivrez-vous', he insists that man should always be intoxicated with wine or with poetry in order to escape from everyday life. Sometimes he seeks to lose himself, to refresh himself in a crowd. To enjoy the crowd is an art; and the only human being who can do so is the one endowed from birth with a taste for disguise, a hatred of home and a passion for travel and exploration. The poet has an incomparable privilege: he can, when he chooses, enter the character of someone else. Baudelaire does not touch the poetic intensity of Keats: 'I do not live in this world alone but in a thousand worlds.'[7] 'If a Sparrow come before my Window I take part in its existince [*sic*] and peck about the Gravel.'[8] Yet there is much of Baudelaire himself in 'Les Foules'. Baudelaire, the solitary, pensive wanderer is intoxicated by communion with the multitude, by this sacred prostitution of the soul which abandons itself to the unknown.

> It is good sometimes to teach the fortunate in this world, were it only for a moment to humble their stupid pride, that there are felicities superior to their own, vaster and more refined. The founders of colonies, the pastors of nations, the missionary priests who are banished to the ends of the earth, no doubt know something of these mysterious intoxications; and, in the bosom of the vast family which their genius has created for them, they must sometimes laugh at those who pity them for a fortune so disturbed and a life so chaste![9]

The poet, too, knows endless and refined felicities; he, too, like the missionary priests, can laugh at the world's scorn.

Sometimes he seeks refreshment in a crowd; sometimes he seeks it in silence and in retreat. 'À une heure du matin' recalls the hôtel Voltaire, the hôtel de Dieppe: every seedy furnished room in which he has been obliged to live in Paris. Night has fallen. He is alone. The sound of the last belated cab has died away in the distance, and, for a few hours, the tyranny of the human face has vanished.

> Discontented with everyone, discontented with myself, I long to be compensated and to make myself a little proud in the silence and the solitude of night. Souls of those whom I have loved, souls of those whom I have sung, give me strength, support me, banish from me the lies and the corrupting vapours of the world, and You, oh Lord my God! grant me the grace to produce a few fine poems which prove to me that I am not the least of men, that I am not inferior to those whom I despise![10]

It is a moment of self-doubt: one of the most famous, most bitter moments when he bares his soul. It is a moment of absolute honesty, absolute despair.

In 'La Chambre double', which is linked to 'L'Invitation au voyage', 'La Mort des pauvres', and 'L'Horloge', the room of the poet's dreams becomes the squalid room of reality, where the phial of laudanum seems to be his only friend. 'L'Idole, la souveraine des rêves' (she is Jeanne, yet more than Jeanne), disappears, with the room of his dreams, when the tipstaff knocks at the door.[11] Jacques Crépet links this poem with the letters in which Baudelaire expressed the need to have a home of his own, not the eternal hotel room in which he was pursued by *ennui* and by his creditors.[12]

There are other escapes from life. One of them is the coming of night. Another is the sight of the sea. 'Le Port', which was presumably inspired by Honfleur, shows the poet tranquil and resigned. In 'Le CONFITEOR de l'artiste', no doubt written at Honfleur, Baudelaire meditates on the artist's condition. He loses himself, with delight, in the fathomless sky and sea; only a tiny, distant ship recalls the smallness and the isolation of his own irremediable life. Then his feelings grow too intense, he becomes afraid of the depth of the sky, and rebels against the insensibility of the ocean. Nature is pitiless, ever victorious. The study of beauty is a duel in which the artist cries out in fear before he is defeated.

Woman remains uncomprehending and trivial (in 'La Femme sauvage et la petite-maîtresse' and, again, in 'Les Yeux des pauvres'); among the few women who move Baudelaire are the lonely widows in 'Les Veuves', and the toothless crone in 'Le Désespoir de la vieille', who can no longer even win the affection of a child. Baudelaire always felt benevolent towards old women, since they were rid of the animal passions found in the young. Another woman to touch his heart is la belle Dorothée, whom he had known, years earlier, in the île Bourbon. She gives her name to one of the richest, most personal, most lyrical prose poems in the collection. 'Un hémisphère dans une chevelure' is the pendant to 'La Chevelure' in *Les Fleurs du mal*: indeed, its seven paragraphs correspond to the seven stanzas of the earlier poem. Here, yet again, is a tribute to Jeanne.

Le Spleen de Paris records some of the poet's less engaging qualities: his contempt for the public (in 'Le Chien et le flacon' and in 'Un Plaisant'); his sinister suppressed violence in 'Le Galant Tireur', and his savagery in 'Une Mort héroïque'. Fancioulle, the prince's favourite actor, is found to be involved in conspiracy. He gives a superb performance on stage, but, at a certain moment, on the prince's orders, a loud, prolonged whistle interrupts his inspiration. Perhaps the prince has determined to cheat the executioner. Perhaps he knows that Fancioulle will die of shame at the thought that his guilt is recognised, or die of grief at his loss of inspiration. Whatever the reason, Fancioulle drops dead. Baudelaire is here the prince, the actor and the narrator. The prince has Baudelaire's love of the arts, his sensibility and cruelty. Fancioulle has 'les rayons de l'Art et la gloire du Martyre', he proves that the intoxication of Art can hide the terror of the abyss.[13]

Baudelaire says much about himself in this savage tale. So he does in 'Le Mauvais Vitrier', an anecdote which has contributed not a little to the legend of his cruelty. It is an answer to Houssaye's 'La Chanson du vitrier', and it is overwhelmingly superior. Most of the characters in the poem want to escape – either from someone else or from reality. One of them hesitates to go home for fear of receiving bad news from his concierge; another keeps a letter for a fortnight without daring to open it, he waits six months to take an action which had been necessary for a year. Such whims are beyond their control, and Baudelaire – who had known them himself – seems to have had an intuition of their profundity. Some men, he also recognised, were dreamers, overcome by boredom, and they made sudden, desperate attempts to relieve *ennui*. The narrator of 'Le Mauvais Vitrier' sees a glazier in the street below, selling his wares. He summons him up to the sixth floor; then he upbraids him for not selling coloured glass through which he could take a roseate view of life. As the glazier emerges into the street, the narrator drops a flower-pot on him. The glazier falls, and breaks 'all his small and ambulatory fortune'.[14] The narrator shouts in triumph. What, he wonders, 'does the eternity of damnation matter to the man who has found in a second the infinity of delight?'[15] It is a vicious story, but Baudelaire's black humour must not be discounted. This would mean a failure to understand his genius.

'Le Mauvais Vitrier' is not the last of the prose poems to reveal his violence and cynicism. In 'La Fausse monnaie', a man gives a counterfeit coin to a beggar. Baudelaire finds it strange that the man should enjoy compromising the poor; but while it is never excusable to be wicked, he concludes, there is some merit in knowing that one is wicked. The irreparable vice is to sin out of stupidity. In 'La Corde', the most macabre and one of the most unfeeling of the poems, Baudelaire suggests that maternal love, said to be the purest of emotions, could be corrupted. The poem is dedicated to Manet; its hero, Alexandre, is the boy who had posed for *L'Enfant aux cerises*, and had hanged himself in Manet's studio. In 'La Corde', the artist threatens to dismiss the boy if he continues to steal his sugar and liqueurs. The boy hangs himself. The artist is deluged with requests for pieces of the rope; finally the boy's mother begs to be given it, because it has commercial advantages. Baudelaire's disappointment in Mme Aupick may help to explain his choice of theme.

It would be illuminating to consider the literary sources of *Le Spleen de Paris* (the opening of 'Le Joueur généreux', a poem much admired by André Gide, owes a patent debt to Tennyson's *The Lotos-Eaters*).[16] Yet it is more rewarding to find, in the prose-poems, the reflection of Baudelaire himself. In 'Le Fou et la Vénus', a clown stands by the statue of the goddess, and begs her to have pity upon him; but the implacable statue gazes into the distance with marble eyes. In the clown, 'the last and the most solitary of human beings, deprived of love and friendship,'[17] one is tempted to recognise a likeness of the poet. Sometimes a sudden insight into life in Paris gives Baudelaire a disturbing vision of the future that could be in store for him. On a public holiday, he sees an aged juggler, spurned by the crowd at a fair:

> Obsessed by this vision, I tried to analyse my sudden grief. I said to myself: I have just seen the image of the old man of letters who has outlived the generation which he once amused so brilliantly: of the old poet without friends, or family, or children, degraded by his poverty and by the ingratitude of the public, the old poet to whose stall the forgetful world will not now come.[18]

There remains escape – which is one of the most persistent themes in the work of Baudelaire. In 'L'Invitation au voyage' he enlarges, not always to advantage, on the poem of the same title in *Les Fleurs du mal*. In 'Déjà!', the voyagers delightedly sight land; he alone regrets the grandeur and vastness of the sea, which seems to contain within itself all the agonies and ecstasies of every human soul, past, present, and to come.

> As I bade farewell to this incomparable beauty, I felt overwhelmed by grief, and sick at heart; and that is why, when all my companions said: 'At last!', I could only cry: 'Already!'
> And yet it was the earth, the earth with its sounds, its passions, its amenities, its festivals; it was a rich and splendid land, full of promises, which sent us a mysterious aroma of rose and musk, a land from which the music of life came to us in a murmur of love.[19]

'Any Where Out of the World' is related to both 'Invitations au voyage' and to two other *Fleurs du mal*: 'Rêve parisien' and 'Le Voyage'. Here, again, in the antepenultimate *Poème en prose*, the restless poet constantly asks his soul where it would choose to be. 'Finally, my soul burst out, and, in its wisdom, cried to me: "Anywhere! Anywhere! As long as it is out of this world!"'[20]

It was on 9 February 1861, in a letter to Armand du Mesnil, that Baudelaire had first mentioned his prose poems.[21] He had already published several in *Le Présent*, but henceforward he was to publish many in various periodicals. They were to be his chief poetic preoccupation. Twenty prose poems appeared in *La Presse* in August and September 1862; another thirty, most already published, were to appear with them in 1869, in the fourth volume of the *Œuvres complètes*.

The parallels between *Les Fleurs du mal* and *Le Spleen de Paris*, the close relationship between the poetry and the prose, the questions of variants and sequences, are themselves a subject for a substantial work. Yet it is clear that, from his first years as a writer, Baudelaire had wanted to arrange the same melody for different instruments. Now he was realising new creations on old themes. *Le Spleen de Paris* is full of echoes and recollections. It presents the eternal Baudelaire: his compassion and his brutality, his fascination with Paris, his nostalgia for the East, and his desperate longing to escape. He is afraid of growing old, of being misunderstood and of being abandoned by the world, and yet he finds a certain peace in solitude. He needs to lose himself in literature, in music, wine or love; he remains a sharp observer of modern life, an acute interpreter of significant detail. He is aggressive, shocking, and at times, when he speaks of the bereaved, the poor and the old, he is heartrending. Never, for a moment, is he content. As Hiddleston observes, in *Baudelaire and LE SPLEEN DE PARIS*, there had been few references to the poet as fool in *Les Fleurs du mal*; such references were much more developed and important in the prose poems. Perhaps the shift reflected a sense of failure after the trial of

1857, a sense of social defeat, and increasing fears about the waning of his creative powers.[22] The prose poems of Baudelaire were a literary adventure; they were also, perhaps, a sign that his poetic energy was spent.

Georges Blin remarks that, when one looks closely at *Le Spleen de Paris*, when one studies the list of poems to be written,

> ... one ascertains that it is a work which has not reached – at least in extent – its full flowering. It is the work of a sick man, a work which is set on the borders of sterility ... He himself was physically exhausted, and, at moments, these poems give a presentiment of paralysis. A good many of them were written after the fateful date of 23 January 1862, when, 'a singular warning', Baudelaire ... felt 'the wind of the wing of madness' pass over him ... Some of them must have been written in that vaporous state which led the poet to question his faculties. He complained to his mother of his difficulties in conceiving and in expressing himself. And one can believe that the work he was obliged to do to create these 'poems to be done' finally exhausted his Muse ... All great poetry finally opens on to silence or nonsense. Rimbaud leaves for Abyssinia, ... Baudelaire sinks into aphasia. As for us, ... we never tire of questioning their *Ultima verba*, which are already moving into darkness. So it is with the *Petits Poèmes en prose*, ... which are clearly Baudelaire's last great work. Whoever claims to determine what irony and humour can mean on the verge of this renunciation, has only to return to the case of Fancioulle, 'that strange buffoon' who 'played the buffoon with death.'[23]

Some of Baudelaire's prose poems are little more than additional entries for his *Journaux intimes*. Some are miniature novellas, vignettes, which owe much to their concentration. Baudelaire found it difficult to write at any length; in *Le Spleen de Paris* he discovered a variable formula which suited him.

> Fiction [explained Banville] is only a pretext in the *Petits Poèmes en prose*, where what is not seen, the intentions and desires, the weakness, cowardice and heroism of our souls, finds a clear and definite form ... Always a likeness of himself, it is the portrait of the inner man, a mixture of the degraded and the divine, dominated by evil and obsessed by good, a man who cannot be unfaithful to his destiny without creating dismal tragedy or irresistibly comic buffoonery in his own existence.[24]

Le Spleen de Paris is the final expression of Baudelaire's evocatory magic. It is the last expression of his vision of the world. Some have called it – perhaps mistakenly – the centre of his work.[25] Borgal observes: 'That the miracle [of poetic prose] did not always happen in *Le Spleen de Paris*, there can be not the slightest doubt. None the less, the path was open down which Rimbaud and Lautréamont were to go.'[26]

Les Fleurs du mal remains the undoubted masterpiece of Baudelaire, and its author did not equal, let alone surpass it, in his prose poems. Yet in *Le Spleen de Paris*, as in *Les Fleurs du mal*, he contributed to the development of modern poetry.[27]

95

In the late summer of 1862, Baudelaire had reason to be satisfied with the reception of his *Poèmes en prose*. This momentary satisfaction had its shadow side. He was about to lose the most devoted and the most understanding of publishers.

The house of Malassis and De Broise had for some time ceased to exist. De Broise had been apprehensive about Malassis' future, and he had decided to separate from him. He had therefore resigned his licence as a bookseller in Paris, and Malassis had resigned his licence as a printer in Alençon. De Broise was eventually to save the printing works, but on 28 August Malassis warned the engraver Félix Bracquemond that he was in liquidation, and would no doubt be declared bankrupt.[1] Next day he called on Bracquemond, and left a few boxes of belongings with him.[2]

Baudelaire was well aware of Malassis' situation. He recognised that, by the terms of his most recent contract, he owed him 5,000 francs. As he had explained to him, the copyright of *Les Fleurs du mal* and *Les Paradis artificiels* might not now be worth that sum, but it could in time be worth much more. It was also possible that his debt to Malassis could be paid by selling *Les Fleurs du mal* alone. There were other means of raising money and of ensuring publication. He could sell one or two of his works for a limited period, or for a single edition, or – which he himself preferred – he could sell all his works to one publisher for a number of years or in perpetuity. In the latter case, he would choose to be published by Michel Lévy. Baudelaire asked Malassis to negotiate with Lévy. If Lévy were not interested, he suggested Hetzel or Didier.[3] Pierre-Jules Hetzel was one of the most intelligent French publishers of the century, and the publisher or friend of everyone who counted in French literature. Malassis would, of course, negotiate for himself as well as Baudelaire.

On 1 September, Leconte de Lisle announced to his sister that Malassis had vanished. He was anxious about this, because Malassis had a stock of his books.[4] Next day, Malassis was declared bankrupt, as he had expected.

He had already left his celebrated bookshop on the corner of the passage des Princes and the rue de Richelieu; by 13 September he was in the route Militaire, Montrouge.

> Your Montrouge is a great obstacle to our seeing one another as easily as we used to do [this from Baudelaire, later in the month]; but I have the greatest need to talk to you at some length, you know why.
> Would you like me to order an appropriate dinner at my hotel on Sunday? We could completely settle the Michel question, and consider it from every point of view. *Whatever happens*, we need a lot of cash, you and I.[5]

Baudelaire himself was lost in literary affairs. He quarrelled with Eugène Crépet over two volumes of Victor Hugo which he had borrowed from him, and had not yet returned. Crépet resented 'the nearly always disdainful, imperious and quasi-dictatorial tone' of his letters.[6] It is not clear whether he recovered the two octavo volumes of *Les Contemplations*, but there was to be no further correspondence between them. The relationship was, so to speak, resumed after Baudelaire had died. In 1887, Crépet published the poet's *Œuvres posthumes*, and introduced them with a biographical notice. The volume established Crépet as a Baudelaire scholar; it confirmed the poet's entrance into literary history.

Now, in the early autumn of 1862, once again, Baudelaire deferred his journey to Honfleur. On 22 September, he apologised to his mother:

> I owe you numerous explanations. Why I haven't left, what's become of me, when I shall leave, etc. But the days are full of such diverse events, and they are so short; a few pages written, some errands done, and then the day is over. Besides, I need a certain serenity to write to you. And anger is my usual state. And so today I'm writing to you from the offices of *La Presse*, . . . where I'm enduring torture, *real torture*, and it may well be that I shall give up publishing the remaining *Poèmes en prose*, which made fifteen articles [*sic*] . . .
> But *money!*
> For that's what it's all about. I don't want to leave problems behind me, which might have repercussions at Honfleur . . .
> My plan for coming back to Honfleur is completely settled; but it is constantly thwarted by events which are impossible to foresee.[7]

Fifteen articles was an excessive calculation for the number of prose poems which he had in mind; but the third instalment appeared in *La Presse* on 24 September, and a fourth instalment was written. On 1 October, *L'Artiste* reprinted Banville's praise of Baudelaire's new venture.

It was characteristic of Baudelaire that, even now, he turned his situation to disadvantage. He needed money so desperately that he had sold some of his prose poems twice over. On 8 October, he felt obliged to explain to Houssaye how he had come to give *La Presse* some 'unpublished' poems which had already appeared in *La Revue fantaisiste.*[8] Houssaye was extremely well disposed towards Baudelaire; and certainly, had it not been for internal problems at *La Presse*, he would have shown less intransigence. As it was, his days as editor-in-chief were already numbered. As a result of an action brought by the shareholders of *La Presse* against its administrators, the paper was soon to return to its founder, the Press magnate, Émile de Girardin. Houssaye published no more of the *Petits Poèmes en prose*.

This was not the only misfortune to befall Baudelaire. On 12 November, Malassis was arrested, and sent for preventive detention to the debtors' prison at Clichy. The following month, he was transferred to Les Madelonnettes. Not until 22 April, after more than five months' preventive detention, was he brought before the eighth correctional court, and – despite his long incarceration – he was sentenced to a month's imprisonment for 'a very venial little offence'.[9]

Meanwhile, on 13 December 1862, Baudelaire wrote to his mother. She had asked him for the 500 francs which she had advanced to him in June; she told him how disturbed she was by the continued crumbling of the cliff at Honfleur. She was anxious about the damage that might be done to her garden and her little house, anxious about the costs that might be incurred, anxious about her personal safety. Baudelaire answered churlishly:

> How hard you were to me in one of your last letters! Those cruel 500 francs! The only serious thing which struck me in your letter was *the cliff*. But I always suppose that you imagine a lot of things. Could I conceive that so many misfortunes were going to befall me at the moment when I was planning my departure? – the Malassis bankruptcy, for example, which you have no doubt heard mentioned – in which I was almost implicated, and which in any case has caused a great upheaval in my life. I owe 5,000 francs [to Malassis, by the terms of our agreement]. I have decided to hide them from justice, so as to be able to give them to Malassis or his mother later. And then *Les Fleurs du mal* and the *Paradis* abandoned to the hazards of being reduced! But you don't understand anything about all that . . .
>
> I sent you some books to amuse you. Some good books . . . But you didn't even guess why I'd sent you the POÈTES FRANÇAIS; it wasn't in the least, as you thought, to show you some old things of mine, it was to make you read Gautier's article about me, that is to say the part which he accorded me in the history of poetry. Perhaps you didn't see it. And your spies? What shall we say about them? What imbeciles! They told you that I was happy. Never. Is it possible? If I'm happy, I am happy in a way that frightens people, and rids me of them quickly. They told you that I was well? None of my infirmities has left me; neither the rheumatism, nor the nightmares, nor the torments, nor this unbearable

faculty for hearing every sound strike me in the stomach; nor the fear, above all: the fear of dying suddenly; the fear of living for too long, the fear of seeing you die, the fear of going to sleep, and the horror of waking up! and this prolonged lethargy which makes me postpone the most urgent matters for months – bizarre infirmities which, I don't know why, intensify my hatred of everyone.[10]

His life's hopes had collapsed; he had failed because he had tried to grasp the infinite. He had found little justice; and, for all his mother's concern, for all her generosity, he felt isolated and unloved. When he was younger and stronger, poetry had come to him even in his moments of apathy. Now his habitual melancholy and inertia made it almost impossible to finish anything. The splendid epilogue he had planned for *Les Fleurs du mal*, an apostrophe to Paris, remained in his portfolio, a series of unmatched and fragmentary lines.

The year 1862 had been a bitter year; and its bitterness was reflected in the poem which appeared in *Le Boulevard* on 28 December: 'Les Plaintes d'un Icare':

> Les amants des prostituées
> Sont heureux, dispos et repus;
> Quant à moi, mes bras sont rompus
> Pour avoir étreint des nuées.
>
> C'est grâce aux astres nonpareils,
> Qui tout au fond du ciel flamboient,
> Que mes yeux consumés ne voient
> Que des souvenirs de soleils.
>
> En vain j'ai voulu de l'espace
> Trouver la fin et le milieu;
> Sous je ne sais quel œil de feu
> Je sens mon aile qui se casse;
>
> Et brûlé par l'amour du beau,
> Je n'aurai pas l'honneur sublime
> De donner mon nom à l'abîme
> Qui me servira de tombeau.[11]

96

The new year, 1863, seemed no less depressing than the last. His mother sent him money as a new year gift. On 3 January, he acknowledged it:

Really you are extraordinary. First you send me two very harsh, very
bitter letters (cold justice is not your concern), and then, lo and behold,
there are more presents . . .

Dear mother, you are very bored. We shall see each other in the middle
of the month; I want to come and find some contracts which are still
somewhere or other among my huge mass of old papers. Because I'm not
giving up my business. In a couple of words, this is what it is: I want a
lump sum of 25,000 francs, in exchange for *the complete, absolute and
permanent* transfer of all my author's rights in my works, such as they are
today . . .

My friends say that it is very lucky that I have not succeeded, because
my works are worth much more, and because one must never sell the
unforeseen, the unknown and the possible. But my friends talk about it in
very easy circumstances. They are rich and prudent, and they can wait.
A publisher [Hetzel] offered me 2,000 francs for *a single edition* of the *Fleurs*
and the [prose] poems. But I wanted to impose my five volumes, and to
sell for ever. I refused, proudly; it offended him; and, to be honest, I rather
regret it . . .

If you have understood my letter properly, you must see that it is
impossible for me to come to you immediately. I shall come and see you
in January, the 15th or the 20th, and, if all goes well, I shall come and do
four volumes at Honfleur (two volumes of Poe and two volumes of
criticism) . . .

It is fifteen months since we embraced each other, and my hair is quite
grey, so much so that I am thinking of powdering it to make it white.
Don't laugh at me, when you see this vanity in an old man.[1]

Baudelaire was forty-one.

One of his fears had recently been realised. On 11 January, after the
closure of Malassis' bookshop, *Le Boulevard* announced that copies of
Les Fleurs du mal, *Les Paradis artificiels* and *Théophile Gautier* were now
available at reduced prices. Baudelaire remained bound by contract to
Malassis, but, not for the first time, he chose to forget his obligations.
Without a word to Malassis, he also decided to negotiate, once again,
with Hetzel. Two days later, for 1,200 francs, little more than half the
previous offer, he assigned to Hetzel, for five years, the exclusive
right to publish *Les Fleurs du mal* and *Petits Poèmes en prose*. Hetzel
undertook to publish, on the same conditions, the first volume of short
stories that Baudelaire proposed to him, and other volumes provision-
ally entitled *Mon Cœur mis à nu*.[2] Baudelaire received his advance.
Hetzel was to wait, in vain, for his manuscripts.

Amid all this unhappiness, uncertainty and poverty, Baudelaire was,
it seems, still writing poetry. On 25 January, in *Le Boulevard*, there
appeared an unpublished poem, 'L'Imprévu'. Baudelaire's belief in the
Devil gave him a dizzying panorama of the world's corruption,

although he ended with a Catholic acceptance of the need for suffering, a Catholic aspiration towards salvation.

> . . . — Cependant, tout en haut de l'univers juché,
>   Un Ange sonne la victoire
>
> De ceux dont le cœur dit: 'Que béni soit ton fouet,
> Seigneur! que la douleur, ô Père, soit bénie!
> Mon âme dans tes mains n'est pas un vain jouet,
>   Et ta prudence est infinie.'
>
> Le son de la trompette est si délicieux,
> Dans ces soirs solennels de célestes vendanges,
> Qu'il s'infiltre comme une extase dans tous ceux
>   Dont elle chante les louanges.[3]

'L'Imprévu' was the poet's epilogue to *Les Fleurs du mal*, it was the crucifix at the end of his pilgrim's progress through the garden of sin. It emphasised the Catholic inspiration of his work. All the poems of revolt which had preceded it had merely been its prelude. They had related the battle in which Baudelaire had spent his strength.

Although he was now translating *Le Mystère de Marie Roget* for Mario Uchard, of *Le Nord*, he chose this particular moment to do what he had promised to do for many months: to visit his ill-used mother at Honfleur. On 19 February he announced to Uchard, with a sad lack of feeling: 'I am obliged to go to Honfleur, and I'm leaving in a moment. I am coming back the day after tomorrow. As for your *Marie Roget*, have no fear; I am working at it slowly, it's true, but I am working at it everywhere, even in the restaurant.'[4]

No doubt he went to Honfleur to ask his mother for some money.[5] His visit also gave him a chance to unpack the boxes of belongings which had been waiting for him for months; it gave him a chance to sort out some of his many papers. It gave him little time to rest, and little time to spend with Mme Aupick. Her love for her son must have been severely tried. Baudelaire left for Honfleur on 19 February; he returned to Paris two days later.

Soon afterwards, a significant figure entered his correspondence. Malassis called him the last man for whom Baudelaire was to feel an eager friendship.[6] 'It seems to me very difficult', Baudelaire confessed, 'not to admire his character as much as his gifts.'[7] That month, at the Galerie Martinet, Manet exhibited his picture, *La Chanteuse des rues*: it was to inspire Baudelaire's poem, 'Les Promesses d'un visage'. Manet also showed his grand tribute to the Second Empire. *La Musique aux Tuileries* presented all the world of the arts assembled elegantly in the summer gardens. Ostensibly they were listening to a military band, but patently they were lost in their own individual pursuits. There, among them, engaged in conversation with Baron Taylor, Inspector of Museums, and Théophile Gautier, was the author of *Les Fleurs du mal*.[8]

On 14 March, he invited Auguste de Châtillon to *déjeuner* next day with Édouard Manet.[9]

The year 1863 did not mark the beginning of Baudelaire's acquaintance with Manet. In *Baudelaire, critique d'art*, Pierre Castex writes that since 1858 they had had an excellent relationship.[10] Some say that Baudelaire had called on the artist in the early summer of 1861. Certainly they had met in 1862. That summer, Baudelaire had taken Jeanne Duval to Manet's studio in the rue Guyot, and Manet had painted that hard and sinister picture, *La Maîtresse de Baudelaire*, the only known portrait of Jeanne, now in Budapest. Castex records: 'Tradition has it that the poet had suggested the subject of his *Buveur d'absinthe*, as well as the negress and the black cat in *Olympia*.'[11] The influence was mutual. With Baudelaire, wrote Antonin Proust, Manet had a close relationship, and it was Manet who remained an influence on his friend.[12]

It was the time when, to hide his pallor, or to play the dandy, to show his disdain for public opinion, Baudelaire resorted to cosmetics. Alcide Dusolier, the malicious journalist, reported in *Le Nain jaune*: 'He powders himself, so his intimates assert, and he even paints his face.'[13] Manet saw beyond such behaviour. Antonin Proust recorded:

> At a time when the poet made himself up outrageously – 'he has a coat of paint', exclaimed Manet, 'but there is so much genius beneath it!' – Baudelaire was his constant companion when Manet went to the Tuileries, and, in the open air, under the trees, made sketches of the children who were playing, the groups of nurses lolling on the chairs.[14]

It could well be that Manet was trying to portray what Baudelaire called the heroism of modern life; and it could be that he did so on Baudelaire's advice. Manet was eleven years younger than Baudelaire, yet, despite their difference in age, they shared many aspirations; and Manet, like Baudelaire, maintained that the artist should be of his time, and paint what he saw with his own eyes. With him, as with Baudelaire, this meant the sublimation of the commonplace, the discovery of beauty in ordinary things. Many of Manet's pictures, it has been rightly said, could be the subjects of poems by Baudelaire.

It has been alleged that Baudelaire did not appreciate Manet at his true worth. Pierre Castex writes: 'One regret remains: that Baudelaire did not devote a large-scale study to Manet, a study on the same level as his studies of Delacroix ... [But] Baudelaire was already ill, and debilitated . . . It is doubtful whether, now, he still had the necessary vigour to define and characterise the temperament of a new artist.'[15] Baudelaire was vigorous enough to write at length about Delacroix, and to lecture on him; he was also to write a substantial appreciation of Constantin Guys. It might indeed be said that Delacroix concealed the modernity and the stature of Manet from him.

However limited his public appreciation of Manet, he supported him warmly in private, and sent him letters of encouragement. He gave him confidence in his ambitions and in his powers. Manet himself – unlike Delacroix – was and remained a devoted friend.[16]

Late in May or early in June 1863, in spite of his obligations to Malassis, and in spite of his contract with Hetzel, Baudelaire suggested to Ancelle the idea of selling his author's rights for several thousand francs. Ancelle rejected the idea, and said that Baudelaire would lose by it. However, at the request of Namslauer, a banker, Baudelaire drew up an account of his literary income; and Namslauer agreed to discuss an arrangement by which Baudelaire would receive between 10,000 and 20,000 francs for his author's rights.[17]

On 3 June, he told his mother about his negotiations.

Once this operation is over [he wrote], . . . I shall come back to Honfleur, stay there for six months, and try out a few *short stories* which obsess me, do the whole of *Mon Cœur mis à nu*, which has become my real intellectual passion, and will be different from the famous *Confessions* of Jean-Jacques, and then just come back to Paris to conclude a great affair which I mentioned to you only casually, a few years ago. I have such a horror of the theatre, that I'd rather control plays than write them. There is one theatre in Paris, *the only one where one can't become insolvent*, and where one can make a profit of 400,000 francs in four years. I want that theatre. If, in the regular course of politics, M. Fould comes back to the Ministry of State, as is probable, I shall have this theatre, thanks to my friends, thanks to Pelletier, Sainte-Beuve and Mérimée. Before I leave Paris, I shall have an exact account of the expenses and receipts and the time when the licence of the present director expires. I want that, and I shall have it. The years are passing by, and I mean to be *rich*. It would be such a little thing, what I call *wealth!* You can imagine that, in this case, in spite of all my plans to save, I should have to furnish a small house in Paris, and you would have to spend some months of the year with me. Besides, at this theatre, there are three months' holiday. I think that the director has seen his licence extended for two or three years, but, by giving him 100,000 or 150,000 francs, one might decide him to go.[18]

It was one of the moments in his life which lead one to ask if Baudelaire suffered from manic depression. He often showed depressive symptoms: loss of zest, withdrawal, loneliness, impaired concentration,

and thoughts of suicide. Now he seemed in a manic mood, full of
grandiose, impossible plans. He had, so he had said himself, a horror
of the theatre. He had had no experience of directing one; he had not
even had a play performed. He was incapable of managing his own
financial affairs. For nineteen years he had suffered the humiliation of
a *conseil judiciaire*: a fact which was doubtless known to all his friends.
He had been obliged, repeatedly, to ask for grants, to pawn his
belongings, to borrow money, to demand advances for unwritten
works, even to sell his writing twice over. Twenty-two years after he
had come of age, he still had no fixed address. He was usually living
in poverty, and constantly escaping his creditors. In spite of this, in
spite of the court case of *Les Fleurs du mal*, in spite of the controversy
which he aroused, and frequently elected to create, he dreamed, now,
of directing the Théâtre de l'Odéon, the second theatre of France.
Charles de La Rounat – whom he had known at the *Corsaire-Satan* –
had become its director in 1856. He was to remain in office until 1867,
and to be recalled in 1880.

Yet Joseph-François Baudelaire had been involved in the rebuilding
of the Odéon, and he had been a member of the reading committee.
Baudelaire was perhaps encouraged by this family connection; he continued to indulge in his dream. 'It is a quite enormous dream,' he
continued, to his mother. 'I shall pursue it carefully, perhaps I shall
realise it, and, in all the turmoil of administration, I even expect not
to abandon the cultivation of my own mind.' In the meanwhile, he
asked her for 500 francs.[19]

Mme Aupick sent him the money. She also sent him three volumes
of the works of Poe, and some letters written by his father. She had,
she confessed, no hope of seeing Baudelaire direct the Théâtre de
l'Odéon. ('My son', she would one day tell Ancelle, 'is sometimes as
credulous as a child.')[20] She expressed such admiration for the art of
Poe that Baudelaire felt hurt: he thought that she disregarded his own
work.

My dear mother [he replied on 5 June],
. . . What you tell me about *Mon Cœur mis à nu* is as disagreeable to me
as your reluctance to see me in control of some great concern.
Well, yes, this book I have so dreamed of will be a book of rancours.
My mother and even my stepfather will certainly be respected in it. But
as I describe my education, the manner in which my ideas and feelings
were formed, I want to make it constantly clear that I feel foreign to the
world and to its creeds. I shall turn my real talent for insolence against
the whole of France. I need revenge like a tired man needs a bath.
And then your admiration for Edgar Poe makes you rather forget
my own works, which would seem much more considerable if I could

reprint them all. I shall never again let you see the wounds that you inflict on me . . .

As for the theatre: within a month, within six weeks, I shall have verified the patronage, and in three years, in a year, perhaps, I shall go through your *conseil judiciaire* like a circus clown through a paper hoop.

I shall certainly not publish *Mon Cœur mis à nu* until I have an adequate fortune to take shelter out of France, if that is necessary.[21]

If his mother wounded him, he in turn wounded her: he no longer thought of Honfleur as his ultimate refuge.

On 10 June, *La Revue nationale et étrangère* published two prose poems; on 14 June, *Le Boulevard* published two more. On 7 July, Baudelaire announced to Michel Lévy that he had finished *Eureka* and that he would soon send him the final chapters of *Histoires grotesques et sérieuses*. He protested at a printing error in the preface to the second volume of Poe, 'for I have', he wrote, 'made Poe a matter of glory, and I have taken so much care with it.' He then asked for a statement of his account, since he needed money to travel abroad. 'I am very weary of France, and I want to forget it for a while.'[22]

It was the first reference in his letters to his departure for Belgium.

97

Baudelaire was later to protest that it was time 'to tell the truth about *Belgium*, and about *America*, that other Eldorado of the French riff-raff.'[1] Belgium was, in fact, far from enchanting. There was no sign, yet, of the literary renaissance which was to flower there at the end of the century. Brussels – or Bruxelles-en-Brabant – was still like a provincial town, sparsely populated, sullen and suspicious. All the French exiles who had settled there after the coup-d'État of December 1851 had hastened to leave it after the imperial amnesty of 1859.[2] Yet now, in 1863, Baudelaire still believed in the Eldorado. Belgium was recognised as the country where Frenchmen could make a fortune. In Paris, official permission was needed for a public reading; and, even when this was given, the Government frequently withdrew it. But Baudelaire had heard, recalled Asselineau, 'of the great success enjoyed in Brussels by French men of letters who had given readings and public lectures . . . He had dreamed of the splendid profits earned in England and America by Dickens, Thackeray, Longfellow and Edgar Poe himself, who had come home rich after a tour which had been spent in going from town to town, exploiting a single book or a single theme.'³

Early in August (the letter has not survived), Baudelaire wrote to the Cercle artistique et littéraire in Brussels, and proposed himself as a lecturer. D. J. L. Vervoort, the advocate, was president of the Cercle (and president, too, of the Belgian Chambre des représentants); he noted Baudelaire's offer for November. On 3 August, Baudelaire asked Maréchal Vaillant, Ministre des Beaux-Arts, for a Government grant in order to go to Belgium. In his determination to obtain it, he even reminded the Minister: 'I am the stepson of General Aupick, who, if I remember rightly, had the honour of knowing you.'⁴ That day, he also drafted a letter to Victor Duruy, Ministre de l'Instruction publique, and asked him, urgently, for an interview. 'I am on the point of leaving France for some time, in order to give some public lectures to foreign societies on subjects associated with painting and literature.'⁵ The letter was drafted, but apparently not sent. On 7 August, he wrote again to Duruy:

> I propose to make an excursion to Belgium for two or three months, especially in order to see *the rich private [art] galleries* in that country, and to write a good book with my personal impressions. I am leaving with someone [Arthur Stevens, the picture-dealer] whose profession and contacts would enable him to see what few people see. But I have no money, and I hope that Your Excellency might continue the kindness that M. Rouland showed me, and provide me with the means to go and travel. I suppose that, even if I should be unable to earn some money in Belgium, a sum of 600 or 700 francs would be enough for me.⁶

An official noted on the letter: 'I am against, *a priori.*'⁷ Baudelaire did not receive a grant.

In the meanwhile, before he had heard from the Minister, Baudelaire sent a note to Malassis.

Malassis, now released from prison, was living in a little house in the boulevard Brune, near the porte d'Orléans. He was 'still spirited, ironic, treating life as it deserves to be treated . . . It was summer,' remembered Maxime Rude. 'Sunday mornings brought the guests to the weekly *déjeuners* . . . Babou and I were the regulars, but how many others there were around us! Baudelaire, Champfleury, Alcide Dusolier, Lemercier de Neuville, &c., &c., then the latecomers who were obliged to be diners – Delvau, Monselet, Courbet . . .'⁸ In the intervals of social life, Malassis was attempting to put some order into his affairs, and transferring his bookshop to René Pincebourde, who had been his senior assistant. He still had debts to settle, and he asked Baudelaire to delay an order to pay.

Baudelaire did not merely refuse to delay it, he insisted that Malassis should pay him early. Some weeks later, in a letter to Asselineau, Malassis explained: '[He] made me pay him in cash before the date an order to pay for 600 francs which I had to reimburse. In the extremities in which I find myself, this base act brought me very much to my senses where he is concerned.'9 Baudelaire had, once again, shown ruthless disregard for his friend.

He himself was still in turmoil.

My dear mother [this on 10 August],
I am overwhelmed by anxieties and errands. You must not reproach me if I answer [your letter] briefly.

The big affair [the agreement with Namslauer] has failed, or, rather, it has been postponed. I was in the hands of rogues, and, taking one rogue with another, I should rather do business with Michel Lévy, and deal directly with him. He is coming back on the 25th.

The question of public lectures is postponed until November . . .

However, I think I am leaving for Belgium on Friday or Saturday, to write some articles for *L'Indépendance belge*, and above all to finish my unfinished books; I have acquired a horror of Paris and of France. If it were not for you, I should like never to come back.

If I leave on Friday, I shall return to Paris when I have tied up affairs in Belgium, I shall negotiate the Poe affair with Michel, and I shall come to Honfleur to wait for November to arrive.

No reproaches, I beg of you . . .10

Like all his plans, or so it seemed, this Belgian plan was not to be realised.

98

On 13 August, Delacroix died. On 15 August, Baudelaire learned of his death. 'I remained in a state of stupor,' he was to remember. 'It was only two hours later that I felt overcome by a desolation which I shall not try to describe. It can be summarised like this: *I shall never, never, never see him again, the man I have loved so dearly, the man who has deigned to love me and has taught me so much.*'1

It is doubtful whether Baudelaire had loved Delacroix the man; but there was no doubt of his desolation. He was mourning the loss of the artist whom he had long admired as a hero. Delacroix had been an artist-poet. Like Baudelaire he had been a classic in his technique and a romantic in his inspiration. He, too, had seen the grandeur of modernity; he, too, had seen the world as a dictionary full of symbols. Perhaps he had taught much to Baudelaire. He had, above all, allowed him to recognise him as a fellow-spirit.

He had not, however, '_deigned to love him_'. There had been none of the chemistry of a close relationship. There remains a sad disparity between Baudelaire's constant, generous acclaim and the artist's cursory acknowledgment.

Yet now, on 15 August 1863, when he learned that Delacroix had died, Baudelaire hurried to his rooms in the place de Furstenberg. He 'stayed for two hours talking about him with Jenny, one of those servants of another age who create themselves their own nobility by their adoration of illustrious masters.'[2] For twenty-eight years she had tended Delacroix, concerned herself about his fragile health, defended him against the inopportune. Now she spoke freely to Baudelaire. 'We stayed there for two hours,' he repeated, 'talking and weeping, beside the coffin. It was lit up by two small candles, and on top of it lay a paltry copper crucifix. For, alas, I had arrived too late to contemplate the face of the great artist-poet one last time.'[3]

That day he also called on the Belgian picture-dealer, Arthur Stevens. Stevens had his _hôtel particulier_ in Paris, as well as his house in Brussels. He had been the intermediary between Baudelaire and Léon Bérardi, the editor of _L'Indépendance belge_, and Baudelaire needed his advice before he went to Belgium.[4] Stevens was not at home, but there proved to be no need for his advice. Bérardi refused _Le Peintre de la vie moderne_ and _Le Spleen de Paris_. Baudelaire suggested two stories by Poe. Bérardi seems to have declined; nor was he interested in articles on Belgian picture galleries. Bérardi was French by birth, and he was himself a man of letters; he had made _L'Indépendance belge_ one of the leading newspapers of Europe. It is sad that he did not show more vision.

For the moment, Baudelaire remained at the hôtel de Dieppe, rue d'Amsterdam. On 17 August, at the church of Saint-Germain-des-Prés, he attended the funeral of Delacroix. Among the congregation was Henri Fantin-Latour.

> With Baudelaire and Manet [recalled Fantin's biographer], . . . he was coming back from Père-Lachaise, . . . when they were joined by some undertakers' men. These undertakers, like old clothes dealers, were wearing Delacroix's complete Academician's dress: the family had forgotten to take it back. At the sight of this, the artist of twenty-seven shook with righteous anger; he thought of protesting with a public tribute against the indignity of this funeral.[5]

Hommage à feu Eugène Delacroix was shown at the Salon of 1864.

Baudelaire, too, was determined to pay tribute. He wrote *L'Œuvre et la vie d'Eugène Delacroix*. The first of the three instalments was published in *L'Opinion nationale* on 2 September.

L'Œuvre et la vie d'Eugène Delacroix owed much to Baudelaire's earlier comments on the artist, and it implied a more intimate and more assiduous friendship than the two men had in fact enjoyed. Baudelaire's admiration and affection for Delacroix had not diminished over the years. Yet, writing to Eugène Crépet at the end of the century, Jules Buisson tried to explain the artist's reserve towards the most fervent, loyal and perceptive of his critics.[6] Some said that he felt a certain humiliation when he recognised that Baudelaire's criticism went beyond his own conception of his work. Delacroix, it seems, did not only complain of Baudelaire's criticism; he also disapproved of *Les Fleurs du mal* and of their author. The comments on the poetry in the artist's letters were eloquent in their reserve. Baudelaire was aware of such reserve; he described Delacroix as an egoist. Whatever he proclaimed in print, he recognised in private that his affection and admiration were not reciprocated.[7] However, in *L'Œuvre et la vie d'Eugène Delacroix*, he paid impassioned tribute to an artist whom he had admired since his days at Louis-le-Grand. His study is written with fervour and understanding, with a sense of Delacroix's character and achievement, and with a fine appreciation of his significance in art.

> What, then, is this mysterious quality which Delacroix, for the glory of our century, has translated better than anyone else? It is the invisible, the impalpable, it is the nerves, the *soul*; and he has done this, remember, . . . with line and colour alone; he has done it like no one else; he has done it with the perfection of a consummate artist, with the rigour of a subtle man of letters, with the eloquence of a passionate musician. It is, moreover, one of the symptoms of the spiritual state of our century that the arts aspire, if not to replace each other, at least to lend one another new powers.[8]

Delacroix had, in fact, understood the correspondences between the arts, between the very senses; he had maintained the theory which was held by Gautier and Baudelaire, and by many writers after them. The theory had been suggested by Balzac, mentioned by Poe, it had been implicit in the work of Wagner. Baudelaire's heroes, in all the arts, had been concerned with it; and in *Baudelaire et Delacroix* Lloyd Austin maintains that, in the most admired works of others, Baudelaire was seeking himself.[9]

Baudelaire's appreciation of Delacroix was intellectually searching. He noted that Delacroix was not only an artist in love with his vocation, but – unlike other modern artists – a man enamoured of poetry, and widely educated. Delacroix had insisted on consummate technical skill. His imagination was always burning, but he had always found the day too short to study the means of expression. He was constantly examining the quality of colours, the chemistry of paint. He had to be instantly prepared to translate his conceptions. The most visible mark of Delacroix's style was, said Baudelaire, conciseness and a kind of quiet intensity, the usual result of the total concentration of spiritual power on a single point.

Delacroix was clearly a man after Baudelaire's own heart: 'A curious mixture of scepticism, politeness, dandyism, ardent determination, cunning, despotism, and finally a particular sort of kindness and gentle affection which always accompany genius.'[10]

Delacroix's father, like Joseph-François Baudelaire, had been a sceptical eighteenth-century figure. Delacroix, said Baudelaire, had inherited this scepticism. He had had the same outward coldness, slightly affected, 'the same cloak of ice which covered a modest sensibility and an ardent passion for the good and beautiful . . . There was, in Eugène Delacroix, much of the *savage*; it was the most precious part of his soul, the part which was entirely devoted to the painting of his dreams and to the cult of his art. There was in him much of the man of the world; that part was meant to conceal the first and to win forgiveness for it. It was, I think, one of the great preoccupations of his life to hide the anger in his heart and not to look like a man of genius.'[11]

Repeatedly, in his study of Delacroix the man, Baudelaire seems to be painting a self-portrait. 'I have to say this, because I find it a new cause for praise: though E[ugène] Delacroix was a man of genius, or because he was a complete man of genius, he had much in him of the dandy.'[12]

Beneath this outward appearance there had lain a nature of extraordinary energy. To Baudelaire, the artist's dusky complexion, his fierceness of expression, suggested some exotic origin; he reminded him of Montezuma 'or one of those Hindu princes who, among the splendours of the most gorgeous feasts, bear in the depths of their eyes a kind of unassuaged avidity and an inexplicable nostalgia, something like the memory and the regret of things unknown.'[13] There was an oriental colour in his canvases. His whole work had borne witness against the eternal and incorrigible barbarity of man.

Baudelaire's appreciation of Delacroix is inspired by a real, informed love of his painting. It is a searching portrait of a man who had had much in common with himself; a passion for perfection, a nostalgia for the unknown, a sense of duty to his art, a sense of solitude among mankind. Delacroix hid his true nature – as Baudelaire had done – under the appearance of a dandy. Delacroix was Romantic as Baudelaire was Romantic. This appreciation was more than a study of an artist: it was, above all, a portrait of the artist as hero.

99

Not for the first time, Mme Aupick felt abandoned by her son, and she found her solitude unbearable. In the second week of September, undeterred by a discouraging letter from Baudelaire, she arrived in Paris.

> It's very hard [he confessed to her] to see as little of each other as if we were separated by many miles! I promise you that it is not my fault. Yesterday evening, and this very evening [Friday, 11 September], I wanted to be with you. Your extraordinary kindness and indulgence often make me ashamed, and I should like to make amends with boundless attention and affection for the moments when I have shown myself so unjust to you. But what can one do, when one is overwhelmed with business and with anxieties? ...
> Love me dearly, untiringly, because I have an awful need of it...
> If tomorrow, Saturday, I am not with you at 6, I shall be there at 8. *Never* worry about dinner; I dine on a piece of bread and a little wine.[1]

Soon after he wrote this letter, Baudelaire discussed the sale of his rights in the Poe translations with Michel Lévy. He asked for a five-year contract, and either for payments for the volumes already published, or for a lump sum representing the expected number of volumes. Lévy asked for a week in which to consider the proposals.

In the meanwhile, anxious to escape Second-Empire Paris, Malassis prepared to leave for Brussels. Despite his own despicable behaviour to Malassis, Baudelaire still chose to ask him for advice and favours.

> My dear friend [this on 15 September].
> ...When you leave, I shall entrust you with a note for M. Vervoort, president of the Chambre des députés and president of the Cercle artistique, *containing the titles of the lectures that I want to give.* I want a *contract,* 200 francs a lecture, and I shan't leave, at the end of October, unless I have this contract.
> I've talked to Michel. He wants a week to consider what he can offer me when he has checked our accounts.

Now should I, plagued by so many needs, try to sign two new contracts with him *Paradis, Contemporains*, 3 volumes [in all]? Or should I be patient until November, in the hope that the lectures in question will excite desire in MM. Lacroix and Verboeckhoven?

I also think that Michel doesn't like to hear one talk of thirty-six things at once, and that I mustn't let my penury be obvious . . .

An answer, please.[2]

On about 26 September, Malassis left for Belgium. In his brief six years as a publisher, he had brought out *Poèmes barbares* and the *Poésies complètes* of Leconte de Lisle, two editions of *Les Fleurs du mal*, *Les Paradis artificiels* and *Théophile Gautier* by Baudelaire, *Émaux et Camées* and *Balzac* by Gautier, and the poetry of Sainte-Beuve. Had he possessed the sum which these works were eventually to fetch, he would have been a wealthy man. As it was, he had been guaranteed by a bank in Alençon, and after the court case of *Les Fleurs du mal* and the departure of De Broise, the bank had withdrawn its support.[3] Authority had no doubt been aware of the irreconcilable republican as well as the controversial publisher; but Malassis 'had ruined himself by publishing *Les Fleurs du mal* . . . That is his glory.'[4] Now, in 1863, he hoped to escape his remaining creditors and, if possible, to make his fortune in Brussels. He travelled under the name of M. Duport, professor of mathematics. He settled in the rue du Midi, in the suburb of Ixelles – the *quartier* for refugees and exiles.[5] He took with him the list of lectures which Baudelaire suggested to Vervoort, and the authority to negotiate the financial arrangements.

In Paris, Baudelaire remained beset by literary problems. Other writers seemed, now, to be exploiting his popularisation of Poe. Hetzel published the *Contes inédits*, translated by William Hughes; on 1 October, Charles de Nouy discussed Poe at length in the *Revue française*.[6] Baudelaire continued to create financial troubles for himself. On 8 October, he explained to Hetzel:

I owe you 1,200 francs, and I don't think I'll be able to deliver your two volumes until ten months after the time agreed. The only way for me to make amends to you will be to deliver something excellent. *Les Fleurs du mal* are completely ready, and the new poems have been put in place.

There will be a hundred pieces in *Le Spleen de Paris* – I still need another thirty. I have recklessly allowed myself to take so many tasks in hand, and I have so many troubles in Paris that I have decided to go and write your thirty poems in Honfleur. I shall leave on the 16th, I shall come and say goodbye to you. I shall come back on the 30th; you will be able to publish in November, and as I leave on the 1st for Brussels, where I am going to give about fifteen public lectures, I shall ask you to give me a mass of advice to guide me in a city where I don't know a soul.[7]

Baudelaire was less than frank. There were to be only fifty *Petits Poèmes en prose*, and some of these were to be written in Belgium. He was not to give 'about fifteen public lectures' in Brussels. Nor was it true that he had no friends in Brussels; he knew Alfred Stevens, and Malassis had just settled there.*

Baudelaire had hoped to return with his mother to Honfleur; but, late that month, she left Paris without him.

> Did the journey pass without troubles and mishaps, and above all how are you [he enquired on 28 October]?
>
> Yes, the Lévy affair is settled. Tomorrow I give up all my future rights for the sum of 2,000 francs payable in ten days. It isn't even half what I need. And so Belgium must pay the rest . . .
>
> The *Poe* gave me an income of 500 [francs] a year. So Michel has treated the matter as one would treat the sale of a grocer's stock in trade. He is simply paying for four years of the profit.[8]

It was in fact on 1 November that Baudelaire signed the contract. For the sum of 2,000 francs, Michel Lévy frères became the sole proprietors of all the Poe translations, and of the prefaces which Baudelaire had written. This leonine treaty was an eloquent proof of his penury, and of the commercial sense – or ruthlessness – with which Michel Lévy exploited him. By 1869, when the first volume of his translations took its place among his *Œuvres complètes*, the *Histoires extraordinaires* had run through six editions, the *Nouvelles Histoires extraordinaires* had run through four, and *Aventures d'Arthur Gordon Pym* had reached its third printing.

100

Whatever his bitter comments on Michel Lévy, Baudelaire's own behaviour was not beyond criticism. On 3 November, he asked the editor of *Le Pays* to return the manuscript of his study of Guys. 'I haven't the least intention', he wrote, 'of taking it back from you. But I absolutely must have it, because I am leaving for Brussels in two or three days, and this work is to be the subject of a public lecture. Now I have no copy. I should be most obliged if you would give it to the bearer of this letter.'[1]

Baudelaire was not in fact about to leave for Brussels. Although *Le Pays* had bought the work, he wanted to give it to *Le Figaro*, which had

already shown an interest in it. On 12 November he wrote to his old
antagonist Gustave Bourdin, son-in-law of Jean-Hippolyte de Villemessant, the owner and editor of the paper.

> Dear Sir, the day before yesterday I met M. de Villemessant, who told
> me that he was printing *Le Peintre de la modernité* [*sic*].
>   I am anxious to have as much printed matter as possible, and as soon
> as possible, so that I can re-read it properly, at leisure . . .²

His dishonesty was palpable.

Despite such expedients, his poverty and his debts remained. He had
owed substantial sums to Arondel for some twenty years. On 12
November, Raymond Matigny, a businessman, assured Arondel that
he had a friend who had known Baudelaire since his college days.
Matigny (who has no other claim to remembrance) told Arondel that
this friend undertook to compel Baudelaire to pay his debts. Soon
afterwards, Matigny and the unidentified friend called on Baudelaire
in the rue d'Amsterdam.

In the meanwhile, no doubt under pressure from the Émons, Mme
Aupick asked her son if he were keeping for her some of the 2,000
francs he received from Lévy.

> My dear mother [came the answer],
>   . . . You have no reproach to make to me about M. Lévy's 2,000 francs.
> I shan't touch even 20 francs of them. Lévy has undertaken to divide the
> money among some of my creditors, when he has the last page of his fifth
> volume, and I am in the process of finishing it.
>   The fourth [*Eureka*] has appeared, I think; but I haven't time to go out
> to concern myself with the distribution.
>   I shall send you a copy – just to prove to you that this terrible book is
> finished; for I doubt whether you can read two pages of it without going to
> sleep. I doubt whether there are ten people in France who can appreciate it.
>   M. Émon is mistaken; I certainly hope that I shan't stay in Brussels for
> more than six weeks (even that is a long time). I shall leave at the
> beginning of December . . .
>   I think that no good at all can come from my journey. I believe that
> I'm well paid for my lectures. But you know that my journey has another
> purpose: that is to say to sell *three* volumes of criticism to the firm which
> bought *Les Misérables*; now, everyone tells me that these people are stupid,
> and that they're very mean. It might be that I should be obliged to sell
> the books in Paris, when I come back, and rather miserably. But *the money
> from the lectures is not to be dismissed* . . .
>   The pieces I am sending you will form part of the three volumes in
> question.
>   The *Delacroix* [the study from *L'Opinion nationale*] has aroused a great
> deal of anger and approval. I am used to that.
>   I attach a certain importance to [*Le Peintre de la vie moderne*].³

So did the editor of *Le Pays*, who had paid Baudelaire for the work, and had recently returned the manuscript to him. On 30 November, after the second instalment had appeared in *Le Figaro*, he sent him a letter of justified reproach.

Baudelaire made no apology, but offered him another manuscript.[4] On 3 December, the third and final piece on Constantin Guys appeared in *Le Figaro*.

It was in about 1859 that Baudelaire had become friends with 'a very strange man', 'a fantastic character', the draughtsman of *The Illustrated London News*, who had recently settled in Paris.[5] Constantin Guys, a Frenchman, had been born in Holland. He was sixteen years older than Baudelaire, who called him 'old Guys', but he was to survive Baudelaire by twenty-five years. He was indeed an original man, unusual for his time: he was cosmopolitan, he spoke several languages, he had travelled widely, and he was retiring to a quite extraordinary degree. A journalist by profession, he had a horror of personal publicity; and when Baudelaire, enthralled by his drawings, expressed the wish to write about them, Guys was as angry as if it had been a betrayal, and almost broke with him. However, Baudelaire persisted, and finally obtained his consent, on condition that Guys was not named.

In *Le Peintre de la vie moderne*, he was the first critic to declare Constantin Guys – or 'M.G.', as he called him – a great artist: great in expression and significance, and in comprehension of life. Baudelaire's appreciation remains an exemplar of art criticism. He is in sympathy with the man, he understands his intentions and his methods, he has, as it were, watched him drawing and painting, and – so it seems – he has studied in depth the whole corpus of his work. In Baudelaire's essay on Guys one senses not only his sympathy but his absolute, all-embracing understanding.

Gaëtan Picon was later to express surprise that Baudelaire devoted so significant a study to an artist of secondary importance. The title of the essay – *Le Peintre de la vie moderne* – suggested, so he wrote, that Baudelaire had largely chosen Guys in order to set down his personal aesthetic of modernity. This essay was, said Picon, linked to the theory which Baudelaire had proclaimed in his *Salon de 1845*: 'The artist, the true artist, will be the one who can extract what is epic from modern life.' It was the theory which he had proclaimed again in his second *Salon*: 'Parisian life is rich in wondrous and poetic themes...'[6] Guys illustrated the wonder and the poetry of modern life which, since the age of twenty-four, Baudelaire had urged artists to express.

One may doubt if Baudelaire had consciously chosen Guys as a pretext to express his personal creed; but it is not surprising that he should discuss him with such sympathy. Guys, like himself, was concerned with the contemporary, with metropolitan life in the days of the Second Empire. The sepias of Guys seemed the illustration of the poet's Paris, the fascinating décor of the age. Baudelaire's poem, 'À une passante', has been called a Guys; and the unknown woman it recalls, the *demi-mondaine* seen in a Paris street, was no doubt caught on paper, recognisably, by the artist who set down the essentials of the Parisian scene. Guys caught not only the *demi-monde*, but the prostitute and the amazon whom Baudelaire celebrated in his poetry. These incarnations of vice were beautiful but corrupt; they touched Baudelaire the dandy and Baudelaire the coenobite, who saw woman as the instrument of the Fall.

In his pictures of the Crimean War, indeed in his roughest sketches, Guys caught not only the atmosphere of Balaclava and Inkerman, but the contrast between East and West, between the patrician and the plebeian, he caught the violence and the grief of conflict. Yet, more important to Baudelaire, he also understood the pomp of the Imperial Court in Paris; he understood the aristocratic soul of the dandy, whose reticence and elegance were a protest against vulgar society. Baudelaire's eulogy of the dandy in Guys is a personal apologia. For Guys the dandy was – like himself – an idealist in love with distinction, and not so far removed from the stoic. The dandy was the last hero possible in an egalitarian age. Above all, Guys appreciated that beauty was both eternal and contemporary, that it was sure to change with passing time, and that his task was to record, sharply and swiftly, the reality of the age in which he lived. Guys, in fact, gave Baudelaire the opportunity to discourse on long-held theories, to transcend what might have been a mere commentary on a chronicler of the contemporary scene. Guys may not have been as great as Baudelaire insisted; but rarely can a critic have been so much in sympathy with an artist. Baudelaire wrote of Guys with an energy, a comprehension and a brilliance which still astonish us. His portrait of Guys the artist, drunk with the visual splendours of Paris, is in itself a prose poem. With Guys, as with Edgar Allan Poe, he felt an instant fraternity. His relationship with Guys himself was not, it seems, to outlast the writing of this article; but there are an intellectual vigour, a self-assurance, a profound conviction in this work which contrast to a singular degree with the tone of Baudelaire's correspondence. Here is Baudelaire as he might always have been, had *le guignon* not been against him. *Le Peintre de la vie moderne* would, alone, have marked him as an outstanding critic of art.

101

On 3 December, the day that the last instalment of *Le Peintre de la vie moderne* appeared in *Le Figaro*, Raymond Matigny told Arondel that he had seen Baudelaire, who had seen Ancelle. Baudelaire had insisted to Ancelle that his debt to Arondel must be paid. Ancelle was to consult Mme Aupick.[1] Other creditors were also growing impatient. On 7 December, the bailiffs arrived at the hôtel de Dieppe, and seized some of Baudclaire's few belongings.[2] Time and again, in Baudelaire's life, one notices a pitiful contrast between the squalor of his existence, the distinction of the man and of his work. While the bailiffs descended on the hôtel de Dieppe, Dr Henri Cazalis, the physician and poet, reported to Mallarmé: 'I dined the other evening with Baudelaire ... I found myself in the presence of a man who was infinitely gentle, gentle as a priest or a child: with a look and a voice which charmed me, full of suavity.'[3]

On 10 December, three unpublished prose poems appeared in the *Revue Nationale et Étrangère*. That day, *Le Monde illustré* announced that Baudelaire, their contributor, had just published *Eureka*. It was, explained *La Petite Revue*, 'a purely scientific work whose laborious statements are beyond all their readers ... We needed the meditative and devoted patience of M. Baudelaire to give us this new translation of the remarkable author whom he has made known in France.'[4] *Eureka* was unlikely to bring its translator a fortune.

However, the Brussels publishers, Lacroix and Verboeckhoven, had recently published *Les Misérables* on terms so generous that they astonished French men of letters; and Baudelaire had taken it into his head to sell them *Les Paradis artificiels* and the two volumes which he foresaw for *Réflexions sur quelques-uns de mes contemporains*. On 17 December, once again forgetting his dislike of the man and his ambivalent feelings about his work, he boldly asked Victor Hugo to support him.

Monsieur,
    Although I always hesitate to ask anything whatever from the people for whom I have the most affection and esteem, I am writing today to ask you a *great* favour, an *enormous* favour. Dissatisfied with Parisian publishers, and thinking, not without reason, that they do not do me absolute justice, I have decided to go and look for a publisher abroad, for three volumes – one of these is *Les Paradis artificiels*, and the other two are *Les Réflexions sur mes contemporains* (fine arts and literature). I have decided to draw attention sharply to these works, by giving some public lectures in Brussels, with some well chosen extracts ...
    Now I hear that M. Lacroix is going to pay you a visit. The great favour would be to tell him anything agreeable which you may think about my

work and about myself, and to inform him of my intention with regard
to the lectures . . .

Goodbye, Monsieur; rest assured always of my affection and my
admiration. You are a mighty lord; but you have, as you see, all the
disadvantages of sovereignty. Everyone has something to ask of you.[5]

Hugo's answer has not survived; but on 22 December he asked
Meurice to forward it. 'They tell me,' he added, 'that [Baudelaire] is
almost hostile to me. However, I will do him the favour that he asks
of me.'[6] It is not clear whether he intervened.

.

102

Early in January 1864, Matigny informed Ancelle that he was tired of
Baudelaire's promises, and that he intended to sue him. Matigny had
protested two bills of 14,900 francs each. He urged Arondel to send
him every letter that Ancelle might write to him on the subject, and
promised that he would force Ancelle to pay. Matigny then informed
Baudelaire that he would be sued for his debts to Arondel. 'Monsieur,'
answered Baudelaire, 'the surest way to get something from me is to
leave me all the necessary *time* and *especially the peace* to act as I choose.'[1]

The poet who found himself obliged to write such a letter was
increasingly aware of his literary achievement. That month, the *Revue
nouvelle* discussed the fashionable series of public lectures which were
bring held in the rue de la Paix. 'Today, thanks to his translator, Ch.
Baudelaire, Poe is popular in France, and *The Gold Bug* . . . and a score
of other curious tales are sufficiently well known for the idea developed
by Félix Foucon, at the evening in the rue de la Paix, to be easily
understood.'[2]

In the early weeks of 1864, Baudelaire had further occasion to be
recalled by the literary public. On 7 February, *Le Figaro* published four
of his prose poems. They were introduced, unexpectedly, by Gustave
Bourdin, who had shown such malice towards *Les Fleurs du mal*. He had
since changed his opinion, or perhaps his loyalties. He now published
a study, doubtless inspired by Baudelaire, of *Le Spleen de Paris*. It was
the title that Baudelaire had chosen for his *petits poèmes en prose*. It
was the first time that this title had appeared in print.

On 14 February, *Le Figaro* published two more prose poems, with the
announcement 'to be continued'. No further poems appeared.

Quite simply, my poems bored everyone [Baudelaire explained to his mother on 3 March]. The editors of the paper told me so. That is why they have been discontinued.

I have fallen into a hideous lethargy. Not only am I late with books, and with articles of every kind (promised and paid for), but I am overwhelmed by urgent affairs, three of them in Belgium. On the other hand, I suffer excessively from never seeing you. I am going to try to restore my willpower, consider what is most urgent, and get hold of a little money from two or three sources, so that I can come and spend a few days with you. Then finally I shall make for Brussels, where new vexations may await me, but perhaps a good deal of money, too.

If only I could stay in Honfleur from the 10th to the 12th, it would do me so much good.[3]

He was constantly raising his mother's hopes only to dash them. The next precisely dated letter in his correspondence was written on 22 March. There is no record that, in the interval, Baudelaire paid a visit to Honfleur.

In Paris, he was concerned with art. Late in February, it seems, he attended the sale of Delacroix's paintings and drawings, which fetched 360,000 francs. Alfred Stevens observed to him that the spirit of Delacroix must be consoled for forty years' injustice. Baudelaire replied that Delacroix would only be confirmed in his contempt for human nature. Three months earlier, he himself had received 2,000 francs for the rights in his translations of Poe. Such inequality could not pass unnoticed.[4]

Yet Baudelaire was not concerned exclusively with the past. In March, in a letter to Philippe de Chennevières, who was organising the Salon, he recommended two of his friends, Manet and Fantin-Latour. Fantin was submitting two paintings: *Tannhäuser au Vénusberg* and *Hommage à feu Eugène Delacroix*. 'Do your utmost', urged Baudelaire, 'to see that they are well hung.'[5] *Hommage à feu Eugène Delacroix* was accepted for the Salon; it showed a number of the artist's admirers grouped round his portrait. They included Whistler, Manet, Fantin, brush in hand, and Baudelaire. Years later, when Baudelaire had died, Fantin thought of painting a sequel. He would show a number of poets assembled in homage to the author of *Les Fleurs du mal*. After a quarrel between two of his sitters, he was obliged to abandon his plan. *Coin de Table* had no connection with Baudelaire; it was exhibited in the Salon of 1872.[6]

The spring of 1864 was not to be entirely serene. On 11 April, a number of friends and admirers of Victor Hugo decided to organise a Shakespeare Banquet. This was ostensibly to mark the tercentenary of Shakespeare's birth. Since the anniversary was to fall on 23 April, less than a fortnight later, the enterprise seemed somewhat ill-conceived; but it was patently to be not so much a tribute to Shakespeare as a tribute to Victor Hugo, who chose to remain in political exile. Hugo, who knew not a word of English, was about to publish his *William Shakespeare* – and he was asked to preside, at least in spirit, over the banquet.[7]

Baudelaire wrote an open letter to *Le Figaro*. It appeared, unsigned, on 14 April. He protested against the committee's commercial intentions. The real reason for this celebration was, he insisted, 'to prepare and further the success of V. Hugo's book on Shakespeare, a book which, like all his books, full of beauties and absurdities, may once again distress his most genuine admirers.'[8]

It was a sharp attack on Hugo, 'in whom, by some impenetrable spirit of mystification, God has combined stupidity and genius.'[9] It may well have been justified, but it was unwise. In literary circles in Paris, its author's identity was soon discovered. Once again, Baudelaire had needlessly damaged his own interests; consciously or not, he had sabotaged his own enterprise. On the eve of his departure for Brussels, he had angered Hugo's publisher, Lacroix, whom he was so anxious to cultivate, and he had ensured his lasting enmity. He himself believed that his authorship was known to those of the Hugo family who were in Brussels, and that they later tried to discredit him.[10] When he and Hugo met in Brussels in 1863, there were to be reservations on both sides.

As for Baudelaire's Belgian enterprise, it seemed already to be doomed to failure. Malassis had not reached agreement with Vervoort about the fee for Baudelaire's lectures, and Baudelaire asked Arthur Stevens to settle matters once and for all. He accepted Stevens' decision in advance. 'My body and my willpower are failing,' he continued. 'I need a change of surroundings. I mean to work like a Devil in Brussels. I mean to finish my *Spleen de Paris* there, and my *Contemporains*. If it is too late to give my ten or twelve lectures in Brussels, I shall go to Antwerp afterwards. I'm told that the lecture season lasts longer, there.'[11]

'I must do something new,' he wrote in his *Journaux intimes*. '[I must] leave Paris, where I am dying.'[12] At five o'clock in the evening on Sunday, 24 April, Baudelaire left from the Gare du Nord for Brussels.

PART FIVE

The Exile

1864–1866

103

At eleven o'clock that night his train arrived at the Gare du Midi where, perhaps, Arthur Stevens was waiting for him. Possibly Baudelaire spent the first three nights with Stevens in the rue du Musée. The register of foreign visitors records that he arrived at the hôtel du Grand Miroir three days later.

The hôtel du Grand Miroir, 28, rue de la Montagne, took its unusual name from its first proprietor, Englebert de Speculo, in 1286. It was an ancient hotel, now somewhat dilapidated, but the clientele were almost exclusively French, and largely Parisian, and they included a number of men of letters – among them, on occasion, Victor Hugo. It was owned by a Parisian, Lepage, and his hardheaded wife, who came from Picardy.[1]

Baudelaire asked for a big room in which he could stretch his legs, with a big table on which he could work. He was given room 39, on the second floor, looking over the courtyard. It was a seedy room, with seedy furniture. He was doubtless disappointed, but he was accustomed to discomfort.

A Belgian friend recorded him, this year, for posterity. Charles Neyt photographed him holding a half-smoked cigar. Baudelaire's shirt and handkerchief are immaculately white, he wears his coat with style, he has combed his long and greying hair; and yet Neyt's photograph suggests a priest rather than a dandy, a priest who knows and suffers from all the sins of the world. Arthur Symons wrote: 'It is always the soul which cries out from those insatiable eyes.'[2] André Suarès went further. In *Trois grands vivants* he declared that Baudelaire 'was the fallen angel, and he had his face.'[3]

In the last nine years, since Nadar had recorded his youthful elegance, Baudelaire had grown immeasurably old. He was forty-three; but, in this photograph, he seems a man of another generation. A second photograph by Neyt shows the same fierce gaze; a copy of it was inscribed 'to my friend Auguste Malassis, the only person whose laughter lightened my sadness in Belgium.'[4]

Baudelaire's lecture on Delacroix, originally planned for 30 April, was postponed until 2 May. He invited Albert Lacroix and Gustave Frédérix to attend it. The publisher was in Paris, but Frédérix came. The literary critic on *L'Indépendance belge*, he had recently written an obituary of Delacroix which Baudelaire had read with interest. He was also one of the earliest admirers of Wagner.

On the evening of 2 May, at the Cercle artistique, Baudelaire gave the first of his lectures. It was, indeed, the first time that he had spoken in public. His opening words assured him of the goodwill of his audience: an audience which was inquisitive rather than intellectual. 'Gentlemen, I have long wanted to come here, and to make your acquaintance. I felt instinctively that I should be well received.'[5] Baudelaire praised 'the sense of wellbeing' which he professed to have found in Brussels, 'this kind of beatitude, fostered by an atmosphere of friendliness to which we French are scarcely accustomed, especially those whom, like myself, France has never treated as favourite sons.'[6] He recalled the death of Delacroix, and the sale of his paintings; he then read his study of Delacroix, which had appeared in *L'Opinion nationale.*

The account which Frédérix published in *L'Indépendance belge* on 4 May, attests 'the very lively and very justified success' which Baudelaire enjoyed for his first lecture.[7] A few days later, another account confirmed this impression. 'Everyone went away very happy with their evening.'[8] As the critic wrote: 'M. Baudelaire is not an orator in the accepted sense of the word; he does not have the manner or the voice. He is very nervous, and the audience finds it rather tiring to follow him. But he has the tact not to aim at oratorical effects, and he succeeds all the better for that. It is said that he will give one more lecture before his departure.'[9]

Baudelaire was to give five more, in less agreeable conditions; but, if the first was not a triumph, it was at least encouraging.

After this lecture, he spent two days at Stalle-sous-Uccle, just south of Brussels. It is not clear whether he stayed with Mme Joseph Stevens or with Mme Collart, who was a friend of the Stevens family. Both the Stevens and the Collarts had country houses there. Léopold Collart was a rich industralist, and his wife was interested in French culture. Whoever his hosts were on this occasion, Baudelaire's visit to Stalle-sous-Uccle was not to be his last.

When he returned to Brussels on the evening of 5 May, he found a letter from his mother. Considering the favourable reception of his lecture, he answered with unexpected disenchantment.

> Here is a note which has appeared about my first lecture. They say here that it was a huge success. But, between ourselves, everything is going very badly. There is great avarice here, an infinite slowness in everything, a vast mass of empty heads; in a word, all these people are more stupid than the French.

No credit, no credit whatever; which perhaps is very fortunate for me.

I am giving another lecture next Wednesday. Since the winter funds of the Cercle were exhausted, so they told me, I have accepted a fee of 50 francs a lecture (instead of 200 or 100). Unfortunately Lacroix was in Paris. I have just *requested* the right to give *three other lectures free* when he is back, but I am not telling anyone.

I have also got them to write to the Cercles in Antwerp, Bruges, Liège and Ghent, to inform them of my presence here. The answers haven't come yet . . .

The lectures in the provinces will be for 80 francs and 100 francs.

I shall achieve all my aims, or at least I shall do all I have to do. I want to have nothing with which to reproach myself . . .

I accept your offer of 50 francs, because there is a distrust here which only allows one to live if one pays cash . . .

I love you with all my heart, and [I love you] all the more since I know how much I make you suffer.[10]

He knew that his own aggressive, demanding behaviour, his desperate life, his frequent inability to work, were the main causes of her suffering. He deliberately made her suffer. It was part of his revenge for the past, it was a means of proving his importance to her. As a boy, he had tried to make her weep; as a man of forty-three he had not changed. He heaped his constant miseries upon her. Yet, as he said, he still loved her to capacity; she was all his past, and the only real love of his life.

Baudelaire had not yet been in Brussels for a fortnight, and he had been warmly welcomed by the Stevens and the Collarts; but his fundamental impression had already been formed. He had thought that he was leaving France; he had found it again, only worse, in Belgium. It was a country to which his hate would henceforth attach him.

He was soon to learn that there would be no provincial lecture tour. The Société d'émulation in Liège had closed its list of speakers; the Cercle d'Anvers was rebuilding its premises. On 11 May he invited Mme Collart, Eugène Verboeckhoven and Albert Lacroix to his second lecture in Brussels. He chose to send these invitations on the very day of the lecture. Once again, it was as if he courted disaster.

His lecture on Théophile Gautier, like the previous lecture, was a reading of a published work: in this case the booklet on Gautier of 1859. May is not the best month for lectures, especially if the weather is fine. The audience was smaller than it had been before, but Nadar maintained that it included some Belgian girls of good family.[11] This was not a trivial observation, for it is said that Baudelaire began with the words: 'It was in your presence, at my first lecture, that I lost what might be called the virginity of speech. This is, incidentally, no more to be regretted than . . . the other.'[12] If the words were not apocryphal, then Baudelaire had already begun to publish his contempt for Belgium; whether he was simply reckless, or whether – as so often before – he was intent on destroying his prospects, he alienated his public, and damaged his desperate hopes of literary and financial success. If Lacroix had accepted his invitation, he could hardly have been favourably impressed.

In their life of Baudelaire, Claude Pichois and Jean Ziegler maintain that the lecture was a failure.[13] The three other lectures, which Baudelaire had offered to give free, were also failures. They took place at the Cercle artistique on 18, 21 and 23 May; they consisted of long extracts from *Les Paradis artificiels*. At the end of the last lecture, he said: 'It remains for me, gentlemen, to thank you warmly for your generous hospitality and for the wonderful attention you have paid to these lectures, which were sometimes rather long.'[14] Charles Tardieu recalled that, at one of these lectures, 'as ill luck would have it, Baudelaire was overcome by terrible stage fright, shuddering and clattering his teeth, burying his face in his manuscript. It was a disaster.'[15] Malassis had attended all five of the lectures. He confessed to Asselineau that the last three had been tedious, and that the final lecture had been given to an audience of eight.[16]

Baudelaire maintained that he had expected 100 francs for each lecture. The Cercle artistique et littéraire sent him 100 francs for all five. It was not enough to pay his hotel bill. The money was accompanied by a letter to explain that the funds of the Cercle were exhausted, but that they would remember him kindly and make amends to him next year. Baudelaire had forgotten that he had offered to give the last three lectures free; he had hoped on these occasions to meet the publishers Lacroix and Verboeckhoven, and they had not even appeared.

His literary failure in Belgium, his aversion to Belgian life, and his constant penury conspired together to affect his health. He was ill, depressed, and in a state of nervous tension, in which unimportant questions assumed undue significance. On 11 June there came a letter from his mother, asking if he had forgotten her.

My dear mother, you aren't forgotten in the least [he answered], but you are a woman, you are nervous. And personally I have a horror of writing to you when I have only miserable things to tell you. Besides which, I am horribly preoccupied; I am weighed down with anxieties about the future, anxieties about Paris, *about a book* which is being printed *in my absence*, I only get the proofs of it *irregularly*; and finally, apart from all my tribulations, in the last six weeks I have constantly been ill, *physically* and at heart . . .

Besides, I think that my affairs are taking a turn which will make me stay rather longer than I had thought. I wanted to leave on the 20th; but I am obliged to earn my living, and I cannot cross Paris without distributing money. I have thought of making a book of my visit, divided into a series of letters which will no doubt appear in *Le Figaro*. Then I shall re-sell the book. There's courage for you! But I shall have to hurry to Antwerp, Ghent, Liège, Namur, Ourdenaarde and Bruges. I must see and question; and if you only knew what brutes I'm dealing with!

(Can you, once again, without turning your poor budget upside-down, send me a little money, 200 or 100 or even 50?)

Once we are together again, I want to do everything, everything possible, to improve my destiny, and *to save myself*; because *I don't want a conseil judiciaire* any more; I want to spend my life working, and giving you pleasure, and *I do not want to die in poverty*.

Now here is the account of my sad saga (sad so far), and you can judge if it has been my fault.

I came here for *a publisher*, to offer him the vol[umes] for five years, and to ask him for 20,000 francs for them, or for the biggest possible sum for each edition, supposing there were a series of editions.

The five lectures were given for him. He received five invitations, he didn't come . . .

However, I must settle things, and I want to stake my all on Monday, on a *lecture* which I have organized myself, at a stockbroker's, who is lending me his salon.[17]

The stockbroker was Prosper Crabbe, of 52, *bis*, rue Neuve: one of the twenty stockbrokers at the Brussels Bourse; he was also a serious collector of pictures. That day, Baudelaire invited Gustave Frédérix to the 'little literary soirée, of a purely private character', at nine o'clock on Monday, 13 June.[18]

On 17 June, he reported to his mother:

Fifteen people invited by me, of whom five came, the best – and of whom only two, the Minister and the editor of *L'Indépendance belge*, sent their apologies in writing – fifteen people invited by the master of the house, of whom five came. Can you imagine *three enormous salons*, lit by *chandeliers and candelabra*, adorned with magnificent pictures, an *absurd* profusion of cakes and wine; all that for ten or twelve *melancholy* people? . . .

There are Belgian intelligence and manners for you.

Seeing that I was boring everyone, I broke off my lecture, and I began to eat and drink. My five friends were ashamed and dismayed. I was the only one who was laughing . . .

I am in an unbearable state of nerves; but I think about the horrible future, and I want to put God and good fortune on my side.[19]

Lacroix had not come to this final lecture. Whatever Hugo had said to him in favour of Baudelaire, he was no doubt aware of the court case of *Les Fleurs du mal,* and of Baudelaire's reputation. He must have known that Baudelaire had condemned the Shakespeare Banquet in *Le Figaro.* He must have thought that Baudelaire was strangely naive to persist with his approaches and invitations. However, on 16 June Baudelaire had a meeting with his partner Verboeckhoven, and offered him three volumes of his works. In the publishers' offices he caught sight of Lacroix; he was so vexed by Lacroix' dismissal of his six invitations, that he pretended not to recognise him. Although he saw Verboeckhoven, he remained convinced that he would need the goodwill of Lacroix, who was patently the senior partner.

On 23 June he learned that Lacroix had rejected his suggestion. Verboeckhoven asked him for a novel. 'What hypocrisy!' said Baudelaire. 'He knows that I don't have one.'[20]

When Asselineau later suggested that Lacroix might publish the complete works of Baudelaire, Malassis replied:

> It is important that you should know about the relationship between Baudelaire and Lacroix, before you decide who shall publish the works.
>
> Baudelaire came to Brussels with the idea of compensating Hetzel and me, and of reaching an agreement with Lacroix.
>
> He gave *lectures* for *Lacroix.*
>
> He personally invited Lacroix to come and hear him.
>
> Lacroix did not come.
>
> Crabbe, a stockbroker and a friend of Stevens, gave a soirée with the sole purpose of bringing Baudelaire and Lacroix together. Lacroix did not deign to appear. He never wanted to meet Baudelaire in any circumstances, and he always behaved to him in the most stupidly offensive manner. Baudelaire had a horror of him, and he had good reason for it.[21]

104

'My dear Ancelle [this from Baudelaire on 14 July], everything has failed . . . I have been ill (continual diarrhoea, palpitations of the heart, violent stomach pains) for *two and a half months!* What a delightful visit! But I want it to be some use to me, and I'm writing a book on Belgium.'[1] He asked Ancelle to send him the 150 francs which were due to him for August. He would, he said, divide the sum between himself and his hotel, he would keep just enough to visit five Belgian cities; as soon as the money came, he would set out. The lectures had been a failure, agreement with Lacroix had proved impossible, Belgium was indifferent to literature, but something might still be salvaged from the Belgian expedition. This 'little book on Belgium' would, he told Noël Parfait, 'be quite unlike anything which has been done on the same subject.'[2] It was indeed to be different; for Baudelaire was affected, now, not only by his disappointments and his failed ambitions, his literary problems and his poverty, he was also affected by illness. The hatred of Belgium which he had begun to express was a kind of mania which was caused by the progress of his syphilis, and perhaps by the effect of years of laudanum, years of rough living and constant stress, on his frail constitution. It was not merely Belgium which was now in question: the same rage would have driven him wherever he had been.

His existence in Brussels was unendurable: it was and was not life. His financial needs had grown so desperate that he was obliged to pawn some of his few personal belongings. His only hope of earning money from his Belgian visit seemed to be by writing his book. He was kept in Belgium by his poverty, by the need to salvage something from the expedition, and by the fear of his Parisian creditors. At times he felt that the only place where he might find serenity was the little house on the clifftop on the Côte de Grâce.

> I need to stay another month in Belgium before I settle in Honfleur [so he told his mother on 31 July]. I have begun this wretched book, and I must finish it. I have taken all my notes on Brussels; five chapters are sketched out; but I must hurry to the provinces. A fortnight will be enough. Liège, Ghent, Namur, Antwerp, Malines, and especially Bruges, will be a relaxation for me. I have calculated that I shan't spend much on the journey; 150 francs will be enough. The railways are expensive, but the distances are short.
>
> I am obliged to call upon your kindness yet again, if the thing is at all possible (because with you I am always in the position of a shameful child). I shall do *what I can* to bring you back part of the money for the *letters* [on Belgium] in September . . .
>
> To go to Paris frightens me, and yet that is the bravest and perhaps the safest thing. I write so many letters which remain unanswered. If you only knew what anger one feels when one is completely isolated, locked up in hostile surroundings, without conversation, without any possible pleasure, and when none of the people you need will answer you! . . .[3]

His mother sent him 50 francs at once, by registered post.

> Those fifty francs had an infinite grace [he told her], and they deeply touched me . . .
>
> How I long to be in my room! And to see all my scrawled-on papers, and all my engravings! But sometimes I become so sad, that I imagine

that I shall never see Honfleur again. Don't go and take this as an omen. These are ideas which come to me only in moments of depression . . .

I embrace you not only as my mother, but as the only person who loves me.[4]

He felt deprived of a tenderness and a normality for which he thirsted, while he vituperated about them.

Mme Aupick was moved by his affection, by his anxiety to work, by his depression and ill-health, and by his abstemious way of life. He was spending, at most, seven francs a day, for, though he was drinking wine, he was scarcely eating. He had not asked her for more money, but she sent him more, immediately.

But, my dear mother [he confessed], it is *more than I expected*. There will now be enough for the three things (some money for the hotel, a visit to Paris, and a sum on account for Arondel). Thank you a thousand times.

It is very easy for you to talk about a diet. Everything is bad, except the wine. The *bread* is bad. The meat is not bad in itself. It becomes bad because of the way it is cooked. People who live at home don't live so badly. But the hotel, the restaurant and the English tavern are all bad. I should, however, tell you that, in my present state of disgust, I find everything even worse.

Malassis has taught his cook a little cooking. If I didn't live so far from him, I really think I should pay him for his board, so that I could eat at his house.

I am going to begin some cold enemas with laudanum.

What is unbearable about these complaints in the stomach and intestines, is the physical weakness and the depression that they bring with them.[5]

A few days later, Baudelaire visited Malines. He was delighted by the tranquillity, the bell-towers and the carillons, and with a certain wine from the Moselle, which left him with a vague recollection of musk and honey.[6] He would willingly have lived there. He bought some old Delft crockery: two fan-shaped bouquet-holders which his mother later treasured at Honfleur.[7]

It was, it seems, in Belgium that Baudelaire had met the artist and engraver Félicien Rops:[8] 'the Baudelaire of the graving-tool', as Claretie was one day to call him.[9] The two men were no doubt introduced to each other by Malassis, whose books Rops was to illustrate. Malassis found Rops almost charming enough for the ultimate honour of being French. 'The truth is', he decided, 'that Rops was born in Belgium by accident.'[10] Rops had, in fact, been born in Namur in 1833.

Despite the unfortunate accident of his Belgian birth, he was in sympathy with Baudelaire.[11] It was hard to come close to a man who mistrusted almost everyone he saw, and Rops – twelve years his junior – had no illusions of intimacy. 'I was, I think, not a friend,' he wrote, 'but I was the most faithful and the most respectful companion.'[12] Nonetheless, their sympathy must have been immediate, because, in May, Baudelaire had spent a week with Rops in Namur. For all his bitter comments on women and on domesticity, he was not averse to the comforts of family life. Rops was living, now, with his wife Charlotte and his mother, in his childhood home, 13, rue Neuve: the imposing *hôtel privé* built for his father. Rops's father-in-law, Théodore Polet de Faveaux, vice-president of the court of Namur, was at once stern and gentle. He delighted Baudelaire by quoting Horace and *Les Fleurs du mal*. He was, noted his visitor, 'the only Belgian who knew Latin and could talk French.'[13] What most impressed Baudelaire in Namur were the three baroque churches: the cathedral of Saint-Aubin, Les Récollets, and, above all, Saint-Loup: '*Saint-Loup*: a sinister and elegant marvel . . . An interior like a catafalque embroidered with *black* and *pink* and *silver* . . . *Saint-Loup* is a terrible and delectable catafalque.'[14] It was not to be the only time that he would see it.

Now, in August 1864, he had visited Malines; he also went to Antwerp, which delighted him after the provincial tone of Brussels. 'At last, a city with the air of a capital!'[15] The domestic architecture reminded him of the architecture of Cape Town, which he had seen twenty-three years earlier. He admired the sixteenth-century pink marble Hôtel de Ville. He was elated by the port, and by the majestic river Scheldt. 'In Antwerp you can breathe at last.'[16]

It was, perhaps, this month that he went to Bruges. He found it a phantom city, with a medieval air, a feeling of death.[17]

Now, at the end of August, he was working on his book on Belgium; but he was still in acute financial straits. Arondel announced that he had borrowed a massive sum, 24,000 francs, from Matigny on a promissory note from Baudelaire. Matigny had asked for money from Ancelle. Baudelaire wrote to Arondel that he had been completely deceived about his Belgian prospects, and that he would have to make a series of payments, quarterly, perhaps, to clear his debt, and to settle matters with Matigny. However, if Matigny threatened to sue him, he would finally elect to live in Belgium, if only to escape his letters and his longwinded speeches.[18]

Arondel had been waiting for twenty years and more. He had lent money to Baudelaire before the days of the *conseil judiciaire*, he had lent him money on the strength of stuffed crocodiles at the hôtel Pimodan, he had accepted countless promissory notes, accumulating constant interest. He knew that he had trapped Baudelaire, and that Baudelaire

could not free himself. Now, in 1864, he continued to wait for payment;
he continued to receive stubborn refusals to pay from Ancelle. On
Baudelaire's death he was to demand 14,000 francs; on the death of
Mme Aupick, Ancelle was to give him 1,500 francs in final settlement.[19]

Meanwhile, on 26 August 1864, from the hôtel du Grand Miroir in
Brussels, Baudelaire confessed to his mother:

> I am bored beyond anything you could imagine in this icy (and completely
> white) room, and though I am generally afraid of your letters, because I
> always fear to find sermons and reproaches in them (and I sermonize and
> reproach myself), I still wait impatiently for *these same letters* . . . Even the
> sight of your writing does me good. You know that I am going back to
> Paris on 1 or 2 September . . . To go back to Paris is, for me, going back
> to Hell, but I shall go.[20]

He had in fact hoped to leave for Paris on the morning of 31 August,
and to dine that evening with Ancelle; but, predictably, as the time
approached, he lacked the courage to set out.

> I want to drag out another fortnight of vegetable existence here [so he
> explained to the patient Ancelle]; and, in a word, I am singularly
> weakened by four months of the colic . . .
>   Seriously, I have a longing to return [to France]; but I must still see
> and work a little. And then my mother! And my garden! And my books,
> and my collections! . . .
>   If, by chance, I were still here on the 25th [of September], which is very
> doubtful, I should leave with Nadar, who has kindly offered me a place
> in the basket [of his balloon]. To escape these foul people by balloon, to
> go and drop in Austria, perhaps in Turkey: every lunacy pleases me,
> provided that it drives away my tedium.[21]

105

Nadar had not been content to be the pre-eminent French photographer of the century. In recent years he had earned new fame as an
aeronaut, and he had been invited to take part in the national
celebrations of the independence of Belgium. These celebrations
marked the four days in 1830 when Belgium had cast off the yoke of
the Netherlands. On 26 September, in his famous balloon, *Le Géant*,
Nadar was to make an ascent from Brussels. He arrived there with a
few friends and an assistant, Georges Barral. Barral, who was twenty-

two, was one of the secretaries of the Société de Locomotion aérienne, which Nadar had just founded in Paris. He was to make a small name for himself in the history of science. More than once, he was to record his *cinq journées avec Charles Baudelaire*; but his memoirs of these five days, 26–30 September 1864, were set down over forty years later, they varied from one version to another, and his memory was not reliable. It is with some reservations that one follows the final version, which was published by Maurice Kunel in 1932.[1]

On the morning of 26 September, said Barral, at Nadar's request, he fetched Baudelaire from his hotel, and took him to *déjeuner* at the Globe Tavern. Then they went to the Jardin botanique, from which the balloon was to make its ascent. *Le Géant* rose into the Belgian sky; it later came to earth between Ypres and the coast. Next day, according to Barral, the aeronauts returned to Brussels. Nadar's wife and son, Bérardi and Baudelaire went to meet them at the railway station. Barral had *déjeuner* with Baudelaire at his hotel. On 28 September, the two of them made an expedition to Waterloo, visited the battlefield, and had *déjeuner* at the hôtel des Colonnes where, three years earlier, Hugo had written the final pages of *Les Misérables*. Next day, with Barral, Baudelaire attended the banquet given by Nadar at the hôtel des Étrangers. Among the guests were Charles Hugo and Dumas *fils*. After dinner, the French guests visited the brothel in the rue Pachecho. Barral and Baudelaire went no further than the salon. On 30 September, Barral once again met Baudelaire, who walked with him round Brussels, and told him about his Academic visits. That evening, Barral left for Paris, full of recollections.

In the presence of Nadar, Baudelaire must have found a lively contrast with the soporific tedium of Brussels. Yet perhaps he found this Parisian interlude disturbing. Nadar himself observed that 'Baudelaire's escape to Belgium was extended and prolonged beyond what had been foreseen. In his tormented life, it would be explained by an unspoken need to escape himself. Two symptoms disturbed me when I met him again in Brussels: his increasing taste for solitude, . . . and an exasperation with the gentle and industrious country which perpetually intensified . . .'[2]

Yet Baudelaire had his Belgian friends. Among them were not only the Rops and Collart families, but the Stevens brothers, noted in the history of Belgian art. The youngest of the trinity, Arthur, had organised his lectures in Brussels, escorted him round the art collections, and introduced him to his brothers: Joseph, the animal painter, and Alfred, the *peintre de genre*. He also gave him financial help. Baudelaire did not merely accept such generosity, he appears to have demanded it. He so vexed him by his incessant comments on his velvet waistcoat, that Stevens gave it to him for the sake of peace.³ In Brussels, Baudelaire also knew the artists Louis Dubois and Edmond Lambrichs, and the photographers Louis Ghémar and Charles Neyt. It is to Neyt, as we have seen, that we owe two photographs of Baudelaire in these bitter years.

The bitterness is plain from the recollections which Camille Lemonnier – then a student – was later to record in *La Vie belge*.

> Henry de Groux, with a gift of strange divination, was, later, to fix it on canvas: that hermetic and hallucinated face, tight-lipped with scorn and irony. The countenance had the ruined beauty of the fallen angels of Burne-Jones. Some obsession, some unknown commerce with the powers of evil, visibly impressed a mystic, sombre stigma on the features . . .
>
> Baudelaire, affectedly, cultivated a taste for funereal and grotesque mystification, a taste which he had nurtured with Poe: it was like a poor performance of his Satanism. He exercised it like fencing, with the cold correctness and the fine subtlety of a skilful fencer. It seemed to clothe his sensibility with the envelope and the defence of a coat-of-mail.⁴

106

One of those in France to whom he turned with most gratitude was Ancelle. 'I thank you very warmly', he wrote, 'for all the affection you have always shown me, which I have sometimes repaid with a little bitterness.'¹ On 13 October 1864, he explained his long delay in answering Ancelle's letter. He had, he said, 'been ill again (but you mustn't write that to my mother, if indeed you do write to her). This time, it isn't the stomach any more, it's a fever which wakes me up at one or two o'clock in the morning, and doesn't let me go back to sleep until about seven.'² This nightly fever and insomnia left him exhausted throughout the day. He was not only exhausted, but increasingly in debt. He needed 979 francs to pay all his debts and expenses in Brussels. He needed to go back to France to get money; he needed money to go there, and to revisit Namur, Bruges and Antwerp. It was a vicious circle. If, when he returned to Paris, he found that his literary agent had sold four volumes of his work, he would, he said, be able to repay his mother or Ancelle.³

Ancelle, sympathetic and practical, sent Baudelaire 200 francs. Baudelaire gave 180 francs to Lepage, the proprietor of the hôtel du

Grand Miroir. Soon afterwards, again from Ancelle, he received a promise to pay for 600 francs. He would, he said, use it only in the last extremity. However, he still owed the hotel 547 francs. 'It is impossible to give the hotel anything whatever this morning [this to Ancelle, on 23 October]. I'm going to get rid of some small debts and the pawnbroker, and I shall still have 20 francs which I shall spend on running to Paris on 1 [November].'[4]

Once again, his intentions changed. He did not go to Paris. He postponed his visit to Honfleur. On 3 November, he confessed to his mother: 'I can only send you the affirmation of my wish to live with you. We have never been bored together, and I think that we shall be as happy as it is possible to be.'[5] By a kind of symbiosis, more or less unconsciously, Baudelaire had always lived with his mother. Now, as the real Honfleur became more and more unattainable, so the Honfleur of the mind strengthened its hold on his imagination. As time went on, he preferred the dream to the realization.

On 13 November, Baudelaire wrote once again to Ancelle. He asked him to send him 600 francs before the following Sunday. If he could have them by Sunday morning, he could pay his hotel bill, and be in Paris at nine o'clock that evening.[6]

> I cannot get over my surprise at so much money being squandered on this [Belgian] journey! It's unheard of [this from Mme Aupick to Ancelle, on 14 November]! I should accustom myself to this life, which is so bizarre, and beyond all received ideas, *I should resign myself.* But I cannot do so, because I cling stupidly, fiercely to the idea that, before I die, I absolutely must have a little satisfaction through him. And now it's becoming urgent, I'm getting very old and rather frail. He has very little time left, now, for the satisfaction of which I dream. I shall never have it. I might have consoled myself with great literary successes (he has the right stuff in him for that), but, there again, there are cruel disappointments (for Charles has adopted a style as absurd and bizarre as himself, one which brings him few admirers). It is true that he has *his originality* in his favour, which is something. He will never write anything trite. He will never borrow other people's ideas, he has such a wealth of his own. I must tell you that he would like to see us attach more importance to his literary affairs. He maintains that, although they are going slowly, even badly, they are still progressing a little.[7]

Ancelle himself was troubled by Mme Aupick's anxiety, by the endless demands of Baudelaire, and by the need to show sympathy and commonsense to mother and son. He could hardly now have believed in Baudelaire's intention to come to Paris, but once again he answered his request, and he sent him 600 francs. Once again, predictably, he was to be disappointed.

On 17 November, Malassis told Bracquemond:

> Baudelaire is well [*sic*]. He comes to dinner with me nearly every other
> day, and I had him again yesterday evening. Although he cannot exactly
> be enjoying himself in Brussels, and even, to be honest, though he is bored
> here most of the time, I find it difficult to foresee when he will be able to
> leave. I'm afraid that he may be stuck with his hotel, because of his
> habitual lack of foresight. He may be short for a long while of some
> hundreds of francs to pay the bill. That, unless I'm mistaken, is why he is
> prolonging his stay.[8]

It was also, perhaps, one of many reasons why he dined so often with
Malassis. Lemercier de Neuville, who was then in Brussels, recorded:
'When we weren't dining with Malassis, we used to spend the evening in
a tavern which he had adopted because of its sign: *Au Vieux Voleur bizarre.*
There we used to talk, while each of us drank a glass of beer, a small glass
of gin, and nibbled some nuts. Our combined bills came to 13 sous!'[9]
   Malassis himself was now attempting to restore his fortunes by
publishing pornographic works 'picked up from goodness knows where,
and often attributed to writers who had not committed them.'[10]
Resilient and daring as ever, he also published pamphlets against the
Second Empire. However, he still kept in touch with the literary world
in Paris. Until November 1866, he remained the editor-in-chief of *La
Petite Revue*, which his former colleague, Pincebourde, was publishing
in France.[11] He 'fed' it with works by Baudelaire; and it was *La Petite
Revue* which announced, on 17 December:

> M. Baudelaire has a big book in hand which he is to publish under the
> title of *Pauvre Belgique!*
>   He went into exile to advise against exile, he embraces Belgium in order
> to stifle it the better.
>   A friend of ours, who has been in Brussels, tells us that one is constantly
> meeting M. Baudelaire, always in the company of his old publisher,
> Malassis.[12]

Le Bibliophile ornais observed: 'They had been friends in France, they
became inseparable abroad.'[13] Malassis was all the closer to Baudelaire
as he had failed to make his ideal marriage. In 1863, in Brussels, he
had met Françoise Daum, but it was to be seven years before he
married her.[14]
   Now, in November 1864, in the kindness of his heart, Ancelle
appears to have sent yet more money to Brussels.

> Thank you [answered Baudelaire, on 18 November]. I feel ashamed as
> regards my mother. How happy I should be to bring her back some

money! In a few days, I shall know if this is possible . . .

In two days, I shall have no more debts in Brussels. I shall leave on Wednesday [23] (either at 9.30, if my fever allows me to get up very early, or at 2.30) – and so I shall be with you, either on *Wednesday, at 6 o'clock in the evening, or on Thursday morning, at 10 o'clock.* You can be sure of that.[15]

Ancelle could not be sure. Once again Baudelaire failed to appear. As he explained to the long-suffering lawyer: 'At the last moment, the moment of departure, . . . *a terror came over me, a blue funk,* the horror of seeing my hell again – of crossing Paris without being certain of making a liberal distribution of money, which would ensure me real peace at Honfleur.'[16]

107

The new year, 1865, began predictably, with more financial problems. Baudelaire had asked Ancelle to retrieve some drawings and a gold repeater watch which were still in pawn in Paris. He had also asked him for 100 francs, and sent him a signed receipt in advance; but he only learned on the evening of 1 January that the letter from Paris had arrived, and he did not get it until next day. He had felt the lack of money acutely.[1] He remained buried in his hotel. 'Short of an act of munificence from Madame Aupick,' Malassis confided to Asselineau, 'I don't see how he will get out of a situation which seems to me increasingly stretched.'[2]

On 3 January, Baudelaire sent his new year wishes to a friend in Paris, the engaging Mme Meurice. Éléonore Meurice, the wife of the dramatist Paul Meurice, was the daughter of Jean-Pierre Granger, who had been a pupil of David, and a fellow-pupil of Ingres at the École de Rome. Ingres had drawn the young girl's portrait on the eve of her marriage; and the pencil drawing – like the portrait painted of her later – reflects her grace and gravity, her inner life, her sense of independence. These qualities were evident, now, while she indulged in virtuous flirtation with Baudelaire; and Baudelaire responded with respect and affection. For all his professed misogyny – Nadar called it sexual nihilism[3] – an intimate friendship with an intelligent woman still remained a necessity to him.

Chère madame [he told Mme Meurice],

I should find it very disagreeable, indeed impossible, to allow a new year to begin without *wishing that it should be good and happy for you* . . .

Should I tell you how much I love you? Should I tell you how much I
wish you peace, prosperity, and those tranquil pleasures which are
necessary even to the most robust of souls?

Should I also tell you how often I have thought of you (every time I
obliged a Belgian to perform a passage from Wagner, every time that I
had to argue about French literature, every time that a new example arose
to prove this Belgian stupidity which you talked about so often to me)?

I have passed here for *a policeman (it serves me right!)* (thanks to that fine
article I wrote about the Shakespearean banquet), – and then for a *pederast*
(I spread that rumour myself; *and they believed me!*), and then I passed for
a proof-corrector, sent from Paris to correct the proofs of *infamous publications*.
As I was *exasperated that they always believed me*, I spread the rumour that I
had *killed* my father, and that *I had eaten him*; and also, that, if they had
let me escape from Paris, that was because of the services I did for the
French police, AND THEY BELIEVED ME! *I am immersed in dishonour like a
fish in water.*

Chère Madame, do not answer this. You would find it hard, for all your
wit, to answer such a letter. Forgive a mind which sometimes needs a
confidant, and has never ceased to think of your grace and kindness.[4]

Cher Monsieur [she replied at once], . . . it is not my *wit* which claims to
answer you, it is my usual simplicity and good nature . . .

What are you doing in Brussels? Nothing. You are dying of boredom
there, and, here, you are impatiently awaited. What is the thread which
holds you, then, attached by the wing, to this stupid Belgian cage? Just
tell us. The little group which misses you would ask no better than to cut
this thread, if it is possible. What is needed? Is it a job? We shall get you
one.[5]

Camille Mauclair was to write that French society had no need to
reproach itself for the destiny of Baudelaire.

Baudelaire flogged himself into making his existence, which, after all, was
rather ordinary, something exceptional, monstrous, solemnly complicated.
Even his stubbornness in staying in Brussels betrays his wish to imitate
Poe. He thought that there he would endure the torture of the isolation
of genius . . . But Poe, without resources, was as imprisoned in America
as Napoleon on St Helena. Baudelaire was a few hours from Paris, from
intellectual life, from friends who would not have left him in destitution.[6]

Baudelaire was not concerned with imitating Poe. He was sick in body
and in mind; he could not summon up the effort of will that he needed
if he was to write.

Paul Meurice was devoted to Hugo, the exile in Guernsey; he was,
with Auguste Vacquerie, his most faithful acolyte. Éléonore Meurice
shared Baudelaire's dislike of *le père Hugo* – or, as he called him

privately, 'that ass of genius.'[7] However, if Hugo still remained in Guernsey, it was impossible, now, in Brussels, to avoid his family. On 18 January, with her younger son, François-Victor, Mme Hugo had left to join her other son in Belgium. Henceforward, they were to spend their lives largely in Brussels. She hoped that, with time, she might create a second home there for her husband: a home where he would be closer to the great sweep of events.[8]

Almost at once, the Hugos began to assemble a French circle in Brussels. On 27 January, Baudelaire refused an invitation to call on them. 'No one', he told Charles Hugo, 'is more overwhelmed with work than idle people, when they have a sense of forgotten duty.'[9]

The excuse was not an empty one. That day he authorised Henry de La Madelène, the editor of the *Revue de Paris*, to publish the prose poems in his possession, and announced that he would send him more. La Madelène had owed him money since Christmas; he had confessed that he could not make any payment until 20 February. The *Revue de Paris* was in a critical condition (indeed, it was to disappear in March). 'It would really be deplorable', answered Baudelaire, 'if a review which everyone wants to see alive should die so soon. Anyway, publish those *Poèmes en prose* which remain with you; then I shall send you others, and on 20 February you will send me some money if you can.'[10] Baudelaire, in poverty, showed a patrician disregard for money, and affectionate loyalty to his friend. He also asked La Madelène to send certain translations from Poe to Louis Marcelin, the editor of *La Vie parisienne*; 'but I don't want Marcelin to see that I'm taking his review as a last resource, and that this packet comes from you.'[11] It was a pitiful note from a man who now earned the homage of the young Stéphane Mallarmé. On 1 February, in *L'Artiste*, in his *Symphonie littéraire*, Mallarmé sang his praise of 'the beloved *Fleurs du mal*.'[12]

Baudelaire lived, now, in increasing isolation. He suffered not only from the financial problems of his editors, but also from their silence. On 3 February, he wrote to his old friend Julien Lemer. Since his days as a journalist, Lemer had been a publisher and a literary agent, and now, at the age of fifty, he was a bookseller in Paris. He managed the Librairie centrale, 24, boulevard des Italiens; the shop stayed open so late that some called it the Librairie de minuit. Lemer himself had been described by the *Revue anecdotique* as 'a living advertisement, an itinerant puff, and also a man of wit and taste, and gastronome emeritus.'[13] Baudelaire asked him, directly, if he would be his literary agent in Paris.[14]

Baudelaire had been suffering from a feverish cold, which had made it impossible to think or to write; now, on 3 February, he dealt energetically with his correspondence. That day he also wrote to his mother. Once again Mme Aupick was depressed by her isolation, and once again she had thought of going to Paris.

> I know quite well what a horrible torture boredom is [he told her]. I consider myself as being in prison, or doing penance here. I hope to stop doing penance. I assure you that this Belgian prison is harder for me than your Honfleur prison is for you. You are in a pretty house, and you don't see *anyone*. As for me, I have no books, I am poorly lodged; I am deprived of money, I only see people whom I detest, boorish people who seem to have invented a special stupidity for themselves, and every morning I go, trembling, to the concierge, to see if there are any letters, if my friends are concerned with me, if my articles are appearing, if the negotiations for my books have been completed – and there's nothing, always nothing . . . I should give anything to clink glasses in a tavern in Le Havre or Honfleur with a sailor, even with a convict, provided that he was not Belgian. As for seeing, once again, that bright and cheerful little house where my mother, books and collections live, that is a joy of which I dare not dream . . .[15]

That day, Baudelaire also sent Mme Meurice a belated answer to her new year letter. He explained the delay by saying that he had often been ill, and that he was too inclined to abuse the indulgence of his friends.

> Why do I stay in Brussels – although I hate it? *In the first place, because I'm here*, and because in my present state I should be unhappy anywhere – and then because I am making myself do penance. I am making myself do penance, until I am cured of my vices (this is going very slowly), and also until a certain person, whom I have entrusted with my literary affairs in Paris, has decided certain matters.[16]

The question of penance was to recur, and it is fundamental to an understanding of Baudelaire. It underlines the essential Catholicism of his nature, the belief that man must be punished for his sins. Yet Baudelaire did more than re-affirm man's need for suffering, the need he had expressed in *Les Fleurs du mal*. He also confessed his own self-destructive nature. Repeatedly, throughout his life, he had created situations which he had known must be disastrous for him; he had sought both private and public humiliation. Perhaps this conduct had owed something to his religious creed; no doubt it had owed much to his intense relationship with his mother, and to the traumatic effect of her second marriage. He had deliberately sought to damage his own prospects, although he longed, with all his heart, for glory. Obscurely, perhaps unwittingly, he still had to take revenge on his mother, though he had always longed to make her proud of him. She, too, needed expiation. Suffering was God's remedy for human imperfections, and to refuse it to human beings was to reduce their chances of salvation. Baudelaire felt forced to complete his penance in Belgium, although he knew that it led to his destruction.

108

On about 7 February, his mother wrote to him. She was sorry, now, that seven years ago she had not given him a substantial sum to pay his debts; it would, she said, have let them have some happiness together at Honfleur. She mentioned the theory of bad luck – *le guignon* – which he later said he knew all too well.

Misfortune continued to follow him. His physical condition was now disturbing.

> I am writing to you in the respite allowed by one of my attacks [he told Ancelle on 8 February]. They are sometimes so violent, that this morning it took me more than an hour to decipher your letter . . .
>
> You congratulate me on my good health. For the past week, I have suffered diabolically. I have had both eyes blocked up, in turn, by a cold, neuralgia or rheumatism. I had begun, as you know, with four months of troubles with my stomach and intestines. In August and September, there was just a little light and warmth here. And then I was well. But for the last two months I have generally been seized by a fever at midnight. The long hours pass in continual shuddering and cold; finally, when morning comes, I go to sleep exhausted, having been unable to take advantage of my insomnia to write, and I wake up later, in a dreadful sweat, quite exhausted by my sleep. For the past week, especially, there has been an increase of pain. And you know that there is no possible courage, except passive courage, in pain. It is an absolute abdication of willpower.
>
> In these conditions, I beg you to allow me to abandon my plan of economy, at least for two months. I shall resume the execution of this project at Honfleur . . .
>
> As for the important affair, the sale of the *Paradis*, *Mes Contemporains*, and *Pauvre Belgique!*, I am waiting.
>
> I cannot suppose that my name is so insignificant and that my friends have so forgotten me that I cannot get at least 600 francs from the first printing of each volume, which would make 2,400. But my sufferings have interrupted my work, which was already very erratic. There are four chapters missing from the *Belgique*, and three from the *Contemporains* . . .
>
> I am suffering and I am bored. And yet, if I had a lot of money, *I should not leave. I am doing penance, and I shall do penance*, until the reasons for penance disappear. It is not only a question of books to be finished, and of books to be sold, which assure me several months of peace in France . . .

Do not delay, I beg you, not only because I need some money, but because your letters are a distraction for me. I do not stir from my room. And besides, where should I go, if I could go out?[1]

It was a desperate letter, and Baudelaire was increasingly desperate. It was some measure of his condition that he now confided completely in Ancelle, and that even a letter from his *conseil judiciaire* had come to be a welcome distraction. He was suffering from his penury and from the progress of his syphilis. He was suffering from his inability to work. Above all, he was suffering from the long, grim, needless penance which he resolutely imposed upon himself.

His concern for his work remained. On about 10 February he wrote to Manet, asking him to call on Lemer and Marcelin, with the aim of finding him a literary agent in Paris. It was a week since he himself had written to Lemer, and Lemer had still not answered him.

Have I chosen the right man [he asked his mother]? That is the great question. I have chosen someone who has long done this work for other men of letters, a man who is a publisher himself, and is not a very successful one. It is precisely because he is short of money that I chose him, hoping that he would see my literary destiny as a means of getting money for himself. (I am convinced − perhaps you will find my pride very great − that, however few works I leave, they will sell very well after my death. As for the author's rights, unless I go before you do, there won't be anyone to touch them. It will be a good affair for the publishers.)

I don't dream of fortune any more. I only dream of the payment of my debts, and of being able to do about twenty books which are frequently reprinted, and assure me a more or less regular income.[2]

He was aware, more than ever, of his true distinction, and, now, of his limited creative powers. He knew that his dream of producing twenty books could not be realized. He acknowledged his limitations with despair.

I don't know how many times you've talked to me about my *facility* [he continued, to his mother] . . . Facility in conception? Or facility in expression? I have never had either one or the other, and it must be as clear as noonday that the little that I have done is the result of very painful work.

From time to time I settle down again to my *Poèmes en prose*. I must finish with them. I know that the publishers won't reprint *Les Fleurs du mal* until after the *Poèmes en prose*. Books which are not reprinted are forgotten, and that's wasted money. But one needs a certain peace of mind to combine ideas and images and words. And I'm very far from having such peace . . .

I cannot describe what I have as a cold − and it has still not quite gone. I do not even dare to go down into the courtyard. It is a kind of acute rheumatism in the head, with attacks, and successive recurrences of pain.

Several times I have thought that I was free of it, and then, without apparent reason, there was a recurrence the next morning . . .

As for the fever, it has gone, thank God! But I beg you not to worry about these infirmities. Mere infirmities, which would vanish very fast, if I were happy.[3]

As usual, he wrote to his mother with disturbing frankness; he was deeply troubled by his state of health. He must have known that his 'mere infirmities' would not vanish with a change of mood or place. He could not reassure Mme Aupick, or indeed himself.

Next day, he wrote to thank Ancelle for sending him some money, Once again, although he chose to stay there, he lamented his life in Brussels. There was, he said, only one person whom he could see with pleasure, and that person (no doubt Malassis) lived in the remotest suburb. He still remained without news of his literary affairs in Paris, there was nothing that he could do, and he felt intensely frustrated.

Next day, in Paris, Manet went to see Lemer and Marcelin on behalf of Baudelaire. Mme Paul Meurice wrote to Baudelaire again; she reproached him, once again, for staying in Belgium. 'I should very much like', she wrote, 'not to regret you, and to be like Paris, which is beginning to reconcile itself to your absence; but no, I can't. I shall never forgive that great simpleton Stevens for sending you off to drink the beer of his native land.'[4]

In Belgium, Baudelaire laboured on. Once again he was ill.

This terrible wintry February played a dirty trick on me [this to his mother, on 9 March]. Even after I recovered, I still had a dull pain over my right eyebrow; but my impatience urges me on to activity.

Yes, I am going on with the *Poèmes en prose*, . . . but I am going on slowly, very slowly. The atmosphere of this country makes one dull, and then, you may have guessed, from reading the forty or fifty which have appeared, that the confection of these little trifles is the result of a great concentration of mind. However, I hope I shall succeed in producing a singular work . . .[5]

On 15 March, Michel Lévy announced the imminent publication of *Histoires grotesques et sérieuses*: the fifth volume of Poe in Baudelaire's translation. Baudelaire asked Lévy for three copies of the book for himself and one for his mother.[6] In a note sent with the copy intended for Sainte-Beuve, he told him, touchingly, that he and Malassis were reading *Joseph Delorme* after dinner. 'You were certainly right,' he told *l'oncle Beuve*, '*Joseph Delorme* is the *Fleurs du mal* of an earlier age. The comparison is glorious for me. You will be kind enough not to find it offensive for yourself.'[7]

On 27 March, in a dictated letter, Sainte-Beuve acknowledged his copy of the book.

My dear friend, my dear child,
      Thank you for your remembrance . . . You are right: my poetry was like your own; I had tasted the same bitter fruit, deep down full of ashes. Hence your very kind, very faithful sympathy for me. I return it to you, dear friend.[8]

There was no mention whatever of Poe, no question of a review; but Baudelaire was touched by the critic's profession of affection. 'When you call me *my dear child*,' he answered, 'you touch me and make me laugh at the same time. Despite my long white hair, I greatly need someone who is fond enough of me to call me their child . . .'[9] He was too distracted to post his letter. He was to find it some weeks later, and send it to Sainte-Beuve, with apologies for his thoughtlessness.

In March, remembering his professed admiration for Poe, he also asked Taine to write an article.[10] Taine, too, was ungenerous. He had, he said, received *Histoires grotesques et sérieuses*, and he had already read half of it with admiration. He added that his poor health and his many occupations prevented him from writing a review.[11] Others were less self-absorbed. Manet wrote to Baudelaire: 'My mouth watered at the thought of reading something new of yours.'[12] Early in May, he wrote again, regretting that Baudelaire had not yet come back to Paris; the poet's deliberate exile deprived him of both a friend and a defender.[13] Baudelaire answered with a rough letter which was calculated to arouse Manet's fighting spirit.[14]

109

His own pain and grief, his spiritual odyssey, were reflected, now, in his *Journaux intimes*. It is impossible to judge the exact date of his comments; one section is, however, written on the paper of the hôtel du Grand Miroir. Many of his reflections show his desperate wish to work, his increasing concern with his physical condition, his state of mind. 'To be cured of everything, of poverty, illness and melancholy, the one and only thing that is needed is a *Liking for Work*.'[1] And again: 'Too late, perhaps! – My mother and Jeanne. My health out of charity and duty! – Jeanne's illnesses. My mother's infirmities and solitude.'[2] On 27 February, according to Malassis, he had made a pen-and-ink drawing of Jeanne, sly and heavy-breasted. It was Jeanne as he remembered her, many years ago, but she still remained a predator. He could still entitle her portrait: 'Quærens quem devoret.'[3]

He tried, now, to forgive her: to think only of charity:

> Without charity, I am only a tinkling cymbal.
> My humiliations have been graces from God.
> Is my phase of egoism over?[4]

More and more he felt an imperious need for conventional morality, indeed for religion. Arthur Stevens was later to remember how Baudelaire had once proclaimed his faith. On 8 January, the feast-day of St Gudule, the patron saint of Brussels,

> ... he had taken his friend Baudelaire to the rue des Paroissiens, to see [the procession] pass by. It was just the dilettantism of an artist who was fascinated by folklore and by the picturesque ...
>
> The procession went past. Baudelaire was deeply moved at the sight of the innocent little girls who were dressed in white, and carried placards with the words of the litanies: 'Virgin most pure, pray for us.' The emancipated citizens chuckled. Then there came the bearers of candles, and the muttered insults increased. Pale with indignation [the account continued], the poet suddenly left Arthur Stevens, pushed his way through the crowd, and, noticing an old man who was carrying a candle and hobbling, bare-headed, in front of the Holy Sacrament, he gently took his candle from him and offered him his arm. At first, astonished and amazed, the old man created a certain difficulty; then, suddenly, understanding the gesture, he took Baudelaire's arm. And Baudelaire, very proud of his behaviour, walked away with the Catholic procession... And so the author of *Les Fleurs du mal* went round old Brussels with his old man and the candle, beside the baldachin which protected the *Corpus Christi* ...[5]

Meanwhile, in his *Journaux intimes*, Baudelaire recorded:

> I vow to myself henceforward to take the following rules as the eternal rules of my life:
>
> Every morning, say *my prayer to God, the fount of all strength and all justice, to my father, to Mariette and Poe*, as intercessors; pray to them to impart to me *the necessary strength* to accomplish all my duties, and to grant my mother *a long enough life* to take pleasure in my transformation; to work all day or at least *as much as my strength allows me to*; to trust in God, that is to say in Justice itself, for the success of my plans; to say a new prayer every evening, to ask God for life and strength for my mother and for me.[6]

His choice of intercessors says much about his deep affections. In 1865 it was thirty-eight years since his father's death; it was, no doubt, almost as long since Mariette had gone out of his life. Yet he still trusted in their goodness, in the power of their love for him. Edgar Allan Poe he had not encountered face to face; and it was, said Asselineau, eighteen years since Baudelaire had discovered him.[7] Yet the discovery had changed his career. It had been, to him, as if he had discovered a second self.

Such intercessors would, he knew, understand his needs. Yet at times his trust in God, his prayer still seemed ineffectual. Among his papers was an uncompleted draft of a preface for a third edition of his poems.

> I have no desire [he wrote] to demonstrate or to astonish, to amuse or to persuade. I have my nerves and my indispositions. I aspire to absolute repose and to unending night. I have sung the wild pleasures of wine and opium, I only thirst for a liquor unknown on earth, a liquor which the pharmacopoeia of heaven itself could not offer me: a liquor which would contain neither life nor death, nor excitation, nor oblivion. Not to know anything, not to teach anything, not to wish anything, not to feel anything, to sleep and just to sleep, that is today my only aspiration.[8]

On 9 April, Baudelaire was forty-four. A few days later, he was obliged, yet again, to ask Ancelle for funds.[9] There is no indication that Ancelle sent the money. On 4 May, Baudelaire felt compelled to break his new year resolutions, and to ask his mother for money.

> I am obliged to resort once again to your kindness [he confessed], *if the thing is at all possible.* For nearly a month, I've been thinking of this necessity, it humiliates me, and, if I have hesitated so long, it is not only because of the repugnance I felt at telling you, but because I didn't want to disturb you in your Easter devotions.
>
> I have to go to Paris, to discuss my affairs myself; I have to go to Honfleur to find the beginning of one of the works (I shall bring the ending with me); I shall have to go back to Paris to settle things in some or other way (I am not content with the offers which have been made me, and I hope to extract more), and finally I must return to Belgium, where, this time, I shall only stay for about ten days.
>
> This journey will take at least eight days. But what am I to do? The manageress of the hotel torments me, and, *not knowing what I was saying* [*sic*], I promised her some money on *Saturday.* And then, I lack *everything,* especially *linen.* I will not and cannot approach Ancelle [*sic*]. In the first place it would be useless, and then I am eager to remain on the strict terms on which I have been with him for four months [*sic*] . . .[10]

The letter was desperate, and in part dishonest. Perhaps Mme Aupick knew of the dishonesty, and chose to overlook it. She recognised the desperation, and made him a 'half-offer'. She wanted a complete list of her son's requirements. 'I feel such a desire and indeed such a need to go to Paris and Honfleur, that I am hanging on the half-offer which you made me,' Baudelaire answered. '. . . I am giving you the figures that you ask for.'[11]

On 10 May, Mme Aupick sent him 200 francs. Baudelaire received them next day, and immediately spent 60 francs on personal necessities.[12] Next day, there came a note from his mother, enclosing a further 500 francs. 'I am writing very briefly,' he answered, 'for a grateful son; but that is not to criticise your letter, in which I should rather have found reprimands than a style so cruelly curt.'[13] If she was curt, it was hardly surprising.

Others were more talkative. Mme Meurice announced to Baudelaire:

> Manet says that you are asking for me. Well, here I am! As I am tired of not seeing you, I am taking advantage at once of your summons, to chat to you for a moment . . .
> Ah! If you were in Paris, you would come and smoke your cigarette *in my flower-pot* – my garden is so small, it doesn't deserve any other name. I am often sitting there, as I was the first time you came to see me, do you remember? My husband has been on a journey in Italy; since he has come back, he often goes to the country . . . for dinner.
> When he enjoys his pastoral fugues, I dine alone, tête-à-tête with somebody or other. I have sometimes had you [to dinner]; probably you haven't noticed it. So come and turn these illusory dinners into real ones . . .[14]

'Quite seriously, quite definitely,' Baudelaire replied, 'I shall come and grasp your hands between the first and the fifth of June.'[15]

On 27 May, Mme Aupick wrote, once again, to her son. She asked him if he still intended to come to Paris and Honfleur.

> My dear good mother [he replied], there has been no change at all in my plans. Besides, I absolutely must talk to several people in Paris, and I must also go and look through all my papers at Honfleur. I shall leave very soon . . .
> If I achieve my aim, and settle at Honfleur at the end of June, I absolutely swear to you that I shall not stir from it for at least six months.[16]

He wrote twice to Ancelle to ask him for the 150 francs which were due to him for June; he needed them for his travel expenses to Paris and Honfleur. The long-promised visit was once again deferred. On 28 June, Baudelaire explained to him: 'The terror of not succeeding, the dilly-dallying, a genuine weakening of resolve, prevented me from going to Paris to discuss an important matter at the beginning of this month. But it must be settled; so send me [my allowance for] July (for which I enclose the receipt), and, if I don't leave the day after tomorrow, when I get your answer, I will leave on 5 July.'[17]

He had been away for fifteen months, and he had postponed his visit eight times. On the evening of 4 July he finally arrived at the Gare du Nord.

110

He settled at the hôtel du Chemin de fer du Nord, in the place du Nord. Next day he sent a letter to Hetzel, saying that he would come and explain why the rights of certain works had been sold twice over, to Hetzel and to Malassis.[1] An explanation was needed. Hetzel had waited two and a half years for manuscripts which had not been delivered. Now he found that he had paid an advance on an illegal contract. He agreed to relinquish his rights, provided that, when Baudelaire found another publisher, he returned the twelve hundred francs which had been paid to him on signature.[2] Baudelaire happily announced the news to Lemer.[3] He sent the contract to Ancelle, in the hope that the lawyer could appeal against the repayment.[4] He borrowed 500 francs from Manet. He visited the engaging Mme Meurice, and no doubt smoked a cigarette in her flower-pot of a garden. On the evening of 6 July, he went to the avenue de la Révolte, at Neuilly, to see Ancelle, and to discuss his substantial debt to Malassis.

> You have Baudelaire's contract with me in your hands [Malassis was to write, later, to Ancelle]. It specifies the amount which Baudelaire owed me in 1865, guaranteed by his works which were also *my property* . . . I seem to recall that it was 5,500 francs.
> Despite the existence of this contract, Baudelaire had been imprudent enough to sell M. Hetzel two volumes which belonged to me, for 1,500 francs [*sic*], which he had already received. His situation was false with regard to me, although our friendship never suffered from it, because we virtually spent our lives together in Brussels, and besides, I saw such a great desire on his part to try to contract with M. Lévy [*sic*], that I thought that, to ease his conscience and satisfy his intentions, I should suggest giving up my contract to him for 2,000 francs.
> He accepted with enthusiasm, and went to Honfleur to procure the 2,000 francs.[5]

He left for Honfleur on 7 July. It was two years and five months since he had been there. It was a year and nine months since he had seen his mother in Paris. He was determined, so he said, later, not to make any regrettable confidences to her. It was a disingenuous statement, since one of the chief objects of his visit was, as usual, to procure some money. He was obliged to tell her about his financial situation.

> As he felt that I was making a sacrifice to friendship [Malassis added, to Ancelle], he apparently declared to Mme Aupick that, should he die [before her], she was to consider this debt as sacred. It was not, however, he who confided this to me, but Mme Aupick herself, one evening when we were talking of the long and faithful friendship which had bound me to Baudelaire, a friendship in which the question of money did not exist.
>
> Between ourselves, I never kept proper accounts with him, and the contract only specifies the sums *which I advanced for the publication of works.* But our lives were, and always had been, so involved with each other, that I never kept, or chose to keep, a note of the money lent from person to person.
>
> Baudelaire was for me like a chosen brother.[6]

In July 1865, Malassis behaved indeed with brotherly love. On 8 July, Baudelaire reported to him from Honfleur:

> Yesterday evening the matter in question came up in conversation. I didn't ask her for anything. It was she who said to me, spontaneously: 'You must get out of this. Thanks to you, I am very short of money. I can't pay 5,000 francs, or even 2,000. But I am going to urge M. Ancelle to lend me the money – to destroy the possible effect of this debt; and you yourself will pay the remaining 3,000 francs later on, when you can.' And so, in two minutes, she settled an affair which had made me shudder every time I thought of it. My mother *has written today* to this gentleman – whom I shall see again when I pass through Paris . . .
>
> I am leaving for Paris again tomorrow; and I think I shall be in Brussels on the 12th.[7]

He was delighted and relieved by the settlement.[8] He said nothing about his pleasure in revisiting Honfleur, in rediscovering the *maison joujou,* his room with the view across the Channel, with the Guys drawings and the Meryon etchings.[9] He did not mention his happiness at being, once again, with his mother. He was to spend much more time in Brussels, which he detested, than he had spent in Honfleur, which he insisted was his dream. Next morning, 9 July, after only forty-eight hours, he left Honfleur. That evening he arrived in Paris.

He made amends for all his months of absence. He spent half a day with Asselineau and Banville.

> In spite of the rumours which had already circulated about his health, I did not find him changed in the least [so Asselineau was to remember].

Perhaps rather fatter, or rather heavier, which could be the effect of the Belgian diet, otherwise he looked all right; he was cheerful and talkative. His eyes were bright, his voice was unaffected and strong. He did complain of some troubles at the beginning of the year: fits of giddiness and headaches; but as he only spoke in the past tense, and as, moreover, he seemed to me in good form, I thought he was cured . . . I exhausted my arguments to persuade him not to go back. But he resisted. It was essential, he told me, absolutely essential to go back to Brussels . . .

He said goodbye to me, and assured me that it could not be more than two months before he returned [to Paris].

That day, ended Asselineau, was the last day that Baudelaire's friends had really known him.[10]

On 11 July, Baudelaire wrote to Sainte-Beuve whom, apparently, he had missed:

I couldn't pass through Paris without coming to shake you by the hand. I shall see you soon – in a month's time, probably.

I saw Julien Lemer three days ago, when I was leaving for Honfleur. Lemer said then that he was going to broach an important affair for me [the reprinting of my works] with M. Garnier. If you could intervene in my favour, with two or three authoritative words, you would make me happy . . .

I am leaving again for Hell *tomorrow evening*; until then, I am at the *hôtel du Chemin de fer du Nord. Place du Nord.*[11]

He was not to leave for Hell so soon. Catulle Mendès chanced to meet him at the Gare du Nord: shabby, sullen, almost menacing. He explained that he had come to Paris on business, and that he was going back to Brussels, but that he had missed the evening train. Mendès lived near the station, in the rue de Douai. He offered him a bed for the night. Baudelaire accepted the offer.[12]

In the rue de Douai, he stretched himself out, fully dressed, on the sofa, asked for a book, and began to read. Suddenly he dropped his book, and asked: 'Do you know, *mon enfant*, how much money I have earned since I began to work, since I was born?'

There was in his voice a heartrending bitterness of reproach and, as it were, of protest. I shuddered [Mendès remembered]. 'I don't know,' I said. 'I'm going to count it out to you,' he cried. And his voice grew exasperated as if with rage . . . He listed, with their payments, the articles, the poems, the prose poems, the translations, the re-publications, and, adding them all up, in his head, . . . he announced: 'The total profits of my whole life: fifteen thousand eight hundred and ninety-two francs and sixty centimes!' He added, with chattering teeth: 'Note those sixty centimes – two Havana cigars!'[13]

Jacques Crépet was later to calculate that Baudelaire had earned 10,000 francs; Claude Pichois and Jean Ziegler were to put the sum at 9,900 francs.[14]

On that summer night in Paris, in 1865, Mendès' increasing sadness turned to anger:

I thought of the famous novelists, the prolific melodramatists, and . . . I thought of this great poet, this strange and delicate thinker, this perfect artist who, in twenty-six years [*sic*] of laborious existence, had earned about one franc seventy centimes a day. He burst out laughing. Then he put out the lamp. 'Now let's go to sleep,' he said. He did not sleep.

No, he began to talk again . . . And, suddenly, he asked: 'Did you know Gérard de Nerval?' 'No,' I said. 'He wasn't mad,' he continued. 'Talk to Asselineau about it. Asselineau will explain to you that Gérard was never mad; and yet he committed suicide, he hanged himself. You know, at the door of a hovel, in an infamous street. He hanged himself – yes, he hanged himself!'[15]

Then, suddenly, he changed his views. Haunted by the fear of madness and the thought of suicide, Baudelaire seems to have had a fit of delirium, and identified himself with the author of *Le Rêve et la vie*. He knew in his heart of hearts, whatever Asselineau said, that Gérard had sometimes been insane. He was desperate, now, to believe that he was wrong, and that Gérard had not taken his own life.

Mendès did not dare to speak.

'But it isn't true,' Baudelaire continued, raising his voice, and almost shouting, 'it isn't true, he didn't kill himself, they were wrong, they lied! No, no, he wasn't mad, he wasn't ill, he didn't kill himself! Oh, you will tell everyone, won't you, that he wasn't mad, and that he didn't kill himself? Promise me you'll say that he didn't kill himself!' I promised everything he asked [added Mendès], and I trembled in the darkness. He stopped speaking . . . I was frozen stiff with fear. I was shattered. I shut my eyes, so as not to see the shadow, before me, in the mirror.

When I woke up, Baudelaire had gone.[16]

He had not yet gone back to Hell. He remained in Paris two days longer, drank a glass of beer with Troubat, *fidus Troubates*, in the rue Royale, and saw Sainte-Beuve in the rue Montparnasse. No doubt Sainte-Beuve advised him to stay in Paris; but Baudelaire clung to the pretext of his Belgian book. If Belgium seemed to him like Hell, Paris and his creditors seemed to him a Hell more fearful still. On 15 July, he took the evening train from the Gare du Nord, and, at midnight, he arrived in Brussels.

111

On his return, he called on Prosper Crabbe. The kindly stockbroker had lent him his salon for his final lecture; he now agreed to serve as intermediary between Ancelle and Malassis. As Baudelaire explained to Ancelle: if he, Ancelle, were to send Crabbe the 2,000 francs for Malassis and a copy of the contract, Crabbe would check the copy against the original contract, and release the money to Malassis. Baudelaire added that Malassis had just sold his pictures to Crabbe. He was clearly in financial straits.[1] Since he was no more prudent in Belgium than he had been in France, Malassis had also been tried, *in absentia*, in Paris, for continuing to publish obscene books, and for contriving to send them across the border. He had been sentenced to a year's imprisonment, and fined 500 francs. As long as the Second Empire lasted, he would be unable to go home.

A note by Malassis, on his most recent contract with Baudelaire, confirms that Ancelle released the necessary money.[2]

> The Malassis affair is settled [Baudelaire reported to his mother on 26 July]. It was arranged on the 20th. Now I am free!!!! *thanks to you.* I can sell my books to whoever I please, and for as much as I can. That same day, 20 July, M. Ancelle announced to me that he had just seen my friend M. Julien Lemer, and that [Lemer] had told him that, on the 20th or 21st, he was definitely going to make a transaction for me, and that he had some hope of drawing up an advantageous contract. But since the 20th, no news at all.
>
> Sainte-Beuve, whom I saw the second time that I passed through Paris, told me that he would take something of a hand in the affair.[3]

On 7 August, Lemer called on the Garniers. Hippolyte Garnier seemed inclined to publish Baudelaire; but Lemer did not draw up a contract with him. In the meanwhile, Auguste Vacquerie, no doubt encouraged by Mme Meurice, determined to find a French publisher for Baudelaire, and to rescue him from Brussels. He had left a 'very significant' note for Lemer.[4] Lemer reported the situation to Baudelaire, who felt much encouraged, for 'the need of money was making itself cruelly felt.'[5]

He was increasingly desperate, and he was increasingly difficult. On 30 August, Malassis confessed to Asselineau: 'I hardly ever see Baudelaire. I am not too sorry about it. I never see him without pleasure. But his failings: his procrastination, his obstinacy and his drivel have reached such proportions that it would be more than tiresome if he visited every day.'[6] In September, Malassis observed the first signs of Baudelaire's mental deterioration.[7] Years later, Alfred Stevens told Edmond de Goncourt that he had seen Baudelaire, 'when he first lost his memory, coming back from a tradesman from whom he had bought something, and to whom he had been unable immediately to give his name, and he added that the poor devil's desolation was pitiful.'[8]

On 3 September, Baudelaire wrote to Sainte-Beuve: 'It would help me a great deal in my conjectures to know *if you have been consulted*. Do tell me, please, that's all I ask. If you have been consulted, that will be a proof to me that there has been some progress.'[9]

> Dear friend [replied Sainte-Beuve, next day],
> You *will be answered*, immediately. M. Hippolyte Garnier spoke to me, only once, about you and the Lemer overture. I said what needed to be said about your talent and your distinction. But these gentlemen usually decide only for sales reasons. The idea of *complete works* may have alarmed them. They are great sceptics when they don't see a clear profit in advance. They have probably neither said yes or no. It is postponed until M. Hippolyte comes back . . .
> I often think of you, and I talk about you to Troubat (who wields the pen). I am really overwhelmed with heavy work . . .
> I grasp your hand, my dear *child*.[10]

'He knew him to be reduced to the last extremity,' so Vandérem was to emphasise in *Baudelaire et Sainte-Beuve*. 'He knew him to be gravely ill, and more than poor . . . It does seem, though it is not certain, that he gave him a hand with the publisher Garnier for a complete edition of his works. But as for articles and quotations, nothing whatever.'[11]

Baudelaire now found himself in increasing financial difficulties. He still owed Manet 500 francs, and he could only promise to repay the debt as soon as possible. Nonetheless, he asked another favour of him. He wanted Manet to concern himself with his literary affairs in Paris, together with Lemer and the Garniers.[12] 'Believe me,' answered Manet, 'your affairs will never be well managed except by yourself. Don't depend on other people. Nothing good can happen to you as long as you are in that accursed place.'[13]

On about 25 October, Ancelle sent Baudelaire an apprehensive letter.

> My dear Ancelle [he answered],
> . . . I guessed, when I read your letter, that you were very alarmed by my situation, and that you were afraid of one of those demands for funds which, naturally, you must resist – those demands which have so impoverished me . . .
> However, here is a receipt prepared in advance . . .

The sum is minimal; but, with 200 or 300 francs which I may receive from *Le Monde illustré*, it will serve *to bribe* my unbearable proprietress . . .

Let me add that, this time, you should *send [your letter] to me poste restante*, that woman's curiosity irritates me so much! I shall go to the post in the morning, on Saturday, the day after tomorrow, but I shall be very anxious if, on Sunday morning, there is still nothing . . .[14]

There was nothing in the post from Ancelle on Saturday or Sunday. On Sunday evening, Baudelaire confessed: 'I don't know what to think, or what I shall become.'[15]

He was increasingly disturbed. At the beginning of November, the editor of a Parisian paper offered him three or four hundred francs for some of his prose poems. Baudelaire did not even answer him.[16] However, he began the summary of his book on Belgium for Lemer.

His mother wrote, accusing him of neglecting her. He did neglect her, he replied, but he did not forget her:

. . . It is you who occupy my thoughts always, all the day . . .

I so long to see you that I should like to go to Paris and Honfleur, do some errands in Paris, and then spend two days with you. But what is the use of spending 200 francs on travelling, when the matter is pending? My journey wouldn't advance it. I am waiting.

Victor Hugo, who was living in Brussels for some time, wants me to go and spend a while on his island; he really wearied me, really tired me. I should not accept his glory or his fortune if I had, at the same time, to *possess* his enormous ridiculousness. Mme Hugo is half mad, and her two sons are great idiots. – If you want to read his latest book [*Chansons des rues et des bois*], *I should send it to you at once*. As usual, an enormous success as a *sale*. All intelligent people are disappointed when they have read it.[17]

Hugo had been in Brussels, in October, for the wedding of his son Charles. On 6 October, Baudelaire had dined with him. That was presumably the last time that Hugo saw him. 'He brought me an article he had written on *La Légende des siècles*, published in 1859 . . . As he handed me these pages, he said to me: *You will recognise that I am with you*. I was leaving. We said goodbye. I did not see him again. He is one of the men whom I miss.'[18] The comment was made to Asselineau, when Baudelaire had died. It was patently insincere. As Hugo confessed in the same letter: 'I met Baudelaire, rather than knew him. He often shocked me, and I must often have offended him.'[19]

112

On 14 November, Victor Hugo asked his son, François-Victor, to find out why Baudelaire had not reviewed his new book of poems.[1] Twelve days later, Mme Hugo answered his letter. 'We very often see Baudelaire. Like [Gustave] Frédérix, [of *L'Indépendance belge*], he is our regular guest. I think that Baudelaire is mentally rather ill. He unearths and revives unknown talents, he is offended by the brilliance and the renown of the living. That, I believe, is why he is silent about the *Chansons des rues et des bois*.'[2] Mme Hugo was tactful to her difficult husband, rather than perceptive about her guest. Yet though she herself was suffering from a heart condition, and she was nearing the end of her life, she continued to show an almost maternal concern for Baudelaire, and this despite his extraordinary rudeness. Frédérix recalled their evenings in the rue de l'Astronomie:

> Baudelaire hardly spoke, except to Mme Victor Hugo . . .; Charles Hugo's sparkling verve displeased him visibly; and François-Victor's rather dry conversation had little interest for him. But, with Mme Victor Hugo, he seemed to find contentment and confidence, to appreciate this warm hospitality as it deserved . . . He did not utter a word to the two or three young women of quite good appearance and quite keen intelligence, whom he used to meet there . . . He kept his pursed lips, his sharp glance, his disdainful politeness, he remained carefully dressed, neat and silent.
>
> His Wagnerism was sometimes satisfied in this house, where music was little appreciated. For Victor Hugo, who spoke powerfully about Beethoven in his *William Shakespeare*, was rarely influenced by music . . . But the young Mme Charles Hugo . . . had boldly brought her piano, a small Érard piano, to her new home, and Baudelaire, with no concern for the probable boredom of his hosts, sometimes said, after dinner, to a friend of the Hugo family [possibly Frédérix himself], who had studied and remembered *Tannhäuser*: 'Let's have a few fine chords from Wagner.' That was his usual formula for getting himself played the Pilgrims' Chorus, the March of the Knights, or the prayer of Elisabeth, from that *Tannhäuser* which he had so passionately defended, so well analysed in Paris.[3]

> How are you, cher Monsieur [Mme Hugo enquired of him, now]? I am sending you this note to soothe your anxiety, not that I think you are seriously ill, but it is already too much not to be quite well. May your cares be lightened at least by the conviction that you have completely devoted friends in us.
>
> Your place is always laid here, so don't leave your chair unoccupied.[4]

Baudelaire was not enamoured of Hugo's family, but he was still grateful for a taste of domesticity, for an hour or two in French

company, and, perhaps, for food and drink. On 30 November, he sent
a pitiful letter to Ancelle:

> Please forgive me for making you pay 12 sols for an unpleasant demand
> for money. *I cannot do otherwise.* I have a trinket, here, which I got for my
> mother a long time ago, and I can't send it to her, because I can't afford
> the postage . . .
>   My dear Ancelle, I'm going to make my habitual request. When I am
> waiting for a little money, I am *physically ill* with impatience. I beg you,
> don't wait till next day to send these miserable 150 francs. That witch [the
> proprietress of the hotel] is making me quite ill with rage and shame . . .
>   I'm weary, and I am enduring martyrdom. I have broken off every kind
> of acquaintance [*sic*]. I still prefer absolute solitude to brutish, stupid,
> ignorant company.
>   And my mother? Have you any news of her? I sometimes imagine that
> I shall not see her again.[5]

Early in December, a friend in Paris, Hippolyte Lejosne, asked
Baudelaire to send Lemer the plan of *Pauvre Belgique*! Baudelaire was
ill, and did not answer. Lemer later wrote: 'The negotiations for the
publication of his original works did not succeed. This may have been
because of my failure to communicate the *argument* of *Pauvre Belgique!*;
he always promised to send it to me, and he never did so.'[6]
    There was little that he could send him, now. It is extraordinary to
compare the declarations, the promises, the confidences in his letters
– so full, for these two years, of the book on Belgium – with the notes
and drafts which are published in the Pléiade edition of his *Œuvres
complètes*. Interspersed with newspaper cuttings, these are rough, repetit-
ive, sometimes gross, and almost entirely antagonistic. *Pauvre Belgique!*
is not the basis for a balanced book; it is the *déversoir* for a man who
had chosen exile, a man who was sinking into impotence and indignity.
It is an expression of his hatred of the world. In these final years of
poverty and illness and isolation, Baudelaire found relief in his savage
comments on Brussels and the Belgian character. Among the possible
titles for the book he listed *Une capitale pour rire, Une capitale de singes*.
Perhaps, he reflected, he had been too critical of France. 'One must
always take ones native land on the soles of ones shoes. It is a
disinfectant.'[7]
    Every city, every country had, it was said, an aroma of its own. To
Baudelaire, Brussels smelt of strong soap. Life in Brussels was insipid,
sad and sluggish. There was no elegance, no life: no point in the *flânerie*
so dear to the imaginative Parisian. As for the Belgians, they had 'the
heads of big yellow rabbits, with yellow eyelashes',[8] their faces had 'a
menacing stupidity'.[9] They had 'obscure, unseeing faces, like that of a
cyclop: a cyclop who was not one-eyed, but blind.'[10] Their mouths,

said Baudelaire, were gaping latrines of imbecility. Their eyes were staring, big and insolent. The Belgians could not understand beauty. Women did not exist, there were only males and females. Belgian females had flat feet and elephantine legs, and they often smelt.

It was as hard, wrote Baudelaire, to define the Belgian character as it was to rank the Belgian in the scale of humankind. The Belgians only thought *en bloc*, and they had a horror of wit. Belgian stupidity was 'French stupidity cubed';[11] but then, perhaps, there was no such thing as a Belgian, and Belgium itself was just 'the result of an alchemical experiment in diplomacy'.[12]

Only when he discussed art and architecture, only when he wandered round the provincial cities, did Baudelaire look on Belgium with any favour. His passionate indictment of the country says more, perhaps, about his own state of mind than it does about Belgium itself. Gustave Charlier, a Belgian critic, later made a study of Baudelaire in Belgium. His country, he concluded, 'was in no way responsible for the pamphleteer's wrath. This cruelly revealed the progress of an illness which was, itself, to remain implacable.'[13] Since 1862 Baudelaire had ceased, in part, to be himself. 'The wind of the wing of madness' had passed over him. Had he finished *Pauvre Belgique!*, his book would have been a blot on his work, and we can only record it as a curiosity. Deep down, he must have known, himself, that it would not be finished. Perhaps he did not want to finish it. He wanted to keep his *déversoir*, to continue his intolerable penance. Silvestre de Sacy wrote perceptively: 'Let us try to imagine the problem solved: it loses all its significance at once. One cannot imagine the book on Belgium finished . . . It may be that there were only a few weeks of elaboration between such advanced notes and the final writing; but it was a space which for Baudelaire – well or ill, it hardly matters – remained essentially uncrossable.'[14]

On 1 December, Ancelle sent him 150 francs, and advised him not to spend too much time alone. A few days later, Léon Massenet de Marancour, the man of letters, called on Baudelaire to report Lemer's progress with the Garniers. Lemer would try to get 5,000 or 6,000 francs instead of the 4,000 anticipated. This was cheerful speculation rather than a contract; it also came too late. Baudelaire's acute neuralgia – if such it was – had returned, and he was taking pills to combat it; they consisted of belladonna, opium, valerian and digitalis. Early in December his health began to deteriorate sharply. His attacks of 'neuralgia' became more frequent and, each time, more acute.

On 21 December, he confessed to Ancelle: 'I have been seized by neuralgia in the head, which has lasted for more than a fortnight. You know that this drives one stupid and mad; and, in order to write to you, Lemer, and my mother today, I have been obliged to swaddle my head in a pad which I soak every hour in cooling water. The attacks are not as violent as they were last year, but the pain lasts very much longer.'[15] He asked Ancelle to retrieve his gold repeater watch from the pawnbroker's in the rue Joubert in Paris. He was much attached to it; he also had a mania for constantly wanting to know the time, and he could not work without a clock. There was no clock in his hotel room, and he had been obliged to return a watch which he had borrowed. He asked Ancelle to pack his watch with care, and to send it to Brussels. He enclosed a receipt for 150 francs. Fifty francs would cover the redemption of the watch and the necessary expenses; he needed the remainder for new year presents.[16]

Ancelle sent Baudelaire the money which he had asked for. Mme Aupick also wrote; she wanted to refuse the presents that he had bought her. His physical condition remained disturbing.

> I am a little vague in mind, I have a mist in the head. I feel an intellectual apathy [he told Ancelle on 26 December]. That is because of a long series of attacks, and also because I have used opium, digitalis, belladonna and quinine. A doctor, whom I called, did not know that I had once made protracted use of opium. That's why he treated me with such caution, and that is why I have been obliged to double and quadruple the dose. I have managed to change the times of the attacks; that is a lot. But I am very tired.[17]

Next day he sent his mother her presents. 'What a strange idea,' he wrote, 'to refuse my trinkets!'[18]

Early in January, Baudelaire dined with Malassis. Malassis had now moved to the rue Mercelis, in the suburb of Ixelles, where his mistress, Françoise Daum, who was said to have been an Alsatian maid, displayed remarkable culinary talents. The other guests on this winter evening were the itinerant actor and poet Albert Glatigny ('there is', wrote Malassis, 'the soul of a nightingale in that giraffe'),[19] and Gilles Nasa, the director of the Théâtre Molière in Brussels.[20]

It was presumably now, on his way back from Louvain, that 'sinful pleasures' kept Glatigny for two days in the company of Malassis and Baudelaire.[21] As far as Baudelaire was concerned, his sinful pleasures could only now have been excessive drink. In 1865 Rops engraved a menu for a dinner given by Neyt and attended by Baudelaire, Malassis, Glatigny and Arthur Stevens; during this dinner, with Baudelaire in mind, they served a *bordeaux retour de l'Inde,* 1842 (the legend of the visit to India was still, it seems, accredited). They served wine – no doubt constantia – from the Cape of Good Hope. Apparently this was not enough to satisfy Baudelaire. Malassis, the most loyal of friends, later told Troubat 'that he no longer left the brandy-bottle on the table within his reach.'[22] Troubat thought that 'this love of brandy was in fact an illness.'[23] It was, more probably, an escape from a life which had now become unendurable.

On 6 January, Baudelaire went to the *poste restante* to collect his watch. It had not yet arrived, and, troubled as he was, he waited for the next delivery, and stood outside for four hours in the wind and rain. Again he was overcome by migraine. Next day, on an empty stomach, he collapsed, and rolled on the floor like a drunkard. He suffered from cold sweats and repeated vomiting. His doctor was to diagnose hysteria.[24] The diagnosis was extraordinary. Yet, whatever the doctor knew about Baudelaire's current symptoms, it is doubtful if he knew of his psychological condition, his medical history, his refusal over the years to consult physicians, his refusal to follow their prescriptions. Medical science left much to be desired; but Baudelaire was perhaps already beyond salvation.

In the second week of January, Ancelle obligingly called on Auguste Garnier, and discussed the publication of the poet's works. Garnier said that he would like to deal directly with him.

> One must consider this carefully [wrote Baudelaire to Ancelle, on 12 January]. I think that in two days you will receive the plan, or, rather, the summary, the *compendium* of the book on Belgium, to transmit to J. Lemer, *who seems to want this book*. It would be too brutal to cast him aside immediately. You will receive the letters from Lemer and the letter from Sainte-Beuve which relate to this affair. Decide *what you want* and *do as you like about my advice* . . .
>
> My greetings to you. Thank you. And remember that, whatever my mother says about it, I have guessed and appreciated all the strength of your friendship.[25]

The friendship had been almost paternal, and Ancelle was to recall it with generosity and enduring pleasure. It left him, he later told Eugène Crépet, with ineffaceable memories 'which are infinitely precious to me. Baudelaire did not always behave as I expected of him, and as my attentions deserved, but I cannot forget the happy moments that he led me to spend in conversations which were full of wit, and by the deep affection which he always showed me [*sic*].'[26] Now, in 1866, Ancelle, the notary, the *conseil judiciaire*, the mayor of Neuilly, so imbued with the dignity of his functions, made himself the literary agent of Baudelaire. 'He hasn't the slightest idea about publishing,' Asselineau confessed to Malassis;[27] yet he showed uncommon delicacy and devotion.

Another friend – less faithful – was Sainte-Beuve, who wrote to
Baudelaire again.

I shall follow your advice [Baudelaire replied], I shall go to Paris, and I
shall see the Garniers myself. And then, perhaps, I shall commit the
indiscretion of asking you to give me more support. But when? For
the past six weeks, I have been immersed in pharmacy. Beer must be
foregone. I ask no better. Tea and coffee, that's more serious, but it's still
all right. Wine? That's bloody cruel! But here is a brute who is harder
still, [Dr Léon Marcq]. He tells me not to read or to study. It is a curious
medicine, that suppresses the principal function![28]

The letter – written on 15 January – was interrupted by dizzy spells,
and falls. On 18 January, sending Ancelle the plan of the book on
Belgium, Baudelaire confessed:

I have been ill again, very ill. Vertigos and repeated vomiting for three
days. I was obliged to lie on my back for three days; for, even when I
crouched on the floor, I fell . . . The doctor only recommended me Vichy
water; but I haven't got a sou! . . .
   I'm very worried about my mother's health.
   As for me, I can't smoke any more without feeling sick. For a smoker,
that is a really discouraging sign. A moment ago, I was obliged to break
off this letter and throw myself on my bed, and that's a great problem,
because I'm always afraid of dragging down the furniture I cling to.
   And then, besides, I have dismal thoughts; it sometimes seems to me
that I shall not see my mother again.[29]

On 20 January, the 'brutal' Dr Marcq – a friend of Malassis and
Félicien Rops – visited Baudelaire at his hotel. Baudelaire gave him
some notes on his condition.

I've noticed that all the attacks have come when I've had an empty
stomach. The recurrences are not at all regular. The first time (on the
night of Sunday to Monday), I had several attacks.
   I think that food and fasting have no effect on it at all. But I am never
hungry; I can go for several days without wanting to eat.
   Order of sensations.
   Vagueness in the mind. Suffocating fits. Horrible headaches. Heaviness;
congestion; complete dizziness. If I'm standing, I fall. If I'm sitting, I fall.
This is all very rapid.
   When I come round again, I want to be sick. Extreme heat in the head.
Cold sweats . . .[30]

It is significant that Baudelaire made no reference to his previous
illnesses, or to any treatment for syphilis; either he wanted to hide his
past, or he saw no connection between his past and present. Nor do

the doctors seem to have made a thorough examination. Baudelaire gave Dr Marcq a draft of his poem, 'Le Rêve d'un curieux' – possibly in lieu of his fee.[31] It is doubtful whether he paid him or Dr Oscar Max, the young hotel physician.

He also authorised Catulle Mendès, in Paris, to publish some of his poems in the newly founded *Parnasse contemporain*. He was usually concerned about what he published; now he virtually gave Mendès a free choice, provided that he himself was sent the proofs.[32] Mendès had offered to lend him 100 francs; Baudelaire confessed that he needed the money, urgently, to pay for his medicines.[33] On 22 January, writing to Ancelle, he announced that he had not yet finished 'the heavy task of classification'.[34] It is unclear what he was classifying; but the fact that the task was onerous was some indication of his frailty. His work, he said, had been interrupted 'by a recurrence of nervous attacks, vertigo, nausea and falls. I even had an attack at the doctor's. He is constantly asking me if I'm following his treatment. I dare not tell him *the reasons why I am doing nothing at all*. (Baths, ether, valerian, Vichy water.) But I think, myself, that all this would be inadequate. *Don't say anything* about this to my mother.'[35]

Ancelle did not answer at once. On 29 January, Baudelaire wrote again, urgently:

> Either you haven't received my packet of last Monday, consisting of *a plan of BELGIQUE* in sixteen pages, *a long letter* for you, *two letters from Lemer, a letter from Sainte-Beuve*, and *a receipt for 100 francs*, or you haven't understood all the sadness of my situation – or, finally, your answer has gone astray or been stolen.
>
> *My attacks, vertigos, convulsions have become less frequent; but I'm not safe unless I'm lying on my back. Perhaps the doctor thinks I'm cured. He no longer comes, and I no longer dare to get the medicines paid for by the hotel.*
>
> Indeed, I am worried not only about the hundred francs, but also about everything else.[36]

It was about now that Ancelle wrote to him, describing his visit to the Garniers. He told Baudelaire the print runs which the publishers had mentioned. He also suggested that Baudelaire should allow Charles Nisard – a friend of the Ancelle family – to help him in his affairs. He warned him that he had cut some of the plan for *Pauvre Belgique!*, so as to soften the language. It was some measure of Baudelaire's condition that Ancelle could act and write like this, and that Baudelaire did not castigate him. Ancelle also advised Baudelaire to come back to France – one can only presume that his hotel bill was to be settled after his departure.

On 30 January, Baudelaire replied. He found the suggested print-run too small; he wanted to keep the right to correct his proofs. He agreed that Nisard should help him.

> My courage is returning now, I am going to re-do the *Spleen*, and also re-do *Les Contemporains* (just relying on my memory, alas! because the manu-script is with Lemer). I shall have finished by 20 February, if my fainting-fits and vomiting don't start again . . .
>   As for your final advice, I cannot follow it. Never shall I find the courage, first of all to announce to the proprietress of my hotel that I am going to leave without paying her, and then to steal more money from my mother, whose kindness I have shamefully abused . . .
>   N.B. I am going to have 20 francs left. On Sunday [4 February] I am going back to Namur to see Rops and once again admire that Jesuits' church of which I shall never tire.[37]

113

He was not to go to Namur. The day before his intended visit, he confessed to Rops that he had had further, frequent attacks of vertigo and nausea. He was now afraid of travelling. In Paris, Asselineau offered to consult a doctor, if Baudelaire would describe his symptoms and the treatment which he was receiving. On 5 February, Baudelaire sent a pitiful account of himself:

> It isn't an easy thing for me to write. If you have some good advice to offer, you will give me pleasure. To be honest, I've been ill almost all the time for the past twenty months . . . In February last year, I had violent neuralgia in the head, or acute twinges of rheumatism; for about a fortnight. Perhaps it's something else. Recurrence of the same trouble in December. In January, a different affliction: one evening, on an empty stomach, I began to roll about and fall down like a drunkard, clutching on to furniture and bringing it down with me. Vomiting bile or white foam. This is the invariable sequence of events:
>   I am perfectly well, I haven't eaten anything, and suddenly, without warning and without apparent reason, I feel a vagueness, an absence of mind, a stupor; and then an atrocious pain in my head. I absolutely have to fall, unless at that moment I am lying on my back. Then a cold sweat, vomiting, a long stupor. For the neuralgia, they had made me take pills which consisted of quinine, digitalis, belladonna and morphine. Then apply cooling water and oil of turpentine [*sic*] – which incidentally I believe quite useless. For the vertigo, Vichy water, valerian, ether, Pullna

water. The trouble continued. Now [I am taking] pills which I remember include valerian, or zinc oxide, asafoetida, etc, etc. So it's an anti-convulsant, then? The trouble still continues . . . Do you know this kind of illness? Have you seen it before?[1]

Asselineau took Baudelaire's letter to Dr Piogey, whom Sainte-Beuve considered 'a real doctor for men of letters'.[2] Piogey made a depressing diagnosis.

Mme Aupick reproached her son for alarming his friends. He sent her some notes on his health to show Lacroix, her doctor at Honfleur.[3] On the one hand he claimed that he did not know what was wrong with him; and yet he was anxious enough to consult a doctor himself, to ask Asselineau and Mme Aupick for medical advice, and he seems to have suspected that he might be on the verge of apoplexy or paralysis. Despite all his assurances that his troubles were not serious, he wrote the same day to Ancelle: 'I have been obliged to go back to bed, for the last few days, and I don't think I shall stir from it again. I am too afraid of my attacks of vertigo, and sometimes, even in bed, my head feels heavy. But I am out of harm's way. As for the proprietress of the hotel, I no longer dare to think of her.'[4] Baudelaire enclosed a note for Hippolyte Garnier, in case Lemer should have ceased to be concerned with publication. He was, however, anxious that Lemer should not lose his commission on this affair, because he had worked on it for a long while. Malassis was now printing *Les Épaves*. The small collection of poems included those suppressed by the judges of *Les Fleurs du mal*. Baudelaire was correcting the proofs. He took pleasure in the publication.

His mother sent him 50 francs; she offered him more financial help, and asked him the total sum of his debts in Brussels. She suggested that she might approach Ancelle; and – after a discussion, no doubt, with Dr Lacroix – she showed how disturbed she was by Baudelaire's condition. On 10 February he answered:

. . . You have had a very bad night, *thanks to me. I was therefore very wrong indeed to talk to you about my infirmity and even about my neuralgia.* Now think of all the nervous troubles and all the migraines which you have suffered for so many years. Is it surprising if I take after you a little, and if, with a splenetic nature and a violent sensibility, I should have some troubles?

I do not want you to write to Ancelle. I do not want you to disturb him. He knows that I have been ill several times. He knows how I long to come back, and to pay what I owe here . . .

I absolutely refuse your help. I want no money from you.[5]

His 'absolute refusal' of her help was shortlived.

Yes [he continued], the 50 francs will be useful to me. I don't intend to
pay the doctor until I leave; but I am often very humiliated to get my
drugs paid for by the assistant manageress of the hotel.

And now, to reassure you, let me tell you that for the past three days I
have had no vertigo or vomiting. It is true that I'm not strong. But the
doctor says: 'Hysteria! Hysteria! You must conquer yourself; you must
force yourself to walk.' Walk, in this weather, in these terrible streets and
worn-down roads! Sauntering is impossible in Brussels.

A really *ridiculous* thing, a man walking behind me, a passing child or
dog, makes me want to faint. It really is ridiculous, isn't it? Yesterday, I
went to see an exhibition of drawings. But, after a few minutes, like when
I am obliged to apply my attention to something (*this won't last for ever*), I
felt a few bad symptoms coming, and, in spite of the rain, I hastily sought
refuge in the open air.

You see that all this is simply a question of nerves. The fine weather
will drive it all away . . . [6]

Mme Aupick wrote to him, in acute anxiety:

I'm really distressed that I talked to you about my state of health [he
answered]. I can see how much I've disturbed you . . . I can tell you now
that I enjoy smoking again (even tobacco used to nauseate me), and that
yesterday I felt not only a great disgust at all the pills, but also a great
hunger, which hadn't happened to me for three weeks . . . I must say that
I don't understand a thing about what's happened to me, and I should
be very glad if at least a doctor who knew me prescribed a way of life for
me once and for all . . .

There is a man in Paris who could have done me a service. I shall see
him next time I pass through. He is Charles Lasègue, who was my tutor
in philosophy when I was a boy. He gave up philosophy. He became a
doctor, and he has now become a famous doctor. He specialises in *madness*
and *hysteria*.[7]

Baudelaire was increasingly disturbed by his own condition. Even
Sainte-Beuve – who was himself far from well – felt some concern.
Perhaps, now that literature was not in question, he could afford to
show affection. 'I have talked about you more than once', he wrote,
'with M. Piogey . . . You must follow a fairly strict regimen . . . Don't
do anything which overexcites you. I know just how overwhelming
boredom can be. But it is necessary in life and for life to know how to
be a little bored.'[8] Sainte-Beuve was not the only person in the world
of letters to feel concerned about Baudelaire. Mme Hugo sent her
physician, Dr Frédéric Jottrand, to see him.[9]

Mme Aupick, in Honfleur, felt increasing frustration and despair.
She sent her son a further hundred francs, and offered to send more,
should he need it. Baudelaire replied with as much perversity as
gratitude.

Still more money. Why? I don't want any more. I had 20 francs left out
of the 50 francs, and I wanted to spend them all on the showers. I'm sure
that I'd offend you if I sent you back these 100 francs. I'm going to put
them on one side, and, when I get a little money from France, I shall add
it to these 100 francs to give a decent sum to my proprietress, and to make
her patient until my affair is settled . . .

No, I don't want your money. I certainly owe you 30,000 francs
already. Am I a cad or a coward, that I should agree to cut down your
pension? . . .

Mme Victor Hugo, who had appeared to me only in a ridiculous light,
is really and truly a good woman. But she rather likes to mother all her
friends. She demanded that her doctor should come and see me. He
approves of the treatment which has been followed until now, but he
maintains that one must add a diet which is very high in iron, because,
he says, the predominance of the bile and nerves proves *an impoverishment
of the blood.* I should never have thought of that. Apparently some people
have heard my ridiculous infirmity discussed in Paris. Sainte-Beuve has
consulted his doctor, and sent me advice. All these opinions roughly
agree.[10]

Mme Aupick was not appeased; indeed, she suggested that she might
be able to send him more money if she gave up her gardener and
dismissed her maid. 'Give up the pleasure of your garden,' Baudelaire
replied, 'and dismiss Aimée, at your age! And you think that I should
let you! It would be shocking.'[11]
On 18 February he wrote to Ancelle, advising him on the approach
to Garnier. He also sent him an explanatory letter for the publisher
Édouard Dentu. Ancelle was to visit him. Though Baudelaire had
professed not to want money from Ancelle, he also asked him for 100
francs, since he had just had an angry scene with *le monstre du Grand
Miroir.* These hundred francs (to be deducted from his March allowance), and the hundred he already had would be an acceptable sum
to offer her.[12]
Just as he was about to send his letter, a note arrived from Ancelle,
to say that the Garniers refused to publish him. Hippolyte Garnier,
said Ancelle, maintained that he had not seen Baudelaire's agent,
Lemer, for a year. Ancelle suggested that Baudelaire should approach
Hetzel.[13] The Garniers' rejection was a rejection of everything that
Baudelaire had done; above all it was a rejection of *Les Fleurs du mal,*
the book which he acknowledged as his spiritual history. In his
exasperation, he confessed to Ancelle the secret which he had always
jealously kept: 'Do I have to tell you, because you haven't guessed it
any more than the rest, that in that *atrocious* book, [*Les Fleurs du mal*],
I put all my *heart,* all my *affection,* all my *religion* (disguised), all my *hate*?
It is true that I'll write the opposite, that I'll swear to all the gods that
it is a book of pure art . . .'[14] The lines were the testament of a lucid

mind. It was ironic that he made the confession to a man whom he
had once despised as a classic bourgeois, a Monsieur Prudhomme.

That night, he wrote again to Ancelle:

> My dear friend, there is still one thing which you should weigh up
> carefully in your mind, it is that if it were possible to resume with Michel
> Lévy, . . . although his manners and his *hideous avarice* inspire me with great
> repugnance, there might be an advantage, because of the influence of his
> firm . . .
> But how can one sound out Michel? Yet another reason for me to go
> to Paris.[15]

The note was written on the night of 18–19 February. On 19
February, Baudelaire received a letter from Troubat, telling him that
Alphonse Lemerre, '*a very zealous and very intelligent publisher*', had
expressed a wish to reprint *Les Fleurs du mal*.[16] Baudelaire replied that
Ancelle was placing everything.[17] 'Does this information demand that
you should break off every approach?' he asked Ancelle. 'I think not.
But perhaps one ought to know what sort of man M. Lemerre is (47,
passage Choiseul).'[18] Lemerre was the publisher of *L'Art* and of *Le
Parnasse contemporain*; he was to be the publisher of the Parnassian poets.
As Laurent Tailhade, the poet and man of letters, was to write, his
dark and airless office 'deserves to be recorded among the illustrious
corners of Paris.'[19] Lemerre himself was said, in time, to be a
millionaire.[20]

'Life is becoming more and more intolerable for me here,' Baudelaire continued, to Ancelle.[21] He waited, in despair, for an answer. Two
days later, he wrote again:

> I waited for your reply [about the 100 francs] yesterday morning at 8
> o'clock, at 3 o'clock, and then at 6 o'clock in the evening, and then at the
> same times today. No doubt you want to send me news of Dentu *at the
> same time*. But, in that case, I risk waiting a long while. You don't know
> *just how difficult my situation is*. I did, as you asked, send you some notes on
> possible publishers; but, except for Dentu, whom you went to see anyway,
> I beg you to leave it all on one side, for the moment . . . Don't be cross
> with me, my dear friend, for saying this to you, and believe that I am very
> grateful for all the friendship and all the devotion which you have shown
> me . . .
> Come wind or tide, I shall go to Paris on 15 March . . .
> Three days ago, I began to cut into the 100 francs which were carefully
> set aside. And so, when your hundred francs arrive, I shall only be able
> to give 190 francs. And suppose they are rejected with contempt?[22]

That day he wrote to the proprietor of the hôtel de Dieppe, in Paris,
to say that he could not pay his longstanding debt; he mentioned his

illness and what he called the betrayal of his literary agent.[23] He also wrote to his mother. He was relieved to hear that her health had improved.

> As for me [he told her], *I am well*, apart from some recurrences of fever, and a permanent background of neuralgia, as in December. I am weak; I am stiff; I am timid and clumsy, that's all . . .
> They say (and I believe it, now), that other nations are even more stupid than the French. And so one must come back and live in France, despite the stupidity of the place, or else depart for the other world.[24]

114

Late that month, or early in March, Malassis published *Les Épaves de Charles Baudelaire*. The title *Les Épaves* had already been given to a collection of poems by Auguste Lacaussade, the editor of the *Revue européenne*, and the periodical had reviewed it on 1 November 1861: on the day it published Baudelaire's *Recueillement*. This may have been an unconscious reason why the title had lingered in his mind. Baudelaire 'considered these scattered pieces, juvenilia or condemned poems, as superfluous in his poetic baggage,' Malassis was to tell Asselineau. 'This will explain to you why he abandoned them to me.'[1] Baudelaire was anxious that these 'bagatelles' should not bring him into conflict with Belgian law.[2] 'Be careful to point out', he had added to Malassis, 'that this collection has been made without the participation of the author.'[3] Malassis duly informed the public, with excessive zeal, that Baudelaire had not considered these poems worthy of inclusion in *Les Fleurs du mal*.[4]

Both publisher and poet spoke less than the truth. Baudelaire would not have sanctioned the publication of any work with which he was dissatisfied. He knew the worth of the poems which had been condemned, and of a handful of others, some of which had appeared in periodicals, and one of which now appeared for the first time. He was much concerned with *Les Épaves*. He had not only sent Malassis his instructions for publication, he had made a number of notes on the proofs, and he had posted several copies of the book to Paris. He had drawn up a press list of 48 copies.[5]

The collection opened with 'Le Coucher du soleil romantique', which had been published in *Le Boulevard* in 1862. It expressed nostalgia for the Romantic age of 1830, a certain piety for the past. Then came the six poems which, on the judges' orders, had been withdrawn from *Les Fleurs du mal*. Among them were 'Lesbos' and 'Femmes damnées', in which Baudelaire wrote with sympathy and dignity of a love which he knew to be condemned. In 'Le Léthé', he sought for oblivion from the all-powerful and heartless Jeanne. In 'Les Bijoux' he described her, like a tigress, in her physical majesty. Some have rightly seen this poem as a Delacroix in poetry.

The first of the 'Galanteries' was 'Le Jet d'eau', one day to be set to music by Debussy.[6] The second, 'Les Yeux de Berthe', was inspired, it has been suggested, by a little actress whom Alfred Stevens recorded as Baudelaire's last mistress: the Berthe who inspired him with a prose poem and probably received the dedication of another.[7] There followed a poem which had been worthy of *Les Fleurs du mal*; if Baudelaire had not included it, this was no doubt because he had thought that it would duplicate 'Que diras-tu ce soir . . .'. The poem had been sent to Mme Sabatier in the early summer of 1854. Pichois maintains that she had been a mere pretext for the poem;[8] yet there seems no doubt of its sincerity. Baudelaire had genuinely loved her, and he had been in love with the image which he had created of her.

> À la très chère, à la très belle
> Qui remplit mon cœur de clarté,
> À l'ange, à l'idole immortelle,
> Salut en l'immortalité! . . .[9]

This hymn to his spiritual love, a love, alas, destroyed by the flesh, remains among the supreme love poems in French literature.

'Les Promesses d'un visage' have a humbler inspiration: perhaps, again, the poem was suggested by Berthe, or by Manet's painting *La Chanteuse des rues*. The manuscript is said to date from Baudelaire's Belgian years. 'Les Promesses d'un visage', a catalogue of a woman's physical charms, is no stronger than some of the early poems to Jeanne; but it had been rejected by Catulle Mendès for *Le Parnasse contemporain*, the first number of which was soon to appear. Mendès himself had already been imprisoned at Sainte-Pélagie for offending public morals in his verse-drama, *Le Roman d'une nuit*. He was hardly entitled to preach morality.[10] However, he had also refused 'Le Monstre'. The poem, recently written, was a baroque account of an ageing and macabre prostitute. In the last days of his literary existence, Baudelaire had returned for stimulus to the poems which he had enjoyed in his youth.[11] There followed three epigraphs, some *Pièces diverses*, and three *bouffonneries*.

'Although the book is very short, it is too long,' Glatigny wrote to Banville. 'Apart from the six suppressed poems from *Les Fleurs du mal*, there are hardly more than 3 or 4 pages worthy of Baudelaire. The rest did not deserve the honour of publication.'[12] Glatigny passed a harsh verdict on *Les Épaves*; and it is true that the *Épigraphes* and the *bouffonneries* reflect Baudelaire in sharp and irreversible decline. Other poems reflect him in his splendour; and if *Les Épaves* contained only the poems banned in 1857, and six other poems, including the resplendent 'Hymne', it would still be a collection to eclipse the work of the Parnassians. *Poèmes saturniens* was published later in the year. Verlaine's first book of poems showed the influence of Baudelaire, instinctive and profound. 'It is to Baudelaire', Verlaine was to write, 'that I owe the awakening of poetic feeling, and what is deep in me.'[13]

Les Épaves, like *Les Fleurs du mal*, was to be condemned by French justice. On 6 May 1868, while Malassis was still in Belgium, the court at Lille condemned the new edition to be destroyed. It also sentenced Malassis to a year's imprisonment and to a fine of 500 francs.

115

On 1 March 1866, Mme Victor Hugo wrote from Brussels to her husband in Guernsey: 'We very often see Baudelaire. He is a rare spirit: noble and, I think, unhappy. His mind has gone a little odd, and he has a nervous illness – the combination makes him a hypochondriac.'[1]

Baudelaire had lamented to his mother that, for the moment, his books were '*dormant*, worthless securities.'[2] This was untrue. In Paris, where the first number of *Le Parnasse contemporain* appeared two days later, Baudelaire was now recognised as a literary master. As Sainte-Beuve had told him, in a rare moment of generosity: 'If you were here, you would become, whether or not you wanted to, an authority, an oracle, a consultant poet.'[3] In Brussels, he learned how he had been praised by Mallarmé. On 5 March, he sent his mother two issues of *L'Art*: they and a third, which he had not seen, had appeared late the previous year. They contained an article on him by Verlaine. Considering the author's age (he was not yet twenty-two), and the usual weakness of his criticism, the article was remarkable for its perception.

> The profound originality of Charles Baudelaire is, as I understand it [wrote Verlaine], to represent modern man, powerfully and in his essence; and, by the term modern man, I do not mean . . . emotional, political and social man. All I mean here is physical man, as he is today, as he has

been made by the refinements of an excessive civilization: modern man, with his sharpened, vibrant senses, his painfully subtle mind, his brain saturated with tobacco, his blood burnt with alcohol: in short, as M. Taine would say, the *bilio-neurotic* par excellence. It is, I repeat, this character of what one might call a sensitive man, that Charles Baudelaire represents as an actual type, or, if you prefer, as a *hero*. Nowhere, not even in Heinrich Heine, will you find it as strongly marked as in certain passages of *Les Fleurs du mal*. And so I believe that, if he is not to be incomplete, the future historian of our age must leaf attentively through this book, which is the quintessence and, as it were, the extreme concentration of a whole element of this century.[4]

'It seems', Baudelaire announced to his mother, 'that *the Baudelaire school* exists.'[5] He was glad to send the news to her, because in her last letter she had reproached him once again for his imprudence. He had, he said, been cheated by Belgium, cheated by Lemer; he had been deprived of his mother for two years longer than he had expected. Now he must extricate himself from his misery, and undo the harm that had been done. 'You could surely abandon me to my fate,' so he pleaded, 'without adding your reproaches. And yet I still prefer reproaches to nothing at all. For your silence is always the most alarming thing to me. You don't mention your health. That's because it's all right, *isn't it?*'[6] Mother and son remained dependent on one another. They knew the power of affection and the power of reproach. They knew, above all, the power of silence. Even now, their relationship contained an element of cruelty.

> Do you really think [he asked her, now], that I enjoy living in a place inhabited by fools and enemies, where I have seen several Frenchmen ill like myself, a place where I think that the spirit deteriorates like the body, *not to mention that I am making myself forgotten*, and that, without wanting to, *I am undoing all my relationships in France?*
> To settle in Honfleur has always been the dearest of my dreams.[7]

A dream. The word, perhaps, said more than Baudelaire intended. He loved his mother best at a distance. He could not, when he felt strong and ambitious, or even now, when he felt far from strong, imagine the rest of his life in Honfleur. He could not conceive the permanent exchange of Paris and his friends – '*all my relationships in France*' – for the *joujou* villa on the cliff, the reading of *L'Écho Honfleurais*, the exclusive, overwhelming, and now provincial society of his mother.

That day, 5 March, Baudelaire also wrote to Troubat: 'I shall follow Sainte-Beuve's advice: I shall go and try my fortune in Paris, in about three weeks . . . I do hope that one evening we shall dine in Paris with him . . . I was very glad to learn that Sainte-Beuve was better. I have never felt this sort of concern about anybody's health, except about that of E. Delacroix. He was, however, a great egoist. But my affections come largely from the mind.'[8] Baudelaire was aware that the relationship with Sainte-Beuve – like that with Delacroix – remained one-sided. Troubat answered, promising that they would dine with him.[9]

Mme Hugo remained concerned about Baudelaire; but she saw him, even now, in relation to her husband: not as a poet in his own right, but as a potential reviewer of Hugo's work. Baudelaire had not reviewed *Les Chansons des rues et des bois*; nor, it seems, had he acknowledged his complimentary copy. Hugo asked his wife if he should now send a copy of his novel. On 11 March she answered:

[If you] have given Baudelaire *Les Chansons des rues et des bois* and he hasn't written to you about it, don't give him *Les Travailleurs [de la mer]*. I am sure that he sets you among the greatest masters, but his unhealthy mind makes its choice. He has a certain twist in his understanding which makes him paradoxical. He is sick in mind and in body. He also has shadow sides in his life which he doesn't mention, but one can easily divine them . . .'[10]

It is difficult to divine what shadow sides she meant.

Later that day, in *L'Indépendance belge*, she read an unacceptable comment on her husband's novel; it was unsigned, but it was the work of her brother, Paul Foucher. That evening, Baudelaire came to dinner. He read the offending passage in the newspaper and, she reported, 'split his sides with laughter.'[11] He told her 'that she would be wrong to take this buffoonery seriously, that it was best to make a joke of it.'[12] They spent a cheerful evening together. Baudelaire not only reassured her; he drafted a reply to Foucher, which she sent to her husband in Guernsey. On 15 March, she announced to Hugo: 'I am having Baudelaire given a copy of *Les Travailleurs*. He has just had *déjeuner* with us, he would like to do an article on the book.'[13] The book was given; Baudelaire began to make notes. His notes are largely factual, and give no indication of his opinions; but they are of interest since they are the last literary notes in his hand.[14]

It was, it seems, that day or the next, 15 or 16 March, that he went, at last, to Namur. He had been invited there by Rops; he was eager to see the family again, and to revisit the church of Saint-Loup: that 'terrible and delectable catafalque', that church of which, he wrote, 'I never tire.'[15] Eugène Crépet was to describe what followed:

As he was admiring the confessionals, so richly and profusely carved, and sharing his admiration with Poulet-Malassis and Rops, who were with him, he was seized by a sudden giddiness, staggered, and collapsed on a step. His friends helped him up; he did not seem to be alarmed, and he maintained that his foot had slipped. They pretended to believe him; but next day, when he got up, he showed signs of mental disturbance. They quickly took him back to Brussels. He had hardly got into the carriage before he asked them to open the window. It was already open. He had said the opposite of what he had meant to say. One must recognise that as an unmistakable preliminary symptom of aphasia, and aphasia soon declared itself.[16]

116

On his return to the hôtel du Grand Miroir, Baudelaire was still able to move and to write; but his friends did not underestimate the gravity of his condition. On 17 March, Eugène Lefébure told Mallarmé of his sadness at the news. 'How many poems I should give for Baudelaire still to be Baudelaire!'[1] On 18 March, Asselineau offered Baudelaire the money he would need to return to Paris. Baudelaire refused, as he thought that he would still be able to return unaided.[2]

In Brussels, he dined with Neyt. He was not only taciturn and gloomy, he also showed occasional signs of confusion. 'He spoke little and with difficulty,' Pierre Dufay recorded, 'he was preoccupied, seized by fits of shuddering, his eyes sometimes wild, and as if lit up by a flash of terror. Then there was a desperate escape into the night.'[3] After he and his guest had parted, Neyt suddenly regretted that he had not taken Baudelaire back to his hotel. He set out to find him.

> At one o'clock in the morning, near the Grand' Place, M. Neyt found the poet again at a table in the Taverne Royale, which was already empty of customers. He had collapsed in a heap on a bench, and he had not finished the small glass of brandy set in front of him. He was far, far away from the café, where the waiters were beginning to stack the chairs on the tables ...
>
> He was taken back to his hotel room, hoisted up to it with great difficulty. With an imperative 'Get out! Get out, I say!', he dismissed his friend. A few hours later, Neyt returned, to find him stretched out on his bed, fully clothed, half dozing, and bereft of speech.[4]

The precise dates of these events are uncertain, but it was probably on about 20 March that Baudelaire had an attack. That day he wrote the last letter which he was to write in his own hand.

> My dear mother, I am neither ill nor well. I find it hard to work and to write. I shall explain why. Because I have intended to write to you for a

long time, and I think that this evening or tomorrow morning I shall answer you, and reply to all your questions. I am compelled to postpone my visit to Paris. But I shall make it, because it's absolutely necessary . . .

Poor darling mother, I am the reason why you are *woried! (with one 'r').* Spelling has so often varied in France that, anyway, you can allow yourself a few little oddities, like Napoleon and Lamartine . . .

If you want to read *Les Travailleurs de la mer*, I will send it to you in a day or two . . .[5]

That day he had another attack, which left him more disabled; and yet, it seems, he spent a night reading Hugo's novel. He even called again on Mme Hugo, and – since the power of speech had returned – he discussed the book with enthusiasm. He told her, again, that he meant to review it.[6] However, on 22 March he was obliged to keep to his bed. He suffered not only from giddiness, but from ataxy, which affected the whole of his right side.[7] On the night of 22–23 March, there was a marked deterioration in his condition. Soon afterwards, while Arthur Stevens sat at his bedside, Baudelaire asked to dictate the article on *Les Travailleurs de la mer*. Stevens dissuaded him.[8]

He could no longer hold a pen; but on 23 March he dictated a letter for his mother. Either he was not aware of the gravity of his condition, or he was anxious not to disturb her. '[Dr. Léon Marcq] is kind enough to write at my dictation. *He begs you not to get excited*, and says that in a few days I shall be ready to resume my work.'[9] The prognosis soon proved to be wrong. On 26 March, Baudelaire was forced to explain: 'All my friends, and the doctors, too, consider that I should drop all literary affairs for six months, and that I should lead a country life.'[10] There is infinite sadness in the words.

He rejected the suggestion that Ancelle should come to Brussels. He was impatient for his hotel bill to be settled; Mme Aupick duly sent him money. He was still concerned with literature. Frédérix recalled: 'At the end of March 1866, we learned that Baudelaire was very ill at the hôtel du Grand Miroir, rue de la Montagne. In fact he was lying on his bed, fully dressed and very despondent, reading a small, well-bound edition of *Les Liaisons dangereuses*. It was no doubt the last book that he held in his hands.'[11] On 28 March, he received the proofs of his poems from *Le Parnasse contemporain*. Mendès suggested the general title *Nouvelles Fleurs du mal*. Baudelaire corrected the proofs with the help of Gustave Millot, an expatriate French journalist, and sent them back to Paris that evening.[12] Next day he dictated a note to Mendès, adding further corrections, and happily accepted the title which Mendès had suggested.[13] He also dictated a letter to Ernest Prarond, thanking him for a copy of his collected poems, *Airs de flûte*;

he suggested one or two corrections.[14] His mind was active. He remained a faithful friend; he had not forgotten the days of the École normande and the Quartier Latin.

It was, perhaps, at Baudelaire's request that Malassis had kept Ancelle informed of events. On 29 March, from Neuilly, after consultation with Mme Aupick, Ancelle replied:

Monsieur,
  I thank you very sincerely for the letters which you have been good enough to send me. They bear witness to your concern for our friend, a concern which deeply touches me. I have sent Mme Aupick your opinion of her son's condition, but I have softened it here and there so as not to alarm her. She is in correspondence with her son, he has told her something about it. She has written to the doctor, Dr Léon Marcq. She is waiting for a reply.
  She would be glad to go and fetch her son herself, but her state of health does not permit it, and she has asked me to make the journey in her stead.
  As you know, I was disposed to do so independently of her, but I shall wait for the opportune moment so that her son's condition allows him to travel home without too much fatigue.
  I have written to Baudelaire to prepare him to see me, but I have also told him to write to me so that my journey is as far as possible in agreement with him.
  I am sending him a hundred francs by registered letter. I presume that they will therefore take this letter to him . . .[15]

Baudelaire's condition has not worsened [Malassis replied next day], but one cannot say that there is an improvement.
  . . . This morning I saw Dr Marcq, who is going to answer Mme Aupick *so as not to increase her anxiety* . . .
  I have just left Baudelaire. He did not tell me that he had received anything from you. I see him every day, twice rather than once, and it has gradually appeared to me that he has ceased to feel repugnance at the idea of leaving.
  The sooner the departure is, the better it will be.[16]

That day, Baudelaire himself dictated two further letters, one addressed to Ancelle, and the other to Mme Aupick. It was, he told her, 'useless, or at least premature', for Ancelle to come to Brussels:

  1. Because I am not in a condition to move.
  2. Because I have debts.
  3. Because I have six towns to visit, which will take, let us say, a fortnight.
     I don't want to lose the fruits of so much work.
  I know that, above all, he has it at heart to please you and obey you; that is why I am writing to you about it. Besides, I am ready to come back as soon as possible.[17]

That day, his right side became paralysed, and aphasia declared itself. Presumably his abuse of drugs, and his recent abuse of alcohol, had contributed to arterial damage. (Dr Augustin Cabanès later maintained, in his study *Grands névropathes*, that Baudelaire had sclerosis of the cerebral arteries.)[18] That day, 30 March, Dr Oscar Max, the hotel physician, was summoned to his bedside, and found him unable to move or to speak. Baudelaire, it seems, had suffered a series of attacks that progressively reduced his powers.[19]

Dr Max advised telling his family and friends that Baudelaire would have to be moved to a *maison de santé*. Next day, Malassis told Dracquemond that Baudelaire's condition was '*most extremely grave*', and that he, Malassis, had sent a telegram to Ancelle.[20] Charles Hugo called on Baudelaire, and found him 'too ill to be left alone'.[21] Mme Hugo told her husband that Baudelaire was 'doomed'.[22]

That day, 31 March, under the title *Nouvelles Fleurs du mal*, *Le Parnasse contemporain* published sixteen poems by Baudelaire. They were, in a sense, his farewell to literature.

> Sois sage, ô ma Douleur, et tiens-toi plus tranquille.
> Tu réclamais le Soir; il descend; le voici:
> Une atmosphère obscure enveloppe la ville,
> Aux uns portant la paix, aux autres le souci.
>
> Pendant que des mortels la multitude vile,
> Sous le fouet du Plaisir, ce bourreau sans merci,
> Va cueillir des remords dans la fête servile,
> Ma Douleur, donne-moi la main; viens par ici,
>
> Loin d'eux. Vois se pencher les défuntes Années,
> Sur les balcons du ciel, en robes surannées;
> Surgir du fond des eaux le Regret souriant;
>
> Le Soleil moribond s'endormir sous une arche,
> Et, comme un long linceul traînant à l'Orient,
> Entends, ma chère, entends la douce Nuit qui marche.[23]

117

On 3 April, on the recommendation of Dr Max, Ancelle (who had arrived in Brussels), Malassis and Arthur Stevens took Baudelaire to the Institut Saint-Jean et Sainte-Élisabeth. The hospital, in the rue des

Cendres, was managed by Augustine nuns. It had been a handsome
private *hôtel*. Indeed, it was here that the Duchess of Richmond had
given her famous ball on the eve of the Battle of Waterloo. According
to the register of new patients, Baudelaire was suffering from apoplexy.

Mme Aupick was seventy-two; she had almost lost the sight of her left
eye, she suffered from nervous troubles and migraines, and Crépet says
that her legs were half paralysed.[1] She found it difficult to walk, let
alone to travel to Brussels. Besides, her son's friends – Ancelle among
them – were not anxious that she should make the journey. A frail old
lady would be an encumbrance rather than a help, and they were not
sure that her presence would be good for him. She therefore stayed in
her seaside villa, and she continued to be disturbed by the details which
she was sent. She remembered that the doctors had failed to diagnose
her first husband's condition, and that he need not have died when he
did. She also remembered that her stepson had died, paralysed, in
middle age, and she was afraid that history might repeat itself. She had
little faith in the medical profession.

> He must be very ill, then, my poor son, since you have had to put him
> in a nursing-home! I have tears in my eyes [she told Ancelle]. How I hate
> this infirmity which keeps me here, so far away from him! I'm afraid I'll
> go mad! *I don't have a good head.*
>   The doctor writes to me that he is suffering from a nervous disease.
> This manifests itself in fits which are liable to recur, and he needs a
> complete change of life . . .
>   At Louis-le-Grand, his friend and tutor in *rhétorique*, M. Lassègue [*sic*] –
> he used to tell the General and me that his pupil was cleverer than he
> was – became a doctor, and a specialist in *mental derangement*. Charles has
> always remained friends with him. Charles wrote to me at the beginning
> of his attack (neuralgia, dizziness, vertigo), that he was mad and that he
> would go and consult Lassègue in Paris.[2]

Baudelaire had not told his mother that he was mad. In his letter of
12 February, he had said that he would consult Lasègue, who
specialised in madness and hysteria.[3]
    Gustave Kahn maintained that 'nowhere, in her verbose letters, did
Mme Aupick give the impression of intelligence.'[4] The observation was
unkind, and it was unjust. She was widowed, now, and alone, and she
was far from well; she was living among a restricted circle of neighbours,
in the depths of the French provinces. Turned in on herself, she was
desperately anxious about her son. To Ancelle she wrote:

> He must leave, without stopping in Paris, for our final reunion, a reunion
> which I hope will be for ever and ever; under his mother's roof, in
> Honfleur, he will find a comfortable life, indeed an easy one: order and

economy are natural to me. I should rather *let him dip into my purse* than diminish his own small means . . .

Please say many affectionate things to Charles for me. Does he show surprise or regret at not seeing me?[5]

She remained in touch with Malassis. On 4 April, she assured him:

I am full of gratitude, Monsieur, for all your kindness to my son, and for the affectionate concern you show for him . . . Do you think that I can write to him? Will he be able to read me? Perhaps he is completely unconscious, if the paralysis has reached his brain. Oh, my God! What an ordeal! It's more than I can bear.

I am very glad that he is with Nuns; but, on the other hand, I'm afraid that they may torment him with excessive or misplaced zeal.

M. Ancelle tells me in his letter that, while he is in the process of writing to me, my son is busy reading a letter from me, and that he is very touched by it. Is that really true? M. Ancelle knows my nervous and impressionable nature, and perhaps he is deceiving me. Enlighten me, monsieur, oh enlighten a poor mother who is crazed with grief and anxiety.[6]

There was apprehension, now, not only in Honfleur, but among the poet's friends in Brussels and in Paris. That day, Malassis sent a note of warning to Asselineau: 'Baudelaire cannot express two related ideas – he seeks for words, to join one to the other, and he can't find them. The intellectual effort is too great.'[7] Dr Crocq, at the Institut Saint-Jean et Sainte-Élisabeth, had spoken to Ancelle 'in such a way that M. Ancelle left with no doubt of a fatal end.'[8] Malassis was despondent, but tactful. Baudelaire wanted him to take home his trunk of books and papers. 'I refused', explained Malassis, 'out of discretion, and also because I was afraid that he might take my consent as a sign that his condition was hopeless.'[9] On 5 April, from Paris, Asselineau wrote to Malassis:

News is awaited here impatiently. You can well imagine that, for the past three days, there has hardly been any other subject of conversation among us.

It is a desolating loss, whether our friend should finally die, or whether he survives in a state in which we shall no longer recognise him.

In your own concern with him and with his affairs, we all recognise the warmth of devoted friendship, and, as you so rightly say, the important question is the literary question. All Baudelaire's friends agree with you on this point, and they will help you with all their might.

Théodore [de Banville] had a letter from Glatigny a week ago; urge him to continue writing.[10]

Glatigny, that sad character from *Le Roman comique*, was on tour with a troupe of actors in Brussels. In the last few weeks, until the attack at

Namur, he had seen much of Baudelaire. It was, presumably, about now that he reported:

> ... Baudelaire is growing worse and worse. I am very much afraid he won't last the week.
>
> He doesn't recognise anyone any more, his tongue is enormously swollen and it has the effect of a gag.
>
> His friends would like to have him taken to a more appropriate place than the one where he is now, but he can't even be moved from his bed in order to change his sheets ... His condition is quite hopeless. He is hardly lucid for five minutes a day, and he has been like this for a week.[11]

The letter was addressed to a friend who remains unidentified; it was later found inserted in a copy of Glatigny's poems, in the possession of the Parnassian poet Albert Mérat.[12]

On the last day of March, Mme Hugo told her husband: 'Baudelaire is finished ... The illness has almost entirely destroyed his brain, they despair of the invalid, and they are afraid, above all, that he will outlive his mind. It is very sad, for Baudelaire was a rare spirit.'[13] The Hugos sent for news of him every day.[14] 'And poor Baudelaire?' the journalist La Fizelière enquired of Malassis. 'Is it true that the hope of saving him, intellectually speaking, is not lost? French literature has a desperate need of the note that he can sound.'[15]

On 7 April, Dr Lequine, the head physician at the hospital, confirmed the diagnosis of aphasia. Two days later, Malassis took it on himself to describe the situation for Jules Troubat, so that the Parisian literary world might be informed of Baudelaire's dreadful fate.

> ... For six months the whole of his nervous system had been greatly endangered. He failed to take account of the serious symptoms and warnings, and, despite the advice of his doctors and the entreaties of his friends, he continued to use and to abuse excitants. Contrary to his habits, his willpower was so weak in this regard that brandy was no longer put on the table in my house, to stop him drinking it. Otherwise the urge was irresistible.
>
> A fortnight ago – eighteen days ago – he had to take to his bed. Dizzy spells, ataraxia [*sic*] of the right side, arm and leg. I should have liked to take him back to Paris, or, better still, to his mother's. He refused this in a sort of fury. A week ago on Friday, he developed paralysis of the right side, as well as softening of the brain ...
>
> He is sinking visibly. The day before yesterday, he mixed up his words in expressing the simplest ideas; yesterday he could not speak at all.
>
> If Baudelaire recovered physically, the doctors say that he would just be reduced to a vegetable existence – short of a miracle, they were saying a week ago, and, since then, they have ceased to speak of miracles.[16]

Baudelaire, said Le Vavasseur, had not drunk excessively in youth; many of his friends had noted his moderation.[17] Malassis did not record the tension and despair that had finally reduced him to intemperance; he therefore implied that Baudelaire had destroyed himself with drink and drugs. Besides, such a phrase as 'softening of the brain' suggested idiocy. In fact, though Baudelaire may have been paralysed and mute, his eyes revealed that his intelligence remained.

There has been much debate about his condition; many of his contemporaries took a syphilitic infection for granted. The issue was whether the infection had reached the tertiary stage, cerebral syphilis; or whether syphilis was merely one of several factors that led to a softening of the brain and to endarteritis of the left cerebral artery – an inflammation of the inner coat of the artery wall – and to a cerebral haemorrhage or stroke. Since most of the disputants were aware that Baudelaire never suffered from megalomania, or from the final madness of general paralysis – such as Jules de Goncourt was to experience – they reached a rough agreement in the 1930s that Baudelaire's paralysis and aphasia had resulted from a cerebral haemorrhage.

Yet, to speak of a cerebral haemorrhage as being the cause of Baudelaire's death, might lead us to forget that the cerebral haemorrhage itself was an effect of some other condition. In the first place, an hereditary predisposition to stroke was indicated in the deaths of Baudelaire's mother and half-brother, who both died partially paralysed, with some degree of aphasia. Baudelaire's own death, however, attested to the existence of factors in this case which led to premature decay: not the orgies of Baudelairean mythology, but a life of almost unrelieved tension and anxiety. Consumed by shame and hatred, imbued with a sense of damnation from an early age, he had come to have a horror of life.[18] No doubt he knew, since he had contracted syphilis as a youth, that he might not live his normal span. Dr Christian Dedet, writing in 1967, saw his early death as 'the biological conclusion of what one might call "an old story".'[19]

118

On 9 April, the forty-fifth birthday of her son, Mme Aupick addressed herself, once again, to Malassis:

Thank you, Monsieur, for your letter, which contains such precious details for me. From what you say I see that [Charles] is not happy with the food. And personally I am not happy about this harshness of manner from the Sisters. I thought that he was surrounded by gentle, affectionate doves, as I always imagine that Nuns must be. We cannot re-educate them, but I thought that one could change the food if one paid more, and I have just written to M. Ancelle about it . . .[1]

There was no doubt of Mme Aupick's concern or her generosity, or of her desire to do what was right for her son. Yet, deep inside herself, she was alarmed at the thought of caring for him in her old age. 'I am afraid', she added, 'that he may be distressed not to have me beside him. Indeed, what must he think when he does not see me hasten to his bedside? He doesn't know my own state of health. If it were a question of going to embrace my dying son, I should go, were I never to arrive! But, since I have been given the hope that he may be brought back to me, it seems to me sensible to wait.'[2]

The problem of where Baudelaire should go was made more acute by a letter from the Mother Superior of the Institut Saint-Jean et Sainte-Élisabeth. Next day, Mme Aupick wrote, once again, to Malassis:

I have heard from the Mother Superior, whom I had asked for news, and she has sent me a letter which overwhelms me. Having talked to me about my poor son's state of health, she says that *it is very hard for her to give shelter to a man without religion, and she asks me to come and help him.* This is what gives me cause to fear that she does not want to keep him there. What should I do if that were so, where should I put him? And there is another fear, which is no less great, it is that the nuns, inspired no doubt by good intentions, are tormenting him; and, by talking to him too soon about God's concerns, they are harming him . . . Since he is not in danger, from what the Mother Superior tells me herself, why torture him in advance? I should certainly be very unhappy if my son were to die without the help of religion; but we haven't reached that point. In any case, I don't know what has caused this complaint against him. Perhaps in Religious Establishments they demand that the sick should recite forms of prayer aloud. I hope that, after what I have written to the Mother Superior, she will keep him; I have written to her in terms as persuasive as my poor maternal heart could suggest.[3]

Perhaps, after all, she considered, she should visit her son; but she was set in her ways, she needed her faithful maid, Aimée Falaise, who had been with her for seven years,[4] and she was anxious about her living conditions in Brussels. 'If I go there with my maid, what shall I do? How shall I be able to settle down? I must have lodgings very near, as near as possible to Charles, since I find it very difficult to drag myself along . . .'[5]

In mid April, writing to Banville to announce his own return to Paris, Glatigny told him: 'Baudelaire is still in the same condition. If you want precise information about his illness, get the second volume of clinical medicine at the Hôtel-Dieu, by M. Armand Trousseau, and look up the chapter headed *aphasia*. M. Trousseau quotes fifty to sixty cases of this horrible thing, and not a single cure.'[6]

Malassis, uniquely devoted, sat with Baudelaire by the hour. Ancelle, paternal as ever, had come to Brussels, and departed. The correspondence between them continued. On 11 April, from Neuilly, Ancelle announced:

Monsieur,

I have received your two letters of the 8th and 9th. Although they are profoundly sad and make me foresee an inevitable calamity, I thank you for the details which they contain . . .

I have had letters from Mme Aupick nearly every day. She disturbs me a great deal, because she has moments of despair . . .

In a letter of the 7th, she tells me that she has written to you and that she is waiting for your answer. You have no doubt sent this answer. (I have just seen that you have written to her.) In this same letter she says to me:

Must I abandon the hope that you will bring him back to me? Remember that I will not, must not let him die without embracing him, while he is conscious. Enlighten me, then. I must know the truth.

I have told her roughly what she asks, but with an attenuation as far as one can judge about his illness; that is to say that I have left her a hope that her son will be brought back to her.

She also thought of undertaking the journey to Brussels despite the weakness of her legs. She expected to be accompanied by her maid, who is devoted to her, and either to stay at the nursing-home or as close as possible to it . . .

I made a few objections to her about this journey. Charles knows that his mother is kept back by her legs. Wouldn't this poor lady's arrival in Brussels make a great impression on her son?

But because of the content of your last letters, and because Mme Aupick would suffer too much grief and would greatly reproach her friend, if she lost her son without seeing him again, as she has told me that she wants to do, I have passed on to one of her friends and neighbours whom I know at Honfleur, [no doubt Émon], the passage in your letter which reveals Baudelaire's true condition, and I have engaged this friend to turn her thoughts towards a journey which seems to me urgent and important in view of what you tell me . . .

I am speaking of this journey as if she could undertake it, but I am afraid that she may be prevented by her health. In her last letter she tells me that she is very unwell. I am uncertain as to what she will be able to do. Baudelaire's sister-in-law was saying yesterday that, if need be, one could bring Baudelaire to Paris. That depends, I told her, on the doctor's advice, of the result which one might fear from such exhaustion. There would be a heavy responsibility in giving such advice. You will be kind enough to [let me] know if it is absolutely impossible. This lady lost her husband – Baudelaire's brother – from paralysis, too!

Mme Aupick spoke to me with very real gratitude about you and M. Stevens, who are caring for her son and love him so dearly. She will have occasion to say so to you both.

If you can improve the food by increasing the payment, please do so, Monsieur. Write and tell me what must be sent and I will send it to you at once. The Sister Superior does not want anything to be brought in from outside, but no doubt she can make an exception and provide what one wants if she is paid . . . I leave that to you.

I am rather puzzled by the letter which [Baudelaire] dictated to you for me. I know what his fantasies can be. He sometimes has moments of hostility towards me. I very readily forgive him for them.

Today I went to M. Asselineau's. I was sorry not to find him in. I left him a card with a message to say that it was about Baudelaire. Perhaps he will come and see me. He seems to me to be most elusive.

As far as the copies of the *Épaves* are concerned, do as the inspiration moves you. It is in fact a duty to fulfil the wish that our friend expressed, and don't worry about this or about any other [wish] that you may have fulfilled on this sad occasion, the same for all the advances either from you or from M. Stevens, expenses of every kind – Mme Aupick begs and implores me to ask you both for your accounts . . .

I shall be very happy to repay such sacred debts.

I strongly suspect that Charles could not refrain from swearing when the idea came to him. I deplore it, but the [Sister] Superior will certainly have to make the best of it.

Kindly present my compliments to M. Stevens, Monsieur, and believe me,

Yours sincerely,

ANCELLE[7]

The question of Mme Aupick's visit was settled sooner than expected. Next day, 12 April, Ancelle duly telegraphed to Malassis: 'Mme Aupick leaves today 11 o'clock arrives Gare St Lazare 5 o'clock. Stays overnight.'[8] There followed a second telegram: 'Aupick and maid arrive [Brussels] 2 o'clock tomorrow. Meet at station take to hotel near son.'[9] That day the tireless Ancelle also wrote a letter to Malassis, and asked him: 'Please would you have the kindness – and I'm sure you've thought of it – to prepare the son to see his mother?'[10] Malassis and Ancelle understood each other.

It was also a question of preparing the mother to see her son. Mme Aupick had not seen Baudelaire for nine months – since his hurried visit to Honfleur in July 1865. She could not have imagined his deterioration. On 14 April, Malassis explained to Asselineau:

Baudelaire's present condition is this. In the last week he has had two severe [attacks] of softening of the brain [*sic*] . . . He could, apparently, die at any time should he have another, but his condition could also continue for months and years. Which I do not wish.

For three days, Baudelaire has not said a single word, he cannot express an idea, however simple it may be. How far does he understand what is said to him? That is a mystery. I spend two hours a day with him, looking at him, and trying to make out his mental state, and really I shouldn't dare to say whether or not he still thinks, *to any degree whatever*. On this point, the doctors do not see more clearly than I do. I have had to conclude, from their conversations, that nothing is more uncertain than signs of intelligence in a softened brain.

The face is still intelligent, and it seems to me that ideas flash through it *like lightning*. I don't think he hears a friend's name *without pleasure*.

His mother arrives in Brussels today [*sic*]. She should really have stayed at home, because it is a heartrending sight.

Against my advice, Baudelaire was put into a hospital which is managed by nuns, *without a controller*. These sisters are moved by excessive zeal, and I am afraid that they have tormented the invalid. Baudelaire has so far refused to give satisfaction with the most elementary signs of belief. They have not been able to get a sign of the Cross from him. Hence a great irritation in the establishment. If I hadn't heard last night about Mme Aupick's arrival, I should, on my own initiative, have had Baudelaire moved today to another nursing-home.

This is not, my dear friend, because of a spirit of opposition and unbelief, you know my respect for cases of conscience. I would go and find a priest for whom Baudelaire had asked in complete awareness of his condition. But you will understand that I cannot allow them to torment and distress a man who has nothing, now, to ask from his fellow men except that they should leave him in peace.

I'm not too sure how I shall get on with Mme Aupick, who has written to me that she would be sorry if her son should die without the help of religion. I imagine that some or other emotion could bring on the third acute attack of softening – and as perhaps there is still one chance in 10,000 that Baudelaire may recover, I am quite determined, as far as I am concerned, not to lose it; and I shall fight to the very end any behaviour which might over-excite him.[11]

It was a letter which revealed Malassis' warmth of heart, his integrity, and his independence of mind.

Champfleury had told him: 'Baudelaire is doomed, there can be no doubt of that. He will die like a poet, and it is better that he should die quickly.'[12] Some Parisians believed that he was already dead. That day, 14 April, in *L'Événement*, Georges Maillard announced the death of Baudelaire. On 17 April Henry de La Madelène was to deny the statement in *Le Temps*. Next day, however, *L'Écho Honfleurais* reprinted a note by Jules Claretie from *L'Avenir national*: 'M. Charles Baudelaire, whose illness we announced the other day, died last week in Brussels. He was forty-five ... M Charles Baudelaire has left in manuscript a work on Belgium, *Pauvre Belgique*, a novel and some new poems.' Nothing more is known of the novel, if it existed; as for the new poems,

they were possibly *poèmes en prose*. But it was now, it seems, that
Swinburne paid tribute to their author's memory in *Ave atque vale*.[13]
Baudelaire was already erased from the list of living men.

On 14 April, a day later than Ancelle had announced, Mme Aupick
arrived in Brussels and settled at the hôtel du Grand Miroir. She paid
her son's arrears of rent. As she reported to Ancelle: 'The doctors have
not concealed from me the gravity of his condition, not physical, but
mental: *his mind has overworked*, it is worn out *before its time*. His tongue
is not paralysed, but he has lost the memory of sounds.'[14] He could
not even utter his own name.

> *Non, quie, quie* are the only words he utters [so she continued, to Ancelle],
> and he shouts them at the top of his voice . . . There is a softening of the
> brain, that's obvious. When he isn't angry, he listens and he understands
> all you are saying to him. And then, when he wants to answer, he is
> enraged by his powerless efforts to express himself. The doctors say that
> his mind has gone and want me to leave; what drives him insane is to be
> unable to speak . . . No extravagant behaviour, no hallucinations . . . He
> eats and sleeps, he goes out in a carriage with Stevens and me, or on foot,
> with a stick, on the public promenade, in the sun. But there are no more
> words . . . I shan't leave him, I shall keep him *like a little child*.
>
> He is not *insane*, as the doctors say. Malassis maintains that a poet's
> nature is so different from other people's that it can sometimes lead the
> doctors astray. What an excellent young man, that Malassis [Malassis was
> forty-one]! He was crying bitterly. How good he is! That young man must
> have a noble soul!
>
> I don't think that Charles can read, or he would always have a book in
> his hand; if he picks up a book, he can't make out the letters any more,
> and he throws it down.
>
> When he sees me, he is moved. Aimée says *that he seems to refrain from
> being pleased* . . . He isn't ill-natured. I have some control over him. He
> grows calm when I speak to him gently. Never any anger with me, not
> even sulkiness . . . He lost his temper with me this morning for the first
> time . . . He is very changeable . . . His nerves have a great deal to do with
> it. After he has lost his temper, he sometimes has prolonged bursts of
> laughter, which frighten me . . . He is very angry when I write . . . He is
> never angry without a reason.
>
> He points out something in the corner of the room, and he does so with
> distaste. They bring him everything. He continues to point it out, and he
> is in a terrible rage. They bring him some dirty linen which was
> underneath a bed. He calms down. He is excessively concerned with
> cleanliness.
>
> They have used electricity with success, but they have stopped because
> they're afraid of excitement and violence.
>
> He listens carefully, he laughs, he ridicules himself, he clearly makes his
> thoughts understood, there is still so much intelligence and animation in
> his eyes . . . He had my letters on his bedside table. And in the pockets of

his overcoat, which is made of some coarse, cheap material, there were many small photographs of himself by Nadar.

Some of his Paris friends want to get up a subscription to take him back there and look after him ... He himself doesn't want to leave, or to go out: he wants to speak.

He is certainly not in a condition to be deprived of his freedom, that would be inhuman, it would be a crime. He has only one fixed idea: *not to be dominated* ... He does not want to wear a hat in the courtyard, in the sun ... The nuns impose habits on him; when he eats, they would like him to cross himself; *then he is mild and gentle*, and wonderfully patient: he shuts his eyes, or turns his head away, but he doesn't lose his temper. He pretends to be asleep when they worry him, but they could provoke a scene that would kill him.

He could live for thirty years, and remain aphasic all his life.[15]

Baudelaire was now able to utter only one word, *crénom*, and that word was understood as an abbreviation of *sacré nom*. He did not use the word in order to offend the Augustines; it was the only expression left to him, and he had to use it to express every kind of meaning. But the nuns were dismayed by what they took to be a frequent blasphemy, and it was clear that he must be removed from their care. On 19 April – just over a fortnight after he had entered it – Malassis told Asselineau that he and Arthur Stevens had taken Baudelaire from the nursing-home, and back to the hotel, to be with his mother.[16]

119

Monsieur [wrote Ancelle to Malassis on 23 April],

I have received your letter of 17 April, containing details of the condition of our poor friend Baudelaire, and I thank you for it. Almost at the same time I received another letter from Mme Aupick, and what she told me roughly agreed with what you said yourself...

I had sent you word by telegraph to find a hotel near the rue des Cendres, to make it easy for Mme Aupick to pay frequent visits to her son. I was pleased to see that you had installed her at the hôtel du Grand Miroir, where she finds them sympathetic. I was afraid of the distance from the rue des Cendres...

So Charles is now settled once again in this hotel ... I should be very glad to know if this change seems to give him pleasure, and if it has had some or other effect on the poor invalid.

What you have done me the honour of telling me is hardly reassuring, but, considering the symptoms which appeared, it is hard to be able to hope for a recovery.

I should, however, view it with great satisfaction if Mme Aupick could take her son to Honfleur, where she will have many facilities for the care that he demands, and, personally, she will have more safeguards from the point of view of her own health.

I cannot help being afraid that this poor mother will be ill. She is showing a great deal of strength and courage, but she is shattered by everything she sees, and I'm afraid that she may not get over so many painful things . . .

I don't want to abuse your kindness, Monsieur, but you would give me pleasure if you wrote to me from time to time.

I beg you to give my compliments to M. Stevens, and to remember me kindly to him, and to believe me, Monsieur,

Yours very sincerely,

ANCELLE

I have consulted a doctor here whom I know, a specialist in mental illnesses, about the fact that Charles says nothing now except *non*. He had a patient in the same situation; he told me that I could hardly hope for anything else, and that it was *very serious*.[1]

Malassis not only continued his correspondence with Ancelle; he and Stevens often went to visit Baudelaire at the hôtel du Grand Miroir. Sometimes they took him, speechless and half paralysed, on carriage-drives round the outskirts of Brussels. They were now concerned both with him and with his mother. To Malassis, she was not the mother whom Baudelaire deserved. On 26 April, he reported to Asselineau: 'Madame Aupick carries a horror of her son's literature a long way, for yesterday she refused to read *Le Parnasse [contemporain]*. I am quite determined that, if she does not behave as she should when the question of the works is discussed, I shall take no notice of her ownership.'[2] She later thanked Banville effusively for his *Nouvelles Odes funambulesques*, but confessed to Asselineau ('*this between ourselves*') that she did not understand them.[3] It was small wonder that *Les Fleurs du mal* remained beyond her comprehension. Mme Aupick, said Nadar, 'was cultivated, and she had a most delicate understanding; but the Work remained inaccessible to her.'[4]

Malassis was still determined that Mme Aupick should appreciate her son's distinction. Despite her refusal to read *Le Parnasse contemporain*, he had given her the issue which contained the *Nouvelles Fleurs du mal*. His patience and resolve were to be rewarded. On 1 May, in another letter to Asselineau, he continued:

I left her the fifth number of *Le Parnasse contemporain*, and she simply had to have a look at it. One poem pleased her, the one which ends:

Entends, ma chère, entends la douce Nuit qui marche.

She read it to me, and I was surprised to see that she read very well, and also like someone who knew that she read well.[5]

It was, perhaps, in answer to this letter that Asselineau wrote, that month, with family news:

Yesterday I dined at M. Ancelle's, with the sister-in-law of Baudelaire. She had once been a pretty woman, and she was very prim. I was even promoted to the honour of escorting her home, since she is a neighbour of mine. [At M. Ancelle's] I found myself, in a sense, in the midst of the enemy . . . These good people have no idea that dear Baudelaire is the illustrious person in the family, and one of the most remarkable spirits of the modern age. They seemed quite astounded to hear me talk about him as you and I do.

I cannot guarantee that I did not pass for a charlatan and a poseur. There was only one person there who was really fond of Charles, and that was good papa Ancelle, he's a worthy man. He makes strange mistakes about our friend; but, when all is said, he loves him . . .

Mme Baudelaire irritated me with her petty dignity as a judge's wife [*sic*]. When I listened to her, I understood all that poor Charles must have suffered from his family.

The general opinion is that Mme Aupick adores her son, but that she would have liked him to be engaged in a more lucrative kind of work. Good papa Ancelle said, innocently: *He would never have thought of investing.*[6]

And Asselineau added: 'If our friend recovers from this, he will be able to take a splendid revenge, because, my dear fellow, it's ridiculous to say so, *his illness will have done him good.* People have grown accustomed to talking seriously about him.'[7]

In the early summer of 1866, the condition of Baudelaire, and the question of his future, were recorded in intensive correspondence. Directly and indirectly, the letters also revealed the characters of his mother and his friends. Some time in May, Asselineau wrote again to Malassis:

I have seen M. and Mme Ancelle several times this week. They insist that Mme Aupick will never agree to part from her son. They read me several letters from this lady, dictated by the most touching maternal feeling, but on the infantile or senile side.

'Since my son grew up, he has not been mine any more, it seems to me that he has now become a little child again, etc, etc.' That sort of stuff.

Since things are as you describe them, I completely agree with you. If B. cannot stay near you in Brussels, he must come back to Paris to be near me, among us. But shall we be believed? I shall urge on M. Ancelle with all my might.

Besides, the question seems to have changed a great deal recently. Doesn't this physical recovery augur something good? I am quite astonished that B. can walk and that he can follow a conversation intellectually.

Do we need after that to press so hard for publication?[8]

Baudelaire's condition augured nothing good. On 23 May, Malassis announced to Champfleury: 'Baudelaire will no doubt be brought back to France in a fortnight. To Honfleur, of course, to his mother's. His paralysis has almost vanished, and his physical health is good. He eats, digests, sleeps, and goes out for walks. But he does not go out alone.'9 Almost at once, the plans to take him back to Honfleur were put in doubt. Four days later, Malassis sent a revealing letter to Asselineau:

It had been decided that Baudelaire would soon be taken to Honfleur, and that his mother would engage a servant to control him a little. Not that he behaves badly: he is simply abrupt, impatient and irascible, just as he has always been, but more so. His mind has, alas, deteriorated in the last month, although there are the most surprising flashes of memory. Madame Aupick was very hostile to the idea of taking him to Honfleur, and was postponing it till the day when Baudelaire had recovered the use of speech, in other words never, and this decided the doctors to leave her no further illusions about the future. The poor lady confessed to me that to go home with her son in such a condition was a very hard blow to her self-esteem . . .

The same self-love explained why Madame Aupick agreed delightedly to the publication of his works, *assuming that it did not cost anything.* Don't be too surprised at this condition, because the good lady's resources are reduced to her pension, and Baudelaire regularly took half of it every year. The money she had on her husband's death had been used up in paying our friend's debts.10

That day, 27 May, Malassis added, to the engraver Bracquemond: 'Physically, Baudelaire is well [*sic*]. As for his mind, it is almost destroyed.'11

Mme Aupick now accepted that her son would need to go to a nursing-home in Paris. On 30 May she announced to the faithful Malassis:

If things got worse to the point where they reached this cruel extremity, I should put him in Monsieur Blanche's home, because he knows Charles and he's fond of him . . .

My compliments to your nice young wife [Malassis was still unmarried], and I send you my gratitude and the assurance of unchangeable affection.12

Malassis deserved her affection and her gratitude. His concern for Baudelaire had long been that of a brother. He could not do enough to ensure his comfort. On 2 June, he explained to Asselineau:

. . . The doctors consider that circumstances are favourable for moving Baudelaire . . .

They will have to take a whole compartment [on the train]. A great expense for Mme Aupick, among so many other unexpected and excessive expenses, not to mention the debts which have had to be paid. Wouldn't there be a way of having a compartment through the Société des gens de lettres, if not free, at least at a reduced price, from the French frontier? . . . Here, [in Brussels], Stevens is going to busy himself to get a reduction to the border.[13]

As Malassis had recognised, illness had not modified Baudelaire's character. It had simply accentuated certain traits. He now took a violent dislike to his mother's maid:

Charles has been very irritable today [Mme Aupick told Malassis on 5 June]: he has been in a furious temper with poor Aimée, for no reason except that he found her in my room, when he came to speak to me, and he would have liked to find me alone. He has just gone to bed (it is five o'clock), and refused to have dinner. Is it tiredness after the scene this morning, or because he tried to write with his left hand under my direction, or quite simply because he had a big *déjeuner*? I can't understand it at all, and I'm worried as you can imagine.[14]

Mme Aupick had complained to Malassis about her son's violent outbursts. It was clear that she herself had a unique gift for disturbing him.

I had always liked the idea of his going back to his mother [so Malassis wrote, again, on 7 June], because of the dignity of the family; but what I have seen, especially during the last month, in other words since Baudelaire has regained his physical health [*sic*], puts me off this idea more and more. Mme Aupick doesn't understand anything about her son's character, and she has never understood anything. There's no question that, despite the excellence of her maternal feelings, she is one of the people least qualified to be concerned with him, and to understand his wishes . . .
To let Baudelaire and his mother live with each other is to poison the lives of both of them.[15]

As time went on, Malassis and Asselineau both became increasingly determined that mother and son should be kept apart. As for M. Émon, who constantly advised Mme Aupick, he remained opposed on principle to their reunion. In an undated letter, addressed to Ancelle, she confessed: 'M. É[mon] is making unheard-of efforts to prevent me from having Charles with me, and he is talking about him in terms which are not only severe, but quite hard, talking about his egotism and extravagance. None of this will make the slightest difference to my determination.'[16] Her determination was not as strong as she suggested; she felt an overwhelming apprehension. Émon might not even cut the pages of *Les Fleurs du mal*; yet, as she later told Asselineau: 'The affection I feel for this old friend is for me a real religion.'[17] She was not only concerned about his low opinion of her son. Her other neighbours in Honfleur were sure to be malicious about the ruined man whom they called *le fils Aupick*.

Meanwhile, in Paris, Émile Blanche showed his sympathy. A famous specialist in mental illness, he had treated more than one man of letters in his private asylum in Passy. He had no doubt known Baudelaire since the early 1850s, when Gérard de Nerval had been among his patients. He was one day to attend Maupassant. Now, early in June 1866, Asselineau reported to Malassis:

> My friend Dr Blanche, to whom I spoke at length about B., generously offered to go and see him in Brussels. I did not think that I should accept.
>
> But today he offers something which might be acceptable, that is to send Mme Aupick a servant whom he has trained, accustomed to looking after the infirm. He could send him at once, either to Brussels, or to Honfleur, and so, if need be, you only have to write to him, and mention my name, in order to negotiate conditions.[18]

On 10 June, in a letter to Malassis, Ancelle confirmed: 'Dr Blanche offered Asselineau to send a special manservant (40 fr. a day, plus fares and expenses). The doctor is also ready to go and see the invalid in Paris at the first opportunity.'[19]

Matters could not be so simply settled. If they accepted the doctor's offer, it would, perhaps, mean putting Baudelaire in his asylum; and, as Asselineau wrote: 'What seems to me clearest about all this is, first and foremost, that B. is not mad in the least.'[20]

It became increasingly evident that, although Baudelaire did not need an asylum, he would have to go to a nursing-home in Paris. There remained financial considerations. Asselineau and Ancelle approached the Société des Gens de Lettres to obtain a train compartment at reduced rates for the journey through France. Arthur Stevens assured Mme Aupick that she would have the same facility as far as the Belgian frontier. Malassis was once again in trouble with French justice, for the publication of *Les Épaves*. He could not risk returning to France. It was finally decided that Mme Aupick and her maid would go with Baudelaire, and that Arthur Stevens would escort them as far as Paris. Ancelle inspected two hotels near the Gare du Nord: the hôtel Cailleux, where Mme Aupick had stayed on her way through Paris, and the hôtel du Chemin de fer du Nord, where Baudelaire had stayed on his last visit. He found them both acceptable for mother and son.[21] Asselineau arranged to meet their train.

On the evening before Baudelaire's departure, Malassis told Asselineau,

> . . . we had dinner together in my room. He had not been there since the eve of his severe attack. He pointed out certain curiosities which I had recently bought, observing their good qualities and their approximate artistic worth with his old sureness of taste [*sic*]. Before we parted company, I spoke to him at length of the pleasure he might find in putting his works in order with a friend – you, for example – until the day when he could work again. I reminded him that the definitive edition of *Les Fleurs du mal* was quite ready, and should be published. He gave me a sign of assent . . . The hope of completely recovering his intellectual health is certainly there . . .
>
> I packed the trunk myself, in the presence of M. Ancelle, when they had to take Baudelaire to hospital. It contains the books and papers which he had brought to Brussels, and a few books sent to him by friends . . . Among other books there is a copy which is all prepared for the printing of the definitive edition of the *Fleurs*, there are some manuscript *Poèmes en prose* and a farrago of notes on Belgium, which would never in any case have seen the light of day. Work had become impossible for Baudelaire. In the two years he spent in Brussels, his work came down to a few prose poems, usually short, and inferior to the first.[22]

On 29 June, accompanied by his mother, her maid, and Arthur Stevens, Baudelaire returned at last to Paris. He had been away for two years and three months. He had wanted to return with his financial problems settled, his fortune made, his penance done. 'I do not want to come back to France,' he had told his mother, 'unless I come with glory.'[23] Of all his failures, the journey to Belgium had, without question, been the most complete.

PART SIX

The Returning Poet

1866–1867

120

On the arrival platform, Mme Aupick remembered, 'he was glad to find Monsieur Ancelle, and especially Monsieur Asselineau.'[1] Asselineau himself recalled:

When I saw him coming towards me, supported by M. Stevens, he was leaning on his *left* arm, and carrying his cane, which was fastened to a button on his coat. It broke my heart, and the tears rose to my eyes. He caught sight of me, and let out a burst of laughter, long, loud and persistent, which froze me. Was he really mad? I hadn't spent fifteen minutes with him before I was – alas! – completely reassured on this point. I acquired the conviction that – a sad advantage, no doubt, for him – Baudelaire had never been more lucid, or more aware.[2]

He and Mme Aupick spent the next few days in a hotel near the Gare du Nord. Asselineau was almost always with them.[3] It was Asselineau who now undertook a delicate mission. On Mme Aupick's authority, he told Baudelaire that, '*since he had a horror of Honfleur, and showed such great repugnance to go there, and since in his present state he could not live alone in Paris, he would do well to go into a nursing-home where he would be perfectly comfortable, and enjoy great freedom, and where, so they said, he would feel at home.* Charles accepted this eagerly,' Mme Aupick reported to Malassis, 'and he is *very willing*, at least so far, but will he change his mind?'[4]

There was, she continued, no improvement in his speaking, 'and there are still rages, from which I suffer cruelly.'[5] Dr Blanche came to see him; so did Dr Piogey and Dr Lasègue. Gérard Piogey was a friend to artists and men of letters; Banville always spoke warmly of him, and Asselineau was one day to give him the portrait of Baudelaire by Deroy. Mme Aupick was to give him a Persian desk that had belonged to her son. As for Charles Lasègue, he had once prepared Baudelaire for his *baccalauréat*. He was now a specialist in mental illness, and Baudelaire himself had thought of consulting him. More than once Lasègue paid a visit to his former pupil, and he repeatedly refused a fee.

All the doctors, presumably, agreed that Baudelaire was not insane, and that he should be put 'into a nursing-home, where there are no lunatics'.[6] On Wednesday, 4 July, he was finally settled in the nursing-home to which, a few years later, Courbet would be taken: the

Clinique hydrothérapique de Chaillot, at 2, rue du Dôme, rond-point de l'Arc de Triomphe.

He was given an airy, ground-floor room in the lodge at the end of the garden. It was high-ceilinged, and it looked over the summer flowers and trees. He insisted on keeping his wooden trunk with him. It was put in a cupboard in his room, but some of its contents were removed: among them a number of books, which were arranged on a table, and a lacquered desk, which he was incapable of using.

On 5 July, the day after Baudelaire's installation, Asselineau reported to Malassis:

> I spent nearly every day with him before he was settled there . . . I found him much less ill than I had feared, that is to say completely lucid, intelligent and calm, except for the moments when Mad. Aupick or her maid exasperated him.
>
> Mme Aupick is going back to Honfleur in a few days. She finally understood that her presence was a source of irritation rather than consolation for her son. B. has been very good to me. He talks about you (talks, you understand!) with affection and regret. Mme Aupick extols you to the skies.
>
> It is now a matter of getting a ministerial grant to relieve the maternal purse.
>
> M. Ancel[le] thought that the affair should be arranged without telling Mme Aupick. Sainte-Beuve is going to set to work. As for the plan of publication, there's no question of it. I mentioned it briefly to B., who answered with a gesture of impatience. Is it discouragement? Is it that he hopes one day to arrange things himself?
>
> I should be very glad to have your opinion about this, or rather to know how you feel, because to my mind you are still the publisher, the proper and legitimate publisher.
>
> Baudelaire attaches great importance to the trunk. He refuses to give up the key, and he even refused to let it be taken up to the attic at Dr Duval's. Is it because this trunk contains his papers?[7]

The contents of the trunk had already been noted by Malassis; they were to be used in the preparation of the *Œuvres complètes*.

In July 1866, the most urgent problem remained the continuing presence of Mme Aupick. Malassis had unkindly noted in Brussels:

> The poor woman is feather-brained . . . She has never appreciated the sad effect of her habits and her attitude on her son. She understands him less than anyone. I can easily imagine that she could have lived with him for thousands of years without understanding him in the least. She wanted to pamper him, coddle him, cajole him. And then she set about it with all her maternal love, in such a way as to keep him in a state of irritation.[8]

Now, with the best intentions, she postponed her return to Honfleur, and she settled in furnished rooms at 8, rue Duphot, near the Madeleine. She remained anxious to do right, anxious to rise to the situation, but she exasperated Baudelaire by her fussy good intentions, her meticulous activity, her concern for trivialities, her failure to understand his deeper needs. She could not give him moral support; she was too concerned with respectability. Malassis judged her harshly: he deplored her 'lack of simplicity', and dismissed her letters, 'full of the spirit of conformity'.[9] Yet, as Arthur Symons was to write, it would have taken a very profound experience of life to have been a good mother to Baudelaire;[10] and, for all her faults, there was no doubt of her devotion. She loved him as much as her bourgeois nature and her limited faculties allowed. She was intent on ensuring his well-being.

On 11 July, she announced to Malassis: 'I have mentioned to Charles the names of some of his friends, to find out if he would like to see them.'[11]

121

Baudelaire had warmly greeted the name of Sainte-Beuve; and, on 10 July, in a letter which revealed her agitation, her anxiety to justify herself, Mme Aupick had sent *l'oncle Beuve* an account of events, 'well persuaded,' so she wrote, 'that you will not be indifferent to them.'[1]

I was at home at Honfleur [she explained], when I learned that [Charles] had been struck by Paralysis. I immediately [*sic*] hastened to his side, in Brussels, where I looked after him for three months [*sic*]. The whole of his right side, and the right side of his face, had twice been paralysed; and twice with softening of the brain. The Paralysis of the arm and leg has continually decreased, but the *Aphasia*, which resulted from it, still persists. My poor son can only utter two or three words: *ah! non, crénom, non*. I am sure, Monsieur, that you understand my regrets and my grief. I wanted – and it would have been a consolation for me – to keep him always with me, to undertake a loving task which might perhaps be permanent, and to devote my attention to him for the little time that remains to me; but the doctors in Brussels told me that, in his interest, I should put him into a nursing-home. In Paris, they said the same thing to me, including *Mr Lassègue* [*sic*]. I suspect that they have given me this advice because of the Sympathy which I inspire in them; they have pity on me when they see me, old and infirm, with this unfortunate man. At certain moments, when he cannot make himself understood, he turns violent, and becomes enraged, especially with me. So I gave in, and, *of his own free will*, having shown a great repugnance to go to Honfleur, Charles let himself be taken, *calm and resigned*, to Dr Duval's nursing-home, 2, rue du Dôme (a street leading into the rue Lauriston), near the Arc de Triomphe. He is comfortable there, and more serene ... Dr Lassègue, who is famous for his knowledge of mental illness, sometimes goes to see him. But Charles is not insane: he has kept a certain lucidity of mind; besides, one cannot know just how far his intellect (that fine, exceptional intellect) has been impaired, because he doesn't speak. I go and see him every day, between one o'clock and four ... In this nursing-home you can visit the patients at any time, any day. Some of his friends go and visit him, which gives me great pleasure, not only because it is a distraction for him, but because Mr Duval thinks that this ought to help him to learn to speak. Dare I ask you, Monsieur, to urge his friends, whom you must know, to go and see him? That would be an act of charity, because conversation with him is impossible, but he hears and understands everything, and likes to hear talk of *art* and *literature*. I dare not ask you, Monsieur, overburdened with work, as you are, to go and see him, but, should you do so, I offer you my gratitude now, in advance ...[2]

Madame [replied Sainte-Beuve].
    You are quite right to think that nothing has interested or concerned me more than the condition of our dear poet ... I shall certainly go and see him, and soon. There is not a man in literature who has shown me more friendship and for whom I in turn feel so much. I enter into everything that is cruel in your grief. Rest assured, Madame, that it is shared by everyone who feels the worth of his distinction and the value of his extraordinary talent.[3]

It was a well-turned and dishonest letter. Sainte-Beuve did not visit Baudelaire – because, so it was said, of his own ill-health; he had always failed his *cher enfant*: the poet who still, in the rue du Dôme, kept *Les Poésies de Joseph Delorme* beside him. Nonetheless, it seems, his name remained deep in Baudelaire's consciousness. Étienne Charavay records that two visitors called on Baudelaire, and 'one of them, ignoring the invalid's presence, began to talk maliciously about Sainte-Beuve. Baudelaire tried in vain to express his displeasure. His powerlessness made him furious, and, with his invalid's stick, he tried to hit the man who had wounded him in his affections and sympathies.'[4]

Sainte-Beuve did not visit Baudelaire; but his secretary, Troubat, went to see him. Baudelaire, he recorded, had lost the gift of speech,

    ... but his memory had not deteriorated ... He showed me everything he loved: the poetry of Sainte-Beuve, the works of Edgar Allan Poe, in English, a little book on Goya – and, in the garden of the Duval nursing-home, a succulent, exotic plant, whose pinking he made me admire. There was the shadow of the Baudelaire of former days, with his unchanged tastes and antipathies. He showed the greatest anger at the name of Courbet (again, as in former days). I talked to him about the success of the *Femme au perroquet*. 'Non, cré non!' But when I talked to him about Richard Wagner, and Manet, he smiled with pleasure.[5]

Champfleury, too, had walked in the garden with Baudelaire.

Until his last day, flowers remained important to him . . . But Baudelaire's favourite flowers were not the marguerite, the carnation or the rose; with eager enthusiasm he stopped in front of the fleshy plants which seemed like crouching hedgehogs, or serpents casting themselves before their prey . . . Speckled plants with twisted shapes: these were his ideal.
    Any flower that was red and garish, loud, capriciously jagged, Baudelaire immediately liked. He was not concerned about its scent. He preferred the dahlia to the violet. I could not explain the man better. If he liked a flower whose shape seemed to me too geometric, that was because it came from overseas. It reminded him of India [*sic*], which was dear to his imagination.[6]

Among the friends of Baudelaire whom Mme Aupick had approached was Maxime du Camp, who was now in Baden-Baden.

Madame [he replied on 13 July],
    They have just sent on to me here the letter which you did me the honour to write to me. I am deeply touched by your appeal . . . Unfortunately I am in Germany until December; but as soon as I return to Paris, I shall make my first visit to poor Baudelaire. I thought he was still in Belgium, otherwise I should have done my utmost to seek him out and to greet him before I left. The very warm friendship that I feel for him, the boundless admiration that I profess for his incomparable gifts made this a duty in which I should certainly not have failed. I hope that the concern which everybody feels for him will soon restore his health: a health which is doubly precious for his friends and for Literature.[7]

Some months later, he went to see him:

He was sitting in a big armchair, his hands white, and his face of that cadaverous pallor which is the paint of madness, his eyelids puffy and his eyes searching and fixed. No trace of emotion on his gaunt face; sometimes he seemed to raise himself up, with the greatest difficulty, to reply to what one said to him: 'Non, non, cré non!' These were the only words – the only two notes – which he managed to articulate.[8]

Du Camp then asked the question which was asked by many friends of Baudelaire: 'What remained of the poet? What faculty had his mind retained? Could he still create poems which he found it impossible to dictate or to write? . . . Did he understand the horror of the torture to which he was condemned?'[9]

He could, it seems, understand his state. Judith Gautier recalled that, once, when her father went to visit him,

> . . . he was looking through the drawer in which Baudelaire kept his manuscripts [*sic*], to see if he could find anything that could be offered to a publisher or editor. He saw his friend was watching him, with the tears streaming down his face. Baudelaire was stricken with paralysis and it was thought that his brain had quite gone. But the sight of my father looking at his cherished writings, poems and essays, . . . seemed to have awakened memory and consciousness in the poet's mind, and the utter wretchedness of his position had been forced upon his understanding. For the rest, this lucid interval was of the briefest, and, before Gautier left the room, Baudelaire had relapsed into idiocy and he sat huddled there in his armchair, repeating over and over again the horrid word in which he summed up his opinion on the lives of men.[10]

Mme Aupick remained convinced of her son's lucidity. 'Charles will not be able to answer you,' she explained to Banville, 'but he will understand all you say to him.'[11]

Banville was shocked by what he found: a man who was already old at the age of forty-five, a poet who had cruelly lost the memory of words. Baudelaire 'had really given his blood, his fluid, the very substance of his mind; he was dying exhausted, broken, defeated; having received no recompense which marked him out for the respect of the common man, having been nothing, not even an Academician; but he left his work, . . . his immortal work.'[12]

Nadar, too, went to visit Baudelaire. Sometimes Manet went with him. One day, when Manet failed to arrive, Nadar admonished him: 'Baudelaire is clamouring for you. Why didn't you come with us and him, today? Will you make amends for this next Friday? He missed you, and he surprised me, when I went to fetch him, by shouting to me from the bottom of the garden: "Manet!! Manet!!" That took the place of *crénom*.'[13]

Years later, an almost unknown French writer, Charles Buet, was to recall how, with a friend, he had visited Baudelaire in the rue du Dôme:

> All the eloquence, all the splendour, all the power of his speech was summed up in the sad words which he uttered, in a tone of happiness, when he saw us: '*Cré nom!*' And that meant, and had the illusion of meaning: 'You are welcome.' . . . His pallid face, the face of a dying man, lit up with pleasure. He looked at my companion with eyes which were open wide, very limpid, very innocent, and he made the sign of the Cross

several times, with an expression of unutterable delight, of majestic serenity, thus proclaiming that he had received the sacraments. And in making this sign of the Cross, . . . with the ample gesture of a Breton peasant, he murmured: '*Cré nom! Cré nom! Cré nom!*' I was choking with agony, my companion had dissolved into tears, and Baudelaire tried to console us, an ecstatic smile on his bluish lips, and murmured gently: '*Cré nom! Cré nom!*'

When we left, Baudelaire said goodbye to us: '*Cré nom!*' It meant that he wanted to keep us . . . I shall never see him again, and I shall no more forget that *Cré nom* than if I had heard it on Mount Sinai.[14]

These descriptions came from friends. The most brutal and, perhaps, the most touching came from the left-wing novelist and journalist, Jules Vallès, who had long detested Baudelaire. After the poet's death, Vallès remembered:

One of our friends saw him, several months ago, in the house [*sic*] in which he died. His left hand [*sic*], inert and twisted, hung against his chest; from time to time, with his right hand, he tried to raise the fingers, which were not yet rotten, but dead.

Only one eye remained a fraction open in this head which hung down too heavily on the shoulder, and in this eye, like a fading gleam, memory kept watch.

He could only articulate one word, like a child, but this word he moaned, and sneered, and, with little cries of anger and pleasure, he translated his ultimate impressions . . .[15]

Meanwhile, on 21 July 1866, *La Petite Revue* published optimistic comments on Baudelaire's condition.[16] The optimism was shared by a visitor, B. Maurice, who so far remains unidentified. His account of Baudelaire, late this July, appeared in a paper, also unidentified; the cutting remains among the Crépet papers:

I was finishing dinner the other day [recorded Maurice] at my friend Dr Émile Duval's, at his hydrotherapy establishment, 2, rue du Dôme, a few yards from the Hippodrome, when he said to me: 'You know Charles Baudelaire?' 'Of course.' 'You take an interest in him?' 'I deplore the misfortune which has befallen him.' 'Then you'll be very pleased to hear that he's recovering. It was De Lasseigle [*sic*] . . . who sent him to me from Belgium [*sic*].' 'What exactly is his illness?' 'Hemiplegia of the right side, together with aphasia, but he is better, much better. In a few days he will dine at table with everyone else . . . Would you like to see him?' 'Indeed I should . . .'

We found our dear invalid in a corridor opening on to the garden, in company with several other patients, smoking a cigar, and smoking it with evident pleasure. This may seem a futile remark, but it is a diagnosis which is rarely mistaken; when smokers and snufftakers no longer ask for tobacco, it is a bad sign; when they come back to it, one is entitled to augur for the best.

I had never been a close friend of Baudelaire's, I had just met him occasionally in the hall of *Le Figaro*, when they were publishing his article on Delacroix [*sic*]. However, when he saw me, his face took on an expression of childlike delight, he uttered cries which instantly reminded me of the educated deaf and dumb. He rushed up to me, and affectionately held out his left hand. A few moments later, at the doctor's suggestion, . . . he also grasped my hand in his right hand; but, although he did so with vigour, one saw that it cost him an effort.

What will save Baudelaire is that his brain, and therefore his intelligence, have remained intact. Today, after less than a month's treatment, the paralysis of the legs has completely gone; he walks straight, and he can go up and down stairs. He is the first to get up in the nursing-home, he arrives for his cold bath at 8 o'clock, and he takes it with evident satisfaction; he is clearly grateful for all the attention which is given. His sight is still very poor, and it does not allow him to read the papers, but he is interested when they are read to him.

In the past few days, he has begun to utter polysyllables: *Encore, voyons, allons, entrez, c'est ça.* When by chance we exchanged a few words in English in front of him, he continued to listen, and to understand, and [we were astonished] to hear him exclaim: *Yes, all right.*

He keeps, to a supreme degree, the memory of the heart. His face lights up when one mentions the names of his most assiduous visitors: Asselineau, Champfleury, Nadar; they are very busy people, but distance has not prevented them from coming.

My deep and personal conviction is that Charles Baudelaire will be restored to us, as we have known him, and that, after God, we owe our thanks to the intelligent and affectionate care of Dr Émile Duval.[7]

Mme Aupick felt less happy. On 23 July, she observed to Malassis:

He has always been gentle and polite with everyone. I alone have had to suffer his great bursts of anger; certainly because he has things to tell me which he does not tell other people, or else because he restrains himself less with me and he knows my weakness. His book of poems [*Les Épaves*] has often been the cause of terrible outbursts: he has something to tell me about this work which I can't make out. The other day he picked up this wretched book, and thrust it into my face to the point where I had to recoil. He flew into a furious rage because I didn't understand, and stamped his foot as hard as he could; finally, worn out with fatigue, he threw himself on his sofa. A few minutes later he began to shout again at the top of his voice, waving his legs in the air and howling like a wild animal. When I described the scene to M. Duval, he said to me: *You must avoid this: it's enough to give him cerebral congestion. I have wanted to ask you to stop coming for a long time, because he is only excited and enraged with you.* Some days later, in spite of this advice, I went back to see him, he was better with me, and at times even affectionate. But I have finally decided to go back to Honfleur.[18]

122

It was the decision which the poet's friends and, no doubt, Baudelaire himself wanted her to make. Dr Duval had helped to ensure it by his harsh, uncompromising warning that she should not visit her son. He had also, paradoxically, helped to ensure it by the hope of recovery he gave her. In the same letter to Malassis, she announced with delight:

> Here it is at last, the good news which has been so ardently desired! There is *a marked improvement* in Charles's condition. M. Duval told me yesterday *that he was on the road to recovery.* He did say that he couldn't answer for the future; but, for the moment, there is a great change . . .
>
> I am leaving Charles perfectly settled in this nursing-home, comfortable and happy [*sic*], receiving many visits, and making friendships with people in the home, and, which is very important to me, he is not far from M. Ancelle. M. Duval has promised to keep me well informed, and, if he was unfortunate enough to have a relapse, I should hasten to his side at once. So I am leaving tomorrow, and I am much less anxious than when I came. Charles has got a few more words; he always says *oui* pertinently now, and *très bien.* They once heard him say *Piogey* when they were looking for the doctor's name; but he hasn't repeated it. May it continue, this improvement! It quite amazes me!'[1]

Asselineau was less amazed: 'He says four new words: *Bonjour, monsieur, Bonsoir,* monsieur, *Adieu* and his doctor's name. The said doctor is triumphant about this result, which doesn't seem so glorious to me [this to Malassis] . . . It is clear that, if he were cured, he would speak; but whatever he says when he's ill will just be parrot-talk.'[2] And again he wrote: 'Dr Duval is only an *officier de santé* [a public health officer licensed by the government]. He is stupidly triumphant, it seems to me.'[3]

The comment on Duval was curious; but, in giving him the inferior title, which had been that of Charles Bovary, Asselineau was only expressing his personal dislike and dissatisfaction. No mere *officier de santé* would, presumably, have been in charge of a 'very extensive' clinic in Paris.[4] Duval, now forty-eight, had presented his thesis in Paris in 1845, and was in fact a doctor of medicine.[5] In *La Vie artistique au temps de Baudelaire,* Tabarant records that 'Dr Émile Duval, Duval *fils,* was a specialist in hydrotherapic cures, the author of numerous papers on the action of cold water in diseases of the marrow and of the nervous system, a former editor of the journal *Hydrothérapie,* editor-in-chief of its successor, *Médicine contemporaine,* and contributor to the *Moniteur des hôpitaux.'*[6]

Yet, whatever his qualifications and his published work, Émile Duval was not ideally suited to his post. Despite his optimistic comments to

his friend Maurice, his protestations of triumph to Mme Aupick and
to Asselineau, he took no particular interest in his patient. He told
Eugène Crépet that Baudelaire ate at table with the other *pensionnaires*,
listened to their conversations, and often intervened with signs of
approval or violent irritation. For some time he tried to set down his
thoughts on a slate, but his hand would waver before he had completed
a word.[7] These were the only other comments which Duval is known
to have made. Dr Augustin Cabanès, who knew him well, later asked
him more than once for his observations on Baudelaire. Duval would
make none; he only told him, recorded Cabanès, 'that he had kept
some manuscripts of his temporary guest's, manuscripts which revealed
his incoherence; but death overtook our colleague before he had had
occasion to show them to us.'[8]

If in fact Duval had kept some of Baudelaire's manuscripts, they
might have been the pathetic scrawls of an aphasic patient; they would
indeed have proved – if proof were needed – that he had lost the use
of words, and the use of his right hand. If the manuscripts were more
than mere remedial exercises, Duval had presumably taken them out
of Baudelaire's trunk. They could have been poems or prose poems,
notes on Belgium, notes for a review of Hugo's novel, pages from the
Journaux intimes. It is difficult to see how they could have revealed
Baudelaire's incoherence while he had the use of his hand and mind.
They would however have revealed Duval's dishonesty.

Towards the end of July, Mme Aupick returned to Honfleur. Soon
afterwards, Asselineau sent her a bulletin. On 6 August she answered,
in a letter which suggested all her feverish concern.

> Thank you, my dear Monsieur Asselineau, for having gone to see my son
> and for hastening to send me news of him . . .
>   Charles ought not to need pills yet. I gave him 60 on 23 July; that should
> last two months, since he ought to take about one a day. He mustn't take
> too many of them: that might purge him too much; but if he is anxious
> about the prescription, I confirm it, now, for his peace of mind.
>   Charles complained to M. Émon about his teeth, which are giving him
> much pain. M. Émon believed, like Dr Duval, that one of his teeth had
> decayed; and they both insisted urgently that he should have it out.
> Charles protested and got angry; it isn't surprising, because as you know
> he has splendid teeth. As a result of his paralysis, he had neuralgia in the
> mouth [*sic*], and he suffered greatly from his gums, which made chewing
> very difficult for him. The doctor in Brussels prescribed a soothing gargle
> for this. I have just written about it to Dr Duval . . .[9]

She was determined to be practical; she left no detail unremarked, no
error uncorrected. Her solicitude was touching, but her constant

agitation disturbed Duval and Ancelle, Malassis and Asselineau, just as it had long disturbed her son. Baudelaire could not have been wholly sorry that his mother had returned to Honfleur.

In the rue du Dôme, his friends continued to visit him. Asselineau was painfully aware of Baudelaire's deterioration. On one occasion he asked him to sign a receipt for a sum which had just been given to him. Baudelaire struggled to recall his name. Asselineau put one of his own books in front of him, so that he could copy the name on the title-page. He also had to see the names of the friends who came to visit him, but he could only repeat them when someone had told them to him.[10]

Catulle Mendès did not find 'the real Baudelaire', but a man who was 'haggard, vague and weak, uttering only the oath which people took for blasphemy'.[11] Manet, ever faithful, arrived with his wife. Champfleury suggested to Éléonore Meurice that she should play the piano for Baudelaire. Mme Meurice, he told Malassis, 'bravely took the score of *Tannhäuser*, and the effect was what I had expected. I was not at the meeting, but Mme Meurice told me about the vivid impressions on Baudelaire. Unfortunately she has just left for the seaside, and so has Mme Manet, whom one might have asked to replace her, and Baudelaire will remain without music until the end of the autumn.'[12]

Baudelaire's friends had, from the first, been aware of his financial problems. They now sent a petition to Victor Duruy, the Minister of Public Instruction, asking him to grant Baudelaire a pension. The petition was signed by Champfleury, Banville, Asselineau and Leconte de Lisle, and by three Academicians: Sandeau, Sainte-Beuve and Mérimée. Sainte-Beuve observed that more than half of Mme Aupick's pension was being spent on the treatment and subsistence of her son, 'one of the finest and most distinguished writers to have appeared in the last fifteen years.' It was qualified praise; nonetheless, Sainte-Beuve supported the petition 'with all his might'.[13] Asselineau told Armand du Mesnil that Mme Aupick was spending '*more than two-thirds*' of her pension on her son.[14] Mérimée, a favourite at Court, declared that 'never has a man of letters been more unfortunate than Baudelaire, and I do not know of anyone who has more claims to the benevolence of Monsieur le Ministre.'[15] On 25 August he assured Banville: 'I should consider myself very happy, if my testimonial could be of some use to your poor friend . . . I had some dealings with M. Baudelaire, whose gifts have been known to me for a very long while.'[16] Mérimée was not optimistic. 'It is rare', he told Sainte-Beuve, 'for a Ministerial coffer not to be empty in the month of August. Besides, it might be that His

Excellency's jurisprudence was opposed to his generous impulses.'[17]
The judgment on *Les Fleurs du mal* might have been remembered.

For Ancelle, it had been an eventful spring and summer. On 17 April,
as Mayor of Neuilly, he had, by a quirk of history, married Catulle
Mendès and Judith Gautier. On 30 July his own daughter, Louise-
Eugénie, had married Ferdinand Oreille, an army captain and a
natural son of the Duc de Berry.[18] A Bourbon son-in-law no doubt
warmed Ancelle's heart. On 24 August, his long years of public service
had been rewarded by the cross of the Légion-d'honneur – the cross
for which Baudelaire had hoped in vain.

Ancelle deserved to be rewarded. As an admirer had explained:

> Since M. Ancelle has been in office, the town of Neuilly has prospered,
> it has grown more beautiful, it has undoubtedly become one of the
> prettiest places in the vicinity of Paris . . .
> M. Ancelle has ordered the opening and the transformation of a great
> number of roads; thanks to him, new *quartiers* have sprung up . . .
> A man of progress, he dreamed of building communal schools for both
> sexes, and these schools exist, and function in the most satisfactory
> manner.
> He demanded and obtained gas lighting, as well as a water supply for
> two-thirds of the town . . .
> Everyone appreciates his admirable good sense; his integrity, his
> absolute clearsightedness in business . . .
> As a private person, M. Ancelle does good; his advice is there for
> everyone, and his purse is open for all deserving cases of misfortune.'[19]

One continual demand upon him had been his care of Baudelaire.
For this, too, and for his patience with Mme Aupick, he deserved some
reward.

Malassis, as usual, took a broad view of events. He concerned himself
with the poet's future. On 3 September he reminded Asselineau:

> The duty of those who have been his friends . . . is to do everything to
> lighten the half-existence which remains to him. I am sorry not to be in
> Paris; I am very sorry . . .
> There is another duty to fulfil, in my opinion, and one that is more
> imperious, if that is possible: it is not to let him be forgotten . . .
> There is no edition of *Les Fleurs du mal* in the bookshops, and we owe
> it to our friend to publish it: not a definitive edition, because we cannot
> let people think, *ourselves*, that we think him *finished*.[20]

In his first months at the rue du Dôme, Asselineau was to remember,
Baudelaire

... took pleasure in carriage drives, in making visits in town, and in going out to dinner. Nadar, who cherished him as an old and excellent friend, felt not only affection for him, but real admiration. In order to divert him and to give him a change from his diet at the nursing-home, he contrived to go and fetch him regularly, once a week, and to take him home to dine with a few other guests. These were old friends who were accustomed to his sign language, and they gave him an affectionate welcome. At first, Baudelaire seemed to be enchanted by these little gatherings, and, when his host went to fetch him, he found him ready and dressed up, and impatient to get into the carriage. Soon, however, to our great astonishment, he refused to come. He conveyed, by gestures, that these meetings tired him, and that he paid for an evening's pleasure by insomnia and [over-] excitement which counteracted his treatment. He had clearly not lost his awareness of his condition, or the hope of cure.[21]

Yet, even if he believed it possible that he might recover, he could not write. His chief preoccupation, for years, had been the publication of his complete works. It now became his only concern. At the end of this summer of 1866, he indicated to Asselineau that he would like to reach an agreement with Michel Lévy. In order to make himself understood, Baudelaire took a volume, published by Lévy, from his desk, and underlined the publisher's name with his finger. On learning this, Malassis explained to Asselineau:

Baudelaire would like to have a contract for all his works, just as he wanted before his aphasia. He had spent his time seeking this contract, and setting out figures about the profits, but he did not apply himself to finishing his books. However, it must be said that Baudelaire could not finish them. His intermittent intellectual impotence, which he must have mentioned to you as he did to me, had become almost continuous.[22]

Meanwhile, on 4 October 1866, after a delay of several weeks, Victor Duruy, the Minister of Public Instruction, made Baudelaire a grant of 500 francs. It was only a grant, and not the pension which his friends had wanted. As Champfleury explained to Banville, 'the sum was miserable enough.'[23] The sum was miserable indeed; it did not begin to cover the cost of Baudelaire's board and lodging and treatment at the rue du Dôme. However, when Champfleury called to tell him of the grant, Baudelaire was happy with this sign of esteem. When he learned that Mérimée had been one of his supporters, he stammered out the name in surprise.[24]

As for Mme Aupick, she remained perpetually apprehensive.

It is a long time since I wrote to you, my dear Monsieur Asselineau, because I am always afraid of being importunate [she confessed on 6

October]; but today I cannot resist the wish to hear from you . . . I have many questions to ask you. You'll be kind enough to answer them, I'm sure; you have been so good to me! And then you take such an interest in my poor Charles! *Is he continuing the showers, in spite of the cold? Is he still complaining about his right eye? Is he practising writing with his left hand? Can he read?*

Are they warming up, or will they soon warm up the heating apparatus, which has hot-air vents opening into all the rooms? (Charles feels the cold, he may be suffering from the cold.) Is he saying any new words?

In short, what progress have you noticed?[25]

Nadar, devoted as ever, had not lost hope of progress. One day, in mid-November, he took Baudelaire to the Grand Gymnase in the rue des Martyrs; the director, Eugène Paz, was an ardent believer in physiotherapy.

My dear Nadar [wrote Paz on 17 November],
   Why didn't you wait for me when you came to the Gymnase with Baudelaire?
   I am all the more anxious to have him as a patient since I have treated several similar cases with the greatest success.
   So do bring him back to me, please, and as soon as possible . . .[26]

It is not known if Baudelaire returned.

Late in October, or early in November, Mme Aupick was once again in Paris. On 22 November, on her return to Honfleur, she reported to Malassis:

I have just spent three weeks in Paris, and I am delighted that I can give you good news of our dear invalid, especially about his health and mind. The leg is virtually all right, there is still some stiffness in the right arm and hand; as for speaking, progress is slower. Recently, however, to the general stupefaction of the people who were at table with him, he pronounced these words quite distinctly: *Passez-moi la moutarde.* This gives me cause to hope that, perhaps, his speech may suddenly come back to him. But what makes me despair, is that he is still unable to read, he does not even know his letters; as he often points to his right eye, I think that there is still Paralysis in this eye [*sic*], and that this is what prevents him from making out printed letters. It is heartrending. However, when I look at the past, I must appreciate the present improvement . . .

My [own] health would be excellent were it not for my poor legs. It was certainly time the other day to come back from Paris, because they couldn't carry me any more. My visits to the Arc de Triomphe to go and see Charles were killing me, and yet I made them by carriage with my faithful Aimée.[27]

Presumably Baudelaire was now having no regular treatment at the rue du Dôme, and he had abandoned hydrotherapy, for late this year there was talk of a holiday in the South of France. 'Yes, I know about this plan to go to Nice,' Mme Aupick told her daughter-in-law, on 2 January. 'It has thrown me into absolute confusion. It worries me very much, because it casts me into indecision. I wonder if I should go with him, if I should have the strength . . . On the other hand, it seems to me that my duty is to go. It will be a terrible expense . . .'[28] The plan for a visit to Nice was abandoned. Three days later, she told Asselineau that she felt 'relieved of a great burden.'[29]

Asselineau, too, had much to bear. More than once he was obliged to talk to Ancelle. Even Mme Aupick recognised that this could try ones patience. 'I suspect, my dear, that Mr Ancelle bores you and tires you to such an extent that you're afraid to find yourself with him. He is ponderous in conversation. The words come with difficulty, one strains every nerve until a sentence is finished. But he is so good! Remember that he is a father to Charles, and a help to me. Bear with him for us both.'[30] At times Asselineau must have felt that Mme Aupick was more of a burden than the Mayor of Neuilly. She was constantly addressing letters to him. She was frail, and she was frightened; but 'in Charles's interest,' she wrote, 'I must be strong and brave, because, old and ailing as I am, I want to live for him and I am so necessary to him.'[31]

Asselineau, too, was necessary to him. One day this month, intent on publishing his friend's *Œuvres complètes*, he took Michel Lévy to the rue du Dôme.

> Baudelaire showed that he much appreciated this gesture. He talked, through me, about the publication of his works; but when M. Lévy suggested that a new edition of *Les Fleurs du mal* should be begun at once, he stubbornly refused. He took an almanack from his desk, and counted out three months, . . . conveying that at this date he hoped that he himself would be able to oversee the printing of his book. This operation had always been of the greatest importance to him, and I think that he would not have entrusted it to the care of his closest friends.
>
> This fixed time of three months appears to have been the limit of his hopes. On the almanack which he had shown us, the thirty-first of March was marked by a line.[32]

It would then be a year to the day since he had been struck by hemiplegia: a year since Mme Hugo had written: 'Baudelaire is doomed.'[33]

123

Baudelaire's future in literature had long since been assured; the present plans for him were constantly changing. Mme Aupick was soon confronted by a daunting prospect: once again there was talk of her son moving to Honfleur. Once again she was torn between her maternal love and the thought of the burden that she might have to bear.

> I am delighted to learn of Charles's eager wish to come here [this to Asselineau on 13 February]. Thank you, Monsieur and friend, for telling me. The repairs to this house are finished, I don't have workmen here any more. I have no objection to make in this respect. But it is the bad weather we are having here at the moment which alarms me for him . . . This hateful wind is very cold, and it plagues and irritates the nerves. I think it would be wise to wait for the weather to improve . . . [1]

Four days later, she confessed her growing apprehension:

> M. Asselineau, that excellent friend of my son's, tells me that Charles needs a change of surroundings, and that he wants to come here. You can imagine [this to Malassis] that I should be very glad to have him, and as soon as the weather is less bad and we can see the fine days dawning, he will be brought here, either by M. Ancelle, or by M. Asselineau, nothing has been decided about this yet. M. Ancelle wants to avoid a journey for me, which I should find tiring; and though I long to see Charles here, I tremble at the thought that he may be bored in this solitude, which he put up with, once upon a time, *because he was working hard, and he was reading.* We used to spend our evenings sensibly, doing English together, I gave him lessons, just for the pronunciation, because he knew the language better than I do, he liked to spend his evenings in this way. But now, in the inaction in which he has to live, how will he bear the continual tête-à-tête with an old woman, especially after being used to receiving so many visits from friends at the nursing-home? Anyway, I shall do my best, I shall lavish so much care and love on him that perhaps our reunion will be happy . . . [2]

One wonders if Baudelaire had really expressed the wish to go and live with his mother. He had long been unable to speak or to write, and the mere suggestion of Honfleur had, before now, moved him to anger. He loved his mother at a distance. Eugène Crépet observed: 'He only loved her when she was far away.'[3] Whether he was still capable of thought, or whether he depended, now, on instinct, he must have known that living in Honfleur would be impossible.

In Mme Aupick's letter to Malassis, one may detect a careful conspiracy to comfort her and to keep her at Honfleur. Yet, as Jacques

Crépet has observed, there is something in this letter which is even more remarkable than Baudelaire's alleged wish to live at Honfleur: it is Mme Aupick's fear and disenchantment and lassitude when she thinks at last that he might come.[4] She not only dreads the burden of an ailing son, she shows her own awareness of her ineffectual love, of all her many failed attempts to live with him. It seems as if she has become suddenly aware of her failure as a mother.

On 25 February, she confessed to Asselineau:

> I am extremely surprised and anxious about M. Ancelle's silence. On 15 February he wrote to me about Charles's wish to come here in March· *You don't need to come and fetch him.* M. Asselineau and I can avoid this journey for you. M. Ancelle might want to escort Charles here himself, and, should this be the case, I should conform with his wish . . . You know what deference I have for him: he is so precious to me! But I have heard nothing more from him . . .
>
> I must know if Charles is to undergo hydrotherapy here. I am very anxious to know *if he can read.* M. Ancelle, to whom I had sent a little note to give him, wrote to me that Charles had read it without difficulty. Didn't he pretend to? If he can really read, how is it that I have not been told? I don't understand it at all.[5]

It is true that her son's friends had conspired to encourage her: they had given her optimistic but unjustified accounts of his progress. Yet one still remains surprised at her powers of self-delusion.

Perhaps she continued to wait for her son; but, as March went by, she must have recognised that he would not come. In his almanack, he had underlined the date, 31 March, as the limit of his hopes. 'When the limit was reached,' said Asselineau, 'he no doubt understood that he was no longer in a condition to travel.'[6] There could be no question, now, of Honfleur. Nor could there be a question of his recovery. As Asselineau recalled: 'He surrendered to the enemy which he had fought so valiantly and for so long . . . Soon he refused to leave his bed . . . His will was broken; but his spirit was still awake . . . He was outliving himself, and he survived only to be aware of all that he had lost.'[7]

On 10 May, Mme Aupick addressed herself, yet again, to Asselineau:

> I want to send you a word of remembrance before I leave for Paris . . .
>
> For a long time I have been feverishly impatient to see my poor son, but I have always been kept back by my poor legs, which are so weak and shaky, and also because for a long while I have been deluded by the hope that he would be brought here; but now that it seems impossible that he should come back for some time, I really must drag myself to his

side, just at the moment when there are all the crowds and everything is so difficult in Paris because of this wretched exhibition. M. Ancelle has booked rooms for me, a ground-floor apartment at 10, rue de Rome, which goes up to the Arc de Triomphe. I am leaving on Tuesday, 21 May. I shall be very comfortable there. I plan to spend only a fortnight there, because of the excessive cost of the lodging and of everything else.[8]

The International Exhibition had opened on 1 April. The capital was full of tourists, and the cost of living had risen. On 21 May, Mme Aupick left for Paris; she settled in the apartment near the nursing-home. It was presumably now that she wrote to an unidentified correspondent: 'There is an improvement in Charles's condition . . . But he is still a long way from being what he was six months ago, when I made my other journey. Will he ever be the same?'[9] She had much to make her anxious. She was disturbed by the expense of living in Paris, and, no doubt, by the gaiety and the excitement around her. She was deeply disturbed by her son's condition. However, on about 5 June, since Baudelaire grew no worse, she went back to Honfleur, as she had planned.

On 20 July, when the Exhibition was over, and the city was less crowded and expensive, she returned to Paris, and this time she settled in furnished rooms at 31, place de la Madeleine. She found a marked difference in her son. 'My son now absorbs all my time,' she told an unidentified friend, possibly Mme Émon.

> I need to give him much more attention than before. He is sinking visibly from day to day. Every time he has an attack, his intelligence and his strength diminish. He had one recently (I was alone with him), luckily I called M. Duval from the window, he came and attended to him and brought him round. Oh, it was terrible! And yet for two days I have been more hopeful, not for a complete cure, but for a more bearable condition in which he can get up and walk in the garden. Forgive me, my dear, for not telling you more about it, I am going back to my poor son, who likes to have me beside him; he shows by his glances and sometimes by a grasp of the hands that he is touched by my attention . . .[10]

And again she wrote:

> I now only leave the nursing-home late, to go home and go to bed. Charles showed such regret, he cast me such woeful looks when he saw me leave at half-past five, that I thought that I should make this decision . . . He is sinking very fast. I find that he is deaf, or at least that he takes a long time to understand what I say to him. Our long intimate conversations have become very painful. During the first fortnight I spent in Paris, they were not without their charm for me [*sic*]; I amused him, spurred him on to talk, to repeat a few words after me. When he spoke

well, I clapped; when he spoke badly, I imitated his gibberish [*sic*]. Now
there is the silence of death between us.'[11]

By mid August, Baudelaire was manifestly dying. His last days,
recorded Banville, 'were only a long agony. He was one of those great
poets to whom terrestrial martyrdom is never refused, so that their soul
and their work, all that was imperishable within them might enter at
once into serenity and light.'[12] In *Mon Cœur mis à nu*, Baudelaire himself
had written: 'It would be impious to give chloroform to a man who
was condemned to death, because it would take away his own sense of
his greatness as a victim, and destroy his chances of gaining Paradise.'[13]
Villon apart, no French poet had lived as intensely as Baudelaire on
intimate terms with death.

In mid August, Asselineau warned Malassis:

He probably won't last another month.
   Mme Aupick still deludes herself. She talks about a possible improvement. But the doctors and we, his friends, who don't see him every day,
notice deterioration every time. For two or three months [*sic*], Baudelaire
has no longer wanted to leave his bed. He is motionless, and as if asleep,
and he now only shows by glances – alas, what melancholy glances! – that
he notices the presence of his friends. Yesterday, after an absence of three
weeks, he only acknowledged me with a heartrending stare, and he
couldn't give me his hand until I had freed it from the bedclothes.
   They sit up with him every night. It is Albert, the publisher, who has
undertaken this nursing, and I must say that he acquits himself with the
most assiduous devotion.'[14]

Edmond Albert was said to have been a childhood friend of Baudelaire's. He had also, briefly, been his factotum. Now he gave him a
final proof of friendship: a proof so constant and so touching that Mme
Aupick later sent him her son's gold watch as a memento.[15]

Since Baudelaire never moves [Asselineau continued, to Malassis],-a sore
has developed on his loins, and it threatens to become gangrenous. And
so the next letter you receive from me will probably be to tell you the
fatal news.
   My dear friend, we shall have to think seriously about the question of
the works.[16]

Posterity had begun before Baudelaire had died. His deterioration continued. Trial says that he was covered with scabs, and he
mentions tabes (though Dr Cabanès maintained that there was no
sign of this).[17] Mme Aupick later recalled: 'My son suffered cruelly in
his last days from several sores which had been caused by his long stay
in bed, and they sometimes made him cry out, when he had to be

moved. However, in his final days he had grown very gentle and resigned.'[18]

Pious as she had always been, she had wanted him to die in peace with God, fortified by the rites of the Catholic Church. She had finally achieved her end. Late in July he had received the sacraments, 'well aware of what he was doing, and with fervour. I was lucky', she recorded, 'to find a good moment.'[19] Now he could no longer fight, perhaps he did not want to fight, against religion. Ancelle's son was later to give Féli Gautier 'the name of the priest who attended Baudelaire in his last moments: it was the abbé Miramon.'[20] Louis Veuillot, a fervent Catholic, was to write to Mme Aupick: 'I had a kind letter from M. Asselineau, telling me that [Baudelaire] had asked for [*sic*] and received the sacraments. It gave me one of the purest delights that I have known, and ... I blessed the infinite mercy of God.'[21]

On the morning of Saturday, 31 August, in a trembling hand, Mme Aupick wrote to an unidentified correspondent: 'My poor son is still alive, but he has been in a very extraordinary state for two days and two nights, in a kind of sleep with open eyes, and with open mouth. After great suffering, he no longer suffers, and he can die like this, peacefully, at any moment. But I pray to keep him for a few more days just as he is.'[22] A postscript in another hand added: 'Our poor friend has just uttered his last breath.'[23]

The end had come at about eleven o'clock.

> He died quite peacefully [wrote his mother], without agony or pain. I had held him in my arms for an hour, waiting to receive his final breath. I said a thousand loving things to him, convinced that, despite his exhaustion and his speechlessness, he must understand me and might answer me. Aimée, who was with me, agreed with me in this, she said to me: *Oh, madame, he is looking at you, of course he understands you, and he is smiling at you.*[24]

The son had found his mother. The mother had at last regained her child.

Epilogue

That day, Saturday, 31 August, Asselineau drafted a note for the Press. That evening, he and Nadar (who had learned the news by telegram from Albert)[1] wrote a *faire-part* which was sent to the poet's friends. 'M. Charles Baudelaire, the author of *Les Fleurs du mal* and *Les Paradis artificiels,* the translator of Edgar Poe, died this morning. The funeral service will be held in the church of Saint-Honoré, in Passy (place de l'Hippodrome), at 11 o'clock, precisely, on Monday, 2 September.' A second, formal *faire-part* announced that Baudelaire had died 'fortified by the rites of the Church.'[2]

Baudelaire was to be buried forty-eight hours after his death. Owing, perhaps, to the August heat and to the fact that the body remained in the rue du Dôme, the arrangements had been made with uncommon haste. Many of the poet's friends were no doubt away from Paris during that week-end at the height of summer. They might well not have received the *faire-part* until after the funeral had been held.[3] Mme Aupick was not, it seems, consulted about all the arrangements. As she later told Malassis: 'I'm afraid that [M. Arthur Stevens] hasn't had a note [about Charles's death]. I don't know how these notes were written.'[4]

They were written with deep feeling, but not always with effect. It was Asselineau who informed the world of literature, asking them to send their sympathy to Mme Aupick, or to publish praise of the poet of *Les Fleurs du mal.*[5] It was Asselineau who wrote to Hugo:

Charles Baudelaire is dead. His friends have done their best to do him literary honour.
 But he leaves an old mother, who is very desolate.
 A word or two from your glorious pen would be balm to this aching heart. Madame Aupick will be staying for another week at no 66, rue Lauriston [*sic*] . . .[6]

Hugo did not write. Some time later, Asselineau felt obliged to tell him: 'Mme Aupick has returned to Honfleur; a word from you would be a great consolation to her.'[7]

Meanwhile, on the last day of August, in the rue du Dôme, the incompetence continued, and the posthumous legend began. One admirer claimed that he was given a last sight of Baudelaire, after death. 'When they lifted the sheet that covered his face,' wrote Alfred d'Aunay, 'I saw his great questioning eyes turned towards me. He had

kept in death, as in illness, that same, strange, searching look, the look
of a man who lives in a world of fantasy, and is constantly pursued by
a vision.'[8] It was a haunting recollection; yet it is difficult to believe
that no one had closed the poet's eyes.

On 1 September, Asselineau wrote to Malassis to announce that
Baudelaire had died. 'The service is on Tuesday [*sic*]. I have tried to
see that we have as many people as possible ... We are still awaiting
the arrival of M. Ancelle, who was somewhere or other, taking the
waters ...'[9] Ancelle returned that day to Neuilly; that day, he and
Asselineau officially recorded the death of Baudelaire.[10]

At eleven o'clock next morning, the funeral service was held in the
little chapel of Saint-Honoré d'Eylau, in Passy:

> A village church [recorded Georges Maillard in *Le Figaro*], with a timbered
> roof, red curtains, and primitive decorations. A simple catafalque, with
> white stripes, stands in the middle.
>   A mass is sung. The voices are rustic, the organ half barbaric. These
> chants surprise you, for they have no melancholy shades of meaning, no
> notes of emotion. But then it is more of a deliverance than a separation
> which they must express.[11]

Maillard wrote with scant regard for truth. He had already announced
in *Le Figaro* that Baudelaire had died in Dr Blanche's asylum.[12] Now
the curé of Saint-Honoré, the abbé P.-P. Chéruel, was moved to assure
the paper

> ... [that], if the church was not decorated with hangings, and if the choir
> was not larger, that was because it had not been requested, but what had
> been agreed was faithfully observed. There were neither rustic voices nor
> a half barbaric organ. My chapelmaster is renowned as one of the finest
> in Paris; the organ was built by Cavallié-Coll, and the organist who plays
> it won a first prize at the Conservatoire ...[13]

After the service, 'in a Senegalese heat, which hurt both the eyes and
the nerves',[14] the funeral procession set out for the cimetière Montparnasse. Auguste Vitu recorded that Ancelle, as the family notary, was
chief mourner.[15] Verlaine recorded – improbably – that he and
Alphonse Lemerre walked immediately behind the coffin, followed by
Louis Veuillot, Arsène Houssaye, Charles Asselineau and Théodore de
Banville.[16] By the ultimate irony, Baudelaire was buried for all eternity,
not beside his father, whose grave remains unknown, but beside
General Aupick. As the coffin was lowered into the grave, there was a
clap of thunder. It was followed by torrential rain.

Mme Aupick, reported Maillard, 'was brave and dignified.'[17] Ancelle
could not restrain his tears. Asselineau and Banville delivered the

funeral orations, but their grief made them barely audible. 'If glory begins today for Charles Baudelaire,' Asselineau said, 'history also begins with it . . . People have talked too much about the *legend* of Charles Baudelaire, not knowing that this legend only reflected his contempt for stupidity and for arrogant mediocrity.'[18] It was that day that Banville spoke, for the first time, with the voice of posterity:

The man whom death has just taken from us bears a large part of my heart away with him . . .

For want of those of our masters who would have been qualified to accomplish this act of justice, I have to find within myself the necessary strength to assess the poet . . .

Yet, to praise Charles Baudelaire as he deserves, the truth is enough, and his memory needs nothing more . . . The man has just died; the lasting triumph has begun . . .

In fact, and the near future will say so for all time, the author of *Les Fleurs du mal* is not a poet of talent, but a poet of genius.[19]

Sainte-Beuve did not attend the funeral, on the grounds of his ill-health. He sent 'a trite letter of condolence' to Mme Aupick.[20] 'Now [Baudelaire] has finally entered the pure region of memory and of poetic recollection . . . His profile must remain engraved upon the medallions of the present age.'[21] He himself was not to engrave it. He assembled a *dossier Baudelaire*, which remains among his papers. The dossier consists of eight articles which appeared at the time of the poet's death. Some of them are dated or identified by the critic, but there is only one comment in his hand. It is contained in a single sentence, and it expresses all his jealousy: 'Baudelaire, in romantic art, is *the Aloysius Bertrand* of the Decadence.'[22]

Mme Aupick was not aware of Sainte-Beuve's essential meanness. His florid letter of condolence had convinced her of his admiration for her son. 'The poor woman', Asselineau wrote to Malassis, 'had come to us still imbued with the prejudices against her son which had been given to her by a lot of artillery officers, friends of her husband's who were neighbours of hers at Honfleur. But . . . the letter from Sainte-Beuve carried her away.'[23]

Monsieur [she replied],

I was very grieved to learn that you were ill. You were so benevolent to my son, and took such an interest in his literary triumphs, how can I be indifferent to the ill health which you describe to me? Of course I infinitely regret that you could not attend his funeral, but how deeply grateful I am for the praise and the Recollection that you bestow upon my son! He professed a real cult for you, the deepest admiration and the most profound devotion . . .[24]

Troubat, the critic's secretary, had received a *faire-part*, but there
is no evidence that he was present at the poet's funeral. Dr Duval,
noted Mme Aupick, had chosen to go shooting rather than attend.[25]
'There were about a hundred people at the church, and fewer at the
cemetery,' Asselineau was to calculate. 'The heat prevented many
people from following to the end. A clap of thunder burst just as we
were going into the cemetery, and it almost led the rest to make
their escape.'[26] Alfred Stevens recalled that the coffin was lashed by
the wind, and covered with leaves that had blown down from the
trees. 'Like you, I find great poetry in that,' he told his brother. 'I am
sure that Baudelaire would have asked no better for his entrance
into death.'[27] Perhaps the scene was reflected in Manet's painting,
L'Enterrement.

It was a very different funeral from the grandiose and largely
attended funeral of Aupick. Asselineau recalled:

> The Société des Gens de Lettres was not represented, although I had
> written on the Saturday to Paul Féval, the president, to tell him that I
> counted on him and on his committee. No one came from the Ministry,
> either, nor Doucet nor Du Mesnil. The addresses were given in the
> presence of sixty people. Théodore de Banville was very moved; I was still
> more moved, and in a rage. We hurried through it like people who were
> anxious to be finished. I noted among those present: Houssaye and his
> son, Nadar, Champfleury, Monselet, Wallon, Vitu, Manet, Alfred Ste-
> vens, Bracquemond, Fantin, Pothey, Verlaine . . .[28]

It was Verlaine who wrote, that day:

> We have just come from the cimetière Montparnasse, where a few friends
> and admirers had gone to take [Charles Baudelaire] to his final resting-
> place . . . This death did not surprise anyone. It grievously impressed
> everyone who has at heart the love of literature and great poetry . . .
>   A somewhat limited group, as we said, gathered round the coffin, and
> we record this without bitterness, for each of those who attended . . . was
> eminent in art or literature . . .
>   It is regrettable that the absence of a famous personage should have
> been observed, and considered as improper. It is even more regrettable
> that this comment should be fair.[29]

The famous personage might have been Sainte-Beuve; more probably it was *le parfait magicien ès lettres françaises*, to whom Baudelaire had
paid a signal honour: the dedication of *Les Fleurs du mal*. On 26 August,
Gautier had left to stay at Saint-Jean, near Geneva, with Carlotta
Grisi.[30] It might be argued that the man who would one day return
from Switzerland for the funeral of Jules de Goncourt could have
returned for that of Baudelaire. It might well be that the *faire-part* did

not reach him in time, or that the Sunday trains did not make the journey possible. Whatever the reason for his absence, Gautier remained at Saint-Jean, writing his official report on French poetry: *Rapport sur le progrès des lettres depuis vingt-cinq ans*. 'Tomorrow', he told his daughter, Estelle, early in September, 'I must resume my work as an undertaker's man and write an obituary of poor Baudelaire. *Crénom!* as he used to say, it's tiresome to bury all ones friends like this and to make copy out of their corpses.'[31] He stayed on at Saint-Jean to finish his 'patriotic chore'.[32] He also wrote the tribute to Baudelaire which appeared in *Le Moniteur universel* on 9 September. The tribute was strangely lacking in warmth; but next day Estelle assured him: 'Your article on poor Baudelaire was very good, you were born to write obituaries for Gazettes . . . It is said that, at the time of his death, he asked for a confessor, how credible that is, he could only say *Crénom* in his latter days, they had managed to make him say *bonjour*, like a child, but that's all . . . The most ridiculous stories are beginning to rain down on every side.'[33]

> People have said strange things about Baudelaire, especially in these last few days [confirmed Charles Durand in *L'Illustration*]. They have endowed him with bizarre tastes, repugnant sympathies and singular habits. They have woven him a life of fantastic adventures . . .
>   None of all this is true, thank God, or at least it is singularly exaggerated . . . Our poet was good; he was gentle; those who claim the contrary never saw him with his mother, or his friends, never grasped his hand . . .[34]

That day, 14 September, Charles Yriarte paid a substantial tribute to Baudelaire. Writing in the *Revue Nationale et Étrangère*, he expressed his affection for the man, his sadness at his life, and his admiration for his work. 'The author of *Les Fleurs du mal* was', he concluded, 'one of the most distinguished writers of the present age.'[35]

Nadar, writing in *Le Figaro*, also emphasised the loss which literature had suffered in the early death of his friend.[36] Mme Aupick was moved by his generosity: 'I have been very deeply touched by it,' she told him, 'especially by what you say about his religious beliefs, which you were in a position to appreciate, since you were close to him. No one could deny his fine, distinguished intellect, his most superior mind, but was it the same with his noble soul? You who understood it, you who have made it known, be blessed.'[37]

La Présidente had completely lost Baudelaire from sight since his departure for Belgium. She was spending the summer at Mosino, on Lake Como; she was shocked and saddened, on her return to Paris, when she learned of his death.[38] Mallarmé's summer holidays, in a

peaceful village in Franche-Comté, were clouded by the news. He
mourned the loss of 'a magician of language.'[39]

On 9 September, Malassis confessed to Ancelle:

> Baudelaire's expected end moved me as much as that of my brother,
> whom I lost suddenly, four years ago . . .
>   But he is the author of *Les Fleurs du mal*, and sure to be remembered as
> long as the French language is spoken and written.[40]

125

In the meantime, there followed the practical and legal complications
which often follow death. In Baudelaire's room in the rue du Dôme,
his possessions had been valued, among them his clothes, assessed at
40 francs.[1] Mme Aupick was harassed, now, by the question of his
estate. She made no attempt to find Jeanne Duval, and to give her
money, as Baudelaire would have wished. 'That infamous Jeanne,' she
told Ancelle,

> . . . tortured him in every way. I have an enormous pile of letters from
> her to Charles, I found as many here [at Honfleur] as were brought back
> from Brussels. In all of them, I see incessant demands for money. Never
> a word of affection, or even of thanks. It is always money that she wants,
> and wants immediately. I have a letter here, the last, dated April 1866,
> when my poor child was on his sickbed, paralysed, and I was setting out
> to be with him. And in this last letter, as in the earlier letters, she plagued
> him, tormented him for money which had to be sent to her without delay.[2]

Jeanne was ignored, but Mme Aupick settled her son's debts,
including his long-standing debt to Malassis. She ensured that memen-
toes were sent to his friends. 'Of course I should have been glad, I
agree [this to Ancelle], if, after Charles's debts had been paid, there
had been a residue that I could have touched, which would have
increased my income; but, at my age, as I already have one foot in the
grave, so to speak, should I be greedy? I don't want to think about it.'[3]
Since Baudelaire had died intestate, the rights to his *Œuvres complètes*
were put on sale, and on 22 November they were bought – as he had
wished – by Michel Lévy.

Absorbed in her grief, Mme Aupick did, however, delight in the
progress of his fame. She remained flattered by the visits that she
received, the sympathy that was shown her, the glory which, already,

rose about the name of Baudelaire. 'I see', she wrote, 'that my son, for all his faults, has his place in literature.'[4] In March and April 1868, in seven instalments in *L'Univers illustré*, Gautier published the study of Baudelaire which was to appear later that year as a preface to *Les Fleurs du mal*, in his *Œuvres complètes*. 'He was himself a master,' so Gautier proclaimed, 'a master who had a kingdom of his own, a nation, and struck money with his image.'[5]

The first of Gautier's articles appeared on 7 March. Mme Aupick acknowledged it with delight,

> Monsieur [this on 10 March],
>
> I knew from Mr Charles Asselineau that you had written an introduction to the new edition of *Les Fleurs du mal* which is a masterpiece. In my grief, in the wretched life to which I am condemned, this news brought me boundless joy, the like of which I believed I could never feel again. Were it not for the fear of annoying you, I should have written to you at once; but I thought that I should wait until it was published. I imposed silence on my heart, which was crying out to you constantly, and at every moment: '*Thank you.*' I have at last received this wonderful article, and, without waiting for the other pleasures promised for Saturday, I come to you, monsieur, an affectionate and devoted friend of my son's, I come to tell you that I am filled with gratitude for what you are doing for his memory. And he himself, you must believe, thanks you for your kind recollection, he smiles at you from above, he hovers over you, he is watching over your happiness (at least, I like to think so), and he loves you, as he has loved you for many years.[6]

As Baudelaire had said to her after Aupick's death, he was now the only person who bound her to life. 'When I am dead', he had told her, 'you will no longer live.'[7] She did live on; but 'nothing interests me,' she wrote, 'unless it is related to his memory. Sometimes, so as not to make myself unbearable to the people I see, I make unheard-of efforts to seem to listen to them and to take an interest in what they say, while, in the depths of my heart, which is indifferent and alien to anything but him, most of the time I talk to him, and I am entirely his.'[8] It was the belated answer to Baudelaire's confession: 'I belong to you absolutely, and I belong only to you.'[9]

Frail as she was – she found it hard to climb the stairs at Honfleur – she visited Paris. She could not bear the sight of the maison Duval from the lodgings in the rue Lauriston, but she settled in her familiar rooms at 8, rue Duphot. It was from here that she wrote to Banville, asking for assurance that nothing, not even the problems of Baudelaire's estate, would prevent the publication of his works, and that the printing costs would be covered by the sales. 'Oh, shall I have time to enjoy the publication and the success? Make haste, my friends.'[10]

Banville and Asselineau had undertaken to prepare this first edition of
the *Œuvres complètes*. In August 1868, Asselineau stayed with her for a
fortnight at Honfleur, and studied the documents which she possessed,
the trunk of manuscripts which Baudelaire had brought back from
Brussels.

She was happy to further the fame of her son, glad to talk about him
with his friends. 'I have just put my little drawing-room back in its
winter dress,' she told Asselineau. 'I mean the little room where there
are views of Constantinople, the one which leads into the Mirador.
There will be no question of using it before next spring, it is too cold
to live in during the winter. My little drawing-room, which you saw at
its simplest, barely furnished, with its plain muslin curtains, is quite
elegant at the moment, dressed in pale yellow silk . . . My Charles, who
never came here in winter [*sic*], never saw this arrangement. I am so
very sorry. It would have pleased him. And I myself would have liked
to rest my gaze where he had rested his.'[11]

She lived in the past, and in the everyday occupations of the present;
but she was old and increasingly apprehensive. 'There is not the
slightest doubt', she reminded Banville, 'of my *boundless confidence* in M.
Asselineau. I am only too glad that I can rely on such a devoted friend
of my son's, a man endowed with such eminent moral and literary
qualities. If you see him before I do, please be good enough to tell him
so, and to say that I am quite prepared to be guided by him, should I
need to give him some authority . . .'[12]

Her position was not to be so simple, for she was obliged to give her
consent to the posthumous edition of *Les Fleurs du mal*. They asked
her for permission to reprint it, that is to say to sanction the blasphemies
which – to her pious mind – it contained. 'Listen,' she wrote to
Asselineau, 'after a long sleepless night in which I thought a great
deal about *Les Fleurs du mal*, in which I considered them scrupulously,
I must ask you to suppress the poem called 'Le Reniement de Saint
Pierre'. As a Christian, I CANNOT, I MUST NOT let that be reprinted
. . .'[13] Asselineau answered that, if she insisted on suppressions, he and
Baudelaire's other friends would cease to concern themselves with his
fame.[14] 'You have written me a very harsh letter,' Mme Aupick
reproached him,

> . . . since it contains the word *resignation*. This terrible and sudden threat
> would no doubt have shaken me, if those magic words: *Charles is not there
> to defend himself,* had not instantly produced a sudden change in my ideas;
> and instantly, too, before his picture, I sacrificed my scruples and
> promised myself that his thought would remain intact and would be
> published as he expressed it. And it is still in this solemn mood that I ask
> you to keep the poem.[15]

The first two volumes of the *Œuvres complètes* were published that December.

Mme Aupick – 'a good and valiant soul', decided Asselineau[16] – died at Honfleur on 16 August 1871. She was seventy-seven. Partly paralysed and partly aphasic, she had witnessed the decline of her faculties. She had been stricken like her son. She was buried, with her second husband and with Baudelaire, at the cimetière Montparnasse. She had divided her estate between Émon (now eighty-one years old), Ancelle (now nearly seventy), and Félicité Baudelaire. Hostile, silly and pretentious, Félicité inherited the private papers of a poet far beyond her comprehension. They came in time into the possession of people who had not known Baudelaire, and were ashamed to be connected with him. Some letters were destroyed by the prudish and the philistine; a few survived as if by miracle.[17] As for the *maison joujou*, it was demolished in 1901, and part of the local hospital was built on the site.[18]

Notes

ABBREVIATIONS

B du B	–	*Bulletin du Bibliophile et du bibliothécaire*
BET	–	Pichois, Claude (ed.): *Baudelaire. Études et Témoignages* (1967)
BN	–	Bibliothèque Nationale, Paris
BP	–	Bandy, W.T., & Pichois, Claude: *Baudelaire devant ses contemporains* (1967)
CB	–	Charles Baudelaire
Corr.	–	Baudelaire: *Correspondance* (Bibliothèque de la Pléiade, 1973)
EJC	–	Crépet, Eugène et Jacques: *Charles Baudelaire*. Étude biographique d'Eugène Crépet revue et mise à jour par Jacques Crépet. (Éditions Messein. s.d.)
LAB	–	Pichois, Claude (ed.): *Lettres à Charles Baudelaire* (1973)
M de F	–	*Mercure de France*
MU	–	*Le Moniteur universel*
NRF	–	*Nouvelle Revue Française*
Œs. cs.	–	Baudelaire: *Œuvres complètes* (Bibliothèque de la Pléiade, 1975, 1976)
PZ	–	Pichois, Claude, & Ziegler, Jean: *Baudelaire* (1987)
RDDM	–	*Revue des Deux Mondes*
RDF	–	*Revue de France*
RDP	–	*Revue de Paris*
RHLF	–	*Revue d'Histoire littéraire de la France*
RNE	–	*Revue Nationale et Étrangère*
RSH	–	*Revue des Sciences Humaines*

1

1 Raynaud: *Les Parents de Baudelaire* (M de F, 15 août 1921, 106 sqq.). Claude Pichois and Jean Ziegler give the most complete account of Joseph-François Baudelaire in *Baudelaire*, 21 sqq.

2 For the question of Joseph-François' priesthood, see Pichois: *Le père de Baudelaire fut-il janséniste?* (RHLF, octobre–décembre 1957, 565–8), and Orcibal: *Joseph-François Baudelaire était-il prêtre?* (RHLF, octobre–décembre 1958, 523–7)

3 PZ: op. cit., 24

4 Mme Aupick to Asselineau, 24 mars [1868]. Ibid, 26
5 Orcibal: op. cit., 527; PZ: op. cit., 28
6 Mme Aupick to Asselineau, 24 mars [1868]. EJC, 263
7 EJC: 4, note
8 Raynaud: op. cit., 112
9 EJC: 264
10 Mme Aupick to Asselineau, 24 mars [1868]. Ibid, 260
11 Ibid, 264–7
12 PZ: op. cit., 52
13 CB to Mme Aupick, 30 déc[embre] 1857. *Corr.*, I, 439
14 PZ: op. cit., 631
15 Ibid, 36
16 Ibid.
17 EJC: op. cit., 6, note
18 Ibid, 5–6, note. CB: *Fusées.* (*Œs. cs.*, I, 661). See also J.-F. Desjardins: *Les Origines familiales de Baudelaire.* (RDDM, 15 décembre 1964, 569–78)
19 Porché: *Baudelaire. Histoire d'une âme*, 244.
20 PZ: op. cit., 38
21 Feuillerat: *Baudelaire et sa mère*, 10
22 Banville: *Lettres chimériques*, 280
23 Mme Tirlet to General Tirlet, 17 août 1814. PZ: op. cit., 45
24 For a detailed account of the apartment, see PZ: op. cit., 52–4
25 Anon: *Baudelaire* (LE CURIEUX, juin 1886, 95–6)
26 PZ: op. cit., 51–2

2

1 CB: 'La Voix'. (*Œs. cs.*, I, 170)
2 CB: *Mon Cœur mis à nu.* (*Œs. cs.*, I, 706)
3 CB: *Notices bio-bibliographiques.* (*Œs. cs.*, I, 785)
4 'Les Vocations'. (*Œs. cs.*, I, 332)
5 'Les Vieux Saltimbanque'. (Ibid, I, 295)
6 *Mon Cœur mis à nu.* (Ibid, I, 702)
7 Ibid, I, 706
8 Ibid, I, 680
9 Ibid, I, 703
10 CB: 'La Voix'. (*Œs. cs.*, I, 170)
11 Pichois: *Lettres à Eugène Crépet sur la jeunesse de Baudelaire* (M de F, 1er septembre 1954, 8–9)
12 Loncke: *Baudelaire et la musique*, 22
13 Mme Aupick to Asselineau, 24 mars [1868]. EJC: op. cit., 265–6
14 PZ: op. cit., 54
15 Ibid.
16 Ibid, 55
17 Ibid.
18 Crépet: *Quelques documents inédits sur Baudelaire* (M de F, 15 mars 1937, 632–3)
19 PZ: op. cit., 55
20 Quesnel: *Baudelaire solaire et clandestin*, 129 and note, 132; see also Bandy et Pichois: *Le Tombeau de François Baudelaire* (BULLETIN BAUDELAIRIEN, 9 avril 1968); Robb:

Baudelaire and the Case of the Empty Grave (FRENCH STUDIES BULLETIN, Winter 1991–92, 17–20)

21 To Asselineau, 24 mars 1868. EJC, op. cit., 259
22 Ruff: *L'Esprit du mal et l'esthétique baudelairienne*, 149
23 PZ: op. cit., 609

3

1 CB: 'Je n'ai pas oublié . . .' (*Œs. cs.*, I, 99)
2 Du Bos: *Approximations*, 5e série, 41
3 Bounoure: *Les Écrits intimes de Baudelaire* (M de F, 1er octobre 1955, 269)
4 Prévost: *Baudelaire*, 192–3
5 CB: 'La servante au grand cœur . . .' (*Œs. cs.*, I, 100)
6 For the date of this poem, see Pichois: *Lettres à Eugène Crépet sur la jeunesse de Baudelaire* (M de F, 1er septembre 1954, 16)
7 CB: *Journaux intimes* (*Œs. cs.*, I, 692–3)
8 Ibid, I, 661
9 [6 mai 1861.] CB: *Corr.*, II, 150
10 Ibid, II, 153
11 Jouve: *Le Tombeau de Baudelaire*, 43–4
12 Laforgue: *L'Échec de Baudelaire*, 17
13 Ibid, 18
14 Ibid, 56, 73
15 Ibid, 49
16 PZ: op. cit., 66
17 Ibid.
18 Ibid.
19 Ibid.
20 Caussy: *La Jeunesse de Baudelaire* (LES ANNALES ROMANTIQUES, tome viii, 1911, 380)

4

1 The most complete account of Aupick's early career is given by Pichois, in *Le Beau-père de Baudelaire* (M de F, 1er juin 1955, 261–81), on which this chapter is largely based. For Jacques-Joseph's origins, see PZ, 56
2 G. de Nouvion: *La famille de Charles Baudelaire*, 159
3 A. Zeloni: *Vie de la princesse Borghèse, née Guendaline Talbot, Comtesse de Shrewsbury* (Aug. Vaton. 1843), 273
4 *Dictionary of National Biography*. Edited by Sidney Lee. Vol. LV (Smith, Elder, & Co., 1898), 322
5 Zeloni: op. cit., 283
6 PZ: 56
7 Boylan: *A Dictionary of Irish Biography*. 2nd edition, 378
8 Pichois: op. cit., 262. In a note to *L'Esprit du mal et l'esthétique baudelairienne*, p. 421, Marcel Ruff writes that Aupick had no birth certificate, but an *acte de notoriété* of 1808 attests that witnesses saw the young Aupick 'in about the middle of 1790,

when the aforesaid Berwick-Irish Regiment was stationed there [in Gravelines], that Jacques Aupick and Amélie Talbot were considered as legally married, the young Aupick as their legitimate child and treated by them as such. . . . On the muster-roll of the Berwick Regiment there figures not only his father Jacques-Joseph, born in 1735, died a captain in 1793, but another Aupick, called Jacques-Éloi, born in Béthune in 1772. He had enlisted as a volunteer in 1790, and retired as a captain in 1816, as the result of a wound received in Spain. This latter Aupick might well be a half-brother of ours, since he is described as the son of Jacques and of Marie-Catherine Caron'.

 9 Pichois: op. cit., 262
10 Pichois: *Le vrai visage du Général Aupick*, 4, note
11 Pichois: *Le Beau-père de Baudelaire* (M de F, 1er juin 1955, 266)
12 Ibid, 267
13 Ibid, 268
14 Caussy: op. cit., 379
15 G. de Nouvion: op. cit., 155
16 Aupick died on 27 April 1857. Mme Aupick spoke of 'the thirty years we spent together' (letter to Asselineau, 24 mars [1868]. EJC, 260)
17 Pichois: op. cit., 270
18 PZ: 68
19 Pichois: op. cit., 270, note. Anon: *Baudelaire* (LE CURIEUX, juin 1886, 96)
20 For an illuminating account, see Quesnel: op. cit.
21 Quesnel: op. cit., 39
22 Féli Gautier: *Baudelaire*, vi
23 B.N. N.A. Fr. 25013 f 11
24 Pichois: *Lettres à Eugène Crépet sur la jeunesse de Baudelaire* (M de F, 1er septembre 1954, 26)
25 To Asselineau, 24 mars [1868]. EJC, 259–60
26 Raynaud: op. cit., 125

5

 1 PZ: op. cit., 69–70
 2 Ibid, 71
 3 Pichois: *Le Beau-père de Baudelaire* (M de F, 1er juin 1955, 269 and 275, note)
 4 PZ: op. cit., 63
 5 *Bulletin de la Société de Géographie*. Tome Second (Au Secrétariat de la Société, 1824), 187
 6 *Bulletin de la Société de Géographie*. Tome 3e. (Arthus Bertrand, 1825), 286–7
 7 MU: 1er août 1827
 8 MU: 11 juin 1827
 9 Séance du 1er juin 1827. *Bulletin de la Société de Géographie*. Tome 7e (Arthus Bertrand, 1827), 269
10 PZ: op. cit., 619
11 Aupick to Thouvenel: 6 mars 1849. Pichois: *Le Beau-père de Baudelaire* (M de F, 1er juin 1955, 280)
12 PZ: op. cit., 71–2
13 Caussy: op. cit., 380

14 9 janvier 1832. CB. *Corr.*, I, 3
15 Le 1er février 1832. Ibid, I, 4
16 Anon: *Guide Historique et pittoresque de Lyon à Châlon, sur la Saône*, 27
17 Ibid, 26
18 Jal: *Lyon en 1835.* (REVUE DU LYONNAIS, 1836, tome 3, 19)
19 See also *Notices bio-bibliographiques*, III. CB: *Œs. cs.*, I, 784
20 1er avril 1832. CB: *Corr.*, I, 6
21 25 avril 1832. Jeudi. Ibid, I, 7
22 Mouquet, quoted by Pichois in CB: *Œs. cs.*, I, 1419–20
23 Borgal: *Charles Baudelaire*, 38
24 F. Gautier: op. cit., vii
25 Ibid, viii
26 [6 mai 1861.] CB: *Corr.*, II, 153
27 Le 6 [septembre] 1832. CB: *Corr.*, I, 9–10, 10
28 Le 9 novembre 1832. Ibid, I, 11
29 Le 27 décembre [1832]. Ibid, I, 13
30 [12 mars 1833.] Ibid, I, 15–16
31 Le 23 novembre 1833. Ibid, I, 22
32 Le 1er jour de l'an 1834. Ibid, I, 22–3
33 Quinet: *Histoire d'un enfant*, 147–8
34 Le 1er jour de l'an 1834. CB: *Corr.*, I, 23
35 CB: *Notices bio-bibliographiques.* (*Œs. cs.*, I, 784)
36 CB: *Edgar Allan Poe: sa Vie et ses ouvrages* (Ibid, II, 257)
37 Le jeudi [6 février 1834?]. CB: *Corr.*, I, 24
38 [Mi-février 1834 (?)]. Ibid, I, 25
39 Le 25 février [1834]. Ibid, I, 25–6, 26, 27
40 Lundi 24 mars [1834]. Ibid, I, 29
41 Le 2 mai [1834] au soir. Ibid, I, 30
42 [1834 ou 1835 (?)] Ibid, I, 31
43 Mme Aupick to Alphonse Baudelaire, 1834. Bandy et Pichois: *Baudelaire devant ses contemporains*, 40–41
44 Le 21 X^{bre} au soir [1834]. CB: *Corr.*, I, 32
45 Hignard: *Charles Baudelaire.* (REVUE DU LYONNAIS, juin 1892, 419)
46 25 mars [1835]. Institut de France. 4740 A 21325. See also Joanna Richardson: *Colonel Aupick: an unpublished letter* (FRENCH STUDIES BULLETIN, Winter 1991–2, 10–11)
47 [Fin août ou début septembre 1835.] CB: *Corr.*, I, 34

6

1 Mme Aupick to Charles Asselineau, 24 mars [1868]. EJC: op. cit., 258
2 Caussy: op. cit., 381
3 Ibid.
4 Deschanel: JOURNAL DES DÉBATS, 15 octobre 1864. Quoted by BP, 43
5 Hignard: *Charles Baudelaire* (REVUE DU LYONNAIS, juin 1892, 420)
6 [23 ? avril 1837 ?]. CB: *Corr.*, I, 39
7 17 mars [1871]. Auzas: *Lettres de Mme Veuve Aupick à Charles Asselineau* (M de F, 16 septembre 1912, 250)
8 [Vendredi 7 ou samedi 8 juillet 1837.] CB: *Corr.*, I, 41–2

9 [Environ 15 août 1837.] Ibid, I, 42

10 Jeudi 2 novembre [1837]. Ibid, I, 43–4

11 [7 novembre 1837.] Ibid, I, 46

12 [5 décembre 1837.] Ibid, I, 48

13 Feuillerat: *Baudelaire et sa mère*, 72

14 For Émon, see CB: *Corr.*, II, 1001–2; Marielle: *Répertoire de l'École impériale poly-technique*, 80

15 Mardi [19 juin 1838?] CB: *Corr.*, I, 54

16 [27 juin 1838.] Ibid, I, 55

17 [2 juillet 1838.] Ibid, I, 57

18 [17 juillet 1838.] Ibid, I, 57–8, 58, 59

19 3 août [1838]. Ibid, I, 60

20 Le 23 [août] 1838. Ibid, I, 62

21 Ibid.

22 CB: *Œs. cs.*, I, 199–200

23 Mardi [23 octobre 1838]. CB: *Corr.*, I, 64

24 [3 (?) décembre 1838.] Ibid, I, 65

25 [31 décembre 1838.] Ibid, I, 65

26 26 février [1839]. Ibid, I, 66–7

27 Ibid, I, 67

28 The letter from the *proviseur*, on 5 July 1886, records: 'Je n'ai pas découvert pour quelle raison Baudelaire a quitté le Lycée le 21 avril 1839.' (B.N. N.A. Fr.15819 f 459)

29 Lemonnier: op. cit., 10

30 18 avril 1839. CB: *Corr.*, I, 68–9, 69

7

1 CB to Mme Aupick [10 (?) juin 1839]. CB: *Corr.*, I, 70–1

2 Ibid, 71

3 Pommier et Pichois: *Baudelaire et Renan à l'ombre de Saint-Sulpice* (M de F, septembre 1958, 164)

4 Ibid.

5 31 juillet 1839. Ibid, 166

6 CB to Mme Aupick [10 (?) juin 1839.] CB: *Corr.*, I, 71

7 CB to Mme Aupick [16 juillet 1839]. Ibid, 74–5

8 R. Laforgue: op. cit., 161

9 Pommier et Pichois; op. cit., 167

10 Mme Aupick to Ancelle, 8 avril 1868. Quoted by F. Gautier: *Documents sur Baudelaire* (M de F, 1er février 1905, 343). See also Mme Aupick to Asselineau, 24 mars [1868], quoted by BP, 42–3

11 CB to General Aupick [13 août 1839]. CB: *Corr.*, I, 77

12 CB to Alphonse Baudelaire [vendredi 23 (août 1839)]. Ibid, I, 78, 79

13 Jules Buisson, quoted by Pichois in *Lettres à Eugène Crépet sur la jeunesse de Baudelaire* (M de F, 1er septembre 1954, 27)

14 Claretie: *La Vie à Paris, 1896*, 271: See also Pommier: *Du nouveau sur la Pension Bailly* (REVUE D'HISTOIRE LITTÉRAIRE DE LA FRANCE, avril–juin 1967, 227–38)

15 Pichois: *Lettres à Eugène Crépet sur la jeunesse de Baudelaire* (M de F, 1er septembre 1954, 6)

16 F. Gautier: *Charles Baudelaire*, XLII
17 CB: *Notices bio-bibliographiques* (*Œs. cs.*, I, 784)

8

1 CB: *Fusées. Œs. cs.*, I, 661; and see Baudelaire's comments to Georges Barral in 1864: EJC, 155–6, note
2 Trial: op. cit., 69–70
3 [6 mai 1861.] *Corr.*, II, 150, 153
4 Laforgue: *L'Échec de Baudelaire*, 49–64
5 Jeudi 13 mars 1856. *Corr.*, I, 338–9
6 L. Daudet: op. cit., 207
7 Peyre: *Connaissance de Baudelaire*, 39
8 Bricon: *Baudelaire et la mort* (LE GAULOIS, 4 novembre 1921)
9 Nadar: *Baudelaire intime*, 11
10 B.N. N.A. Fr.25013 f 14
11 B.N. N.A. Fr.25013 f 39
12 LE GAULOIS, 30 septembre 1886
13 LE FIGARO, 15 août 1890
14 CB: *Journaux intimes*. (*Œs. cs.*, I, 683)
15 Ibid, I, 651
16 Ibid, I, 652
17 Ibid, I, 702
18 Ibid, I, 661
19 Ibid, I, 677
20 Ibid, I, 686
21 Ibid, I, 688
22 Ibid. Silvestre de Sacy wrote: 'One cannot imagine him a good husband and a good father. His star at birth had made him otherwise.' (*'Pauvre Belgique' ou l'échec parfait*. M de F, 1er juin 1955, 293)
23 CB: *Journaux intimes*. (*Œs. cs.*, I, 682–3)
24 Ibid, I, 700
25 Nadar: op. cit., 127
26 Quoted by Trial: op. cit., 48
27 Ibid.
28 'La femme est *naturelle*, c'est-à-dire abominable.' CB: *Journaux intimes*. (*Œs. cs.*, I, 679)
29 The comment recalls the last lines of the poem 'Je t'adore a l'égal de la voûte nocturne':

> ... Et je chéris, ô bête implacable et cruelle,
> Jusqu'à cette froideur par où tu m'es plus belle!

(CB: *Œs. cs.*, I, 27)
30 Barrès: *Cahiers*, IX, 166
31 G. de Reynold: *Charles Baudelaire*, 38
32 C. du Bos: *Approximations*, I, 231
33 Ibid, 222
34 Ferran: *L'Alchimie amoureuse de Baudelaire* (L'ARCHER, 3 mars 1930, 161)

9

1 Mercredi [20 novembre 1839]. CB: *Corr.*, I, 79
2 Ibid, I, xxx
3 Hérisson: *À propos des 'lettres inédites aux siens.' Quelques aspects de la vie de Baudelaire de 1839 à 1842.* (RSH, janvier–mars 1969, 65, 66, 68)
4 Dedet: *'Sois sage, ô ma douleur . . .'* (LE FIGARO LITTÉRAIRE, 9 mars 1967)
5 [Lundi, 2 décembre 1839.] CB: *Corr.*, I, 80
6 Jeudi [31 décembre 1840]. Ibid, I, 83
7 Pichois: BET, 27–8
8 'Je n'ai pas pour maîtresse . . .' CB: *Œs. cs.*, I, 203
9 'Tu mettrais l'univers entier . . .' Ibid, I, 27–8
10 Jeudi [31 décembre 1840]. CB: *Corr.*, I, 84

10

1 Mercredi soir [20 janvier 1841]. CB: *Corr.*, I, 85
2 25 Jan[vier] 1841. Ibid, I, 732–3
3 [Lundi 1er février 1841.] Ibid, I, 86
4 3 février 1841. Ibid, I, 733, 734
5 Crépet: *Quelques documents inédits sur Baudelaire.* (M de F, 15 mars 1937, 630–2)
6 Ibid.
7 Du Camp: *Souvenirs littéraires*, II, 80–1
8 Ibid, 81
9 CB: *Corr.*, I, 87
10 30 avril 1841. Ibid, I, 734, 735–6
11 Crépet: op. cit., 632–3. Poggenburg dates this letter 4 May, Crépet dates it 5 May
12 F. Gautier: *Documents sur Baudelaire.* (M de F, 15 janvier 1905, 191)
13 Hignard: *Charles Baudelaire. Sa Vie, son œuvre, souvenirs personnels.* (REVUE DU LYONNAIS, juin 1892, 421–2)
14 Mercredi [9] juin 1841. CB: *Corr.*, I, 88
15 F. Gautier: loc. cit.
16 Crépet: op. cit., 632
17 Hérisson: op. cit., 69
18 To Asselineau, 1868. BP, 49–50
19 Undated. Institut de France. Lovenjoul C 491 f 124
20 F. Gautier: *Documents sur Baudelaire.* (M de F, 15 janvier 1905, 191)

11

1 Pichois: *Lettres à Eugène Crépet sur la jeunesse de Baudelaire* (M de F, 1er septembre 1954, 27)
2 LA CHRONIQUE DE PARIS, 13 septembre 1867
3 Rosenmark: *Le Voyage de Baudelaire à l'île Maurice* (RDF, 15 septembre 1921)
4 F. Gautier: *Documents sur Baudelaire* (M de F, 15 janvier 1905, 191–4)
5 Le 20 octobre 1841. CB: *Corr.*, I, 89

6 'À une dame créole'. CB: *Œs. cs.*, I, 62–3

7 Hérisson: *Le Voyage de Baudelaire* (M de F, avril 1959, 637–73)

8 CB: *Œs. cs.*, I, 784

9 For Baudelaire and this famous wine, see Mouquet: *Baudelaire: le constance et 'L'Invitation au Voyage'* (M de F, 1er mars 1934, 305–12). See also Joanna Richardson: *Dr Melchior Yvan: an influence on Baudelaire?* (FRENCH STUDIES, Vol. XLVI. October 1992, No 4, 406–11)

10 *Pauvre Belgique!* CB: *Œs. cs.*, II, 823

11 Ibid, II, 950

12 *Any Where Out of the World.* Ibid, II, 357

13 Nnadi: *Visions de l'Afrique dans l'œuvre de Baudelaire*, 135

14 *Salon de 1859.* CB: *Œs. cs.*, II, 650

15 Proust: *À propos de Baudelaire* (NRF, janvier–juin 1921, 660)

16 Yriarte: op. cit., 163

17 Undated. Institut de France. Lov. C 491 ff 124–5

18 Théophile Gautier: *Histoire du Romantisme*, 302

19 Gautier maintained that Baudelaire had been born in India (*Portraits contemporains*, 159)

20 Levallois: *Mémoires d'un critique*, 93 sqq.

21 Du Camp: op. cit., II, 81

22 Pichois: *Lettres à Eugène Crépet sur la jeunesse de Baudelaire* (M de F, 1er septembre 1954, 7)

23 Hérisson: *Le Voyage de Baudelaire dans l'Inde* (M de F, octobre 1956, 295)

24 Hérisson: loc. cit.

25 Mme Aupick to Asselineau, 1868; quoted by BP: 51. Hérisson: loc. cit.

26 16 février [1842]. CB: *Corr.*, I, 91

27 PZ: 156. Ruff: *L'Esprit du mal et l'esthétique baudelairienne*, 465. Hérisson: *À propos des 'Lettres inédites aux siens'* (RSH, janvier–mars 1969, 62)

28 Mme Aupick to Asselineau, 1868. BP, 51

29 Pichois: *Lettres à Eugène Crépet sur la jeunesse de Baudelaire* (M de F, 1er septembre 1954, 7–8)

30 Pommier: op. cit., 348 sqq.

31 'À une Malabaraise' was to be changed considerably before it appeared in *Les Épaves* in 1866

32 'La Musique'. CB: *Œs. cs.*, I, 68

33 Fairlie: *Baudelaire. LES FLEURS DU MAL*, 26

34 Symons: *Charles Baudelaire*, 11

35 Ibid, 29

36 Ibid, 39

12

1 Mme Aupick to Asselineau [1868]. EJC: op. cit., 255

2 Ibid, 257

3 Malassis to Asselineau, 7 juillet 1866. Richer et Ruff: op. cit., 58

4 Du Camp: op. cit., II, 82, 84

5 For an obituary of Prarond, see L. Séché: *Nécrologie: Ernest Prarond* (LES ANNALES ROMANTIQUES, tome vi, novembre–décembre 1909, 392–4)

6 Pichois: *Lettres à Eugène Crépet sur la jeunesse de Baudelaire* (M de F, 1er septembre 1954, 8, 10–11)

7 [Fin mars ou début avril 1842.] CB: *Corr.*, I, 92–3
8 PZ: op. cit., 157
9 Cousin: *Voyage dans un grenier*, 12
10 Cousin: op. cit., 13; see also Jacques Patin: *Charles Baudelaire et Louis Ménard* (LE FIGARO, 14 décembre 1930)
11 Cousin: op. cit., 12
12 Ibid, 15
13 North Peat: *Gossip from Paris during the Second Empire*, 190–1
14 Levallois: op. cit., 93 sqq.
15 Troubat: *Nouveaux témoignages d'un survivant de Baudelaire* (B.N. N.A. Fr.25013 f 565)
16 Cabanès: *Grands névropathes. Malades immortels*, I, 304
17 Champfleury: *Souvenirs et portraits de jeunesse*, 144
18 Rude: *Confidences d'un journaliste*, 164 sqq.
19 Gautier: *Charles Baudelaire*. Introductory notice to CB: *Les Fleurs du mal* (6e edition, 1878), 57–8

13

1 [28 mai 1842.] LAB, 137–8
2 'Je t'adore à l'égal de la voûte nocturne . . .' CB: *Œs. cs.*, I, 27
3 Du Camp: *Souvenirs littéraires*, II, 81
4 J. Crépet: *Baudelaire et Jeanne Duval* (LA PLUME, 15 avril 1898, 242–4)
5 J. Crépet: *Propos sur Baudelaire*, 155
6 J. Crépet: *Baudelaire et Jeanne Duval* (LA PLUME, 15 avril 1898, 242)
7 Nadar: op. cit., 7–8
8 Banville: *Mes Souvenirs*, 74–5; see also his *Lettres chimériques*, 281–2
9 F. Gautier: *Charles Baudelaire*, xxi–xxii
10 Rioux de Maillou: *Souvenirs des autres*. Quoted by BP, 131
11 Ibid.
12 Ruff: *L'Esprit du mal et l'esthétique baudelairienne*, 187
13 G. de Reynold: *Charles Baudelaire*, 42
14 EJC: op. cit., 267
15 F. Gautier: fascicule, 20
16 Baudelaire repeated the idea in *La Fanfarlo*. Samuel Cramer, in love with La Fanfarlo, 'a été puni par où il avait péché'. (CB: *Œs. cs.*, I, 579)
17 Butor: *Histoire extraordinaire*, 93
18 Nadar Papers. B.N. N.A. Fr.25013 f 11
19 Porché: *Baudelaire. Histoire d'une âme*, 188
20 Ibid, 282
21 Prévost: *Baudelaire*, 239, 240
22 'Sed non satiata'. CB: *Œs. cs.*, I, 28

14

1 [Printemps ou été 1842 (?)] CB: *Corr.*, I, 94
2 [Vers le 20 avril 1842 (?)] Ibid, I, 93

3 [12 juillet 1842.] Ibid, I, 95
4 State Archives, The Hague. Photocopy kindly sent by Baron H. J. van Asbeck
5 Quoted by Bassim: *La femme dans l'œuvre de Baudelaire*, 14
6 [4 décembre 1842.] CB: *Corr.*, I, 97
7 Banville: op. cit., 73 sqq.
8 Auguste Vitu: 'Petits Profils contemporains – Pierre Dupont.' (LA SILHOUETTE, 2 septembre 1849. Quoted by Bandy and Pichois in *Baudelaire devant ses contemporains*, 136)
9 Champfleury: *Souvenirs et portraits de jeunesse*, 132–4
10 Quoted by BP: op. cit., 137–8
11 [Samedi 11 février 1843.] CB: *Corr.*, I, 97
12 Pichois: *Lettres à Eugène Crépet sur la jeunesse de Baudelaire* (M de F, 1er septembre 1954, 28)
13 Ibid; and EJC: op. cit., 37–8, note
14 [19 avril 1843.] CB: *Corr.*, I, 98
15 [22 mai 1843.] Ibid, I, 98
16 Undated. Ibid, I, 98
17 Le 11 juin [1843]. Ibid, I, 98–9, 748
18 [31 août 1843.] Ibid, I, 100
19 [Fin octobre 1843 (?)] Ibid, I, 101
20 For Arondel (1809–1881), who also had pretentions as an artist, see Ziegler: *Gautier–Baudelaire*, 48
21 B.N. N.A. Fr.15814 f 62

15

1 The hôtel Pimodan, recorded by Gautier and Banville, was also the subject of Roger de Beauvoir's book: *Les Mystères de l'île Saint-Louis. Chroniques de l'Hôtel Pimodan* (1859)
2 R. de Beauvoir: op. cit., I, 4–9
3 Mme Paul de Molènes: loc. cit. Quoted by BP, 258–9. For an appreciation of her husband, see Edmond Taigny: *Un romancier idéaliste: M. Paul de Molènes* (REVUE EUROPÉENNE, 1er mai 1861)
4 Mme Aupick to Ancelle. Undated, but 1868 [?]. F. Gautier: *Documents sur Baudelaire* (M de F, 1er février 1905, 344)
5 Hignard: *Charles Baudelaire*. (REVUE DU LYONNAIS, juin 1892, 427)
6 Th. Gautier: *Souvenirs romantiques*, 268 sqq. In 1859, Baudelaire described his first encounter with Gautier: 'I had presented myself to give him a small volume of poetry on behalf of two absent friends . . .' (L'ARTISTE, 13 mars 1859, 162). Pichois and Ziegler note (op. cit., 633) that *Vers* had three authors, and they date the meeting 1845. For the influence of Gautier on Baudelaire, see Pommier: *Dans les chemins de Baudelaire*, 179 sqq.
7 Pichois: *Lettres à Eugène Crépet sur la jeunesse de Baudelaire* (M de F, 1er septembre 1954, 23)
8 Asselineau: *Charles Baudelaire*, 7–8; in his unpublished notes, Asselineau records that Baudelaire's rooms were on the fifth floor (B.N. N.A. Fr.25013 f 406)
9 Banville: *Charles Baudelaire*. (Galerie contemporaine, littéraire, artistique, 1876. Press-cutting. Taylor Institution, Oxford. Pages un-numbered.)

10 Asselineau: op. cit., 8
11 Cousin: op. cit., 12
12 Champfleury: op. cit., 135
13 Yriarte: *Portraits cosmopolites*, 121–3. This version differs from the one that Yriarte had given in RNE, 14 septembre 1867
14 Yriarte: *Courrier de Paris*. (LE MONDE, 24 septembre 1867)

16

1 Barrès: op. cit., IX, 383
2 Nicolardot: *L'Impeccable Théophile Gautier*, 6–7: Baudelaire also claimed to be the son of a defrocked priest (Audebrand: *Derniers jours de la Bohème*, 205)
3 Pichois: *Lettres à Eugène Crépet sur la jeunesse de Baudelaire* (M de F, 1er septembre 1954, 20)
4 CB: Preface to Cladel: *Les Martyrs ridicules*. (*Œs. cs.*, II, 187)
5 For Baudelaire's irreverence, see also BP: op. cit., 256
6 Prévost: *Baudelaire*, 73
7 Jouve: *Tombeau de Baudelaire*, 21
8 R. de Bonnières: *Mémoires d'aujourd'hui*, 3e série, 292
9 Crépet: *Propos sur Baudelaire*, 535
10 CB: *Journaux intimes. Œs. cs.*, I, 649
11 Ibid, I, 659
12 Ibid, I, 705

17

1 Pichois: *Lettres à Eugène Crépet sur la jeunesse de Baudelaire* (M de F, 1er septembre 1954, 16, 17)
2 Ibid, 27–8
3 Yriarte: RNE, 14 septembre 1867
4 Nadar: *Charles Baudelaire intime*, 39, 40
5 Ziegler: *Émile Deroy (1820–1846) et l'esthétique de Baudelaire* (GAZETTE DES BEAUX-ARTS, mai–juin 1976, 153–60)
6 Banville: *La Lanterne magique. Camées parisiens*, 282. See also *Notes pour une iconographie du poète Charles Baudelaire*. (LA PLUME, undated. Press-cutting. Taylor Institution, Oxford.)
7 Asselineau: *Charles Baudelaire*, 13. The friend was Asselineau himself; on his death the picture became the property of Dr Gérard Piogey, who had attended Baudelaire.
8 Asselineau: op. cit., 8
9 [5 janvier 1844.] CB: *Corr.*, I, 104
10 Ibid.
11 [3 mars 1844.] Ibid, I, 105–6
12 [15 juillet 1844.] Ibid, I, 112

18

1 Troubat: *Souvenirs du dernier secrétaire de Sainte-Beuve*, 207–8
2 Ibid, 208
3 Troubat to E. Crépet, 16 août 1886. Quoted by J. Crépet in *Baudelairiana* (B du B, février 1946, 62–3)
4 Cousin: *Voyage dans un grenier*, 17
5 Pichois: *Lettres à Eugène Crépet sur la jeunesse de Baudelaire* (M de F, 1er septembre 1954, 28)
6 PZ: op. cit., 162–4
7 J. Crépet: *Quelques documents inédits sur Baudelaire* (M de F, 15 mars 1937, 686)
8 For Ancelle, see CB: *Corr.*, II, 981; Dufay: *Un ami de Baudelaire: M. Ancelle, beau-père d'un fils du duc de Berry* (M de F, 15 octobre 1934, 421–5). See also B.N. N.A. Fr.15814 ff 41, 42–3
9 'Samedi 14'. J. Crépet: *Les derniers jours de Charles Baudelaire . . .* (NRF, novembre 1932, 665)
10 J. Crépet: *Les derniers jours de Charles Baudelaire* (B du B, 1er avril 1925, 202); see also Dufay: *Un ami de Baudelaire: M. Ancelle, beau-père d'un fils du duc de Berry* (M de F, 15 octobre 1934, 421–5)
11 Quesnel: *Baudelaire solaire et clandestin*, 11
12 Jouve: *Tombeau de Baudelaire*, 41
13 Ibid, 47

19

1 [Début 1845 (?)] CB: *Corr.*, I, 119
2 [Début 1845 (?)] Ibid, I, 120, 120–1
3 3 août [1838]. Ibid, I, 61
4 PZ: op. cit., 183–4
5 [Fin 1844 ou début 1845.] CB: *Corr.*, I, 116–8
6 Ibid, I, 118
7 Barrès: *Cahiers*, IX, 98–9
8 Rude: op. cit., 164 sqq.
9 27 mars 1865. Sainte-Beuve: *Corr. gén.*, XIV, 132–3
10 J. Crépet: *Baudelairiana.* (B du B, février 1946, 66–7)
11 Pichois: *Lettres à Eugène Crépet sur la jeunesse de Baudelaire* (M de F, 1er septembre 1954, 12)
12 Gilman: *Baudelaire the critic*, 3
13 [Premiers jours d'avril 1845.] CB: *Corr.*, I, 122
14 [Mi-avril 1845 (?)] Ibid.

20

1 *Salon de* 1845. CB: *Œs. cs.*, II, 353
2 PZ: op. cit., 632: Gilman: *Baudelaire the critic*, 10. In *Baudelaire et Delacroix*, p. 16, Lloyd Austin suggests that Prosper Richomme may have introduced them to each other.

3 Prévost: *Baudelaire*, 50, 51
4 Ibid, 88, 132, 137
5 CB: *Œs. cs.*, II, 356
6 CB: *Corr.*, II, 996
7 Ibid.
8 Carter: *Baudelaire et la critique française*, 30
9 CB: *Œs. cs.*, II, 359
10 Baudelaire was well aware of his audacity in publishing this 'éloge violent' (ibid, II, 358)
11 Ibid, II, 375
12 Ibid, II, 377
13 Lawrence had paid his last visit to France in 1825, when George IV had commissioned him to paint Charles X for the Waterloo Chamber at Windsor; he also seems to have painted two versions of a portrait of the Duchesse de Berry.
14 CB: *Œs. cs.*, II, 407
15 B.N. N.A. Fr.25013 f 19
16 Monselet: *La Lorgnette littéraire*, 7. Asselineau's contributions to L'ARTISTE included *Retour des paysagistes* (15 décembre 1851) and *Beaux-Arts* (15 mars 1852); he reviewed art books (28 novembre, 19 décembre 1858, 13 février 1859). On 26 August 1855, L'ARTISTE recorded him as secretary of the Société des Gens de Lettres. Jacques Crépet and Claude Pichois pay him tribute in their introduction to *Baudelaire et Asselineau*.
17 Ch. de Ricault d'Héricault: *Murger et son coin*, 276-8
18 Poem of September 1852. Quoted by Delvau: *Histoire anecdotique des Cafés et Cabarets de Paris*, 189
19 EJC: op. cit., 289
20 Ibid, 290

21

1 Borgal: *Charles Baudelaire*, 32
2 Du Bos: *Approximations*, I, 184
3 Le 30 juin 1845. CB: *Corr.*, I, 124-6
4 Cousin: *Voyage dans un grenier*, 17. See also L'ILLUSTRATION, septembre 1867, 147: 'As for suicide, Baudelaire liked to say that he dreamed of it for a long while. But he did not find any [means of suicide] which was sufficiently atrocious or bizarre. The truth was that he was attached to life; his ironic humour got the better of his romanticism.'
5 [Début juillet 1845 (?)] CB: *Corr.*, I, 126-7, 127
6 CB: *Corr.*, I, 768-9
7 Rioux de Maillou: *Souvenirs des autres*. Quoted by BP: 79. For the two versions of Ménard's account, see BP: 73-80
8 [Juillet 1845 (?)] CB: *Corr.*, I, 129
9 [1845(?)] Ibid, I, 129-30
10 Du Camp: op. cit., II, 79-80
11 Aupick to Thouvenel, 6 mars 1849. Pichois: *Le Beau-père de Baudelaire* (M de F, 1er juin 1955, 280)
12 Trial: op. cit., 17

13 Samedi 26 mars 1853. CB: *Corr.*, I, 214
14 28 juillet 1854. Ibid, I, 285
15 Samedi 26 mars 1853. Ibid, I, 214
16 Pichois: *Le Beau-père de Baudelaire* (M de F, 1er août 1955, 673)
17 Berthelot: *Louis Ménard.* Quoted by BP, 75. See also Rioux de Maillou: op. cit., quoted by BP, 80
18 Undated. CB: *Corr.*, I, 131
19 Undated. Ibid.
20 CB: *Œs. cs.*, I, 662
21 Undated. CB: *Corr.*, I, 132

22

1 *Comment on paie ses dettes quand on a du génie.* (CB: *Œs. cs.*, II, 8)
2 [20–22 février 1846.] CB: *Corr.*, I, 133
3 [Fin février 1846.] Ibid, I, 134
4 Bandy: *Baudelaire et Croly. La vérité sur LE JEUNE ENCHANTEUR* (M de F, 1er février 1950)
5 [Environ 3 mars 1846.] CB: *Corr.*, I, 135
6 9 janvier 1856. Ibid, I, 335
7 Poggenburg: op. cit., 77
8 [Seconde quinzaine de mars 1846.] CB: *Corr.*, I, 135–6
9 [Avril 1846.] Ibid, I, 137
10 [Début mai 1846.] Ibid, I, 138

23

1 *Salon de 1846.* CB: *Œs. cs.*, II, 417–9
2 Ibid, 420–2
3 Ibid, 425–6
4 See pp. 225–229 of the present book
5 Shanks: *Baudelaire. Flesh and Spirit*, 79
6 *Salon de 1846.* CB: *Œs. cs.*, II, 430, 431, 432
7 Ibid, 440
8 Ibid, 494, 496
9 Quennell: *Baudelaire and the Symbolists*, 55

24

1 Barrès: preface to Ménard: *Rêveries d'un Païen Mystique*, viii–ix
2 LAB: 206
3 Calmettes: *Leconte de Lisle et ses amis*, 94–5, 95
4 Dornis: *Leconte de Lisle intime*, 20
5 Calmettes: op. cit., 95–6, 96
6 Ibid, 96

7 [Octobre 1846 (?)] CB: *Corr.*, I, 139
8 Ibid.
9 [Décembre 1846 (?)] Ibid, I, 140
10 Asselineau: *Charles Baudelaire*, 11
11 *La Fanfarlo*. CB: *Œs. cs.*, I, 577
12 Ibid, I, 578
13 Borgal: op. cit., 20
14 *La Fanfarlo*. CB: *Œs. cs.*, I, 579–80

25

1 Pichois and Ziegler record (op. cit., 636) that the date is a hypothetical date for the portrait, now in the Musée Fabre, Montpellier. For the history of this picture, see Joanna Richardson: *L'Homme à la pipe. Some Correspondence about Courbet's Portrait of Baudelaire* (FRENCH STUDIES BULLETIN, No 45, Winter 1992–93, 9–11).
2 Champfleury: *Souvenirs* . . ., 135
3 Ibid; PZ: op. cit., 137
4 Champfleury: op. cit., 144
5 Albalat: *Souvenirs de la vie littéraire*, 82–3
6 Champfleury: op. cit., 136
7 Levallois: *Mémoires d'un critique*, 93 sqq.
8 Jollivet: *Souvenirs de la vie de plaisir sous le Second Empire*, 229
9 Rude: op. cit., 164–5
10 Ibid.
11 Ibid. See also Champfleury: *Les Chats*, 110
12 Marx: *Une figure étrange* (L'ÉVÉNEMENT, 14 juin 1866; quoted by BP, 286). See also North Peat: op. cit., 191
13 Levallois: op. cit., 93 sqq.
14 Mendès: *Le Mouvement poétique français de 1867 à 1900*, 102–3
15 Barrès: *Cahiers*, VI, 260
16 CB: *Journaux intimes*. *Œs. cs.*, II, 661
17 Nadar Papers. B.N. N.A. Fr.20513 f 363

26

1 [13 mars 1847.] CB. *Corr.*, I, 141
2 R. Laforgue: op. cit., 175
3 [1847.] CB: *Corr.*, I, 141
4 Samedi 4 décembre 1847. Ibid, I, 142, 143
5 Ibid, 145
6 Ibid.
7 Ibid, 146–7
8 Ibid, 147
9 Pichois: BET: 233
10 Dimanche 5 décembre [1847]. CB: *Corr.*, I, 147
11 16 décembre 1847. Ibid, I, 148

27

1 2 janvier 1848. CB: *Corr.*, I, 148–9
2 Champfleury to E. Crépet. Quoted by Poggenburg: op. cit., 91
3 Loncke: *Baudelaire et la musique*, 42–3
4 Toubin: *Souvenirs d'un septuagénaire*. Quoted by PZ: op. cit., 253
5 Alfred Cobban: *A History of Modern France*. Vol. II. 1799–1871. (Pelican Books. 1965, 130–1.) An account of the episode is also found in Vicomte de Beaumont-Vassy: *Histoire de mon temps*. Tome IV. (Perrotin. 1858, 63–6)
6 Buisson: quoted in Pichois: *Lettres à Eugène Crépet . . .* (M de F, 1er septembre 1954, 29)
7 Massin. *Baudelaire 'entre Dieu et Satan'*, 119–20
8 Pinet: *Histoire de l'École Polytechnique*, 239
9 Freycinet: *Souvenirs, 1848–1878*, 6–7
10 Pinet: op. cit., 239, 240, 241–2
11 Ibid, 244
12 Freycinet: op. cit., 7
13 Lemer: op. cit., 143
14 EJC: op. cit., 79–80
15 Pichois: *Le Beau-père de Baudelaire* (M de F, 1er juin 1955, 273–4)
16 O'Callaghan: *History of the Irish Brigades in the Service of France*, 633–4
17 Pinet: op. cit., 239
18 Bonde: *Paris in '48*, 89, 90
19 Lamartine: *Histoire de la Révolution de 1848*, II, 162–3
20 CB: *Corr.*, I, 149
21 Ibid.
22 To A.-A. Cuvillier-Fleury. Thouvenel: *La Grèce du Roi Othon*, 192

28

1 *Mon Cœur mis à nu*. CB: *Œs. cs.*, I, 679
2 21 août 1848. CB: *Corr.*, I, 150
3 *Mon Cœur mis à nu*. CB: *Œs. cs.*, I, 680
4 Simon Brugal (Firmin Boissin). (LE FIGARO, 19 janvier 1887. BP, 107)
5 Sherard: *Twenty Years in Paris*, 358
6 25 janvier 1887. B.N. N.A. Fr.15815 f 296
7 8 décembre 1848. CB: *Corr.*, I, 153–4, 155

29

1 CB: *Corr.*, I, 157–8
2 Delacroix: *Journal*, I, 258–9
3 CB: *Corr.*, I, 158
4 Ibid, I, 160
5 Asselineau: *Charles Baudelaire*, 36–7
6 Coppée: *Souvenirs d'un Parisien*, 83

7 Firmin Maillard: *La Cité des intellectuels*, 62. For Malassis, see also Un Bibliophile ornais: *Auguste Poulet-Malassis*. One hundred and fifty letters from Malassis, many of them concerning Baudelaire, were listed in 1891, in the *Catalogue des autographes composant la collection Champfleury*, 25

8 Monselet: *Curiosités littéraires et bibliographiques*, 69

9 H. d'Alméras: *La Littérature au café sous le Second Empire*, 347

10 Delvau: *Histoire anecdotique des Cafés et Cabarets de Paris*, 17

11 Lemercier de Neuville: *Souvenirs d'un Montreur de Marionnettes*, 143‒4

12 A. Daudet: *Trente ans de Paris*, 248

13 Rude: op. cit., 121‒3

14 Ibid, 121

15 Lundi, 15 juillet [1850]. CB: *Corr.*, I, 165

16 25 novembre 1849. Pichois: *Le vrai visage du Général Aupick*, 23

17 Pichois: *Le Beau-père de Baudelaire* (M de F, 1er juillet 1955, 482)

18 Asselineau: *L'Italie et Constantinople*, 187‒8. Asselineau sent a signed copy of the book to Mme Aupick. A copy of the first edition, with a pencilled inscription to Philippe Burty, was listed in Burty's library as no 593. For another account of Therapia, see Théophile Gautier: *Constantinople* (Michel Lévy. 1853), 354

19 Pichois: *Le Beau-père de Baudelaire* (M de F, 1er juillet 1955, 480)

20 Flaubert: *Voyages*, II, 330, 338

21 4 décembre 1850. Flaubert: *Corr.*, IIe série, 266

22 Flaubert: *Voyages*, II, 343

23 Du Camp: op. cit., II, 77‒9

24 Flaubert: *Voyages*, II, 347

30

1 Pichois: *Le Beau-père de Baudelaire* (M de F, 1er juillet 1955, 481)

2 Aupick to Thouvenel, 25 avril 1851. (Ibid, 482, note)

3 Aupick to Thouvenel, 26 juin 1851. (Ibid, 483)

4 'Ce vendredi 15'. Auzas: *Lettres de Madame Veuve Aupick à Charles Asselineau* (M de F, 16 septembre 1912, 246)

5 Aupick to Thouvenel, 24 mai 1849. Pichois: *Le Beau-père de Baudelaire* (M de F, 1er juillet 1955, 476)

6 Letter undated and unsigned. B.N. N.A. Fr.15826 f 59. Brenier and the other new Ministers had been appointed by the Prince-President on 24 January 1851.

7 Aupick to Thouvenel, 11 février 1853. Pichois: *Le Beau-père de Baudelaire* (M de F, 1er août 1955, 661)

8 Aupick to Thouvenel, 26 juin 1851. Pichois: *Le Beau-père de Baudelaire* (M de F, 1er juillet 1955, 483‒4). For a summary of Aupick's career to this point, see Duckett: *Dictionnaire de la conversation*. Seconde édition. Tome II, 236

9 Samedi 7 juin 1851. CB: *Corr.*, I, 170

10 Quoted by Babuts: *Baudelaire et J.G.F.* (BULLETIN BAUDELAIRIEN, Hiver 1979, Tome 14, No 2, p. 3.)

11 Jeudi 12 juin 1851. CB: *Corr.*, I, 171

12 Mme Aupick to Asselineau, 24 mars [1868]. EJC: op. cit., 266

13 Mercredi 9 juillet 1851. CB: *Corr.*, I, 173‒4

14 Despatch of 29 July 1851. Pichois: *Le vrai visage du Général Aupick*, 37

31

1 Samedi 30 août 1851. CB: *Corr.*, I, 175–6, 176, 177, 178
2 Le 15 octobre 1851. Ibid, I, 179–80

32

1 Mauclair: *Charles Baudelaire*, 22
2 Ibid, 23
3 Shanks: *Baudelaire. Flesh and Spirit*, 120
4 EJC: op. cit., 93–4
5 For Pichot, who sometimes published under the signature of Alphonse Borghers, see W. T. Bandy: *Amédée Pichot: Premier Traducteur de Poe* (BULLETIN BAUDELAIRIEN, 31 août 1966. Vol. 2, No 1)
6 15 octobre 1851. CB: *Corr.*, I, 179–80
7 Lemonnier: *Les Traducteurs d'Edgar Poe en France*, 97
8 RDP: octobre 1851
9 CB: *Œs. cs.*, II, 1103
10 [C. 19 février 1852.] LAB, 140. Pichois dates the letter 19 or 20 February, but Du Camp would surely have written 'demain', not 'samedi, 21 courant', if he had been referring to next day.
11 Yriarte: *Courrier de Paris* (RNE, 24 septembre 1867, 162)
12 Lundi, 23 février 1852. CB: *Corr.*, I, 187
13 Ibid, I, 808
14 Ibid, I, 809
15 Théophile Gautier: *Portraits contemporains*, 160–1
16 Vendredi 5 mars 1852. CB: *Corr.*, I, 188
17 Edmond Richard: *Notes sur la Présidente*, 282 (Bibliothèque municipale de Fontainebleau)
18 Ibid.
19 Samedi 27 mars 1852. CB: *Corr.*, I, 190

33

1 Audebrand: *Un Café de journalistes sous Napoléon III, 295–6*. The café de Robespierre was demolished when the avenue de l'Opéra was built (ibid, 2)
2 For the Brasserie des Martyrs, see Delvau: *Histoire anecdotique des cafés et cabarets de Paris*; Firmin Maillard: *Les Derniers Bohèmes*, passim
3 Delvau: op. cit., 103
4 Audebrand: op. cit., 209
5 B.N. N.A. Fr.25013 f 37
6 Delvau: op. cit., 9
7 Maillard: *La Cité des intellectuels*, 400
8 Delvau: op. cit., 86
9 [30 janvier 1862.] CB: *Corr.*, II, 224
10 Dreyfous: *Ce que je tiens à dire*, 124–5

11 Delvau: loc. cit.
12 F. Brunetière. Quoted by G. Rodenbach, LE FIGARO, 6 septembre 1892. (B.N. N.A. Fr.25013 f 521)
13 For the café Lemblin, known for its billiards and its excellent coffee, see Delvau: op. cit., 69–70•
14 Le Petit: *Notes sur Baudelaire* (LA PLUME, 1er juillet 1893, 285); Monselet: *Catalogue . . .*, 37

34

1 27 mars 1852. CB: *Corr.*, I, 192
2 Ibid.
3 Ibid.
4 Ibid, 193–4
5 Porché: *Baudelaire. Histoire d'une âme*, 290
6 27 mars 1852. CB: *Corr.*, I, 194
7 Ibid, I, 814
8 Dimanche 18 avril 1852. Ibid, I, 196–8
9 Lundi 19 avril 1852. Ibid, I, 198
10 Ibid, I, 814
11 Nadar Papers. B.N. N.A. Fr.25013 f 4
12 Bassim: *La femme dans l'œuvre de Baudelaire*, 99

35

1 Du Camp: *Souvenirs littéraires*, II, 84 sqq.
2 Lundi, 30 août 1852. CB: *Corr.*, I, 202
3 Poggenburg: op. cit., 129
4 Monselet: *La Lorgnette littéraire*, 20–1
5 Du Camp: op. cit., II, 10–11
6 Poggenburg: op. cit., 132
7 Jeudi 9 décembre 1852. CB: *Corr.*, I, 205–6

36

1 For the most complete account of Mme Sabatier, see Billy: *La Présidente et ses amis*; see also Ziegler: *Baudelairiana. Alfred Mosselman et Mme Sabatier* (B du B, 1975, III, 266–73); *Baudelairiana. Madame Sabatier (1822–1890). Quelques notes biographiques* (B du B, 1977, III–IV, 366–82). The present account is also based on Edmond Richard's manuscript, *Notes sur la Présidente* (Bibliothèque municipale de Fontainebleau)
2 In his *Meissonier*, Gustave Larroumet lists two portraits of Mme Sabatier (pp. 38, 39)
3 Ziegler: *Baudelairiana. Madame Sabatier . . .*, loc. cit., 371
4 Théophile Gautier praised her portraits in *Abécédaire du Salon de 1861* (Dentu, 1861), 324
5 Ziegler gives a useful account of Mosselman in *Alfred Mosselman et Mme Sabatier (supra)*
6 Richardson: *Théophile Gautier. His Life and Times*, 87

7 [29 juin 1866.] Goncourt: *Journal*, VII, 187

8 For Mosselman's friendship with Musset, see P. d'Ariste: *La Vie et le monde du boulevard (1830–1870)*, 35. Some of Mosselman's collection of paintings were sold in 1849; for an account of them, see L'ARTISTE, 15 décembre 1849, 62

9 For further details about Bébé, see Ziegler: *Gautier–Baudelaire. Un carré de dames . . .*, passim

10 Théophile Gautier: *Souvenirs romantiques*, 277

11 RDDM, 1er mai 1847

12 Billy: op. cit., 67; see also Delacroix: *Journal*, 7 mai 1847

13 Billy: op. cit., 59

14 The poem was entitled 'Devant une statue du Salon de 1847. À Madame —.' In the index it was called 'Devant la femme piquée par un serpent'.

15 Billy: op. cit., 63–4

16 31 août 1862. Goncourt: *Journal*, V, 165

17 16 avril 1864. Ibid, VI, 197–8

18 Edmond Richard: *Notes sur la Présidente*, 136 (Bibliothèque municipale de Fontainebleau)

19 19 octobre 1850. Théophile Gautier: *Œuvres érotiques* (Arcanes. 1953), 95–116

20 Théophile Gautier: 'Émaux et Camées', 53–4

21 Richard: op. cit., 122 (Bibliothèque municipale de Fontainebleau)

22 Quoted by Richard: ibid.

23 Ibid, 154

24 Richardson: *Théophile Gautier. His Life and Times*, 161

25 J. Gautier: *Le Collier des Jours. Le Second Rang du Collier*, 180

26 Ibid, 180–4

27 Billy: op. cit., 137

28 E. About: *Voyage à travers l'exposition des beaux-arts . . .*, 197

29 Porché: *Baudelaire. Histoire d'une âme*, 316

30 'Confession', CB: *Œs. cs.*, I, 45

31 Richard: op. cit., 282 (Bibliothèque municipale de Fontainebleau)

32 Borgal: *Charles Baudelaire*, 44

33 CB: *Œs. cs.*, II, 59

34 Gilbert Maire: *La personnalité de Baudelaire et la critique biologique des FLEURS DU MAL* (M de F, 1er novembre 1910, 231 sqq.). B.N. N.A. Fr.15820 f 23. See also Nadar Papers: B.N. N.A. Fr.25013 f 5

35 B.N. N.A. Fr.25013 f 5

36 Quesnel: op. cit., 197, 198

37

1 Pichois: *Le vrai visage du Général Aupick*, 45–6, 46–7

2 Aupick to Thouvenel, 16 août 1852. Ibid, 47

3 Aupick to Thouvenel, 31 janvier 1853. Ibid, 48

4 Aupick to Thouvenel, 11 février 1853. Ibid, 51

5 Pichois: op. cit., 49

6 Ibid, 54

7 For Aupick's career in Spain, see Pichois' pamphlet: an enlarged version of the articles published in the *Mercure de France* in 1955.

8 Samedi 26 mars 1853. CB: *Corr.*, I, 210
9 Ibid.
10 Ibid, 210–11, 212, 212–3, 213, 213–5, 217
11 20 avril 1853. Ibid, I, 218
12 [Avril 1853 (?)]. Ibid, I, 221

38

1 Rude: op. cit., 170
2 Du Camp: *Souvenirs littéraires*, II, 69–74
3 CB: *Corr.*, I, 833
4 Quoted in M de F, 1er octobre 1924, 230–3
5 Ibid, 232–3
6 CB: *Corr.*, I, 224
7 Ibid.
8 [Mai 1853 (?)] Ibid, I, 224. One might recall Baudelaire's comment in *Hygiène* (*Œs. cs.*, I, 668): 'After debauchery, one always feels more alone, more abandoned.'
9 CB: *Corr.*, I, 224
10 3 mai 1853. Ibid, 223
11 Lundi 9 mai 1853. Ibid, 225–6
12 Lundi, 27 juin 1853. Ibid, 227
13 1er juillet 1853. Ibid, 228

39

1 Dimanche, 18 sept[embre] 1853. CB: *Corr.*, I, 230
2 Lundi 31 oct[obre] 1853. Ibid, 232–3
3 Quesnel: op. cit., 131
4 18 nov[embre] 1853. CB: *Corr.*, I, 234
5 18 nov[embre] 1853. Ibid, 235
6 19 [novembre] 1853. Ibid, 235–6
7 1er décembre 1853. Ibid, 236, 236–7
8 Samedi 10 décembre 1853. Ibid, 237
9 Vendredi, 16 décembre 1853. Ibid, 238–40
10 Lundi 26 décembre 1853. Ibid, 241–2, 243
11 Lundi [26] décembre 1853. Ibid, 243
12 31 décembre 1853. Ibid, 244, 244–5, 245–6
13 Midi, 31 décembre 1853. Ibid, 247

40

1 Mardi 3 janvier 1854. CB: *Corr.*, I, 253–4
2 Mercredi 4 janvier 1854. Ibid, 254
3 *Carnet*. CB: *Œs. cs.*, I, 742
4 Samedi 28 janvier 1854. CB: *Corr.*, I, 257

5 29 janvier 1854. Ibid, 262
6 31 janvier 1854. Ibid, 263–4
7 Ibid, 264
8 6 février 1854. Ibid, 264
9 Mardi 7 février 1854. Ibid, 266. The sonnet begins: 'Ils marchent devant moi, ces Yeux extraordinaires . . .'. Fontainas, in *Lignée*, p. 31, notes the resemblance to Poe's poem 'To Helen'
10 Jeudi 16 février 1854. CB: *Corr.*, I. 267

41

1 23 février 1854. CB: *Corr.*, I, 268
2 Ibid.
3 Ibid.
4 Ibid.
5 8 mars 1854. Ibid, 269, 269–70
6 Ibid, 271
7 20 mars 1854. Sainte-Beuve: *Corr. gén.*, IX, 416
8 13 mars 1854. CB: *Corr.*, I, 272
9 Jeudi 13 avril 1854. Ibid, 274

42

1 Lundi 8 mai 1854. CB: *Corr.*, I, 275–6, 276–7
2 Ibid, 276
3 Bourcau: *L'État civil de Marie Daubrun* (RHLF, janvier–mars 1958. 60–1)
4 Hervey: *The Theatres of Paris*, 198
5 Feuillerat: *Baudelaire et la Belle aux cheveux d'or*, 82
6 MERCURE DES THÉÂTRES, 19 août 1847
7 Lyonnet: *Dictionnaire des comédiens français*, I, 438
8 Feuillerat: op. cit., 20
9 Ibid, 22–3
10 Ibid, 33
11 Ibid.
12 Ibid, 34
13 CB: *Corr.*, II, 995
14 Poggenburg: op. cit., 153
15 'L'Invitation au voyage'. CB: *Œs. cs.*, I, 53
16 Jeudi 18 mai 1854. CB: *Corr.*, I, 278–9
17 LAB: 27 and note
18 For Barbey d'Aurevilly's dandyism, see Maillard: *La Cité des intellectuels*, 360–11; Calmettes: *Leconte de Lisle et ses amis*, 313–6
19 23 X^bre 1905. Féli Gautier Papers. Ms 8° F 40/58. (Taylor Institution, Oxford.)
20 Firmin Boissin to Eugène Crépet, 25 janvier 1887. B.N. N.A. Fr.15815 f 296
21 3 juin 1854. CB: *Corr.*, I, 279–80
22 Samedi 10 juin 1854. Ibid, 280

23 LAB: 140
24 EJC: 46, note
25 25 juin 1854. CB: *Corr.*, I, 281
26 28 juillet 1854. Ibid, I, 285–6, 286

43

1   [28 juillet 1854.] CB: *Corr.*, I, 285
2   1er août 1854. Ibid, I, 286, 287
3   Aupick to Thouvenel, 11 mars 1853. Pichois: *Le Beau-père de Baudelaire* (M de F, 1er août 1955, 661)
4   Jean-Aubry: *Un Paysage littéraire. Baudelaire et Honfleur*, 14, 15–16
5   Undated. Auzas: *Lettres de Madame Veuve Aupick à Charles Asselineau* (M de F, 16 septembre 1912, 243)
6   CB: *Corr.*, 11, 777
7   14 août 1854. Ibid, I, 288, 288–9
8   Mardi 22 août 1854. Ibid, I, 289, 290
9   Mardi 26 septembre 1854. Ibid, I, 292
10 Vendredi. [29 septembre 1854.] LAB, 351–2
11 CB: *Corr.*, I, 293
12 14 oc[tobre 18]54. Ibid, I, 293
13 Ibid, I, 868
14 Mardi 17 oct[obre 18]54. Ibid, I, 294
15 Mercredi 8 novembre 1854. Ibid, I, 298–300
16 Le 14 novembre. Lundi. 1854. Ibid, I, 300
17 Lundi 4 décembre [1854]. Ibid, I, 300, 301, 302

44

1   Crépet et Pichois: *Petites Énigmes baudelairiennes* (M de F, 1er juillet 1952)
2   Dimanche 7 janvier 1855. CB: *Corr.*, I, 306–7
3   Jeudi 18 janvier 1855. Ibid, I, 308–9
4   Ibid, I, 309
5   3 février 1855. Ibid, I, 310
6   5 avril 1855. Ibid, I, 310–11, 311
7   [7 avril 1855]. Ibid, I, 312
8   Morcredi 13 juin 1855. Ibid, I, 313
9   Du Camp: *Souvenirs littéraires*, 11, 89
10 'L'Ennemi'. CB: *Œs. cs.*, I, 16
11 Gide: *Baudelaire et M. Faguet.* (NRF, 1910, Vol. 11, 499 sqq.)
12 'Mœsta et errabunda'. CB: *Œs. cs.*, I, 64
13 *Richard Wagner et TANNHÄUSER à Paris.* CB: *Œs. cs.*, 11, 781–2
14 Gide: op. cit., 506, 510, 512

45

1 *Exposition universelle,* 1855. Beaux-Arts. 1. Méthode de critique. De l'idée moderne du progrès appliquée aux beaux-arts. Déplacement de la vitalité. CB: *Œs. cs.,* 11, 575–83

2 Ibid, 576–7

3 Ibid, 582

4 *Salon de 1845.* CB: *Œs. cs.,* 11, 377, 386

5 *Salon de 1846.* Ibid, 11, 464

6 *Exposition universelle, 1855* . . . Ibid, 11, 582, 1371

7 Ibid, 11, 1384–5

8 *Eugène Delacroix.* Ibid, 11, 590–7

9 Ibid, 592

10 Ibid, 593

11 Ibid, 594–5

12 10 juin 1855. LAB: 114–5

13 Ibid, 112

14 Ibid, 116

15 Ce 17 février 1858. Ibid, 116

16 *[Exorde de la conférence faite à Bruxelles en 1864]* sur Eugène Delacroix. CB: *Œs. cs.,* 11, 774

17 Ce 10 juin 1855. LAB: 114–5

18 Mercredi 13 juin 1855. CB: *Corr.,* I, 313–4

19 Ibid, 879

20 Poggenburg: op. cit., 169

21 CB: *Œs. cs.,* 11, 1344

22 *De l'essence du rire.* Ibid, 11, 525

23 *Quelques caricaturistes français.* Ibid, 11, 556

24 Ibid, 558

25 Ibid, 559

26 Ibid, 560

27 Burton: *Baudelaire en* 1859, 4

28 [Été 1855?] CB: *Corr.,* I, 318

29 Ibid, 319–20; Drouot catalogue, 29 mai 1968, no 15

46

1 Environ 7 août 1855. CB: *Corr.,* I, 320

2 Mardi 14 août 1855. Ibid, I, 321

3 Feuillerat: op. cit., 86

4 Mardi 14 août 1855. CB: *Corr.,* I, 320

5 Marix-Spire: *La femme Sand* (EUROPE, avril–mai 1967, 213)

6 Feuillerat: op. cit., 64; LAB: 353–4

7 Feuillerat: op. cit., 65

8 Ibid, 66

9 Ibid, 67

10 9 janvier 1858. LAB: 25. The Drouot catalogue for 29 mai 1968 has this letter as no 24. It is Banville's only known letter to Baudelaire.

11 *Revue fantaisiste,* 1er août 1861

12 Feuillerat: op. cit., 67
13 Ibid, 67–8
14 4 octobre 1855. CB: *Corr.*, I, 323–4
15 Louis Goudall: LE FIGARO, 4 novembre 1855

47

1 Raynaud: *Les Parents de Baudelaire* (M de F, 15 août 1921, 126)
2 Pichois: *Le Beau-père de Baudelaire* (M de F, 1er août 1955, 655)
3 3 juin 1895. Goncourt: *Journal*, XXI, 63
4 B.N. N.A. Fr.15826 f 59; Pichois: *Le vrai visage du Général Aupick*, 30; Pichois et Ziegler: *Le Testament de Mme Aupick* (BULLETIN BAUDELAIRIEN, décembre 1985, tome 20, no 3, 64–5). On 9 April 1840 the Duc d'Orléans had specified in his will: 'Je désire qu'Hélène donne un souvenir de moi...au Général Aupick.' Ferdinand-Philippe, Duc d'Orléans: *Lettres, 1825–1842.* 2e édition, (Calmann Lévy, 1889), 321. Anon: *Le Livre d'or de l'Ordre de Léopold et de la Croix de fer*, (Bruxelles. Ch. Lelong. 1858), 11, 512. Lacrosse: *Éloge de M. le Général Aupick*, 31. Photocopies of documents from the State Archives in The Hague, sent to the author by Baron H. J. van Asbeck.
5 Aupick to Thouvenel, 26 janvier 1856. Pichois: op. cit., 35–6, note
6 24 octobre 1855. Pichois: op. cit., 665 and note
7 Trial: op. cit., 18–19
8 *Bulletin de la Société de Géographie.* 4e série. Tome XIV, 520
9 Séance du 17 janvier 1851. *Bulletin de la Société de géographie.* 4e série. Tome 1er, 93–4:

> M. le général Aupick, ministre plénipotentiaire de France auprès de la Porte Ottomane, écrit de Péra (25 décembre 1850) au secrétaire-général de la Commission centrale pour lui désigner, en réponse à sa lettre du 7 novembre précédent, M. Ch. Schefer, l'un des drogmans de sa légation, comme la personne qui paraît réunir à un plus haut degré [*sic*] les conditions nécessaires à un correspondant de la Société de géographie en Turquie. Il transmet en même temps à M. de la Roquette une lettre portant la date du 20 décembre, par laquelle M. Schefer témoigne le désir d'être nommé correspondant de la Société...
>
> Des remerciements seront adressés à M. le général Aupick, et la lettre intéressante de M. Schefer sera transmise au comité du Bulletin.

10 *Bulletin de la Société de Géographie.* 4e série. Tome IX, 326
11 *Bulletin de la Société de Géographie.* 4e série. Tome X, 386:

> M. le général Aupick, vice-président de la Société, occupe le fauteuil en l'absence du président,...auquel des affaires urgentes n'ont pas permis d'assister à la séance...M. le général Aupick exprime le regret d'avoir été informé trop tard des fonctions qu'il avait à remplir, et de ne pouvoir rappeler au public les services que la Société a rendus à la Science dans le cours de l'année qui vient de s'écouler.

12 Pichois: loc. cit.; Prévost et d'Amat: op. cit., 651; *L'Écho Honfleurais*, 17 mai 1857

13 The notes on Aupick's colleagues at the Senate are taken from two anonymous books: *Galerie historique et biographique des membres du Sénat* (À la Librairie nouvelle, 1852); *Biographie des membres du Sénat* (Michel Lévy frères, 1852). They are also indebted to Un Vieil Écrivain: *Profils critiques et biographiques des sénateurs...* (Garnier frères, 1852). The Senators mentioned in the present book were among the many who attended Aupick's funeral.

14 Vendredi 21 déc[embre 18]55. CB: *Corr.*, I, 330

15 Jeudi 20 décembre 1855. Ibid, I, 325, 325–8

16 This letter is mentioned by Pichois in his notes to Baudelaire's correspondence (I, 887). Another letter from Mme Aupick to Ancelle is given by F. Gautier in his *Documents sur Baudelaire* (M de F, 15 janvier 1905, 194–5). Gautier dates this letter 'about 1842'. This could not be correct, since it deals with Baudelaire's finances, and Ancelle was not concerned with them at the time.

48

1 Poggenburg: op. cit., 175

2 Ibid, 176

3 *Études sur Poe*. CB: *Œs. cs.*, II, 260

4 Ibid, 262

5 For a further tribute to Maria Clemm, see ibid, II, 308–9

6 24 mars [1868]. EJC, 266–7

7 Théophile Gautier: *Portraits contemporains*, 159 sqq.

8 Jeudi 13 mars 1856. CB: *Corr.*, I, 338–41

9 Butor: *Histoire extraordinaire. Essai sur un rêve de Baudelaire*, 42

10 R. Laforgue: *L'Échec de Baudelaire*, 165

11 [Environ 15 mars 1856.] CB: *Corr.*, I, 342

12 Ibid.

13 19 mars 1856. Ibid, I, 343

14 24 mars 1856. Sainte-Beuve: *Corr. gén.*, X, 235–6

15 CB: *Corr.*, I, 895

16 Delacroix: *Journal*, III, 437

17 LE FIGARO, 23 avril 1856

18 JOURNAL DES DÉBATS, 20 avril 1856

19 8 mai 1856. CB: *Corr.*, I, 348

49

1 Vendredi 6 juin 1856. CB: *Corr.*, I, 349–50

2 Vendredi 6 [juin 18]56. Ibid, I, 350

3 Mardi 22 juillet 1856. Ibid, I, 353–4, 354

4 Jeudi 11 septembre 1856. Ibid, I, 355

5 Ibid, I, 355–6

6 [Environ 10 juin 1838.] Ibid, I, 52–3. 3 août [1838]. Ibid, I, 61. See also [10 (?) juin 1839.] Ibid, I, 70

7 Jeudi 11 septembre 1856. Ibid, I, 356–7, 357, 357–8

8 Samedi 13 sept[embre] 1856. Ibid, I, 358

50

1 Aupick to Thouvenel, 9 octobre 1856. Pichois: *Le Beau-père de Baudelaire* (M de F, 1er août 1955, 669)
2 Aupick to Thouvenel, 24 octobre 1856 (Ibid, 669–70)
3 4 novembre 1856. CB: *Corr.*, 359–60
4 Ibid, 360
5 Mercredi, 12 novembre 1856. Ibid, I, 361–2
6 Jeudi 11 septembre 1856. Ibid, I, 355
7 Jeudi 4 déc[embre] 1856. Ibid, I, 363
8 Mardi, 9 décembre 1856. Ibid, I, 364
9 Pichois: *Documents nouveaux sur Charles Baudelaire* (M de F, février 1961, 262)
10 Le 11 décembre 1856. CB: *Corr.*, I, 365–6
11 [30 décembre 1856.] Ibid, I, 368. This contract was auctioned by Drouot as No 17 in their sale on 29 May 1968

51

1 Jeudi 29 janvier 1857. CB: *Corr.*, I, 369
2 Théophile Gautier: *Souvenirs romantiques*, 268
3 Pichois: *Lettres à Eugène Crépet sur la jeunesse de Baudelaire* (M de F, 1er septembre 1954, 23)
4 Gautier: op. cit., 277
5 J. Prévost: *Baudelaire*, 57–68
6 Raynaud: *Baudelaire et Théophile Gautier* (M de F, 16 octobre 1917, 580)
7 Ibid, 589
8 Ibid.
9 CB to Malassis. Mardi 10 février 1857. CB: *Corr.*, 1, 374
10 CB to Mme Aupick. Dimanche 8 février 1857. Ibid, 371
11 Aupick to Thouvenel. 8 janvier 1857. Pichois: *Le Beau-père de Baudelaire* (M de F, 1er août 1955, 670, note)
12 CB to Mme Aupick. Lundi 9 février 1857. CB: *Corr.*, I, 372, 373

52

1 Mardi 10 février [18]57. CB: *Corr.*, I, 374
2 Théophile Gautier: *Portraits contemporains*, 159
3 Vendredi 20 février 1857. CB: *Corr.*, I, 377
4 *Ville de Neuilly et de Ternes. Annuaire 1857*. B.N. N.A. Fr.15814 f 41
5 [Mars–avril 1857.] LAB: 376
6 Samedi, 7 mars 1857. CB: *Corr.*, I, 378
7 9 mars 1857. Ibid I, 380. For a sidelight on the dedication, see Bandy: *Edgar Poe et la dédicace des FLEURS DU MAL* (REVUE DES SCIENCES HUMAINES, janvier–mars 1957, 99)
8 Malassis' threat is evident from Baudelaire's reply on 30 March, *infra*
9 Lundi 30 mars 1857. CB: *Corr.*, I, 391
10 4 avril 1857. Ibid, I, 392, 393

53

1 Aupick to Thouvenel, 23 janvier [1857]. Pichois: *Le Beau-père de Baudelaire* (M de F, 1er août 1955, 670)

2 Lacrosse: *Éloge de M. le général de division Aupick*, 1

3 Ibid, 23

4 F. Gautier: *Documents sur Baudelaire* (M de F, 15 janvier 1905, 195–6)

5 Lacrosse: op. cit., 24

6 Ibid; and ibid, 1

7 CB to Mme Aupick, 30 déc[embre] 1857. CB: *Corr.*, 1, 438–9

8 *L'Écho Honfleurais*, 5 mai 1857

9 Ibid, 17 mai 1857

10 MU, 30 avril 1857

11 MU, 1er mai 1857; *La Presse* gave no account of the funeral. On 29 April it had simply announced: 'Vient de mourir: à Paris, M. le général Aupick, sénateur.'

12 *Bulletin de la Société de Géographie*, 4e série, tome XIII (Arthus Bertrand, 1857), 415. At the same meeting, it was announced that Dr David Livingstone had accepted the Society's grand gold medal for his travels across Southern Africa.

13 *Bulletin de la Société de Géographie*, 4e série, tome XIV (Arthus Bertrand, 1857), 519–20

14 MU, 8 mai 1857

15 CB: *Œs. cs.*, I, 898

16 Quesnel: op. cit., 79, 80, 81, 82, 91

17 CB: *Œs. cs.*, I, 36

18 20 mai 1857. CB: *Corr.*, I, 401

19 G. de Nouvion: op. cit., 172–3

20 Poggenburg: op. cit., 199

21 CB to Mme Aupick, 3 juin 1857. CB: *Corr.*, I, 403

22 CB: *Corr.*, I, 930

23 The most complete accounts of Aupick are given by Baron de Lacrosse in *Éloge de M. le général de division Aupick* (1858), and by Pichois in *Le Beau-père de Baudelaire* (M de F, 1er juin, 1er juillet, 1er août 1955). Numerous details are given by the obituary in *Le Moniteur de l'armée*, reprinted by *L'Écho Honfleurais* on 17 May 1857.

24 26 juin [1868]. To Asselineau. Auzas: op. cit. (M de F, 16 septembre 1912, 239)

25 Undated. Ibid, 233

26 CB to Mme Aupick, [6 mai 1861]. CB: *Corr.*, II, 151

27 Charles Michaud to Charles Asselineau, 16 août 1871. Auzas: op. cit., 257

28 B.N. N.A. Fr. 15819 f 236

29 Ibid.

30 Poggenburg: op. cit., 197

31 R. Laforgue: *L'Échec de Baudelaire*, 189, 192

32 CB to Mme Aupick, 3 juin 1857. CB: *Corr.*, I, 403

33 Ibid, 403–4, 404

34 Ibid, 404

35 The inscription on the General's tomb is quoted by F. Gautier: *Documents sur Baudelaire* (M de F, 1er février 1905, 346)

54

1 Samedi 13 juin 1857. CB: *Corr.*, I, 406–8. The copy inscribed to Champfleury was later acquired by Arthur Symons (Symons: *Charles Baudelaire*, 110–11)

2 Charles Tennyson: *Alfred Tennyson* (Macmillan, 1950, 460 and note). Tennyson's copy of *Les Fleurs du mal* seems to have vanished during his lifetime. When, in 1887, his daughter-in-law Audrey Tennyson listed his library at Farringford, she made no mention of Baudelaire. There are no copies of his books in any of the family libraries now at the Tennyson Research Centre in Lincoln, and the name of Baudelaire does not figure in the index to the correspondence. (Letter to the present author from the Senior Librarian, Lincolnshire County Reference Service, 17 May 1989.)

3 In 1935, Gautier's copy of *Les Fleurs du mal* was listed in the library of Louis Barthou. I, 80

4 Ibid, I, 79

5 20 [juin 1857]. Sainte-Beuve: *Corr. gen.*, X, 422–3

6 'Au Lecteur'. CB: *Œs. cs.*, I, 5, 6

7 *Mon Cœur mis à nu*. Ibid, I, 682–3

8 'Bénédiction'. Ibid, I, 7

9 'Élévation'. Ibid, I, 10

10 'Correspondances'. Ibid, I, 11

11 Picon: op. cit., 277

12 To Ernest Delahaye, 15 mai 1871. Quoted by Borgal: op. cit., 17

13 Richardson: *Théophile Gautier. His Life and Times*, 298–301

14 Ibid, 298

15 Comte Gustave de la Moussaye had discussed correspondences in two articles: *Les Couleurs et les sons* (L'ARTISTE, 15 janvier 1853, 189–90); *Harmonies des sensations* (L'ARTISTE, 1er septembre 1853, 33–5). He was to publish a further article, *Les Couleurs et les sons*, in LA GRANDE REVUE (25 juillet 1889, 193 sqq.)

16 Richardson: loc. cit.

17 *Théophile Gautier, I*. CB: *Œs. cs.*, II, 117

18 Richardson: op. cit., 301

19 17 mars 1861. Quoted by Cabanès: op. cit., I, 273

20 Banville: *Petit Traité de la poésie française*, 8

21 Ibrovac: op. cit., 345

22 Ghil: op. cit., 25

23 Raynaud: *Baudelaire et la religion du Dandysme*, 45–6

24 Borgal: op. cit., 78

25 Quoted by Eigeldinger: op. cit., 13

26 Borgal: op. cit., 81–2; see also Raymond: *De Baudelaire au surréalisme*, 20

27 Vouga: *Baudelaire et Joseph de Maistre*, 188

28 'Les Phares'. CB: *Œs. cs.*, I, 14

29 'La Beauté'. Ibid, I, 21

30 'Les Bijoux'. Ibid, I, 158

31 L. Daudet: *Flambeaux*, 218

32 'Parfum exotique'. CB: *Œs. cs.*, I, 25–6

33 Porché: *Baudelaire. Histoire d'une âme*, 351–2

34 Prévost: op. cit., 217–8

35 'Que diras-tu ce soir . . .' CB: *Œs. cs.*, I, 43

36 Ruff: *L'Esprit du mal et l'esthétique baudelairienne*, 188
37 Turnell: *Baudelaire*, 140
38 'L'Invitation au voyage'. CB: *Œs. cs.*, I, 53
39 'Epipsychidion'. (Shelley: *Selected Poetry, Prose and Letters*. Edited by A. S. B. Glover. The Nonesuch Press, 1951, p. 540.)
40 Richardson: *Dr Melchior Yvan: an influence on Baudelaire?* (FRENCH STUDIES, Vol. XLVI. October 1992. No 44, pp. 406–11)
41 'L'Invitation au voyage'. CB: *Œs. cs.*, I, 53–4
42 'Mœsta et errabunda'. Ibid, I, 63–4
43 Pichois: *Lettres à Eugène Crépet sur la jeunesse de Baudelaire* (M de F, 1er septembre 1954, 26)
44 [13 juillet 1857.] LAB: 150
45 R. de Gourmont: *Baudelaire et le songe d'Athalie* (M de F, 1er juillet 1905, 30)
46 Ibid.
47 CB: *Œs. cs.*, I, 1069–70
48 'Un Voyage à Cythère'. Ibid, I, 119
49 Barrès: *Cahiers*, XI, 304
50 'Le Reniement de Saint Pierre'. CB: *Œs. cs.*, I, 121–2
51 Prévost: op. cit., 119
52 *Les Fleurs du mal*. Texte de 1861 . . . précédé d'une étude sur Baudelaire par Théodore de Banville. Étude, xxv
53 L. Daudet: *Baudelaire à la Salle Pleyel* (ACTION FRANÇAISE, 8 juin 1931). B.N. N.A. Fr.15816 f 78.
54 Jackson: *La Mort Baudelaire. Essai sur LES FLEURS DU MAL*, 10

55

1 Lanier to Malassis, 4 juillet 1857. Crépet: *Baudelairiana*. (B du B, Série de Guerre, 207, note.)
2 Dufay: *Le Procès des FLEURS DU MAL* (M de F, 1er avril 1921, 86). For Bourdin, see also Audebrand: *Un Café de journalistes sous Napoléon III*, 60–73
3 Bergerat: *Souvenirs d'un Enfant de Paris. I, Les Années de Bohème.* (Charpentier, 1911, 141)
4 Dufay: loc. cit. 11 juillet 1857. CB: *Corr.*, I, 412 3
5 B.N. N.A. Fr.25013 f 504
6 11 juillet 1857. CB: *Corr.*, I, 412–3
7 Malassis to an unidentified correspondent, 8 juillet 1857. Crépet: *Baudelairiana*. (B du B, Série de guerre, 207)
8 Jeudi 9 juillet 1857. CB: *Corr.*, I, 410
9 Ibid, 410–11
10 Ibid, 411
11 11 juillet 1857. Ibid, I, 412–3
12 [11 juillet 1857 (?)] Ibid, I, 413
13 12 juillet 1857. Ibid, I, 414
14 Dufay: op. cit., 87. On 1 August 1859, in L'ARTISTE, Léon Magnier reviewed *Les Fleurs du bien*: 'un honorable écho de la lyre lamartinienne.'
15 12 juillet 1857. CB: *Corr.*, I, 414
16 12 juillet 1857. Ibid, I, 414
17 EJC: 298–9
18 MU: 14 juillet 1857

19 14 juillet 1857. CB: *Corr.*, I, 415
20 Flaubert: *Corr.*, XIII, 594, 595. (Édition du Club de l'Honnête Homme, 1974.)
21 Du Bos: *Approximations*, I, 236
22 Quoted by Crépet: op. cit., 319
23 Quoted by PZ: op. cit., 348
24 [Environ 20 juillet 1857.] CB: *Corr.*, I, 415–6
25 20 juillet 1857. Ibid, I, 417
26 Malassis to an unidentified correspondent, 13 juillet 1857. Crépet: op. cit, 208

56

1 Samedi [25 ? juillet 1857]. LAB: 45
2 27 juillet 1857. CB: *Corr.*, I, 418
3 Richardson: *Judith Gautier*, 60–2
4 27 juillet 1857. CB: *Corr.*, I, 419
5 [Fin juillet ou début août 1857.] Ibid, I, 419
6 Poggenburg: op. cit., 205
7 14 août 1857. Flaubert: *Corr.*, XIII, 602
8 12 juin 1857. Doudan: *Mélanges*, II, 283
9 Poggenburg: op. cit., 207
10 Lundi matin 17 août 1857. LAB: 47
11 Ce 20 [juillet 1857]. LAB: 332–4
12 Mardi 18 août 1857. CB: *Corr.*, I, 420
13 B.N. N.A. Fr.25013 f 496
14 B.N. N.A. Fr.25013 ff 503–4
15 Vandérem: *Baudelaire et Sainte-Beuve*, 19
16 Rude: op. cit., 173
17 F. Gautier: *Documents sur Baudelaire* (M de F, 15 mars 1906, 202)
18 Mardi 18 août 1857. CB: *Corr.*, I, 421–3
19 Edmond Richard: op. cit., 284 (Bibliothèque municipale de Fontainebleau)
20 Poggenburg: op. cit., 208

57

1 Pinard: *Mon Journal*, I, 57
2 Ibid, 56
3 Ibid, 55–6
4 Dufay: *Le Procès des FLEURS DU MAL* (M de F, 1er avril 1921, 90)
5 CB: *Œs. cs.*, I, 1206
6 Ibid, I, 1206–7
7 Dufay: op. cit., 92
8 CB: *Œs. cs.*, I, 1207
9 Ibid, I, 1207, 1208
10 Ibid, I, 1209
11 Ibid, I, 1210
12 Ibid.

13 Ibid, I, 1224
14 Malassis to an unidentified correspondent, late August 1857. J. Crépet: *Baudelairiana* (B du B, Série de Guerre, 212)
15 To Ancelle, 18 février 1866. CB: *Corr.*, II, 610
16 Asselineau: *Charles Baudelaire*, 63. Asselineau himself reviewed *Les Fleurs du mal* in the REVUE FRANÇAISE (septembre 1857, 236–47). An editorial note explained: 'It is understood that nothing which is said in this article applies to the poems which have been suppressed.'

58

1 Ce 25 août 1857. LAB: 48, note
2 Champfleury: *Souvenirs et portraits de jeunesse*, 138
3 Malassis exhibition catalogue, 34
4 De La Fizelière et Decaux: *Essais de Bibliographie contemporaine. I. Charles Baudelaire*, 19: Malassis to an unidentified correspondent, 13 juillet 1857. Crépet: op. cit., 208–9
5 9 octobre 1857. CB: *Corr.*, I, 429
6 The catalogue is bound with *La Foire aux artistes*, by Aurélien Scholl, published by Malassis in 1858
7 23 août 1857. Flaubert: *Corr.*, XIII, 603
8 Samedi, 7 mars 1857. CB: *Corr.*, I, 378
9 To Banville, 27 août 1866. J. Crépet: *Propos sur Baudelaire*, 51
10 Raitt: *Prosper Mérimée*, 301
11 To Banville, 27 août 1866. J. Crépet: loc. cit.
12 Mérimée: *Corr. gén.*, XIV, 531
13 30 août 1857. LAB: 186
14 [Fin août 1857.] CB: *Corr.*, I, 424
15 6 novembre 1857. Ibid, I, 432
16 Ibid, I, 951
17 For an account of this final judgment, see Flottes: *Les Deux Procès des FLEURS DU MAL* (RSH, janvier–mars 1957, 101–10). The official file on the case of 1857 was destroyed on 24 May 1871, when the Palais de Justice was set on fire during the Commune (PZ, 648).

59

1 Undated. B.N. N.A. Fr.15835 f 73. There is no further mention of Narc in the 'N' volumes of the Crépet Papers.
2 LE JOURNAL, 3 mars 1902
3 Quoted by CB in his letter to Mme Sabatier, 31 août 1857. CB: *Corr.*, I, 425
4 LAB: 322
5 Mauclair: *Charles Baudelaire*, 27, 28, 29
6 Porché: *Baudelaire et la Présidente*, 226
7 Mercredi 3 juin 1857. CB: *Corr.*, I, 404
8 Bassim: op. cit., 18

9 Thibaudet: op. cit., 37

10 Ibid, 39, 41

11 Du Bos: *Approximations*, I, 227–8

12 Quesnel: op. cit., 200. For a curious footnote, see Delahaye: *Le Tableau que personne ne veut voir* (M de F, 1er octobre 1955, 292–8)

13 *Journaux intimes*. CB: *Œs. cs.*, I, 694. Max Maurey assured Féli Gautier, in the early years of the twentieth century: 'It has always seemed certain to me that C.B.'s love for La Présidente was entirely platonic, from first to last.' (12 janvier 1906. Féli Gautier Papers. Ms 8° F 40/174. Taylor Institution, Oxford.) Trial wrote (op. cit., 42): 'The two great liaisons of his life, Jeanne Duval and Mme Sabatier, were platonic.'

14 PZ: op. cit., 364

15 31 août 1857. CB: *Corr.*, I, 425

16 Eigeldinger: *Le Platonisme de Baudelaire*, 54–5

17 31 août 1857. CB: *Corr.*, I, 425–6

18 *Journaux intimes*. CB: *Œs. cs.*, I, 649

19 31 août 1857. CB: *Corr.*, I, 426

20 CB: *Corr.*, I, 947

21 'Semper eadem'. CB: *Œs. cs.*, I, 41

22 LAB: 322–3, where it is tentatively dated 1er septembre 1857

23 Trial: op. cit., 51

24 Dimanche [6 septembre 1857 (?)]. CB: *Corr.*, I, 427

25 Mardi 8 septembre 1857. Ibid, I, 427

26 10 septembre 1857. Ibid, I, 428

27 Dimanche 13 septembre 1857. Ibid, I, 428

28 [13 septembre (?)1857.] LAB: 323–4

29 Mauclair: *Charles Baudelaire*, 32

30 Vendredi 25 sept[embre] 1857. CB: *Corr.*, I, 429

31 17 nov[embre 18]57. Ibid, I, 433

32 Porché: *Baudelaire et la Présidente*, 240–1

60

1 *MADAME BOVARY. Par Gustave Flaubert.* CB: *Œs. cs.*, II, 76–7, 77

2 Ibid, 81

3 Ibid.

4 Ibid, 83–4

5 [21 octobre 1857.] Flaubert: *Corr.*, XIII, 610–611

6 17 novembre 1857. CB: *Corr.*, I, 433

7 Mercredi 9 décembre 1857. Ibid, I, 434–5

8 17 décembre [1857]. Ibid, I, 435

9 14 juin 1857. Crépet: *Baudelairiana* (B du B, Série de Guerre, 211)

10 CB: *Corr.*, I, 435–6, 437

11 Thibaudet: op. cit., 54

12 Scouras: *La Maladie et la mort de Baudelaire* (ÆSCULAPE, I, janvier 1930, 28)

13 CB: *Corr.*, I, lxxxv, note

14 30 déc[embre] 1857. Ibid, I, 437–8, 438–9, 439

61

1 Lundi 11 janvier 1858. CB: *Corr.*, I, 443–4, 444
2 Mardi 12 janv[ier 18]58. Ibid, I, 445–6
3 Mercredi 20 janvier 1858. Ibid, I, 447, 448
4 Samedi 20 février 1858. Ibid, I, 454–6
5 Ibid, I, 457
6 Ibid, I, 457, 458, 458–9
7 Ibid, I, 963
8 Vendredi 26 février 1858. Ibid, I, 460

62

1 Samedi 27 février 1858 [matin]. CB: *Corr.*, I, 464
2 Ibid, I, 465
3 Samedi 27 février 1858 [vers midi]. Ibid, I, 466–7
4 Ibid, I, 467
5 [Samedi 27 février 1858.] 4 heures du soir. Ibid, I, 467, 468
6 Samedi 27 février 1858. 5 h[eures] du soir. Ibid, I, 468, 369
7 Samedi 27 février 1858. Ibid, I, 470
8 Samedi 27 février 1858. Ibid, I, 470, 471
9 Dimanche 28 février 1858. Ibid, I, 472, 472–3, 473
10 [1er mars 1858.] Ibid, I, 968–9
11 Vendredi 5 mars [1858]. [Matin.] Ibid, I, 479
12 [8 mars 1858.] Ibid, I, 488–9
13 Poggenburg: op. cit., 228

63

1 7 mai [1858]. BP, 116–8
2 Jeudi 13 mai 1858. CB: *Corr.*, I, 494, 496
3 Ibid, I, 495
4 Vendredi, 14 mai 1858. Ibid, I, 496–7
5 Dimanche 16 mai 1858. Ibid, I, 498
6 Mercredi, 19 mai 1858. Ibid, I, 499
7 9 juin 1858. Ibid, I, 502
8 11 juin 1858. Ibid, I, 503, 504
9 14 juin 1858. Ibid, I, 505, 506
10 Lemonnier: *Enquêtes sur Baudelaire*, 31
11 14 août 1858. CB: *Corr.*, I, 510
12 Vandérem: *Baudelaire et Sainte-Beuve*, 33

64

1 Jeudi 13 mai 1858. CB: *Corr.*, I, 495. 9 juin 1858. Ibid, I, 503
2 Dimanche 22 août [18]58. Ibid, 512. A note to Eugène Crépet, from the Bureau du Secrétariat Général, Grande Chancellerie de la Légion-d'honneur, records that

they have found no dossier for a member of the Order in the name of Charles Baudelaire. (B.N. N.A. Fr.15819 f 356)

3 *Mon Cœur mis à nu.* CB: *Œs. cs.*, I, 689
4 Lundi 4 oct[obre 18]58. CB: *Corr.*, I, 516
5 Letter dated only 'ce samedi'. Auzas: *Lettres de Madame Veuve Aupick à Charles Asselineau* (M de F, 16 septembre 1912, 243)
6 Mardi 19 oct[obre 18]58. CB: *Corr.*, I, 516
7 Samedi 23 oct[obre 18]58. Ibid, I, 517
8 Ibid.
9 Burton: *Baudelaire en 1859*, 21. On 16 March 1868, Mme Aupick explained to Asselineau: 'Je n'ai que trois chambres à coucher: celle du Général, la mienne, celle de Charles.' (Auzas: op. cit., 235)
10 Mercredi 27 octobre 1858. CB: *Corr.*, I, 517, 518
11 Mme Aupick's hopes of reforming Baudelaire confirm Malassis' opinion that 'she doesn't know anything about her son's character'. (Richer et Ruff: op. cit., 52)
12 29 oct[obre 18]58. CB: *Corr.*, I, 518
13 Ibid.
14 31 oct[obre 18]58. Ibid, I, 519
15 Mercredi 17 nov[embre 18]58. Ibid, I, 525
16 Jeudi [18?] novembre [18]58. Ibid, I, 526
17 31 décembre 1858. Ibid, I, 534

65

1 27 janvier 1859. CB: *Corr.*, I, 541
2 1er février 1859. Ibid, I, 544
3 Burton: *Baudelaire en 1859*, 21
4 Ibid, 22, 25–6
5 Emmanuel: *Baudelaire*, 26–7
6 Burton: op. cit., 29
7 *Journaux intimes.* CB: *Œs. cs.*, I, 689
8 Burton: op. cit., 182
9 'Le Balcon'. CB: *Œs. cs.*, I, 37

66

1 Bréard: *Vieilles rues et vieilles maisons de Honfleur . . .*, 150–1
2 Jean-Aubry: *Eugène Boudin*, 26
3 Quoted by Cahen: *Eugène Boudin. Sa Vie et son œuvre*, 28–31. Schanne does not merely give Baudelaire a bachelor room in the rue Mazarine, he still gives Mme Aupick's address as the place Vendôme (B.N. N.A. Fr.15824 f 153)
4 Cahen: loc. cit.
5 Ibid.
6 Jean-Aubry: op. cit., 30–1; Pichois, however, questions the authority of the inscription (PZ: op. cit., 651)
7 Jean-Aubry: loc. cit.

8 Baudelaire was in advance of his time. Writing of 1865, Jean-Aubry notes: 'Since Baudelaire had written his lines in 1859, the chroniclers of Salons had not felt themselves obliged to devote part of their articles to this marine artist.' (Op. cit., 60)

9 CB: *Œs. cs.*, II, 665

10 Ibid, I, 344‑5

11 CB: *Corr.*, I, 545

12 LAB: 56

13 Jean-Aubry: *Un Paysage littéraire. Baudelaire et Honfleur*, 50, 51

14 Pommier: *Dans les chemins de Baudelaire*, 351, 342‑4

15 23 février 1859. CB: *Corr.*, I, 554

16 *Childe Harold's Pilgrimage*. Lord Byron: *Works* (Paris. A. & W. Galignani, 1826, 47‑8)

17 Le Dantec: '*Le Beau Navire*' ou *Baudelaire maritime* (LE BEAU NAVIRE, 10 novembre 1934, 16, where the date is wrongly given as 1858)

18 CB: *Fusées. Œs. cs.*, I, 655

19 23 février 1859. CB: *Corr.*, I, 554‑5

20 Abé: *Baudelaire et Maxime du Camp* (REVUE D'HISTOIRE LITTÉRAIRE DE LA FRANCE, avril‑juin 1967, 274)

21 CB: *Œs. cs.*, I, 134

22 Prévost: *Baudelaire*, 112, 124, 125

67

1 As Pichois explains (LAB: 339), the poems may have been accompanied by a note from Baudelaire which has not survived

2 5 mars 1859. Sainte-Beuve: *Corr. gén.*, XI, 239

3 *Théophile Gautier, I*. CB: *Œs. cs.*, II, 104

4 Ibid, 106

5 Ibid, 117, 118

6 *Comment on paie ses dettes quand on a du génie*, CB: *Œs. cs.*, II, 8

7 Vendredi, [23?] septembre 1859. CB: *Corr.*, I, 597

8 *L'Œuvre et la vie d'Eugène Delacroix*. CB: *Œs. cs.*, II, 765

9 26 mars 1859. CB: *Corr.*, I, 563

10 Ibid, 1019

11 1er avril 1859. Ibid, 564

12 LAB: 155, note

13 [Février 1859.] Flaubert: *Corr.*, XIII (Club de l'Honnête Homme, 1974), 573‑4. Mistakenly dated avril 1857

14 17 février 1907. Féli Gautier Papers. Ms 8° 40/122. (Taylor Institution, Oxford)

15 Vendredi 29 avril 1859. CB: *Corr.*, I, 567

16 Mercredi, 4 mai 1859. Ibid, 571

17 Dimanche, 8 mai 1859. Ibid, 572

18 14 mai 1859. Ibid, 573

19 Ibid, 1025; Temkine: *De Baudelaire à Michaux*, 236

20 16 février 1859. CB: *Corr.*, I, 551

21 Lemonnier: *Enquêtes sur Baudelaire*, 20‑1

22 16 mai 1859. CB: *Corr.*, I, 576

23 Quoted by Milner: op. cit., 12

24 Symons: *Charles Baudelaire*, 2
25 'La Chevelure'. CB: *Œs. cs.*, I, 26

68

1 *Salon de* 1859, CB: *Œs. cs.*, II, 649–50
2 Ibid, 665
3 Ibid, 666
4 Ce 27 juin 1859. LAB: 116, 117

69

1 29 juin [18]59. CB: *Corr.*, I, 585–6
2 [Fin juin ou début juillet 1859?] Ibid, I, 586
3 E. Daudet: *Souvenirs de mon temps*, 198
4 Mercredi 20 juillet 1859. CB: *Corr.*, I, 588–9, 589
5 Pichois notes that Baudelaire's room was later divided into three (PZ: op. cit., 384)
6 Porché: op. cit., 426, 427
7 Vendredi, [23?] septembre 1859. CB: *Corr.*, I, 596
8 Ibid, I, 597–8
9 J. Crépet: *Miettes baudelairiennes* (M de F, 15 septembre 1935, 522)
10 PZ: op. cit., 390
11 LA REVUE INTERNATIONALE, mars 1860
12 1er oct[obre 18]59. CB: *Corr.*, I, 604
13 6 octobre 1859. LAB: 187–8
14 Poggenburg: op. cit., 259; but this statement is not substantiated by the correspondence
15 [Environ 15 octobre 1859] CB: *Corr.*, I, 609

70

1 Feuillerat: *Baudelaire et la Belle aux cheveux d'or*, 71
2 Ibid.
3 Ibid, 71
4 Ibid, 71–2
5 CB: *Œs. cs.*, I, 934
6 Ibid, I, 57
7 Turnell: *Baudelaire*, 143
8 Ibid.
9 Le 6 9bre 59. LAB: 289
10 Feuillerat: op. cit., 75
11 Trial: op. cit., 46
12 'À une Madone'. CB: *Œs. cs.*, I, 59
13 Feuillerat: op. cit., 78. Du Bos: *Approximations*, I, 230

14 'Causerie'. CB: *Œs. cs.*, I, 56
15 Lyonnet: loc. cit.
16 J. Crépet: *Propos sur Baudelaire*, 216–7, 220–1

71

1 Poggenburg: op. cit., 261
2 24 novembre 1859. LAB: 191
3 7 décembre 1859. CB: *Corr.*, I, 623
4 18 X^bre 1859. LAB: 189–90
5 [15 novembre 1859.] CB: *Corr.*, I, 616
6 16 9bre 59. LAB: 305
7 [15 novembre 1859.] CB: *Corr.*, I, 617
8 8 déc[embre 18]59. Ibid, I, 623–4
9 15 déc[embre 18]59. Ibid, I, 632
10 J. Crépet: op. cit., 134
11 Mercredi 21 déc[embre 18]59. CB: *Corr.*, I, 643
12 28 déc[embre 18]59. Ibid, I, 643–4
13 Crépet: op. cit., 334
14 28 déc[embre 18]59. CB: *Corr.*, I, 644

72

1 CB: *Corr.*, I, 648–9. Baudelaire's copy of this contract was sold at the Hôtel Drouot on 29 May 1968. (*Précieux Manuscrits et Lettres autographes.* 1re partie. No 18.)
2 CB: *Corr.*, I, 653
3 Dimanche 15 janvier [18]60. Ibid, I, 660, 661
4 Porché: op. cit., 386–7
5 Pichois: BET, 241
6 Ch. Michaud to Ch. Asselineau, 25 juillet [1871]. Auzas: *Lettres de Mme Veuve Aupick à Charles Asselineau* (M de F, 16 septembre 1912, 255)
7 [Environ 20 janvier 1860.] CB: *Corr.*, I, 661, 662
8 Trial: loc. cit.
9 [Environ 10 février 1860.] CB: *Corr.*, I, 664–7; *Œs. cs.*, I, 75–6
10 [Environ 10 février 1860.] CB: *Corr.*, I, 666, 667
11 16 février 1860. Ibid, I, 671
12 Vendredi 17 février 1860. Ibid, I, 672–3, 673–4
13 Suarès: *Trois grands vivants*, 293
14 CB: *Corr.*, I, 1080
15 Porché: op. cit., 390

73

1 19 février 1860. CB: *Corr.*, I, 677
2 [4 mars 1860.] Ibid, II, 5

3 Dimanche 2 mai 1858. Ibid, I, 494
4 [4 mars 1860.] Ibid, II, 5–6
5 Ibid, II, 6
6 4 mars 1860. Ibid, II, 6, 7
7 Ziegler: *Baudelairiana. I. Alfred Mosselman et Mme Sabatier.* (B du B, 1975, III, 272). For Meissonier's portraits of Mme Sabatier, see G. Larroumet: *Meissonier* (Ludovic Baschet, 1895)
8 J. Gautier: op. cit., 184
9 9 novembre 1871. Goncourt: *Journal*, X, 41
10 31 août 1862. Ibid, V, 165
11 Richard: *Notes sur la Présidente*, 282 (Bibliothèque municipale de Fontainebleau)
12 A. Augustin-Thierry: *La Fin de la Présidente* (LE TEMPS, 23 août 1932)
13 Richard: op. cit., 280, 282
14 In an undated and unidentified article, *La Vérité sur la Présidente* (B.N. N.A. Fr.15823 f 353), André Billy maintains that La Présidente died of influenza on 31 December 1889.
15 Augustin-Thierry: loc. cit.
16 Richard: op. cit., 32
17 Archives André Billy (Bibliothèque municipale de Fontainebleau)
18 B.N. N.A. Fr.15835 f 3

74

1 23 février 1860. LAB: 252–3
2 [28 février 1860.] CB: *Corr.*, I, 683
3 26 mars 1860. Ibid, II, 18
4 Ibid, II, 17
5 [2 avril 1860?] Ibid, II, 20

75

1 [14 avril 1860.] CB: *Corr.*, II, 22
2 CB: *Œs. cs.*, I, 742
3 PZ: op. cit., 467
4 [Environ 10 avril 1860.] CB: *Corr.*, II, 21
5 Ibid, II, 22
6 Samedi [14 avril 1860.] Ibid, II, 23
7 [19 avril 1860.] Ibid, II, 23–4
8 19 avril 1860. Ibid, II, 24
9 [20 avril 1860.] Ibid, II, 25
10 CB to Mme Alphonse Baudelaire, dimanche 11 [mai] 1862. Ibid, II, 242
11 CB: *Lettres inédites aux siens*. Présentées . . . par Philippe Auserve. Préface, 13–14
12 Kopp et Pichois: *Les Années Baudelaire*, I, 54 sqq.
13 Auserve: op. cit., 14

76

1 29 avril 1860. Hugo: *Corr.*, II, 334–5
2 [Mercredi 9 (?) mai 1860.] CB: *Corr.*, II, 40
3 [Environ 15–20 mai 1860.] Ibid, II, 46
4 [18 mai 1860.] Ibid, II, 48
5 22 mai 1860. E. Daudet: *Souvenirs de mon temps*, 199. See also B.N. N.A. Fr.15823 f 65
6 *Les Paradis artificiels. 'Le Poème du hachisch'*. CB: *Œs. cs.*, I, 416
7 Ibid, I, 419
8 *Le Hachich.* (LA PRESSE, lundi 10 juillet 1843)
9 CB: *Œs. cs.*, I, 426
10 Ibid, I, 428–9
11 Ibid, I, 438
12 B. N. N.A. Fr.15817 f 377
13 CB: *Œs. cs.*, I, 441
14 Champfleury: *Souvenirs*, 136. Maxime du Camp observed that 'Baudelaire looked like a doctor who sought a cure for an incurable disease, the disease of an ill-ordered existence.' (Du Camp: op. cit., II, 88)
15 MU: 9 septembre 1867
16 CB: *Œs. cs.*, I, 499

77

1 LAB: 194
2 Ibid, 192–3
3 Flaubert: *Corr.*, XIV, 52–3, where it is wrongly dated 22 octobre 1860
4 Baudelaire had also sent a copy to Jules Janin, inscribed in pencil: 'À M. J. Janin. C.B.' This figured as no 1443 in the *Catalogue des livres rares et précieux formant la bibliothèque de M. Jules Janin.* (1877)
5 LAB: 111
6 Dimanche, 1er juillet 1860. CB: *Corr.*, II, 55–6
7 3 juillet 1860. Sainte-Beuve: *Corr. gén.*, XI, 522–3

78

1 12 juillet 1860. CB: *Corr.*, II, 63
2 At the time of his brother's death, Baudelaire had not seen him for twenty years (Auserve: op. cit., 20)
3 14 juillet 1860. CB: *Corr.*, II, 67
4 [28 juillet 1860.] Ibid, II, 69
5 Samedi [4 août 1860]. Ibid, II, 70–1
6 Dimanche matin [5 août 1860]. Ibid, II, 71
7 7 août 1860. Ibid, II, 72
8 Ibid.
9 Ibid, II, 72, 73

10 Mardi soir 7 août [1860]. Ibid, II, 75
11 [21 août 1860.] Ibid, II, 84
12 [Fin août 1860.] Ibid, II, 85–8
13 27 septembre 1860. Ibid, II, 92–4

79

1 11 octobre 1860. CB: *Corr.*, II, 96–7, 99
2 [14 octobre 1860.] Ibid, II, 99–100
3 'Un Fantôme'. CB: *Œs. cs.*, I, 40
4 Jeudi 18 [octobre] 1860. CB: *Corr.*, II, 100

80

1 LA REVUE ANECDOTIQUE, quoted by Un Bibliophile ornais, III, 7–8
2 Ibid, 7
3 *Notes pour une iconographie du poète Charles Baudelaire.* (Undated cutting from LA PLUME. Taylor Institution, Oxford.)
4 Un Bibliophile ornais, II
5 Troubat: op. cit., 209 (note)
6 Mendès: *La Légende du Parnasse contemporain*, 92–3; the first issue of *La Revue Fantaisiste*, on 15 February 1861, contained the first instalment of a story by Poe, translated by William Hughes.
7 Claretie: *Charles Baudelaire. L'homme.* (LES ANNALES POLITIQUES ET LITTÉR-AIRES, 26 octobre 1902.) B.N. N.A. Fr.25013 f 535
8 Ibrovac: *José-Maria Heredia. Sa Vie – son œuvre*, 319
9 Ibid, 126

81

1 Jeudi 18 [octobre 1860]. CB: *Corr.*, II, 101
2 [Octobre–novembre 1860.] Ibid, II, 102
3 For Stoepel, see letter dated [mardi, 20 novembre(?)]. Ibid, II, 106–7, 697–8, and CB: *Œs. cs.*, I, 1279–81
4 1er janvier 1861. CB: *Corr.*, II, 113, 113–4
5 [Environ 5 janvier 1861.] Ibid, 117–9

82

1 Pichois: *Lettres à Eugène Crépet sur la jeunesse de Baudelaire* (M de F, 1er septembre 1954, 7)
2 CB: *Œs. cs.*, I, 836
3 Ibid, I, 837

4 Ibid, I, 835
5 Joanna Richardson: *Dr. Melchior Yvan: an influence on Baudelaire?* (FRENCH STUDIES, vol. XLVI, October 1992, No.4, 406–11)
6 CB: *Œs. cs.*, I, 316–7
7 Yvan: *De France en Chine*, 118
8 CB: *Œs. cs.*, I, 53
9 Ibid, I, 28
10 CB: *Les Fleurs du mal.* Edited by Enid Starkie. (Oxford, Blackwell, 1942, 202–3)
11 Yvan: op. cit., 125
12 CB: *Œs. cs.*, I, 880
13 [8 mars 1858.] CB: *Corr.*, I, 488
14 CB: *Œs. cs.*, I, 40
15 Prévost: op. cit., 235
16 Massin: op. cit., 32
17 CB: *Œs. cs.*, I, 937
18 Ibid, I, 938
19 Prévost: op. cit., 231
20 CB: *Œs. cs.*, I, 1004
21 Ibid, I, 86–7
22 Ibid, I, 88
23 Ibid, I, 1011
24 Vendredi, [23?] septembre 1859. CB: *Corr.*, I, 598
25 CB: *Œs. cs.*, I, 91
26 Ibid, I, 92
27 [6 mai 1861.] CB: *Corr.*, II, 151
28 Hiddleston: *Essai sur Laforgue . . .*, 79
29 CB: *Œs. cs.*, I, 192

83

1 [Mercredi], 20 février 1861. LAB, 71
2 Poggenburg: op. cit., 309
3 For Baudelaire's criticism of Wagner, see Servières: *Richard Wagner jugé en France*, passim
4 [Début de mars 1861.] CB: *Corr.*, II, 132
5 [15 février 1861.] LAB: 396
6 *Richard Wagner et TANNHÄUSER à Paris.* CB: *Œs. cs.*, II, 780–1
7 M. Wilhelm: *Revue musicale.* (REVUE CONTEMPORAINE, 15 mars 1861, 159)
8 [Environ 20 mars 1861?] CB: *Corr.*, II, 135
9 Ibid, II, 135–6
10 Ibid, II, 136
11 [Mars 1861?] LAB: 309
12 [25 mars 1861.] CB: *Corr.*, II, 137
13 21 mars 1861. LAB: 396
14 [4 avril 1861.] CB: *Corr.*, II, 144
15 J. Gautier: *Le Collier des jours. Le Second Rang du Collier*, 178
16 *Reliquat et dossier des FLEURS DU MAL. Projets de préfaces. III.* CB: *Œs. cs.*, I, 183

17 For Baudelaire as a critic of Wagner, see Servières: op. cit., and Loncke: *Baudelaire et la musique*, passim.

84

1 [Février ou mars 1861.] CB: *Corr.*, II, 139–40
2 1er avril 1861. Ibid, II, 140–1, 141
3 T. Bassim: *La femme dans l'œuvre de Baudelaire*, 99
4 1er avril 1861. CB: *Corr.*, II, 141, 142
5 [3 avril 1861.] Ibid, II, 143, 144
6 Picon: op. cit., 271
7 15 avril 1861. LAB: 399, 400

85

1 Hiddleston: *Essai sur Laforgue . . .*, 257
2 CB: *Œs. cs.*, II, 784
3 Ibid, II, 785
4 Ibid, II, 793
5 Ibid, II, 795
6 Ibid, II, 1459
7 Ibid, II, 1468
8 [6 mai 1861.] CB: *Corr.*, II, 150–1, 151
9 Ibid, II, 151–2, 152–3
10 R. Laforgue: *L'Échec de Baudelaire*, 28
11 [6 mai 1861.] CB: *Corr.*, II, 153
12 Ibid, II, 153–4, 154
13 Ibid, II, 154–5, 155, 156–7
14 7 mai [1861]. Ibid, II, 157
15 7 mai [1861]. Ibid, II, 158
16 8 mai 1861. Ibid, II, 159–60

86

1 Mardi 21 mai 1861. CB: *Corr.*, II, 163
2 *Baudelaire et Asselineau*, 181–2
3 [24 mai 1861.] CB: *Corr.*, II, 167–8
4 [Environ 25 mai 1861?] Ibid, II, 169
5 [27 mai 1861.] Ibid, II, 170
6 Feydeau: *Théophile Gautier. Souvenirs intimes*, 155
7 Ibid, 165
8 Richardson: *Baudelaire and the Origins of Feydeau's SYLVIE* (FRENCH STUDIES BULLETIN, No. 15, Summer 1985, 4)
9 Ibid, 7

87

1 Banville: *Baudelaire*, Étude, x
2 Hugo was well aware of such hostility. On 22 December 1863 he told Paul
  Meurice: 'On dit qu'il [Baudelaire] m'est à peu près ennemi.' LAB: 195
3 *Réflexions sur quelques-uns de mes contemporains. I. Victor Hugo.* CB: *Œs. cs.*, II, 130
4 Ibid, II, 135
5 CB: *Corr.*, II, 178. Mendès records that when he asked him how, if elected, he
  would pay his statutory tribute to his predecessor, Baudelaire replied: 'Je dirai:
  M. Scribe était homme de lettres, et il fut riche!' (Mendès: *La Légende du Parnasse
  contemporain*, 180)

88

1 Nadar: *Charles Baudelaire intime*, 120
2 25 juillet 1861. CB: *Corr.*, II, 181
3 27 juillet 1861. Ibid, II, 184
4 CB: *Œs. cs.*, II 171
5 Pontmartin: *Nouvelles Semaines littéraires*, 262. This *causerie* from the RDDM, 1861,
  was reprinted here in 1863, and re-dated and re-titled *La Poésie en 1862.*
6 Ibid, 263
7 Ibid, 265
8 Leconte de Lisle: *LES FLEURS DU MAL, par M. Charles Baudelaire, 2e édition.* (REVUE
  EUROPÉENNE, 1er décembre 1861, 596–7)
9 Dimanche 1er septembre [1861]. CB: *Corr.*, II, 187–8
10 13 novembre 1861. Ibid, II, 191

89

1 CB to Flaubert: 31 janvier 1862. *Corr.*, II, 225
2 11 décembre 1861. Ibid, II, 193–4. There is no fair copy of this letter, or of the
  letter of withdrawal, in the archives of the Académie-Française. Perhaps Villemain
  kept the letters with his personal correspondence, which is not available.
3 [Décembre 1861?] CB: *Corr.*, II, 194
4 [Environ 16 décembre 1861.] Ibid, II, 195
5 Ibid.
6 CB: *Corr.*, II, 750–1
7 [Environ 16 décembre 1861.] Ibid, II, 195–6
8 Noël 25 déc[embre] 1861. Ibid, II, 202, 206
9 Ibid, II, 203
10 Lemercier de Neuville: *Souvenirs d'un Montreur de Marionnettes*, 146
11 [Vers le 20 décembre 1861.] CB: *Corr.*, II, 196
12 Noël 25 déc[embre] 1861. Ibid, II, 202–3
13 Ibid, II, 755
14 Lundi 23 décembre 1861. Ibid, II, 199
15 Ibid.

16 1er mai 1859. CB: *Corr.*, I, 569
17 CB: *Corr.*, II, 755
18 LE SIÈCLE, 23 décembre 1861

90

1 Noël 25 déc[embre] 1861. CB: *Corr.*, II, 200, 200–1, 202, 206
2 Mauclair: *Charles Baudelaire*, 24
3 Noël 25 déc[embre] 1861. CB: *Corr.*, II, 205
4 Noël. 1861. Ibid, II, 207–8

91

1 REVUE ANECDOTIQUE. 2e semestre. Année 1862. Tome V, 18
2 LE BOULEVARD, 5 janvier 1862
3 For Claretie on Baudelaire and the Académie, see also Claretie: *Souvenirs d'un Académicien.* (LES ŒUVRES LIBRES, janvier 1934, 24)
4 Sainte-Beuve: *Des prochaines élections à l'Académie.* (LE CONSTITUTIONNEL, 20 janvier 1862)
5 Vandérem: *Baudelaire et Sainte-Beuve*, 17, 20
6 Antoine et Pichois: *Sainte-Beuve, juge de Stendhal et Baudelaire* (REVUE DES SCIENCES HUMAINES, janvier–mars 1957, 30)
7 [Environ 24 janvier 1862.] CB: *Corr.*, II, 219
8 Ibid, II, 220, 221
9 10 juillet 1866. Institut de France. Lov. D 597 f 210
10 26 janvier 1862. Sainte-Beuve: *Corr. gén.*, XII, 273
11 [Environ 24 janvier 1862.] CB: *Corr.*, II, 220
12 Pichois: BET, 43 and note
13 CB: *Œs. cs.*, I, 668
14 [24 janvier 1862.] CB: *Corr.*, II, 218
15 Flaubert: *Corr.*, XIV, 99
16 CB: *Corr.*, II, 766
17 Lundi 3 février [18]62. Ibid, II, 227
18 Dimanche 26 janvier [18]62. Ibid, II, 221–3
19 L[un]di 27 janvier [18]62. LAB, 382–3
20 Lundi soir [3 février 1862]. CB: *Corr.*, II, 228
21 Ce 9 février 1862. Sainte-Beuve: *Corr. gén.*, XII, 284
22 Lundi, 10 février 1862. CB: *Corr.*, II, 229
23 CB: *Œs. cs.*, I, 142–3

92

1 17 mars 1862. CB: *Corr.*, II, 232
2 Ibid, 233–4
3 Ibid, 234

4 29 mars 1862. Ibid, II, 236–7
5 Ibid, II, 237, 238
6 31 mars [1862]. Ibid, II, 240
7 3 juin 1895. Goncourt: *Journal*, XXI, 63. Laure Dulong (b. 1847) was married in 1868 to Auguste Sichel, who sold oriental *objets d'art*. Pichois dates Mme Aupick's observation 1864, when the young girl was seventeen (PZ: op. cit., 655–6)

93

1 [Lundi 1er février 1841.] CB: *Corr.*, I, 86
2 9 janvier 1856. Ibid, I, 335
3 Pichois: BET, 45
4 Ibid, 52–3
5 29 décembre 1854. CB: *Corr.*, I, 306
6 Pichois: op. cit., 54
7 Ibid, 55
8 G. de Nouvion: op. cit., 157
9 Trial: op. cit., 16
10 Pichois: *Lettres à Eugène Crépet sur la jeunesse de Baudelaire* (M de F, 1er septembre 1954, 9)
11 G. de Nouvion: op. cit., 157
12 Ibid.
13 The most complete accounts of Baudelaire's brother are given by Pichois in *Alphonse Baudelaire ou le magistrat imprudent* (BET: 44–58), and G. de Nouvion in *La Famille de Charles Baudelaire* (Bulletin de la Société historique du VIe arrondissement de Paris, 1901).
14 Dimanche 11 [mai] 1862. CB: *Corr.*, II, 242–3
15 Samedi 24 mai [1862]. Ibid, II, 246–7
16 Dimanche [10] août 1862. Ibid, 255
17 *LES MISÉRABLES par Victor Hugo.* CB: *Œs. cs.*, II, 224
18 Dimanche [10] août 1862. CB: *Corr.*, II, 254
19 B.N. N.A. Fr.25013 f 504
20 Samedi 24 mai [1862]. CB: *Corr.*, II, 247
21 15 mai 1862. Ibid, II, 245
22 31 mai 1862. Ibid, II, 247, 249
23 Convention. [1er juillet 1862.] Ibid, II, 251
24 4 août 1862. Ibid, II, 253. On 15 August, the REVUE FRANÇAISE (p. 327) classed Baudelaire, as a modern poet, with Arsène Houssaye and Auguste Vacquerie.
25 [Été 1862?] CB: *Corr.*, II, 252–3
26 Dimanche [10] août 1862. Ibid, II, 253, 254, 255
27 18 août 1862. Ibid, II, 255
28 Quoted by Parménie et Bonnier de la Chapelle: op. cit., 408
29 See also Banville: *Charles Baudelaire* (GALERIE CONTEMPORAINE, LITTÉRAIRE, ARTISTIQUE, 1876. Press-cutting, pages un-numbered. Taylor Institution, Oxford.)

94

1 CB: *À Arsène Houssaye. Œs. cs.*, I, 275–6
2 CB: *Petits Poèmes en prose. (Le Spleen de Paris).* Chronologie et introduction par Marcel Ruff. Introduction, 19
3 CB: *À Arsène Houssaye. Œs. cs.*, I, 275
4 Ibid, 276
5 Théophile Gautier: *Charles Baudelaire.* (MU, 9 septembre 1867)
6 CB: 'L'Étranger'. *Œs. cs.*, I, 277
7 To George and Georgiana Keats, 14–31 October 1818. (*The Letters of John Keats.* Edited by Maurice Buxton Forman. Second Edition. Oxford University Press. 1942, 241)
8 To Benjamin Bailey, 22 November 1817. Ibid, 69
9 CB: 'Les Foules'. *Œs. cs.*, I, 291–2
10 CB: 'À une heure du matin.' Ibid, I, 288
11 CB: 'La Chambre double'. Ibid, I, 280, 281
12 Ibid, I, 1312
13 CB: 'Une Mort héroïque'. Ibid, I, 319–20, 321
14 CB: 'Le Mauvais Vitrier'. Ibid, I, 287
15 Ibid.
16 Ibid, I, 1337
17 CB: 'Le Fou et la Vénus'. Ibid, I, 284
18 CB: 'Le Vieux Saltimbanque'. Ibid, I, 297
19 CB: 'Déjà!' Ibid, I, 338
20 CB: 'Any Where out of the World'. Ibid, I, 357
21 [9 février 1861.] CB: *Corr.*, II, 128–9
22 Hiddleston: *Baudelaire et LE SPLEEN DE PARIS*, 12
23 Blin: *Le Sadisme de Baudelaire*, 176, 177
24 Banville: *Charles Baudelaire.* (GALERIE CONTEMPORAINE, LITTÉRAIRE, ARTISTIQUE, 1876. Press-cutting, pages un-numbered. Taylor Institution, Oxford.)
25 Shanks: op. cit., 216
26 Borgal: op. cit., 118
27 Ruff: op. cit., 25

95

1 Pichois: *Documents nouveaux sur Charles Baudelaire* (M de F, février 1961, 269)
2 Ibid.
3 [Août–septembre 1862?] CB: *Corr.*, II, 256–7
4 *Bibliothèque de M. Louis Barthou.* Catalogue, II, 742
5 Vendredi [19 ou 26 septembre 1862?] CB: *Corr.*, II, 260
6 14 sept[embre 18]62. LAB: 106
7 Lundi 22 septembre 1862. CB: *Corr.*, II, 261, 262
8 8 octobre 1862. Ibid, II, 263–4
9 Jules Pelpel: DIOGÈNE, 10 mai 1863
10 13 déc[embre] 1862. CB: *Corr.*, II, 273, 273–4
11 LE BOULEVARD, 28 décembre 1862. CB: *Œs. cs.*, I, 143

96

1 3 janvier 1863. CB: *Corr.*, II, 283, 283–4, 284, 285
2 The title *My Heart Laid Bare* had appeared in Poe's *Marginalia*, published in New York in 1856
3 'L'Imprévu'. CB: *Œs. cs.*, I, 172
4 Jeudi 19 février 1863. CB: *Corr.*, II, 292
5 Ibid, 806
6 PZ: 582
7 28 mars 1863. CB: *Corr.*, II, 296
8 *La Musique aux Tuileries* is now in the National Gallery, London
9 [14 mars 1863.] CB: *Corr.*, II, 294
10 Castex: *Baudelaire, critique d'art*, 74
11 Ibid, 74–5
12 A. Proust: *Édouard Manet. Souvenirs*, 39
13 LE NAIN JAUNE, 27 avril 1864
14 A. Proust: loc. cit.
15 Castex: op. cit., 75
16 LAB: 228–9
17 See *Note pour M. Namslauer.* [Fin mai ou début juin 1863.] CB: *Corr.*, II, 298–9
18 3 juin 1863. Ibid, II, 302–3
19 Ibid, 303
20 Undated, but 1866. F. Gautier: *Documents sur Baudelaire.* (M de F, février 1905, 340)
21 5 juin 1863. CB: *Corr.*, II, 305
22 [7 juillet 1863.] Ibid, 308, 309

97

1 18 février 1866. CB: *Corr.*, II, 607
2 Kunel: *Cinq journées avec Ch. Baudelaire*, 13
3 Quoted by Silvestre de Sacy: '*Pauvre Belgique' ou l'échec parfait* (M de F, 1er juin 1955, 284)
4 3 août 1863. CB: *Corr.*, II, 309–10
5 3 août 1863. Ibid, II, 310
6 7 août 1863. Ibid, 310–11
7 Ibid, II, 818
8 Rude: op. cit., 33, 123
9 26 octobre 1863. CB: *Corr.*, II, 818
10 Lundi 10 août [1863]. Ibid, II, 312

98

1 [*Exorde de la conférence faite à Bruxelles en 1864*] *sur Eugène Delacroix.* CB: *Œs. cs.*, II, 774
2 Ibid.
3 Ibid.

4 15 août 1863. CB: *Corr.*, II, 312–3
5 Jullien: *Fantin-Latour. Sa vie et ses amitiés*, 62–3
6 LAB: 112
7 Ibid.
8 *L'Œuvre et la vie d'Eugène Delacroix.* CB: *Œs. cs.*, II, 744
9 Lloyd Austin: *Baudelaire et Delacroix* (Actes du Colloque de Nice, 19)
10 CB: *Œs. cs.*, II, 756
11 Ibid, II, 757–8
12 Ibid, II, 759
13 Ibid, II, 760

99

1 [Vendredi, 11 septembre 1863?] CB: *Corr.*, II, 318, 319
2 [15 septembre 1863.] Ibid, II, 319
3 Gaucheron: *Poulet-Malassis éditeur et républicain* (EUROPE, avril–mai 1967, 177)
4 Ibid, 182
5 Dufay: *Autour de Baudelaire*, 95
6 REVUE FRANÇAISE, 1er octobre 1863, 145 sqq.
7 8 oct[obre 18]63. CB: *Corr.*, II, 323–4
8 Mercredi [28 octobre 1863]. Ibid, II, 327–8

100

1 3 nov[embre] 1863. CB: *Corr.*, II, 329
2 12 novembre 1863. Ibid, 330
3 25 novembre 1863. Ibid, 332, 332–3
4 2 déc[embre 18]63. Ibid, 334–5
5 Porché: op. cit., 391. Baudelaire sent a copy of the first edition of *Les Fleurs du mal*, with a faux-titre of 1861 inscribed 'À M. Constantin Guys. Témoignage d'amitié et d'admiration.' (*Bibliothèque de M. Louis Barthou*, 1935, I, 78)
6 Picon: op. cit., 278

101

1 CB: *Corr.*, II, 841
2 [Mardi,] 8 décembre 1863. Ibid, II, 338
3 Undated, but December 1863. Mondor: *Vie de Mallarmé*, 103
4 LA PETITE REVUE, 10 décembre 1863, 78. On 1 July 1865, A. Arnould announced in the REVUE MODERNE: 'The translated works of Edgard Poe [*sic*] now fill five volumes, of which the four most important are due to the intelligent initiative of M. Baudelaire.' (B.N. N.A. Fr.15822 f 12)
5 17 déc[embre] 1863. CB: *Corr.*, II, 338–9, 340
6 CB: *Corr.*, II, 836

102

1 12 février 1864. CB: *Corr.*, II, 347
2 REVUE NOUVELLE, 1er février 1864, 141–4
3 3 mars 1864. CB: *Corr.*, II, 350
4 *[Exorde de la conférence faite à Bruxelles en 1864] sur Eugène Delacroix* . . . CB: *Œs. cs.*, II, 774–5
5 [Mars 1864.] CB: *Corr.*, II, 351
6 Jullien: *Fantin-Latour. Sa vie et ses amitiés*, 75–6, 81–2; Goncourt: *Journal*, X, 80
7 CB: *Corr.*, II, 847. See also Richardson: *Victor Hugo*, 184
8 *Anniversaire de la naissance de Shakespeare.* CB: *Œs. cs.*, II, 229
9 Ibid.
10 Samedi 11 juin 1864. CB: *Corr.*, II, 377–8. See also Mauron: *Le dernier Baudelaire*, 149–50
11 21 avril 1864. CB: *Corr.*, II, 355–6
12 CB: *Journaux intimes. Œs. cs.*, I, 756

103

1 PZ: op. cit., 501
2 Symons: *Charles Baudelaire*, 4
3 Suarès: *Trois grands vivants*, 304
4 F. Gautier: *Charles Baudelaire*, LXVIII. Letter from Baudelaire, addressed to Malassis at '35, bis, rue de Mercelis, dans le faubourg d'Ixelles'.
5 PZ: op. cit., 504
6 Ibid.
7 L'INDÉPENDANCE BELGE, 4 mai 1864
8 PZ: op. cit., 504
9 JOURNAL DES BEAUX-ARTS ET DE LA LITTÉRATURE, 15 mai 1864. BP, 210
10 [Vendredi] 6 mai [1864]. CB: *Corr.*, II, 362, 363
11 B.N. N.A. Fr.25013 f 33
12 LA PETITE REVUE, 21 janvier 1865
13 PZ: op. cit., 509
14 Ibid.
15 Kunel: op. cit., 36
16 PZ: op. cit., 664
17 Samedi 11 juin 1864. CB: *Corr.*, II, 376–7, 378
18 Samedi 11 juin 1864. Ibid, 380
19 Vendredi 17 juin 1864. Ibid, 384
20 31 juillet [1864]. Ibid, 391
21 18 septembre 1867. Richer et Ruff: op. cit., 115–6

104

1 14 juillet [1864] – *Jeudi.* CB: *Corr.*, II, 387
2 Jeudi 16 [juin 1864]. Ibid, II, 382
3 31 juillet [1864]. Ibid, II, 390, 391–2

4 8 août [1864]. Ibid, II, 393, 394, 396
5 Dimanche matin 14 [août 1864]. Ibid, II, 396–7
6 *Pauvre Belgique!* CB: *Œs. cs.*, II, 948
7 Mme Aupick: undated letter to Ancelle. J. Crépet: *Miettes baudelairiennes* (M de F, 1er février 1940, 324, note)
8 CB: *Corr.*, II, 1030
9 Claretie: *La Vie à Paris, 1898*, 428
10 Pichois: *Documents nouveaux sur Charles Baudelaire* (M de F, février 1961, 260)
11 L. Daudet: *Écrivains et artistes*, II, 23–4
12 Quoted by Ruff, in introduction to Richer et Ruff: *Les Derniers mois de Charles Baudelaire*, 12
13 *Pauvre Belgique!* CB: *Œs. cs.*, II, 951
14 Ibid, II, 951, 952
15 Ibid, II, 949
16 Ibid, II, 950
17 Ibid, II, 952
18 26 août 1864. CB: *Corr.*, II, 399
19 Ibid, II, 982
20 Vendredi 26 août [1864]. CB: *Corr.*, II, 400
21 Vendredi 2 sept[embre 18]64. Ibid, II, 403, 404, 404–5

105

1 Kunel: *Cinq journées avec Ch. Baudelaire.* (Propos recueillis à Bruxelles par Georges Barral et publiés par Maurice Kunel.) (Liège, Aux Éditions de 'Vigie 30', 1932.)
2 Nadar Papers. B.N. N.A. Fr.25013 f 33
3 Maillard: *La Cité des intellectuels*, 362–3
4 Lemonnier: op. cit., 67

106

1 Vendredi 2 sept[embre 18]64. CB: *Corr.*, II, 405
2 Jeudi 13 octobre [18]64. Ibid, 407
3 Ibid, 408–10
4 Dimanche, 23 octobre 1864. Ibid, 414
5 [5 novembre 1864.] Ibid, 417
6 Dimanche soir, 13 novembre [1864]. Ibid, 420, 421
7 BP, 120–1
8 Pichois: *Documents nouveaux sur Charles Baudelaire* (M de F, février 1961, 271)
9 Lemercier de Neuville: loc. cit.
10 Du Camp: op. cit., II, 91
11 Dufay records (op. cit., 99): 'In the *Petite Revue*, . . . the former publisher took his mother's name as a pseudonym, and (when they were not anonymous) he signed his contributions Emmanuel Rouillon, E. R., or just plain R. Many of them are concerned with Baudelaire's stay in Brussels, and with his health.'
12 LA PETITE REVUE, tome V, 71

13 Un Bibliophile ornais, III, 28
14 CB: *Corr.*, II, 1028
15 18 novembre 1864. Ibid, 422
16 Dimanche 18 décembre 1864. Ibid, 425

107

1 1er janvier 1865. CB: *Corr.*, II, 434–5
2 3 janvier 1865. Richer et Ruff: op. cit., 18
3 Nadar Papers. B.N. N.A. Fr.25013 f 10
4 Mardi, 3 janvier 1865. CB: *Corr.*, II, 437
5 Undated. F. Gautier: *Documents sur Baudelaire. III. Baudelaire et Mme Paul Meurice.* (M de F, 15 mars 1906, 209 sqq.) Mme Meurice died in 1874, but at the turn of the century the proposed publication of her letters still caused certain problems with her husband. Among Féli Gautier's correspondence at the Taylor Institution, Oxford, are two letters from Paul Meurice (MS 8° F 40/177–178). In the first, dated 5 April 1903, Meurice writes:

> Monsieur et cher confrère,
> J'ai été l'ami et je suis l'admirateur de Baudelaire, et je serai charmé d'apporter ma contribution au monument que vous lui élevez et de souscrire à votre intéressant ouvrage. Vous me dites que vous possédez des lettres de ma femme et que vous comptez les publier; vous n'ignorez pas que pour cela mon autorisation vous est nécessaire. Je ne demande pas mieux que de vous la donner, je voudrais simplement que vous eussiez la bonté de me communiquer ces lettres avant la publication . . .

On 18 October 1903, Meurice continues, firmly:

> Je ferai honneur à votre reçu, mais je vous rappelle que, de votre côté, vous m'avez promis de me communiquer les lettres de Mme Paul Meurice, que je suis tout disposé à vous racheter et pour la publication desquelles mon autorisation vous est en tout cas nécessaire. J'ai moi-même des lettres inédites de Baudelaire dont je pourrai vous faire part . . .

Féli Gautier also had problems with Mme Paule Montargis, whose help he acknowledged in his article. On 14 January 1906, she wrote to him:

> Mes sœurs ont trouvé pas mal de billets de Baudelaire, (acceptations ou refus de dîners, demandes de places de théâtre, etc), qui n'ont d'autre intérêt que d'avoir été écrits par lui; et les deux lettres ci-jointes dont je vous envoie la copie . . .
> Nous vous serions obligées de ne pas mentionner Madame Stevens dans la lettre écrite par Mme Paul Meurice, nous connaissons particulièrement sa fille et nous sommes d'avis que dans ce genre de publication on doit éviter de blesser les sentiments de famille. Ce n'est pas Ed. que signait Mme Meurice, mais É. P. (Éléonore Palmyre) . . .
>
> PAULE MONTARGIS

(MS 8° f 40/187)

That day, in a second note marked 'p/m 14 janv. soir 06' (MS 8° f 40/191), Mme Montargis added:

> Mon beau-frère me dit qu'il a été copié par inadvertence dans la lettre de 1845 [*sic*] un mot choquant et qu'il est préférable de ne pas trouver dans une correspondance adressée à une femme; nous vous serions donc très obligées de bien vouloir le supprimer en le remplaçant par des points . . .

There are no letters to Mme Paul Meurice, dated 1845, in the Pléiade edition of Baudelaire's correspondence. The earliest published letter is the one given here, dated 3 January 1865.

6 Mauclair: *Charles Baudelaire*, 24–5
7 See also CB: *Œs. cs.*, I, 665
8 For Mme Hugo in Brussels, see Richardson: *Victor Hugo*, 187 and *passim*
9 Vendredi 27 janvier 1865. CB: *Corr.*, II, 439
10 Vendredi 27 janvier 1865. Ibid, 440
11 Ibid.
12 L'ARTISTE, 1er février, 1865
13 REVUE ANECDOTIQUE, 1857, 228
14 Vendredi 3 février 1865. CB: *Corr.*, II, 441–3
15 Vendredi 3 février 1865. Ibid, 446
16 Vendredi 3 février 1865. Ibid, 448

108

1 Mercredi 8 février [18]65. CB: *Corr.*, 452, 453–4, 455
2 Samedi 11 février 1865. Ibid, 456–7
3 Ibid, 457–8, 458
4 Undated. F. Gautier: *Documents sur Baudelaire. III. Baudelaire et Mme Paul Meurice.* (M de F, 15 mars 1906, 211–3)
5 Jeudi 9 mars 1865. CB: *Corr.*, II, 473
6 Ibid, 478, 482
7 15 mars [18]65. Ibid, 474
8 Sainte-Beuve: *Corr. gén.*, XIV, 132–3
9 Jeudi 30 mars 1865. CB: *Corr.*, II, 490
10 Ibid, 477
11 30 mars 1865. LAB: 367–8
12 For Manet's friendship with Baudelaire, see LAB: 228–39
13 [Début mai 1865.] LAB: 233
14 Jeudi 11 mai 1865. CB: *Corr.*, II, 496–7

109

1 CB: *Œs. cs.*, I, 669
2 Ibid, I, 670
3 Pia: *Baudelaire*, 48

4 CB: *Œs. cs.*, I, 671

5 Léopold Levaux: *Les Masques de Baudelaire* (LES CAHIERS DU JOURNAL DES POÈTES, 1938, 51–2). The incident had been described to Levaux's father.

6 CB: *Œs. cs.*, I, 673

7 The first mention of Poe in Baudelaire's surviving correspondence occurs on 15 October 1851 (CB: *Corr.*, I, 180)

8 Projet de préface pour *Les Fleurs du mal*. CB: *Œs. cs.*, I, 185–6

9 Mardi 18 avril 1865. CB: *Corr.*, II, 484

10 Jeudi 4 mai 1865. Ibid, II, 486–7

11 Lundi 8 mai [1865]. Ibid, II, 494

12 Jeudi soir 11 mai [1865]. Ibid, II, 498

13 Vendredi 12 mai [18]65. Ibid, II, 499

14 Undated. F. Gautier: *Documents sur Baudelaire* (M de F. 15 mars 1906, 213–5)

15 Mercredi, 24 mai 1865. CB: *Corr.*, II, 501

16 Mardi 30 mai [18]65. Ibid, II, 503, 504

17 Mercredi 28 juin [18]65. Ibid, II, 508–9

110

1 Mercredi 5 juillet [1865]. CB: *Corr.*, II, 511–2

2 Baudelaire to Lemer, [6 juillet 1865]. CB: *Corr.*, II, 512. Hetzel was not to be reimbursed until after Baudelaire's death.

3 Ibid.

4 Ibid.

5 19 septembre 1867. J. Crépet: *Miettes baudelairiennes.* (M de F, 1er février 1940, 325–6)

6 Ibid, 326

7 Samedi 8 juillet 1865. CB: *Corr.*, II, 513–4

8 Samedi 8 juillet 1865. Ibid, 515

9 Porché: op. cit., 472

10 Asselineau: op. cit., 90–1

11 11 juillet [1865]. CB: *Corr.*, II, 517

12 Mendès: LE FIGARO, 2 novembre 1902, quoted in BP, 157–8, where the date is mistakenly given as 4 July. This was the date of Baudelaire's arrival in Paris, not of his proposed departure for Brussels.

13 Ibid, 159–60, 160–1, 161, 161–2. Butor: op. cit., 259–60.

14 PZ: op. cit., 497

15 Butor: loc. cit.

16 Ibid.

111

1 Lundi 17 [juillet 1865]. CB: *Corr.*, II, 518

2 Ibid, II, 925

3 26 juillet 1865. Ibid, II, 520

4 Lemer to Baudelaire, 7 août 1865. LAB: 220

5 9 août 1865. CB: *Corr.*, II, 521–2

6 PZ: op. cit., 544

7 J. Crépet: *Miettes baudelairiennes.* (M de F, 1er février 1940, 323)

8 10 juin 1889. Goncourt: *Journal*, XVI, 88

9 3 sept[embre].1865. CB: *Corr.*, II, 527, 528

10 4 septembre 1865. Sainte-Beuve: *Corr. gén.*, XIV, 343

11 Vandérem: *Baudelaire et Sainte-Beuve*, 17

12 Baudelaire's letter has not, it seems, survived; but it was answered by Mme Manet in her husband's absence, and then by Manet himself (LAB: 235, 236–7)

13 Jeudi 14 septembre 1865. LAB: 236–7

14 Jeudi 26 oct[obre 18]65. CB: *Corr.*, II, 536, 536–7

15 Dimanche 29 oct[obre 1865]. Ibid, II, 540

16 Lundi 13 novembre 1865. Ibid, II, 542

17 Vendredi 3 novembre [18]65. Ibid, II, 540, 540–1

18 [Mars 1869.] Victor Hugo: *Corr.*, III, 179

19 Ibid.

112

1 14 novembre 1865. CB: *Corr.*, II, 936

2 26 novembre 1865. Maison de Victor Hugo, Paris

3 L'INDÉPENDANCE BELGE, 20 juin 1887. Quoted by EJC: 168–9, note

4 [Fin 1865 ou début 1866.] LAB: 196

5 30 novembre 1865. CB: *Corr.*, II, 546–7, 547, 548

6 Lemer: op. cit., 153

7 *Pauvre Belgique!* CB: *Œs. cs.*, II, 821

8 Ibid, II, 824

9 Ibid, II, 826

10 Ibid, II, 829

11 Ibid, II, 899

12 Ibid, II, 914

13 Charlier: *Passages*, 182

14 Silvestre de Sacy: '*Pauvre Belgique*' ou l'échec parfait (M de F, 1er juin 1955, 290, 291)

15 Jeudi 21 décembre 1865. CB: *Corr.*, II, 548

16 Ibid, II, 549

17 Mardi 26 décembre [18]65. Ibid, 555–6

18 27 décembre 1865. Ibid, 558

19 Dufay: *Baudelaire à Bruxelles* (M de F, 15 novembre 1929, 80); Pichois: *Documents nouveaux sur Charles Baudelaire* (M de F, février 1961, 274)

20 Glatigny: *Lettres . . . à Théodore de Banville*, 18

21 Ibid, 19

22 J. Crépet: *Baudelairiana* (B du B, février 1946, 64)

23 Ibid.

24 [5 février 1866.] CB: *Corr.*, II, 587

25 Vendredi 12 janvier 1866. Ibid, II, 566

26 PZ: op. cit., 610

27 2 mai 1866. J. Crépet: *Les Derniers Jours de Charles Baudelaire.* (B du B, 1er février 1925, 78)

28 15 janvier 1866. [Et 5 février.] CB: *Corr.*, II, 583
29 Jeudi 18 janvier [1866]. Ibid, II, 570, 572
30 [20 janvier 1866.] Ibid, II, 575
31 CB: *Œs. cs.*, I, 1094
32 Dimanche 21 janvier 1866. CB: *Corr.*, II, 575
33 Ibid, 575–6
34 Lundi 22 [janvier 1866]. Ibid, 576
35 Ibid, 576–7
36 Lundi 29 janvier 1866. Ibid, 578–9
37 30 janvier 1866. Ibid, 581, 582

113

1 [5 février 1866.] CB: *Corr.*, II, 586–7
2 15 février 1866. Sainte-Beuve: *Corr. gén.*, XV, 93
3 Mardi 6 février [18]66. CB: *Corr.*, II, 587
4 Mardi 6 février 1866. Ibid, II, 590
5 Samedi matin 10 février [1866]. Ibid, II, 593
6 Ibid, 593–4
7 Lundi 12 février [18]66. Ibid, II, 595, 597
8 Sainte-Beuve: *Corr. gén.*, XV, 93
9 Vendredi 16 février 1866. CB: *Corr.*, II, 599
10 Ibid, II, 598, 599
11 Samedi 17 février 1866. Ibid, II, 602
12 Dimanche 18 février 1866. Ibid, II, 605
13 Dimanche 18 février 1866. Ibid, II, 608
14 Ibid, II, 610
15 Cette nuit, du 18 au 19 [février 1866]. Ibid, II, 612
16 Lundi 19 février [18]66. Ibid, II, 613
17 Ibid.
18 Ibid.
19 Tailhade: *Quelques fantômes de jadis*, 182
20 Hoche: *Les Parisiens chez eux*, 33
21 Lundi 19 février [18]66. CB: *Corr.*, II, 613
22 Mercredi 21 février 1866. Ibid, II, 617–8
23 21 février 1866. Ibid, II, 619
24 21 février 1866. Ibid, II, 619, 620

114

1 13 août 1867. J. Crépet: *Miettes baudelairiennes* (M de F, février 1940, 322–3)
2 CB: *Œs. cs.*, I, 1120
3 Ibid.
4 PZ: op. cit., 546
5 A copy on fine paper, with an autograph copy by Baudelaire of *Le Flambeau*, was listed as no. 657 in the *Catalogue de la bibliothèque de M. Philippe Burty*.

6 In the 1890s, Gustave Charpentier was inspired by *Les Fleurs du mal*. The young Debussy read it at the Villa Médicis in Rome, and in 1890 he finished his setting of *Cinq poèmes de Baudelaire*.

7 CB: *Œs. cs.*, I, 1140–1

8 Ibid, I, 1142

9 Ibid, I, 162

10 [Environ 23 janvier 1866.] LAB: 247. For Mendès' imprisonment, see Richardson: *Judith Gautier*, 30, 60–2

11 CB: *Œs. cs.*, I, 1144

12 Undated. *Lettres d'Albert Glatigny à Théodore de Banville* (M de F, 15 mars 1923, 609–10)

13 For the influence of Baudelaire on Verlaine, see Richardson: *Verlaine*, 22–3 and *passim*

115

1 1er mars 1866. (Maison de Victor Hugo, Paris)

2 Porché: op. cit., 476

3 5 janvier 1866. Sainte-Beuve: *Corr. gén.*, XV, 42

4 Verlaine: *Charles Baudelaire* (*Œuvres posthumes*, II, 8–9)

5 Lundi 5 mars 1866. CB: *Corr.*, II, 625

6 Ibid.

7 Ibid, 625–6

8 Lundi 5 mars 1866. Ibid, 627

9 Ibid, 972

10 11 mars 1866. (Maison de Victor Hugo, Paris)

11 15 mars 1866. (Maison de Victor Hugo, Paris)

12 Ibid.

13 Ibid.

14 CB: *Œs. cs.*, II, 244

15 Ibid, II, 952; *Corr.*, II, 582

16 Nadar, who was far from reliable, wrote in his notes that 'Rops, in whose house Baud. had his attack in Belgium [*sic*], looked after him as a sister of-charity tends a child.' (B.N. N.A. Fr.25013 f 10)

116

1 Mondor: *Eugène Lefébure . . .*, 211

2 Baudelaire to Mme Aupick. Lundi 26 mars 1866. CB: *Corr.*, II, 629

3 Dufay: *Autour de Baudelaire*, 140; Pichois and Ziegler date this dinner 20 March or a little earlier (op. cit., 669–70)

4 Dufay: op. cit., 140–1

5 Mardi 20 mars [1866]. CB: *Corr.*, II, 628

6 Mme Hugo to Victor Hugo, 'samedi [31 mars?] 1866.' (Maison de Victor Hugo, Paris)

7 PZ: op. cit., 557

8 Mme Hugo to Victor Hugo, 'samedi [31 mars?] 1866.' (Maison de Victor Hugo, Paris)

9 Vendredi 23 mars 18[66]. CB: *Corr.*, II, 629

10 Lundi 26 mars 1866. Ibid.
11 Quoted by J. Crépet: *Propos sur Baudelaire*, 172–3
12 29 mars 1866. CB: *Corr.*, II, 630
13 Ibid.
14 29 mars 1866. Ibid, II, 631
15 29 mars [1866]. B.N. N.A. Fr.15814 f 34
16 30 mars 1866. B.N. N.A. Fr.15814 f 103
17 Vendredi 30 mars 1866. CB: *Corr.*, II, 632
18 Cabanès: op. cit., I, 323
19 *La maladie et la mort de Baudelaire.* (CHRONIQUE MÉDICALE, 1er décembre 1907, 771)
20 31 mars 1866. Pichois: *Documents nouveaux sur Charles Baudelaire.* (M de F, février 1961, 272)
21 Poggenburg: op. cit., 463
22 Samedi [31 mars 1866]. (Maison de Victor Hugo, Paris)
23 CB: *Œs. cs.*, I, 140–1

117

1 EJC: op. cit., 196. Raynaud says that she was completely paralysed (M de F, 15 août 1921, 116)
2 Undated. F. Gautier: *Documents sur Baudelaire* (M de F, 1er février 1905, 340–1)
3 CB: *Corr.*, II, 597
4 Kahn: *Charles Baudelaire. Son Œuvre*, 17
5 Undated. F. Gautier: op. cit., 339
6 J. Crépet: *Les Derniers Jours de Charles Baudelaire . . .* (NRF, novembre 1932, 643–4)
7 4 avril 1866. Richer et Ruff: op. cit., 25
8 Ibid.
9 Malassis to Asselineau, 26 avril 1866. Ibid, 37
10 5 avril [1866]. Crépet: *Les Derniers jours de Charles Baudelaire . . .* (B du B, 1er février 1925, 74–5)
11 Cabanès: *Lettre d'Albert Glatigny sur la maladie de Baudelaire.* (L'INTERMÉDIAIRE DES CHERCHEURS ET DES CURIEUX, 20 mars 1913, 376)
12 Ibid.
13 'Samedi' [31 mars]. (Maison de Victor Hugo, Paris)
14 PZ: op. cit., 561
15 Dufay: *Autour de Baudelaire*, 143
16 EJC: op. cit., 190–1
17 See p. 72 of the present book
18 These are the conclusions of Roger L. Williams in *The Horror of Life*, with which the present author largely agrees.
19 Dedet: '*Sois sage, ô ma douleur . . .*' (LE FIGARO LITTÉRAIRE, 9 mars 1967)

118

1 J. Crépet: *Les Derniers Jours de Charles Baudelaire . . .* (NRF, novembre 1932, 644–6)
2 Ibid.
3 Ibid, 646–8

4 For Aimée Falaise, see Pichois and Ziegler: *Le Testament de Madame Aupick* (BULLETIN BAUDELAIRIEN, décembre 1985, 61–9)

5 Crépet: loc, cit.

6 Undated, but April 1866. Reymond: *Albert Glatigny*, 88

7 11 avril 1866. B.N. N.A. Fr.15814 ff 28–30

8 12 avril 1866. B.N. N.A. Fr.15814 f 35

9 B.N. N.A. Fr.15814 f 33

10 PZ: op. cit., 564

11 Richer et Ruff: *Les Derniers mois de Baudelaire . . .*, 28

12 Champfleury to Malassis, 11 avril 1866. PZ: op. cit., 565

13 Porché: *Baudelaire. Histoire d'une âme*, 483

14 EJC: op. cit., 197

15 Ibid, 197–9

16 Richer et Ruff: op. cit., 32

119

1 23 avril 1866. B.N. N.A. Fr.15814 f 32

2 Richer et Ruff: op. cit., 37

3 Mme Aupick to Asselineau, 1869. B.N. N.A. Fr.15826 f 55

4 Nadar Papers. B.N. N.A. Fr.25013 f 11

5 Richer et Ruff: op. cit., 39

6 [Mai, 1866.] J. Crépet: *Les Derniers Jours de Charles Baudelaire . . .* (B du B, 1er février 1925, 78–9)

7 Ibid, 79

8 Quoted by J. Crépet: *Les Derniers Jours de Charles Baudelaire . . .* (NRF, novembre 1932, 650)

9 J. Crépet: *Quelques billets de Poulet- Malassis* (LE FIGARO, 26 août 1933)

10 Riche et Ruff: op. cit., 42–3

11 Pichois: *Documents nouveaux sur Charles Baudelaire* (M de F, février 1961, 272)

12 Mercredi [30 mai 1866]. J. Crépet: op. cit., 650

13 Richer et Ruff: op. cit., 47, 48

14 J. Crépet: op. cit., 651–2

15 Richer et Ruff: op. cit., 52, 53

16 Féli Gautier: *Documents sur Baudelaire* (M de F, 15 janvier 1905). Gautier suggests in his *Baudelaire*, xciv, that this letter was written in 1866, while Baudelaire was ill in Brussels, but the date appears uncertain.

17 10 juin [1868]. Auzas: op. cit. (M de F, 16 septembre 1912, 245)

18 Undated, but early June 1866. J. Crépet: *Les Derniers Jours de Charles Baudelaire* (B du B, 1er février 1925, 81)

19 10 juin [1866]. B.N. N.A. Fr.15814 f 35

20 Asselineau to Malassis. Undated. J. Crépet: *Les Derniers Jours de Charles Baudelaire* (B du B, 1er février 1925, 79)

21 Ancelle to Malassis, 10 juin [1866]. B.N. N.A. Fr.15814 f 35

22 Malassis to Asselineau, 7 juillet 1866. Richer et Ruff: op. cit., 59, 60

23 To Mme Aupick, 1er janvier 1865. CB: *Corr.*, II, 433

120

1　Mme Aupick to Malassis, 30 juin 1866. PZ: op. cit., 574
2　Asselineau: *Charles Baudelaire*, 95–6
3　Ibid, 96
4　J. Crépet: *Les Derniers Jours de Charles Baudelaire. Lettres inédites de Madame Aupick à Poulet-Malassis* (NRF, novembre 1932, 653–4)
5　Ibid.
6　Ibid, 671
7　J. Crépet: *Les Derniers Jours de Charles Baudelaire. Lettres de Charles Asselineau à Poulet-Malassis.* (B du B, 1er février 1925, 81–2)
8　7 juillet 1866. Richer et Ruff: op. cit., 58, 59
9　PZ: op. cit., 609
10　Symons: *Charles Baudelaire*, 76
11　J. Crépet: *Les Derniers Jours de Charles Baudelaire...* (NRF, novembre 1932, 654–6). Mme Aupick's letter to Hetzel, on 15 July 1866, which Bandy and Pichois mistakenly date 1867, was published by Parménie and Bonnier de la Chapelle in *Histoire d'un éditeur et de ses auteurs. P.–J. Hetzel (Stahl),* 473

121

1　10 juillet [1866]. Institut de France. Lovenjoul D 597 f 209
2　Ibid, ff 209–10
3　12 juillet 1866. Sainte-Beuve: *Corr. gén.,* XV, 227
4　Charavay: op. cit., 113
5　16 août 1886 Quoted by J. Crépet in *Baudelairiana* (B du B, février 1946, 63–4); see also Troubat: op. cit., 208–9
6　Champfleury: *Souvenirs...,* 143–4
7　Baden-Baden, allee Haü, 280, 13 juillet 1866. Unidentified press-cutting. B.N. N.A. Fr.15819 f 236
8　Du Camp: op. cit., II, 92
9　Ibid, II, 91
10　Sherard: *Modern Paris,* 194
11　'Mercredi 18'. Couturier: *Lettres de Mme Aupick à Théodore de Banville* (M de F, 1er septembre 1917, 36–7). See also Mme Aupick to Hetzel, 15 juillet [1867]: BP, 229–30
12　Banville: *Étude,* xix–xx
13　'Lundi'. J. Crépet: *Les Derniers Jours de Charles Baudelaire...* (NRF, novembre 1932, 656–7)
14　Charles Buet: DURANDAL, juillet 1894, 129–31. Quoted by Levaux: op. cit., 55–6
15　7 septembre 1867. Reprinted in Vallès: *Les Enfants du peuple,* 115–6
16　LA PETITE REVUE, 21 juillet 1866, 155
17　B.N. N.A. Fr.15814 f 48
18　PZ: op. cit., 579

122

1 J. Crépet: *Les Derniers Jours de Charles Baudelaire* (NRF, novembre 1932, 656–7)
2 [1866] J. Crépet: *Les Derniers Jours de Charles Baudelaire* (B du B, 1er février 1925, 83)
3 Undated. Ibid, 84
4 Tabarant: *La Vie artistique au temps de Baudelaire*, 387
5 PZ: op. cit., 672; but there is a factually different account in the *Dictionnaire de biographie française*, XII, 962
6 Tabarant: op. cit., 387–8. In the first volume of *L'Hydrothérapie*, which appeared without a publisher's name in 1860, Duval contributed a number of articles, including *Affection rhumatismale des enveloppes de la moelle (région lombaire)*, 29; *Quelques remarques sur l'application de l'hydrothérapie, suivie d'un cas de guérison*, 54–6; *Sciatique datant de dix mois. Applications hydrothérapiques. Guérison*, 327 sqq.; *Cas grave d'affection paralytique généralisée*, 375 sqq.; *Paralysie du bras droit et atrophie du deltoïde*, 445–7. In Volume II, 12 janvier 1861, the bibliography includes, p. 1; *De l'hydrothérapie appliquée au traitement de l'épilepsie et aux paralysies, etc.*
7 EJC: 200
8 Cabanès: *Grands névropathes. Malades immortels*, I, 318. Émile Duval died in 1889
9 Auzas: *Lettres de Mme Veuve Aupick à Charles Asselineau* (M de F, 16 septembre 1912, 226–7)
10 EJC, 201
11 Mendès: op. cit. Quoted in BP, 161, 162
12 B.N. N.A. Fr.15814 ff 95–6. Mme Manet, the daughter of an organist, had had a thorough musical education. She had given lessons to her husband and to his brother Eugène. (Loncke: *Baudelaire et la musique*, 45)
13 Sainte-Beuve: *Corr. gén.*, XV, 280
14 Ce 7 juillet 1866. Sagnes: *Baudelaire, Armand du Mesnil et la pétition de 1866. Lettres inédites.* (RHLF, avril–juin 1967, 304)
15 PZ: op. cit., 578
16 Mérimée to Banville, 25 août 1866. J. Crépet: *Propos sur Baudelaire*, 51
17 27 août 1866. Sainte-Beuve: *Corr. gén.*, XV, 280–1. Among the Crépet Papers is a letter from Banville to Asselineau, also written on 27 August 1866:

> Cher ami,
>   Bien induement, Mérimée qui a mal compris ma lettre, quoiqu'elle est excessivement claire, a lui-même envoyé la pétition à M. Duruy après l'avoir apostillée. Il m'écrit cela avec une foule de choses très aimables pour Baudelaire . . .
> (B.N. N.A. Fr.15814 f 236)

18 Dufay: *Un ami de Baudelaire: M. Ancelle, beau-père d'un fils du duc de Berry* (M de F, 15 octobre 1934, 421–5)
19 Jules Vernier: *Le Courrier de Boulogne et de Neuilly*, 30 juillet 1864. (B.N. N.A. Fr.15814 ff 42–3)
20 3 septembre 1866. J. Richer et M. Ruff: *Les Derniers mois de Charles Baudelaire*, 70
21 *Baudelaire et Asselineau*, 147–8
22 27 septembre 1866. Richer et Ruff: op. cit., 78
23 PZ: op. cit., 578
24 Ibid.

25 6 octobre 1866. Auzas: op. cit., 227–8
26 B.N. N.A. Fr.24280 f 592
27 J. Crépet: op. cit. (NRF, novembre 1932, 659–60)
28 Auzas: op. cit., 229
29 5 janvier 1867. Ibid.
30 13 janvier 1867. Richer et Ruff: op. cit., 86
31 6 février 1867. Ibid, 88
32 *Baudelaire et Asselineau*, 148 9
33 [31 mars 1866.] Maison de Victor Hugo, Paris

123

1 Auzas: *Lettres de Madame Veuve Aupick à Charles Asselineau* (M de F, 16 septembre 1912, 229–30)
2 J. Crépet: *Les Derniers Jours de Charles Baudelaire* (NRF, novembre 1932, 661–2)
3 B.N. N.A. Fr.15814 f 406
4 J. Crépet: op. cit., 662
5 Auzas: op. cit., 230
6 Asselineau: *Charles Baudelaire*, 102
7 Ibid, 103
8 Auzas: op. cit., 231
9 Unidentified newspaper cutting. (B.N. N.A. Fr.15819 f 236)
10 Ibid. It is unclear whether the extracts come from the same letter.
11 Undated. Quoted by BP, 225–6
12 Banville: *Charles Baudelaire. Étude*, xxviii
13 CB: *Œs. cs.*, I, 683
14 Undated. J. Crépet: *Les Derniers Jours de Charles Baudelaire* (B du B, 1er mars 1925), 155–6). In *La Mort de Baudelaire* (LE FIGARO, 3 septembre 1867), Alfred d'Aunay says that Albert had sat up with Baudelaire for three months.
15 CB: *Corr.*, II, 981
16 Undated, J. Crépet: op. cit., 156
17 Trial: op. cit., 61, 62; Cabanès: op. cit., I, 319–20
18 To Malassis, 16 septembre 1867. J. Crépet: *Les Derniers Jours de Charles Baudelaire* (NRF, novembre 1932, 662–3)
19 [31 août 1867.] Unidentified newspaper cutting. (B.N. N.A. Fr.15819 f 236)
20 10 février 1914. (Féli Gautier Papers, MS 8° F 42/1. Taylor Institution, Oxford.)
21 Quoted by PZ: op. cit., 591
22 [31 août 1867.] Unidentified newspaper cutting. (B.N. N.A. Fr.15819 f 236)
23 Ibid.
24 J. Crépet; op. cit., 663; see also Mme Aupick's letter to Malassis [1868]: ibid, 668

124

1 Pichois: *Un ami de Baudelaire. Edmond Albert.* (ÉTUDES BAUDELAIRIENNES, 1971, II, 178)
2 Poggenburg: op. cit., 477; PZ: op. cit., 594
3 Asselineau to Malassis [6 or 7 September 1867]. EJC: op. cit., 275

4 J. Crépet: *Les Derniers Jours de Charles Baudelaire*... (NRF, novembre 1932, 663)
5 *Baudelaire et Asselineau*, 25–6
6 Ibid, note
7 Ibid, 26, note
8 Alfred d'Aunay: *La Mort de Baudelaire* (LE FIGARO, 3 septembre 1867). This article had presumably been suggested by Georges Maillard's article in LE FIGARO the previous day, in which he had announced: 'Baudelaire est mort cette nuit chez le docteur Blanche.' D'Aunay, who was an otherwise unknown acquaintance of Baudelaire, recorded:

> La nouvelle de la mort de Baudelaire nous est arrivé hier assez vaguement. On le disait fou. Je courus chez le docteur Blanche:
> – Allons! me dit l'excellent aliéniste, on prétendra encore que j'ai fait mettre cela dans les journaux! Baudelaire n'est jamais venu ici. Un de ses amis, Asselineau, m'en avait parlé. Il m'avait même demandé quelles seraient mes conditions. Je lui répondis que l'honneur de soigner les gens de lettres me suffisait...
> Je n'en entendais pas davantage, et je partis à la recherche de la maison mortuaire. C'est à l'église indiquée pour les funérailles qu'on me donna ce renseignement.

It is remarkable that, thirteen months after Baudelaire had entered the Duval nursing-home, any literary acquaintance in Paris should still have been ignorant of the fact. However, d'Aunay claimed that he was ushered into the room in the rue du Dôme where Baudelaire lay dead.

> [Mme Aupick] n'a pas faibli pendant ces trois jours d'agonie. Elle était encore là, dans cette chambre, aux pieds du Christ, quand je me suis présenté à elle.
> – Vous avez connu mon fils, me dit-elle. Vous l'avez aimé aussi, comme tous ceux qui l'ont connu. Donnez-moi la main!

D'Aunay's account is increasingly suspect and bewildering.
9 J. Crépet: *Les Derniers Jours de Charles Baudelaire*... (B du B, 1er mars 1925, 157)
10 EJC: op. cit., 208
11 Maillard: LE FIGARO, 4 septembre 1867
12 LE FIGARO, 2 septembre 1867
13 LE FIGARO, 7 septembre 1867.
14 LE FIGARO, 4 septembre 1867
15 Vitu: *Nécrologie.* (L'ÉTENDARD, 3 septembre 1867.)
16 Quoted by Raynaud in *Baudelaire et Théophile Gautier*, 589
17 Maillard: loc. cit.
18 Cousin: *Charles Baudelaire*, 139, 140
19 Ibid, 129 sqq.
20 Vandérem: *Baudelaire et Sainte-Beuve*, 17
21 PZ: op. cit., 596
22 Antoine et Pichois: op. cit., 25. Institut de France: Lovenjoul, D 539 ff 379–84
23 Asselineau to Malassis, 6 or 7 September 1867. Quoted by E. Crépet in CB: *Œuvres posthumes*, 329
24 Ce samedi 7 sept. [1867]. Institut de France. Lovenjoul D 597 ff 211–2

25 Ce samedi [1868]. Auzas: op. cit., 245

26 EJC: op. cit., 275

27 4 septembre 1867. PZ: op. cit., 597

28 Asselineau to Malassis, 6 or 7 September 1867. (E. Crépet: loc. cit.) An invitation to the funeral, addressed to Nadar at the boulevard des Capucines, remains among Nadar's papers (B.N. N.A. Fr.25013 f 592)

29 Verlaine: *Œuvres posthumes*, II, 177–9

30 26 août 1867. Diary of Eugénie Fort (Pierre Th. Gautier). See also Raynaud: *Baudelaire et Théophile Gautier* (M de F, 16 octobre 1917, 588)

31 Undated, but early September 1867. Boucher: *Lettres familières de Théophile Gautier* (M de F, 15 mai 1929, 117–8)

32 Ibid.

33 Mardi 10 septembre. (Institut de France. Lov. C 502 *ter* ff 3–4.) For 'the most ridiculous stories', see Crépet: *Miettes baudelairiennes* (M de F, 15 juin 1937, 529 sqq.)

34 L'ILLUSTRATION, 14 septembre 1867

35 REVUE NATIONALE ET ÉTRANGÈRE, 14 septembre 1867, 162

36 LE FIGARO, 10 septembre 1867

37 [Septembre 1867.] J. Crépet: *Miettes baudelairiennes* (M de F, 15 juin 1937, 528)

38 Richard: op. cit., 284, 285 (Bibliothèque municipale de Fontainebleau)

39 Mondor: *Vie de Mallarmé*, 244–5

40 Malassis to Ancelle, 9 septembre 1867. J. Crépet: *Baudelairiana*. (B du B, Série de Guerre, 1940–1945, 209)

125

1 CB: *Corr.*, I, lxxix–lxxx

2 To Ancelle. [24 mars 1868.] EJC, 59, note

3 22 février 1869. B.N. N.A. Fr.15814 f 96

4 To Asselineau. Undated, but 1868? F. Gautier: *Documents sur Baudelaire* (M de F, 1er février 1905, 344)

5 Théophile Gautier: *Souvenirs romantiques*, 278

6 Ce mardi 10 mars [1868]. Institut de France. Lov. C 491 ff 167–8

7 [6 mai 1861.] CB: *Corr.*, II, 151

8 10 juin [1868]. Auzas: *Lettres de Madame Veuve Aupick à Charles Asselineau* (M de F, 16 septembre 1912, 244)

9 Mercredi 3 juin 1857. CB: *Corr.*, I, 404

10 Raynaud: *Les Parents de Baudelaire* (M de F, 15 août 1921, 128–9)

11 'Ce samedi'. Auzas: op. cit. (M de F, 16 septembre 1912, 243)

12 Ce samedi 14. Couturier: *Lettres de Madame Aupick à Théodore de Banville* (M de F, 1er septembre 1917, 38)

13 Raynaud: op. cit., 129–30

14 PZ: op. cit., 606

15 Lundi 28 novembre [1868]. EJC, 270–1

16 J. Crépet: *Les Derniers Jours de Charles Baudelaire* (B du B, 1er mars 1925, 160)

17 See pp. 308–9 of the present book

18 Fournier: *Les 44 domiciles de Baudelaire* (EUROPE, avril–mai 1967, 273)

Select Bibliography

I

BOOKS

The following are among the books consulted. English books are published in London, French books in Paris unless otherwise stated.

Unless indicated otherwise, all quotations from Baudelaire are taken from the Pléiade edition of his works and correspondence:

BAUDELAIRE: *Œuvres complètes*. Texte établi, présenté et annoté par Claude Pichois. 2 tomes. (Bibliothèque de la Pléiade. NRF. Gallimard. 1975, 1976)

BAUDELAIRE: *Correspondance*. Texte établi, présenté et annoté par Claude Pichois avec la collaboration de Jean Ziegler. 2 tomes. (Bibliothèque de la Pléiade. NRF. Gallimard. 1973)

About, Edmond, *Voyage à travers l'exposition des beaux-arts (peinture et sculpture)* (L. Hachette, 1855)
Abse, D. W., *Hysteria and related mental disorders. An approach to psychological medicine* (Bristol, John Wright & Sons Ltd, 1966)
Albalat, Antoine, *Souvenirs de la vie littéraire* (Arthème Fayard, s.d.)
Alméras, Henri d', *Avant la Gloire. Leurs Débuts*. 1re série. (Société Française d'Imprimerie et de Librairie, 1902)
Anon., *Guide Historique et pittoresque de Lyon à Châlon, sur la Saône*. (Maison, 1844)
—— *Biographie des membres du Sénat*. (Michel Lévy frères, 1852)
—— *Galerie historique et biographique des membres du Sénat* (À la librairie nouvelle, 1852)
—— *Le Livre d'or de l'Ordre de Léopold et de la Croix de fer*. Tome second. (Bruxelles, Ch. Lelong, Imprimeur-Éditeur, 1858)
Ariste, Paul d', *La Vie et le monde du boulevard (1830–1870). (Un Dandy: Nestor Roqueplan)*. (Éditions Jules Tallandier, 1930)
Arnold, Paul, *Ésotérisme de Baudelaire*. (Librairie philosophique J. Vrin, 1972)
Asselineau, Charles, *Charles Baudelaire. Sa Vie et son Œuvre*. (Alphonse Lemerre, 1869)

[Asselineau, Charles] *L'Italie et Constantinople*. (Alphonse Lemerre, 1869)

Audebrand, Philibert, *Un Café de journalistes sous Napoléon III*. (Dentu, 1888)

—— *Derniers jours de la Bohème. Souvenirs de la vie littéraire*. (Calmann-Lévy, 1905)

Austin, Lloyd, *L'Univers poétique de Baudelaire. Symbolisme et symbolique*. (Mercure de France, 1956)

—— *Poetic principles and practice. Occasional papers on Baudelaire, Mallarmé and Valéry*. (Cambridge, Cambridge University Press, 1987)

Austin, Lloyd, and Rees, Garnet, and Vinaver, Eugène (ed.), *Studies in modern French literature presented to P. Mansell Jones*, (Manchester, Manchester University Press, 1961)

Badesco, Luc, *La Génération poétique de 1860. La Jeunesse des deux rives*. 2 vols. (Éditions A.-G. Nizet, 1971)

Bandy, W. T., *Baudelaire judged by his contemporaries. (1845–1867.)* (N. Y. Publications of the Institute of French Studies, Inc, Columbia University, N. Y, 1933)

—— et Pichois, Claude, *Baudelaire devant ses contemporains*. Témoignages rassemblés et présentés par W. T. Bandy et Claude Pichois. (Monaco, Éditions du Rocher, 1957)

Banville, Théodore de, *Odes funambulesques*. (Poulet-Malassis et De Broise, 1857)

—— *Petit traité de la poésie française*. (Bibliothèque de l'Écho de la Sorbonne, 1872)

—— *Trente-six ballades joyeuses*. (Alphonse Lemerre, 1873)

—— *Mes Souvenirs*. (Charpentier, 1882)

—— *La Lanterne magique. Camées parisiens. La Comédie-Française*. (Charpentier, 1883)

—— *Lettres chimériques*. (Charpentier, 1885)

Barrès, Maurice, *La Folie de Charles Baudelaire*. (Les Écrivains réunis, 1936)

—— *Mes Cahiers*. (Plon, 1929–57)

Barthou, Louis, *Autour de Baudelaire*. (Maison du Livre, 1917)

Bassim, Tamara, *La femme dans l'œuvre de Baudelaire*. (Neuchâtel, À la Baconnière, 1974)

Baudelaire, Charles, *Œuvres posthumes et correspondances inédites*. Précédées d'une étude biographique par Eugène Crépet. (Maison Quantin, 1887).

—— *Œuvres complètes*. Notices, notes et éclaircissements de M. Jacques Crépet. 3 tomes. (Louis Conard, 1923–1930)

—— *Les Fleurs du mal*. Précédées d'une notice par Théophile Gautier. 6e édition. (Calmann Lévy, 1878)

—— *Les Fleurs du mal*. Texte de 1861 avec les variantes de 1857 et des journaux et revues précédé d'une étude sur Baudelaire par Th. de Banville. (Bibliothèque Charpentier, 1917)

—— *Les Fleurs du mal*. Edited by Enid Starkie. (Oxford, Blackwell, 1942)

—— *Lettres inédites à sa mère*. Préface, notes et index de Jacques Crépet. (Louis Conard, 1918)

—— *Dernières Lettres inédites à sa mère*. Avec un avertissement et des notes de Jacques Crépet. (Éditions Excelsior, 1926)

—— *Lettres inédites aux siens*. Présentées et annotées par Philippe Auserve. (Éditions Bernard Grasset, 1966)

—— *Petits Poèmes en prose (Le Spleen de Paris)*. Chronologie et introduction par Marcel A. Ruff. (Garnier-Flammarion, 1967)

[Baudelaire, Charles] *Petits Poèmes en prose*. Édition critique par Robert Kemp. (Librairie José Corti, 1969)

—— *Causeries*. Illustrations de Constantin Guys. Préface de F.-F. Gautier. (Éditions du Sagittaire, Simon Krâ, 1920)

—— *Intimate Journals*. Translated by Christopher Isherwood. Introduction by T. S. Eliot. (The Blackamore Press, 1930)

—— *Salon de 1846*. Texte établi et présenté par David Kelley. (Oxford, at the Clarendon Press, 1975)

[Baudelaire, Charles] *Le Tombeau de Charles Baudelaire*. (Bibliothèque artistique et littéraire, 1896)

—— *Le Cinquantenaire de Baudelaire*. (Maison du Livre, 1917)

Beauvoir, Roger de, *Les Mystères de l'Île Saint-Louis. Chroniques de l'Hôtel Pimodan*. (Librairie Nouvelle, 1859)

Benjamin, Walter, *Charles Baudelaire*. Translated from the German by Harry Zohn. (Verso, 1985)

Bénouville, Guillain de, *Baudelaire le trop chrétien*. (Éditions Bernard Grasset, 1936)

Bersani, Léo, *Baudelaire and Freud*. (Berkeley, University of California Press, 1977)

Berthelot, Philippe, *Louis Ménard et son Œuvre*. (Félix Juven, 1902)

Bibliophile Ornais, Un (Comte Gérard de Contades), *Auguste Poulet-Malassis. Bibliographie descriptive et anecdotique des ouvrages écrits ou publiés par lui*. (Rouquette, 1883)

Billy, André, *La Présidente et ses amis*. (Flammarion, 1945)

Blin, Georges, *Baudelaire*. Préface de Jacques Crépet. (NRF, Gallimard, 1939)

—— *Le Sadisme de Baudelaire*. (Librairie José Corti, 1948)

Boisson, Marius, *Les Compagnons de la vie de Bohème*. (Éditions Jules Tallandier, 1929)

Bonde, Baroness, *Paris in '48*. Letters from a resident describing the events of the Revolution. Edited by C. E. Warr. (John Murray, 1903)

Bonnet-Roy, Flavien, *Ferdinand-Philippe, duc d'Orléans. Prince Royal, 1810–1842*. (Société d'Éditions françaises et internationales, 1947)

Bonnières, Robert de, *Mémoires d'aujourd'hui*. 2e série. (Ollendorff, 1885)

Borgal, Clément, *Charles Baudelaire*. (Classiques du XIXe siècle. Éditions Universitaires, 1961)

Bourget, Paul, *Essais de Psychologie contemporaine*. (Lemerre, 1885)

Boylan, Henry, *A Dictionary of Irish Biography*. 2nd edition. (Dublin, Gill & Macmillan, 1988)

Bréard, Charles, *Vieilles rues et vieilles maisons de Honfleur du XVe siècle à nos jours*. (Honfleur, Société normande d'Ethnographie et d'Art populaire, 1900)

Brisson, Adolphe, *Portraits intimes*. 2e série. (Armand Colin, 1896)

Brunetière, Ferdinand, *Questions de critique*. 4e édition. (Calmann-Lévy, 1909)

—— *L'Évolution de la poésie lyrique en France au XIXe siècle*. Leçons professées à la Sorbonne. Tome II. (Hachette, 1894)

—— *Nouveaux essais sur la littérature contemporaine*. (Calmann-Lévy, 1895)

Burton, Richard D. E., *Baudelaire in 1859*. A study in the sources of poetic creativity. (Cambridge, Cambridge University Press, 1968)

Butor, Michel, *Histoire extraordinaire*. Essai sur un rêve de Baudelaire. (NRF Gallimard, 1962)

Byvanck, W. G. C., *Un Hollandais à Paris en 1891*. Sensations de littérature et d'art. Préface d'Anatole France. (Perrin, 1892)

Cabanès, Dr Augustin, *Grands névropathes. Malades immortels*. 3 tomes. (Albin-Michel, 1930–1935)

Cahen, Gustave, *Eugène Boudin. Sa Vie et son œuvre*. (H. Floury, 1900)

Caignart de Saulcy, L.-F., *Carnets de voyage en Orient (1845–69)*. Publiés par Fernande Bassan. (Presses universitaires de France, 1955)

Calmettes, Fernand, *Leconte de Lisle et ses amis*. (Librairies-Imprimeries réunies, s.d.)

Calvé, Emma, *Sous tous les ciels j'ai chanté. Souvenirs*. (Plon, 1940)

Carrère, Jean, *Les Mauvais Maîtres*. (Plon, 1922)

Carter, A. E., *Baudelaire et la critique française, 1868–1917*. (Columbia, University of South Carolina Press, 1963)

Castellane, Maréchal de, *Journal, 1804–1862*. Tome III. 1831–1847. (Plon, 1896)

Castex, Pierre-Georges, *Baudelaire critique d'art. Études et Album*. (Société d'Édition d'Enseignement supérieur, 1969)

Champfleury, *Les Chats*. (J. Rothschild, 1869)

—— *Souvenirs et portraits de jeunesse*. (Dentu, 1872)

Champion, Édouard, *Le Tombeau de Louis Ménard*. (Honoré Champion, 1902)

Charavay, Étienne, *A. de Vigny et Charles Baudelaire candidats à l'Académie Française*. (Charavay frères, éditeurs, 1879)

Charlier, Gustave, *Passages*. (Bruxelles, La Renaissance du Livre, 1947)

Cladel, Judith, *La Vie de Léon Cladel*. (Lemerre, 1905)

—— *Maître et Disciple. Charles Baudelaire et Léon Cladel*. (Corrêa, 1951)

Cladel, Léon, *Les Martyrs ridicules*. Avec une préface de Charles Baudelaire. (Poulet-Malassis, 1862)

Clapton, G. T., *Baudelaire. The Tragic Sophist*. (Edinburgh, Oliver & Boyd, 1934)

Claretie, Jules, *La Vie à Paris, 1882*. (Victor Havard, s.d.)

—— *La Vie à Paris, 1896*. (Bibliothèque Charpentier, 1897)

—— *La Vie à Paris, 1901–1903*. (Bibliothèque Charpentier, 1904)

—— *La Vie à Paris, 1907*. (Bibliothèque Charpentier, 1908)

—— *La Vie à Paris, 1908*. (Bibliothèque Charpentier, 1909)

—— *La Vie à Paris, 1911–1912–1913*. (Bibliothèque Charpentier, 1914)

Contades, Comte G. de, *Portraits et Fantaisies*. (Quantin, 1887)

—— *Gustave Le Vavasseur*. Bibliographie de ses œuvres (1840–1896). (Alençon, E. Renaut–De Broise, 1898)

Coppée, François, *Souvenirs d'un Parisien*. (Lemerre, 1910)

Cousin, Charles, *Charles Baudelaire*. Souvenirs – Correspondances. Bibliographie suivie de pièces inédites. (René Pincebourde, 1872)

—— *Voyage dans un grenier*. (Damascène Morgand & Charles Fatout, 1878)

—— *Racontars illustrés d'un vieux collectionneur*. (À la librairie de 'L'Art', 1887)

Crépet, Eugène et Jacques, *Baudelaire*. Étude biographique d'Eugène Crépet revue et complétée en 1907 par Jacques Crépet. (Éditions Messein, s.d.)

Crépet, Jacques, *Propos sur Baudelaire*. Rassemblés et annotés par Claude Pichois. Préface de Jean Pommier. (Mercure de France, 1957)

Crépet, Jacques, et Pichois, Claude, *Baudelaire et Asselineau.* Textes recueillis et commentés par Jacques Crépet et Claude Pichois. (Librairie Nizet, 1953)

Daudet, Alphonse, *Trente ans de Paris.* (Marpon et Flammarion, 1888)

Daudet, Ernest, *Souvenirs de mon temps.* Débuts d'un homme de lettres, 1857–1861. (Plon-Nourrit, 1921)

Daudet, Léon, *Écrivains et artistes.* Tome 2. (Éditions du Capitole, 1928)

—— *Les Pèlerins d'Emmaus.* (Bernard Grasset, 1928)

—— *Flambeaux.* (Bernard Grasset, 1929)

Delacroix, Eugène, *Journal.* Publié d'après le manuscrit original avec une introduction et des notes par André Joubin. 3 tomes. (Plon, 1932)

Delille, Edward, *Some French Writers.* (Chapman & Hall, 1893)

Delmas, Marc, *Gustave Charpentier et le lyrisme français.* (Librairie Delagrave, 1931)

Delvau, Alfred, *Histoire anecdotique des Cafés et Cabarets de Paris.* (Dentu, 1862)

Dornis, Jean, *Leconte de Lisle intime.* (Alphonse Lemerre, 1895)

Doudan, Ximénès, *Mélanges et Lettres.* 4 tomes. (Calmann-Lévy, 1876–7)

Dreyfous, Maurice, *Ce que je tiens à dire.* 2e édition. (Librairie Paul Ollendorff, 1912)

Du Bos, Charles, *Approximations.* I. (Plon, 1922)

—— *Approximations.* V. (Éditions R.-A. Corrêa, 1932)

Du Camp, Maxime, *Souvenirs littéraires.* 2 tomes. (Hachette, 1882, 1883)

Duckett, M. W., *Dictionnaire de la conversation et de la lecture.* Seconde édition. Tome II. (Michel Lévy frères, 1852)

Dufay, Pierre, *Autour de Baudelaire.* Poulet-Malassis, l'éditeur et l'ami. Madame Sabatier, la muse et la madone. (Au Cabinet du Livre, 1931)

Dupuy, Ernest, *Poètes et critiques.* (Hachette, 1913)

Dusolier, Alcide, *Nos Gens de lettres.* Leur caractère et leurs œuvres. (Librairie Achille Faure, 1864)

Eigeldinger, Marc, *Le Platonisme de Baudelaire.* (Neuchâtel, À la Baconnière, 1951)

Emmanuel, Pierre, *Baudelaire.* ('Les écrivains devant Dieu.' Desclée de Brouwer, 1967)

Estignard, A., *Clésinger. Sa vie, ses œuvres.* (Librairie H. Floury, 1900)

Fairlie, Alison, *Baudelaire: LES FLEURS DU MAL.* (Studies in French Literature No 6. Edward Arnold Ltd, 1960)

Ferran, André, *L'Esthétique de Baudelaire.* (Hachette, 1933)

Feuillerat, Albert, *Baudelaire et la Belle aux cheveux d'or.* (New Haven, Yale University Press, 1941)

—— *Baudelaire et sa mère.* (Montréal, Les Éditions Variétés, 1944)

Feydeau, Ernest, *Sylvie.* (Dentu, 1861)

—— *Théophile Gautier. Souvenirs intimes.* (Plon, 1874)

Fizelière, A. de La, & Decaux, Georges, *Essais de Bibliographie contemporaine. I. Charles Baudelaire.* (Librairie de l'Académie des Bibliophiles, 1868)

Flaubert, Gustave, *Correspondance.* Nouvelle édition augmentée. Deuxième série (1847–1852). (Louis Conard, 1926)

—— *Voyages.* Tome Second. Texte établi et présenté par René Dumesnil. (Société Les Belles Lettres, 1948)

—— *Correspondance.* (Œuvres complètes, XIII, XIV.) (Club de l'Honnête Homme, 1974, 1975)

Flottes, Pierre, *Baudelaire. L'homme et le poète*. (Perrin, 1922)

Fondane, Benjamin, *Baudelaire et l'expérience du gouffre*. Préface de Jean Cassou. (Pierre Seghers, 1947)

Fontainas, André, *Dans la lignée de Baudelaire*. (Éditions de la Nouvelle Revue Critique, 1930)

France, Anatole, *Œuvres complètes illustrées*. Tomes VI, VII. (Calmann-Lévy, 1926)

Freycinet, C. de, *Souvenirs. 1848–1878*. 2e édition. (Librairie Ch. Delagrave, 1912)

Gautier, Félix-François, *Charles Baudelaire*. (Bruxelles, E. Déman, 1904)

Gautier, Judith, *Le Collier des Jours. Souvenirs de ma vie*. (Félix Juven, 1907)

—— *Le Collier des Jours. Le Second Rang du Collier*. (Félix Juven, 1903)

Gautier, Theophile, *Portraits contemporains*. (Bibliothèque Charpentier, s.d.)

—— *Histoire du Romantisme*. Suivie de Notices Romantiques et d'une Étude sur la Poésie française, 1830–1868. (Librairie des Bibliophiles, Flammarion, 1929)

—— *Souvenirs romantiques*. Introduction et notes par Adolphe Boschot. (Librairie Garnier Frères, 1929)

—— *Émaux et Camées*. Introduction de Jean Pommier. (Genève, Droz, 1947)

Gheusi, P.-B., *Cinquante ans de Paris*. Mémoires d'un témoin, 1889–1938. 2 tomes. (Plon, 1939, 1940)

Ghil, René, *Traité du verbe*. Avec avant-dire de Stéphane Mallarmé. (Giraud, 1886)

Gilman, Margaret, *Baudelaire the critic*. (N. Y., Columbia University Press, 1943)

—— *The Idea of Poetry in France*. (Cambridge, Mass., Harvard University Press, 1958)

Ginisty, Paul, *L'Année littéraire, 1885*. (Nouvelle Librairie Parisienne, 1886)

—— *L'Année littéraire, 1888*. (Charpentier, s.d.)

—— *L'Année littéraire, 1892*. (Bibliothèque Charpentier, 1893)

Girard, Henri, *Émile Deschamps, 1791–1871*. (Édouard Champion, 1921)

Glatigny, Albert, *Lettres d'Albert Glatigny à Théodore de Banville*. (Mercure de France, 1923)

Goncourt, Edmond et Jules de, *Journal*. Mémoires de la vie littéraire. 22 tomes. (Monaco, Les Éditions de l'Imprimerie Nationale, 1956)

Gosse, Edmond, *French Profiles*. (Heinemann, 1905)

Hart-Davis, Rupert (ed.) *The Letters of Oscar Wilde*. (Hart-Davis, 1962)

Hassine, Juliette, *Essai sur Proust et Baudelaire*. (A.-G. Nizet, 1979)

Hemmings, F. W. J., *Baudelaire the Damned. A Biography*. (Hamish Hamilton, 1982)

Héricault, Charles de Ricault d', *Souvenirs et Portraits*. Œuvres posthumes. (P. Téqui, 1902)

Hervey, Charles, *The Theatres of Paris*. (Mitchell, 1846)

Heylli, G. d', *Gazette anecdotique, littéraire, artistique et bibliographique*. Publiée par G. d'Heylli. 9e année. Tome II. (Librairie des Bibliophiles, 1884)

Hiddleston, J. A., *Essai sur Laforgue et les DERNIERS VERS suivi de LAFORGUE ET BAUDELAIRE*. (Lexington, Kentucky, French Forum, 1980)

—— *Baudelaire et LE SPLEEN DE PARIS*. (Oxford, The Clarendon Press, 1987)

Hoche, Jules, *Les Parisiens chez eux.* (Dentu, 1883)

Houssaye, Arsène, *Les Confessions.* Tome II. (Dentu, 1885)

Hubert, J.-D., *L'Esthétique des FLEURS DU MAL.* Essai sur l'ambiguité poétique. (Genève, Pierre Cailler, 1953)

Hugo, Victor, *Correspondance.* II, III. (Albin Michel, 1950, 1952)

Huret, Jules, *Enquête sur l'évolution littéraire.* (Bibliothèque Charpentier, 1891)

Hyslop, Lois Boe (ed.), *Baudelaire as a love poet, and other essays.* (University Park, Pennsylvania State University Press, 1969)

—— *Baudelaire. Man of his time.* (New Haven, Yale University Press, 1980)

Ibrovac, Miodrag, *José-Maria de Heredia. Sa Vie – son œuvre.* (Les Presses Françaises, 1923)

Jackson, John E., *La Mort Baudelaire. Essai sur LES FLEURS DU MAL.* (Neuchâtel, À la Baconnière, 1982)

James, Henry, *French Poets and Novelists.* (Macmillan, 1908)

Jean-Aubry, G., *Un Paysage littéraire. Baudelaire et Honfleur.* (Maison du Livre, 1917)

—— (avec la collaboration de Robert Boudin) *Eugène Boudin.* (Neuchâtel, Édition Ides et Calendes, 1968)

Jollivet, Gaston, *Souvenirs de la vie de plaisir sous le Second Empire.* (Éditions Jules Tallandier, 1927)

Jones, P. Mansell, *Baudelaire.* (Cambridge, Bowes & Bowes, 1952)

Jouve, Nicole Ward, *Baudelaire. A Fire to Conquer Darkness.* (Macmillan, 1980)

Jouve, Pierre-Jean, *Tombeau de Baudelaire.* (Aux Éditions du Seuil, 1958)

Jullien, Adolphe, *Fantin-Latour. Sa vie et ses amitiés.* (Lucien Laveur, 1909)

Kahn, Gustave, *Charles Baudelaire. Son Œuvre.* (Éditions de La Nouvelle Revue Critique, 1925)

—— *Silhouettes littéraires.* (Éditions Montaigne, 1925)

Kopp, Robert, et Pichois, Claude, *Les Années Baudelaire.* Études baudelairiennes. I. (Neuchâtel, À la Baconnière, 1969)

Kunel, Maurice (ed.), *Cinq journées avec Ch. Baudelaire.* Propos recueillis à Bruxelles par Georges Barral et publiés par Maurice Kunel. (Liège, Aux Éditions de 'Vigie 30', 1932)

—— *La Vie de Félicien Rops.* (Bruxelles, F. Miette, 1937)

Laforgue, Dr René, *L'Échec de Baudelaire.* Étude Psychanalytique sur la névrose de Charles Baudelaire. (Les Éditions Denoël et Steele, 1931)

Lamartine, A. de, *Histoire de la Révolution de 1848.* Tome II. (Perrotin, 1849)

Lang, Georges E., *Charles Baudelaire jugé par Ernest Feydeau.* Avec un portrait-charge de Charles Baudelaire par Ch. Giraud et 2 facsimilés. (Ronald Davis, 1921)

Larroumet, Gustave, *Meissonier.* Étude suivie d'une biographie par Philippe Burty. (Librairie d'Art, Ludovic Baschet, 1895)

Leakey, F. W., *Baudelaire and Nature.* (Manchester, Manchester University Press, 1969)

Lemaître, Jules, *Les Contemporains.* 4e série. (Lecène & Oudin, 1889)

Lemercier de Neuville, Louis, *Souvenirs d'un Montreur de Marionnettes.* (Maurice Bauche, 1911)

Lemonnier, Camille, *La Vie belge.* (Bibliothèque Charpentier, 1905)

—— *Alfred Stevens et son œuvre.* Suivi des *Impressions sur la peinture* par Alfred Stevens. (Bruxelles, G. Van Oest, 1906)

Lemonnier, Léon, *Les Traducteurs d'Edgar Poe en France de 1845 à 1875. Charles Baudelaire.* (Presses Universitaires de France, 1928)
—— *Enquêtes sur Baudelaire.* (Les Éditions G. Crès & Cie, 1929)
Léon-Daudet, François, *Charles Baudelaire et l'esprit classique.* (Pierre Farré, 1946)
Lepage, Auguste, *Les Cafés politiques et littéraires de Paris.* (Dentu, 1874)
Levallois, Jules, *Mémoires d'un Critique.* (À la Librairie illustrée, s.d.)
Le Vavasseur, Gustave, *Poésies complètes.* I. (Alphonse Lemerre, 1888)
Lloyd, Rosemary, *Baudelaire's literary criticism.* (Cambridge, Cambridge University Press, 1981)
Loncke, Joycelynne, *Baudelaire et la musique.* (Éditions A.–G. Nizet, 1975)
Lyonnet, Henry, *Dictionnaire des Comédiens Français (Ceux d'hier).* 2 tomes. (E. Jorel, Librairie théâtrale, 1908)
Maillard, Firmin, *Les Derniers Bohèmes. Henri Murger et son temps.* (Sartorius, 1874)
—— *La Cité des intellectuels.* (H. Daragon, 1905)
Marielle, C.-P., *Répertoire de l'École impériale polytechnique.* (Mallet–Bachelier, 1855)
Massin, Jean, *Baudelaire 'entre Dieu et Satan.'* (René Julliard, 1945)
Mauclair, Camille, *Charles Baudelaire. Sa vie – son art – sa légende.* (Maison du Livre, 1917)
Mauriac, François, *Mémoires intérieurs.* (Flammarion, 1959)
Mauron, Charles, *Le dernier Baudelaire.* (José Corti, 1966)
May, Gita, *Diderot et Baudelaire. Critiques d'art.* (Genève, Librairie E. Droz, 1957)
Ménard, Louis, *Rêveries d'un Païen Mystique.* Préface de Maurice Barrès. (A. Durel, 1909)
Mendès, Catulle, *La Légende du Parnasse contemporain.* (Bruxelles, Brancart, 1884)
—— *Le Mouvement poétique français de 1867 à 1900.* (Imprimerie Nationale, 1903)
Mermaz, Louis, *Un Amour de Baudelaire. Madame Sabatier.* (Éditions j'ai lu, 1967)
Milner, Max, *Baudelaire. Enfer ou ciel, qu'importe?* (Plon, 1967)
Mondor, Henri, *Vie de Mallarmé.* 16e édition. (NRF, Gallimard, 1941)
—— *Eugène Lefébure. Sa vie – ses lettres à Mallarmé.* (NRF, Gallimard, 1951)
Monselet, Charles, *La Lorgnette littéraire.* (Poulet-Malassis et de Broise, 1857)
—— *Curiosités littéraires et bibliographiques.* (Librairie des Bibliophiles, 1890)
Mouquet, Jules, et Bandy, W. T., *Baudelaire en 1848. La Tribune Nationale.* (Éditions Émile-Paul frères, 1946)
Nadar, *Charles Baudelaire intime. Le Poète vierge.* (A. Blaizot, 1911)
Nicolardot, Louis, *L'Impeccable Théophile Gautier et les sacrilèges romantiques.* (Tresse, 1883)
Nnadi, Joseph E., *Visions de l'Afrique dans l'œuvre de Baudelaire.* (Yaoundé (Cameroun), Editions CLÉ, 1980)
O'Callaghan, J. C., *History of the Irish Brigades in the Service of France.* (Glasgow, Cameron & Ferguson, 1870)
Parménie, A., et Bonnier de la Chapelle, C., *Histoire d'un éditeur et de ses auteurs. P.-J. Hetzel (Stahl).* (Albin Michel, 1953)
Peat, Anthony B. North, *Gossip from Paris during the Second Empire.* Correspondence (1864–1869) of Anthony B. North Peat, Attaché au Cabinet du Ministre de l'Intérieur and, later, Attaché au Conseil d'État. Selected and arranged by A. R. Waller. (Kegan Paul, 1903)
Peter, René, *Vie secrète de l'Académie Française.* Cinquième période. (Librairie des Champs-Élysées, 1940)

Peyre, Henri, *Louis Ménard (1822–1901)*. (New Haven, Yale University Press, 1932)
—— *Connaissance de Baudelaire*. (Librairie José Corti, 1951)
—— (ed.) *Baudelaire*. A collection of critical essays. (Englewood Cliffs, New Jersey, Prentice-Hall, 1962)
Pia, Pascal, *Baudelaire*. (Écrivains de toujours, Éditions du Seuil, 1952)
Pich, Edgard, *Leconte de Lisle. Articles-Préfaces-Discours*. (Société d'Édition 'Les Belles Lettres,' 1971)
Pichois, Claude, *Le vrai visage du Général Aupick*. (Mercure de France, 1955)
—— (ed.) *Baudelaire. Études et Témoignages*. (Neuchâtel, Éditions de la Baconnière, 1967)
—— (ed.) *Lettres à Eugène Crépet*. Textes retrouvés par Eric Dayre et publiés par Claude Pichois. (José Corti, 1991)
Pichois, Claude, et Pichois, Vincenette, *Lettres à Charles Baudelaire*. Publiées par Claude Pichois avec la collaboration de Vincenette Pichois. Études Baudelairiennes IV–V. (Neuchâtel, Éditions de la Baconnière, 1973)
—— *Armand Fraisse sur Baudelaire, 1857–1869*. Textes recueillis et présentés par Claude et Vincenette Pichois. (Gembloux, Éditions J. Duculot, S. A, 1973)
Pichois, Claude, et Ruchon, François, *Iconographie de Charles Baudelaire*. Recueillie et commentée par Claude Pichois et François Ruchon. (Genève, Pierre Cailler, 1960)
Pichois, Claude, et Ziegler, Jean, *Baudelaire*. (Julliard, 1987)
Pinard, Ernest, *Mon Journal*. Tome 1er. (E. Dentu, 1892)
Pinet, G., *Histoire de l'École Polytechnique*. (Librairie polytechnique Baudry & Cie., Éditeurs, 1887)
Poggenburg, Raymond, *Charles Baudelaire. Une Micro-histoire*. (Librairie José Corti, 1987)
Poizat, Alfred, *Le Symbolisme de Baudelaire à Claudel*. (La Renaissance du Livre, 1919)
Pommier, Jean, *Dans les chemins de Baudelaire*. (Librairie José Corti, 1945)
Pontmartin, Armand de, *Nouvelles Semaines littéraires*. (Michel Lévy, 1863)
Porché, François, *La Vie douloureuse de Charles Baudelaire*. (Plon, 1926)
—— *Baudelaire et la Présidente*. (Genève, Éditions du Milieu du Monde, 1941)
—— *Baudelaire. Histoire d'une âme*. (Flammarion, 1944)
Poulet, Georges, *Qui était Baudelaire?* Essai critique, . . . précédé de notices documentaires par Robert Kopp. (Genève, Éditions d'Art Albert Skira, 1969)
Prévost, Jean, *Baudelaire*. Essai sur l'inspiration et la création poétiques. (Mercure de France, 1953)
Prévost, M., et Amat, Roman d', *Dictionnaire de biographie française*. Sous la direction de M. Prévost et Roman d'Amat. Tome IV. (Librairie Letouzey et Ané, 1948)
Prinet, Jean, et Dilasser, Antoinette, *Nadar*. (Armand Colin, 1966)
Profizi, Jacques, *Charles Baudelaire*. Essai psychanalytique d'après *Les Fleurs du mal*. (Les Éditions de l'Athanor, 1974)
Proust, Antonin, *Édouard Manet. Souvenirs*. Publiés par A. Barthélemy. (Librairie Renouard, 1913)
Proust, Marcel, *Contre Sainte-Beuve*. Suivi de nouveaux mélanges. Préface de Bernard de Fallois. (NRF, Gallimard, 1954)

Quennell, Peter, *Baudelaire and the Symbolists*. Five Essays. (Chatto & Windus, 1929)

Quesnel, Michel, *Baudelaire solaire et clandestin*. Les données singulières de la sensibilité et de l'imaginaire dans *Les Fleurs du mal*. (Presses Universitaires de France, 1987)

Quinet, Edgar, *Histoire d'un enfant*. (Hachette, 1903)

Raitt, A. W., *Prosper Mérimée*. (Eyre & Spottiswoode, 1970)

—— *The Life of Villiers de l'Isle-Adam*. (Oxford, The Clarendon Press, 1981)

Raymond, Marcel, *De Baudelaire au surréalisme*. Essai sur le mouvement poétique contemporain. (Éditions R.-A. Corrêa, 1933)

Raynaud, Ernest, *Baudelaire et la Religion du Dandysme*. (Mercure de France, 1918)

—— *Charles Baudelaire*. (Librairie Garnier frères, 1922)

Régnier, H. de, *Baudelaire et LES FLEURS DU MAL*. (Les Presses Françaises, 1925)

Reymond, Jean, *Albert Glatigny*. La Vie – l'Homme – le Poète. (Droz, 1936)

Reynold, Gonzague de, *Charles Baudelaire*. (Les Éditions G. Crès & Cie, 1920)

Ricault d'Héricault, Charles de, *Murger et son coin*. Souvenirs très vagabonds et très personnels. (No publisher given, 1896)

Richardson, Joanna, *Théophile Gautier. His Life and Times*. (Max Reinhardt, 1958)

—— *Verlaine*. (Weidenfeld & Nicolson, 1971)

—— *Judith Gautier. A Biography*. (Quartet Books, 1986)

Richer, Jean, et Ruff, Marcel A., *Les Derniers mois de Charles Baudelaire, et la publication posthume de ses œuvres*. Correspondances – documents présentés par Jean Richer et Marcel A. Ruff. (A.-G. Nizet, 1976)

Robb, Graham, *Le Corsaire-Satan en Silhouette*. (Nashville, Tennessee. Publications du Centre W. T. Bandy d'Études baudelairiennes, 1985)

Rodenbach, Georges, *L'Élite*. (Bibliothèque Charpentier, 1899)

Rude, Maxime, *Confidences d'un journaliste*. (André Sagnier, 1876)

Ruff, Marcel A., *Baudelaire. L'Homme et l'œuvre*. (Hatier-Boivin, 1955)

—— *L'Esprit du mal et l'esthétique baudelairienne*. (Librairie Armand Colin, 1955)

Sainte-Beuve, C.-A., *Correspondance générale*. Recueillie, classée et annotée par Jean Bonnerot [et par son fils Alain Bonnerot]. 18 tomes. (Stock; Privat; Didier, 1935–1977)

Sartre, Jean-Paul, *Baudelaire*. Précédé d'une note de Michel Leiris. (NRF, Gallimard, 1947)

Schérer, Edmond, *Études sur la littérature contemporaine*. VIII. (Calmann Lévy, 1885)

Séché, Léon, *La Jeunesse dorée sous Louis-Philippe*. (Mercure de France, 1910)

Seillière, Ernest, *Baudelaire*. (Librairie Armand Colin, 1931)

Servières, Georges, *Richard Wagner jugé en France*. (Librairie Henry du Parc, s.d.)

Shanks, Lewis Piaget, *Baudelaire. Flesh and Spirit*. (Noel Douglas, 1930)

Sherard, Robert Harborough, *Twenty Years in Paris*. (Hutchinson, 1905)

—— *Modern Paris. Some sidelights on its inner life*. (T. Werner Laurie, 1911)

Soupault, Philippe, *Baudelaire*. (Les Éditions Rieder, 1931)

Souriau, Maurice, *Histoire du Parnasse*. (Éditions Spes, 1929)

Spoelberch de Lovenjoul, Charles, Vte de *Les Lundis d'un chercheur*. (Calmann Lévy, 1894)

—— *Bibliographie et littérature*. (Trouvailles d'un bibliophile.) (Henri Daragon, 1903)

[Spoel berch de loven joul] *Charles Baudelaire. Souvenirs – correspondances. Bibliographie. Suivie de pièces inédites.* (René Pincebourde, 1872)

Starkie, Enid, *Baudelaire.* (Faber and Faber, 1957)

Suarès, André, *Trois grands vivants.* Cervantès, Tolstoï, Baudelaire. (Éditions Bernard Grasset, 1938)

Symons, Arthur, *Charles Baudelaire. A Study.* (Elkin Mathews, 1920)

Tabarant, A., *La vie artistique au temps de Baudelaire.* (Mercure de France, 1963)

Tailhade, Laurent, *Quelques fantômes de jadis.* (L'Édition française illustrée, 1920)

Thibaudet, Albert, *Intérieurs. Baudelaire – Fromentin – Amiel.* (Plon, 1924)

Thouvenel, Édouard, *La Grèce du Roi Othon.* Correspondance de M. Thouvenel avec sa famille et ses amis. Recueillie et publiée avec notes et index biographique par L. Thouvenel. (Calmann Lévy, 1890)

Tourneux, Maurice, *Auguste Poulet-Malassis.* Notes et souvenirs intimes. (Aux Bureaux de L'ARTISTE, 1893)

Trial, Dr. Raymond, *La Maladie de Baudelaire.* Étude médico-psychologique. (Jouve et Cie, 1926)

Troubat, Jules, *Souvenirs du dernier secrétaire de Sainte-Beuve.* (Calmann-Lévy, 1890)

—— *Sainte-Beuve et Champfleury.* Lettres de Champfleury à sa mère, à son frère et à divers. (Mercure de France, 1908)

Turnell, Martin, *Baudelaire. A Study of his Poetry.* (Hamish Hamilton, 1953)

Unwin, Timothy A., *Flaubert et Baudelaire.* Affinités spirituelles et esthétiques. (A.-G. Nizet, 1982)

Urruty, Jean, *Le Voyage de Baudelaire aux Mascareignes.* (Port-Louis, 1968. No publisher given.)

Vallès, Jules, *Les Enfants du peuple.* (Administration du journal LA LANTERNE, 1879)

Vandérem, Fernand, *Baudelaire et Sainte-Beuve.* (Librairie Henri Leclerc, 1917)

—— *Le Miroir des Lettres.* 1re série. 1918. (Flammarion, s.d.)

—— *Le Miroir des Lettres.* 4e série. (Flammarion, 1922)

Vanzype, Gustave, *Les Frères Stevens.* (Bruxelles, Nouvelle Société d'Éditions, 1936)

Verlaine, Paul, *Œuvres complètes.* Tome II. (Messein, 1923)

—— *Œuvres complètes.* Tome V. (Messein, s.d.)

—— *Œuvres posthumes.* 3 tomes. (Messein, 1922–1929)

Vieil Écrivain, Un, *Profils critiques et biographiques des sénateurs . . .* (Garnier frères, 1852)

Villemer, Marquis de (Charles Yriarte), *Les Portraits cosmopolites.* (E. Lachaud, 1870)

Villemessant, J.-H.-A.-D. de, *Mémoires d'un journaliste.* 6 tomes. (Dentu, 1872–1878)

Villiers de l'Isle-Adam, Auguste, *Correspondance générale et documents inédits.* Édition recueillie, classée et présentée par Joseph Bollery. 2 tomes. (Mercure de France, 1962)

Vivier, Robert, *L'Originalité de Baudelaire.* (Bruxelles, Publications de l'Académie royale de langue et de littérature françaises, 1926)

Vouga, Daniel, *Baudelaire et Joseph de Maistre.* (Librairie José Corti, 1957)

Vuillaume, Maxime, *Mes Cahiers rouges.* 12e cahier de la 9e série. II. Quand nous faisions le 'Père Duchêne'. Mars–avril–mai 1871. (Cahiers de la Quinzaine, 1908)

Williams, Roger L. *The Horror of Life.* (Weidenfeld & Nicolson, 1980)

Yvan, Dr Melchior, *La Chine et la presqu'île malaise.* (Boulé, 1850)

—— *De France en Chine.* (L. Hachette, 1855)

Ziegler, Jean, *Gautier–Baudelaire. Un carré de dames. Pomaré, Marix, Bébé, Sisina.* (A.-G. Nizet, 1977)

II

ARTICLES, PAMPHLETS AND CATALOGUES

Abé, Yoshio, *Baudelaire et Maxime du Camp.* (REVUE D'HISTOIRE LITTÉRAIRE DE LA FRANCE, avril–juin 1967, 273–85)

Alméras, Henri d', *La littérature au café sous le Second Empire.* (LES ŒUVRES LIBRES, septembre 1932, 337 sqq.)

Anon. *Fragment pour servir à l'histoire de Lyon, pendant les événements d'avril 1834.* (REVUE DU LYONNAIS, tome 3, 1846, 216–32)

—— *Mobilier artistique. Dépendant de la succession de Madame S^{xxx}* (Hôtel Drouot, 1890)

—— *Hôtel Drouot. Précieux Manuscrits et Lettres autographes.* 1re partie. 29 mai 1968. (Hôtel Drouot, 1968)

—— *Chronique.* (L'ARTISTE, 18 mai 1845)

—— *Revue critique des livres nouveaux.* Mars 1857. (Unidentified cutting from Geneva periodical. Taylor Institution, Oxford)

—— *Charles Baudelaire.* (LA PLUME, No 139, 1er février 1895, 72–4)

—— *Les Journaux.* (MERCURE DE FRANCE, 1er octobre 1924, 229–33)

—— *Baudelaire.* (LE CURIEUX, juin 1886, 95–6)

—— *La maladie et la mort de Baudelaire.* (LA CHRONIQUE MÉDICALE, 1er décembre 1907, 770–2)

Antoine, G., et Pichois, Claude, *Sainte-Beuve juge de Stendhal et de Baudelaire.* (REVUE DES SCIENCES HUMAINES, janvier-mars 1957, 7–34)

Arnould, A., *Edgar Poe. (Fin.)* (REVUE MODERNE, 1er juillet 1865, 68–90)

Asselineau, Charles, *LES FLEURS DU MAL par Charles Baudelaire.* (REVUE FRANÇAISE. Tome X. Août–septembre–octobre 1857. Aux bureaux de la REVUE FRANÇAISE, 1857)

Augustin-Thierry, A., *La Fin de la 'Présidente'.* (LE TEMPS, 23 août 1932)

Austin, Lloyd James, *Baudelaire et l'énergie spirituelle.* (REVUE DES SCIENCES HUMAINES, janvier–mars 1957, 35–42)

—— *Mallarmé disciple de Baudelaire: 'Le Parnasse contemporain'.* (REVUE D'HISTOIRE LITTÉRAIRE DE LA FRANCE, avril–juin 1967, 437–49)

—— *Baudelaire et Delacroix.* (Actes du Colloque de Nice. Annales de la faculté des lettres et sciences humaines de Nice, Minard, 1968. 13–23)

Auzas, Auguste, *Lettres de Mme Veuve Aupick à Charles Asselineau.* (MERCURE DE FRANCE, 16 septembre 1912, 225–57)

Babuts, Nicolae, *Baudelaire et J.G.F.* (Nashville, Tennessee. BULLETIN BAUDELAIRIEN, Tome 14, Hiver 1979, No 2, 3–5)

Badesco, Luc, *Baudelaire et la revue JEAN RAISIN. La première publication du VIN DES CHIFFONNIERS.* (REVUE DES SCIENCES HUMAINES, janvier–mars 1957, 55–85)

Bandy, W. T., *Baudelaire et Croly. La vérité sur LE JEUNE ENCHANTEUR.* (MERCURE DE FRANCE, 1er février 1950, 233–47)
—— *Edgar Poe et la dédicace des FLEURS DU MAL.* (REVUE DES SCIENCES HUMAINES, janvier–mars 1957, 97–100)
—— *Le Chiffonnier de Baudelaire.* (REVUE D'HISTOIRE LITTÉRAIRE DE LA FRANCE, octobre–décembre 1957, 580–4)
—— *Amédée Pichot: Premier Traducteur de Poe.* (Nashville, Tennessee. BULLETIN BAUDELAIRIEN, 31 août 1966, tome 2, No 1.)
—— *Baudelaire et Poe: Vers une nouvelle mise au point.* (REVUE D'HISTOIRE LITTÉRAIRE DE LA FRANCE, avril–juin 1967, 329–34)
—— *L'Universalité de Baudelaire.* (Actes du Colloque de Nice. Annales de la faculté des lettres et sciences humaines de Nice, Minard, 1963, 25–30)
Bandy, W. T., and Pia, Pascal, *Le Tombeau de François Baudelaire.* (Nashville, Tennessee. BULLETIN BAUDELAIRIEN, 9 avril 1968. Tome 3, No 2, 10–11)
Bandy, W. T., and Pichois, Claude, *Du nouveau sur la jeunesse de Baudelaire. Une lettre inédite de Banville.* (REVUE D'HISTOIRE LITTÉRAIRE DE LA FRANCE, janvier–mars 1965, 70–77)
Banville, Théodore de, *Charles Baudelaire.* (GALERIE CONTEMPORAINE, LITTÉRAIRE, ARTISTIQUE, 1876.) Press-cutting, pages un-numbered. Taylor Institution, Oxford.
Barral, Georges, *Souvenirs sur Baudelaire. La Maladie et la Mort de Baudelaire.* (Bruxelles, LE PETIT BLEU, 17 octobre 1907)
[Barthou, Louis], *Bibliothèque de M. Louis Barthou.* 4 parties. (Auguste Blaizot, 1935–7)
Bellet, Roger, et Scheler, Lucien, *Vallès et Baudelaire.* (EUROPE, avril–mai 1967, 216–22)
Blanc, Paul, *La Mort de Firmin Maillard.* (Nashville, Tennessee. BULLETIN BAUDELAIRIEN, Hiver 1978, Tome 3, No 2)
Blin, Georges, *La Conspiration.* Texte inédit de Charles Baudelaire. (ESPRIT, février 1951, 161–8)
Bonnefoy, Yves, *Les Fleurs du mal.* (MERCURE DE FRANCE, 1er septembre 1954, 40–7)
Bounoure, Gabriel, *Les Écrits intimes de Baudelaire.* (MERCURE DE FRANCE, 1er octobre 1955, 255–70)
Boureau, Yvon, *L'État civil de Marie Daubrun.* (REVUE D'HISTOIRE LITTÉRAIRE DE LA FRANCE, janvier–mars 1958, 59–61)
Bousquet, J., *Lettre sur Baudelaire.* (REVUE DES SCIENCES HUMAINES, janvier–mars 1957, 5–6)
Bricon, Étienne, *Baudelaire et la mort* (LE GAULOIS, 4 novembre 1921)
Burton, Richard D. E., *Baudelaire and the Agony of the Second Republic: 'Spleen' (LXXV) ('Pluviôse, irrité . . . ')* (THE MODERN LANGUAGE REVIEW, July 1986. Vol. 81, Part 3, 600–11)
[Burty, Philippe], *Catalogue de la bibliothèque de M. Philippe Burty.* Précédé d'une préface par M. Maurice Tourneux. (Émile Paul, L. Huard et Guillemin, 1891)
[Cabanès, Dr A.] *Lettre d'Albert Glatigny sur la maladie de Baudelaire.* Communiquée par le Dr Cabanès. (L'INTERMÉDIAIRE DES CHERCHEURS ET DES CURIEUX, 20 mars 1913, 376)

Cassin, Yolande, *Le Procès des FLEURS DU MAL.* (EUROPE, avril–mai 1967, 183–97)

Caussy, Fernand, *La Jeunesse de Baudelaire.* (LES ANNALES ROMANTIQUES, tome viii, 1911, 376–82)

Cellier, Léon, *'Les Phares' de Baudelaire.* Étude de structure. (REVUE DES SCIENCES HUMAINES, janvier–mars 1966, 97–103)

—— *Baudelaire et George Sand.* (REVUE D'HISTOIRE LITTÉRAIRE DE LA FRANCE, avril–juin 1967, 239–59)

—— *Baudelaire et l'enfance.* (Actes du Colloque de Nice. Annales de la faculté des lettres et sciences humaines de Nice, Minard, 1968. 67–77)

[Champfleury], *Catalogue des autographes composant la Collection Champfleury.* (Étienne Charavay, 1891)

Charpentier, John, *La poésie britannique et Baudelaire.* (MERCURE DE FRANCE, 15 avril 1921, 289–332)

—— *La poésie britannique et Baudelaire.* (MERCURE DE FRANCE, 1er mai 1921, 635–75)

Cladel, Léon, *Souvenirs littéraires. Chez feu mon maître.* (LA REVUE ROSE, août 1887)

Claretie, Jules, *Charles Baudelaire. L'homme.* (LES ANNALES POLITIQUES ET LITTÉRAIRES, 26 octobre 1902)

—— *Souvenirs d'un Académicien.* Mémoires inédites. (LES ŒUVRES LIBRES, janvier 1934, 6–132)

Clavel, Bernard, *Compagnon de voyage.* (EUROPE, avril–mai 1967, 107–12)

Contades, Cte G. de, *Auguste Poulet-Malassis.* (LE LIVRE, 10 mars 1884, 72 sqq.)

Couturier, Claude, *Lettres de Madame Aupick à Théodore de Banville.* À propos du cinquantenaire de Baudelaire. (MERCURE DE FRANCE, 1er septembre 1917, 34–43)

Crépet, Jacques, *Baudelaire et Jeanne Duval.* (LA PLUME, No 216, 15 avril 1898, 242–4)

—— *Les Derniers Jours de Charles Baudelaire. Lettres de Charles Asselineau à Poulet-Malassis.* (BULLETIN DU BIBLIOPHILE, 1er février 1925, 74–84)

—— *Les Derniers Jours de Charles Baudelaire. Lettres de Charles Asselineau à Poulet-Malassis.* (BULLETIN DU BIBLIOPHILE, 1er mars 1925, 155–60)

—— *Les Derniers Jours de Charles Baudelaire. Lettres de Charles Asselineau à Poulet-Malassis.* (BULLETIN DU BIBLIOPHILE, avril 1925, 198–206)

—— *Quelques billets de Poulet-Malassis.* (LE FIGARO, 26 août 1933)

—— *Miettes baudelairiennes.* (MERCURE DE FRANCE, 15 septembre 1935, 514–38)

—— *Quelques documents inédits sur Baudelaire.* (MERCURE DE FRANCE, 15 mars 1937, 629–36)

—— *Miettes baudelairiennes. Baudelaire et Nadar. Deux anecdotes.* (MERCURE DE FRANCE, 15 juin 1937, 525 sqq.)

—— *À propos de FANNY. Baudelaire et Feydeau.* (BULLETIN DU BIBLIOPHILE, 20 mai 1938, 198–208)

—— *Documents baudelairiens. Le mot d'une petite énigme.* (MERCURE DE FRANCE, 1er mai 1939, 700–705)

—— *Baudelaire et Duranty.* (MERCURE DE FRANCE, 15 août 1939, 66–72)

—— *Miettes baudelairiennes.* (MERCURE DE FRANCE, 1er février 1940, 321–35)

[Crépet, Jacques] *LE PONT DES SOUPIRS de Thomas Hood. Traduction inédite par Baudelaire.* (MERCURE DE FRANCE, 1er avril 1949, 599–607)

—— *Les Derniers Jours de Charles Baudelaire. Lettres inédites de Madame Aupick à Poulet-Malassis.* (NOUVELLE REVUE FRANÇAISE, 1er novembre 1932, 641–71)

—— *Quelques documents inédits sur Baudelaire.* (MERCURE DE FRANCE, 15 mars 1937, 629–636)

—— *Baudelairiana. Lettres adressées ou relatives à Baudelaire.* (BULLETIN DU BIBLIOPHILE, 20 décembre 1939, 447–55)

—— *Baudelairiana. Lettres adressées ou relatives à Baudelaire.* (BULLETIN DU BIBLIOPHILE. Série de guerre, 1940–1945, 10–17; 46–52; 86–90; 139–44; 200–16)

—— *Baudelairiana* (BULLETIN DU BIBLIOPHILE, janvier 1946, 34–45)

—— *Baudelairiana. Lettres adressées ou relatives à Baudelaire.* (BULLETIN DU BIBLIOPHILE, février 1946, 58–67)

—— *Baudelairiana. Lettres adressées ou relatives à Baudelaire.* (BULLETIN DU BIBLIOPHILE, mars 1946, 123–7)

Crépet, Jacques, et Pichois, Claude, *Petites Énigmes baudelairiennes.* (MERCURE DE FRANCE, 1er juillet 1952, 432–47)

Daruty de Grandpré, Marquis, *Baudelaire et Jeanne Duval.* (LA PLUME, No 103, 1er août 1893, 329–33)

—— *Baudelaire et Jeanne Duval.* (LA PLUME, No 104, 15 août 1893, 354–5)

Daudet, Léon, *Baudelaire à la Salle Pleyel.* (ACTION FRANÇAISE, 8 juin 1931)

Deauville, Max, *Le Vicomte de Spoelberch de Lovenjoul.* (MERCURE DE FRANCE, 16 décembre 1907, 646–64)

Dedet, Dr Christian, '*Sois sage, ô ma douleur . . .*' (LE FIGARO LITTÉRAIRE, 9 mars 1967)

Delahaye, Louis, *Le Tableau que personne ne veut voir.* (MERCURE DE FRANCE, 1er octobre 1955, 292–8)

Delesalle, Jean-François, *Miettes baudelairiennes.* (REVUE D'HISTOIRE LIT-TÉRAIRE DE LA FRANCE, janvier–mars 1963, 113–7)

Denux, Roger, *LE SPLEEN DE PARIS.* (EUROPE, avril–mai 1967. 112–9)

Dérieux, Henry, *La Plasticité de Baudelaire et ses rapports avec Théophile Gautier.* (MERCURE DE FRANCE, 1er octobre 1917, 416–31)

Desjardins, J.-F., *Les Origines familiales de Baudelaire.* (REVUE DES DEUX MONDES, 15 décembre 1964, 569–78)

Dufay, Pierre, *Le Procès des FLEURS DU MAL.* (MERCURE DE FRANCE, 1er avril 1921, 84–103

—— *Poulet-Malassis à Bruxelles.* (MERCURE DE FRANCE, 15 novembre 1929 38–83)

—— *Dix-huit lettres de Félicien Rops à Poulet-Malassis.* (MERCURE DE FRANCE, 1er octobre 1933, 44–83)

—— *Un ami de Baudelaire: M. Ancelle, beau-père d'un fils du duc de Berry.* (MERCURE DE FRANCE, 15 octobre 1934, 421–5)

—— *Le Monument de Charles Baudelaire.* (MERCURE DE FRANCE, 15 mai 1937)

Duflo, P. *Baudelaire et Constantin Guys. Trois lettres inédites.* (REVUE D'HISTOIRE LITTÉRAIRE DE LA FRANCE, juillet–août 1983, 599–603)

Durand, Charles, *Charles Baudelaire.* (L'ILLUSTRATION, 14 septembre 1867)

Duval, Jean, *Pages sur Baudelaire.* (EUROPE, avril–mai 1967, 31–41)

Eigeldinger, Marc, *Le Symbolisme solaire dans la poésie de Baudelaire.* (REVUE D'HISTOIRE LITTÉRAIRE DE LA FRANCE, avril–juin 1967, 357–74)

Escholier, Raymond, *Baudelaire carabinier.* (EUROPE, avril–mai 1967, 46–52)

Fagus, *Tribune libre.* (LA PLUME, 15 février 1902)

Fairlie, Alison, *Quelques remarques sur les PETITS POÈMES EN PROSE.* (Actes du colloque de Nice. Annales de la faculté des lettres et sciences humaines de Nice, Minard, 1968, 89–97)

Ferran, André, *L'Alchimie amoureuse de Baudelaire.* (L'ARCHER, 3 mars 1930)

Flottes, Pierre, *Les Deux Procès des FLEURS DU MAL.* (REVUE DES SCIENCES HUMAINES, janvier–mars 1957, 101–10)

Fongaro, Antoine, *Sources de Baudelaire.* (REVUE DES SCIENCES HUMAINES, janvier–mars 1957, 89–96)

Fontainas, André, *Baudelaire.* (MERCURE DE FRANCE, 1er avril 1921, 5–27)

Fouchet, Max-Pol, *Baudelaire en question.* (EUROPE, avril–mai 1967, 3–15)

Fournier, Albert, *Les 44 domiciles de Baudelaire.* (EUROPE, avril–mai 1967, 263–75)

Gamarra, Pierre, *L'inquiétude critique.* (EUROPE, avril–mai 1967, 24–30)

Gaucheron, Jacques, *Poulet-Malassis éditeur et républicain.* (EUROPE, avril–mai 1967, 176–82)

Gautier, Félix-François, *La Vie amoureuse de Baudelaire.* (MERCURE DE FRANCE, janvier 1903, 46–86)

—— *Charles Baudelaire.* (LA PLUME, 1er mars–1er juin 1903.)

—— *Documents sur Baudelaire.* (MERCURE DE FRANCE, 15 janvier 1905, 190–204)

—— *Documents sur Baudelaire.* (MERCURE DE FRANCE, 1er février 1905, 329–46)

—— *Documents sur Baudelaire. I. Baudelaire et Barbey d'Aurevilly.* (MERCURE DE FRANCE, 1er mars 1906, 5–21)

—— *Documents sur Baudelaire. II. Baudelaire et la très belle. III. Baudelaire et Madame Paul Meurice.* (MERCURE DE FRANCE, 15 mars 1906, 202–18)

—— *Documents sur Baudelaire. IV. Baudelaire, ses amis, ses ennuis.* (MERCURE DE FRANCE, 1er avril 1906, 367–81)

Gendreau, Georges, et Pichois, Claude, *Autour d'un billet inédit de Charles Baudelaire.* (REVUE D'HISTOIRE LITTÉRAIRE DE LA FRANCE, octobre–décembre 1957, 574–8)

Gide, André, *Baudelaire et M. Faguet.* (LA NOUVELLE REVUE FRANÇAISE, 1910, tome II, 499–518)

Gilman, Margaret, *Baudelaire and Thomas Hood.* (THE ROMANIC REVIEW, XXVI, 1935, 240–44)

[Glatigny, Albert], *Lettres d'Albert Glatigny à Théodore de Banville.* (MERCURE DE FRANCE, 15 mars 1923, 601–30)

Goudall, Louis, *Revue littéraire.* (LE FIGARO, 4 novembre 1855)

Gourmont, Rémy de, *Baudelaire et le songe d'Athalie.* (MERCURE DE FRANCE, 1er juillet 1905, 25–30)

Grojnowski, Daniel, *Baudelaire et Pierre Dupont. La source de l'inspiration de L'INVITATION AU VOYAGE.* (EUROPE, avril–mai 1967, 228–33)

Guinard, Paul, *Baudelaire, le Musée Espagnol et Goya.* (REVUE D'HISTOIRE LITTÉRAIRE DE LA FRANCE, avril–juin 1967, 310–28)

Guiral, Pierre, et Pichois, Claude, *L'ALBATROS de Polydore Bounin*. (REVUE D'HISTOIRE LITTÉRAIRE DE LA FRANCE, octobre–décembre 1957, 570–4)

Hérisson, Charles D., *Le Voyage de Baudelaire dans l'Inde. Histoire d'une légende*. (MERCURE DE FRANCE, octobre 1956, 273–95)

—— *Le voyage de Baudelaire*. (MERCURE DE FRANCE, avril 1959, 637–73)

—— *À propos de Baudelaire en 1841 et 1842*. (MERCURE DE FRANCE, mars 1960, 449–75)

—— *À propos des 'Lettres inédites aux siens.' Quelques aspects de la vie de Baudelaire de 1839 à 1842*. (REVUE DES SCIENCES HUMAINES, janvier–mars 1969, 57–71)

Hignard, Henri, *Charles Baudelaire. Sa Vie, son œuvre, souvenirs personnels*. (REVUE DU LYONNAIS, juin 1892, 418–34)

Hughes, Randolph, *Baudelaire et Balzac*. (MERCURE DE FRANCE, 1er novembre 1934, 476–518)

Jal, M., *Lyon en 1835*. (REVUE DU LYONNAIS, 1836, tome 3, 14 sqq.)

[Janin, Jules], *Catalogue des livres rares et précieux composant la bibliothèque de M. Jules Janin*. Avec une préface par M. Louis Ratisbonne. (Adolphe Labitte, 1877)

Jarry, Paul, *La Présidente et le sculpteur Clésinger*. (FIGARO ARTISTIQUE, 21 février 1924)

J., C., *Courrier de Paris*. (L'ILLUSTRATION, JOURNAL UNIVERSEL. Undated press-cutting, early September 1867. Taylor Institution, Oxford.)

Jouve, Pierre-Jean, *LE SPLEEN DE PARIS*. (MERCURE DE FRANCE, 1er septembre 1954, 32–9)

—— *Anniversaire*. (REVUE D'HISTOIRE LITTÉRAIRE DE LA FRANCE, avril–juin 1967, 225–6)

Joxe, F., *Ville et modernité dans LES FLEURS DU MAL*. (EUROPE, avril–mai 1967, 139–62)

Kunel, Maurice, *Quatre jours avec Baudelaire*. (LES ŒUVRES LIBRES, no 132, juin 1932, 193–244)

Lacrosse, Baron de, *Éloge de M. le général de division Aupick, Sénateur, prononcé dans la séance du 13 mars 1858*. (Ch. Lahure, 1858)

Larroutis, M., *Une source de L'INVITATION AU VOYAGE*. (REVUE D'HISTOIRE LITTÉRAIRE DE LA FRANCE, octobre–décembre 1957, 585–6)

Leakey, F. W., *Pour une étude chronologique des FLEURS DU MAL. 'Harmonie du soir'*. (REVUE D'HISTOIRE LITTÉRAIRE DE LA FRANCE, avril–juin 1967, 343–56)

Leconte de Lisle, Charles-Marie, *LES FLEURS DU MAL, par M. Ch. Baudelaire*. 2e édition. (REVUE EUROPÉENNE, 1er décembre 1861, 595–7)

Le Dantec, Yves-Gérard, *'Le Beau Navire' ou Baudelaire maritime*. (LE BEAU NAVIRE, 10 novembre 1934, 10–16)

—— *Un secret de Baudelaire. L'Héautontimorouménos et l'énigme de J.G.F.* (MERCURE DE FRANCE, avril 1958, 676–90)

Lemer, Julien, *Quelques autographes intimes de Ch. Baudelaire*. (LE LIVRE, 10 mai 1888, 140 sqq.)

Le Petit, Jules, *Notes sur Baudelaire*. (LA PLUME, no 101, 1er juillet 1893, 285–8)

Levaux, Léopold, *Les Masques de Baudelaire*. (LES CAHIERS DU JOURNAL DES POÈTES, 1938)

Lyons, Margaret, *Autour d'un billet de Baudelaire à Gautier.* (Nashville, Tennessee. BULLETIN BAUDELAIRIEN, Hiver 1978, Tome 13, no 2, 9–11.)

Madaule, Jacques, *Baudelaire et Claudel.* (EUROPE, avril–mai 1967, 197–204)

Magne, Émile, *Charles Baudelaire.* (LAROUSSE MENSUEL, no 196, juin 1923, 146–7)

Maire, Gilbert, *La Personnalité de Baudelaire et la critique biologique des FLEURS DU MAL.* (MERCURE DE FRANCE, 1er février 1910, 231–48)

Marix-Spire, Thérèse, *La femme Sand. George Sand et Baudelaire (documents inédits).* (EUROPE, avril–mai 1967, 205–16)

Mauron, Charles, *Le rire baudelairien.* (EUROPE, avril–mai 1967, 54–61)

Milhaud, Gérard, *Baudelaire au sortir de sa jeunesse.* (EUROPE, avril–mai 1967, 41–6)

Monselet, Charles, *Chronique.* (LE JOURNAL ILLUSTRÉ, 20–27 decembre 1868)

[Monselet, Charles], *Catalogue . . . d'une jolie collection de livres rares et curieux dont la plus grande partie provient de la bibliothèque d'un homme de lettres bien connu . . .* (René Pincebourde, 1971)

Mouquet, Jules, *Baudelaire: le constance et 'L'Invitation au Voyage'.* (MERCURE DE FRANCE, 1er mars 1934, 305–12)

Moussaye, Comte Gustave de la, *Les Couleurs et les sons.* (L'ARTISTE, 15 janvier 1853, 189–90)

—— *Harmonies des sensations.* (L'ARTISTE, 1er septembre 1853, 33–5)

—— *Les Couleurs et les sons.* (LA GRANDE REVUE, 25 juillet 1889, 193 sqq.)

Nouvion, Georges de, *La famille de Charles Baudelaire.* (Bulletin de la Société historique du VIe arrondissement de Paris. Année 1901. Siège social: Mairie du VIe arrondissement. Place Saint-Sulpice, Paris. [1901])

Orcibal, Jean, *Joseph-François Baudelaire était-il prêtre?* (REVUE D'HISTOIRE LITTÉRAIRE DE LA FRANCE, octobre–décembre 1958, 523–7)

Ourousoff, Prince Alexandre, *Le Tombeau de Charles Baudelaire.* (LA PLUME, no 148, 15 juin 1895, 267–9)

—— *Iconographie Baudelairienne.* (LA PLUME, no 174, 15 juillet 1896, 533–4)

—— *Extrait du volume 'Le Tombeau de Charles Baudelaire'.* Notes pour une iconographie du poète. (LA PLUME, no 180, 15 octobre 1896, 634–41)

Parturier, Maurice, et Privat, Daniel, *Duranty et Baudelaire.* (BULLETIN DU BIBLIOPHILE, 1953, 1–13)

Patin, Jacques, *Charles Baudelaire et Louis Ménard.* (LE FIGARO, 14 décembre 1930)

Patty, James S., *Baudelaire et Hippolyte Babou.* (REVUE D'HISTOIRE LITTÉRAIRE DE LA FRANCE, avril–juin 1967. 260–72)

Pellegrin, Jean, *Baudelaire et les 'correspondances'.* (REVUE DES SCIENCES HUMAINES, janvier–mars 1966, 105–20)

Petit, Jacques, *Baudelaire et Barbey d'Aurevilly.* (REVUE D'HISTOIRE LITTÉRAIRE DE LA FRANCE, avril–juin 1967, 286–95)

Peyre, Henri, *Remarques sur le peu d'influence de Baudelaire.* (REVUE D'HISTOIRE LITTÉRAIRE DE LA FRANCE, avril–juin 1967, 424–36)

Pichois, Claude, *Lettres à Eugène Crépet sur la jeunesse de Baudelaire.* (MERCURE DE FRANCE, 1er septembre 1954, 5–31)

—— *Le Beau-père de Baudelaire.* Le Général Aupick. D'après des documents inédits. (MERCURE DE FRANCE, 1er juin 1955, 261–81)

[Pichois, Claude] *Le Beau-pere de Baudelaire. Le Général Aupick. D'après des documents inédits.* (MERCURE DE FRANCE, 1er juillet 1955, 472–90)

—— *Le Beau-père de Baudelaire. Le Général Aupick. D'après des documents inédits.* (MERCURE DE FRANCE, 1er août 1955, 651–74)

—— *La première poésie imprimée de Baudelaire.* (MERCURE DE FRANCE, 1er octobre 1955, 286–91)

—— *Documents nouveaux sur Charles Baudelaire.* (MERCURE DE FRANCE, février 1961, 259–76)

—— *Le père de Baudelaire fut-il janséniste?* (REVUE D'HISTOIRE LITTÉRAIRE DE LA FRANCE, octobre–décembre 1957, 565–8)

—— *De Poe à Dada.* (REVUE D'HISTOIRE LITTÉRAIRE DE LA FRANCE, avril–juin 1967, 450–60)

—— *'L'Ivresse du chiffonnier'.* (REVUE D'HISTOIRE LITTÉRAIRE DE LA FRANCE, octobre–décembre 1957, 584–5)

—— *Sur le prétendu voyage aux Indes.* (REVUE D'HISTOIRE LITTÉRAIRE DE LA FRANCE, octobre–décembre 1957, 568–70)

—— *Un ami de Baudelaire. Edmond Albert.* (ÉTUDES BAUDELAIRIENNES, 1971, II, 160 sqq.)

Pichois, Claude, et Kopp, Robert. *Baudelaire et l'opium. Une enquête à reprendre.* (EUROPE, avril–mai 1967, 61–79)

Pichois, Claude, et Ziegler, Jean, *Le Testament de Madame Aupick, 27 mars 1869–13 novembre 1870.* (Nashville, Tennessee. BULLETIN BAUDELAIRIEN, décembre 1985, 61–9)

Picon, Gaëtan, *Les derniers écrits esthétiques de Baudelaire* (MERCURE DE FRANCE, 1er octobre 1955, 271–85)

Pierrot, Roger, LES FLEURS DU MAL *avec envoi à Pincebourde.* (REVUE D'HISTOIRE LITTÉRAIRE DE LA FRANCE, octobre–décembre 1957, 578–80)

Poizat, Alfred, *Charles Baudelaire.* (LE CORRESPONDANT, 25 août 1917, 683–701)

Pommier, Jean, *Baudelaire et Michelet devant la jeune critique.* (REVUE D'HISTOIRE LITTÉRAIRE DE LA FRANCE, octobre–décembre 1957, 544–64)

—— *Du nouveau sur la Pension Bailly.* (REVUE D'HISTOIRE LITTÉRAIRE DE LA FRANCE, avril–juin 1967, 227–38)

Pommier, Jean, et Pichois, Claude, *Baudelaire et Renan à l'ombre de Saint-Sulpice.* (MERCURE DE FRANCE, septembre 1958, 164–8)

[Poulet-Malassis, Auguste], *Bibliothèque, portraits, dessins et autographes de feu M. Auguste Poulet-Malassis.* (J. Baur, 1878)

—— *A. Poulet-Malassis.* Catalogue de l'exposition organisée à la Bibliothèque d'Alençon pour le centième anniversaire de l'édition des *Fleurs du mal*, octobre 1957. (Alençon, Imprimerie Alençonnaise, 2, place Poulet-Malassis, 1957)

Proust, Marcel, *À propos de Baudelaire.* (NOUVELLE REVUE FRANÇAISE, tome XVI, janvier–juin 1921, 641–63)

Raitt, A. W., *On* LE SPLEEN DE PARIS. (NINETEENTH-CENTURY FRENCH STUDIES, Vol. 18, nos 1 and 2. Fall–winter 1989–1990, 150–164)

Raynaud, Ernest, *Baudelaire et Théophile Gautier.* (MERCURE DE FRANCE, 16 octobre 1917, 577–606)

—— *Les Parents de Baudelaire.* (MERCURE DE FRANCE, 15 août 1921, 106–31)

Richardson, Joanna, *Baudelaire and the origins of Feydeau's SYLVIE.* (FRENCH STUDIES BULLETIN, no 15, Summer 1985, 5–7)
—— *Colonel Aupick: an unpublished letter.* (FRENCH STUDIES BULLETIN, no 41, Winter 1991–2, 10–11)
—— *Dr Melchior Yvan: an influence on Baudelaire?* (FRENCH STUDIES, Vol. XLVI, October 1992. no 4, 406–11)
—— *L'Homme à la pipe.* Some Correspondence about Courbet's portrait of Baudelaire. (FRENCH STUDIES BULLETIN, no 45. Winter 1992–3, 9–11)
Robb, Graham, *Baudelaire à la comète.* (BULLETIN BAUDELAIRIEN, décembre 1990, 49–51)
—— *Baudelaire and the Case of the Empty Grave.* (FRENCH STUDIES BULLETIN, no 41. Winter 1991–2, 17–20)
[Rops, Félicien], *Lettres inédites à Félicien Rops.* (MERCURE DE FRANCE, I, 1905, 43)
Rosenmark, Solange, *Le voyage de Baudelaire à l'île Maurice.* (LA REVUE DE FRANCE, 15 septembre 1921)
Rousseaux, André, *L'avenir de Baudelaire.* (FIGARO LITTÉRAIRE, 27 juillet 1933)
—— *Baudelaire et sa mère.* (FRANCE ILLUSTRATION, 8 décembre 1945)
Ruff, Marcel A., *Baudelaire et le problème de la forme.* (REVUE DES SCIENCES HUMAINES, janvier–mars 1957, 43–54)
Sacy, S. de, *'Pauvre Belgique' ou l'échec parfait.* (MERCURE DE FRANCE, 1er juin 1955, 282–95)
Sagnes, Guy, *Baudelaire, Armand du Mesnil et la pétition de 1866. Lettres inédites.* (REVUE D'HISTOIRE LITTÉRAIRE DE LA FRANCE, avril–juin 1967, 296–309)
Savatier, Thierry-Richard, *À propos du portrait de Madame Sabatier par Charles Jalabert.* (Nashville, Tennessee. BULLETIN BAUDELAIRIEN, hiver 1981, tome 16, no 2, 6–9)
Schanne, Alexandre, *Les Souvenirs de Schaunard.* (LE FIGARO, 15 mai 1886)
Scouras, Dr Photis, *La Maladie et la mort de Baudelaire.* (ÆSCULAPE, I, janvier 1930, 29–35)
S., J., *Baudelairiana. Un Billet inédit de Baudelaire.* (BULLETIN DU BIBLIOPHILE, III, 1975, 274–5)
Séché, Léon, *Nécrologie. Ernest Prarond.* (ANNALES ROMANTIQUES, tome vi, novembre–décembre 1909, 392–4)
—— *La Présidente.* (ANNALES ROMANTIQUES, tome vii, novembre–décembre 1910, 357–71)
Spire, André, *Baudelaire esthéticien et précurseur du symbolisme.* (EUROPE, avril–mai 1967, 79–99)
Starobinski, Jean, *Sur quelques répondants allégoriques du poète.* (REVUE D'HISTOIRE LITTÉRAIRE DE LA FRANCE, avril–juin 1967, 402–12)
Suarès, André, *Baudelaire.* (LA GRANDE REVUE, 25 décembre 1911)
Tausserat-Radel, A., *Baudelaire intime. D'après des documents inédits.* (LE FIGARO (supplément), 12 août 1893)
Temkine, Raymonde, *De Baudelaire à Michaux.* (EUROPE, avril–mai 1967, 234–43)
Thébault, Eugène, *Baudelaire disciple de Saint Thomas d'Aquin.* (MERCURE DE FRANCE, 15 juillet 1929, 358–66)

Tourneux, Maurice, *Baudelaire amoureux.* Sept lettres inédites à la Présidente. (LE LIVRE MODERNE, 10 novembre 1891, 265–75)

—— *Auguste Poulet-Malassis. Notes et souvenirs intimes.* (Aux bureaux de L'ARTISTE, 1893)

Troubat, Jules, *Nouveaux témoignages d'un Survivant de Baudelaire.* (Bruxelles, LE PETIT BLEU, 9 novembre 1907)

Uzanne, Octave, *Vieux Airs – Jeunes Paroles.* (LE LIVRE, 10 septembre 1884, 545–50)

Vandérem, Fernand, *Vallès et Baudelaire.* (LE FIGARO, 6 août 1932)

Vivier, Robert, *Critique et métaphysique.* (REVUE D'HISTOIRE LITTÉRAIRE DE LA FRANCE, avril–juin 1967, 413–23)

Wallace, James K., *La violette d'Honfleur était-elle une fleur du mal?* (REVUE D'HISTOIRE LITTÉRAIRE DE LA FRANCE, mars–avril 1969, 245–51)

Wilhelm, M., *Revue musicale.* (REVUE CONTEMPORAINE, 15 mars 1861, 159)

Yriarte, Charles, *Courrier de Paris.* (LE MONDE, 24 septembre 1867)

Ziegler, Jean, *Baudelairiana. Alfred Mosselman et Mme Sabatier.* (BULLETIN DU BIBLIOPHILE, 1975, III, 266–73)

—— *Émile Deroy (1820–1846) et l'esthétique de Baudelaire.* (GAZETTE DES BEAUX-ARTS, mai–juin 1976, 153–60)

—— *Baudelairiana. Madame Sabatier (1822–1890). Quelques notes biographiques.* (BULLETIN DU BIBLIOPHILE, 1977, III–IV, 366–82)

Index

INDEX

Abé, Yoshio: quoted, 280–1

About, Edmond: 156

Académie-Française: CB a candidate for, 341–2, 344–52; CB renounces candidature, 352; mentioned, 94

Albert, Edmond: keeps vigil over CB, 487

Alençon: Poulet-Malassis and, 131, 249; CB visits, 261, 289; mentioned, 241, 261, 310, 313, 343

Allais, M. (pharmacist at Honfleur): 286

Allais, Mme: recalls CB and Mme Aupick, 286

Ancelle, Narcisse-Désiré: character, 91; career, 91, 480; appointed *conseil judiciaire* to CB, 91; relationship with CB, 71, 91–3, 100–1, 210 and *passim*; quoted, 455–6, 459–60; mentioned, 71, 80, 100, 112, 128, 129, 130 and *passim*

Antwerp: CB enjoys, 405; mentioned, 65–6, 401, 403

Archenbaut-Dufays, Caroline: see Aupick, Mme Jacques

Arondel, Antoine: CB indebted to, 81, 97, 106, 177–8, 388, 391, 392, 405–6

Art, L': CB praised in, 443–4

Artiste, L': CB contributes to, 157, 282; mentioned, 235, 347, 348

Asselineau, Charles-François-Alexandre: character, 96–9; appearance, 99; career, 98–9; friendship with CB, 98–9 and *passim*; quoted, 67, 83, 84, 99, 133–4, 237, 243–4, 379–80, 424 and *passim*; mentioned, 45, 61, 87, 113, 131

Athens: the Aupicks visit, 126, 135

Audebrand, Philibert: describes CB in Parisian cafés, 143–4

Augustin-Thierry, A.: talks to Mme Sabatier about CB: 305

Aunay, Alfred d': sees CB after death, 491–2

Aupick, Jacques-Joseph (presumed father of Jacques Aupick): 18, 19

Aupick, Mme Jacques-Joseph (mother of Jacques Aupick): 18, 19

Aupick, General Jacques (stepfather of CB): origins and birth, 18–19; army career, 19–20, 36, 45, 53, 56 and *passim*; liaison with Mme Veuve Baudelaire, 17–18, 20–1; marriage, 21–22; relationship with CB, 23, 28, 29–30, 31–2, 36–7, 38, 39–40, 45–46, 57–61, 70, 88, 93, 103–5, 116–7, 118–9, 121–2, 176 and *passim*; publishes atlases, 27–8; in Algeria, 28; in Lyons, 28–36; returns to Paris, 36; and CB's Eastern voyage, 57–61; and *conseil judiciaire*, 90; final quarrel with CB, 103–5; and 1848 Revolution, 122–5; Minister to Constantinople, 125, 126, 133–5; refuses London Embassy, 136; Ambassador to Madrid, 136, 158; Senator, 158; worsening health of, 193, 204, 209; at Honfleur, 176–7, 192–3; death and funeral of, 211–4; tributes to, 214–5; quoted, 55, 59, 77–8, 133, 135, 136, 158, 192, 193, 211, 212

Aupick, Mme Jacques (mother of CB): appearance, 278, 355; character, 7–8, 9–10 and *passim*; origins and birth of, 7; death of parents, 7; ward of Pierre Pérignon, 8–9; marries J.-F. Baudelaire, 8–9; gives birth to son, 10; death of husband, 13; burial of husband, 13; liaison with Aupick, 17–18, 20–21; marries Aupick, 21–2; birth of stillborn daughter, 22; relations with CB, 10–11, 14–17, 22–23, 34 and *passim*; in Lyons,